AF881168

A knowledge discovery approach to urban analysis

Beyoğlu Preservation Area as a data mine

Ahu Sökmenoğlu Sohtorik
Delft University of Technology, Faculty of Architecture and the Built Environment, Department of Architecture

Architecture and the Built environment

abe.tudelft.nl

Design: Sirene Ontwerpers, Rotterdam

ISBN 978-94-6186-652-3
ISSN 2212-3202

Unless otherwise specified, all the photographs in this thesis were taken by the author. For the use of illustrations effort has been made to ask permission for the legal owners as far as possible. We apologize for those cases in which we did not succeed. These legal owners are kindly requested to contact the publisher.

A Knowledge discovery approach to urban analysis

The Beyoğlu Preservation Area as a data mine

Proefschrift

ter verkrijging van de graad van doctor
aan de Technische Universiteit Delft,
op gezag van de Rector Magnificus prof. ir. K.C.A.M. Luyben,
voorzitter van het College voor Promoties,
in het openbaar te verdedigen op 23 mei 2016 om 15:00 uur
door Ahu SÖKMENOĞLU SOHTORİK
Master of Science in Architectural Design Computing,
Istanbul Technical University, Turkey
geboren te Istanbul, Turkey

This dissertation has been approved by the promotors:

Prof.dr. G. Çağdaş
Prof.dr.ir.arch. I.S. Sarıyıldız
Assoc. Prof.dr. R.M.F.A. Stouffs

Composition of the doctoral committee:

Rector Magnificus,	chairman
Prof.dr. G. Çağdaş	Istanbul Technical University, Turkey
Prof.dr.ir.arch. I.S. Sarıyıldız	Delft University of Technology
Assoc. Prof.dr. R.M.F.A. Stouffs	National University of Singapore

Independent members:

Prof.dr. A. Erdem, Istanbul Technical University, Turkey
Dr.ir. F.D. van der Hoeven, UHD-Bk, Delft University of Technology
Prof.dr.ir. B.D. de Vries, Eindhoven University of Technology
Prof.dr. I. Horvath IO, Delft University of Technology
Prof.dr.ir. H.J. Visscher Bk, Delft University of Technology, reservelid

This research was partially supported by the Netherlands organisation for international cooperation in higher education (Nuffic).

The doctoral research has been carried out in the context of an agreement on joint doctoral supervision between Istanbul Technical University, Turkey and Delft University of Technology, the Netherlands.

To Ali, Ayșe and 'Simba'

Foreword

I would like to express my special appreciation and thanks to my advisors Prof. Dr. Gülen ÇAĞDAŞ and Prof. Dr. Sevil Sarıyıldız. Prof. Gülen ÇAĞDAŞ have been a very supportive mentor for me. You have never stopped encouraging my research even at the hardest moments and you have always respected my thoughts and supported my attempts. You have also showed me the way to the TU Delft by introducing me to Prof. Dr. Sevil Sarıyıldız, who became my second advisor and had a great impact on my life by trusting me for the joint supervision program. You have always pushed the limits of this research and I am grateful that you did this. This research has developed so much thanks to the guidance of my advisors.

There is another important mentor, who guided this research with his extremely valuable advices. Assoc. Prof. Dr. Rudi STOUFFS, I am grateful to you for all the time you have dedicated to me and generous support you have provided. I hope one day I would become a flawless mentor for young researchers, just like you.

I would also like to express my appreciation to my committee members: Prof. Dr. Arzu ERDEM, Assoc. Prof. Dr.ir. Frank Van der HOEVEN, Prof. Dr. ir. Bauke de VRIES, Prof. Dr. Imre HORVATH and Prof. Dr. ir. Henk VISSCHER.

I would also like to especially thank to Prof. Dr. Arzu ERDEM for her generous support together with Prof. Dr. Belkıs ULUOĞLU and Assoc. Dr. Şebnem YALINAY ÇİNİCİ for giving me their valuable time and advices through my research process in ITU.

I would also like to express my gratitude for Nuffic (the Netherlands Institute for Higher Education) for the financial support that allowed me carry out this thesis.

I would especially like to thank to some of my colleagues and friends in Delft. I should express my gratitude for Daniel MULDER for translating the summary of the thesis during the last weekend. Jose Nuno BEIRAO and Pirouz NOURIAN, thank you for helping me to organize and tutor the workshop of the thesis 'Tarlabaşı Datascope'. Bige TUNÇER, thank you for support in Delft. I should especially thank, Sine ÇELİK and İrem and Luc MOERS, who opened their hearts and their homes and made me feel at home in Delft.

I should thank to the two key persons who had a great impact on this research. Ceyhun Burak AKGÜL, my old friend from the high school, who I met in Delft by coincidence just when I was looking for 'something'. I am grateful to you for introducing me data mining. The other key person is Nizam Onur Sönmez, my colleague from ITU, you and I we were the 'lonely' joint PhD students, we bear the heavy load of this process together.

Your endless support in every step, specifically in evolutionary computation, was surely one of the turning points of this research.

I would also like to thank to colleagues in Istanbul: Aslıhan ŞENEL, Zeynep ATAŞ and especially Ozan AVCI. I believe that the first year design studio -'traumatic studio'- that we tutored all together in full energy in ITU during 4 years and our brilliant students lighted my mind whenever it got black overwhelmed by this research process. Above all, thank you for your friendship.

Obviously words will not be enough to express my gratitude to my big family: my cousin and brother-in-law Merve-Micheal CONSTANTINI, my cousin Necla SÖKMENOĞLU and my aunt Deniz ÖNGÖREN, my nephew Öykü and my aunt and uncle Deniz-Mehmet ÖNDER, my nephew Mira, my sister and brother-in-law Simge-Cem SOHTORİK, my parents-in law Zeynep-Selim SOHTORİK, my brother and my sister-in-law Ali Tan-Deniz SÖKMENOĞLU, my grand-parents Gönül-Falih ÖNDER, and my mother Füsun ÖNDER. However, I especially have to thank to the three gorgeous women of my life. My mother-in-law, thank you for loving me as your daughter, this is so precious.My extraordinary grand-mother, I would not decide being an academic without you giving me courage to do so, thank you for lighting my way with my grand-father through my whole life. I will be thinking of you everytime I see a flower and I will always remember the delicious smell of the kitchen while cooking our orange cake together. And my mother, my beautiful soul, thank you for believing in me and loving me unconditionaly. I should also express that without my mother and mother-in-law taking care of my daughter Ayşe, it would have been impossible to find the time required for the completion of this thesis.

Finally, Ali, you know how grateful I am for your endless patience, unconditional support and 'no-ordinary' love. I would not be me without your companion through all those years. Therefore I would surely dedicate this thesis to you, to our little miss sunshine Ayşe and to the one in my belly 'Simba'...

January 2016
Ahu Sökmenoğlu Sohtorik

Contents

List of tables

List of figures

Abbreviations

KDPM	Knowledge Discovery Process Model
GIS	Geographical Information System
SIGKDD	the Association for Computing Machinery Special Interest Group on Knowledge Discovery and Data Mining
CIM	City Information Modeling
BIM	Building Information Modeling
UIM	Urban Information Modeling

Summary

A knowledge discovery approach to urban analysis

Beyoğlu Preservation Area as a data mine

Enhancing our knowledge of the complexities of cities in order to empower ourselves to make more informed decisions has always been a challenge for urban research. Recent developments in large-scale computing, together with the new techniques and automated tools for data collection and analysis are opening up promising opportunities for addressing this problem. The main motivation that served as the driving force behind this research is how these developments may contribute to urban data analysis. On this basis, the thesis focuses on urban data analysis in order to search for findings that can enhance our knowledge of urban environments, using the generic process of knowledge discovery using data mining. A knowledge discovery process based on data mining is a fully automated or semi-automated process which involves the application of computational tools and techniques to explore the "previously unknown, and potentially useful information" (Witten & Frank, 2005) hidden in large and often complex and multi-dimensional databases. This information can be obtained in the form of correlations amongst variables, data groupings (classes and clusters) or more complex hypotheses (probabilistic rules of co-occurrence, performance vectors of prediction models etc.). This research targets researchers and practitioners working in the field of urban studies who are interested in quantitative/ computational approaches to urban data analysis and specifically aims to engage the interest of architects, urban designers and planners who do not have a background in statistics or in using data mining methods in their work.

Accordingly, the overall aim of the thesis is the development of a knowledge discovery approach to urban analysis; a domain-specific adaptation of the generic process of knowledge discovery using data mining enabling the analyst to discover 'relational urban knowledge'. 'Relational urban knowledge' is a term employed in this thesis to refer to the potentially 'useful' and/or 'valuable' information patterns and relationships that can be discovered in urban databases by applying data mining algorithms. A knowledge discovery approach to urban analysis through data mining can help us to understand site-specific characteristics of urban environments in a more profound and useful way.

On a more specific level, the thesis aims towards 'knowledge discovery' in traditional thematic maps published in 2008 by the Istanbul Metropolitan Municipality as a basis of the Master Plan for the Beyoğlu Preservation Area. These thematic maps, which represent urban components, namely buildings, streets, neighbourhoods and their various attributes such as floor space use of the buildings, land price, population density or historical importance, do not really extend our knowledge of Beyoğlu Preservation Area beyond documenting its current state and do not contribute to the interventions presented in the master plan. However it is likely that 'useful' and 'valuable' information patterns discoverable using data mining algorithms are hidden in them.

In accordance with the stated aims, three research questions of the thesis concerns (1) the development of a general process model to adapt the generic process of knowledge discovery using data mining for urban data analysis, (2) the investigation of information patterns and relationships that can be extracted from the traditional thematic maps of the Beyoğlu Preservation Area by further developing and implementing this model and (3) the investigation of how could this 'relational urban knowledge' support architects, urban designers or urban planners whilst developing intervention proposals for urban regeneration.

A Knowledge Discovery Process Model (KDPM) for urban analysis was developed, as an answer to the the first research question. The KDPM for urban analysis is a domain-specific adaptation of the widely accepted process of knowledge discovery in databases defined by Fayyad, Piatetsky-Shapiro, and Smyth (1996b). The model describes a semi-automated process of database formulation, analysis and evaluation for extracting information patterns and relationships from raw data by combining both GIS and data mining functionalities in a complementary way. The KDPM for urban analysis suggests that GIS functionalities can be used to formulate a database, and GIS and data mining can complement each other in analyzing the database and evaluating the outcomes. The model illustrates that the output of a GIS platform can become the input for a data mining platform and vice versa, resulting in an interlinked analytical process which allows for a more sophisticated analysis of urban data.

To investigate the second and third research questions, firstly the KDPM for urban analysis was further developed to construct a GIS database of the Beyoğlu Preservation Area from the thematic maps. Then, three implementations were performed using this GIS database; the Beyoğlu Preservation Area Building Features Database consisting of multiple features attributed to the buildings. In Implementation (1), the KDPM for urban analysis was used to investigate a variety of patterns and relationships that can be extracted from the database using three different data mining methods. In Implementations (2) and (3), the KDPM for urban analysis was implemented to test how the knowledge discovery approach through data mining proposed in this thesis can assist in developing draft plans for the regeneration of a run-down neighbourhood in the Beyoğlu Preservation Area (Tarlabaşı). In Implementation (2), the KDPM for urban analysis is implemented in combination with an evolutionary process to apply a regeneration approach developed by the author; a computational process which generates draft plans for ground floor use, user-profile and tenure-type allocation was developed. In Implementation (3), students applied the KDPM for urban analysis during the course of an international workshop. The model enabled them to explore site-specific particularities of Tarlabaşı that would support their urban intervention proposals.

Among the outputs of the thesis three of them are considered as utilizable outputs that distinguish this thesis from previous studies:

1 *The KDPM for urban analysis.* Although there have been other studies which make use of data mining methods and techniques combined with GIS technology, to the best of our knowledge no previous research has implemented a process model to depict this process and used the model to extract 'knowledge' from traditional thematic maps. Researchers and practitioners can re-use this process model to analyze other urban environments. The KDPM for urban analysis is, therefore, one of the main utilizable outputs of the thesis and an important scientific contribution of this study.

2 *The Beyoğlu Preservation Area Building Features Database.* A large and quite comprehensive GIS database which consists of 45 spatial and non-spatial features attributed to the 11,984 buildings located in the Beyoğlu Preservation Area was constructed. This database is one of the original features of this study. To the best of our knowledge, there are no other examples of applications of data mining using such a comprehensive GIS database, constructed from a range of actual micro-scale data representing such a variety of features attributed to the buildings. This database can be re-used by analysts interested in studying the Beyoğlu Preservation Area. The Beyoğlu Preservation Area Building Features Database is therefore one of the main utilizable outputs of the thesis and represents a scientific contribution to the research material on the Beyoğlu Preservation Area. .

3 *A computational process which generates draft plans for ground floor use, user-profile and tenure-type allocation, using GIS and data mining functionalities with evolutionary computation.* This output of the thesis was generated by Implementation (2), which aimed to investigate Research Question (3). The overall process involved the successive application of Naïve Bayes Classification, Association Rule Analysis and an Evolutionary Algorithm to a subset of the Beyoğlu Preservation Area Building Features Database representing the Tarlabaşı neighbourhood. Briefly, the findings of the data mining analysis were used to formulate a set of rules for assigning ground floor use information to the buildings. These rules were then used for fitness measurements of an Evolutionary Algorithm, together with other fitness measurements for assigning user-profile and tenure-type information (defined by the author according

to the regeneration approach developed by the author). As a result, the algorithm transformed the existing allocation of the ground floor use in the buildings located in Tarlabaşı in accordance with the given rules and assigned user-profile and tenure-type information for each building. This computational process demonstrated one way to use the data mining analysis findings in developing intervention proposals for urban regeneration. A similar computational process can be implemented in other urban contexts by researchers and practitioners. To the best of our knowledge, no prior research has used data mining analysis findings for fitness measurements of an Evolutionary Algorithm in order to produce draft plans for ground floor use, user-profile and tenure-type allocation. This is, therefore, the most original scientific contribution and utilizable output of the thesis.

As a result of the research, on the basis of the data that is available in the thematic maps of the Beyoğlu Preservation Area, the potential of a knowledge discovery approach to urban analysis in revealing the relationships between various components of urban environments and their various attributes is demonstrated. It is also demonstrated that these relationships can reveal site-specific characteristics of urban environments and if found 'valuable' by the the targeted researchers and practitioners, these can lead to the development of more informed intervention proposals. Thereby the knowledge discovery approach to urban analysis developed in this thesis may help to improve the quality of urban intervention proposals and consequently the quality of built environments. On the other hand, the implementations carried out in the thesis also exposed the major limitation of the knowledge discovery approach to urban analysis through data mining, which is the fact that the findings discoverable by this approach are limited by the relevant data that is collectable and accessible.

Samenvatting

Kenniswinning als benadering van stedelijke analyse

Beyoğlu Preservation Area als informatiemijn

Een van de uitdagingen van stedelijk onderzoek is altijd geweest om onze kennis over de complexe aspecten van steden te vergroten, zodat we beter geïnformeerde beslissingen kunnen nemen. Recente ontwikkelingen op het gebied van grootschalige computerberekeningen bieden, samen met nieuwe technieken en geautomatiseerde tools voor gegevensverzameling en -analyse, veelbelovende mogelijkheden om dit probleem aan te pakken. De hoofdzakelijke motivatie en drijvende kracht van dit proefschrift is de manier waarop deze ontwikkelingen kunnen bijdragen aan de analyse van stedelijke gegevens. Die analyse wordt vervolgens gebruikt om onze kennis van stedelijke omgevingen te vergroten met behulp van het generieke proces van kenniswinning door middel van datamining. Dit is een geheel of gedeeltelijk geautomatiseerd proces waarbij gebruik wordt gemaakt van rekentools en -technieken om 'voorheen onbekende en mogelijk nuttige informatie' te onderzoeken (Witten & Frank, 2005) die verborgen ligt in grote, vaak complexe en multidimensionale databases. Deze informatie kan worden verkregen in de vorm van correlaties tussen variabelen, gegevensgroepen (klassen en clusters) of meer complexe hypothesen (probabilistische regels voor gelijktijdig voorkomen, prestatievectoren van voorspellingsmodellen, enzovoort). Dit onderzoek is gericht op onderzoekers en professionals werkzaam in het gebied van stadsonderzoek die geïnteresseerd zijn in kwantitatieve/rekenkundige benaderingen van analyse van stedelijke gegevens en doelt er specifiek op de interesse te wekken van architecten, stedenbouwkundigen en planologen die geen achtergrond hebben in statistiek of in het gebruik van datamining methodes in hun werk.

Het algemene doel van dit proefschrift is dan ook het ontwikkelen van een benadering van stedelijke analyse om kennis te vergaren; een domein specifieke vorm van het generieke proces van kenniswinning door middel van datamining waarmee analisten 'relationele stedelijke kennis' kunnen vergaren. De term 'relationele stedelijke kennis' wordt in dit proefschrift gebruikt voor mogelijk 'nuttige' en/of 'waardevolle' informatiepatronen en relaties die in stedelijke databases kunnen worden ontdekt met behulp van datamining-algoritmes. Door stedelijke analyse te benaderen via de aanpak van kenniswinning door middel van datamining kunnen we meer inzicht in en bruikbare kennis krijgen over locatiespecifieke kenmerken van stedelijke omgevingen.

Op een specifieker niveau, het proefschrift doelt op 'kenniswinning' in traditionele thematische kaarten gepubliceerd in 2008 door de gemeente van Istanboel (Istanbul Metropolitan Municipality) als basis voor het Masterplan voor het Beyoğlu Preservation Area (Beschermd Stadsgezicht Beyoğlu). Deze thematische kaarten, waarop verschillende kenmerken van de stedelijke componenten worden gerepresenteerd namelijk gebouwen, straten, wijken en de verschillende kenmerken daarvan zoals gebruik van begane grond en verdiepingen, landprijs, bevolkingsdichtheid of historisch belang, voegen niet veel meer toe aan onze kennis van het Beschermd Stadsgezicht Beyoğlu naast het documenteren van de huidige staat en hebben geen toegevoegde waarde voor de beslissingen die in het plan worden gepresenteerd. Toch is het aannemelijk dat er 'nuttige' en 'waardevolle' informatiepatronen, te ontdekken door datamining algoritmes, hierin verstopt zitten.

In overeenstemming met de gestelde doelen zijn er drie onderzoeksvragen in het proefschrift die zich bezighouden met (1) het ontwikkelen van een algemeen proces model voor het aanpassen van het generieke proces van kenniswinning door gebruik te maken van datamining voor de analyse van stedelijke gegevens, (2) het onderzoeken van informatie patronen en relaties die onttrokken kunnen worden uit de traditionele thematische kaarten van het Beschermd Stadsgezicht Beyoğlu door middel van het verder ontwikkelen en implementeren van dit model en (3) onderzoeken hoe kan deze 'gerelateerde stedelijke kennis' ondersteuning bieden aan architecten, stedenbouwkundigen of planologen bij het ontwikkelen van voorstellen voor bepaalde ingrepen.

Er is een KDPM (Knowledge Discovery Process Model: model van het proces van het vergaren van kennis) voor stedelijke analyse ontwikkeld als antwoord op de eerste onderzoeksvraag. Het KDPM voor stedelijke analyse is een domeinspecifieke aanpassing van het algemeen aanvaarde proces om kennis te vergaren uit databases dat is beschreven door Fayyad, Piatetsky-Shapiro en Smyth (1996b). Dit model beschrijft een gedeeltelijk geautomatiseerd proces voor het formuleren, analyseren en evalueren van databases om informatiepatronen en relaties uit ruwe gegevens te onttrekken door GIS- en dataminingfunctionaliteiten op een complementaire manier te combineren. In het KDPM voor stedelijke analyse wordt ervan uitgegaan dat GIS-functionaliteiten kunnen worden gebruikt om een database te formuleren en dat GIS en datamining elkaar kunnen aanvullen bij het analyseren van de database en het evalueren van de resultaten. Het model laat zien dat de output van een GIS-platform de input kan worden van een datamining-platform en omgekeerd, wat resulteert in een onderling verbonden analytisch proces dat een meer verfijnde analyse van stedelijke gegevens mogelijk maakt.

Om de tweede en derde onderzoeksvraag te behandelen werd het KDPM voor stedelijke analyse verder ontwikkeld om een GIS-database op te bouwen van het Beschermd Stadsgezicht Beyoğlu op grond van de thematische kaarten. Er werden drie implementaties toegepast met behulp van deze GIS-database; de Beschermd Stadsgezicht Beyoğlu Gebouw Kenmerken Database (Beyoğlu Preservation Area Building Features Database) waarbij er meerdere kenmerken werden toegekend aan de gebouwen. Bij Implementatie (1) werd het KDPM voor stedelijke analyse gebruikt om diverse patronen en relaties te onderzoeken die uit de database kunnen worden gehaald met behulp van drie verschillende dataminingmethoden. Bij Implementatie (2) en (3) werd het KDPM voor stedelijke analyse geïmplementeerd om te testen hoe de in dit proefschrift voorgestelde benadering om kennis te vergaren door middel van datamining de ontwikkeling van concept plannen kan ondersteunen voor het herstel van een vervallen wijk in het Beschermd Stadsgezicht Beyoğlu (Tarlabaşı). Bij Implementatie (2) wordt het KDPM voor stedelijke analyse geïmplementeerd in combinatie met een evolutionair proces om een door de auteur ontwikkelde benadering voor vernieuwing toe te passen; een rekenkundig proces, dat concept plannen voor begane grond gebruik, gebruikers-profiel en eigendoms-type toewijzing genereert, is ontwikkeld. Bij Implementatie (3) hebben studenten het KDPM voor stedelijke analyse toegepast tijdens een internationale workshop. Met dit model konden ze locatiespecifieke bijzonderheden van Tarlabaşı onderzoeken die hun voorstellen voor ingrepen in de stad zouden ondersteunen.

Drie originele bruikbare opbrengsten die dit proefschrift onderscheiden van eerdere studies:

1 *Het KDPM voor stedelijke analyse.* Er zijn eerdere studies geweest die gebruik hebben gemaakt van datamining methodes en technieken gecombineerd met GIS technologie, maar voor zover bekend is er geen onderzoek geweest die een proces model heeft geïmplementeerd om dit proces te beschrijven en het model heeft gebruikt om 'kennis' te onttrekken uit traditionele thematische kaarten. Onderzoekers en professionals kunnen dit proces model hergebruiken om andere stedelijke omgevingen te analyseren. Het KDPM voor stedelijke analyse is dan ook één van de hoofdzakelijk bruikbare opbrengsten van het proefschrift en een belangrijke wetenschappelijke bijdrage van deze studie.

2 *De Beschermd Stadsgezicht Beyoğlu Gebouw Kenmerken Database.* Een grote en begrijpelijke GIS database die bestaat uit 45 ruimtelijke en niet-ruimtelijke kenmerken behorende bij de 11.984 gebouwen in het Beschermd Stadsgezicht Beyoğlu is gemaakt. Deze database is één van de originele aspecten van deze studie. Voor zover bekend zijn er geen andere voorbeelden van toepassingen van datamining die gebruik maken van zo'n begrijpelijke GIS database, geconstrueerd uit een bereik van mirco-schaal gegevens die een variatie aan kenmerken toegekend aan gebouwen representeert. Deze database kan worden hergebruikt door analisten die geïnteresseerd zijn in het bestuderen van het Beschermd Stadsgezicht Beyoğlu. De Beschermd Stadsgezicht Beyoğlu Gebouw Kenmerken Database is daarom één van de hoofdzakelijke bruikbare opbrengsten van het proefschrift en is een wetenschappelijke bijdrage aan het onderzoeksmateriaal over het Beschermd Stadsgezicht Beyoğlu.

3 *Een rekenkundig process dat concept plannen voor begane grond gebruik, gebruikers-profiel en eigendoms-type toewijzing genereert, gebruik maken van GIS en datamining functionaliteit met evolutionaire berekening.* Deze opbrengst van het proefschrift is gegenereerd bij Implementatie (2), die doelde op het behandelen van onderzoeksvraag (3). Het algehele proces omvatte de opeenvolgende toepassing van Naïve Bayes Classificatie, Associatie Analyse en een Evolutionair Algoritme op een subset van de Beschermd Stadsgezicht Beyoğlu Gebouw Kenmerken Database dat de Tarlabaşı wijk representeert. Kort gezegd, de bevindingen van de datamining analyse zijn gebruikt om een set regels op te stellen voor de toewijzing van began grond gebruik informatie aan de gebouwen. Deze regels zijn toen gebruikt voor een fitness meting van het Evolutionaire Algoritme, samen met andere fitness metingen voor het toewijzen van gebruikers profielen en eigendoms-type informatie (gedefinieerd door de auteur op basis van de benadering voor vernieuwing ontwikkeld door de auteur). Dit resulteerde erin dat het algoritme het bestaande begane grond gebruik toewijzingsplan van het Beschermd Stadsgezicht Beyoğlu veranderde in overeenstemming met de regels en toegewezen gebruikers profiel en eigendoms-type informatie voor elk gebouw. Dit rekenkundig proces liet een manier zien voor het gebruik van datamining analyse bevindingen in het genereren van voorstellen voor ingrepen in de stad. Een gelijkwaardig rekenkundig proces kan worden geïmplementeerd in een ander stedelijk context door onderzoekers en professionals. Voor zover bekend is er geen ander onderzoek dat gebruik heeft gemaakt van datamining analyse bevindingen voor fitness metingen van een Evolutionair Algoritme om zo concept plannen te produceren voor begane grond gebruik, gebruikers profiel en eigendoms-type toewijzing. Hierdoor is dit dan ook de meest originele wetenschappelijke bijdrage en bruikbare opbrengst van het proefschrift..

Het onderzoek resulteert, op basis van de gegevens die beschikbaar zijn in de thematische kaarten van het Beschermd Stadsgezicht Beyoğlu, in het demonstreren van de potentie van een kenniswinning benadering naar stedelijke analyse voor het blootleggen van de relatie tussen verscheidene componenten van stedelijke omgevingen en hun kenmerken. Het is ook aangetoond dat deze relaties plek-specifieke eigenschappen van stedelijke omgevingen kunnen blootleggen en als deze als 'belangrijk' worden geacht door de betreffende onderzoekers en professionals, dit kan leiden tot de ontwikkeling van betere voorstellen voor ingrepen. Zodanig kan de kenniswinning benadering voor stedelijke analyse, ontwikkeld in dit proefschrift, helpen bij het verbeteren van de kwaliteit van voorstellen voor ingrepen en zodoende de kwaliteit van bebouwde omgevingen. Aan de andere kant leggen deze implementaties ook de grote beperking van de kenniswinning benadering voor stedelijke analyse door middel van datamining bloot, namelijk het feit dat de bevindingen die gedaan kunnen worden gelimiteerd zijn door de relevante data die toegankelijk is en verzameld kan worden.

Özet

Kent analizinde bir bilgi keşfi yaklaşımı

Bir veri madeni olarak Beyoğlu Kentsel Koruma Alanı

Kentlerin karmaşık yapısına ilişkin mevcut bilgimizi arttırarak kentsel müdahele süreçlerinde daha bilinçli ve bilgiye dayanan kararlar üretebilmek kent araştırmaları için önemli bir çalışma alanı ve mücadele konusu olagelmiştir. Geniş ölçekli hesaplama sistemleri (large-scale computing) ve yeni nesil veri toplama ve analiz etme teknikleri bu alanda çalışan araştırmacılara yeni fırsatlar sunmaktadır.. Bu tez hesaplamalı bilim ve mühendislik alanındaki bu önemli gelişmelerin kentsel veri analizi alanına ne tür katkılar sağlayabileceği konusuna odaklanmaktadır. Tezin hedefi 'veri madenciliği aracılığı ile bilgi keşfi' jenerik sürecini kullanarak kentsel verileri analiz etmek ve böylelikle kente dair bilgimizi arttırabilecek bulgulara erişmektir. 'Veri madenciliği aracılığı ile bilgi keşfi' süreci hesaplamalı araç ve teknikleri kullanarak çok geniş, çoğunlukla karmaşık ve çok boyutlu veri tabanlarında gizli "önceden bilinmeyen ve faydalı/kullanışlı" (Witten & Frank, 2005) enformasyon örüntülerinin (değişkenler arasındaki korelasyonlar, veri gruplamaları (sınıflandırma ve kümeleme) ya da daha kompleks hipotezler) otomatik ya da yarı-otomatik olarak araştırılması sürecidir .

Bu doğrultuda bu tezin ana hedefi 'kent analizinde veri madenciliği aracılığı ile bir bilgi keşfi yaklaşımı' geliştirmektir. Kent analistlerinin bu yaklaşımı, kentsel müdahele süreçlerinde kanıta dayalı ve kentsel bağlama duyarlı kararlar verebilmeyi sağlayabilecek, 'ilişkisel kent bilgisi'ni keşfetmek amacı ile kullanılabileceği düşünülmektedir. İlişkisel kent bilgisi bu tez kapsamında önerilmiş bir kavramdır ve kentsel veri tabanlarını veri madenciliği algoritmaları kullanarak analiz ederek bulabileceğimiz 'kullanışlı' ve 'değerli' enformasyon örüntüleri ve ilişkilerini ifade etmektedir. Kent analizinde veri madenciliği aracılığı ile bilgi keşfi' yaklaşımı kentsel alanların yerel ve özgün karakteristiklerinin daha derinden ve kullanışlı bir şekilde anlaşılmasını sağlayabilir.

Tezin ikincil hedefi ise, 2008 tarihli Beyoğlu Koruma Amaçlı Nazım İmar Planına ilişkin tematik analiz paftalarında gizli olduğu düşünülen 'bilgilerin' keşfedilmesidir. Bir grup temel kentsel bileşenin yani binalar, sokaklar, mahalleler ve bunlara ilişkin çeşitli özelliklerin resmedildiği geleneksel tematik kent analizi paftaları söz konusu Nazım İmar Planı'nın temelini oluşturmaktadır. Bu analiz paftalarının oldukça zengin birer veri kaynağı oldukları ancak mevcut durumu görsel olarak ifade etmekten öteye bir fayda getirmedikleri ve planlama kararlarına doğrudan etki etmedikleri gözlemlenmiştir. Veri madenciliği aracılığı ile bilgi keşfi yaklaşımı kullanılarak tematik analiz paftalarında gizli olduğu düşünülen 'bilgiler'in keşfedilmesi mümkün olabilir ve bu 'bilgiler' kentsel bağlama duyarlı dönüşüm yaklaşımları geliştirmek üzere kullanılabilir.

Bu amaçlar doğrultusunda, tez kapsamında birbiri ile bağlantılı üç araştırma sorusu belirlenmiştir: (1) 'Veri tabanlarında bilgi keşfi' jenerik sürecinin kentsel veri analizi alanına uyarlanmasını sağlayacak genel bir kent analizi süreç modelinin geliştirilmesi, (2) bu modelin geliştirilerek Beyoğlu Koruma Amaçlı Nazım İmar Planı tematik kent analizi paftalarının analizi için kullanılması, (3) Tematik analiz paftalarından elde edilecek 'ilişkisel kent bilgisi'nin kentsel dönüşüm süreçlerinde müdahele önerilerinin geliştirilmesi amacı ile kullanılması.

İlk araştırma sorusuna cevap olarak Fayyad, Piatetsky-Shapiro, and Smyth (1996b) tarafından geliştirilen ve yaygın olarak kabul gören 'veri tabanlarında bilgi keşfi' jenerik süreci kentsel veri analizi alanına uyarlanarak bir 'Kent Analizinde Bilgi Keşfi Süreç Modeli' geliştirilmiştir . Bu süreç modeli ham veriler içerisinde gizli enformasyon örüntüleri ve ilişkilerini ortaya çıkartmak için coğrafi bilgi sistemleri ve veri madenciliği araçlarını bir arada kullanarak 'kentsel veritabanı oluşturulma, analiz etme ve analiz sonuçlarını değerlendirme' alt süreçlerini tarif etmektedir. Modelde, veri tabanı oluşturma süreci için coğrafi bilgi sistemleri kullanılırken, veri tabanı analiz etme ve sonuçları değerlendime süreçleri için coğrafi bilgi sistemleri işlevleri ve veri madenciliği teknikleri birbirini tamamlayacak şekilde kullanılmaktadır. Model, coğrafi bilgi sistemleri ve veri madenciliği platformlarının karşılıklı olarak birbirlerine girdi sağlayabileceğini ve iki farklı işlev platformunun bu şekilde bağlantılanması ile daha incelikli/nitelikli bir veri analizi yapmanın mümkün olabileceğini göstermektedir.

İkinci ve üçüncü araştırma sorularının araştırılması amacı ile öncellikle 'Kent Analizinde Bilgi Keşfi Süreç Modeli' bir miktar daha geliştirilerek tematik kentsel analiz paftalarının çeşitli hesaplamalı platformlarda işlenmesi ile paftaların içerdiği verilerden coğrafi bilgi sistemleri tabanlı bir veri tabanı (Beyoğlu Kentsel Koruma Alanı Bina Özellikleri Veri Tabanı) oluşturulmuştur. Beyoğlu Kentsel Koruma alanı içerisinde yer alan binalar ve binalara ilişkin birçok farklı mekansal ve mekansal olmayan özellikten oluşan bu dijital veri tabanı kullanılarak üç farklı uygulama yapılmıştır. İlk uygulama Beyoğlu Kentsel Koruma Alanı Bina Özellikleri Veri Tabanının veri madenciliği teknik ve yöntemleri kullanılarak analiz edilmesi ile elde edilebilecek enformasyon ilişkileri ve örüntülerininin nasıl çeşitlenebileceğini araştırmak amacı ile yapılmıştır. İkinci ve üçüncü uygulamalarda, tez kapsamında önerilen veri madenciliği aracılığı ile bilgi keşfi yaklaşımının Beyoğlu Koruma alanı içerisinde yer alan Tarlabaşı semtinin dönüşümü sürecine nasıl bir katkı sağlayabileceği sınanmak istenmiştir. İkinci uygulama kapsamında 'Kent Analizinde Bilgi Keşfi Süreç Modeli', evrimsel bir yaklaşımla bir arada kullanılarak, araştırmacı tarafından önerilen alternatif bir kentsel dönüşüm yaklaşımı çerçevesinde ortaya konulan bir dizi kentsel müdahelenin alana nasıl uygulanabileceği gösterilmiştir. Üçüncü uygulama kapsamında ise 'Kent Analizinde Bilgi Keşfi Süreç Modeli' öğrenciler tarafından uluslararası bir çalıştay sürecinde yine Tarlabaşı dönüşümü sorunsalı bağlamında kullanılarak test edilmiştir. Öğrenciler bu modeli kullanarak Tarlabaşı semtinin yerel özelliklerini keşfederek bu analizleri temel alan bir takım kentsel dönüşüm müdahele önerileri ortaya koymuşlardır.

Tezin bilimsel çıktıları arasında özellikle üç tanesinin doğrudan kullanılabilir olduğu ve bu çalışmayı benzerlerinden ayırdığı düşünülmektedir:

1 *Kent Analizinde Bilgi Keşfi Süreç Modeli.* Coğrafi Bilgi Sistemleri ve veri madenciliği tekniklerinin bir arada kullanıldığı başka araştırmalar mevcuttur ancak mevcut literatürde böyle bir süreci tarif eden bir kent analizi süreç modelinine rastlanmamış ve özellikle de böyle bir sürecin geleneksel tematik kent analizi paftalarını analiz ederek bunlar içerisinde gizli enformasyon örüntüleri ve ilişkilerini keşfetmek amacı ile kullanıldığı bir örneğe rastlanmamıştır.

2 *Beyoğlu Kentsel Koruma Alanı Bina Özellikleri Veri Tabanı.* Beyoğlu Kentsel Koruma alanı içerisinde yer alan 11,984 adet bina ve bu binaların mekansal ve mekansal olmayan 45 farklı özelliğini içeren oldukça geniş ve detaylı bir dijital veri tabanı oluşturulmuştur. Mevcut literatürde veri madenciliği tekniklerinin, bina ölçeğinde bu kadar kapsamlı mikro ölçekli veri içeren bir mekansal veri tabanı üzerinde uygulandığı başka bir araştırmaya rastlanmamıştır. Bu veri tabanının Beyoğlu Kentsel Koruma Alanı üzerine çalışmak isteyen araştırmacılar ve pratisyenler tarafından kullanılabileceği için tezin önemli kullanılabilir çıktılarından biri olduğu düşünülmektedir.

3 *Coğrafi Bilgi Sistemleri, veri madenciliği işlevleri ve evrimsel hesaplama yaklaşımlarını bir arada kullanarak bina zemin katlarına işlev, kullanıcı tipi ve mülkiyet tipi atfeden bir hesaplamalı süreç.* Tezin bu çıktısı üçüncü araştırma sorusuna yanıt aranan ikinci uygulama kapsamında üretilmiştir. Beyoğlu Kentsel Koruma Alanı Bina Özellikleri Veri Tabanı içerisinden Tarlabaşı semtine ait veriler ayrılarak sırası ile Naïve Bayes Sınıflandırma analizi ve Birliktelik Kuralları analizi uygulanmıştır. Bu analiz sonuçlarında elde edilen veri madenciliği bulguları binaların zemin katlarına işlev atayan bir dizi kuralın tanımlanması için kullanılmıştır. Bu kurallar, yazar tarafından geliştirilen bir kentsel dönüşüm yaklaşımı çerçevesinde önerilen kullanıcı ve mülkiyet tipi yerleşimi kurallarıyla birlikte evrimsel bir algoritmanın uygunluk (fitness) ölçütü olarak kullanılmıştır. Sonuç olarak evrimsel algoritma binaların zemin katlarının mevcut işlevlerini dönüştürmüş ve binalara birer kullanıcı tipi ve mülkiyet tipi bilgisi atfetmiştir. Bu uygulama, veri madenciliği analizi sonuçlarının kentsel dönüşüm amaçlı müdahele önerileri geliştirirken nasıl kullanılabileceğine dair bir yol örneklemektedir. Bu hesaplamalı sürecin benzerleri araştırmacılar ve pratisyenler tarafından başka kentsel bağlamlar için dönüştürücü müdahele önerileri geliştirmek üzere yeniden kullanılabilir. Mevcut literatürde, veri madenciliği analizi sonuçlarını evrimsel bir algoritmanın uygunluk (fitness) ölçütü olarak kullanarak işlev, kullanıcı tipi ve

mülkiyet tipi yerleşim planları üreten başka bir örneğe rastlanmamıştır. Bu nedenle tez kapsamında geliştirilen bu hesaplamalı sürecin tezin en özgün bilimsel çıktısı olduğu düşünülmektedir.

Sonuç olarak yapılan araştırma, Beyoğlu Kentsel Koruma Alanı Bina Özellikleri Veri Tabanı içerisinde yer alan verilerle sınırlı olsa da, kent analizinde veri madenciliği aracılığı ile bilgi keşfi yaklaşımının, temel kentsel bileşenler ve onların farklı özellikleri arasındaki enformasyon ilişkileri ve örüntülerini ortaya çıkartma potansiyelini ortaya koymaktadır. Bunun yanı sıra, bu araştırma, sözü edilen enformasyon ilişkileri ve örüntülerinin, kentsel mekanların özgün özelliklerini ortaya koyabileceği ve bu özelliklerin, araştırmacılar ve pratisyenler tarafından değerli bulunurlarsa, daha bilinçli ve bilgiye dayalı kentsel müdahele önerileri geliştirmek üzere kullanılabileceğini de göstermiştir. Böylelikle tez kapsamında geliştirilen kent analizinde veri madenciliği aracılığı ile bilgi keşfi yaklaşımının kentsel dönüşüm süreçlerinde yapılan müdahelelerin kalitesini arttırabileceği ve dolayısı ile genel anlamda kentsel alanların kalitesinin arttırılabileceği düşünülmektedir. Bununla birlikte, tez kapsamında yapılan uygulamalar, böyle bir yaklaşımın ortaya çıkarabileceği sonuçların kalitesinin toplanabilen ve erişilebilen veri kalitesi ve miktarı ile sınırlı olduğu da ortaya koymaktadır.

1 Introduction

§ 1.1 Problems and Motivation

§ 1.1.1 Generic problem: 'Knowledge discovery' in urban analysis

Cities are overwhelmingly complex, due to the relationships that exist between their multiple dimensions (physical, social, economic, cultural, political, etc.) operating both on a micro level (between individual urban components and actors) and a macro level (between policy makers, companies, institutions, etc.). Enhancing our knowledge of the complexities of cities in order to empower ourselves to make more informed decisions has always been a central problem for urban analysis research. Recent advances in computer science and ICT which have produced new tools and techniques for capturing, storing and analysing data therefore offer an important opportunity to address this challenge.

Urban data analysis using the new and more advanced analytical methods has therefore gained momentum recently. A new line of research, which is often referred to as urban analytics or urban informatics, has emerged in urban analysis research and new research programmes have been established in leading universities and research institutions. Together with conventional data analysis approaches, urban analytics researchers have sought to implement more sophisticated approaches to analyze large and often complex multidimensional databases.

The central problem of urban analytics is to explore how the new advanced analytical methods can be used to improve our understanding of cities in order to implement more informed decisions about urban design and planning processes. In a similar vein, the main motivation that served as the driving force behind this research is how to use the new and powerful set of data analysis tools and techniques which new developments in computing and information technologies have provided to increase our current knowledge of cities. After a general exploration of these tools and techniques, it was decided that using data mining methods to analyze urban data, which is also referred to as knowledge discovery in databases, is a subject worth investigating and may lead to valuable results and contributions to the fields of urban analysis and urban analytics.

A knowledge discovery process based on data mining is a fully automated (all the steps in the process are automated by a computer) or a semi-automated process (some steps in the process requires human interference) which involves the application of computational tools and techniques to explore the "previously unknown, and potentially useful information" (Witten & Frank, 2005) hidden in large databases. These patterns are often referred to as 'useful knowledge'. Data mining is the essential step in this knowledge discovery process and consists of "applying data analysis and discovery algorithms that, under acceptable computational efficiency limitations, produce a particular enumeration of patterns (or models) over the data" (Fayyad, Piatetsky-Shapiro, & Smyth, 1996b). Data mining methods and techniques are mainly derived from statistics and machine learning.

§ 1.1.2 Particular problem: 'Knowledge Discovery' in traditional thematic maps

On a more specific level, the motivation for this research stems from a real-world planning project, namely the 2008 Master Plan for the Beyoğlu Preservation Area, prepared and published by the Istanbul Metropolitan Municipality. The Beyoğlu Preservation Area is a very important spot in Istanbul, and is part of the historic city centre, which is also the present-day centre of culture and tourism. The area is now changing dramatically due to the top-down planning measures introduced by the 2008 Master Plan for the Beyoğlu Preservation Area. The inadequacies of the Master Plan for the Beyoğlu Preservation Area, have been heavily criticized by a large number of locals and professionals. The Master Plan for the Beyoğlu Preservation Area was developed using an outdated top-down approach which focused on large-scale architectural projects and disregarded the particular characteristics of the district. The planning decisions were almost entirely concerned with providing benefits for those investing in tourism, whilst destroying local life in Beyoğlu.

The municipality essentially published a set of analysis, synthesis and planning maps for the Beyoğlu Preservation Area, together with a plan report. The main data source for the planning decisions was the traditional thematic maps, which represent urban components, namely buildings, streets, neighbourhoods and their various attributes such as floorspace use of the buildings, land price, population density or historical importance. As an investigation of the plan report reveals, the analysis maps do not contribute to the planning decisions beyond documenting the current state of the district. Nevertheless, these analysis maps are quite a rich data source and it is likely that valuable information patterns are hidden in them. Identification of these implicit patterns using data mining could reveal some of the site-specific characteristics of the Beyoğlu Preservation Area and these information patterns could become operational whilst developing urban intervention proposals. Therefore, the specific problem that this research addresses is that of revealing the information patterns and relationships implicitly stored in these thematic maps and discovering how to use these whilst developing regeneration interventions for a run-down neighbourhood in the Beyoğlu Preservation Area (Tarlabaşı).

At this point it is important to make clear that the aim of the thesis is not to generate alternative master plan proposals which can repair the inadequacies of the existing master plan of the Beyoğlu Preservation Area, nor to research about how the problematic decision-making process implemented by the municipalities could be alternatively managed. These issues constituted a motive for the author to set the context of the thesis as Beyoğlu Preservation area but the thesis merely concerned with developing a domain-specific adaptation of the generic process of knowledge discovery through data mining and specifically focused on how data mining can be implemented to extract the 'knowledge' hidden in the traditional thematic maps of the Beyoğlu Preservation Area. On the basis of the data that is available in these thematic maps, the thesis also provides two implementations to demonstrate how such 'knowledge' can provide support in generating intervention proposals for urban regeneration. On one hand, these implementations demonstrate the possible contributions of implementing a knowledge discovery through data mining for architects, urban designers or urban planners, on the other hand they provide concrete suggestions on how some of the shortcomings of the Master Plan could be repaired. Although the aim of the thesis is not to develop an alternative approach for the Beyoğlu Preservation Area Master Plan or Tarlabaşı renewal project, this research can be seen as a limited (because of the limitations of the available data) but significant contribution about what could have been done alternatively in terms of developing context-sensitive interventions for the regeneration of the Tarlabaşı neighborhood in the Beyoğlu Preservation Area.

§ 1.2 Aims and Research Questions

The main goal of this research is the development of a knowledge discovery approach to urban analysis through Data Mining, a domain-specific adaptation of the generic process of knowledge discovery using data mining enabling the analyst to discover 'relational urban knowledge' 'Relational urban knowledge' is a term employed in this thesis to refer to the potentially 'useful' and/or 'valuable' information patterns and relationships that can be discovered in urban databases by applying data mining algorithms. A knowledge discovery approach to urban analysis through data mining can help us to understand the site-specific characteristics of urban environments in a more profound and useful way. On a more specific level, the thesis also aims towards 'knowledge discovery' in traditional thematic maps of the Master Plan for the Beyoğlu Preservation Area.

In order to achieve this goal, three main research questions were formulated:

Research Question (1): Can we develop a general process model to adapt the generic process of knowledge discovery using data mining for urban data analysis?

Research Question (2): What kind of information patterns and relationships can be extracted from the traditional thematic maps of the Beyoğlu Preservation Area by further developing and implementing this model?

Research Question (3): How could this 'relational urban knowledge' support architects, urban designer or urban planners whilst developing intervention proposals for urban regeneration?

This research targets researchers and practitioners working in the field of urban studies (architects, urban designers, urban planners, etc.) who are interested in quantitative/computational approaches to urban data analysis. The simplicity of use and understandability of results, which are the typical differences between data mining and more conventional statistical data analysis methods, are considered important opportunities that enable non-experts to make use of data mining methods. This study therefore implements relatively simple data mining methods to encourage architects, urban designers, urban planners or urban gepgraphers who have no knowledge of statistics or data mining to use data mining methods in their work.

§ 1.3 Research Method

This chapter describes how the research was carried out and presents the outputs produced in the different phases of the thesis.

Highlighted by the generic and specific problems addressed in this thesis, the main goal of the thesis is to develop a domain-specific adaptation of the generic process of knowledge discovery through data mining. And in particular, the research aims to implement this process to explore information patterns hidden in the urban analysis maps of the Beyoğlu Preservation Area in order to investigate how they may provide support for developing urban intervention proposals.

An in-depth research process began after setting the aims of the thesis. From this point onwards, the research was carried out in six main phases: the Background Research Phase (Literature Review), the Data Collection Phase, the Development Phase, the Implementation Phase and the Evaluation Phase. The process including the Development, Implementation and Evaluation phases involve significant iteration. There is also an iterative process between the development phase and the background research and data collection phases. The loops between different phases explain how previously acquired knowledge is incorporated into the whole process of the thesis. Research process is illustrated in Figure 1.1 and Figure 1.2.

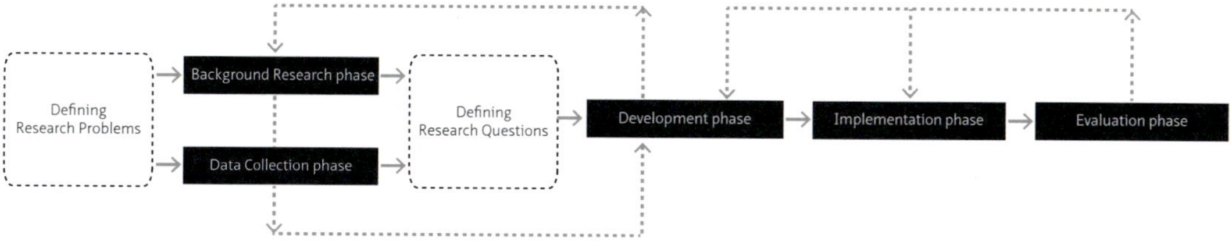

FIGURE 1.1 Research process (solid lines illustrate the main flow of the research process and dashed lines show how the iteration between different phases occurs).

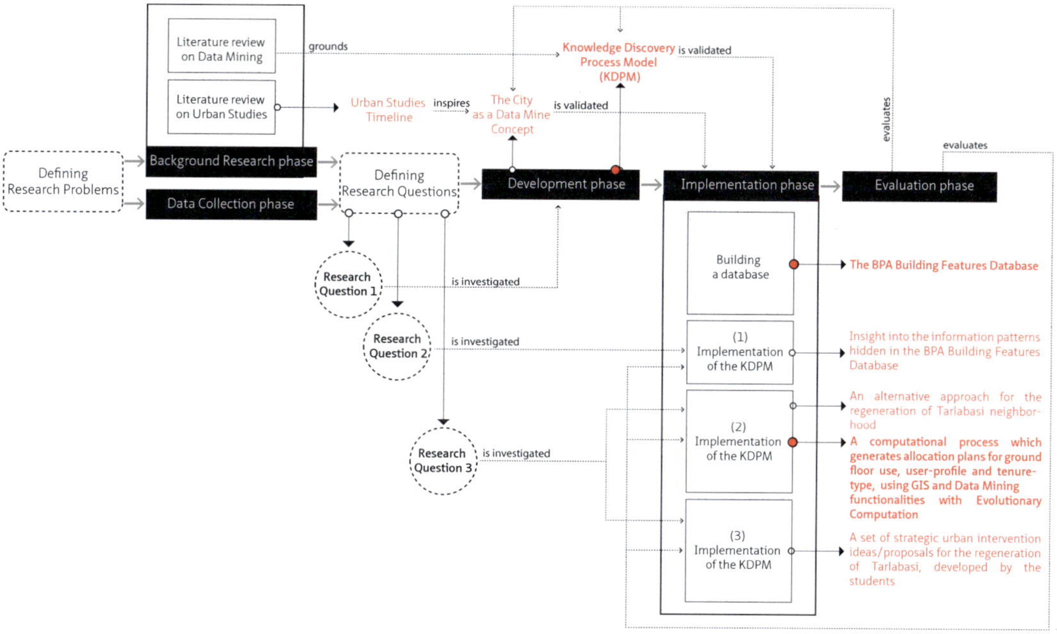

FIGURE 1.2 Research process and outputs (text in red indicates the outputs of the thesis and text in bold red the utilizable outputs).

The Figure 1.2 is a more detailed version of the previously given illustration of the research process (see Figure 1.1); phases are illustrated together with the outputs of the thesis. In Figure 1.2, the text in red indicates the outputs of the thesis and text in bold red the utilizable outputs. Smaller dashed lines explain basic relationships between different outcomes of the thesis and how these are related to the phases and the research questions.

Background Research Phase (Literature Review): This phase started more or less at the same time with the Data Collection Phase and they evolved together. The Background Research Phase began with a parallel investigation of the two main fields that provide the input for this research, namely urban studies and data mining. On the one hand, an urban studies timeline was designed, including the basic literature i.e. the ideas and works that have had the greatest influence on the development of urban theories and practice. This timeline systematized the literature survey and enabled the range of urban concepts and theories to be examined, including the tools, techniques and methods used in urban analysis, and the developments in computer science and ICT that have influenced urban theory and practice. On the basis of this examination a series of inferences were proposed for how conceptual, theoretical and practical approaches to cities have evolved over time. In addition to revealing the new trends in this field, this speculative analysis made three main contributions to the thesis. As a result of this analysis, the approach of the city as 'data mine', which provides a conceptual general basis for this line of research was drawn up. In addition, the relative importance of the this thesis was established; it is becoming increasingly important to investigate new approaches to urban analysis, which can provide better information for targeted researchers and practitioners. The analysis also identified a number of important contributions that data mining methods can make towards solving some of the major problems cited by urban theorists and practitioners. The urban studies timeline and its analysis is therefore the first output of the thesis:

Output (1): Urban studies timeline and a number of inferences about the evolution of urban theory and practice. Although these inferences can be considered speculative and incomplete, it still contributes towards general research on the evolution of approaches, objectives, and focal points in the field of urban theory and practice in general and the field of urban analysis in particular.

A parallel literature survey was carried out for the knowledge discovery through data mining process in order to gain an understanding of this analytical approach, which was used to investigate the general and specific problem addressed in this thesis. On the one hand, ways of implementing data mining algorithms were investigated, which involved an intensive study of the goals, methods and techniques, data types and format of the findings. In addition to the general literature on data mining, a number of recent studies were examined, mainly from the fields of computer science, information science and geographical sciences, providing a more extensive knowledge on the implementation of data mining algorithms. The literature survey on data mining led to the formulation of the KDPM for urban analysis. In addition, previous studies which implemented data mining methods specifically for use with urban data were also examined. In this way the possible original contributions of the thesis were revealed. Overall, the Background Research Phase provided a justification for the importance of the topic of the thesis and, in particular, this phase provided the basis for (1) justifying the overall and specific problem addressed in the thesis (2) formulating the research questions and (3) acquiring the knowledge needed to start the Development Phase.

Data Collection Phase: This phase involved investigating other data types associated with the Beyoğlu Preservation Area. The information provided by the traditional thematic maps of the Beyoğlu Preservation Area focuses mainly on the characteristics of the physical urban components. However, more information about the social, cultural, demographic and economic characteristics of the people living in the Beyoğlu Preservation Area or data on environmental issues such as the energy consumption of buildings, telecommunication could be also incorporated in the research. The relevant governmental and private institutions, such as the Beyoğlu Civil Registry Office, Istanbul Gas Distribution Company (IGDAS) and Telecommunication Company (Turk Telekom), were contacted for access to this type of information but unfortunately none of these institutions were willing to share data. The lack of any 'data sharing culture' in the country is, in fact, a major obstacle for scientific studies in this line of research. Consequently this research had to be carried out using only the information provided by the thematic maps of the Beyoğlu Preservation Area. The research questions were formulated accordingly and the Development Phase began.

Development Phase: This phase involved the investigation of the research question (1) studying how the generic process of knowledge discovery through data mining can be implemented in the field of urban analysis. A conceptual model was developed, together with a Knowledge Discovery Process Model (KDPM) for urban analysis, a domain-specific adaptation of the widely accepted knowledge discovery process in databases defined by Fayyad, Piatetsky-Shapiro, and Smyth (1996b). The KDPM for urban analysis was implemented in the Implementation Phase. Development phase generated two outputs:

Output (2): A concept for approaching the city as a 'data mine'. The city is a source of an enormous variety of data and now that we have new tools and methods for capturing and analyzing this data, it is particularly interesting and promising to research data-driven approaches to the analysis, design and planning of urban environments. Altought the thesis does not implement a city scale analysis, it proposes the approach of the city as 'data mine' to provide a conceptual general basis for this line of research.

Output (3): A KDPM for urban analysis. This model describes a general process, which combines GIS and data mining to extract 'relational urban knowledge' from urban data. To be more specific, this urban data analysis model describes a semi-automated process of database formulation, analysis and evaluation for extracting information patterns and relationships from raw data by combining both GIS and data mining functionalities in a complementary way. In the Implementation Phase, the model was extended and applied to specifically demonstrate how to analyze data contained in traditional thematic maps using data mining methods. Although there have been other studies which make use of data mining methods and techniques combined with GIS technology, to the best of our knowledge no previous research has implemented a process model to depict this process and used the model to extract 'knowledge' from traditional thematic maps. Researchers and practitioners can re-use this process model to analyze other urban environments. The KDPM for urban analysis is, therefore, one of the main utilizable outputs of the thesis and an important scientific contribution of this study.

Implementation Phase: This phase involved investigating the research questions (2) and (3). The concept and the model built in the Development Phase were implemented and validated, involving three different implementations: the first was used to investigate Research Question (2), and the second and third to investigate Research Question (3). This phase generated five outputs:

Output (4): The Beyoğlu Preservation Area Building Features Database. A large and quite comprehensive GIS database was constructed in order to implement the data mining analysis, based mainly on the traditional thematic maps of the Master Plan for the Beyoğlu Preservation Area. This database, which is named the Beyoğlu Preservation Area Building Features Database, consists of 45 spatial and non-spatial features attributed to the 11,984 buildings located in the Beyoğlu Preservation Area and is one of the original features of this study. To the best of our knowledge, there are no other examples of applications of data mining using such a comprehensive GIS database, constructed from a range of actual micro-scale data representing such a variety of features attributed to the buildings. This database can be re-used by analysts interested in studying the Beyoğlu Preservation Area. The Beyoğlu Preservation Area Building Features Database is therefore one of the main utilizable outputs of the thesis and represents a scientific contribution to the research material on the Beyoğlu Preservation Area.

Output (5): An insight into the information patterns hidden in the Beyoğlu Preservation Area Building Features Database. This output of the thesis was generated by Implementation (1), which aimed to investigate Research Question (2): what kind of information patterns and relationships can be extracted from the traditional thematic maps of the Beyoğlu Preservation Area Area by further developing and implementing the KDPM for urban analysis? Three basic data mining methods, i.e., Naïve Bayes Classification, Association Rules and Clustering were implemented using the Beyoğlu Preservation Area Building Features Database and a number of information patterns and relationships between different features of the buildings were discovered. These findings were visualized and used to compare the characteristics of the buildings in the Beyoğlu Preservation Area and its three neighbourhoods (Cihangir, Karaköy and Tarlabaşı).

Output (6): An alternative approach to the regeneration of the Tarlabaşı neighbourhood. The intention behind the development of this approach was to develop a greater sensitivity to the existing social and spatial characteristics of the neighbourhood than the destructive approach developed by the Istanbul Metropolitan Municipality and Beyoğlu Municipality. The main objective was to produce draft plan proposals for ground floor use, user-profile and tenure-type allocation which would create a mixed-use + mixed-user profile + mixed-income Tarlabaşı, whilst preserving the existing patterns of ground loor use in the neighbourhood. This output of the thesis was generated through Implementation (2), which aimed to investigate Research Question (3): how could this 'relational urban knowledge' support architects, urban designers or urban planners whilst developing intervention proposals for urban regeneration? The approach was first developed in theoretical terms, then the draft plan proposals were generated using a computational process which is described below. This output of the thesis contributes to the ongoing discussion on how to approach the problem of urban regeneration in Tarlabaşı in particular and in inner-city contexts in general.

Output (7): A computational process which generates draft plans for ground floor use, user-profile and tenure-type allocation, using GIS and data mining functionalities with evolutionary computation. This output of the thesis was generated by Implementation (2), which aimed to investigate Research Question (3). The overall process involved the successive application of Naïve Bayes Classification, Association Rule Analysis and an Evolutionary Algorithm to a subset of the Beyoğlu Preservation Area Building Features Database representing the Tarlabaşı neighbourhood. Briefly, the findings of the data mining analysis were used to formulate a set of rules for assigning ground floor use information to the buildings. These rules were then used for fitness measurements of an Evolutionary Algorithm, together with other fitness measurements for assigning user-profile and tenure-type information (defined by the author according to the regeneration approach described above in Output (6)). As a result, the algorithm transformed the existing ground floor use allocation plan of the Beyoğlu Preservation Area in accordance with the given rules and assigned user-profile and tenure-type information for each building. This computational process demonstrated one way to use the data mining analysis findings in generating intervention proposals for urban regeneration. A similar computational process can be carried out in other urban contexts by researchers and practitioners. To the best of our knowledge, no prior research has used data mining analysis findings for fitness measurements of an Evolutionary Algorithm in order to produce draft plans for ground floor use, user-profile and tenure-type allocation. This is, therefore, the most original scientific contribution and utilizable output of the thesis.

Output (8): A set of strategic urban intervention ideas/proposals for the regeneration of Tarlabaşı, developed by students. This output of the thesis was generated by Implementation (3), which also aimed to investigate Research Question (3); How could this 'relational urban knowledge' support architects, urban designers or urban planners whilst developing intervention proposals for urban regeneration? However, in this case the investigation was carried out in an educational workshop. Students made use of data mining methods, together with parametric urban analysis techniques, to produce urban intervention proposals for the regeneration of Tarlabaşı. Like Output (6), this output of the thesis also contributes to the ongoing discussion on how to approach the problem of urban transformation in Tarlabaşı in particular and in inner-city contexts in general.

Evaluation Phase: This phase involved a critical review of each implementation and a general evaluation of the entire research. Critical reviews were carried out to identify the achievements and shortcomings of each implementation there was also a discussion of what could have been done to improve the implementations. Furthermore, a more general evaluation was carried out to conclude the research, examining how the research questions were investigated, reviewing the outputs of the thesis and scientific and societal contributions of this study, and discussing the limitations of the approach and highlighting possible paths for future research.

As a result of the research, on the basis of the data that is available in the thematic maps of the Beyoğlu Preservation Area, the potential of a knowledge discovery approach to urban analysis in revealing the relationships between various components of urban environments and their various attributes is demonstrated. It was also demonstrated that these relationships can reveal site-specific characteristics of urban environments and if found 'valuable' by the targeted researchers and practitioners, these can lead to the development of more informed intervention proposals. Thus the major societal contribution of this thesis is that it demonstrates that implementing a knowledge discovery approach to urban analysis which uses data mining may help to improve the quality of built environments by helping the achitects, urban designers or urban planners to develop insights into situations before proposing any intervention.

§ 1.4 Overview of the Thesis

Following the Introduction, Chapter 2 describes the shifting perspectives in urban theory and analysis methods by examining an Urban Studies Timeline designed by the author. This timeline includes important texts, facts, events, scientific developments and planning and design proposals that have been influential in the development of urban studies since the 1880s. Examination of this timeline generated a number of inferences on the evolution of urban studies, including how the approaches, objectives and focal points have transformed over time and the most recent research paths. Through these inferences, the chapter aims to determine the ongoing problems in the field and the possible contributions of developing a knowledge discovery approach to urban analysis using data mining.

Chapter 3 presents the generic concept of knowledge discovery in databases. This is the term used to describe the process of discovering useful knowledge from raw data. Data mining is the major component in this process, employing an advanced set of computational methods and techniques for data analysis. Previous applications of knowledge discovery in databases (by architects, urban planners, urban geographers and social scientists) are briefly mentioned. The concept of knowledge discovery in databases is introduced through its various definitions, and some general information on data mining is provided, based on the types of data that can be mined, types of relationships and patterns to be discovered, the methods and techniques used, and pattern validity measures. Finally, the data mining methods and operators employed in this thesis are presented.

Chapter 4 focuses on the investigation of the Research Question (1) and describes the details of the approach developed in this thesis, namely a knowledge discovery approach to urban analysis through data mining, by establishing its conceptual basis (the city as a 'data mine') and introducing the model designed to implement it (the KDPM for urban analysis combining GIS and data mining). The city as 'data mine' concept aims to fill the gap that was identified in the literature review. There is a need to research the multi-dimensional properties of cities by investigating the relational aspects of components of the urban environments, focusing on micro-scale data. The city is therefore described as a 'data mine' that consists of micro-scale data and contains hidden interrelations between the multiple dimensions of its components. The KDPM for urban analysis, which combines GIS and data mining, provides a means of analysing these aspects of the city. This model enables qualitative and quantitative data gathered from the cities to be stored, represented and analyzed in order to explore 'relational urban knowledge' which can support the development of urban intervention proposals. A theoretical background is provided to clarify the meaning of the term 'relational'. As the research focuses on the discovery of patterns and relationships in urban analysis, a brief theoretical background is also provided to clarify the similarities and differences between this approach and the 'relational thinking' mainly associated with post-structuralist theories of urban geography.

Chapter 5 focuses on the implementation of the KDPM in urban analysis. Three implementations are performed to validate the model and the approach. The model is tested by building a micro-scale GIS database of the Beyoğlu Preservation Area, based mainly on the cartographic/thematic urban analysis maps provided with the Master

Plan for the Beyoğlu Preservation Area, and is first implemented through a comparative study that explores patterns and relationships between features of buildings in the Beyoğlu Preservation Area and its three neighbourhoods, Cihangir, Karaköy, and Tarlabaşı. This implementation enabled Research Question (2) to be investigated. The model is then implemented a second time through a case study in combination with an evolutionary process, with the aim of developing an alternative approach to the regeneration of Tarlabaşı, and a final time in combination with parametric urban analysis techniques in an international workshop in which students aimed to develop urban intervention scenarios for the regeneration of Tarlabaşı. The last two implementations enabled Research Question (3) to be investigated by illustrating how could this 'relational urban knowledge' support architects, urban designers or urban planners whilst developing intervention proposals for urban regeneration.

Chapter 6 concludes the thesis by evaluating its outputs, scientific and societal contributions and limitations. It also sets an agenda for future research in two directions: research in City Information Modeling (CIM) and research in data mining non-conventional urban data (data types that cannot be represented in traditional data tables, e.g. images, texts etc.).

This introductory chapter has provided detailed explanations of the problems and motivations behind the research, its main goal and the research questions addressed to achieve this goal. It then explains the method used to conduct the research and concludes with an overview of the thesis.

Before moving on to the details of the research, it is important to note that knowledge discovery can be accomplished using a variety of methods (i.e. with or without the use of a computer). Within the scope of this thesis, the term 'Knowledge Discovery' is defined in a specific sense as the extraction of knowledge in the form of patterns and relationships through the analysis of a database using data mining methods.

2 Shifting perspectives in urban studies

This chapter presents a brief overview of how the perspectives in the main fields related to urban studies, namely urban theory, urban analysis, urban design and planning, have transformed over time. Undertaking a literature survey of this kind, which does not focus solely on quantitative urban analysis, highlights the importance of constructing a conceptual background for this research which applies an analytical approach. Accordingly, Chapter 4 proposes the concept of the city as a 'data mine' and a brief theoretical examination is also carried out, speculating on a possible convergence between a knowledge discovery approach to urban analysis using data mining and the 'relational thinking' mainly associated with post-structuralist theories of cities. Conducting a literature survey that covers the wide area of urban studies also led to inferences about how a knowledge discovery approach to urban analysis using data mining can contribute, not only to the field of quantitative urban analysis but also to the field of urban studies in general terms.

§ 2.1 An Overview of Shifting Perspectives in Urban Studies

The literature survey section of this thesis reviews the texts, facts, events, scientific developments and planning and design proposals that have been most influential in the development of urban studies since the 1880s, showing the diversity of approaches to the study of the city, its conceptualization, analysis and design and planning. This investigation:

- Covers texts from diverse fields such as urban analysis, urban design, urban planning, urban geography, and urban sociology;
- Includes important facts and events, such as the founding of associations or journals;
- Includes scientific developments which have a direct effect on quantitative studies of the city as well as its conceptualization;
- Comprises planning and design proposals, which are especially common in the first half of the 20th century.

Three main rationales underpin this chapter:

1. In general terms, what differentiates the contributions of a knowledge discovery approach to urban analysis using data mining from other approaches included in the urban studies timeline?
2. How could a knowledge discovery approach to urban analysis using data mining contribute to the other approaches in general terms?
3. How could a knowledge discovery approach to urban analysis using data mining contribute to the knowledge domain of urban studies in general? Is there a gap to be filled?

These questions will be reviewed at the end of this chapter.

An urban studies timeline designed to systematize the literature survey and show the evolution of urban studies i.e. how the approaches, objectives, and focal points have transformed over time. It includes a chronological sequence of events that were influential in the history of urban studies, presented in Appendix A. It is important to note that this urban studies timeline is based on a personal selection and therefore there may be more material to be included.

A number of inferences are derived from the urban studies timeline. These inferences refer to the contents of the urban studies timeline in Appendix A.

Inference (1). Urban studies is a highly multidisciplinary research field because of the multi-dimensional (architectural, social, economic, cultural, political, etc.) nature of the city. This is highlighted by H. Lefebvre (1970), who argues that inter-disciplinary cooperation is essential for studying urban phenomena which cannot be grasped by any specialized science. However, most of the time the different disciplines active in the field of urban studies adopt a domain-specific approach to conceptualising, analysing and developing strategies and formulas for managing and shaping the city. Moreover, there is clearly no consensus in each discipline, and diverse opinions and approaches develop in parallel. On the other hand, inter-disciplinary cooperation is not an easy task: H. Lefebvre (1970) argues that inter- and multi-disciplinary efforts have largely failed and have produced some artificial syntheses.

Inference (2). The city is constantly evolving, driven by micro- and macro- dynamics, which makes it hard for the various disciplines to understand and explain the nature of this complex system. Existing approaches, models, analyses, and planning and design methods soon become invalid or inadequate because of the ever-changing urban conditions and the emergence of new urban phenomena.

It is, therefore, fully acknowledged that it is extremely hard or even impossible to construct a comprehensive and sustainable framework that can conceptualize and analyze the city without simplifying its multi-dimensional complex nature. Nevertheless, this thesis still proposes a knowledge discovery approach to urban analysis using data mining that can be applied to gather new and useful knowledge about the city.

Inference (3). In urban studies, the most frequent approaches are those concerned with the physical structure of the city, which focus on issues such as the morphological, typological, geometric, visual and architectural aspects of the layout of the city. Some of those form-based approaches are concerned with explaining the history of the city and urban phenomena, focusing solely on physical developments. Others are concerned with conceptualizing and analyzing its physical aspects, developing formulas for planning and designing the layout of the city.

Inference (4). Most of the form-based approaches in urban studies, which are concerned with explaining the history of the city and urban phenomena based on the physical developments, adopt a linear understanding of time: the development of the city form over time is essential. Such approaches can be traced in the works of Mumford (1961), Spriergegen (1965), Moholy-Nagy (1968), Kostof (1991) and Hall (1998) (see Appendix A [23], [28], [31], [62], [74]). An alternative view can be found in Patrick Geddes's work (1915), which adopted an evolutionary approach to the physical development of the city and explained the foundations of urban growth based on Darwin's theory of natural selection (see Appendix A [8]).

Inference (5). In urban studies, the form-based approaches concerned with conceptualizing and analyzing the physical aspects of the city and developing formulas for planning and designing the form of the city are diverse in focus. Some scholars, such as Camillo Sitte (1945), Thomas Cullen (1961) and Gordon Cullen (1985), mainly concentrated on the artistic aspects of the city (see Appendix A [2], [25], [57]) whereas others, such as Arturo Soria y Mata (Linear City), Tony Garnier (Une Cite Industrielle), Le Corbusier (Radiant City), Ludwig Hilberseimer (The Hochhausstadt), Sir Leslie Patrick Abercrombie and John Henry Forshaw (the Country of London Plan), Otto Wagner (1896) and Percy Johnson-Marshall (1966) adopted a modernist and rational perspective (see Appendix A [3], [4], [6], [10], [12], [14], [16], [18], [30]). Park, Burgess, and McKenzie (1925), for instance, emphasized visual aspects of the city and constructed a theory of urban ecology shaped by forces of Darwinian evolution (see Appendix A [11]). Wirth (1938) introduced a sociological definition of the city (see Appendix A [15]). The city was also conceptualized as a human ecosystem in the works of scholars such as Doxiadis (1968) and Marshall (2009) (see Appendix A [33], [87]). There is also an important number of studies based on the concepts, tools, and quantitative methods of the hard sciences, including works of Batty and Longley (1994), Batty (1976) and (2005), P. Allen (1997) and Portugali (2011) (see Appendix A [42], [66], [72], [81], [89]). Moreover, there are some form-based approaches which cannot be easily categorized and can therefore be considered unique approaches, such as the works of Howard (1946), Lynch (1960), Archigram, Alexander (1965, 1987), Krier (1979), Hillier and Hanson (1984) (see Appendix A [5], [21], [22], [26], [29], [44], [45], [46], [47], [50], [54], [60]).

Inference (6). It is not possible to claim that form-based approaches totally exclude other aspects of the city, such as social, economic, or cultural dimensions: some form-based approaches are concerned with other dimensions of the city as well. Although they essentially focus on the physical aspects of the city, they adopt a unique perspective. Krier (1979), for instance, rejected the imposition of aesthetic criteria in analyzing urban form (see Appendix A [47]); Lynch (1960) and (1981) took human perception as the basis for evaluating the form of the city, whilst Boyer (1994) emphasized emotions, daily life and collective memory (see Appendix A [21], [50], [56]). Moreover, the individual works of Alexander (1965, 1979, 1987) and some of his works produced with colleagues (Alexander et al., 1977; Alexander, Silverstein, Angel, Ishikawa, & Abrams, 1975) focused on the complexity of physical urban patterns and the processes that create the form of the city (see Appendix A [29], [41], [44], [46], [60]). Hillier and Hanson (1984) based their work on the syntactic organization of the form of the city (see Appendix A [54]). However, most of the form-based approaches generally assume that physical interventions can solve social, economic, or even cultural problems This approach is called "architectural determinism" and is especially prominent in Modernist approaches to urban planning and design, which are based on socialist ideas such as 'Une Cite Industrielle' - the Modernist proposal for utopian city design - by Tony Garnier (see Appendix A [6]). Modernist approaches usually establish a unidirectional relationship between the spatial and social dimensions of the city, assuming that physical and functional planning can create a new social order.

Inference (7). "Architectural determinism" (see Appendix A [3], [4], [5], [6], [10], [12], [16], [18]) in urban studies, as seen in the works of Wagner (1896), Le Corbusier (1933) and Howard (1946) for instance, prevailed for a long time without facing any criticism. In the 1960s, as Modernism waned (see Appendix A [20], [37], [53]) a few key texts appeared, such as Jacobs (1961), Alexander (1965) and Henri Lefebvre (1970) (see Appendix A [24], [29], [36], [41]), and there was also a general move away from reductionist methods of science due to the establishment of general systems theory in 1968 (see Appendix A [35]). This was how an era of rigorous criticism of Modernist approaches to urban studies began, and new approaches such as those of Doxiadis (1968), Krier (1979), Rowe and Koetter (1978) and many others emerged (see Appendix A [21], [22], [29], [33], [41], [44], [45], [46], [47], [50]). Later on, "Architectural determinism" was also associated with top-down approaches (see Appendix A [2], [3,] [4], [5], [6], [10], [11], [12], [14], [18]) in planning, in which planning is undertaken by a central authority and considered solely as an exercise in technical expertise, ignoring political links and social relevance. Even though the top-down approach to planning is seriously criticized today, planning practice is still dominated by top-down theories and is frequently applied worldwide, especially in non-developed or developing countries. The inability of this approach to foresee and fight social, economic, cultural and spatial problems such as spatial and social segregation, poverty and social exclusion resulted in the emergence of bottom-up approaches, which are particularly emphasized in the works of Jacobs (1961), Alexander's individual works (1965, 1987) and some the works he produced with colleagues (Alexander et al., 1977; Alexander et al., 1975) (see Appendix A [24], [29], [41], [44], [46]). Bottom-up planning is an approach governed by local authorities instead of the central government and enables local residents to participate in the planning and decision-making process. Alongside the bottom-up approaches, strategic planning and community development, which can be found in the 'Towards an Urban Renaissance report' by Richard Rogers (1999) or in the work of Healey (2007), gained acceptance by the end of 1990s (see Appendix A [76], [84]). More recently, the arguments of Marshall (2009) concerning the impossibility of planning the city due to its dynamic and complex nature has also started to be discussed (see Appendix A [87]).

Inference (8). Since the 1960s, there has also been a shift in the scale of interest in planning; the macro scale has yielded to the micro, as emphasized in particular in the works of major scholars such as Lynch (1960), Jacobs (1961) and Alexander (1965). An approach to designing the micro components of the city form (paths, edges, nodes, landmarks, and districts) is proposed by Lynch (see Appendix A [21]), the importance of neighbourhood scale and localities was emphasized by Jacobs (see Appendix A [24]), and an approach based on designing the micro-scale patterns of the city was constructed by Alexander (see Appendix A [44], [46]). Collage City by Rowe and Koetter (1978) (see Appendix A [45]) and Urban Space by Krier (1979) (see Appendix A [47]) are among the important works that contain a strong sense of the importance of the micro-scale in designing and planning cities.

Inference (9). By the 1960s, simplistic urban planning concepts which focused on the arrangements of buildings had become outdated and new concepts and strategies specific to the city, such as 'mixed-use' (see Appendix A [24], [65]), 'planning at neighbourhood level' (see Appendix A [24], [75]), 'encouraging walkability and non-car transport' (see Appendix A [24], [65], [76]), 'designing on a human-scale' (Appendix A [24], [65]), 'organicness and wholeness of the city' (see Appendix A [59]), 'community-based planning and participation' (see Appendix A [41], [44], [65], [76]), "improving sustainability" (see Appendix A [65], [76]) and 'design-led urbanism' (see Appendix A [76]) started to appear and gain importance in urban design. For example, 'land use zoning and functional separation of daily activities' started to be criticized, whilst the importance of the concept of 'mixed-use planning' in creating vibrant neighbourhoods began to be emphasized, as seen in Jane Jacobs's (1961) groundbreaking book (see Appendix A [24]).

Inference (10). The social and political relevance of urban planning was first mentioned in the 1970s with the rise of Marxist approaches to urban geography, particularly in the works of Castells (1972; 1989; 1996), Harvey (1973; 1982; 1985; 1996; 2008), Tafuri (1976) and Dickens (1981) (see Appendix A[38], [40], [43], [51], [52], [58], [61], [67], [70], [83], [86]). Urban problems started to be analyzed from a Marxist perspective, criticizing the capitalist structuring of urban space, society and the economy, and their interrelations. The roots of Marxist approaches can be traced back to the "Frankfurt School" (see Appendix A [9]), which introduced an interpretation of architecture as a "code language for processes taking place in society" (Held, 1980). Problems originating in capitalist ideology, such as the "lack of social justice" Harvey (1973) (see Appendix A [40]), "instrumentalization of architectural practice as a tool of ideological pressure" Tafuri (1976) (see Appendix A [43], [51]), "overproduction and overconsumption", "social control through urban planning" Harvey (1982) (see Appendix A [52]), and the "invaded right of the citizens to shape their environments" Harvey (2008) (see Appendix A [86]) are widely discussed in the works of the Marxist urban scholars. By the end of the 1980s, the restructuring of capitalism due to the rise of ICTs resulted in globalization, the new research focus of Marxist scholars such as M. Castells (1989; 1996), who mainly focus on the dramatic change in spatial forms and the social structure of the 'information age' (see Appendix A [61], [70]).

Inference (11). By the end of the 1970s, the move beyond formal and functionalist approaches in urban studies gathered pace and new topics started to emerge: the cultural properties of urban space and its symbolic and semiotic content (Appleyard, 1979) (see Appendix A [48]), the meaning of places (Norberg-Schulz, 1980) and the existential dimension of architecture and the city (Perez-Gomez, 1983) (see Appendix A [49], [55]), the collective memory of the city (Boyer, 1994) (see Appendix A [56]), and recovering architecture from its ideological and capitalist ties (Tschumi, 1996) (see Appendix A [69]) became important lines of research alongside the Marxist perspective.

Inference (12). In its most general sense, urban analysis is applied to obtain knowledge of the urban subject under investigation. Gathering, organizing and analyzing any type of data or information gathered from the city and city dwellers and representing, visualizing and evaluating the findings of the analysis all fall within the scope of urban analysis.

The publication of the first Ordnance Survey map (see Appendix A [1]) was an important phase in the development of urban analysis: traditional urban mapping emerged as a tool to guide urban planning. The need for land regulations emerged as a result of the great economic and social developments that occurred as a consequence of the Industrial Revolution which, in turn, led to the development of new techniques and methods for representing, analyzing and managing cities. Therefore, in the field of urban analysis, analytical tools, together with cartographic representations, began to be applied to support urban planning and decision-making.

As the urban studies timeline shows, quantitative methods which applied mathematical and statistical techniques borrowed from physicists, social scientists and economists to geographical data had begun to be implemented by the 1950s. In fact, the period between the 1950s and 1960s is described as the 'quantitative revolution' by Burton (1963) (see Appendix A [26], [27]). In December 1954, the Regional Science Association (see Appendix A [17]), founded by a group of academics from economics, geography, city planning, political science, rural sociology and American spatial science at the Universities of Washington and Iowa, and later Chicago, Northwestern, Michigan and Ohio, led by economist Walter Isard, marked the beginning of the quantitative revolution (Barnes, 2000, 2003).

In addition to the quantitative trend, the urban studies timeline also shows that the variety of subjects analyzed has increased over time, though it was essentially the physical aspects of the city form which were considered important. By the 1960s, social, economic, cultural, behavioural and cognitive aspects also started to be studied and analyzed. This meant that more attributes of cities were captured and analyzed, both qualitatively and quantitatively. Whereas qualitative analysis focused on non-quantifiable/soft aspects of cities, quantitative analysis focused on the topological, geometric and geographic properties of spatial entities.

Within the quantitative trend, mathematical approaches tailored for spatial data, such as spatial autocorrelation, spatial interpolation, and spatial regression, started to be used, together with descriptive and inferential statistics, and geostatistics emerged as an offshoot of statistics. The particular characteristics of spatial data gave rise to the development of multi-dimensional approaches, implying that a certain variable is characterized by a number of elements, usually measured in different dimensions. Many methods (multivariate statistics) for analyzing multi-dimensional data in urban and geographical research were developed in the 1970s, such as pattern and impact analysis, interdependence analysis, multidimensional scaling analysis, correspondence analysis, canonical analysis, spatial correlation, multidimensional optimization, multicriteria models and interactive decision models.

Alongside the developments in statistical methods, Geographic Information Science-GIS (a synthesis of cartography, statistical analysis and database technology) was introduced in the late 1960s and commercialized in the late 1980s and 1990s (see Appendix A [32]).

The late 1990s are described as the period of data science (Han & Kamber, 2006), resulting from the enormous increase in data enabled by developments in data capturing and storing technologies. This range of data triggered the birth of knowledge discovery through data mining (see Appendix A [59]), a new advanced set of computational methods and techniques for data analysis fed by database technology, artificial intelligence, machine learning, neural networks, statistics, pattern recognition, knowledge-based systems, knowledge acquisition, information retrieval, high performance computing and data visualization (Han & Kamber, 2001).

Recently, the rise of data science has boosted quantitative urban analysis and a new line of research often called urban analytics or urban informatics has emerged. Academic interest in this topic is growing and new research programmes are being offered by leading universities and research institutions (see for example: http://cities.media.mit.edu/about/cities, http://ual.berkeley.edu/, http://mscsmartcities.org/msc-smart-cities/). Urban analytics research mainly focuses on how new advanced analytical methods can be used to improve our understanding of cities in order to make more informed decisions in urban design and planning processes. Two main factors differentiate urban analytics from previous quantitative data analysis approaches:

1. In addition to conventional methods, urban analytics employs more sophisticated data analysis methods (e.g. data mining), involving more types (often complex data types) and large amounts of data. Due to the developments in large-scale computing, our capacity to both generate and collect data has increased enormously and we are now surrounded by a tremendous amount of data and information gathered from cities. The massive amount of both structured (highly organized and readily processed by computers) and unstructured data (which is not organized and needs to be transformed into structured data to be 'understood' by computers), which is difficult to process using traditional database technologies and analytical approaches is often referred as 'Big Data'. Urban analytics usually concentrates on the analysis of 'Big Data' which is collected mainly by the systems that pervade everyday life in cities such as traffic lights and lifts, car park barriers, central heating boilers, security systems in buildings, burglar and fire alarms, accounting software, vehicle fleet maintenance systems, local authority revenue systems, child protection registers, benefit systems, emergency service communication systems, medical equipment, mobile phones, internet, radios, etc. (Nigel Thrift, 2002a). These systems generate data on how people live in cities. Augmented reality interfaces, social computing, computational abilities embedded in clothing and furniture are other important generators of urban data and personal information (Nigel Thrift & French, 2002b).
2. The essence of urban analytics lies in building a data-driven approach to urban analysis, design and planning. In other words, the task of making decisions is based on data and data analytics, often referred to as evidence-based decision-making. Urban analytics researchers study data-driven approaches that can empower us to build better cities. The concept of the "smart city" is directly associated with urban analytics research. By referring to Harrison et al. (2010), Batty et al. (2012, p. 484) mentions that:
The concept of the 'smart city' emerged during the last decade as a fusion of ideas about how ICT might improve the functioning of cities, by improving their efficiency, enhancing their competitiveness and providing new ways to address the problems of poverty, social deprivation and poor environments.

Sassen (2011) refers to the concept of the smart city as intelligent city and instant city. On one hand Sassen (2011) gets excited that smart technologies embedded in cities can guide the management of major urban systems such as the transport, clean energy, water, garbage and security. On the other hand she gets worried that tracking technologies would create a censored city. Indeed, ICT has already seriously transformed cities in architectural, economic, social and cultural terms (Sökmenoğlu & Çağdaş, 2006). The worldwide trend towards the "smart city" shows that these transformations will increase further and that ICT will play a major role in operating the cities of future (Aurigi, 2005).

Moreover, the rise of systems theory in the late 1960s (see Appendix A [35]) and complexity science in the early 1990s (see Appendix A [64]) have also affected the analysis of spatial data and led to the establishment of geocomputation (see Appendix A [68]) in the mid 1990s, an interdisciplinary area employing non-conventional data analysis techniques that differ from statistical methods (computational-intensive techniques such as genetic algorithms, artificial neural networks, cellular automata and agent-based systems).

One of the most recent developments in the field of urban analysis is the concept of CIM (see Appendix A [80]). CIM does not exist yet as a platform but is a conceptual idea that describes an adaptation of the BIM (Building Information Modeling) for cities. CIM, as a concept, first appeared in 2005, and was described by Khemlani (2005) as:

An extension of the BIM concept to neighbourhood and city level which is able to capture all the critical data relating to a city's geographical location, topology, major roads, bridges, buildings, etc. within an intelligent format, creating a highly accurate and detailed digital replica which can be subjected to sophisticated analysis and simulations to support more holistic decision-making.

Conceptually, CIM can be defined as a support platform for urban analysis, design and decision-making, integrating physical, economic, social and environmental attributes as well as the spatial and temporal dimensions of the city. Since then, the concept of CIM as well as UIM (Urban Information Modeling) has begun to be used, and a small number of researchers, such as Hamilton et al. (2005), Gil, Beirão, Montenegro, and Duarte (2010), Beirao, Montenegro, and Arrobas (2012) and Stojanovski (2013) are working on the concept.

Inference (13). The extension of the "quantitative revolution" in geography to the field of urban planning mainly took the form of urban modelling, i.e. the "representation of urban reality through systems of mathematical relationships" (Bernstein & Mellon, 1978) Spatial modelling is concerned with constructing mathematical models to predict spatial outcomes and can be seen as a natural extension of spatial analysis, focussing mainly on employing statistical techniques to interrogate spatial data

(O'Sullivan & Unwin, 2003). The 1970s is described as an explosion in the use of quantitative methods in planning via urban modelling (see Appendix A [39], [42]). Bernstein and Mellon (1978) argue that this explosion took place when it was seen that quantitative methods used in business or military-oriented research are not appropriate for applying in urban research and it was also around that time that urban researchers were not satisfied with the traditional methods of planning and urban urban management. The roots of urban modelling can be traced back to the late 19th century with the emergence of the Location Theory, but since the 1950s it has made use of three distinct sets of techniques: macro-static models (1960-1970), aggregate dynamics (1970-1980s) and, since the 1990s, models based on cells (cellular automata) and agents (agent-based) (Batty, 2008). Modelling techniques have evolved from static to dynamic, from aggregate to disaggregate (modelling individuals instead of the population as a whole), from macro to micro and from deterministic to stochastic (Batty, 2008).

Inference (14). A 'relational approach' to urban studies, which focuses on the "interrelations running through different spatial scales" (Massey, 1998) (see Appendix A [73]) instead of studying only the physical space of the city, has taken over from the object-based approach which focuses on the design of buildings and urban planning through the arrangements of the buildings in urban space (see Appendix A [3]). This represents a shift in focus from unidirectional relationships between the physical and social dimensions of the city, which assumes that physical and functional planning can solve social problems (see Appendix A [13]) or vice versa (see Appendix A [51]), to bidirectional ones, which assumes that spatial and social dimensions are intertwined and influence each other and the shape of the city (See Appendix A [15] and [63]). The study of interrelations between the physical and social dimensions of the city has now become central to many contemporary urban studies. The establishment of general systems theory (see Appendix A [35]) in the late 1960s, which introduced the idea of studying systems without reducing them to their parts, focusing instead on the relations between parts, may have had an influence on the rise of the 'relational approach' in urban studies.

Inference (15). By the 1990s, the notion that the city is not a static object but is in constant transformation gained importance in urban concepts and analysis. In other words, there was a shift from a static-passive to a dynamic-active concept of space. This shift is particularly observed in post-structuralist approaches to urban studies in several arguments, such as the impossibility of representing urban space due to its ever-changing composition (Nigel Thrift, 1999) (see Appendix A [75]), and the idea of the inseparability of time and space which counters the notion of society as a kind of 2D or 3D slice moving through time (Massey, 1992) (see Appendix A [63]).

Inference (16). Even though the mapping of the cities had begun by the early 1800s (see Appendix A [1]), the profession of town planning was only institutionalized and recognized as a distinctive area of expertise in 1914 in the United Kingdom (see Appendix A [7]). It took 40 years for urban design to move away from urban planning and become an independent field of research and practice: 'urban design' was first used as a distinctive term at the 1st Conference of Urban Design in the USA (see Appendix A [19]) and it took another 40 years for urban design to acquire an international journal (see Appendix A [71]). The reason for this delay may be due to the multi-disciplinary nature of the field, given that each individual discipline could publish its research in its domain-specific journals without the need for a journal that focused solely on the field of urban design.

Inference (17). The failure of the domain-specific approaches of diverse disciplines to solve urban problems makes cooperation between the various disciplines necessary. Thus, there was a shift away from single-discipline perspectives towards interdisciplinary ones from the 1950s onwards, with the rise of spatial science. The establishment of the Regional Science Association (see Appendix A [17]), for instance, is an indicator of this trend. In the case of the spatial sciences, this convergence mostly materialized by adopting hard science methods in urban studies, as examined by Portugali (2011) (see Appendix A [89]), although there may be other ways to establish alternative collaborations, as explored by Nigel Thrift (2002a) (see Appendix A [79]). This is, in fact, one of the major challenges for the forthcoming years, reflected in the founding of the interdisciplinary journal of Urban Design and Planning in 2008 (see Appendix A [85]).

Inference (18). The divergence between urban theory and practice has been evident since the appearance of the first books on urban studies, although this issue first began to be criticized in the early 1960s, and it is nowadays seen as a major obstacle to solving urban problems. Some scholars, such as Bunge (1962) and Harvey (1969), criticized the lack of a scientific theoretical approach based on quantitative methods (see Appendix A [26], [34]), while others, such as Jacobs (1961) and Alexander (1965; 1979), claimed that this divergence arises from the oversimplified study of urban phenomena using deterministic methods (see Appendix A [24], [29], [46]), a lack of urban epistemology, as claimed by Henri Lefebvre (1970) (see Appendix A [36]), or an appropriate normative theory for cities as argued by (Lynch, 1981) (see Appendix A [50]), or a disregard for the qualitative aspects and multi-dimensionality of urban environments, as discussed by scholars such as Doxiadis (1968), Henri Lefebvre (1970), Rowe and Koetter (1978) and Appleyard (1979) (see Appendix A [33], [36], [45], [48]).

The gap between urban theory and practice is even greater in the period of post-modern theories (Doel, 1999) (see Appendix A [78]), which strongly oppose deterministic methods of analysis that oversimplify the complex nature of urban environments.

One remarkable development that has the potential to create a new rapprochement between urban theory and practice is the rise of complexity science (see Appendix A [72], [77], [82], [88], [89]) together with ICT-based approaches (see Appendix A [79]). In this sense, smart city research (see Appendix A [90]) which explores ways of improving the functioning of cities and solving their social and spatial problems through the use of ICT, can be seen as a promising new line of research.

Computational intelligence is embedded into cities through a wide range of mobile, embedded, wearable, networked, distributed, and location-aware devices that collect data and information based on everyday experiences. This means that it is possible to collect an enormous variety of context-based data derived from social-spatial behaviour. Analysis of this type of non-conventional data can dramatically change our existing knowledge of the way in which cities function and offer insights into solving urban problems.

Complexity science, on the other hand, provides a totally new theoretical foundation and a new set of methods and techniques for studying cities beyond the traditional linear and reductionist approaches. The study area that addresses urban complexity by applying the complexity sciences has been termed "Complexity Theories of Cities" i.e. CTC (see Appendix A [82], [88], [89]). As also highlighted elsewhere (Portugali, 2006, 2011), Portugali (2012, pp. 60-61) claims that "CTC have the potential to bridge the two cultures of cities: the "quantitative" science of cities and the "qualitative" social theory-oriented study of cities". Portugali (2011, p. 101) states that CTC shares common ground with "social theory-oriented urban studies", which argue that the "human-urban domain" cannot be understood by scientific methods of positivism.

§ 2.2 Possible Contributions of a Knowledge Discovery Approach for Urban Studies

This section presents a discussion on the most general and conceptual level of how a knowledge discovery approach to urban analysis through data mining could be valuable for the domain of urban studies. More specific and technical information regarding this approach will be provided in the next section.

As the inferences derived from the urban studies timeline illustrate, the history of urban studies is the history of the shifting ideas in our understanding of 'the kind of thing a city is'. It should be also be acknowledged that the distinction between these different perspectives of cities is not always clear-cut: sometimes they intersect in certain ways, but differ in others. However, from our perspective, what is really important is that throughout the history of urban studies, urban theories and analytical methods have reciprocally framed the way in which we conceptualize and intervene in cities. In other words, there is always a close interrelation between how researchers conceptualize and analyze cities, although this is not always framed explicitly. It is important to draw up a framework for this relationship in order to contribute to the whole domain of urban studies. Therefore, this thesis not only considers applying an analytical approach in the domain of urban analysis, but also developing a conceptual background for this analytical approach. In addition, a brief theoretical survey was carried out to reveal the possible links between this approach and the most recent concepts highlighted by post-structuralist urban theories (see Chapter (4)). Thus, learning more about the interaction between the development of urban theories, analysis methods, planning and design practices provided a deeper insight into how the approach adopted in this thesis can contribute to the whole domain of urban studies, rather than just the field of quantitative urban analysis.

Returning to the questions raised at the beginning of this chapter:

– In general terms, what differentiates the contributions of a knowledge discovery approach to urban analysis using data mining from other approaches included in the urban studies timeline?

Most (qualitative or quantitative) urban analysis approaches and their theoretical backgrounds adopt perspectives with a particular focus which, to a certain extent, force the researcher to accept a series of predefined conditions. However, in principle, the knowledge discovery approach to urban analysis through data mining developed in this thesis does not restrict the researcher's perspective by imposing a certain direction in terms of 'what to focus on'. Since it is data-driven, such an approach might be considered to offer a substantially neutral analytical perspective that is free from predefined conditions and preconceptions. Rather than simply verifying a priori hypotheses, this approach may allow for an exploratory analysis with no a priori expectations of the nature of the relationships to be examined.

– How could a knowledge discovery approach to urban analysis using data mining contribute to the other approaches in general terms?

As previously discussed in the detailed analysis of the urban studies timeline, cities are multi-dimensional and a vast range of data can be gathered from them. In addition to hard facts (i.e. the quantifiable attributes) of cities, there are also "soft" aspects (i.e. qualitative attributes concerning social, cultural, behavioural, cognitive aspects, etc.), which are extremely important. Now that our capability to capture soft data has increased, thanks to the developments in ICT, the analysis of this type of soft data has become important. In principle, a knowledge discovery approach to urban analysis through data mining is able to deal with any type of qualitative and quantitative data, and may therefore support both qualitative and quantitative approaches to analyzing specific data types. Thus, a knowledge discovery approach to urban analysis through data mining may help the existing approaches to acquire more knowledge of the urban characteristics that they are exploring.

– How could a knowledge discovery approach to urban analysis using data mining contribute to the knowledge domain of urban studies in general? Is there a gap to be filled?

The analysis of the urban studies timeline shows that there is a general tendency to seek new methods to deal with the multi-dimensional properties of cities, investigate the relational aspects between components of urban environments, and focus on micro-scale data (see section (4.1) for more details). In principle, a knowledge discovery approach to urban analysis through data mining can be used to analyze relationships between large amounts and wide varieties of data. In addition, the findings of urban analysis are often criticized as inadequate in supporting the development of urban interventions. The findings of a knowledge discovery approach to urban analysis through data mining are, in general, capable of becoming readily operational. In these respects, this approach could provide important benefits for the general knowledge domain of urban studies.

§ 2.3 Conclusion

This chapter has provided an overview of the relevant literature. This enabled a conceptual background to be constructed for the analytical approach used in this study and inferences to be made concerning the possible contributions of applying a knowledge discovery approach to urban analysis through data mining for the whole domain of urban studies.

The next chapter provides technical information on the knowledge discovery approach through data mining, adapted to the problem of urban analysis addressed in this thesis.

3 A perspective for computational data analysis: knowledge discovery through data mining

Han and Kamber (2006) describe the 1950s-1990s, when most disciplines developed a third computational branch, as the period of computational science, and denote the period starting in 1990 as the period of data science. On the one hand, developments in computing and ICT allow us to capture, store and process massive quantities of data; on the other hand, making sense of the sheer amount of data constitutes one of the major challenges of the information age, which may be formulated as transforming data into information and information into knowledge (Gray, 2005). To distinguish between data and information, data can be defined as "recorded facts", whereas information can be described as "the set of patterns or expectations underlying the data" (Witten & Frank, 2005, p. 37). Databases contain an enormous amount of potentially important information waiting to be revealed. (Witten & Frank, 2005, p. xxiii). Knowledge discovery through Data Mining, also called Knowledge discovery in databases, emerged during the late 1980s and is a very promising and active research area which aims to reveal this hidden useful content in the form of patterns and relationships, and turn it into knowledge (the discovery of useful knowledge). Data mining is the main component of the Knowledge discovery in databases process and is popularly referred to as Knowledge discovery in databases. Data mining is defined by Gray (2005 p. v) as "the synthesis of statistics, machine learning, information theory, and computing; a solid science with a firm mathematical base and very powerful algorithmic tools". Han and Kamber (2001, p. 1) note that the development in information technologies naturally led to the science of data mining.

This chapter provides basic information on the process of knowledge discovery and introduces the goals and methods of data mining. It then explains the specific issues concerning data mining spatial data and provides a brief overview of a number of previous applications of data mining methods in urban studies. Finally, it describes the methods (i.e. classification, association rules and clustering analysis) and operators implemented used in this thesis and briefly reviews a number of studies that have used the same methods.

§ 3.1 Definitions of Knowledge Discovery through Data Mining

One of the most widely used definitions of knowledge discovery through data mining or knowledge discovery in databases is proposed by Fayyad, Piatetsky-Shapiro, and Smyth (1996a, p. 30) as the "nontrivial process of identifying valid, novel, potentially useful, and ultimately understandable patterns in data". According to Fayyad et al. (1996a, p. 39), knowledge discovery "refers to the overall process of discovering useful knowledge from data", and data mining is the key component, which "refers to a particular step in this process", namely the "application of specific algorithms for extracting" informative patterns and generalizable rules. Miller and Han (2001), on the other hand, define knowledge discovery approaches as the task of determining unknown patterns and relationships within large amounts of data that cannot be uncovered through simple queries or reports. Han and Kamber (2001, p. preface) note that data mining is popularly referred to as knowledge discovery in databases and involves the "automated or convenient extraction extraction of patterns representing knowledge implicitly stored or captured in large databases, data warehouses, the Web, other massive information repositories, or data streams.". Witten and Frank (2005, p. xxiii) define it as the "extraction of implicit, previously unknown, and potentially useful information from data" by building "computer programs that sift through databases automatically, seeking regularities or patterns". In a knowledge discovery process using data mining, the data is analysed by a software program running on a computer; it is either fully or semi-automated, i.e. the whole process may require human interaction and/or supervision.

Knowledge discovery in databases and data mining differ from classical statistics since they constitute a multidisciplinary field, closely linked to many areas such as database technology, artificial intelligence, machine learning, neural networks, statistics, pattern recognition, knowledge-based systems, knowledge acquisition, information retrieval, high performance computing and data visualization (Han & Kamber, 2001).

One key question concerns how data mining differs from statistics. According to Chawla, Shekhar, Wu, and Tan (2000), the major difference is that data mining, in exploring data, allows for the discovery of patterns that can lead to the formulation of new hypotheses, whereas statistics are used to validate or verify hypotheses. On the other hand, according to Witten and Frank (2005), we cannot isolate machine learning (one of the major fields contributing to data mining) from statistics, since there is a continuum in terms of data analysis techniques. Some data analysis techniques used in data mining are derived from standard statistics and others are more closely associated with machine learning, which has emerged from computer science Witten and Frank (2005). Witten and Frank (2005, p. 29) also argue that historically, statistics and machine learning have had rather different traditions, since "statistics has been more concerned with testing hypotheses, whereas machine learning has been more concerned with formulating the process of generalization as a search for possible hypotheses". However, they also note that this statement oversimplifies the scope of the both fields. Three important differences are:

- Algorithmic models applied in Data Mining treat the data mechanism as unknown. Breiman (2001, p. 200) argues that the relationships and information patterns found by algorithmic models used for data mining can be more reliable than data models typically applied in statistics,
- Data mining aims at tackling databases with huge amount of data consisting of a large number of instances and variables (or attributes),
- The form and the understandability of the results of data mining applications may be very different from conventional statistics. Some output formats, which can be easily translated into rules and parameters, may be more informative and supportive whilst developing urban intervention proposals.

Looking for patterns and relationships is not a new task; it is, in fact, the core of any human activity. However, it is becoming increasingly complicated to conduct these operations, given the incredible amount of data emerging from such a complex world. Hence, as the world grows in complexity, knowledge discovery in databases is becoming more and more popular in various fields of science and research. As Witten and Frank (2005, p. 5) note, knowledge discovery in databases has become our "only hope" for revealing the hidden patterns in databases. Witten and Frank (2005) also emphasize that information patterns found in databases can be of great importance since these can provide new and valuable insights.

According to the well-known definitions, a knowledge discovery process must discover valid patterns that have some degree of certainty, are previously unknown or new to the analyst, offer benefits to the user, can be understood by the user, cannot be revealed by simple queries or the human eye and can be automatically generated. Therefore, the basic goal of a knowledge discovery process through data mining is to generate evidence-based new insights that can be used in making decisions.

§ 3.2 The Knowledge Discovery Process and Data Mining as its Essential Component

Most of the approaches that have been proposed for the knowledge discovery process through data mining tend to be variations of the same scheme, consisting of an iterative sequence of the following steps: data preparation, data mining, evaluation of patterns and interpretation of these patterns (if found valid) as knowledge. The first basic process model was the one proposed by Fayyad et al. (1996b) which has subsequently been improved/modified or adapted by others for several application domains (see Cios, Pedrycz, Swiniarski, and Kurgan (2007) and Kurgan and Musilek (2006) for an overview of some other knowledge discovery process models). The basic steps in the knowledge discovery process defined by Fayyad et al. (1996b) are shown in Figure 3.1.

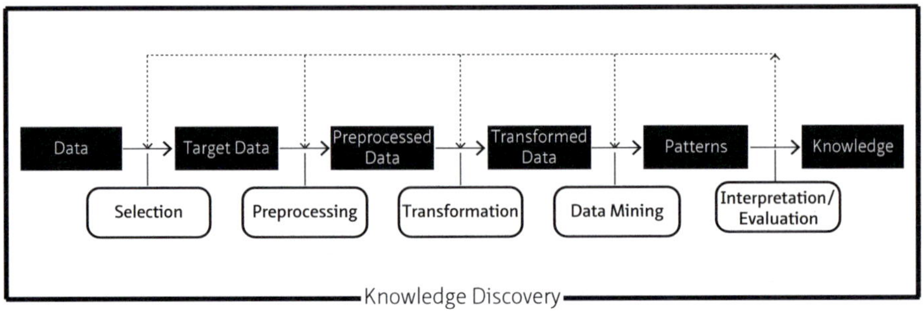

FIGURE 3.1 The basic steps in the knowledge discovery process, redrawn from Fayyad et al. (1996b, p. 41).

The knowledge discovery process depicted above involves the following five general steps: data selection, data pre-processing, data transformation, Data Mining, and interpretation/evaluation of the findings. A brief analysis of the knowledge discovery process will now be presented, based on Fayyad et al. (1996b) and Han and Kamber (2001):

Data Selection: The first step is the selection of data, involving identification of the target dataset and focusing on a subset of variables, on which the discovery methodology will be implemented. There are also some automated techniques for data reduction or 'focusing'.

Data Pre-processing: The second step concerns data cleaning and pre-processing. Basic operations include removing noise (incorrect data types, outliers), handling missing data fields, accounting for time-sequence information and known changes, (Fayyad et al., 1996b) and enhancement of data by combining the selected datasets with external data (Han & Kamber, 2001).

Data Transformation: The transformation step involves consolidating the data into forms appropriate for Data Mining. This step involves the reduction of data and its transformation, projection and aggregation (Fayyad et al., 1996b). In this step the analyst focuses on identifying the useful features which represent the data (Fayyad et al., 1996b). Dimensionality reduction or transformation methods help the analyst to decrease the number of variables, or to identify the invariant representations for the data (Fayyad et al., 1996b).

Data Mining: This is the essential step in the knowledge discovery process, in which advanced automated data analysis methods are applied to extract patterns in large and complex datasets. As Han and Kamber (2001) explain, the data mining step involves identifying the type of generic data pattern of interest and applying the matching data mining technique to explore this pattern. The particular pattern types, which can be searched by applying data mining techniques, are classes (objects sharing similar characteristics), associations (objects related to, or depending on, each other), rules, clusters (object grouping), outliers (inconsistent or distinct objects), and trends (Han & Kamber, 2001).

Interpretation and evaluation: This is the final step in the knowledge discovery process, involving representations and visualization of the extracted patterns and relationships or visualization of the data provided by the models. Patterns discovered by a data mining algorithm are evaluated as knowledge if determined as valid by the analyst. This step may also involve documenting the knowledge to further incorporate it into another system.

As noted by Fayyad et al. (1996b, p. 42), knowledge discovery in databases process is highly iterative and loops can occur between any two steps.

§ 3.3 Data Mining Goals and Methods

This section presents general information on data mining, based on the types of data that can be mined, types of relationships and patterns to be discovered, the methods and techniques used, and measures of pattern interestingness.

Data mining can be explored on the basis of the different types of data that can be mined. In principle, data mining can be performed on any type of information repository, such as relational databases, data warehouses, transactional databases, the World Wide Web, spatial databases, time-series databases, and text and multi-media databases. However, the challenges and techniques may differ for each system (Han & Kamber, 2001).

Data mining can be examined from the perspective of the type of patterns to be mined. According to Fayyad et al. (1996b, p. 43), "verification and discovery" are two main general goals in data mining. Verification occurs if the analyst implements data mining to verify a hypothesis and discovery occurs if he or she implements data mining for finding new information patterns. Fayyad et al. (1996b) add that the goal of discovery can be divided into prediction and description. Prediction, is concerned with seeking "for patterns for predicting the future behaviour of certain entities", whereas description is concerned with finding "patterns to present to the user in a human-understandable form." (Fayyad et al., 1996b, p. 43). The goals of prediction and description can be achieved using a variety of data mining methods, and there are various schemes for classifying data mining methods in the literature. The classifications used by Han and Kamber (2001) for the description of the main data mining methods are: characterization and discrimination (concept/class description), association analysis, classification and prediction, clustering, outlier analysis and evolution analysis.

Characterization and discrimination: Han and Kamber (2001) define characterization of data as the task of providing a summary of the general characteristics of the data class under study (target class). Han and Kamber (2001, p. 16) note that data discrimination involves comparing "the general features of a target class data object against the general features of objects from one or a set of contrasting classes."

Classification and prediction: Classification is defined by Han and Kamber (2001, p. 18) as "the process of finding a set of models (or functions) that describe and distinguish data classes or concepts" so that the model can predict the class of records with unknown class label. Classification can also be used to predict missing or unavailable values. Prediction is a different task than classification; it "may refer to both data value prediction and class label prediction" (Han & Kamber, 2001, p. 15). Decision trees, neural networks and Bayes classifiers are among the most widely used classification techniques (Duda, Hart, & Stork, 2000).

Association analysis: This is the discovery of Association Rules showing attribute-value conditions that frequently occur together in a database. Han and Kamber (2001) note that Association Rule Analysis is commonly used for market basket analysis which examines market customer buying habits in order to detect the sets of items that are frequently purchased together or in sequence.

Clustering: This method is different than classification and prediction. As noted by (Han & Kamber, 2001, p. 19) clustering can be used to generate previously unknown class labels. Clustering analysis groups objects according to the "principle of maximizing intraclass similarity and minimizing interclass similarity" (Han & Kamber, 2001, p. 20). In other words, clusters of objects are formed in such a way that objects in a cluster are very similar to each other but highly dissimilar to the objects gathered in other clusters (Han & Kamber, 2001, p. 20). (Han & Kamber, 2001) note that clustering can also be applied for building taxonomies.

Outlier analysis: This method is concerned with the detection of outliers, which is data that does not conform to the "general behaviour" of the data (Han & Kamber, 2001, p. 20).

Evolution analysis: This method is used to analyze how the behaviour of objects changes over time by looking for the regularities or trends. Han and Kamber (2001). It may include the clustering, classification, discrimination or characterization of time-based data but may also involve similarity based data analysis, sequence or periodicity pattern matching and time-series data analysis (Han & Kamber, 2001).

The most critical issue concerns how to measure pattern interestingness. A very large number of rules or patterns can be generated through a Data Mining analysis but not all of these outputs are interesting to the analyst (Han & Kamber, 2001). Han and Kamber (2001, p. 21) state that a pattern can be accepted as interesting on the basis of five main criteria: (1) if it is "easily understood by humans", (2) if it is "valid on new or test data with some degree of certainty", (3) if it is "potentially useful", (4) if it is "novel" and (5) if it "validates a hypothesis that the user sought to confirm". "An interesting pattern represents knowledge" Han and Kamber (2001, p. 21) and this depends on the interpretation of the analyst. Pattern interestingness can be objectively measured. Different measures (e.g., support, confidence and correlation) are used with different data mining analysis methods and these measures are generally adjustable by the analyst Han and Kamber (2001, p. 21). Following objective measures, subjective human judgement is needed to validate the results of knowledge discovery through data mining. It should also be noted that background knowledge of the application domain is crucial to guiding the knowledge discovery process. The types of patterns to be explored within a database and the evaluation criteria used to measure the interestingness of the patterns all depend on the knowledge domain that is used to guide the database knowledge discovery process.

§ 3.4 Data Mining with Spatial Data

Knowledge discovery is widely applied in many fields of science, engineering and business but also has applications in geographical information systems, remote sensing and many other areas related to spatial data, under the name of geographic knowledge discovery or spatial data mining. Spatial data mining uses the same functions as data mining, the main objective being to find information patterns in spatial databases.

Spatial databases include spatial and non-spatial information on spatial objects, i.e. entities related to space (Güting, 1994). Geographic space, which is the two-dimensional abstraction of (parts of) the surface of the earth, is the most typical example of space (Güting, 1994). Mining data related to geographic space is more difficult than mining traditional numerical and categorical data, due to the complexity of spatial data types, spatial relationships and spatial autocorrelation (Shekhar, Zhang, Huang, & Vatsavai, 2003). In spatial databases, spatial objects are represented by shape; points, lines and polygons. These spatial objects have non-spatial attributes (e.g., name, population, colour, material etc.) and spatial attributes (geographic coordinates, geometric features, spatial relationships). Three types of spatial relationships are defined by Güting (1994): topological (adjacent, inside, disjoin, etc.), distance (metric relationships) and direction (above, below, or north_ of, southwest_ of, etc.). Due to these relationships, spatial objects can affect each other (Bogorny, Palma, Engel, & Alvares, 2006). Moreover, "the values of the attributes of nearby spatial objects tend to systematically affect each other" and this is called spatial autocorrelation (Chawla, Shekhar, Wu, & Ozesmi, 2001, p. 1). The well-known first law of geography: "everything is related to everything else but nearby things are more related than distant things" (Tobler, 1979) refers to the concept of spatial autocorrelation. Mostly, databases do not "explicitly store" the spatial relationships of objects therefore these relationships need to be computed via "spatial operations" (Bogorny et al., 2006, p. 2). These relationships differentiate geographic/spatial data mining from conventional data mining (Bogorny et al., 2006). Spatial relationships can computed before the data mining process (the data pre-processing phase) or can be integrated into the data mining process. Therefore, there are two approaches to exploring spatial data using data mining algorithms:

(1) One possible way to explore spatial data is to first compute the spatial relationships in the data pre-processing phase and then apply conventional data mining methods (Agrawal & Srikant, 1994; Barnett & Lewis, 1994; Jain & Dubes, 1988; Quinlan, 1993) (as cited in Shekhar et al., 2003, p. 3). In this way, implicit relationships between spatial objects can be explicitly stored in traditional data formats suitable for classic data mining algorithms. This operation is called materialization (Sahli & Jabeur, 2010; Shekhar, Gandhi, Zhang, & Vatsavai, 2009). Materialization of spatial relationships can be carried out by using GIS operations and functions and some data mining toolkits offer support for running automated operations. The Weka, data mining toolkit, for instance, provides a module to support automated geographic data pre-processing, named GDPM (Geographic Data Pre-processing Module). Weka-GDPM enables topological features to be computed ("the type of intersection between two spatial features"), which can then be categorized as "Equal, Disjoint, Touches, Within, Overlaps, Crosses, Contains, and CoveredBy") and distance (Euclidian distance between two spatial features) relationships (Bogorny et al., 2006, p. 3).

(2) Another possible way of dealing with spatial data is to apply data mining algorithms that have been adapted or designed to deal with specific spatial data features. This approach incorporates the calculation of the spatial relationships as part of the algorithm: the algorithms can be termed "spatially aware algorithms" (Demsar, 2006). Spatial data mining is a developing branch of data mining, mainly researched and applied by an expert community of computer scientists. Scientists working in this line

of research tend to use data mining query languages or invent new spatial data mining algorithms (Bogorny et al., 2006). The GeoMiner software prototype (Han, Koperski, & Stefanovic, 1997), for example, uses a spatial data mining query language named GMQL and provides three data mining modules; characteristic rules, comparison rules and association rules. Another software prototype, INGENS 2.0 (Malerba, Esposito, Lanza, Lisi, & Appice, 2003; Malerba, Lanza, & Appice, 2009), is a GIS prototype that uses an object-oriented data mining query language named SDMOQL for classification and association rule discovery. However these two prototypes are no longer available (Bogorny et al., 2006). ARES (Appice, Berardi, Ceci, & Malerba, 2005), a spatial association rule discovery system, represents another solution. It is argued that ARES is not very practical for mining real databases since the spatial feature extractor function calculates all spatial relationships of all the spatial objects (Bogorny et al., 2006, p. 2). Another disadvantage of ARES is that it only implements the SPADA algorithm (Bogorny et al., 2006). SPIN! (May & Savinov, 2003), another spatial data mining software prototype, also integrates GIS and data mining functionalities. Developed as part of an EU research project ("Spatial Mining for Data of Public Interest") between 2000 and 2002, SPIN! is no longer available. Further information on different spatial data mining techniques (co-location mining, spatial outliers, etc.) and software tools (Oracle Spatial, GeoDa, R, etc.) can be found in Shekhar, Evans, Kang, and Mohan (2011).

Computing spatial relationships in the data pre-processing phase is more straightforward than developing approaches for integrating them into the data mining process. The former approach therefore seems to be more convenient for non-expert data mining users, whereas data mining professionals generally prefer the latter. Although it is argued that pre-processing spatial relationships can result in loss of information[1] and spatial data mining algorithms can perform better than the conventional ones in the presence of spatial data (Shekhar et al., 2003), the existing works on data mining do not really support analysts on the choice between classic and spatial data mining techniques for mining spatial data (Shekhar et al., 2003; Sumathi, Geetha, & Bama, 2008). Shekhar et al. (2003) argue that it is difficult to tell whether we should develop new algorithms specifically designed to mine spatial data or modify the existing data mining algorithms to compute implicit properties and relationships of spatial objects. According to Shekhar et al. (2003), both approaches are gaining momentum. Comparing the effectiveness and computational efficiency of these approaches would therefore appear to be an important line of research (Shekhar et al., 2003; Sumathi et al., 2008).

1 Conventional data mining algorithms require a single table (a classical double-entry table with rows and columns) and this can be a factor which can cause some information to be lost while mining spatial data. For instance, Malerba et al. (2009) argue that single table representation is not suitable for data characterized by geometry mainly because spatial relationships cannot be naturally represented.

In the author's opinion, the choice between applying conventional or spatial data mining methods and techniques mainly depends on the scope of the research, the intended audience and the background of the researcher. In this thesis, the decision was made to use the former approach, namely computing spatial relationships (certain topological and distance relationships) in the data pre-processing phase by means of GIS functionalities, then applying conventional data mining methods, for the following reasons:

- Conventional data mining algorithms are easy to access. There is a variety of free and powerful software tools (e.g., RapidMiner, R, Weka, Orange, KNIME etc.) (Jović, Brkić, & Bogunović, 2014). Due to their visual qualities and user-friendly interface, some of these software packages are especially suitable for non-experts wishing to explore data mining methods and techniques (e.g., RapidMiner). However, spatial data mining toolsets are rare (Bogorny & Tietbohl, 2006) and scarcely accessible to non-professionals. In addition, spatial data mining toolsets usually require an advanced knowledge of data mining and statistics, since these toolsets are mostly aimed at geoscientists and computer scientists specializing in spatial data analysis. Spatial data mining toolsets are therefore not very easy for a non-data mining expert community of architects, urban designers and urban planners to use.
- Whereas there is quite a wide variety of conventional data mining algorithms, spatial data mining methods and techniques have not yet been highly diversified. Therefore one important advantage of measuring spatial relationships in the data pre-processing phase is that this also allows for the use of any conventional data mining algorithm.

This thesis investigates the potential of the major data mining methods to support urban designers, urban planners or architects (with no expertise in data mining) in the course of generating intervention proposals for urban regeneration. The development of special techniques to improve the performance of the data mining algorithms in terms of analyzing spatial data does not fall within the scope of this thesis, which instead aims to encourage non-GIS, statistics and data mining specialists to implement data mining algorithms in urban analysis and utilize the outcomes. Its main concern is, therefore, to employ easily accessible and usable software that can assist non-experts in applying basic data mining methods. For this reason, the decision was made to use the conventional data mining algorithms available in RapidMiner, an open-source, user-friendly data mining software package for the implementations, details of which will be provided in section (5.1).

§ 3.5 Knowledge discovery through data mining applications in Urban Studies

To date, data mining methods and spatial data techniques with have mostly been used by geoscientists and/or computer scientists. Nevertheless, the number of studies that have applied data mining in the context of architectural and urban research has begun to increase recently. Some works that use architectural and/or urban data are briefly reviewed below in order to provide an overview of the applications, as well as the possible types of data and data mining methods:

- In her PhD thesis, Demsar (2006) explored methods for finding relationships between the locations of incidents and other factors, using fifty-one different temporal and non-temporal attributes (such as location of eating/drinking places and proximity to different geographical features including roads and railways) in Helsinki between 2001-2003. This research in geoinformatics, which is entitled "Data mining of geospatial data: combining visual and automatic methods", was developed together with the Helsinki University of Technology and the Stockholm Royal Institute of Technology and implements an approach which combines spatial and visual data mining methods to investigate why incidents occur in certain locations. Demsar (2006) notes that this approach is similar to the spatial data mining approach that applies classic data mining algorithms to spatially pre-processed data. The difference is that visual data mining was used instead of a classic mining algorithm.
- In the article entitled "Automated Representation of Style by Feature Space Archetypes: Distinguishing Spatial Styles from Generative Rules", Hanna (2007) implemented several techniques from machine learning (Principal component analysis, Nearest-neighbour algorithms, Support Vector Machine, Neural Networks, etc.) and space syntax to define architectural archetypes (for the plans of modern and neoclassical museums). Hanna (2007, p. 3) proposed that a style can be characterized by utilizing an "ideal model" containing the elements that embody the style and he invented an algorithmic method which can automatically extract these elements from examples and assign a "stylistic definition" (Hanna, 2007, p. 20). He also demonstrated that this method can be used to for producing new designs. Spatial features gathered from the plan layouts of modern and neoclassical museums were used as the input for the proposed method.
- Reffat (2010) developed a data mining system which facilitates the utilization of data mining techniques for architects without a technical background. Using this system, the researcher investigated "the patterns of architectural features" (e.g. features about the form, circulation system, façade treatment of the buildings) in a database consisting of six hundred buildings representing a contemporaray style (houses and commercial office buildings) located in the three main cities in Saudi Arabia (Riyadh, Jeddah and Dammam). Six data mining methods included in this system are Apriori, Bayesian Network, Cobweb, J48, ID3 and Simple K means. The system outputs both

textual and graphical results. The background of the research was first presented in 2008 in the paper entitled "Investigating Patterns of Contemporary Architecture using Data Mining Techniques" and then the implementation of the data mining system was introduced in 2010 in the paper entitled "A Decision Support System of Discovering Architectural Patterns using Data Mining". The researcher argued that the patterns discovered by data mining methods can be used as design guidelines and inform decision-makers.

– Behnisch and Ultsch (2008) explored the phenomena of shrinking and growing in cities in Germany. Their article, entitled "Urban Data Mining Using Emergent SOM" presents an application of Emergent SOM and U*C-Algorithm for clustering communities in Germany with the same dynamic characteristics using four variables, namely statistics on inhabitants, migration, employment and mobility. An Emergent SOM is a type of artificial neural network and allows for the "visualization of high-dimensional data as a projection from high dimensional space onto two dimensions. This projection onto a grid of neurons is called SOM map." (Behnisch & Ultsch, 2008, p. 313). The article provided a geographic map of the 'localization of shrinking and growing municipalities in Germany'. A year later Behnisch and Ultsch (2009) analyzed multi-dimensional characteristics of German communities between 1994-2004 using six variables, namely statistics for inhabitants, migration, tax capacity, dwellings, employment and commuters. Their article, entitled "Urban data-mining: spatiotemporal exploration of multidimensional data", also presented the implementation of Emergent Self Organizing Maps (ESOM) together with the U*C-Algorithm to perform clustering and classification of the 12,430 German communities. Six main clusters with the same multi-dynamic characteristics were discovered through examination of the data.
– Liu and Seto (2008, p. 297) built a model for urban growth that "uses historical urban growth data to 'learn' urban growth patterns and then predicts urban growth." Their article, entitled "Using the ART-MMAP neural network to model and predict urban growth: a spatiotemporal data mining approach", presented a spatiotemporal ART-MMAP neural method to simulate and predict urban growth. The probability of urban growth in a pixel was described as a function of proximity factors, neighbour factors, historical land use data and slope. The neural network model was applied to predict how the St Louis metropolitan region in the United States will expand in the future and to study the possible future scenarios of land development.
– In her PhD thesis entitled "A Geographic Knowledge Discovery Approach to Property Valuation", Christopoulou (2009) investigated how location affects property prices. The thesis presented a method which used association rule mining and associative classification algorithms to investigate the interrelationships between location and price. This method was based on the Apriori algorithm and extended it with an implementation of a 'Best Rule' classification scheme based on the Classification Based on Associations (CBA) algorithm. The method was validated through a case study with data from three central London boroughs.

– Gil, Montenegro, Beirao, and Duarte (2009) implemented a data mining method to extract descriptions of street and block typologies using attributes related to the morphology and density of urban blocks and street mobility for use in a parametric rule-based urban design process. Their article, entitled "On the discovery of urban typologies: data mining the many dimensions of urban form", presented an application of the k-means clustering technique to classify urban block and street types. A test case was conducted on the data of two neighbourhoods in Lisbon which are adjacent but different in character, namely the Expo 98 PP4 site and Moscavide.

As this overview shows, data mining has only been applied in architectural and urban research mainly during the last decade. However, data mining can have a serious impact on these fields of research. Knowledge discovery is a promising approach for extracting valuable information, initially to develop a better understanding of the urban environment under investigation and subsequently to assist whilst developing urban intervention proposals.

In terms of analyzing the characteristics of buildings, this research is similar to the work of Hanna (2007), Gil, Montenegro, Beirao, and Duarte (2009) and Reffat (2010), which are reviewed above. However, there are also important differences. Hanna's study focused mainly on architectural features and architectural design. Reffat's work also focused on architectural design but his system looks flexible enough to implement with other features but he does not demonstrated how the outputs of data mining can be utilized in the course of architectural design. Gil and his colleagues produced an interesting typology study of certain buildings features using a clustering method, but did not use any implementation to illustrate how to make use of these outputs in urban design or planning. This thesis first investigated the kind of outputs that can be achieved using three basic data mining methods including classification, association rules, and clustering. It then used implementations to demonstrate how the results can be employed in generating intervention proposals for urban regeneration: (1) a computational framework was developed to produce ground floor use, user-type and tenure-type allocation plans for a neighbourhood in the Beyoğlu Preservation Area subject to regeneration, using an Evolutionary Algorithm with the outputs of the data mining analysis; (2) a workshop was organized in which students made use of data mining methods to develop urban intervention proposals for the same neighbourhood in the Beyoğlu Preservation Area. In addition, a relatively large GIS database consisting of the 45 features attributed to the buildings was constructed and used for these implementations. In this sense, in addition to the size of the database used for the data mining, the most important factor that distinguishes this study from others is that this thesis demonstrates how the findings of a data mining analysis using urban data can support the development of intervention proposals for urban regeneration.

§ 3.6 Data Mining Methods and Operators Implemented in the Thesis

As previously stated, the computational platform used for urban feature analysis in this thesis is RapidMiner Community edition (RapidMiner 5.3). RapidMiner's open source, code-free Analytics platform does not require programming skills and offers a variety of data mining solutions for business and research purposes. The RapidMiner project has an academic background, originating in the University of Dortmund in 2001, and has been further developed by Rapid-I GmbH since 2007 (https://rapidminer.com). The first commercial version of RapidMiner (RapidMiner 6) was released in autumn 2013. However, the developers have announced that whenever they release a new major version of RapidMiner, all previous versions will become free for open source community members.

The RapidMiner platform offers data mining techniques that are used by various disciplines such as computer science, statistics and mathematics, physics, mechanical engineering, medicine, chemistry, linguistics and the social sciences. The developers state that the software has over 250,000 users around the world. In addition, the annual RapidMiner Community Meeting and Conference - RCOMM, where researchers using RapidMiner share their scientific work, has been held since 2010.

The main reasons for the use of RapidMiner in this thesis are that it is one of the most comprehensive data mining platforms that enables researchers without a statistical or technical background to use data mining technologies, it does not require programming skills, it has an easy-to-grasp graphical user interface, it is an open-source solution and its scientific reliability has been proved in EU supported and funded research projects (e.g., e-LICO, ViSTA-TV, SustainHub, ProMondi, Healthy Greenhouse) (Land & Fischer, 2013).

RapidMiner uses a modular concept and each step of the analysis is illustrated by an operator (Land & Fischer, 2013). Operators have input and output ports via which a data flow is created among the operators throughout the analysis process. In RapidMiner, operators communicate with each other to receive input data or transmit processed data and generated models to the next operators (Land & Fischer, 2013).

This thesis implements three types of data mining methods: classification, association rule analysis, and clustering. The main RapidMiner operators applied in these methods are the Naïve Bayes Operator and FP-Growth Operator, together with Association Rule Operators and the DBSCAN Clustering Operator, which will be explained in following sections.

§ 3.6.1 Classification

The task of classification is implemented to find out the predefined class in which an item belongs. Tan, Steinbach, and Kumar (2005, p. 146) explains that the input of a classification process is a set of records and:

Each record, also referred to as an instance or an example, is characterized by a tuple (x, y), where x is the attribute set and y is a special attribute designated as the class label (also known as category or target attribute. Tan et al. (2005, p. 146).

Accordingly, classification is defined by Tan et al. (2005, p. 146) as "the task of learning a target function f that maps each attribute set x to one of the predefined class labels y", as illustrated in Figure 3.2.

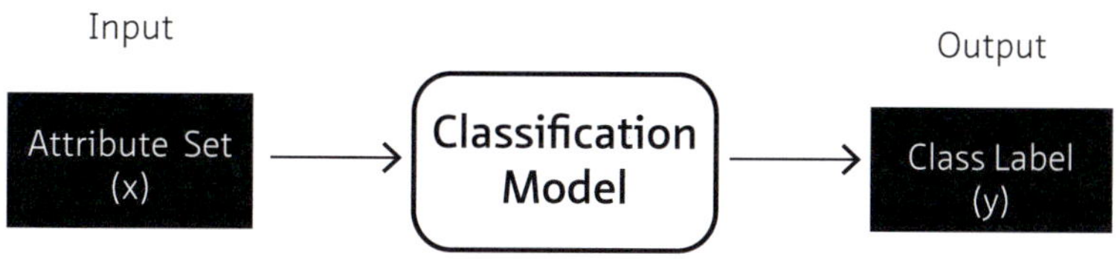

FIGURE 3.2 Classification, redrawn from Tan et al. (2005), p. 146.

The target function f is also referred to as a classification model which can be implemented for the task of description and prediction. A classification model that serves as a descriptive model helps the analyst to recognize objects that fit in with distinctive classes (Tan et al., 2005, p. 147). Classification models that serve as a predictive model, on the other hand, predicts "the class label of unknown records." (Tan et al., 2005, p. 147). The target function is learnt from a set of instances whose class labels are known beforehand (the training set). The learnt function can then be used to classify (or predict the class label of) new instances (in the so-called test set).

Tan et al. (2005, p. 148) note that there are various classification techniques-classifiers, which apply different "learning algorithms to identify a model that best fits the relationships between the attribute set and class label of the input data." In general, a classification model can be built as illustrated in Figure 3.3.

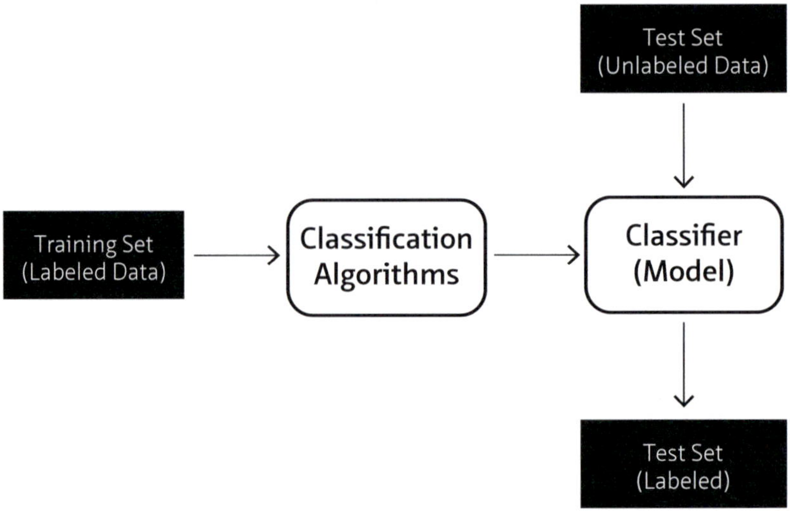

FIGURE 3.3 General approach to building a classification model, adapted from Tan et al. (2005) p. 148.

A learning algorithm builds a classification model from the training set (a set of data with records whose class labels are known) and applies this model to the test set (a set of data with records whose class labels are unknown) to predict the unknown class labels. The amount of correctly and incorrectly predicted records of a test set can be used to evaluate the performance of a classification model and these results can be presented in a table known as a "confusion matrix" (Tan et al., 2005, p. 149). There are performance metrics such as *accuracy*, *error rate*, *precision* and *recall* (also referred to as sensitivity or true positive rate) for the classification model, namely:

Accuracy= Number of Correct Predictions / Total Number of Predictions

Error rate = Number of Wrong Predictions / Total Number of Predictions

Precision= Number of Correctly Classified Positive Predictions / Number of Predictions Labelled by the Model as Positive

Recall = Number of Correctly Classified Positive Predictions / Number of Positive Records in the Data

The Naïve Bayes Classification technique, which basically exploits the probabilistic characteristics of data (based on applying Bayes' theorem, developed by Thomas Bayes in 1763), is one of the data mining methods implemented in this thesis. Naïve Bayes is a very well known classifier with a high predictive ability and is available in almost every open source data mining tool. The Naïve Bayes classifier is relatively easy to implement compared to other machine learning techniques but despite its simplicity, it is known to be a powerful technique (Kononenko, 1993; Možina, Demšar, Kattan, & Zupan, 2004). Han and Kamber (2001) note that the performance of the Bayes classifiers in terms of prediction accuracy and speed is comparable with neural network and decision tree classifiers and Bayes classifiers perform very well with large databases.

The probability for an object being in a particular class can be predicted by using a Bayes classifier, which is one of the most frequently employed statistical classifier in pattern recognition and classification (Cios et al., 2007). The Naïve Bayes Classification technique can be also used to understand "the structure of the training data" and how the independent variables influence the output class. (Breskvar Zaucer, Zupan, & Golobic, 2010, p. 169).

The Naïve Bayes classifier is a type of Bayes classifier with "naïve" independence assumptions, meaning that in a Naïve Bayes classification, it is assumed that all the attributes of an object independently contribute to the probability for this object being in a particular class. For instance, an orange can be classified based on its shape, colour and dimensions. While assigning a class label for this fruit (orange or not), Naïve Bayes classifiers assume that all of these features are independent from each other even if they might be dependent.

This assumption of independence greatly reduces computation costs, since the estimation of the individual probability structure of independent variables requires much less training data than the joint probability structure of many dependent variables. Although from a theoretical perspective this may be an oversimplification of the actual statistical dependence relationship between the variables involved, in practical data-analytics applications it has been observed that the Naïve Bayes assumption leads to satisfactory or even better predictive performance. Despite the assumption of independence, the Naïve Bayes classifier is known for its high predictive ability with independent and highly correlated data attributes (Ibrahim & Bennett, 2014). Many scientific domains working with highly dependent variables has applied this classifier and the results have confirmed that it performs very well and can often achieve better results than more powerful classifiers (Qi & Zhu, 2003). The study of Domingos and Pazzani (1997) demonstrated that the prediction accuracy of the Naïve Bayes classifier can be very high even with statistically dependent variables (Ceci, 2005). However, one limitation of the Naïve Bayes classifier is that it does not provide a description about how the results were created, it only classifies future samples (Qi & Zhu, 2003).

The analysis process involved in applying a Naïve Bayes operator to perform a classification application in RapidMiner is illustrated in Figure 3.4.

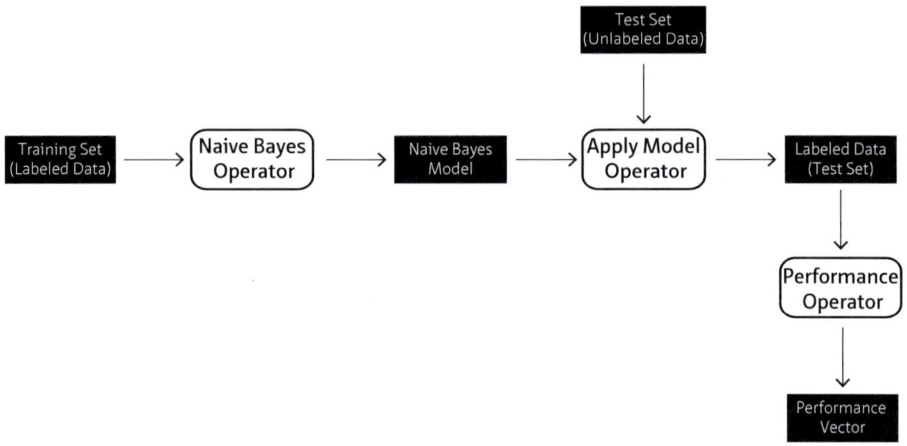

FIGURE 3.4 Naïve Bayes operator performing a classification application in RapidMiner.

The Naïve Bayes operator builds a Naïve Bayes Classification model by learning the training set and this model is then applied to the test set using the Apply Model Operator. The output of this operation is labelled test set data. The Performance Operator evaluates test records that are correctly and incorrectly labelled (predicted) and generates a performance vector.

Although the assumption of independence between some of the predictor variables is probably not valid for our database, the Naïve Bayes Classification is still one of the data mining techniques implemented in this study. This is because, despite the assumption of independence, the Naïve Bayes classifier is known for its high predictive ability with highly correlated data attributes (Ibrahim & Bennett, 2014) and it is a relatively simple technique for non-experts to apply. These implementations of the Naïve Bayes Classification were applied to the Beyoğlu Preservation Area Building Features Database, which includes 11,984 buildings and their 45 non-spatial (e.g., floorspace use, land-price, building maintenance conditions) and spatial (e.g., the distances from the buildings to the important transportation nodes and pedestrian meeting points) attributes.

(1) One implementation of the Naïve Bayes Classification was performed to explore the effects of each spatial and non-spatial variable on the use of ground floor (i.e. accommodation, business-shopping, empty, open space, other, residential, sociocultural infrastructure, technical infrastructure) of the buildings in the Beyoğlu Preservation Area and in its three neighbourhoods (Tarlabaşı, Cihangir and Karaköy) and vice versa. In other words, the predictive power of one variable over different categories of the ground floor land- use was postulated as a measure of the relationship between these two variables. This analysis indicates that there is a certain relationship between ground- floor land- use and relevant predictors for this attribute. Details of these implementations will be provided in subsection (5.1.2).

(2) A second implementation of the Naïve Bayes Classification was performed to explore the combined effects of a set of multiple variables with the highest level of prediction accuracy, i.e. 1st floor use, 2nd floor use, 1st basement use, neighbourhood and population density, in predicting ground floor use categories. This analysis provided the highest possible prediction power (with the data included in the Beyoğlu Preservation Area Building Features Database) in predicting the use of ground floor for buildings in the Beyoğlu Preservation Area. This application, with multiple variables, also enabled us to examine how much the prediction accuracy for different ground categories of ground floor use could be increased. In this analysis, accounting for spatial autocorrelation would be likely to increase the prediction accuracy of the Naïve Bayes classifier in predicting the categories of ground floor use. However, this was beyond the scope of the research, as it was not primarily concerned with the problem of prediction but with exploring the data extracted from the thematic maps of the Beyoğlu Preservation Area. An exploration of the effect of spatial autocorrelation on the occurrence of the categories of ground floor use of buildings in the Beyoğlu Preservation Area can be investigated in a future study. Details of this implementation are provided in subsection (5.1.2).

(3) The Naïve Bayes Classification was implemented again to select the most relevant attributes to which the association rule would be applied, as explained in subsection (3.6.2).

(4) The Naïve Bayes Classification was implemented by students during the course of the Tarlabaşı Datascope workshop, explained in subsection (5.3.3). A team of students implemented the Naïve Bayes Classification for a prediction task. The Naïve Bayes model was trained with the existing floorspace use data and then applied to an unlabeled dataset. The model predicted the floorspace use categories for empty ground floors. This implementation enabled students to assign new functions to the empty ground floors based on the existing floorspace use patterns in Tarlabaşı.

A number of studies are briefly reviewed below to illustrate the wide-range of applications of the Naïve Bayes technique with spatial and non-spatial data:

- Altartouria and Jolmaa (2013) from the Department of Civil and Environmental Engineering at the Aalto University in Finland, examined the potential of the Nave Bayes classification method for modelling the distribution of the common reed Phragmites australis. The authors developed a Naïve Bayes classifier to predict occurrences of Phragmites australis in a site on the Southern Finnish coast. All the analyses were performed using a raster data model. The authors used three types of explanatory variables (depth of water, openness, and distance to a river mouth) to predict presence/absence of the reed. The authors also tested the potential of the Naïve Bayes classifier to provide input for a cellular automaton for modelling the spread of Phragmites australis. In this phase, the authors also accounted for spatial autocorrelation by incorporating the spatial neighbourhood composition in the classification process as a new variable and discovered that this increased the prediction accuracy for future distributions of Phragmites colonies. According to the results of this research the authors concluded that the Naïve Bayes classifier has significant potential in predicting occurrences of the species and providing transition rules for the dynamic modelling of species distribution.

- Ibrahim and Bennett (2014) from the School of Computing at the University of Leeds in the UK researched distribution models used to predict the potential locations of alluvial minerals. The authors investigated the performance of five classification algorithms: "Naïve Bayes (NB), Support Vector Machine (SVM), K-Nearest Neighbour (KNN), Decision Tree Bagging (DTB) and Discriminant Analysis (DA)." Alluvial deposit mining points (present and past points) in the Jos Plateau State area of the Nigeria Younger Granite region was used to carry out the research. The authors examined how spatial autocorrelation occurs with different data splitting techniques. To prevent the dependecy between attributes that are used for the prediction of the alluvial deposit mining points, they applied "longitudinal spatial data splitting (strips and halves)" technique while splitting data for training and testing the classifiation model. The authors found out that the effect of spatial autocorrelation was reduced by applying "a systematic spatially segregated split" instead of no splitting or random splitting.
- In her PhD thesis work, Ceci (2005), from the Department of Informatics at the University of Bari in Italy, investigated the problem of Naïve Bayesian learning with structured data (data structured into a hierarchy of categories and data that contains dependencies between variables). This study introduced methods for hierarchical and multi-relational classification with Naïve Bayes. It also integrated Naïve Bayesian classification with multi-level spatial Association Rules method. This classification method is based on a multi-relational approach that takes spatial relations into account. The method performs the classification at different levels of granularity (the hierarchy of objects based on the inside relationship between locations) and takes advantage of domain-specific knowledge expressed in form of rules to support qualitative spatial reasoning. In this way, Ceci (2005) argues that the proposed method can deal with the implicit definition of spatial relations and the granularity of spatial objects. This work did not account for spatial autocorrelation, as far as the author can determine.
- Kumar, Venkatesan, and Prabhu (2014), from the Computer Science Department at the VIT University in India, analyzed landslide susceptibility using a classification-based clustering approach. The factors considered in the analysis were geology, geomorphology, soil type, slope, land use and land cover, and rainfall. These factors were analyzed using the Bayes Classification, then k means to classify the landforms into different classes according to their probability of landslides, using zones ranging from "Very High" to "Low". The authors used RapidMiner to implement their research. This study did not account for spatial autocorrelation.
- Qi and Zhu (2003) from the Department of Geography at the University of Wisconsin-Madison, and the State Key Laboratory of Resources and Environmental Information

System Institute of Geographical Sciences and Natural Resources Research at the Chinese Academy of Sciences, developed a knowledge discovery process using data mining to examine the knowledge embedded in a soil map. They investigated the learning accuracy and result comprehensibility of three inductive learning algorithms: the See5 decision tree algorithm, Naïve Bayes, and an artificial neural network. The soil type was seen as a function of climatic, biotic, topographic, time and parent material. In addition to those factors, this study also computed spatial information (topological, distance and spatial neighbourhood information) in the data pre-processing phase, incorporated this information into the process of knowledge discovery and found that this improved the accuracy of the knowledge extracted. The authors aimed to design an automated soil inference system and model spatial autocorrelation as a future project.

- Breskvar Zaucer et al. (2010), from the Biotechnical Faculty and the Faculty of Computer and Information Science at the University of Ljubljana in Slovenia, implemented data mining to interpret preference maps (cartographic maps indicating the preferences of people regarding future spatial development) of Komenda in Ljubljana using data from a 2001 public survey. This study used nine types of spatial variables including some distance relationships, visibility and land use. They implemented Naïve Bayes and classification tree algorithms available in Orange software. As a result, they were able to identify some of the main factors that affected people's views on spatial development in their region.
- Karthikeyan and Manikandaprabhu (2015), from the PSG College of Arts and Science in India, focus on the classification of satellite images using data mining methods. This work specifically dealt with classifying high-resolution images of an urban land cover area (Landsat image of Coimbatore city in India, acquired in 2014). The aim of the study was to classify the image data into nine classes (asphalt, buildings, cars, concrete, grass, pool, shadows, soil and trees) using relevant features (such as texture, shape, size and spectral information). Three different classification algorithms (Naïve Bayes, K Nearest Neighbors, a Decision Tree and Random Tree algorithms) were implemented and evaluated in terms of their performance. In this study, neighbourhood relations between pixels were also taken into consideration (calculated and processed in the form of a feature type) using a method commonly used in remote sensing analysis, namely the Gray Level Co-occurrence Matrix (GLCM).
- Shekhar et al. (2003), from the Department of Computer Science and Engineering at the University of Minnesota in the USA, developed the Spatial Autoregressive Model and the Markov Random Field-based Bayesian classifier methods to be used for location prediction. These two different methods of spatial data mining allowed for modelling of spatial dependencies, namely the "the relationships between spatially adjacent pixels in a small neighbourhood" (Shekhar et al., 2003, p. 7), during the classification process.

As can be seen from the examples listed above, most of the applications of the Naïve Bayes Classification with spatial data were performed by geoscientists and/or computer scientists working with geographical data (geographic vector data or raster data). Some of this research accounted for the effects of spatial autocorrelation on the accuracy of the Naïve Bayes Classification model, but some did not. These examples also show that there are different approaches to incorporating the issue of spatial relationships (and spatial autocorrelation in particular) into the data mining process.

The most important differences between the Naïve Bayes Classification implementations carried out in this study and the examples reviewed above are the following:

- Whereas most of the implementations listed above aim both ta prediction problem and develop techniques for incorporating spatial relationships into the data mining process, the goal of the implementations used in this is to explore the effects of a set of variables on a specific variable. In this sense, our implementations are similar to the work of Breskvar Zaucer et al. (2010) reviewed above, which applied the Naïve Bayes Classification to interpret preference maps. Instead of solving a prediction problem, both studies implement the Naïve Bayes Classification to explore relationships between attributes.
- Whereas most of the implementations listed above used geographical data (geographic items with climatic, geologic, topographical features etc.), this study uses a database representing spatial and non-spatial features attributed to buildings in a historic inner-city neighbourhood. Moreover, it uses a relatively large database (11,984 buildings) with a high number of variables (45 attributes) in comparison to the works reviewed above. To the best of our knowledge, there are no other examples of data mining with such a large database consisting of building features. In particular, it has not been possible to find a data mining application with such a comprehensive database in terms of floorspace use data (the floorspace use data in this study covers all the floors in the buildings).

§ 3.6.2 Association rule analysis

Association rule analysis is the second data mining method applied in this thesis. This is a useful method for discovering relationships hidden in large datasets and representing them in the form of association rules or frequent item sets. Basically, association rules is a classification approach applied to find items in a database that occur together. Association rule mining is one of the most important data mining techniques that has been frequently applied and researched since the important work by Agrawal, Imielinski, and Swami (1993), which implemented an algorithm that generates all significant association rules between item sets in a customer transaction database of a large retailing company. The aim of association rule mining is "to extract interesting correlations, frequent patterns, associations or casual structures among sets of items in the transaction databases or other data repositories" (Kotsiantis &

Kanellopoulos, 2006, p. 71). Association rules are widely used in diverse areas such as the telecommunications industry, retail industry and finance, and a variety of techniques and algorithms are used in association rule mining.

Association rules are if/then statements that expose implicit relationships between data. An example of an association rule would be: 90% of the customers who bought bread and butter also bought eggs. An association rule has the form of "X –>Y", where X and Y are set of items co-occurring in a given tuple (record in a database) (Agrawal et al., 1993). Accordingly, an association rule has two parts: X is an antecedent (if) and Y is a consequent (then). In other words, an association rule is detected in a dataset when an item or itemset (an antecedent) is found together with another item or itemset (a consequent). There are also spatial association rules, as defined by Koperski and Han (1995, p. 48), which are rules in the form of "X –>Y, where Y and X are sets of predicates, some of which are spatial ones". More recently Verhein and Chawla (2006) provided a definition of spatio-temporal association rules that describe the movement patterns of objects in space and time.

Frequent if/then patterns found in data are used to create association rules. Algorithms used for mining association rules may generate an excessive number of patterns and it is therefore important to eliminate some by applying objective measures for interestingness, such as support, confidence and correlation (Tan et al., 2005). Support is an indication of how frequently the items appear in the database and confidence indicates the number of times the if/then statements have been found to be true (Tan et al., 2005). The usefulness (strength) and certainty of an association rule can be judged by the support and confidence values (Cios et al., 2007). In addition to the traditional methods which are used to measure support and confidence, support and confidence for an association rule can olso be measured using fuzzy-logic theory ("fuzzy association rules") Kuok, Fu, and Wong (1998). Subjective measures, which depend on the knowledge and intention of the analyst, are also important in the pattern discovery task, since a rule with low occurrence values could also be considered interesting (Tan et al., 2005).

The results of association rule analysis should be interpreted carefully, since it is not certain that there is a causal relationship between the antecedent and consequent of an association rule. An association rule only designates a strong co-occurrence relationship between items (Tan et al., 2005). Causality would require more evidence and, typically, a systematic occurrence of the rules over time (Tan et al., 2005).

The two main operators required to perform association rule analysis in RapidMiner are an FP-Growth operator to mine the patterns and a Create Association Rules operator to generate a set of association rules from the given set of frequent itemsets. Frequent itemsets are groups of items that often appear together in the data. Figure 3.5 illustrates this process in RapidMiner.

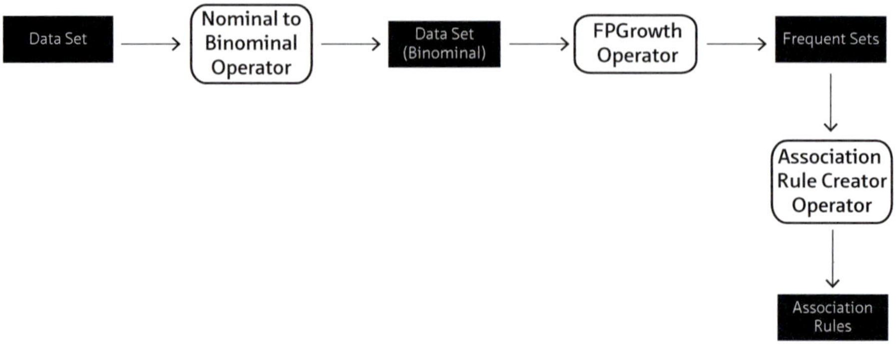

FIGURE 3.5 FP-Growth and association rule operators performing an association rule analysis process in RapidMiner.

As explained in the RapidMiner Operator Reference Manual by Akthar and Hahne (2012), the FP-Growth operator efficiently calculates all frequent itemsets from the given data set containing only binominal attributes, using the FP-tree data structure. Therefore a Nominal to Binominal operator is often applied before the FP-Growth operator to change the type of selected attributes and map all these attribute values to binominal values i.e. true and false. This FP-tree generates all frequent itemsets . Many other algorithms to mine frequent itemsets also exist, such as the Apriori algorithm. However Akthar and Hahne (2012) note that FP-Growth has an important advantage: it can be applied to large data sets since it uses only two data scans.

The frequent itemsets are often confused with association rules. However association rules are generated using the frequent itemsets and postulate a more complex description of data (Akthar & Hahne, 2012). In RapidMiner, frequent itemsets are generated using the FP-Growth operator, whilst the association rules are derived from the frequent itemsets using the Create Association Rules operator (Akthar & Hahne, 2012).

Association rule mining is one of the techniques used in this study because; (1) it is a relatively simple method for non-data mining experts to apply, (2) it generates highly descriptive quantitative outputs, (3) given their form, association rules are suitable for use as input for other computational methods. This implementation will be presented in section (5.2). The aim of the implementation is to investigate how data mining methods can assist architects, urban designers and urban planners whilst developing intervention proposals for urban regeneration. For this purpose, the study focuses on a regeneration problem in the Tarlabaşı neighbourhood, located in the Beyoğlu Preservation Area. An alternative approach is proposed for the regeneration of the Tarlabaşı neighbourhood, which aims to preserve the original patterns of ground floor use in Tarlabaşı whilst transforming the neighbourhood. A computational process that implements this approach is developed to generate ground floor use, user profile and tenure-type allocation plan layouts for Tarlabaşı. This computational process involves the successive application of Naïve Bayes Classification, Association Rule analysis and an Evolutionary Algorithm, using a subset of the Beyoğlu Preservation Area Building Features Database. The subset, representing the Tarlabaşı neighbourhood, consists of 45 spatial and non-spatial attributes of 2,136 buildings.

In this implementation, association rule analysis is mainly used to formulate the intervention decisions about the allocation of the ground floor use. In particular, this method enables the original patterns of the ground floor use to be identified. Since association rule algorithms usually generate an excessive amount of rules and the database used in this study contains a large number of attributes, it would have been very time-consuming to directly implement this method with all the attributes in the database. For this reason, the Naïve Bayes was first implemented to eliminate the attributes that were irrelevant to an association rules analysis. The most powerful attributes for predicting the use of ground floor identified with the Naïve Bayes classifier were postulated as the most relevant ones for an association rules analysis. Following this, the FP-Growth algorithm was implemented, revealing each relevant attribute's associations with the categories of the ground floor use. These association rules are described in the form of probabilistic rules. Association rules with the rule consequent "ground floor use: residential" and "ground floor use: business-shopping" were considered to represent the important site-specific patterns of ground floor use in the Tarlabaşı neighbourhood which should be preserved. In addition, the association rules with the rule consequent "ground floor use: empty" were used to allocate a new category for empty ground floors, based on the existing ground floor use allocation patterns in Tarlabaşı. Existing trends of ground floor use are determined by associating each attribute associated with empty ground floors to other use categories. In this way, new rules were determined which allocated business-shopping, residential or other uses to the empty floors of the buildings, based on the existing patterns of ground floor use allocation. These selected association rules were then used for fitness measurements of an Evolutionary Algorithm (together with other fitness measurements defined by the author, according to the regeneration approach) to generate draft plans for ground floor use, user profile and tenure-type allocation for Tarlabaşı.

In order to illustrate the wide range of applications for the association rules technique using spatial and non-spatial data, a number of studies were briefly reviewed:

- Koperski and Han (1995), from the School of Computer Science at the Simon Fraser University in Canada, investigated methods for mining spatial association rules. They studied how the methods used for the discovery of association rules in transaction-based databases could be developed to analyze spatial association rules. In this very early work, they introduced the concept of spatial association rules for the first time. They developed a method to find multilevel (hierarchical) spatial association rules which organize the spatial and non-spatial data into hierarchies. A spatial data query language was implemented to compute spatial relationships (topology and distance), although this method did not account for spatial autocorrelation. The method was implemented in their software GeoMiner, which is no longer available.

- Mukhlash and Sitohang (2007), from the Department of Mathematics and the School of Electrical Engineering and Informatics at the Sepuluh Nopember Institute of Technology in Indonesia, proposed to implement spatial data pre-processing with GIS functionalities and implement conventional association rule algorithms (Apriori and FP-Growth) to discover spatial association rules. Their data pre-processing method was used on spatial data with non-spatial attributes and delivered specific spatial relations (e.g. topological and distance relations) and was implemented to find spatial association rules between demographics data and the number of DBD (Degenerative Bone Disease) disease cases in Surabaya.
- In her PhD thesis on computer science, Bogorny (2006), from the Department of Informatics at the University of Rio Grande do Sul in Brazil, addressed the main technical problems of spatial association rule mining. This thesis introduced a methodological framework to eliminate the extraction of well-known patterns, which is one of the main drawbacks of mining spatial association rules. Additionally, an automated geographic data pre-processing module (GDPM) was developed in the Weka data mining toolkit to compute spatial relationships (i.e. topological and distance relationships).
- Tang and McDonald (2002), from the School of Environmental and Information Science at the Charles Sturt University in Australia, explored the relations between the students registered to a particular course and their demographic features (such as the socio-economic status, the ethnic background of the students or their accessibility and proximity to university campus,) using the association rules method. They used GIS for pre-processing spatial relationships (distance relationships) and combined spatial data mining with spatial statistics and GIS. Tang and McDonald (2001) introduced a method for mining "multi-level association rules" between spatial and non-spatial data through integrating expert knowledge in to the data mining process.
- Motivated by the dramatic increase in geo-referentiation of socio-economic data in recent decades, Appice, Ceci, Lanza, Lisi, and Malerba (2003), from the Department of Informatics at the University of Bari in Italy, investigated the discovery of knowledge in geo-referenced data. In particular, the work focused on how to use spatial data in census data mining. A new method for discovering spatial association rules, grounded on a multi-relational data mining approach, was proposed and a new algorithm for mining spatial association rules was described. The algorithm, named SPADA (Spatial Pattern Discovery Algorithm), was based on an ILP approach to relational data mining and enabled "multi-level spatial association rules" to be mined, i.e. "association rules involving spatial objects at different granularity levels" (Appice et al., 2003, p. 543) In the study, data stored in a spatial database was pre-processed in order to represent it in a deductive relational database. The authors devised a spatial feature extraction module named FEATEX, which was implemented as an Oracle package of procedures and functions in order to generate spatial relationships. The SPADA algorithm was

tested to explore the accessibility to the Stepping Hill hospital in Stockport, Greater Manchester, UK from the five EDs ("enumeration districts, the smallest areal unit for which census data is published") within in the area served by the hospital. Topological and distance relationships between the EDs and the hospital were computed in the data pre-processing phase.

- In their paper, Chen, Chen, Yu, and Yang (2011), from the School of Remote Sensing and Information Engineering at the Wuhan University in China, aimed to compare spatial association rule mining and spatial autocorrelation. The paper explored a dataset including county-level revenue, population, education state, health state and social security state in China from 2000 to 2005 using two different approaches; spatial analysis (spatial autocorrelation and spatial regression methods implemented in GeoDa) and spatial association rules (with the Apriori algorithm and a new improved version of Apriori algorithm). The conclusions of the two analysis processes were then compared and discussed. They concluded that the results of the spatial association rule mining process are compatible with the results of spatial autocorrelation and spatial regression. They explained that many rules generated by both methods are common and therefore spatial statistics output a *priori* knowledge for spatial association rules. They also found that spatial autocorrelation introduces deviation into the results and requires further research on how this can be eliminated. In addition, they argued that it is not easy to use spatial autocorrelation to define the rules to specify the candidate frequent itemsets, concluding that they did not know how the mining procedure is affected by the spatial autocorrelation and proposed to investigate this problem, i.e. when to employ spatial autocorrelation and when to exclude it in the mining procedure, as a future project.
- Shekhar et al. (2003), from the Department of Computer Science and Engineering at the University of Minnesota in the USA, introduced a novel method named the event centric model to discover spatial co-location rules. Spatial co-location rules are defined as a particular form of spatial association rules which "represent the subsets of the boolean spatial features whose instances are often located in close geographic proximity" (Shekhar et al., 2003, p. 12). Boolean spatial features are defined by Shekhar et al. (2003, p. 12) as "geographic object types which are either present or absent in different locations in a two-dimensional or three-dimensional metric space, e.g. the surface of the earth" such as animal species, plant species, crime, disease.

As can be seen from the examples listed above, most of the applications of association rules analysis using spatial data were developed by geoscientists, computer scientists and/or informatics engineers using diverse types of data (geographical data, census data, socio-demographic data. etc.) and include applications of specialized algorithms (spatial association rules) and conventional algorithms to mine association rules. The main approach in association rules mining is to compute topological and distance relationships in the data pre-processing phase and it is not very common to account for the effects of spatial autocorrelation. The incorporation of spatial autocorrelation within the association rule mining process is a relatively new research trend.

Apart from the content of our database, the most important difference between the association rule implementation used in this thesis and the examples reviewed above is the fact that it is applied mainly to demonstrate how data mining findings can become operational in the course developing of intervention proposals for urban regeneration. This implementation of association rules enables the site-specific characteristics of a historical inner-city neighbourhood to be identified. These site-specific characteristics, in the form of association rules, are used as input for another computational method, namely an evolutionary algorithm. To the best of our knowledge, there are no other applications of association rules which investigate how this method can support the development of intervention proposals for urban regeneration and integrate the outputs generated (i.e. association rules) with evolutionary computation.

§ 3.6.3 Clustering

Clustering analysis is the third data mining method applied in this thesis. Clustering is the task of dividing "data into groups (clusters) that are meaningful, useful, or both (Tan et al., 2005, p. 487). As explained by Tan et al. (2005), the goal is to find out items in a dataset that are similar (or related) to eachother and different from (or unrelated) the others. "The greater the similarity (or homogeneity) within a group and the greater the difference between the groups, the better or more distinct the clustering" will be (Tan et al., 2005, p. 490). Figure 3.6 illustrates different ways of clustering the same points.

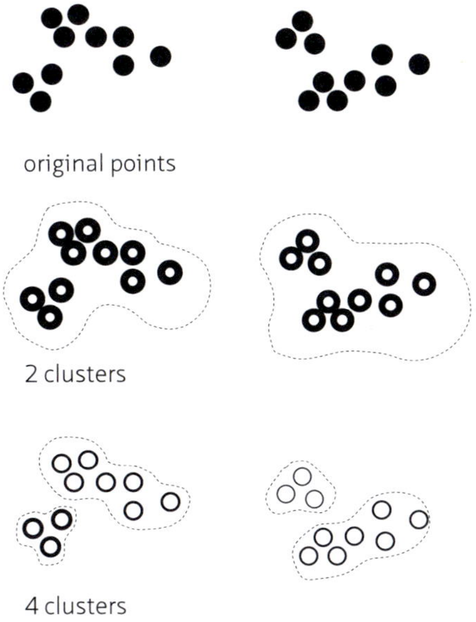

FIGURE 3.6 Different ways of clustering the same set of points, redrawn from Tan et al. (2005), p. 491.

As Tan et al. (2005) state, both classification and clustering are used to label items in a dataset, in this sense clustering might be considered as a form of classification. The main difference is that there are no predefined class labels in a clustering process, class labels are previously unknown. While clustering derives these labels from the data, classification builds a model from objects with known class labels to categorize objects with unknown class labels (Tan et al., 2005). For this reason, classification is referred to as 'supervised learning' and clustering as 'unsupervised learning'.

The main operator employed to perform clustering analysis in RapidMiner is the DBSCAN (Density-Based Spatial Clustering of Applications with Noise) Clustering Operator. As defined by Akthar and Hahne (2012, p. 817), this density-based clustering algorithm "finds a number of clusters starting from the estimated density distribution of the corresponding nodes". The analysis process that applies a DBSCAN Clustering operator to perform a clustering analysis process in RapidMiner is illustrated in Figure 3.7.

FIGURE 3.7 DBSCAN Clustering operator performing a clustering analysis process in RapidMiner.

The DBSCAN algorithm defines clusters based on the notion of "density reachability" and "density-connectedness". As explained in the RapidMiner Operator Reference Manual by Akthar and Hahne (2012, p. 817), basically;

A point q is directly density-reachable from a point p if it is not farther away than a given distance epsilon (i.e. it is part of its epsilon-neighbourhood) and if p is surrounded by a sufficient number of points to enable p and q to be considered part of a cluster. q is called density-reachable (note the distinction between "directly density-reachable") from p if there is a sequence p(1),...,p(n) of points with p(1) = p and p(n) = q, where each p(i+1) is directly density-reachable from p(i). Akthar and Hahne (2012, p. 817).

It should be noted that the density-reachable relationship is not symmetric. In other words a point q located on the edge of a cluster may be reachable from a point p (via other points), yet it cannot reach any other points. This point cannot be considered a dense point because the number of neighbourhood points surrounding it is not sufficient. Therefore, the notion of "density-connectedness", which is a symmetric relationship, is introduced to include such an "edge" point in a cluster: "two points *p* and q are density-connected if there is a point o from which both p and q are density-reachable." Akthar and Hahne (2012, p. 817).

Accordingly, for a subset of the points of the data set to be considered a cluster, it should satisfy two properties: "all points within the cluster are mutually density-connected, and if a point is density-connected to any point in the cluster, it is part of the cluster as well" (Akthar & Hahne, 2012, p. 818).

In RapidMiner, DBSCAN is implemented using the epsilon and the minimum number of points required to form a cluster (MinPts) parameters. As explained by Akthar and Hahne (2012, p. 818) DBSCAN starts a cluster if an arbitrary point's epsilon-neighbourhood contains sufficient number of points (MinPts). All the points located in this epsilon-neighbourhood are added to the cluster and the points found in the epsilon-neighbourhood of these new points are also added if they are also density-connected. The formation of a cluster stops when the density-connected cluster is completely identified. Then the process starts once again with another arbitrary point (a new point, not previously visited) to identify new clusters or find out points that cannot be clustered (noise).

The DBSCAN concepts are illustrated in Figure 3.8.

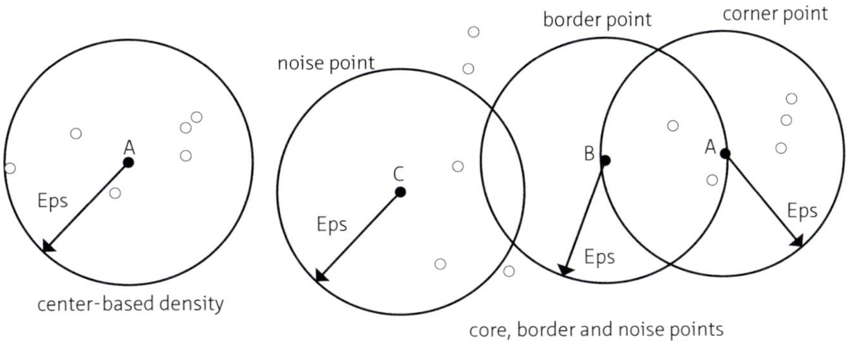

FIGURE 3.8 DBSCAN uses a centre-based approach that allows a point to be classified as being in the interior of a dense region (A: a core point), on the edge of a dense region (B: a border point) or in a sparsely occupied region (C: a noise point) and point A is a core point for the epsilon in question if MinPts ≤7 (Tan et al., 2005), redrawn from Tan et al. (2005), p. 528.

The DBSCAN operator creates an ID (identity) if this is not predefined. The points, which are labelled as noise, are named 'Cluster 0'.

DBSCAN algorithm, a method of choice for clustering applications in the data mining community, was used in this thesis. In 2014, the algorithm was awarded The Test of Time award by the SIGKDD (the Association for Computing Machinery Special Interest Group on Knowledge Discovery and Data Mining) for its important impact on the data mining research community. One of the main attractions of the algorithm is that it does not require the analyst to specify the number of clusters beforehand (Kotu & Deshpande, 2015). Therefore, it is particularly suitable for practical applications when the number of clusters to be discovered is unknown (Kotu & Deshpande, 2015). In addition, RapidMiner facilitates the implementation of DBSCAN with nominal data due to the Nominal Distance measure type (a measure type used for measuring the distance between points, where nominal distance is 0 if two records match exactly, and 1 otherwise).

In this thesis, DBSCAN was implemented with floorspace use data of the buildings:

1 The implementation of DBSCAN with data from the Beyoğlu Preservation Area Building Features Database will be presented in subsection (5.1.2). The aim of this implementation was to investigate floorspace use patterns within buildings (referred as vertical floorspace use patterns) in the Beyoğlu Preservation Area and its three

important neighbourhoods with different land use characteristics, namely Tarlabaşı, Karaköy and Cihangir. The DBSCAN algorithm was implemented with 10 attributes representing floorspace use categories for 10 floors of the buildings (from the ground floor to the 9th floor). The algorithm scanned 11,984 buildings in terms of their functional uses and exposed vertical floorspace use patterns existing in the Beyoğlu Preservation Area.

2 The DBSCAN algorithm was also implemented by students during the international Tarlabaşı Datascope workshop, explained in subsection (5.3.3). The workshop mainly focused on developing intervention proposals for the regeneration of Tarlabaşı neighbourhood, located in the Beyoğlu Preservation Area. Students implemented the DBSCAN algorithm to explore the vertical floorspace use characteristics in the buildings of theTarlabaşı neighbourhood and used the results of the clustering analysis in the course of synthesizing their intervention proposals. In specific terms, they were able to define the potentials and problems concerning allocation of different types of uses in Tarlabaşı by investigating the existing patterns, which were identified by implementing the DBSCAN clustering technique.

In order to illustrate the wide-range of applications of the DBSCAN clustering technique with spatial and non-spatial data, a number of studies are briefly reviewed below:

- Verma, Srivastava, Chack, Diswar, and Gupta (2012), from the GLNA Institute of Technology in Mathura, reviewed six types of clustering techniques- k-Means Clustering, Hierarchical Clustering, DBSCAN Clustering, Density Based Clustering, Optics, EM Algorithm. Their work introduced an implementation of each algorithm with a banking database including information about customers (11 attributes and 600 entries were used), using the Weka tool.
- Santhisree, Damodaram, Appaji, and NagarjunaDevi (2010), from the College of Engineering at the JNTUH University in India, presented a new method which implemented a specialized version of the DBSCAN Clustering algorithm to identify the behaviour associated with user web page visits and the order of occurrence of those visits. They used the MSNBC web navigation dataset to perform a clustering analysis to discover the groups which share common interests while using the www. The dataset included web server logs, queries and mouse clicks.
- Celik, Dadaser Celik, and Dokuz (2011), from the Department of Computer Engineering at the Erciyes University in Turkey, focused on finding of anomalies in monthly temperature data. They implemented the DBSCAN algorithm with a Turkish State Meteorological Service provided dataset, which consisted of daily average temperature data collected at the Develi Station in Kayseri (Turkey) over a 33-year period (from 1975 to 2008).
- Peca, Fuchs, Vrotsou, Andrienko, and Andrienko (2012), from the Institute for Intelligent Analysis and Information Systems (IAIS) at the University of Bonn in Germany, proposed a deterministic density clustering algorithm based on DBSCAN that identified arbitrary shaped clusters of spatio-temporal events. The research

implemented an example application concerning traffic data analysis. A dataset of 17,200 GPS-tracks of cars in Milan collected over one week (2 million position records) was analysed to detect traffic jams in the city during this period and investigate their properties.

- Birant and Kut (2007), from the Computer Engineering Department at the Dokuz Eylul University in Turkey, presented a new density-based clustering algorithm, ST-DBSCAN, which is based on DBSCAN. This algorithm was implemented to cluster objects based on their non-spatial, spatial and temporal features. The article presented three data mining applications to find out the regions that have similar seawater characteristics. The project aimed to discover new insights about the distribution of the physical properties of water (e.g., sea surface temperature, wave height values, bathymetric data) in a marine environment.

One important difference between the DBSCAN implementation carried out in this thesis and the examples reviewed above is that it exemplifies how a clustering analysis can enable the analyst to uncover the site-specific characteristics of an urban setting and inform the development of urban intervention proposals. Additionally, to the best of our knowledge there are no other applications of the DBSCAN algorithm implemented to identify vertical floorspace use patterns within the buildings.

§ 3.7 Conclusion

This chapter has provided general information on the knowledge discovery process in databases using data mining methods, presenting the goals, methods and techniques used in data mining. The branch of data mining known as spatial data mining was briefly introduced and a number of studies which have implemented data mining methods in urban studies were reviewed in order to examine how this study differs from similar works. Finally, the specific data mining methods implemented in this thesis, and their applications in RapidMiner were examined. A number of works that have implemented these techniques with spatial and non-spatial data were also reviewed in order to compare the implementations carried out in this thesis study with other projects.

The next chapter presents the concept of the city as a 'data mine' and the urban analysis process model developed to implement a knowledge discovery approach to urban analysis through data mining.

4 A knowledge discovery approach to urban analysis through data mining

As examined in the second chapter, there are various perspectives for approaching cities and urban analysis. In fact, the history of urban studies is the history of a range of perspectives on how to conceptualize and analyze cities. Acknowledging that different paradigms have complementary strengths in terms of explaining urban complexity, this thesis proposes to conceptualize the city as a 'data mine' and analyze it accordingly, using a knowledge discovery approach to urban analysis through data mining. Chapter (4) presents the conceptual background to this approach and the urban analysis process model developed to implement it. This chapter also discusses the possible links between a knowledge discovery approach to urban analysis through data mining and the most recent concepts underlined by post-structuralist urban theories.

§ 4.1 Conceptual Background: The city as a 'Data Mine'

The approach to this thesis is based on the fact that the city is a source of an enormous variety of qualitative and quantitative data. To some extent, thanks to advances in computation and ICT, this range of data and information can be collected electronically and stored, accessed, visualized and analyzed using databases, information systems, and advanced analysis methods. The development of data and information systems offers an important opportunity for researchers and practitioners to extend the scope of urban analysis. This thesis aims to investigate whether these developments can help us build a perspective that provides a better understanding of cities. Accordingly, the city is conceptually defined as a 'data mine' and it is proposed to analyze urban data by implementing a knowledge discovery approach through data mining. The concept of the city as a 'data mine' suggests that the city is a system of components that generate data and can be represented in a database consisting of micro-scale urban components (e.g., buildings, streets, individual actors etc.) and their multiple features. This conceptual model is an abstraction, which provides a basis from which our approach to urban analysis can be developed. This approach to cities can support urban analysts in dealing with two important features of urban environments, which are often considered to be essential research challenges:

Urban environments contain hidden relationships between their multiple dimensions: In urban analysis, there is a need to progress from the traditional one-dimensional description and classification of urban forms (e.g., land use maps, density maps) (Marshall, 2004) to a consideration of the multi-dimensionality of urban environments (Sökmenoğlu, Çağdaş, & Sarıyıldız, 2011). That is because, in order to decode the complexity of cities we need to move beyond focusing on just a few dimensions and examine the relationships between their multiple dimensions. Obviously, this perspective is not new; it has been recognized as an important challenge for urban studies since the 1960s. Alexander (1979), for instance, explains that the kind of complexity found in cities derives from the interaction and relationships between the different component parts on different scales over time. However, determining how to examine these interactions and relationships and make use of them in design, planning and decision-making processes still remains a challenge and new approaches to urban analysis are needed to address this. Data mining methods and techniques enable a great number of qualitative and quantitative attributes that belong to the components of cities to be considered. In addition, there are methods for mining data collected at discrete points in time which could enable researchers to identify the impact of time on urban environments. Therefore, in principle, a knowledge discovery through data mining approach may have significant potential for supporting urban researchers in exploring the relationships between the multiple dimensions of cities and studying how these relationships change over time.

Urban environments contain micro-scale data: In order to achieve a deeper understanding of an urban environment, it is necessary to address its complexity, which can be attempted by considering (analyzing) micro-scale data. This is also emphasized by Jacobs (1961): a microscopic or detailed view is an important strategy for studying complex urban problems. Hence, one important challenge in the field of urban analysis is to study how to analyze micro-scale - rather than aggregated - data in order to counter urban analysis methods that involve a low level of detail. As the knowledge discovery approach through data mining provides methods that are capable of efficiently analyzing large quantities of data, it may be suitable for analysing a large amount of micro-scale urban data.

Accordingly, this thesis proposes to conceptually define the city as a 'data mine' that can be represented through a database composed of micro-scale urban data with multiple dimensions that are in constant interaction with each other.

Based on this conceptual background, a KDPM for urban analysis which combines GIS and data mining was developed to uncover hidden information patterns and relationships among the features of urban components. The Beyoğlu Preservation Area was chosen as a test context for the KDPM for urban analysis. A micro-scale GIS database was constructed and some data mining methods and techniques (Naïve Bayes Classification, Association Rule Analysis and DBScan Clustering) were applied using the model. The major data source is the thematic maps of the Beyoğlu Preservation Area provided by the Istanbul Metropolitan Municipality. Detailed information on the Beyoğlu Preservation Area and the data resources used in the thesis are provided in the Implementation Phase (see next chapter).

§ 4.2 The Model: A Knowledge Discovery Process Model (KDPM) for Urban Analysis Combining GIS and Data Mining

As previously stated, this thesis conceptually defines the city as a 'data mine' represented in a database, with the aim of exploring hidden information patterns and relationships within this database. In order to accomplish this, a knowledge discovery approach to urban analysis through data mining was used, namely a semi-automated data analysis process which identifies previously unknown information patterns and relationships between data. A KDPM for urban analysis combining GIS and data mining was developed to apply a knowledge discovery approach to urban analysis. Applying data mining methods and techniques in combination with GIS technology is a relatively new and promising area of urban analysis (see, for instance, Malerba et al. (2003); May and Savinov (2003); Mukhlash and Sitohang (2007); Tang and McDonald (2002)). Data mining and GIS have separate technologies, methods, and traditions for analyzing and visualizing data. Whereas GIS offers basic spatial analysis functionalities, data mining involves advanced methods for data analysis derived from various domains (artificial intelligence, machine learning, statistics, database and information systems etc.), and can therefore supplement GIS in developing more sophisticated data-driven approaches to urban analysis. With recent developments in ICT, an immense amount of thematic and geographically referenced data has become available and it is now a more important challenge to capture the hidden information in these databases, since this has great potential for supporting urban design, planning and decision-making. The branch of data mining known as spatial data mining is also growing, and moving towards integrating GIS technologies with data mining methods specifically designed for spatial data (see, for instance, Yang, Ju, and Shao (2012) who proposed integrating spatial data mining with GIS using component technology).

Before elaborating on the KDPM developed for urban analysis, the proposal to implement data mining in urban analysis will be clarified. Data mining can be defined as extracting important patterns and trends from raw data. As also seen in the work of Gil et al. (2009) when applied to discovering relationships between urban attributes, data mining can serve various types of data analysis methods and techniques for the analysis of the multi-dimensional relational complexity of urban environments. In this thesis, data mining of multiple urban attributes is proposed as a promising alternative approach to many multi-dimensional methods (e.g., interdependence analysis, canonical correlation, partial least squares, multidimensional scaling, spatial autocorrelation, correspondence analysis etc.) developed during the 1970s, which are known to be useful for data and decision analysis in urban and geographical research (Nijkamp, 1980). However, as noted by Miller (2004) traditional analytic methods used for spatial analysis were developed to find out useful information from simple datasets (not heterogeneous, scientifically sampled and small). These methods were designed when computational power was weak and data collection was not cheap. However today, the geographic data is stored in very large digital databases and it is highly diverse. Therefore, traditional spatial statistics, which have high computational burdens, can be easily exhausted by this complexity (Miller, 2004).

Certain properties associated with data mining methods and techniques make it particularly interesting and promising in urban data analysis:

- Data mining techniques are data-driven, therefore they counter the confirmatory analytical techniques which require a *priori* hypotheses that restrict the researcher and prevent the discovery of previously unknown, unexpected or surprising information (Miller, 2004; Miller & Han, 2001). Thus, data mining techniques can support the analysis of urban databases without relying on any existing theories and enable previously unknown patterns and relationships to be determined from data. Recent advances in computer science have highlighted the need to move from the confirmatory to the knowledge discovery type of analysis (Christopoulou, 2009). The data-driven nature of data mining analysis makes it an exploratory and context-sensitive approach, which is promising for urban analysis. Moreover, the data-driven nature of data mining can support architects, urban designers, urban planners for making evidence-based decisions.
- Data mining techniques can incorporate a range of variables in large quantities without restricting the analyst to a small data sample and a small number of variables and are therefore appropriate for dealing with the multi-dimensional features of cities. In addition, this feature of data mining makes it possible to deal with individual (disaggregated) data, which enables a micro-scale urban analysis to be carried out.
- Some algorithmic models used for data mining can produce results that can be highly explanatory and suitable for direct use in developing urban intervention proposals. This will be exemplified further in Implementation (2), in which results of data mining are directly translated into rules and support the generation of draft plans for ground floor use, user-type and tenure-type allocation (see chapter 5).

Hence, the knowledge discovery approach to urban analysis through data mining developed in this thesis, involving the combined use of GIS and data mining methods and techniques, offers a computer-based, data-driven, exploratory, context-specific approach that allows for a multi-dimensional analysis of micro-scale urban data without relying on any existing theories. Figure 4.1 depicts the KDPM for urban analysis.

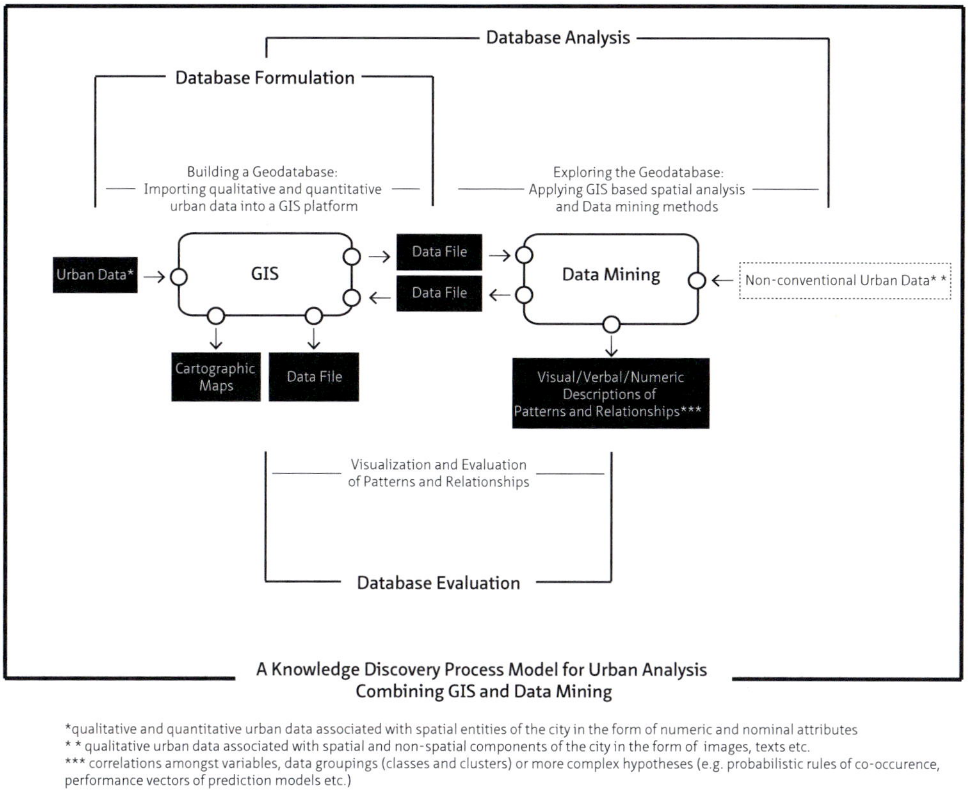

FIGURE 4.1 A Knowledge Discovery Process Model (KDPM) for urban analysis.

The KDPM for urban analysis is a domain-specific adaptation of the widely accepted process of knowledge discovery through data mining proposed by Fayyad et al. (1996b) and provides guidance on how to apply a knowledge discovery process for analyzing micro-scale, multi-dimensional urban data. This model describes a general process of database formulation, analysis and evaluation for extracting patterns and relationships from raw data by combining both GIS and data mining functionalities in a complementary way. The model describes a generic method that can be implemented by analysts using data belonging to different urban contexts. However, it is important to note that the process described by the model is rather abstract and therefore, in order to re-use the model for specific implementations, it will be necessary to develop more detailed versions in accordance with the focus of the research and the available data. A GIS platform is used as a medium for data management, data visualization and data analysis, whilst data mining is used as a complementary method for data analysis and visualization in the context of urban analysis.

The KDPM for urban analysis was constituted in three main steps:

Step 1. Database formulation: this step consists of building a dataset out of micro-scale data (qualitative and quantitative urban data associated with spatial entities in the city in the form of nominal and numeric attributes) using different data sources. In this step, GIS operations can be carried out to compute spatial relationships. The computational platform used in this step is GIS (ArcGIS and PostGIS software is used in this research).

Step 2. Database/data analysis: this is the analysis phase of the urban data. This step consists of applications of the spatial analysis functionalities of GIS and data mining methods (classification, association rule analysis and clustering methods are implemented in this research) using a data mining software application. In this thesis, the computational platform used in this step is the RapidMiner data mining software. If available, non-conventional data (qualitative urban data associated with spatial and non-spatial components of the city in the form of images, text, visual and audio recordings etc.) that cannot be processed in GIS can be also analyzed by applying the appropriate data mining methods and techniques (e.g., image mining, video mining, audio mining, text mining etc.).

Step 3. Database evaluation: this step evaluates the results in the form of verbal or numeric descriptions of information patterns and relationships. These descriptions can be correlations amongst variables, data groupings (classes and clusters) or more complex hypotheses (probabilistic rules of co-occurrence, performance vectors of prediction models etc.). The descriptions can be visualized in the form of cartographic maps using GIS, other visual descriptions provided by the data mining platform (e.g., scatter plots, histograms etc.) or other visualization techniques. Visual representation of information patterns and relationships facilitates the understanding and interpretation of the findings and thus allows further inferences and evaluations to be gathered. If interpreted as 'useful' and/or 'valuable' by the analyst, these information patterns and relationships are considered 'knowledge'. Therefore, the initial input of the model is urban data and the final output is a number of information patterns and relationships found in the data. These outputs can support architects, urban planners or urban designers in the course of urban design, planning and decision-making if interpreted as 'relational urban knowledge'.

In principle, both spatial and non-spatial data can be processed using this model, which may be capable of storing, representing and analyzing a wide range of information and data gathered from cities to explore 'relational urban knowledge'. Information about cities in various categories and multiple levels of abstraction may be processed using the KDPM for urban analysis. Obviously, it cannot be claimed that any type of information on the city can be represented in a database and analyzed with data mining methods. Nevertheless, in theory, this is a holistic approach that may allow for the analysis of both tangible and intangible assets of the city associated with its morphological, functional, economic, social, cultural, temporal, perceptual, visual dimensions, etc.

The terms used in this thesis are defined as follows:

Urban entities/components: components of the city with properties (features or attributes). Although, in principle, in urban analysis, a wide variety of urban entities can be considered (immobile and dynamic components and micro and macro scale components) as exemplified in Table 4.1, the urban entities employed in this thesis are restricted by the data sources that could be accessed: floors of buildings, buildings, blocks, streets and neighbourhoods.

COMPONENT TYPE	COMPONENT CATEGORY
Physical Urban Components	Building components, Parcels, Buildings, Building blocks, Squares, Streets, Roads, Underpasses, Open spaces, Green spaces, Bridges, Neighborhoods, Waterways, Highways, etc.
Actors	Individual people,Architects, Urban Planners, Urban Designers, Public&Private Instituitions, NGOs, Commercial firms, Business-makers, Decision-makers, Administrative agencies, etc.

TABLE 4.1 Urban Components (a proposal for a general categorical picture).

Urban attributes: distinct properties of urban entities. Attributes may be obtained from various data sources on the basis of different levels of observation. In this research, the range of attributes included in the database built to implement the KDPM for urban analysis was restricted by the data source. However, a general categorization of the possible attributes of urban entities that can be analyzed is provided in Table 4.2.

CATEGORY	ATTRIBUTES
Morphological	Gross Floor Area, Built-up Area (Footprint), Perimeter, Ground floor Index (GSI), Floor Space Index (FSI), Proportions, Orientations, Open space ratio, Compactness, etc.
Spatial	Coordinates, Topographical attributes (e.g., View, Slope, Land Height) Topological attributes (e.g., street network connectivity, accessibility), Proximity, etc.
Socio-Demographic	User profiles (Likes and Dislikes, Census attributes etc.), Daily activity profiles, Mobility, Population Density, etc.
Economic	Land value, Property value, Variables concerning trading volume of companies, etc.
Socio-Economic	Land use, Floorspace use in the buildings, Income levels, Vitality, Life expectancy, etc.
Cultural-Historic	Cultural Identity, Historical Importance, Historical Register of buildings, etc.
Architectural	Building style, typologies, etc.
Architectural-Physical	Building size, age, material, height, etc.
Political	Planning regulations, policies, etc.
Environmental	Noise, Pollution, Availability of green space, Sustainability level, Energy consumption, etc.
Urban Infrastructure	Security, Playground availability, Social, Technical and Medical infrastructures, Availability of open space, Availability of street lighting, etc.

TABLE 4.2 Urban attributes (proposal for a general categorisation).

In principle, each basic urban entity is unique in terms of its attributes. All the available qualitative/quantitative, spatial/non-spatial data that is relevant (in the view of the analyst) and suitable for encoding can be coded within the database.

In a diverse urban environment, complexity emerges from the interrelations between all of these urban entities and their multiple features presented in Table 4.1 and Table 4.2 (more aspects could be added to these tables). The existence of various features operating simultaneously results in a unique spatial and social configuration of urban space. The formulation of the city as a 'data mine' and the KDPM for urban analysis represent an attempt to understand more about the relationships between various different features of urban entities in order to address this complexity. Unfortunately, the unavailability and/or inaccessibility of relevant urban data and the high level of complexity found in cities constitute major limitations to this approach. Given present-day technology, it is practically possible to form complete data sets containing all the urban entities and their multiple features in a time-based manner. Therefore this thesis proposes to consider the database representing the city as an open system, to which any data can be added as it becomes available.

The power of this approach lies in its independence from any existing perspective on urban analysis that is limited by specific urban entities and attributes. Moreover, the type of data used as input for the model can be both qualitative and quantitative. However, the most important restrictions may be the unavailability of large amounts of various kinds of data and technical deficiencies in the available data mining algorithms.

As previously stated, in this thesis the Beyoğlu Preservation Area is the main urban context within which the generic KDPM for urban analysis is implemented (the implementations can be found in Chapter 5). The generic process described by the KDPM for urban analysis was further developed to analyze the data contained in the official thematic maps of the Beyoğlu Preservation Area prepared by the Istanbul Metropolitan Municipality as a foundation for the Master Plan for the Beyoğlu Preservation Area (published in 2008 and provided as pdf files). Thus, using the thematic maps, an urban database was built in GIS, namely the Beyoğlu Preservation Area Building Features Database, and analyzed. This database consists of the buildings located in the Beyoğlu Preservation Area, which are represented by their multiple features. Location or position of buildings is the primary reference for data in the Beyoğlu Preservation Area Buildings Features database. Apart from the data gathered from the thematic maps, the database contains some data gathered from Beyoğlu Municipality Internet resources and data measured by means of GIS spatial analysis functionalities. Further information on this implementation is provided in Chapter (5).

Having established the conceptual background and the urban analysis process model, the following section will provide a brief theoretical examination which focuses on the similarities and differences between a knowledge discovery approach to urban analysis and 'relational thinking' mainly associated with post-structuralist theories of cities.

§ 4.3 A Brief Theoretical Examination

As previously argued in Chapter (2), the divergence between the concerns of urban theory and the practices of urban analysis, design and planning is often seen as a major obstacle for solving urban problems and it is claimed that ICT-based approaches have the potential to create a new rapprochement between these fields. In may therefore be argued that a knowledge discovery approach to urban analysis through data mining has significant potential to create such a rapprochement. To be specific, common ground can be found between this approach and post-structuralist theories of cities. Accordingly, this section examines whether a knowledge discovery approach to urban analysis through data mining and the 'relational thinking' mainly associated with post-structuralist approaches towards cities have any concepts in common. This brief examination is conducted both in general terms and in terms of the work carried out in this study. Before proceeding, it is important to note that some readers may consider that the links between a knowledge discovery approach to urban analysis through data mining and 'relational thinking' may be weak and, as such, irrelevant to this thesis. However, since the study of relationships between urban components is the main topic of this research, it is relevant to examine the theoretical aspects of the concept of 'relationships'. Moreover, this may provide new insights and hopefully convince the reader that a convergence between these fields is possible and worth investigating further.

'Thinking space relationally' is one of the most influential concepts of the early 21st century (Jones, 2009). Relational approaches are influential in many disciplines, mainly in economic geography, economic sociology and post-structuralist discourses: however, there is no consistent research agenda which defines the relations in question (Sunley, 2008). Very broadly, in these disciplines relations are defined as all forms of networks between entities and 'relational thinking' replaces "topography and structure-agency dichotomies with a topological theory of space, and place and politics as encountered, performed and fluid" (Jones, 2009, p. 492). 'Relational thinking';

Dissolves the boundaries between objects and space, and rejects forms of spatial totality... does not exist as an entity in and of itself, over and above material objects and their spatiotemporal relations and extensions. In short, objects are space, space is objects, and moreover objects can be understood only in relation to other objects – with all this being a perpetual becoming of heterogeneous networks and events that connect internal spatiotemporal relations (compare Mol and Law, 1994; Dainton, 2001; Massey, 2005). (Jones, 2009, p. 491)

The overall aim of a knowledge discovery approach to urban analysis is to capture 'useful' and 'valuable' interrelations between the features of urban components. The focus of the analysis is the information patterns and relationships that exist within the order of an urban context. Conceptually speaking, it is thereby possible to say that a knowledge discovery approach through data mining and 'relational thinking' have a goal in common: uncovering hidden relationships. Moreover, in principle, a knowledge discovery approach to urban analysis through data mining enables the multiple aspects of urban entities to be considered together in terms of their interrelations. This is a departure from the classic one-dimensional descriptions of urban entities and might encourage researchers to study a large number of relations, as highlighted in post-structuralist discourses.

In the context of this thesis, the holistic view of urban networks and processes conceptualized in post-structuralist theories is acknowledged, although this research focuses on a specific type of relation in the Implementation Phase (interrelations between different features of buildings), rather than the whole network of relations operating in the urban context. Another point that differentiates this thesis from the post-structuralist conceptualization of relations is that a cross-sectional rather than a time-based analysis, as emphasized by post-structuralist theories, was implemented, due to the unavailability of time-based data. Essentially a fragment in time and space is considered and this fragment is analyzed in a relational manner. Finally, again due to the unavailability of the appropriate data, the research does not include relations involving the social aspects of the city, also an important aspect of 'relational thinking' in post-structuralist approaches. However, as previously mentioned, an-open system is proposed in which any type of data (both qualitative, quantitative and time-based data) can be used as input for the KDPM for urban analysis. Thus the variety of information patterns and relationships can be extended.

In addition to the major emphasis on the concept of relations, which is the core of 'relational thinking'; the latter has introduced other important concepts into the research agenda for cities. These concepts might help to establish common ground between a knowledge discovery approach to urban analysis and 'relational thinking':

Contextuality: 'relational thinking' assumes that there is no universal knowledge and that knowledge is context-dependent. No universal generalizations can be made about what the 'city' is and there is no absolute truth. Graham and Healey, for example, emphasize the importance of knowledge which is specific to a particular instance. They discuss that the idea that particular forms found in cities "will lead to particular social, economic and cultural behaviours need to be demonstarted in terms of the relational dynamics of specific instances, not assumed as a universal generalization" (Graham

& Healey, 1999, p. 642) . In this respect, because a knowledge discovery approach to urban analysis through data mining is a data-driven approach, it always suggests a context-specific analysis (since the data is always context-dependent).

Non-territorial orderings: 'relational thinking' constructs a new interpretation of "scale and scalar units"; assuming that "scalar units have no genuine existence" and they are "epiphenomenal" (Sunley, 2008, p. 14). It assumes that spatial boundries between cities and regions are unneccessary (J. Allen, Massey, & Cochrane, 1998) and proposes to understand the world through networks and relations between entities, instead of scalar units. In particular, implementing a knowledge discovery approach to urban analysis through data mining using a multi-relational data mining approach (assuming an object-relational data representation, see Malerba et al. (2009)) may expose the links between different dimensions of urban entities operating on different scales. This might enable researchers to focus on the relationships between entities instead of scalar units. In this thesis, although the KDPM for urban analysis was implemented with categorized data attributed to a scalar unit of analysis i.e. buildings, the extraction of new patterns through data mining enables previously unperceivable new 'territories' to be discovered in other spatial scales. Section 5.1 demonstrates that instead of the official neighbourhood boundaries drawn on the maps by the municipal authorities, new types of natural territories are discovered by applying a clustering method.

Co-existence of several space-time geographies: relational spatio-temporality theory designates "how different processes can define completely different spatio-temporalities, and so set up radically different identification of entities, places, relations" (Harvey, 1996, p. 284). It rejects generalizing "the city as a unitary phenomenon with a single space-time" and advocates "relational rather than absolute theories of time-space" (Graham & Healey, 1999, p. 627) Graham and Healey also refer to Harvey (1996) and Hwang (1996) for a similar approach. Some data mining methods are specifically designed to deal with time-series data. Thus, a knowledge discovery approach to data mining might facilitate exploration of the transformation of certain aspects of urban environments over time, instead of focusing solely on data collected at one discrete point in time. In this thesis however, for reasons previously mentioned, it was not possible to access time-based data of any type and carry out a spatio-temporal analysis.

Micro-scale: 'relational thinking' emphasizes the importance of micro-relations, which have generally been ignored. It highlights the study of the "microlevel social processes and interactions between individual agents rather than spatial representations" (Sunley, 2008, p. 14). Generally speaking, data mining methods are good at tackling very large databases and this makes it possible to analyze disaggregated data. In this study, a micro-scale database consisting of buildings was constructed and the interrelations between multiple dimensions of urban components operating at the micro-scale were analyzed.

To conclude, mainly because time-based data was not being used and a limited number of relations between the multiple dimensions of urban components (relations between building features in different categories) were considered in the Implementation Phase, this thesis does not fully refer to the problems identified in the post-structuralist theories of cities. Instead, 'relational thinking' has been adopted as a conceptual starting point, as argued by Dicken and Malmberg (2001). It serves as a conceptual point of departure for the urban analysis approach developed in the thesis.

Although the contributions of 'relational thinking' to urban research are very important and promising, there have also been important criticisms, mainly based on the avoidance of analytical and operational procedures (Thompson, 2003) and the dismissal of the "importance of regularities, patterns, categories and processes on the assumption that these factors inevitably lead to a nomothetic essentialist science" (Sunley, 2008, p. 17). Relational approaches are also criticized for restricting ontologies and methodologies (Sunley, 2008), thus becoming difficult to test in empirical terms and make operational (Phelps & Waley, 2004). This may explain why Harvey argued for a "dialectical relationalism" (Jones, 2009, p. 15) ;

While I accept the general argument that process, flux, and flow should be given a certain ontological priority in understanding the world, I also want to insist that this is precisely the reason why we should pay so much attention to what I will later call the 'permanences' that surround us and help solidify and give meaning to our lives. Furthermore, while it is formally true that everything can be reduced to flows...we are in daily practice surrounded by things, institutions, discourses and even states of mind of such relative permanence and power that it would be foolish not to acknowledge those evident qualities. (Harvey, 1996, pp. 7-8) (as cited in Jones, 2009, p. 15)

This theoretical examination may be concluded by posing the following question: "Could a knowledge discovery approach to urban analysis through data mining serve as a tool that makes 'relational thinking' operational?"

Based on the theoretical analysis conducted in this section, it can be added that, in theoretical terms, the thesis adopts a post-positivist approach, for the following reasons:

- It uses quantitative methods, allowing for stochastic results in urban data analysis;
- It acknowledges the contextual nature of knowledge and, by using a data-driven approach, draws conclusions directly from context-specific data;
- It acknowledges the limitations on achieving a completely objective reality, due to the fact that cities are complex, and therefore focuses on discovering evidence-based probabilities rather than absolute truths.

§ 4.4 Conclusion

This chapter have mainly presented the concept of the city as a 'data mine' and the urban analysis process model, namely the KPDM for urban analysis, developed to implement a knowledge discovery approach to urban analysis through data mining. The details of this semi-automated data analysis process for extracting patterns and relationships from raw data, namely information about the database formulation, analysis and evaluation by combining both GIS and data mining functionalities in a complementary way, has been given. The terms used in this thesis have also been introduced. Since the study of relationships between urban components is the main topic of this study, this chapter has also examined if a theoretical convergence can be found between this approach and the 'relational thinking' underlined by post-structuralist urban theories.

Having established a conceptual background for applying a knowledge discovery approach through data mining to the field of urban analysis, the KDPM for urban analysis, and a brief theoretical examination, the following chapter will focus on the Implementation Phase of the thesis. It provides detailed information on the construction of the Beyoğlu Preservation Area Building Features Database and the application of the knowledge discovery approach to urban analysis through data mining in three different implementations.

5 Implementations of the KDPM for urban analysis in the Beyoğlu Preservation Area

This chapter explores the implementations of the knowledge discovery approach to urban analysis through data mining applied in the Beyoğlu Preservation Area in Istanbul. Three implementations of the KDPM for urban analysis were executed in order to investigate the research questions underpinning this study and subsequently reviewed in terms of their achievements and limitations. The first section introduces Implementation (1), which focuses on the application of the KDPM for urban analysis in the Beyoğlu Preservation Area. This section provides information on the formulation of the Beyoğlu Preservation Area Building Features Database, the analysis of this database using data mining methods and the evaluation of the results. It is a comparative study that explores patterns and relationships between building features in the Beyoğlu Preservation Area and its three important neighbourhoods. The second section introduces Implementation (2), which implements the KDPM for urban analysis together with Evolutionary Computation. This implementation focuses on developing an alternative approach to the regeneration of Tarlabaşı neighbourhood located in the Beyoğlu Preservation Area. The final section introduces Implementation (3), which implements the KDPM for urban analysis via an educational workshop focusing on the regeneration of Tarlabașı. This implementation investigates how to combine the knowledge discovery approach to urban analysis through data mining with parametric urban analysis techniques and tests the usability of this approach by the students. Each implementation is evaluated at the end of each section.

§ 5.1 Implementation (1) the Beyoğlu Preservation Area Building Features Database

This implementation focuses on Research Question (2) and investigates the kind of patterns and relationships that can be extracted from the traditional thematic maps of the Beyoğlu Preservation Area by implementing a knowledge discovery approach to urban analysis through data mining and how these patterns and relationships can be represented. This section therefore describes how the KDPM for urban analysis, previously introduced in Chapter 4 (see Figure 4.1), was implemented in the context of the Beyoğlu Preservation Area. As described in the previous chapter, the KDPM for urban analysis is a generic model which describes a general process of database formulation, analysis and evaluation for extracting patterns and relationships from raw data by combining both GIS and data mining functionalities. The model uses GIS as a platform for data management, visualization and spatial analysis and data mining for advanced computational data analysis and visualization.

The Beyoğlu Preservation Area, officially housing about 100,000 inhabitants and containing 11,984 buildings, 700 building blocks and 30 neighbourhoods in an area of approximately 3.200.000 m^2 which is an important part of the historic city centre of Istanbul, is the context for the implementation and testing of this approach. This choice was made on the basis of the requirements of the knowledge discovery approach through data mining, which requires a large volume of diverse data. The Beyoğlu Preservation Area meets these criteria. A detailed one-dimensional analysis of the urban features of the Beyoğlu Preservation Area, i.e. the urban analysis maps, was prepared and published by the Istanbul Metropolitan Municipality to inform the preparation of the 2008 Master Plan for the Beyoğlu Preservation Area. However, these analysis maps do not seem to provide enough direct support in the making of the Master Plan for the Beyoğlu Preservation Area. Nevertheless, the urban analysis maps for the 2008 Master Plan for the Beyoğlu Preservation Area are appropriate for testing a knowledge discovery approach to urban analysis through data mining in terms of their rich coverage of micro-scale urban features. These analysis maps are the principal data source in this thesis and enabled a large and high-dimensional database (11,984 buildings with their 45 different features) to be constructed. More importantly, the main reason why the Beyoğlu Preservation Area is appropriate for this thesis is that it is a very good example of a complex urban centre, with great potential for including repetitive and diverse relationships. The Beyoğlu Preservation Area includes both residential and commercial functions and is also one of the most frequently visited leisure areas in Istanbul. Well-known for its heterogeneous local and visitor population, the Beyoğlu Preservation Area is very attractive both as a historical and a contemporary city centre, and is significantly diverse in terms of land use and population characteristics. Hence it is a very good example of an urban environment where relations among diverse features of micro-scale urban entities can be studied by applying data mining methods. Figure 5.1 shows the Beyoğlu Preservation Area in red, located on the European side of Istanbul and connected to the old city (the historic peninsula of Constantinople) by two bridges passing over the Golden Horn (an inlet of the Bosporus connecting the Black Sea with the sea of Marmara).

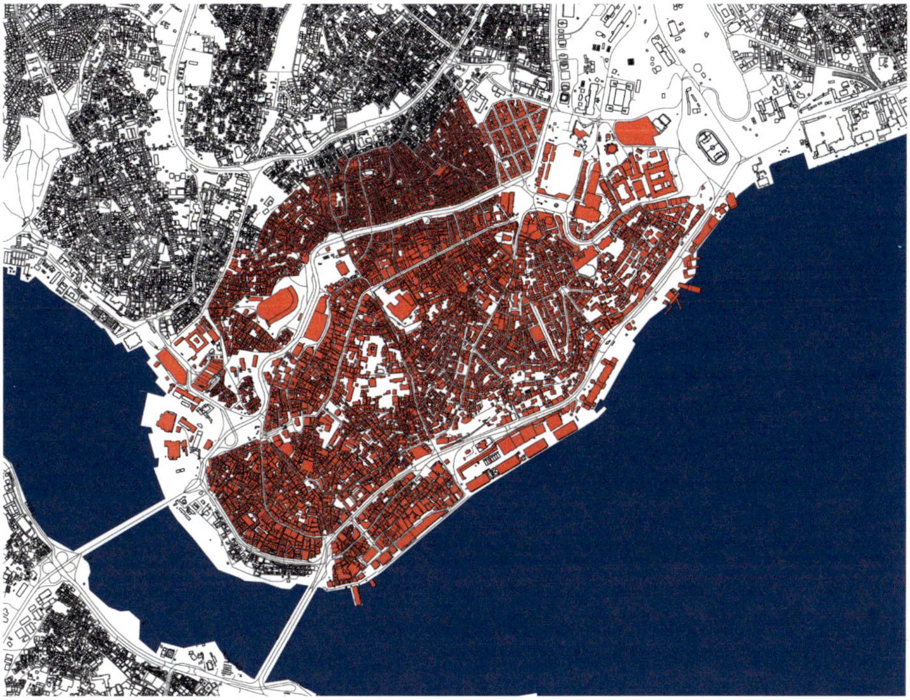

FIGURE 5.1 The Beyoğlu Preservation Area, buildings coloured in red, is approximately 3.200.000 m2 and has 100,000 inhabitants.

Applying the KDPM for urban analysis described in the previous chapter (see Figure 4.1) to an analysis of the Beyoğlu Preservation Area involved the design, analysis and evaluation of the Beyoğlu Preservation Area Building Features Database. Figure 5.2 shows the overall process.

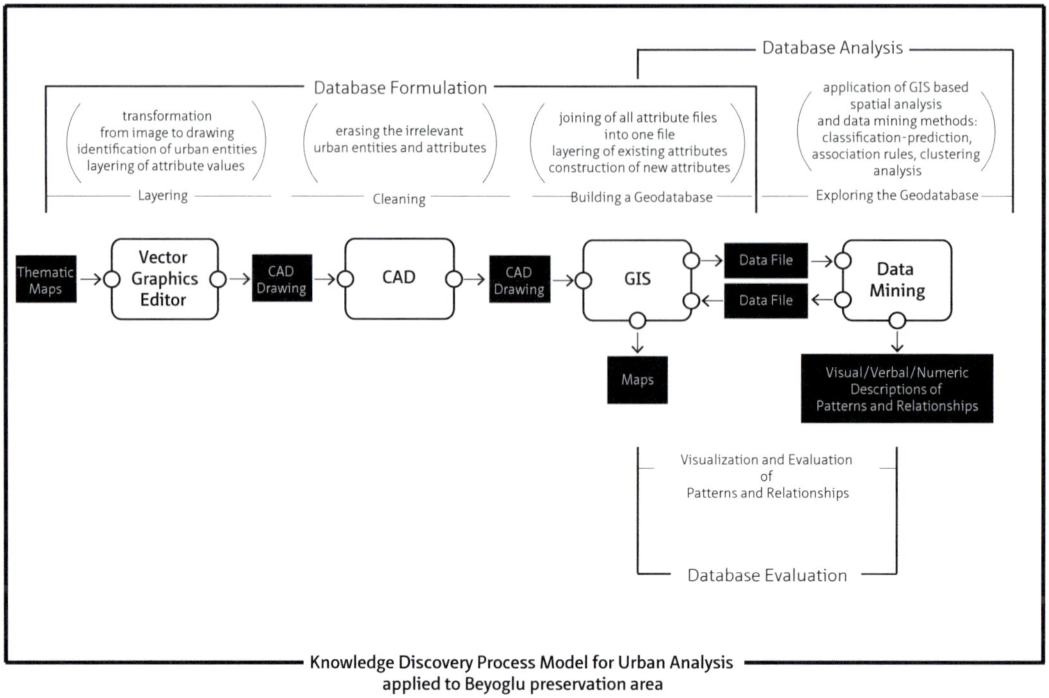

FIGURE 5.2 KDPM for urban analysis applied to the Beyoğlu Preservation Area

Figure 5.2 depicts the following steps in the knowledge discovery approach through data mining applied to the Beyoğlu Preservation Area:

Step 1. Database formulation: This involved the design of the Beyoğlu Preservation Area Building Features Database, in which the traditional thematic maps from the Master Plan for the Beyoğlu Preservation Area (published in 2008 and provided in the form of pdf files) were first processed using vector graphics editor software (Adobe Illustrator) for layering, followed by a CAD (Autodesk AutoCAD) program for cleaning and finally a GIS program (ArcGIS) to build the database. The pdf files were thus transformed into drawing files and exported into GIS to combine all the information layers in a geodatabase. In addition to data gathered from the thematic maps of the Master Plan for the Beyoğlu Preservation Area, land-price data gathered from the Beyoğlu Municipality (the land price for buildings per square meters) was also added and GIS spatial analysis operations were implemented to compute spatial relationships (certain topological and distance relationships). The output of the GIS platform, within which a geodatabase for the Beyoğlu Preservation Area building features was built, is a flat data file which can be exported to the data mining platform (RapidMiner).

Step 2. Database analysis: This phase consists of the application of methods to explore patterns and relationships hidden in the database. Three analysis methods are applied, namely classification, association rule analysis and clustering. These methods are explained in detail in the previous Section 3.5.

Step 3. Database evaluation: This is the phase in which the results discovered in the analysis process are examined. The results of the analytical processes are obtained in various forms depending on the analysis method used (probabilistic relationships, association rules, data groupings etc.) and can either be visualized using different techniques available in RapidMiner (graphical representations) or in GIS (cartographic maps). In order to visualize the results in the form of cartographic maps, the results can be exported from the data mining platform to the GIS in the form of data files or can be directly queried in GIS using Structured Query Language (SQL). This combined use of GIS and data mining extends the analysis and visualization capabilities of both technologies. The output of this final phase is a number of descriptions and visual representations of the relationships and patterns found in the data and, if considered 'useful' and/or 'valuable' by the analyst, some of these results can be interpreted as 'relational urban knowledge'. However, this is a specific type of 'relational urban knowledge' limited by the relationships between the available features of the buildings in the Beyoğlu Preservation Area, hereafter referred to as 'relational urban knowledge' of building features.

The phases of the Beyoğlu Preservation Area Building Features Database formulation, analysis and evaluation are presented in detail in the following sections.

§ 5.1.1 Formulation of the Beyoğlu Preservation Area Building Features Database

The first phase of the knowledge discovery through data mining process involves formulating a database. Three different types of data sources were used in this formulation. The data sources provided various types of data associated with several types of urban entities (building floor, building, building block, neighbourhood), which are called attributes (features) of urban entities. These urban entities, their attributes and attribute categories are listed in Table 5.1.

Data Source	Urban Entities	Attributes of Urban Entities	Attribute Dimensions (Categories)
Thematic maps of the 2008 Master Plan for the Beyoğlu Preservation Area, published by the Istanbul Metropolitan Municipality	Building Floor	Floor space use (of basements, ground floors, 1st- 10th floors, penthouses, 17 attributes in total)	Socio-economic
	Neighborhood	Neighborhood Name	Location Name
	Building Block	Population Density (Person/Ha)	Socio-demographic
	Building	Presence in the Bosporus Silhouette	Cultural-historic-economic
	Building	Building Maintenance Conditions	Architectural-physical
	Building	Building Construction Style	Architectural-physical
	Building	Empty floor ratio	Socio-economic
	Building	Ownership	Socio-economic
	Building Block	Historical Registry of Building Blocks (intensity)	Cultural-historic
	Building Block	Floor Space Index (FSI)	Architectural-morphological
	Building	Historical Registry of Buildings	Cultural-historic
	Building	Slope Code	Spatial-topographical
	Building	Land Height (elevation from sea level)	Spatial-topographical
	Building	Number of Floors	Architectural-physical
	Building	Basement (with or without)	Architectural
	Building	Penthouse (with or without)	Architectural
	Street	Streets	Location Name
	Street	Street Hierarchy	Socio-economic
GIS computation	Building	Ground floor surface area (Footprint)	Geometric-spatial
	Building	Distance to Dolmabahce	Spatial
	Building	Distance to Galata Bridge	Spatial
	Building	Distance to Galata Tower	Spatial
	Building	Distance to Galatasaray	Spatial
	Building	Distance to Kabatas	Spatial
	Building	Distance to Taksim	Spatial
	Building	Distance to Tepebasi	Spatial
	Building	Distance to Tunel	Spatial
	Building	Distance to Unkapani	Spatial
Beyoğlu Municipality - 2008	Street	Land Price	Economic

TABLE 5.1 Urban Entities, Attributes and Attribute Categories.

As Table 5.1 shows, the largest number of attributes (34) was extracted from the thematic maps of the 2008 Master Plan for the Beyoğlu Preservation Area provided by Istanbul Metropolitan Municipality. These maps include information attributed to several urban entities classified under various themes. The maps were processed using various computer applications and finally transformed into the Beyoğlu Preservation Area Building Features Database in GIS, as shown in Figure 5.2. In addition to the 34 attributes gathered from the Istanbul Metropolitan Municipality, 10 attributes were calculated by means of GIS computation. 1 attribute was gathered from the Beyoğlu Municipality web page, transferred into GIS and added to the Beyoğlu Preservation Area Building Features Database. The Beyoğlu Preservation Area Building Features Database, developed in GIS, contains 45 attributes in total. More information about these attributes can be found in Appendix B.

Unfortunately, the Beyoğlu Preservation Area Building Features Database does not contain detailed information on the social, cultural, demographic and economic characteristics of the people living in the Beyoğlu Preservation Area. Other types of information, for example data on environmental issues such as energy consumption in buildings, or the telecommunication behaviour of people living in the Beyoğlu Preservation Area, could not be accessed either. Applications were made to the Beyoğlu Civil Registry Office, Istanbul Gas Distribution Company (IGDAS) and Telecommunication Company (Turk Telekom) for this information but this type of micro-scale data is not shared for security and privacy reasons. However, these issues could have been resolved: the most important difficulty for a researcher who is interested in working in this area is the lack of a 'data sharing culture' in the country. An incremental system is therefore proposed that could incorporate these types of information later, if they ever become available.

The most time-consuming and demanding part of the database formulation was processing the thematic maps from the 2008 Master Plan for the Beyoğlu Preservation Area. Each step of the database formulation process will now be examined. The raw data was gathered in the form of thematic maps (one map for each theme), in the form of pdf files. Figure 5.3 shows the original analysis map depicting the use of ground floors of buildings located inside the Beyoğlu Preservation Area, as provided by the Istanbul Metropolitan Municipality.

Harita 3 - 25 Beyoğlu İlçesi Kentsel Sit Alanı Zemin Kat Fonksiyon Analizi

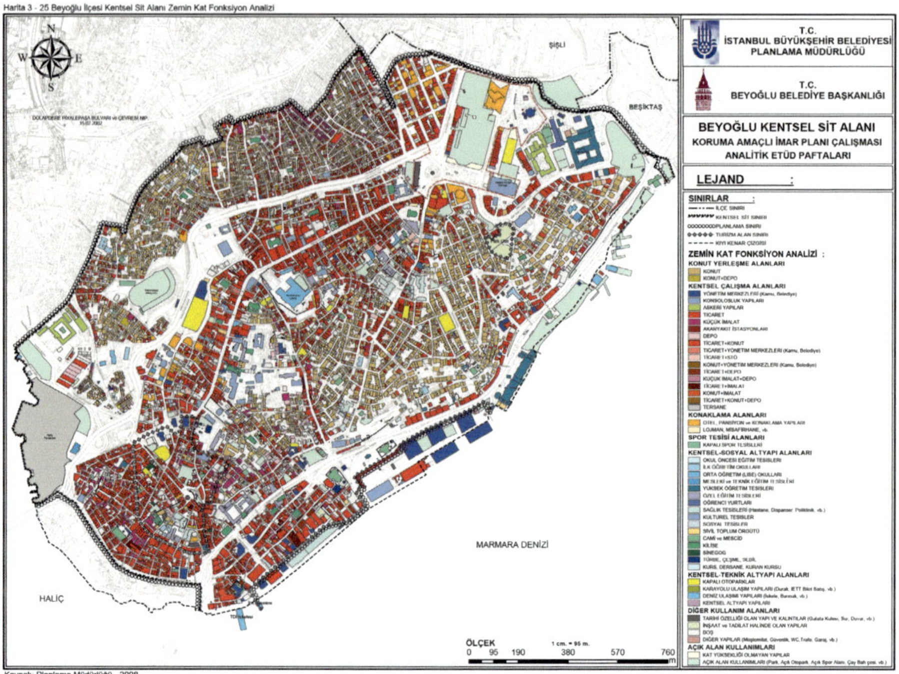

Kaynak: Planlama Müdürlüğü - 2008

FIGURE 5.3 Ground floor use allocation map, provided by the Istanbul Metropolitan Municipality, 2008.

Each cartographic/thematic urban analysis map was separately transformed from a pdf file to a drawing file (dwg) with layers, using vector graphics editor software. The various types of floorspace use supplied by the Istanbul Metropolitan Municipality were classified under more generic labels to simplify the analysis process: residential, business-shopping (including commercial, office and administrative uses); accommodation (including hotels, hostels, guest houses); social infrastructures (including schools, educational, cultural, religious buildings, NGO offices and consulate and embassy buildings); technical infrastructures (including parking areas, sanitary facilities, transportation nodes, sports facilities); empty/other (including warehouses, historical ruins and all other uses) and open spaces (parks, green areas, tea gardens). All these drawing files were then preprocessed and cleaned by erasing irrelevant entities using a CAD application. Next, all the drawing files were individually processed using a GIS application and combined in the form of a GIS file. Each drawing file constitutes a unique layer of this GIS file. This file contains all the data from each thematic map transformed into a database containing buildings as basic entities and their various features as attributes. By performing 'Spatial Join' operations in GIS, some topological relationships between buildings and building block, streets and official neighbourhood boundaries were computed. Features measured on the basis of these urban entities were attributed to the buildings. Accordingly, a database consisting of only one type of urban entity, namely buildings with attributes, was constructed.

The available quantitative and qualitative data was associated with geographical space with the help of GIS and represented both as a cartographic/thematic map and a data file i.e. the Beyoğlu Preservation Area Building Features Database. In GIS, 2D polygon geometry represents urban entities that are basically individual buildings. After formulating the main structure of the database by processing the thematic maps, land price data gathered from Beyoğlu Municipality was added to the database by associating the land price data provided on the basis of the streets in which the buildings were located. The screen shot in Figure 5.4 shows the Beyoğlu Municipality web page where land price data is published.

FIGURE 5.4 The Beyoğlu Municipality web page listing land prices on the basis of the Beyoğlu Preservation Area streets, 2008.

Finally, some distance relationships, i.e. proximity of buildings to important transportation nodes and pedestrian meeting points in the Beyoğlu Preservation Area and the surface area of building floors (building footprints) were calculated using GIS spatial analysis tools. The map in Figure 5.5 shows these nodes in the Beyoğlu Preservation Area.

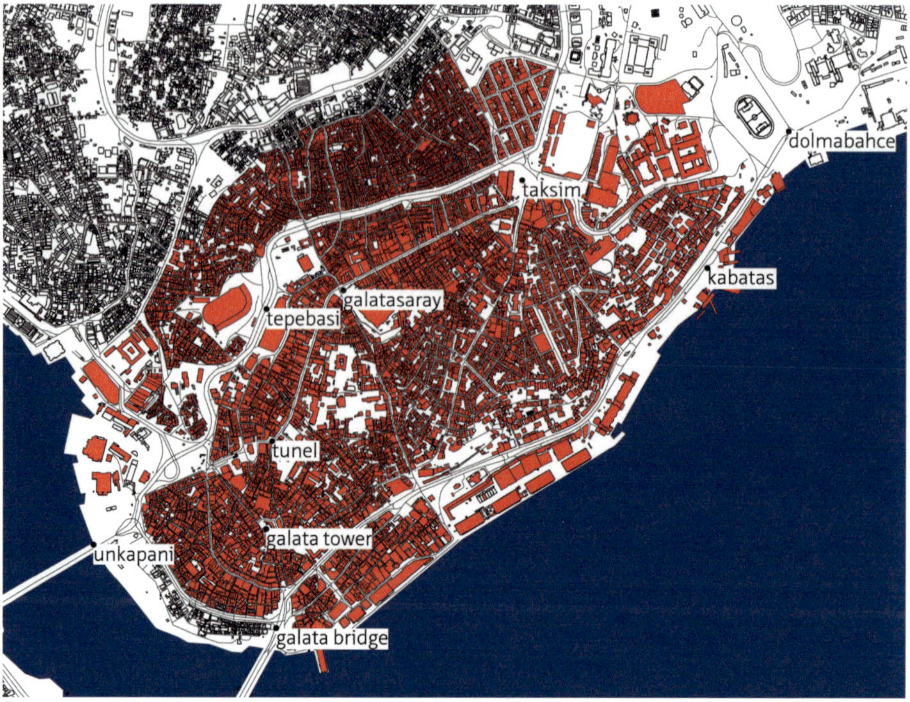

FIGURE 5.5 Important transportation nodes and pedestrian meeting points in the Beyoğlu Preservation Area; Dolmabahce, Galata bridge, Galata Tower, Galatasaray, Kabatas, Taksim, Tepebasi, Tunel and Unkapani.

The Euclidian distance from each building to Dolmabahce, Galata Bridge, Galata Tower, Galatasaray, Kabatas, Taksim, Tepebasi, Tunel and Unkapani were calculated using Hawth's Tools distance calculator. Hawth's Tools (http://www.spatialecology.com/htools) is an add-on created for ArcGIS that provides a set of spatial analysis tools not included in the ArcGIS software. After obtaining distances in meters, in order to prepare the database for classic data mining techniques, the distance values were materialized into categories by applying classification algorithms in GIS. Natural Breaks classification was conducted in ArcGIS, using the Jenks Optimization algorithm to obtain seven classes of distance. This is a "manual data classification method that seeks to partition data into classes based on natural groups in the data distribution" (http://support.esri.com). Natural Breaks classification uses the Jenks Optimization algorithm, "a statistical data classification method that partitions data into classes using an algorithm that calculates groupings of data values based on the data distribution", "seeking to reduce variance within groups and maximize variance between groups" (http://support.esri.com). The values of these classes are given in Appendix B. The map in Figure 5.6 shows the distances of the buildings from Taksim square, based on seven classes calculated in ArcGIS.

FIGURE 5.6 Distances from buildings to Taksim based on seven classes calculated in ArcGIS: buildings closer to Taksim are shaded in darker grey.

Building footprints were calculated using the ArcGIS function for polygon geometry calculation. Quantile classification was conducted in ArcGIS to classify the values obtained for the seven categories. Quantile classification is a data classification method that "distributes a set of values into groups that contain an equal number of values" (http://support.esri.com). The values of these classes are provided in Appendix B. The map in Figure 5.7 shows seven classes of building footprints.

FIGURE 5.7 Map of the Beyoğlu Preservation Area showing seven classes of building footprints, smaller footprints are shaded in darker colours.

Following these methods the formulation of the Beyoğlu Preservation Area Building Features Database, which includes 11,984 buildings and their 45 attributes, was completed and the qualitative and quantitative attributes of the buildings were all stored in the data table available in GIS.

Additional attributes can be calculated using other analysis tools or simply added as they become available. Data that can be gathered from various spatial analysis methods, such as space syntax analysis of street network patterns (Hillier & Hanson, 1984), could be also integrated into this knowledge discovery process using data mining.

This is one of the most important properties of the knowledge discovery approach through data mining developed in this thesis; it proposes an open-ended formulation whereby any new and relevant entities and their qualitative and quantitative attributes can be added to the database as they become available. It is also possible to organize the database in new ways, by building a relational database, for example.[2]

2 Relational data representation is a developing research topic in Spatial Data Mining: see, for instance, Malerba et al. (2009).

Figure 5.8 shows a section of the Beyoğlu Preservation Area, represented in GIS, in the form of a cartographic map, associated with its data table. Buildings are entities with unique IDs (identities) and attributes, such as buildings ID.702.

IDNO	Att.1	Att.2	Att.3	Att.4	Att.5	Att.6	Att.7
700	Residential	Residential	Residential	Residential	No 4th Floor	No 5th Floor	No 6th Floor
701	Residential	Residential	Residential	No 3rd Floor	No 4th Floor	No 5th Floor	No 6th Floor
702	Residential	Residential	Residential	Residential	Residential	Residential	No 6th Floor
703	Other	No 1st Floor	No 2nd Floor	No 3rd Floor	No 4th Floor	No 5th Floor	No 6th Floor
704	Business-Shopping	Empty	Residential	Residential	Residential	Residential	No 6th Floor
705	Business-Shopping	Business-Shopping	Business-Shopping	Business-Shopping	No 4th Floor	No 5th Floor	No 6th Floor

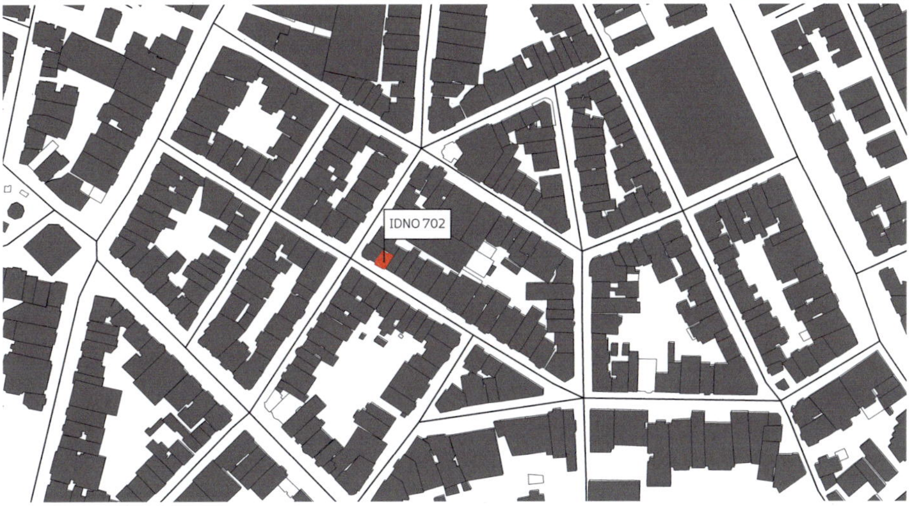

FIGURE 5.8 A GIS based representation of the Beyoğlu Preservation Area as a cartographic map, associated with its data table.

Once it had been formulated, the Beyoğlu Preservation Area Building Features Database was exported into a data mining application software package for analysis. The next section explains the analysis and evaluation process illustrated in Figure 5.2.

§ 5.1.2 Analysis and evaluation of the Beyoğlu Preservation Area Building Features Database using Data Mining

As previously stated, the Beyoğlu Preservation Area Building Features Database was analyzed using RapidMiner open-source software (https://rapidminer.com). The following sections include tests that explore patterns and relationships within the Beyoğlu Preservation Area Building Features Database using data mining methods and techniques. These experiments were designed in order to test different data mining analysis methods using this database and illustrate the different forms of patterns and relationships that data mining can discover, thus investigating of Research Question (2).

§ 5.1.2.1 Test (1): Which attributes of the buildings in the Beyoğlu Preservation Area perform best in predicting the use of ground floor?

In this first test, the problem was to identify attributes of the buildings in the Beyoğlu Preservation Area that perform best in predicting the use of ground floor. A Naïve Bayes learning operator was applied as a data mining method to explore whether the use category of the ground floor (i.e. accommodation, business-shopping, empty, open space, other, residential, sociocultural infrastructure, technical infrastructure) can be predicted using other attributes of the buildings in the Beyoğlu Preservation Area. This is an application of a classification method based on the Bayes theorem, as previously detailed in Section 3.5 (Data Mining Methods and Operators Implemented in the Thesis).

The Naïve Bayes learning operator applies Bayes theorem with strong independence assumptions (assuming independence between features contributing to the probability of the classification procedure), using the method of maximum likelihood. As the predictive power of each attribute of the buildings in the Beyoğlu Preservation Area (44 different attributes) in relation to the use of the ground floor (Att.1) is measured separately in this analysis, the "naïve" independence assumption is not relevant in this case. Each analysis concerns only one attribute's relationship to Att.1, and this is therefore a two-dimensional (one-by-one) implementation of the Naïve Bayes Classification. In essence, the Naïve Bayes learning operator helps to find best predictors of Att.1 for buildings in the Beyoğlu Preservation Area. Accordingly, Att.1 is defined as the label attribute and other attributes are the predictors. The screenshot in Figure 5.9 is taken from RapidMiner and illustrates the data mining process that consists of applying a Naïve Bayes learning operator and a Validation operator performing cross-validation in order to estimate the statistical performance of the learning operator.

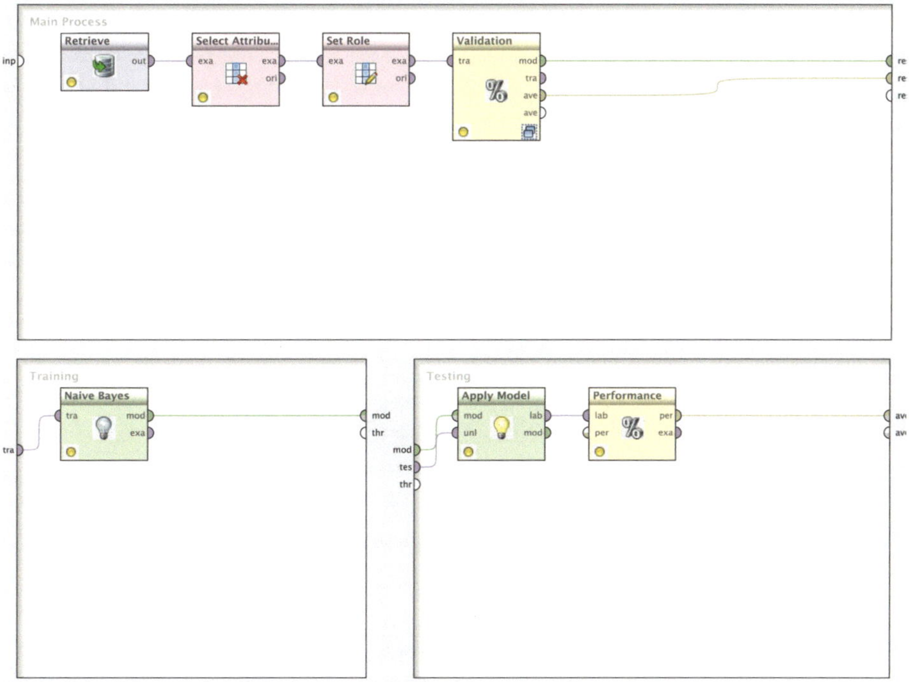

FIGURE 5.9 Data mining process using Bayes Classification in RapidMiner.

The Validation operator named X-Validation is implemented to estimate how accurately the Naïve Bayes Model performs in practice. This operator is;

A nested operator with two subprocesses: a training subprocess and a testing subprocess. The training sub process is used for training a model, which is then applied in the testing sub process. The performance of the model is also measured during the testing phase. (http://docs.rapidminer.com/studio/)

To perform a cross-validation process the X-Validation operator is fed with the dataset and the analyst partitions this dataset into k subsets of equal size. Then;

A single subset from the k subsets is retained as the testing data set (i.e. input for the testing sub process), and the remaining k – 1 subsets are used as the training data set. The cross-validation process is then repeated k times, with each of the k subsets used once as the testing data. The results from the k iterations can then be averaged (or otherwise combined) to produce a single estimation. (http://docs.rapidminer.com/studio/)

Using the number of validations parameter that is provided by the X-Validation operator, the analyst can adjust the value k. In this case, k is defined as 10, meaning that 10 subsets of equal size are created from the Beyoğlu Preservation Area Building

Features Database and 9 of them are used as the training data set. The X-Validation operator can use several types of sampling to build the subsets. Stratified sampling, which builds random subsets and ensures that the class distribution in the subsets is the same in the whole data set, is applied in this analysis.

The confidence of classification rules increases with training set size used to generate the rule. By construction, the cross-validation mechanism mitigates the problem of insufficient training set size; hence the learned classification rules are deemed to be reliable. The standard deviation of the accuracy can be taken as a measure to evaluate the model.

The X-Validation operator outputs a model, which is trained using the input dataset, and a performance vector showing the performance of the model.

Figure 5.10 contains a comparative distribution chart showing the differences between the original dataset and the predicted values of ground floor use by means of 1st floor use (Att.2).

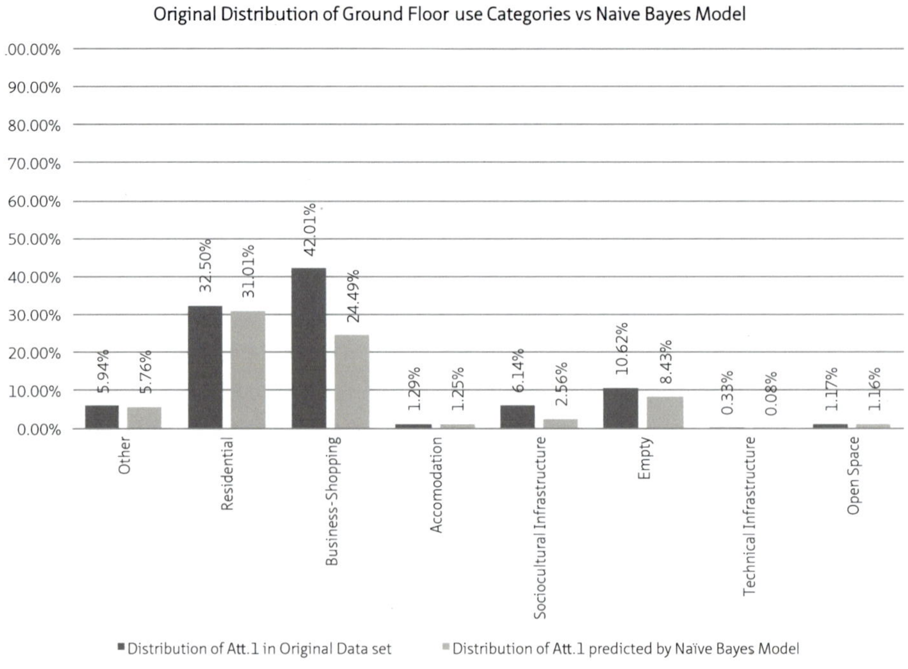

FIGURE 5.10 A comparative distribution chart.

RapidMiner software also outputs a table as a result of the Naïve Bayes Classification process. This table is known as the Confusion Matrix, which exposes the true versus predicted values. The Confusion Matrix which shows the results of the process applied to predict ground floor use by means of 1st floor use are given in Figure 5.11.

accuracy: 74.74% +/- 1.60% (mikro: 74.74%)

	true Other	true Residential	true Business-Shopping	true Accomodation	true Sociocultural Infrastructure	true Empty	true Technical Infrastructure	true Open Space	class precision
pred. Other	690	138	428	4	409	64	19	1	39.36%
pred. Residential	11	3716	1115	0	8	110	1	0	74.90%
pred. Business-Shopping	9	18	2935	0	12	86	1	0	95.88%
pred. Accomodation	1	0	17	150	0	0	0	0	89.29%
pred. Sociocultural Infrastructure	0	2	69	0	307	3	8	0	78.92%
pred. Empty	1	21	470	0	0	1010	0	0	67.24%
pred. Technical Infrastructure	0	0	1	0	0	0	10	0	90.91%
pred. Open Space	0	0	0	0	0	0	0	139	100.00%
class recall	96.91%	95.40%	58.29%	97.40%	41.71%	79.34%	25.64%	99.29%	

FIGURE 5.11 Accuracy Table for Naïve Bayes Classification to predict Att.1 by means of Att.2.

The accuracy of the Naïve Bayes Model is calculated by taking the percentage of correct predictions over the total number of examples. There are also other performance metrics shown in this Confusion Matrix, such as class precision and class recall. Class precision, also called positive predictive value, is the probability that a retrieved class label is relevant. Class recall, also known as sensitivity, is the probability that a relevant class label will be retrieved in a search. A variety of different performance metrics can be applied for different research domains. The value of a model is dependent on the interest of the analyst. Besides, knowing your data is also very beneficial when building a classification model and interpreting its performance.

The overall accuracy of the classifier, the recall and the precision for different classes shown in Figure 5.11 indicate the performance of the Naïve Bayes Model in predicting the unknown class labels, which in this case are the use categories of ground floor of the buildings in the Beyoğlu Preservation Area.

This analysis can be interpreted as follows: according to Figure 5.11, the prediction accuracy for the Naïve Bayes Model is 74.74 %, which means that the model has 74.74 % average accuracy across the 10 validations (with +/-%1.60 standard deviation). This shows that given any building in the database, the probability that the use of its ground floor will be classified correctly by this model is 74.74 % and the margin of error is +/- %1.60. The low deviation here is an indication of the reliability of the model.

In the case of residential use of the ground floor, for instance, out of 3895 buildings with residential ground floor use, the model predicts 3716 of them as residential and 179 of them are predicted incorrectly, which indicates that the class recall for residential is 95.40%. However, in total the model predicts 4961 buildings as residential, 3716 of which are true, indicating that the class precision for residential is 74.90%. The class recall results of the Naïve Bayes model in this analysis is over 50% for the following types of use: other (96.91%), residential (95.40%) business-shopping (58.29%), accommodation (97.40%), empty (79.34%) and open spaces (99.29%). However, it is below 50% for socio-cultural infrastructures (41.71%) and technical infrastructures (25.64%), which means that the probabilities that this model will retrieve a relevant class label in a search for the socio-cultural infrastructures (41.71%) and technical infrastructures (25.64%) uses is below 50%. Therefore, 1st floor use is not a powerful predictor for these two class labels of ground floor use. In conclusion, the prediction accuracy of the Naïve Bayes Model, which is 74.74 % (with +/-%1.60 standard deviation), indicates that for the buildings in the Beyoğlu Preservation Area, 1st floor use is a powerful predictor of ground floor use, and the model performs significantly well for the following class labels; other, residential, accommodation and open spaces (class recall above 90%).

1st floor use is the best attribute for predicting ground floor use (in terms of prediction accuracy measure). The results of the Naïve Bayes Classification in predicting ground floor use by means of all the other attributes of the Beyoğlu Preservation Area Building Features Database are provided in Appendix C.

The findings of 44 different Naïve Bayes Classification applications are filtered in the form of charts. The highest performance measures are found in the cases of Overall (accuracy), Residential (class recall) and Business-Shopping (class recall) uses.

Figure 5.12 lists attributes with over 50% accuracy in predicting ground floor use, in the form of a bar chart.

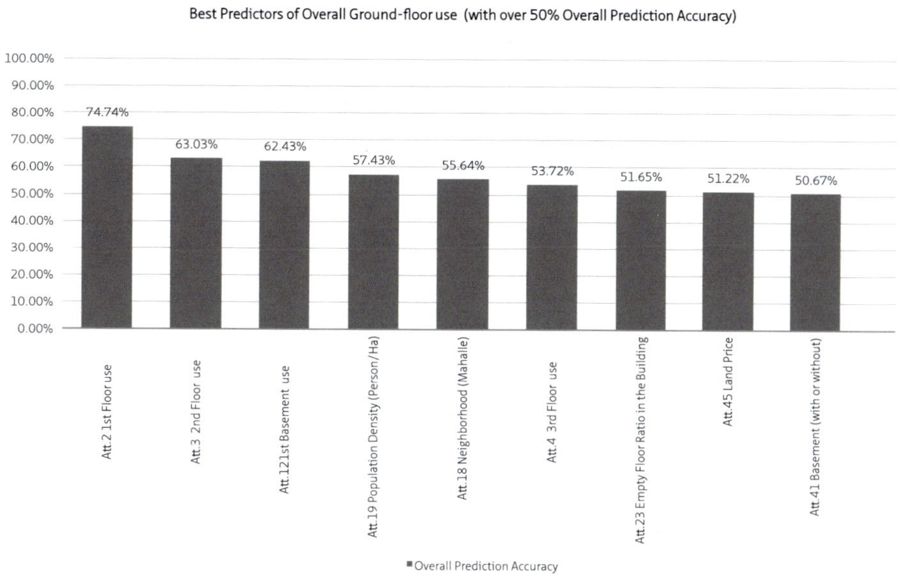

FIGURE 5.12 Best predictors of overall ground floor use with over 50% overall prediction accuracy.

As seen in Figure 5.12, the best predictors of ground floor use, in descending order, are the 1st floor, 2nd floor, 1st basement use, population density, neighbourhood (mahalle), 3rd floor use, empty floor ratio in the building, land-price and basement availability in the building.

The class recall results in predicting residential use of the ground floor using a Naïve Bayes classification are shown in the form of a bar chart in Figure 5.13.

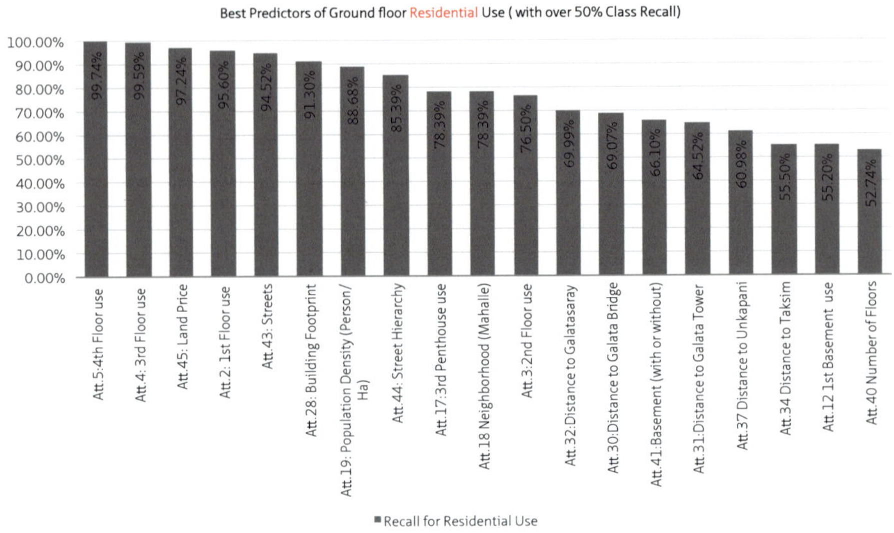

FIGURE 5.13 Best predictors of ground floor residential use, with over 50% class recall.

As seen in the chart above, the best predictors (with over 50% class recall) of ground floor residential use, in descending order, are 4th floor, 3rd floor use, land price, 1st floor use, streets, building footprint, population density, street hierarchy, neighbourhood, the use of 3rd penthouse, 2nd floor use, distance to Galatasaray and Galata Bridge, basement availability, distance to Galata Tower, Unkapani and Taksim, 1st basement use and number of floors. Very high levels of class recall shows that some of the attributes are very informative in predicting whether the ground floor use is residential (although they might not be informative for any other classes).

The class recall results in predicting Business-Shopping use of the ground floor using a Naïve Bayes classification are shown in the form of a bar chart in Figure 5.14.

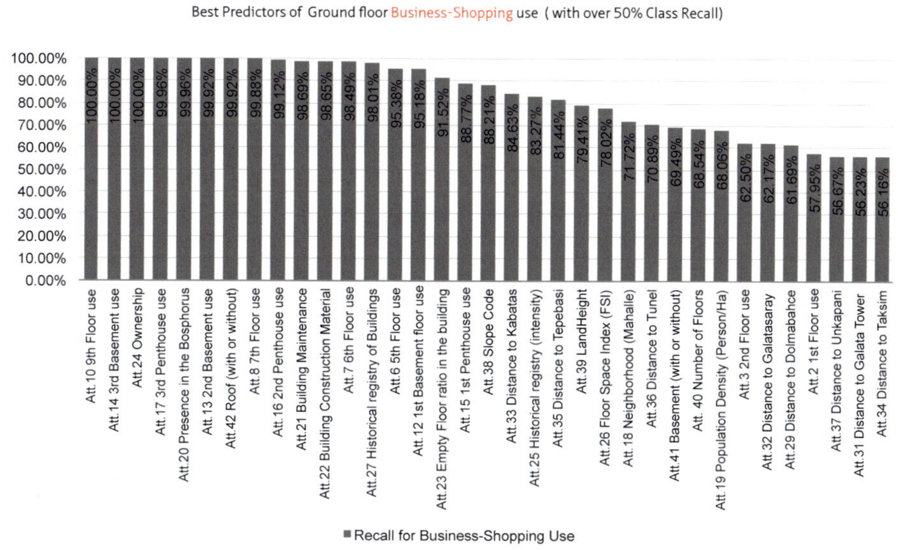

FIGURE 5.14 Best predictors of ground floor Business-Shopping use, with over 50% class recall.

The chart above shows the best predictors (with over 50% class recall) of ground floor business-shopping use, in descending order, namely 10th , 8th , 9th , 3rd basement floor use, ownership, 3rd penthouse use, presence in the Bosphorus silhouette, 2nd basement use, penthouse availability, 7th floor use, 2nd penthouse use, building maintenance conditions, building construction material, 6th floor use, historical registry, 5th use, 1st basement floor use, empty floor ratio, 1st penthouse use, slope code, distance to Kabatas, intensity of historical registration in building blocks, distance to Tepebasi, land height, FSI, neighbourhood, distance to Tunel, basement availability and population density, 2nd floor use, distance to Galatasaray, distance to Dolmabahce, 1st floor use, distance to Unkapani, Galata and Taksim. These results reveals some hidden relationships which can be interesting for an analyst. For instance, while the distance of a building to Kabatas is highly informative in predicting whether its ground floor is used for business-shopping purpose, its distance to Taksim is not very informative. This information can be used to interfere that the nearness/farness of a building to Kabatas influence the probability for its ground floor to be used as business-shopping purpose. On the other hand, this makes the analyst think the reasons why the same does not apply for Taksim. This exemplifies how this information might help to formulate interesting questions that are likely to lead the analyst to carry out a deeper research. Knowledge acquired in this way can result in a better understanding of the urban environment under examination.

In the following two charts (Figure 5.15 and Figure 5.16), only the most powerful attributes (with a class recall of over 90%) for predicting ground floor residential and business-shopping uses are brought together to allow for comparison.

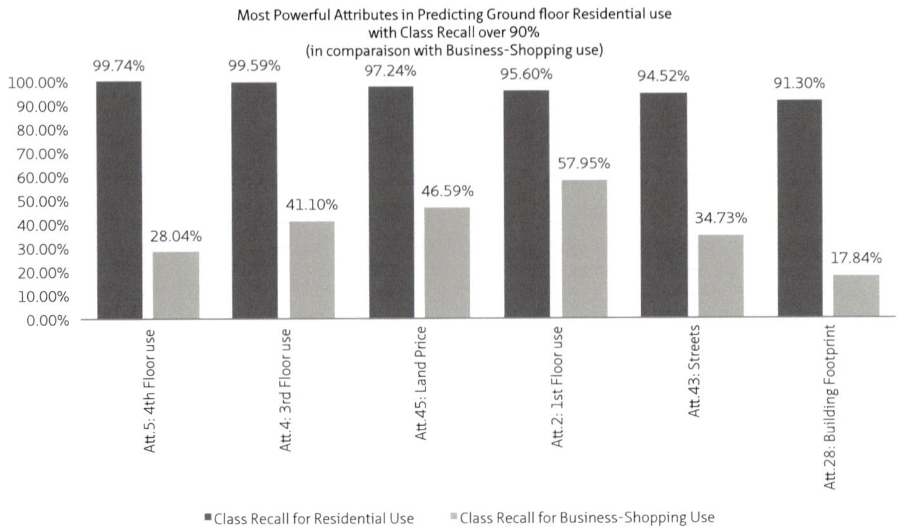

FIGURE 5.15 Most powerful attributes with over 90% class recall in predicting ground floor residential use, compared with their recall in predicting Business-Shopping use.

From Figure 5.15 it can be seen that;

- Although the use of 4th floor of the buildings in the Beyoğlu Preservation Area is a highly powerful attribute in predicting the use of the ground floor for residential purposes, it is not powerful in the case of business-shopping use.
- While the use of 3rd floor of the buildings in the Beyoğlu Preservation Area is a highly powerful attribute in predicting the use of the ground floor for residential purposes, it is not powerful in case of business-shopping use.
- While the land price of buildings in the Beyoğlu Preservation Area is a highly powerful attribute in predicting the use of the ground floor for residential purposes, it is not powerful in the case of business-shopping use (The database shows that if the land price is within a certain range the ground floor category is definitely residential but if it falls within other ranges it is not possible to predict the floorspace use.)
- While the use of 1st floor of the buildings in the Beyoğlu Preservation Area is a highly powerful attribute in predicting residential ground floor use , it is not so powerful in case of business-shopping use (although it still has 50% class recall)
- Although the street in which buildings are located in the Beyoğlu Preservation Area is a highly powerful attribute in predicting the use of the ground floor for residential purposes, it is not powerful in case of business-shopping use.

Although the building footprint in the Beyoğlu Preservation Area is a highly powerful attribute in predicting the use of the ground floor for residential purposes, it is not powerful in case of business-shopping use.

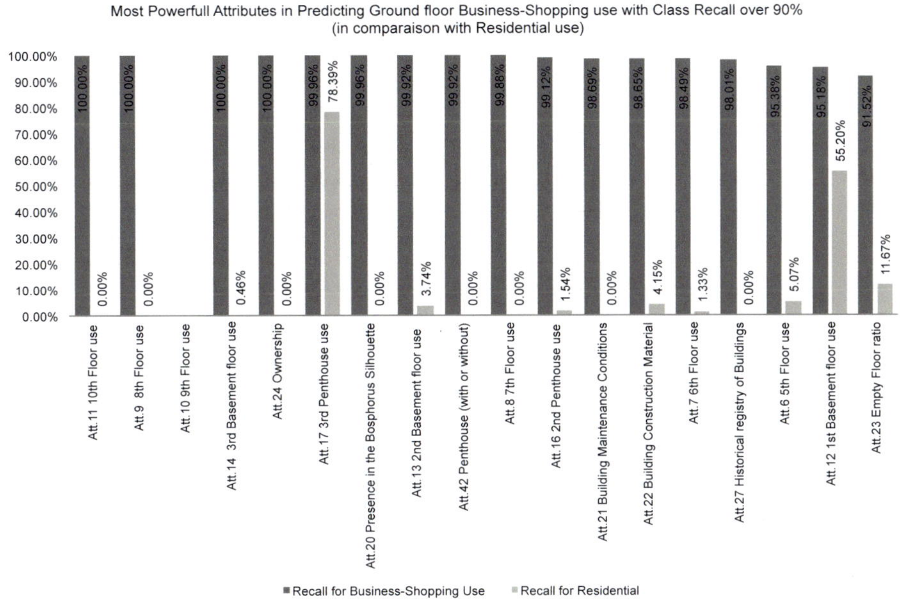

FIGURE 5.16 Most powerful attributes with over 90% class recall in predicting ground floor Business-Shopping use, compared with their recall in predicting Residential use.

From Figure 5.16 it can be observed that:

- Whereas the use of 10th floor of buildings in the Beyoğlu Preservation Area is a very powerful attribute (100% class recall) in predicting the use of the ground floor for business-shopping purposes, the model completely fails to classify residential use.
- While the use of the 8th floor of the buildings in the Beyoğlu Preservation Area is a very powerful attribute (100% class recall) in predicting the use of the ground floor for business-shopping, the model completely fails to classify residential use.
- While the use of the 9th floor of the buildings in the Beyoğlu Preservation Area is a very powerful attribute (100% class recall) in predicting the use of the ground floor for business-shopping, the model completely fails to classify residential use.
- While the use of the 3rd basement floor of the buildings in the Beyoğlu Preservation Area is a very powerful attribute (100% class recall) in predicting the use of the ground floor for business-shopping, the model almost completely fails to classify residential use.
- While ownership of the buildings in the Beyoğlu Preservation Area is a very powerful attribute (100% class recall) in predicting the use of the ground floor for business-shopping, the model completely fails to classify residential use.
- The use of the 3rd penthouse of the buildings in the Beyoğlu Preservation Area is a very powerful attribute in predicting the use of the ground floor, both for business-shopping (very powerful, over 90% class recall) and residential uses.

- While the presence of the buildings in the Beyoğlu Preservation Area in the Bosporus silhouette is a very powerful attribute in predicting the use of the ground floor for business-shopping, the model completely fails to classify residential use.
- While the use of the 2nd basement floor of the buildings in the Beyoğlu Preservation Area is a very powerful attribute in predicting the use of the ground floor for business-shopping, the model almost completely fails to classify residential use.
- While penthouse availability in buildings in the Beyoğlu Preservation Area is a very powerful attribute in predicting the use of the ground floor for business-shopping, the model completely fails to classify residential use.
- While the use of the 7th floor of the buildings in the Beyoğlu Preservation Area is a very powerful attribute in predicting the use of the ground floor for business-shopping, the model completely fails to classify residential use.
- While the use of the 2nd penthouse floor of the buildings in the Beyoğlu Preservation Area is a very powerful attribute in predicting the use of the ground floor for business-shopping, the model almost completely fails to classify residential use.
- While the maintenance conditions of the buildings in the Beyoğlu Preservation Area is a very powerful attribute in predicting the use of the ground floor for business-shopping, the model completely fails to classify residential use.
- While the construction materials used in the buildings in the Beyoğlu Preservation Area is a very powerful attribute in predicting the use of the ground floor for business-shopping, the model almost completely fails to classify residential use correctly.
- While the use of the 6th floor of the buildings in the Beyoğlu Preservation Area is a very powerful attribute in predicting the use of the ground floor for business-shopping, the model almost completely fails to classify residential use correctly.
- While the historical registry of the buildings in the Beyoğlu Preservation Area is a very relevant attribute in predicting the use of the ground floor for business-shopping, the model completely fails to classify residential use correctly.
- While the use of the 5th floor of the buildings in the Beyoğlu Preservation Area is a very powerful attribute in predicting the use of the ground floor for business-shopping, the model almost completely fails to classify residential use correctly.
- The use of the 1st basement floor of the buildings in the Beyoğlu Preservation Area is a powerful attribute in predicting the use of the ground floor for business-shopping (very powerful, over 90% recall) and there is a 55.20% probability that this model will retrieve a relevant class label in a search for residential use.
- While the amount of empty floors in buildings in the Beyoğlu Preservation Area is a very powerful attribute in predicting the use of the ground floor for business-shopping, the model almost fails to classify residential use correctly.

This description of the results of the analysis exemplifies the type of relationships that can be observed based on the use of the Naïve Bayes Classification for the analysis of the Beyoğlu Preservation Area Building Features Database.

In these tests, the predictive power (measured by the overall prediction accuracy and the class recall values) of one variable over another is postulated as a measure of the relationship between these two variables. In other words, this classification-based approach is pragmatically employed as a non-parametric statistical test objectively quantifying the relationships between two scalar variables. This approach avoids explicit functional dependency modelling and/or probabilistic modelling, otherwise, the specific models chosen would have to be justified and validated (a task beyond the scope of this thesis). A further advantage is its ability to rank the relationships between a specific variable and other variables (one-by-one) in terms of their reciprocal predictive powers (for the specific variable). This analysis provides site-specific knowledge about the predictive power of attributes concerning the use of ground floor.

The same data mining process applied to the whole Beyoğlu Preservation Area which consisted of applying a Naïve Bayes learning operator to calculate the predictive powers of the other features of the buildings over the use of ground floor, was also conducted separately for its three most important neighbourhoods; Tarlabaşı, Cihangir and Karaköy. These neighbourhoods are shown in Figure 5.17.

FIGURE 5.17 Map showing Tarlabaşı, Cihangir and Karaköy in the Beyoğlu Preservation Area.

These neighbourhoods were selected because they have different identities in terms of building stock and population. It was therefore assumed that the application of data mining analysis would generate different types of patterns and relationships that would objectively expose their site-specific characteristics and allow for comparison.

Two types of analyses were carried out:

- The predictive power of other building attributes in predicting the use of ground floor in the Beyoğlu Preservation Area (Figure 5.18), Tarlabaşı (Figure 5.20), Cihangir (Figure 5.22) and Karaköy (Figure 5.24) ;
- The predictive power of the use of ground floor in predicting other building attributes in the Beyoğlu Preservation Area (Figure 5.19), Tarlabaşı (Figure 5.21), Cihangir (Figure 5.23) and Karaköy (Figure 5.25);

The results, in the form of predictive powers (prediction accuracy), are illustrated below in a series of polar graphs; the closer the dots are to the centre, the higher the predictive power is, as seen in Figures 5.18-27.

Beyoglu Preservation Area

Attribute 1 : Label

Attributes	Prediction Accuracy for Overall	Attributes	Prediction Accuracy for Overall
Att.2	74.74%	Att.24	41.91%
Att.3	63.03%	Att.25	48.25%
Att.4	53.72%	Att.26	48.53%
Att.5	47.75%	Att.27	44.73%
Att.6	42.69%	Att.28	37.62%
Att.7	42.37%	Att.29	40.05%
Att.8	42.32%	Att.30	44.53%
Att.9	42.19%	Att.31	44.59%
Att.10	41.96%	Att.32	48.87%
Att.11	41.91%	Att.33	42.96%
Att.12	62.43%	Att.34	41.64%
Att.13	43.31%	Att.35	43.76%
Att.14	42.11%	Att.36	44.09%
Att.15	49.40%	Att.37	43.62%
Att.16	42.24%	Att.38	45.39%
Att.17	41.92%	Att.39	48.80%
Att.18	55.64%	Att.40	45.94%
Att.19	57.43%	Att.41	50.67%
Att.20	41.92%	Att.42	41.91%
Att.21	44.28%	Att.43	45.49%
Att.22	44.09%	Att.44	43.96%
Att.23	51.65%	Att.45	51.22%

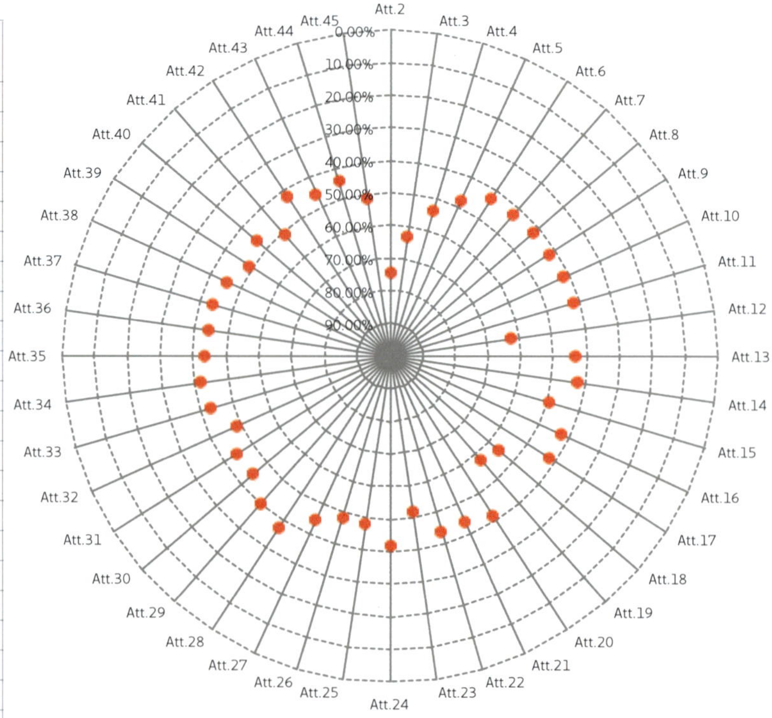

FIGURE 5.18 Predictive power of building attributes in the Beyoğlu Preservation Area in predicting Att.1.

Beyoglu Preservation Area

Attribute 1 : Predictor

Attributes	Prediction Accuracy for Overall	Attributes	Prediction Accuracy for Overall
Att.2	74.69%	Att.24	84.05%
Att.3	61.27%	Att.25	20.62%
Att.4	52.68%	Att.26	37.48%
Att.5	71.75%	Att.27	65.32%
Att.6	88.70%	Att.28	94.64%
Att.7	95.33%	Att.29	45.44%
Att.8	97.85%	Att.30	63.92%
Att.9	99.17%	Att.31	56.51%
Att.10	99.82%	Att.32	41.35%
Att.11	99.97%	Att.33	46.56%
Att.12	66.82%	Att.34	19.54%
Att.13	97.77%	Att.35	20.55%
Att.14	99.59%	Att.36	22.74%
Att.15	73.95%	Att.37	20.73%
Att.16	98.50%	Att.38	40.93%
Att.17	99.91%	Att.39	22.06%
Att.18	8.56%	Att.40	32.45%
Att.19	28.51%	Att.41	69.31%
Att.20	94.82%	Att.42	73.95%
Att.21	68.57%	Att.43	71.99%
Att.22	65.79%	Att.44	71.99%
Att.23	79.13%	Att.45	25.77%

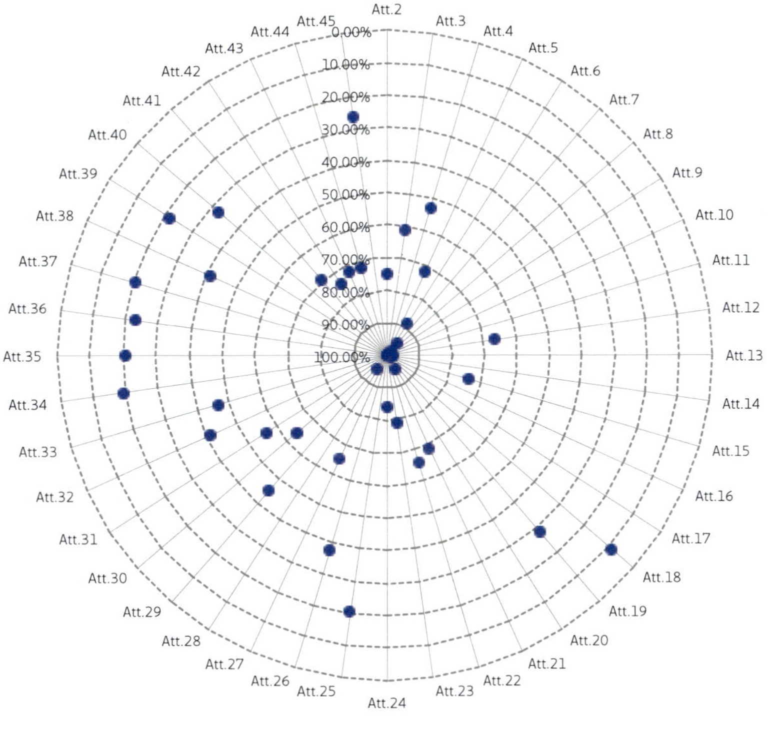

FIGURE 5.19 Predictive power of building attributes in the Beyoğlu Preservation Area in predicting Att.1.

Tarlabasi

Attribute 1 : Label

Attributes	Prediction Accuracy for Overall	Attributes	Prediction Accuracy for Overall
Att.2	73.96%	Att.24	47.34%
Att.3	64.36%	Att.25	47.68%
Att.4	56.22%	Att.26	49.88%
Att.5	51.29%	Att.27	47.54%
Att.6	48.66%	Att.28	49.15%
Att.7	48.22%	Att.29	50.46%
Att.8	47.83%	Att.30	47.44%
Att.9	47.54%	Att.31	47.44%
Att.10	47.54%	Att.32	47.29%
Att.11	47.54%	Att.33	52.07%
Att.12	66.41%	Att.34	51.78%
Att.13	47.54%	Att.35	47.54%
Att.14	47.54%	Att.36	47.54%
Att.15	51.88%	Att.37	47.54%
Att.16	47.73%	Att.38	47.88%
Att.17	47.54%	Att.39	52.95%
Att.18	49.93%	Att.40	53.34%
Att.19	54.31%	Att.41	56.31%
Att.20	47.54%	Att.42	47.54%
Att.21	51.73%	Att.43	54.22%
Att.22	50.51%	Att.44	54.07%
Att.23	58.02%	Att.45	51.88%

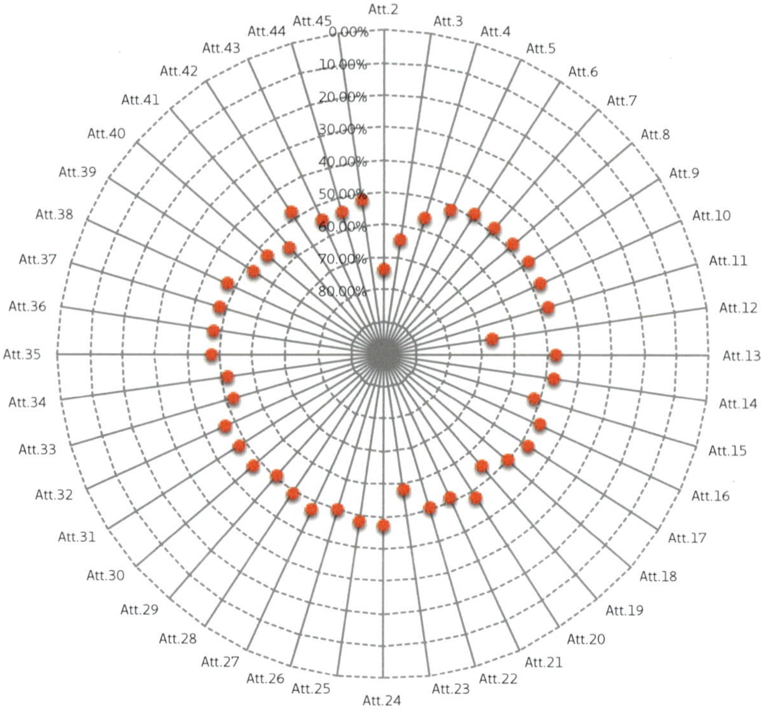

FIGURE 5.20 Predictive power of building attributes in Tarlabaşı in predicting Att.1.

Tarlabasi

Attribute 1 : Predictor

Attributes	Prediction Accuracy for Overall	Attributes	Prediction Accuracy for Overall
Att.2	77.04%	Att.24	92.20%
Att.3	65.38%	Att.25	15.89%
Att.4	63.29%	Att.26	45.59%
Att.5	87.71%	Att.27	61.43%
Att.6	96.73%	Att.28	94.64%
Att.7	98.73%	Att.29	45.44%
Att.8	99.51%	Att.30	63.92%
Att.9	99.85%	Att.31	56.51%
Att.10	100%	Att.32	41%
Att.11	100%	Att.33	47%
Att.12	64.94%	Att.34	41.59%
Att.13	99.66%	Att.35	31.40%
Att.14	100%	Att.36	49%
Att.15	68.89%	Att.37	51.29%
Att.16	98.29%	Att.38	51.29%
Att.17	99.90%	Att.39	27.69%
Att.18	25.16%	Att.40	42.91%
Att.19	31.64%	Att.41	67.72%
Att.20	100%	Att.42	69%
Att.21	66.02%	Att.43	80.01%
Att.22	86.64%	Att.44	80.01%
Att.23	71.72%	Att.45	45.49%

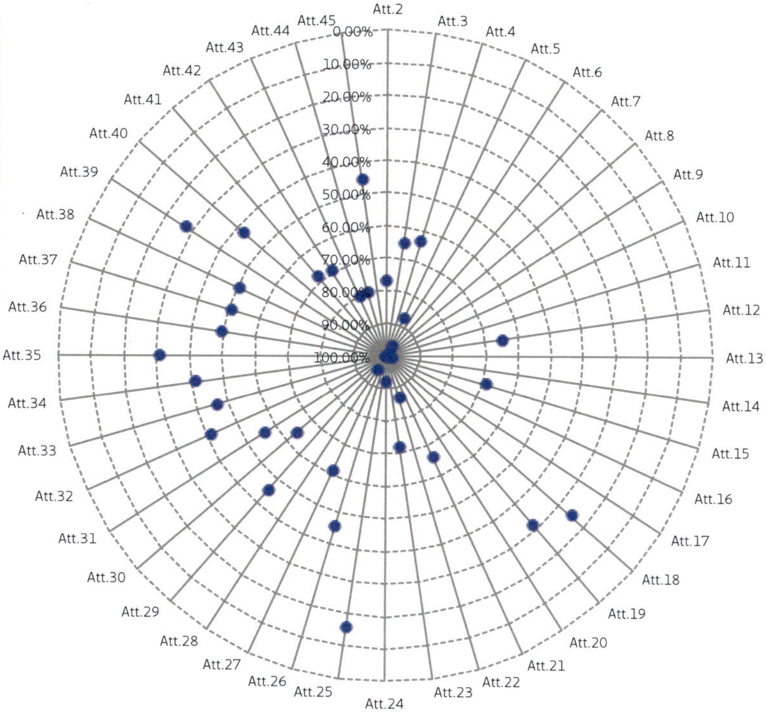

FIGURE 5.21 Predictive power of Att.1 in predicting other building attributes in Tarlabaşı.

Cihangir

Attribute 1 : Label

Attributes	Prediction Accuracy for Overall	Attributes	Prediction Accuracy for Overall
Att.2	75.63%	Att.24	56.28%
Att.3	65.95%	Att.25	54.02%
Att.4	62.80%	Att.26	55.53%
Att.5	60.88%	Att.27	58.61%
Att.6	57.24%	Att.28	54.91%
Att.7	55.39%	Att.29	53.95%
Att.8	54.43%	Att.30	53.95%
Att.9	53.95%	Att.31	54.43%
Att.10	53.95%	Att.32	54.98%
Att.11	53.95%	Att.33	53.95%
Att.12	59.64%	Att.34	54.84%
Att.13	54.08%	Att.35	55.36%
Att.14	53.95%	Att.36	54.36%
Att.15	58.20%	Att.37	53.95%
Att.16	54.02%	Att.38	42.96%
Att.17	53.95%	Att.39	55.46%
Att.18	53.95%	Att.40	58.48%
Att.19	56.21%	Att.41	56.62%
Att.20	53.95%	Att.42	53.95%
Att.21	54.36%	Att.43	60.67%
Att.22	55.66%	Att.44	54.29%
Att.23	59.64%	Att.45	56.83%

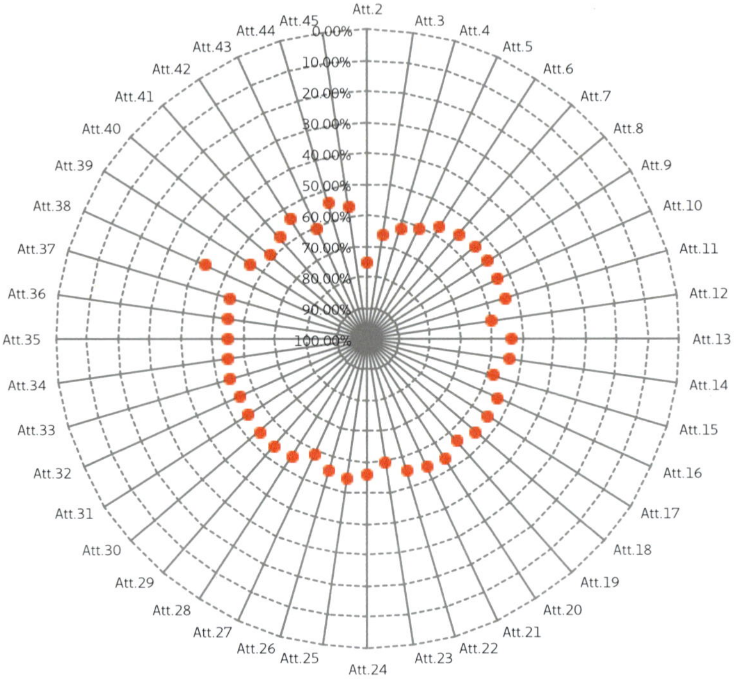

FIGURE 5.22 Predictive power of building attributes in Cihangir in predicting Att.1.

Cihangir

Attribute 1 : Predictor

Attributes	Prediction Accuracy for Overall	Attributes	Prediction Accuracy for Overall
Att.2	77.14%	Att.24	85.72%
Att.3	71.45%	Att.25	34.87%
Att.4	59.92%	Att.26	40.01%
Att.5	62.73%	Att.27	75.70%
Att.6	85.86%	Att.28	63.56%
Att.7	95.61%	Att.29	35.69%
Att.8	98.76%	Att.30	39.93%
Att.9	99.79%	Att.31	37.20%
Att.10	100%	Att.32	27.39%
Att.11	100%	Att.33	42.69%
Att.12	63.42%	Att.34	32.53%
Att.13	93.82%	Att.35	31.02%
Att.14	98.63%	Att.36	32.26%
Att.15	70.42%	Att.37	32.12%
Att.16	99.04%	Att.38	41.87%
Att.17	99.93%	Att.39	23.75%
Att.18	34.59%	Att.40	28.33%
Att.19	27.18%	Att.41	68.29%
Att.20	15.06%	Att.42	70.42%
Att.21	70.35%	Att.43	67.81%
Att.22	53.60%	Att.44	67.95%
Att.23	85.55%	Att.45	44.96%

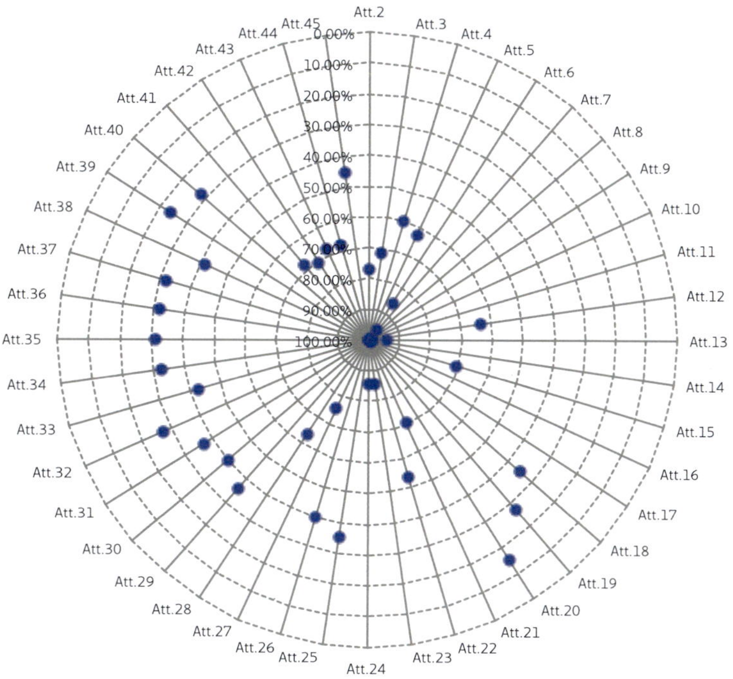

FIGURE 5.23 Predictive power of Att.1 in predicting other building attributes in Cihangir.

Karakoy

Attribute 1 : Label

Attributes	Prediction Accuracy for Overall	Attributes	Prediction Accuracy for Overall
Att.2	76.59%	Att.24	68.17%
Att.3	68.52%	Att.25	68.17%
Att.4	69.57%	Att.26	69.05%
Att.5	69.57%	Att.27	72.03%
Att.6	68.17%	Att.28	68.17%
Att.7	68.17%	Att.29	68.17%
Att.8	68.17%	Att.30	68.17%
Att.9	68.17%	Att.31	68.17%
Att.10	68.17%	Att.32	68.46%
Att.11	68.17%	Att.33	68.17%
Att.12	70.22%	Att.34	68.46%
Att.13	68.17%	Att.35	68.34%
Att.14	68.17%	Att.36	68.17%
Att.15	68.17%	Att.37	68.17%
Att.16	68.17%	Att.38	68.17%
Att.17	68.17%	Att.39	68.17%
Att.18	68.17%	Att.40	69.10%
Att.19	67.82%	Att.41	68.17%
Att.20	68.17%	Att.42	67.70%
Att.21	69.51%	Att.43	68.17%
Att.22	69.10%	Att.44	68.17%
Att.23	78.94%	Att.45	68.11%

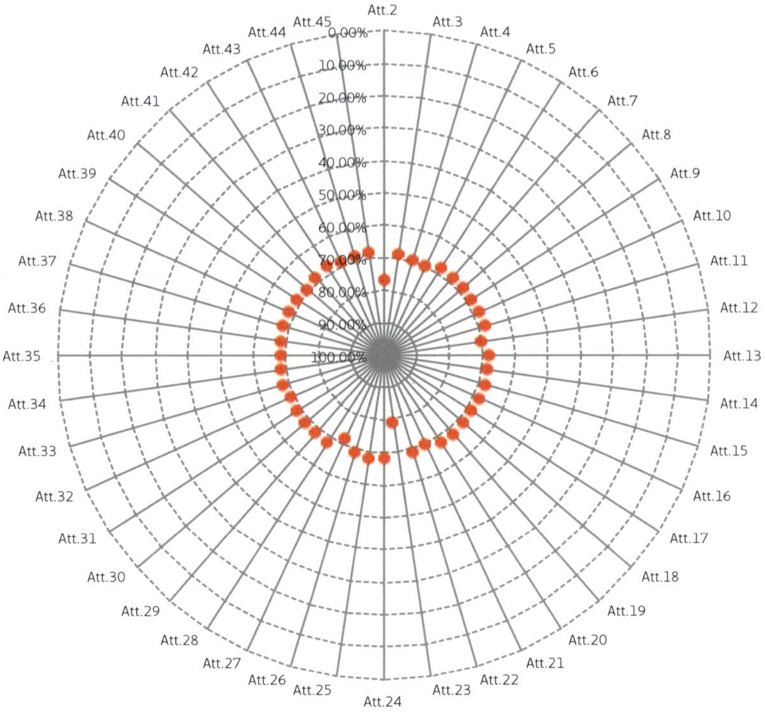

FIGURE 5.24 Predictive power of building attributes in Karaköy in predicting Att.1.

Karakoy

Attribute 1 : Predictor

Attributes	Prediction Accuracy for Overall	Attributes	Prediction Accuracy for Overall
Att.2	77.06%	Att.24	79.52%
Att.3	62.38%	Att.25	18.78%
Att.4	51.43%	Att.26	35.17%
Att.5	67.35%	Att.27	69.57%
Att.6	85.55%	Att.28	66.35%
Att.7	93.10%	Att.29	51.08%
Att.8	96.55%	Att.30	57.81%
Att.9	98.30%	Att.31	63.78%
Att.10	99.30%	Att.32	35.05%
Att.11	100%	Att.33	45.70%
Att.12	77.82%	Att.34	55.12%
Att.13	99.41%	Att.35	43.89%
Att.14	100.00%	Att.36	56.29%
Att.15	87.71%	Att.37	48.27%
Att.16	99.47%	Att.38	48.68%
Att.17	100.00%	Att.39	38.33%
Att.18	24.81%	Att.40	26.55%
Att.19	63.43%	Att.41	77.88%
Att.20	99.82%	Att.42	87.71%
Att.21	59.92%	Att.43	74.20%
Att.22	54.59%	Att.44	74.20%
Att.23	77.30%	Att.45	65.65%

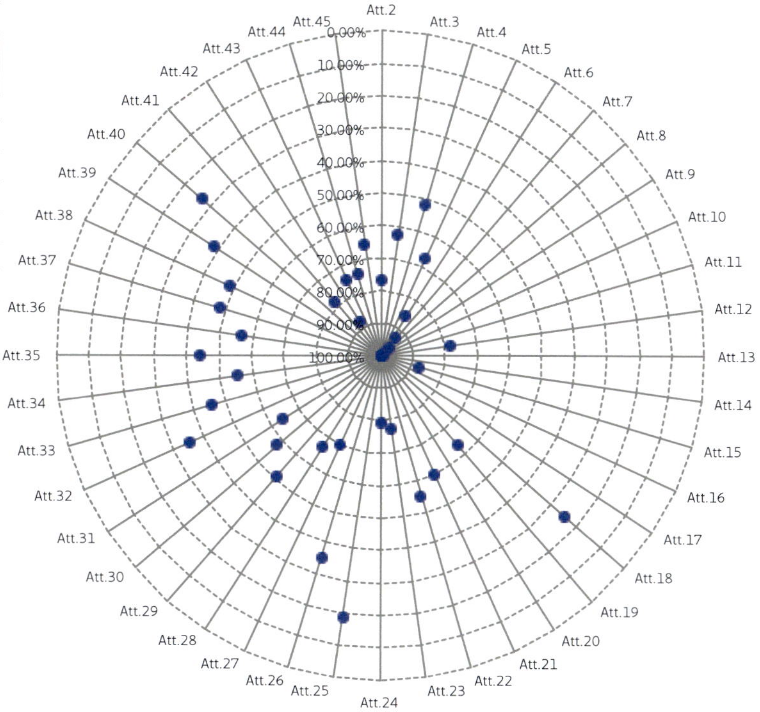

FIGURE 5.25 Predictive power of Att.1 in predicting other building attributes in Karaköy.

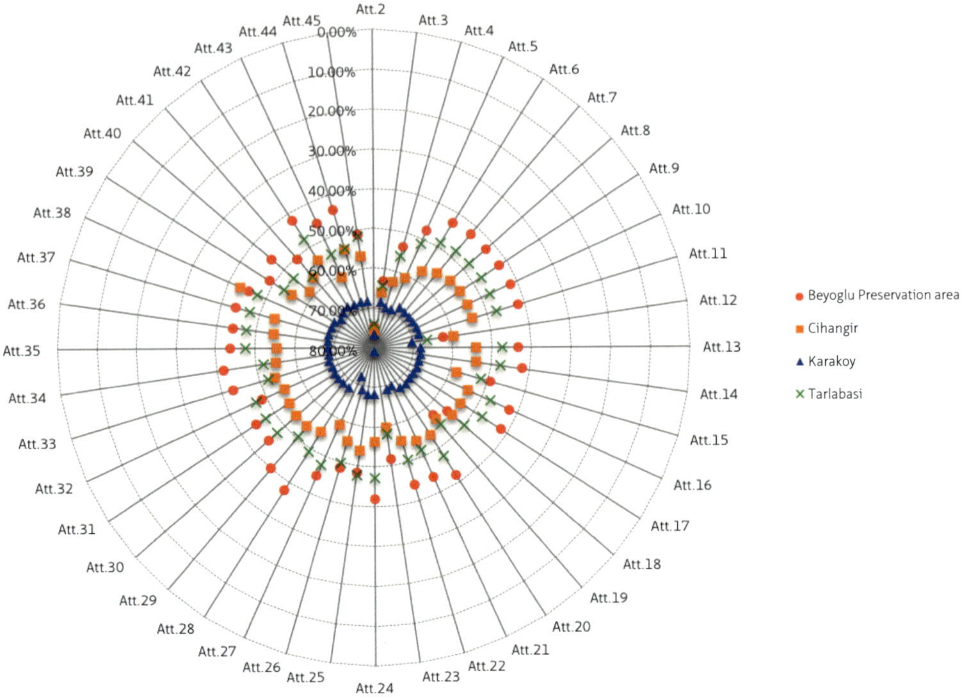

FIGURE 5.26 Predictive power of building attributes in the Beyoğlu Preservation Area, Cihangir, Tarlabaşı and Karaköy in predicting the use of ground floor

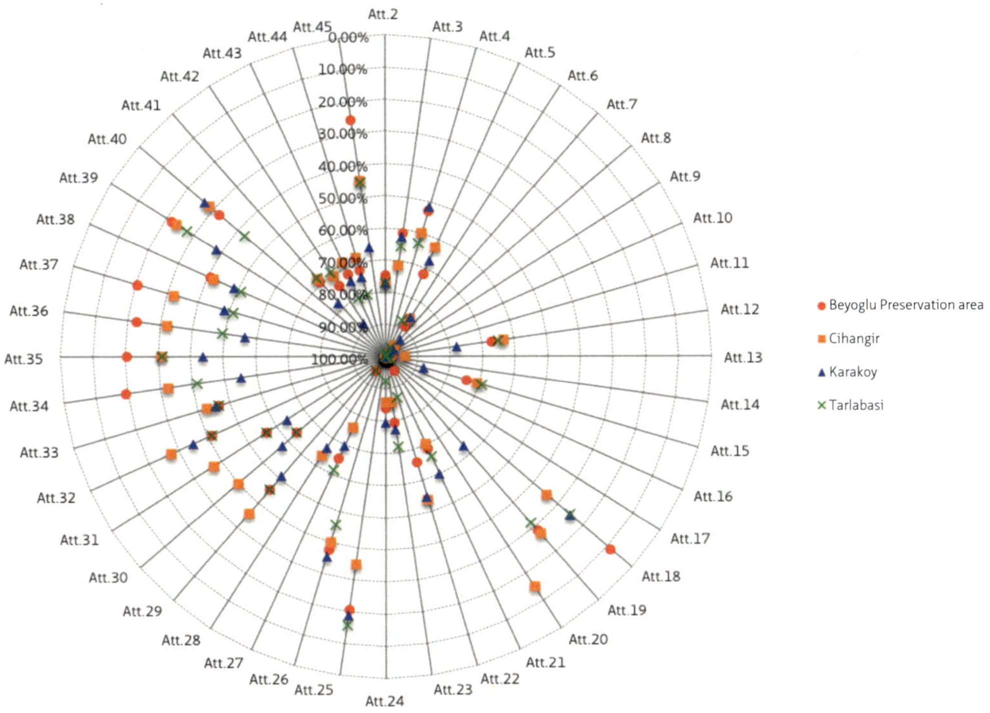

FIGURE 5.27 Predictive power of Att.1 in predicting other building attributes in the Beyoğlu Preservation Area, Cihangir, Tarlabaşı and Karaköy.

The polar graph in Figure 5.26 illustrates the predictive power of building attributes in the Beyoğlu Preservation Area, Cihangir, Tarlabaşı and Karaköy in predicting the use of ground floor. As Figure 5.26 shows, the form of the patterns for the prediction power of the building attributes in predicting the use of ground floor is fairly similar in all cases. However, there is a marked difference in terms of the absolute values of prediction power for building attributes. The ranking for the prediction powers, in descending order, would be: Karaköy, Cihangir, Tarlabaşı, the Beyoğlu Preservation Area.

The polar graph in Figure 5.27 illustrates the predictive power of the use of ground floor in predicting other building attributes in the Beyoğlu Preservation Area, Cihangir, Tarlabaşı and Karaköy. As can be seen in Figure 5.27, the form of the patterns for the prediction power of the use of ground floor in predicting other building attributes is fairly similar in all cases. In terms of the absolute values of prediction power, however, the Beyoğlu Preservation Area-Cihangir and Tarlabaşı-Karaköy are more similar to each other.

In general, on the basis of these results it can be concluded that there is a certain relationship between the use of ground floor and powerful predictors for this attribute (Sökmenoğlu, Çağdaş, & Sarıyıldız, 2010). In other words, these attributes might affect the occurrence of certain categories of the ground floor use. Obviously, there is no argument for causality based on the relative prediction capabilities of the attributes, as this would require further analysis and more evidence. Therefore, the explanation for why these attributes are relevant in predicting the use of ground floor of the buildings in the Beyoğlu Preservation Area demands further exploration, which is beyond the scope of this thesis.

These results give an indication of the composition of data and possible patterns for the co-occurrence of certain attribute values. Naïve Bayes Classification can also be implemented in order to predict unknown values, which, in turn, can be used to predict missing values in the database. Additionally, Naïve Bayes Classification can be used to quantify the existing relationships (in probabilistic terms) between the components of a database and this information can support the development of urban intervention proposals. This will be exemplified in Implementations (2) and (3).

§ 5.1.2.2 Test (2): What combination of building attributes in the Beyoğlu Preservation Area might provide the highest overall prediction power for the use of ground floor?

The question in this case requires multi-dimensional exploration, since it involves analyzing relations between a subset of attributes and the use of ground floor (a one-to-many exploration). Hence, in this case the Naïve Bayes Classification was applied to calculate the combined effects of multiple attributes in predicting the use of ground floor.

Naïve Bayes classifiers assume that "the effect of an attribute value on a given class is independent of the values of the other attributes" (Han & Kamber, 2001, p. 373). This is called "class conditional independence" and simplifies the required computation. It is also the reason why the method is called "naïve" (Han, Kamber, 2001). Therefore, in this case, even if some building attributes are interrelated, the Naïve Bayes classifier considers that all attributes independently contribute to the probability that an entity belongs to a specific class. This test is carried out in full awareness of the fact that this assumption of independence might not be valid for our data. Moreover, as previously noted in subsection 3.6.1, Naïve Bayes classifiers can perform well even with correlated data attributes (Domingos & Pazzani, 1997; Ibrahim & Bennett, 2014; Qi & Zhu, 2003).

The effect of each attribute on predicting the use of ground floor was already observed in Test (1), where a two-dimensional analysis was performed. On the basis of the results of this one-by-one analysis shown in Appendix C, the attributes returning the five highest values for overall prediction power were selected to implement the Naïve Bayes Classification. These attributes are:

- Att.2: 1st floor use, individual overall prediction power over the use of ground floor is %74.74 (with +/-%1.60 standard deviation)
- Att.3: 2nd floor use, individual overall prediction power over he use of ground floor is %63.03 (with +/-%1.84 standard deviation)
- Att.12: 1st basement floor use, individual overall prediction power over the use of ground floor is %62.43 (with +/-%0.82 standard deviation)
- Att.18: Neighbourhood (where the building is located), individual overall prediction power over he use of ground floor is %55.64 (with +/-%1.07 standard deviation)
- Att.19: Population density, individual overall prediction power over he use of ground floor is %57.43 (with +/-%0.92 standard deviation)

Accordingly, four different combinations were formulated using these attributes and a multiple attribute analysis was conducted to explore the extent to which these combined attributes can increase the overall prediction accuracy of the Naïve Bayes model and the prediction accuracy for different categories of the use of ground floor . As the results of these applications show, it is not obvious what the combination of 'best performing' attributes will yield in terms of different categories of the use of ground floor.

The first application analyses the overall accuracy of the Naïve Bayes Model in predicting the use of ground floor, using a combination of 1st floor use and 2nd floor use. As a result, the model is 75.88% accurate (with +/-%1.63 standard deviation) and the details are shown in the Performance Table, in Figure 5.28.

accuracy: 75.88% +/- 1.63% (mikro: 75.88%)

	true Other	true Residential	true Business-Shopping	true Accomodation	true Sociocultural Infrastructure	true Empty	true Technical Infrastructure	true Open Space	class precision
pred. Other	690	136	427	4	409	64	19	1	39.43%
pred. Residential	11	3702	1056	0	8	99	1	0	75.91%
pred. Business-Shopping	9	49	3119	0	14	131	1	0	93.86%
pred. Accomodation	1	0	17	150	0	0	0	0	89.29%
pred. Sociocultural Infrastructure	0	0	52	0	305	1	8	0	83.33%
pred. Empty	1	0	363	0	0	978	0	0	72.44%
pred. Technical Infrastructure	0	0	1	0	0	0	10	0	90.91%
pred. Open Space	0	0	0	0	0	0	0	139	100.00%
class recall	96.91%	95.40%	61.95%	97.40%	41.44%	76.83%	25.64%	99.29%	

FIGURE 5.28 Naïve Bayes Model Performance Table (Att.1 is label, Att.2 and Att.3 are predictors).

The second application analyses the overall accuracy of the Naïve Bayes Model in predicting the use of ground floor, using a combination of 1st floor use, 2nd floor use and 1st basement floor use. As a result, the model is 76.39% accurate (with +/-%1.53 standard deviation) and the details are shown in the Performance Table, in Figure 5.29.

accuracy: 76.39% +/- 1.53% (mikro: 76.39%)

	true Other	true Residential	true Business-Shopping	true Accomodation	true Sociocultural Infrastructure	true Empty	true Technical Infrastructure	true Open Space	class precision
pred. Other	690	100	408	4	398	58	18	1	41.14%
pred. Residential	11	3735	1056	0	9	99	0	0	76.07%
pred. Business-Shopping	9	47	3119	0	14	119	2	0	94.23%
pred. Accomodation	1	0	17	150	0	0	0	0	89.29%
pred. Sociocultural Infrastructure	0	0	52	0	315	1	8	0	83.78%
pred. Empty	1	13	382	0	0	996	0	0	71.55%
pred. Technical Infrastructure	0	0	1	0	0	0	11	0	91.67%
pred. Open Space	0	0	0	0	0	0	0	139	100.00%
class recall	96.91%	95.89%	61.95%	97.40%	42.80%	78.24%	28.21%	99.29%	

FIGURE 5.29 Naïve Bayes Model Performance Table (Att.1 is the label, Att.2, Att.3, Att. 12 are predictors).

The third application analyses the overall accuracy of the Naïve Bayes Model in predicting the use of ground floor, using a combination of 1st floor use, 2nd floor use, 1st basement floor use and the neighbourhood where the building is located. As a result, the model is 76.26% accurate (with +/-%1.47 standard deviation) and the details are shown in the Performance Table, in Figure 5.30.

accuracy: 76.26% +/- 1.47% (mikro: 76.26%)

	true Other	true Residential	true Business-Shopping	true Accomodation	true Sociocultural Infrastructure	true Empty	true Technical Infrastructure	true Open Space	class precision
pred. Other	629	92	337	4	318	51	15	1	43.47%
pred. Residential	9	3653	996	0	9	81	0	0	76.94%
pred. Business-Shopping	13	128	3173	2	17	139	2	0	91.34%
pred. Accomodation	0	0	14	148	0	0	0	0	91.39%
pred. Sociocultural Infrastructure	60	8	120	0	392	8	11	0	65.44%
pred. Empty	1	14	394	0	0	994	0	0	70.85%
pred. Technical Infrastructure	0	0	1	0	0	0	11	0	91.67%
pred. Open Space	0	0	0	0	0	0	0	139	100.00%
class recall	88.34%	93.79%	63.02%	96.10%	53.26%	78.08%	28.21%	99.29%	

FIGURE 5.30 Naïve Bayes Model Performance Table (Att.1 is label, Att.2, Att.3, Att. 12, Att.18 are predictors).

The final application analyses the overall accuracy of the Naïve Bayes Model in predicting the use of ground floor, using a combination of 1st floor use, 2nd floor use, 1st basement floor use, the neighbourhood where the building is located and population density. As a result, the model is 76.63% accurate (with +/-%1.29 standard deviation) and the details are shown in the Performance Table, in Figure 5.31.

accuracy: 76.63% +/- 1.29% (mikro: 76.63%)

	true Other	true Residential	true Business-Shopping	true Accomodation	true Sociocultural Infrastructure	true Empty	true Technical Infrastructure	true Open Space	class precision
pred. Other	586	97	269	4	242	40	12	1	46.84%
pred. Residential	8	3631	950	0	9	77	0	0	77.67%
pred. Business-Shopping	15	147	3219	3	15	154	3	0	90.52%
pred. Accomodation	0	0	14	146	0	0	0	0	91.25%
pred. Sociocultural Infrastructure	103	5	191	1	469	19	14	0	58.48%
pred. Empty	0	15	391	0	0	983	0	0	70.77%
pred. Technical Infrastructure	0	0	1	0	1	0	10	0	83.33%
pred. Open Space	0	0	0	0	0	0	0	139	100.00%
class recall	82.30%	93.22%	63.93%	94.81%	63.72%	77.22%	25.64%	99.29%	

FIGURE 5.31 Naïve Bayes Model Performance Table (Att.1 is label, Att.2, Att.3, Att. 12, Att.18 are predictors).

Table 5.2 compares the prediction powers of individual attributes (two-dimensional Naïve Bayes Classification) and subsets of attributes (multi-dimensional Naïve Bayes Classification) in predicting the use of ground floor.

LABEL: ATT.1	PREDICTOR: ATT.2	PREDICTOR: ATT.3	PREDICTOR: ATT.12	PREDICTOR: ATT.18	PREDICTOR: ATT.19	PREDICTORS: ATT.2, ATT.3	PREDICTORS: ATT.2, ATT.3, ATT.12	PREDICTORS: ATT.2, ATT.3, ATT.12, ATT.18	PREDICTORS: ATT.2, ATT.3, ATT.12, ATT.18, ATT.19
Categories (Values)	Prediction Metrics (Overall prediction accuracy and class recall values)								
Overall	74.74%	63.03%	62.43%	55.64%	57.43%	75.88%	76.39%	76.26%	76.63%
Other	96.91%	13.82%	0.00%	0.00%	0.00%	96.91%	96.91%	88.34%	82.30%
Residential	95.40%	76.50%	55.20%	78.39%	88.68%	95.01%	95.89%	93.79%	93.22%
Business-Shopping	58.29%	62.50%	95.18%	71.72%	68.06%	61.95%	61.95%	63.02%	63.93%
Accommo-dation	97.40%	95.00%	45.00%	0.00%	0.00%	97.10%	97.10%	96.10%	94.81%
Socio-Cultural Infra-structure	41.71%	29.85%	13.01%	0.00%	0.00%	41.44%	42.80%	53.26%	63.72%
Empty	79.34%	64.22%	29.71%	0.00%	0.00%	76.81%	78.21%	78.08%	77.22%
Technical Infrastruc-ture	25.64%	9.52%	0.00%	0.00%	0.00%	25.61%	28.21%	28.21%	25.64%
Open Space	99.29%	100.00%	0.00%	2.90%	0.00%	99.29%	99.29%	99.29%	99.29%

TABLE 5.2 Naïve Bayes Model Performance Table, including all tests.

The overall accuracy increases (albeit slightly) when features are combined. Certain conclusions can be drawn on the basis of Table 5.2:

- Overall, multi-dimensional analyses return higher levels of prediction power than two-dimensional analyses.
- The subset Att.2, Att.3, Att.12, Att.18 and Att.19 returns the highest overall prediction power (76.63%) and this figure is very close to the individual predictive power of Att.2 (74.74%).
- The subset Att.2, Att.3, Att.12, Att.18 and Att.19 implies a balancing effect for the prediction accuracy (class recall) of individual categories; although the accuracy of the model decreases for 'best predicted' categories (other, residential, accommodation, empty), it increases for the less powerful ones (business-shopping and socio-cultural infrastructure).
- Even though the two-dimensional analysis of Att.3, Att.12, Att.18 and Att.19 produces a lower prediction power than Att.2, they do not decrease overall.
- The inclusion of Att.3 in the analysis implies an increase in the overall prediction accuracy (+1.14%) and in the class recall value for business-shopping (+3.60%) category and a decrease in the class recall values for residential (-0.39%), accommodation (-0.30%), socio-cultural (-0.27%), and empty (-2.53%) categories. There is no change in other and open space categories.

- The inclusion of Att.12 in the analysis implies an increase in the overall (0.51%), prediction accuracy and in the class recall values for residential (0.88%), socio-cultural infrastructure (1.36%), empty (1.40%) and technical infrastructure (2.60%) categories. It implies no change in the class recall values for other, business-shopping and open space categories.
- The inclusion of Att.18 in the analysis implies an increase in the class recall values for business-shopping (1.07%) and socio-cultural infrastructure (10.46%) categories and a decrease in the overall prediction accuracy (-0.13%) and in the class recall values for other (-8.57%), residential (-2.10%), accommodation (-1.00%) and empty (-0.13%) categories. It implies no change in the class recall value for technical infrastructure and open space categories.
- The inclusion of the Att.19 in the analysis implies an increase in the overall prediction accuracy (0.37%), and in the class recall values for business-shopping (0.91%) and socio-cultural infrastructure (10.46%) categories and a decrease in the class recall values for other (-6.04%), residential (-0.57%), accommodation (-1.29%), empty (-0.86%), and technical infrastructure (-2.57%) categories. It implies no change in the class recall value for open space category.

According to the analysis of these applications, the answer to the question which frames this test is the combination of five attributes; 1st floor, 2nd floor 1st basement uses, Neighbourhood and Population Density, which provide the highest overall prediction power for the use of ground floor. It should be noted that accounting for spatial autocorrelation in such an analysis would be likely to change the prediction accuracy of the Naïve Bayes classifier in predicting the use categories of the gorund floor. However, as previously clarified in subsection (3.6.1), this was beyond the scope of the research as it was not primarily concerned with the problem of prediction but in exploring the data extracted from the traditional thematic maps of the Beyoğlu Preservation Area.

To conclude, multiple attributes analysis tests whether is possible to obtain a better performing Naïve Bayes Model by combining the individual effects of each attribute. Additionally, comparing individual and multiple attributes reveals the positive/negative effects of each attribute on the performance of the Naïve Bayes Model in predicting different categories.

§ 5.1.2.3 Test (3): Are there any associations between the use of ground floor and other building attributes in the Beyoğlu Preservation Area?

This test applies Association Rule Analysis in order to capture association links between the use of ground floor of the buildings and 44 other attributes, one by one. Once again, this is a two-dimensional exploration of data, since each case concerns only one attribute linked to the use of ground floor.

Compared to Naïve Bayes Classification analysis, Association Rule Analysis introduces different types of observations and results. Whereas Naïve Bayes Classification reveals the relationships between items based on relative prediction power of one or multiple attributes, Association Rule Analysis reveals items in the Beyoğlu Preservation Area Building Features Database that occur together. Association Rule Analysis is a descriptive analysis method and hence is not concerned with classes but focuses instead on the co-occurrence of attribute values. Basically, association rules analysis indicates attribute-value conditions that appear frequently together in the Beyoğlu Preservation Area Building Features Database. Thus, this method allows for the discovery of a different form of 'knowledge' of the database. The Association Rules methodology was explained in detail in Section 3.5 (Data Mining Methods and Operators Implemented in the Thesis).

The RapidMiner screenshot in Figure 5.32 illustrates the data mining process, which consists of applying an FPGrowth Learner algorithm to calculate all frequent items sets from the data set and an Association Rule Generator operator to generate a set of association rules for a given set of frequent item sets.

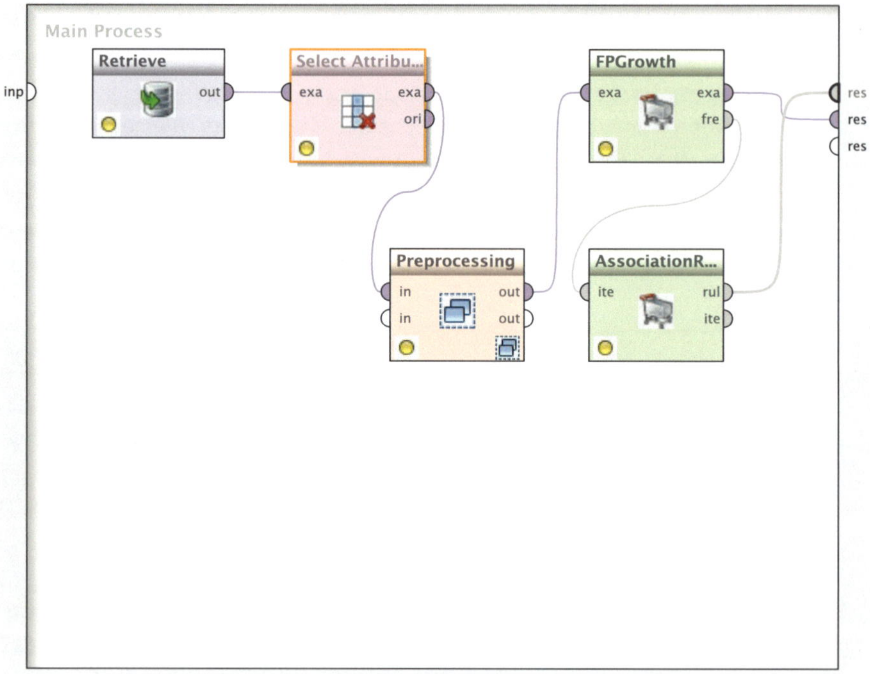

FIGURE 5.32 Data mining process using Association Rules Generator Operator in RapidMiner.

As seen in Figure 5.32, after selecting the relevant attributes from the data set a pre-processing operator is used. This procedure is shown in Figure 5.33.

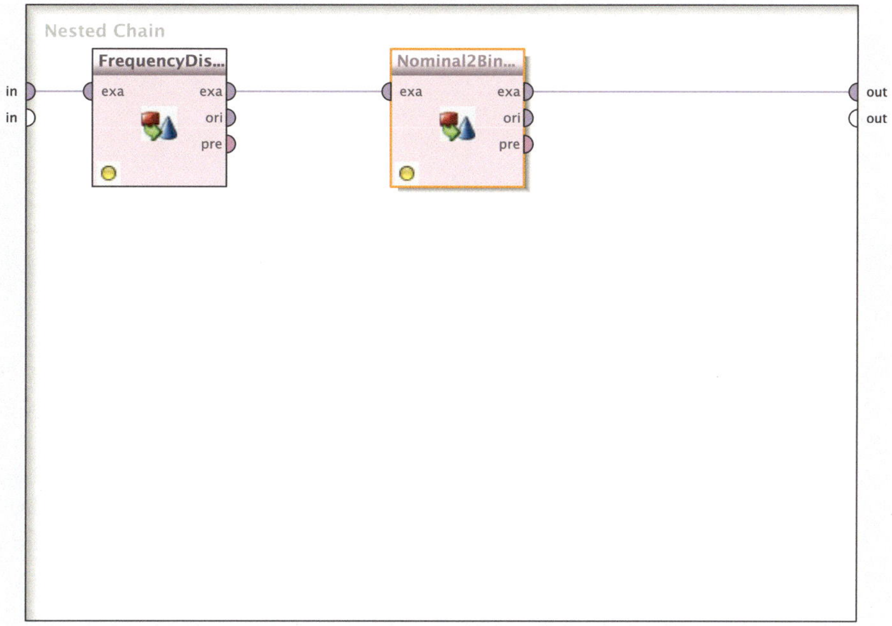

FIGURE 5.33 Pre-processing operator containing Frequency Discretization operator and Nominal to Binominal operator.

The pre-processing operator contains a Frequency Discretization operator for converting "selected numerical attributes into nominal attributes (by discretizing the numerical attribute into a user-specified number of bins)", together with a "Nominal to Binominal operator for changing the type of nominal attributes to a binominal type" (http://docs.rapidminer.com/studio/). The output of the pre-processing process is a data set containing only the binominal values of the selected attributes. The FPGrowth Learner algorithm then calculates all the frequent items sets from the data set, which are then processed by the Association Rules Generator operator to produce a set of association rules.

RapidMiner software provides the results of the analysis in the form of a table stating the rules and their level of support and confidence. The results of this process performed to find association rules between the use of ground floor and 1st floor are given in Figure 5.34.

FIGURE 5.34 Association Rules Table presenting association rules between Att.1 and Att.2.

As stated in Section 3.5 (Data Mining Methods and Operators Implemented in the Thesis), confidence is a measure of the strength of the association rules. As the figure shows, confidence for Association Rule No. 1 is 0.583, meaning that 58.3% of the buildings with ground floor business-shopping also have 1st floor business-shopping. On the other hand, support for Association Rule No. 1 is 0.245, meaning that 24.5% of all buildings have ground floor and 1st floor business-shopping.

Similarly, according to Association Rule No. 2, 74.9% of the buildings with 1st floor residential use also have ground floor residential use and 31% of all buildings have ground floor and 1st floor residential use. According to Association Rule No. 3, 95.4% of the buildings with ground floor residential use also have 1st floor residential use (in other words, if the ground floor of the building is residential, there is a 95.4% chance that the 1st floor is also residential) and 31% of all buildings have ground floor and 1st floor residential use. According to Association Rule No. 4, 95.9% of the buildings with 1st floor business-shopping also have ground floor business-shopping (in other words, if the 1st floor of the building is business-shopping, there is a 95.9% chance that ground floor is also business-shopping) and 24.5% of all buildings have ground floor and 1st floor business-shopping.

Frequent itemsets can be discovered within the database by interpreting the association rules. In addition, the rules found in the exploration above gives some indication of the possible clusters of residential and business-shopping uses within the buildings in the Beyoğlu Preservation Area, which will be another area to explore.

The results of the Association Rule Analysis applied to investigate associations between the use of ground floor of the buildings and 44 other building attributes in the Beyoğlu Preservation Area are presented in Table 5.3, which shows the rules with more than 70% confidence.

RULE	ANTECEDENT	CONSEQUENT	CONFIDENCE	SUPPORT	DESCRIPTION OF RULE
1	Att.19= No residents	Att.1= Business-Shopping	0.7080	0.1120	70% of the buildings that have no residents have ground floor business-shopping. These buildings constitute 11% of the whole Beyoğlu Preservation Area.
2	Att.1= Business-Shopping	Att.21= Medium	0.7100	0.2980	71% of the buildings with ground floor business-shopping are in medium maintenance condition. These buildings constitute 29% of the whole Beyoğlu Preservation Area.
3	Att.1= Residential	Att.21= Medium	0.7240	0.2350	72 % of the buildings with ground floor residential use are in medium maintenance condition. These buildings constitute 23% of the whole Beyoğlu Preservation Area.
4	Att.1= Business-Shopping	Att.23= Fully Occupied	0.7300	0.3070	73% of the buildings with ground floor business-shopping are fully occupied. These buildings constitute 30% of the whole Beyoğlu Preservation Area.
5	Att.1= Business-Shopping	Att.15= No 1st penthouse	0.7340	0.3080	73% of the buildings with ground floor business-shopping have no penthouse floor. These buildings constitute 30% of the whole Beyoğlu Preservation Area.
6	Att.2= Residential	Att.1= Residential	0.7490	0.3100	74% of the buildings with 1st floor residential use also have ground floor residential use. These buildings constitute 31% of the whole Beyoğlu Preservation Area.
7	Att.1= Residential	Att.3= Residential	0.7670	0.2490	76% of the buildings with ground floor residential use also have 2nd floor residential use. These buildings constitute 24% of the whole Beyoğlu Preservation Area.
8	Att.1= Residential	Att.23= Fully Occupied	0.7730	0.2510	77% of the buildings with ground floor residential use are fully occupied. These buildings constitute 25% of the whole Beyoğlu Preservation Area.
9	Att.1= Residential	Att.5= No 4th floor	0.7920	0.2580	79% of the buildings with ground floor residential use have less than 3 floors. These buildings constitute 25% of the whole Beyoğlu Preservation Area.
10	Att.1= Business-Shopping	Att.24= Private	0.8230	0.3460	Private owners own 82% of the buildings with ground floor business shopping. These buildings constitute 34% of the whole Beyoğlu Preservation Area.
11	Att.1 = Residential	Att.43 = 3rd Level	0.8550	0.2780	85% of the buildings with ground floor residential use are located along a 3rd level of street. These buildings constitute 27% of the whole Beyoğlu Preservation Area.
12	Att.1 = Residential	Att.44 = 3rd Level	0.8550	0.2780	85% of the buildings with ground floor residential use are located along a 3rd level of street. These buildings constitute 27% of the whole Beyoğlu Preservation Area.
13	Att.1= Residential	Att.24= Private	0.9220	0.3000	92% of the buildings with ground floor residential use are privately owned. These buildings constitute 30% of the whole Beyoğlu Preservation Area.
14	Att.1= Residential	Att.6= No 5th Floor	0.9480	0.3080	94% of the buildings with ground floor residential use have less than 4 floors. These buildings constitute 30% of the whole Beyoğlu Preservation Area.
15	Att.1= Residential	Att.2= Residential	0.9540	0.3100	95% of the buildings with ground floor residential use also have 1st floor residential use. These buildings constitute 31% of the whole Beyoğlu Preservation Area.
16	Att.3= Business-Shopping	Att.1= Business-Shopping	0.9550	0.1800	95% of the buildings with 2nd floor business-shopping have ground floor business-shopping too. These buildings constitute 18% of the whole Beyoğlu Preservation Area.

>>>

RULE	ANTECEDENT	CONSEQUENT	CONFIDENCE	SUPPORT	DESCRIPTION OF RULE
17	Att.4= Business-Shopping	Att.1= Business-Shopping	0.9550	0.1290	95% of the buildings with 3rd floor business-shopping have ground floor business-shopping too. These buildings constitute 12% of the whole Beyoğlu Preservation Area.
18	Att.12= Residential	Att.1= Residential	0.9570	0.1770	95% of the buildings with 1st basement residential use also have ground floor residential use. These buildings constitute 17% of the whole Beyoğlu Preservation Area.
19	Att.2= Business-Shopping	Att.1= Business-Shopping	0.9590	0.2450	95% of the buildings with 2nd floor business-shopping have ground floor for business-shopping. These buildings constitute 24% of the whole Beyoğlu Preservation Area.
20	Att.1= Empty	Att.7= No 6th Floor	0.9650	0.1030	96% of the buildings with an empty ground floor have less than 6 floors. These buildings constitute 10% of the whole Beyoğlu Preservation Area.
21	Att.1= Business-Shopping	Att.16= No 2nd Penthouse	0.9840	0.4130	98% of the buildings with ground floor business-shopping do not have a 2nd penthouse floor. These buildings constitute 41% of the whole Beyoğlu Preservation Area.
22	Att.1= Empty	Att.16= No 2nd Penthouse	0.9840	0.1050	98% of the buildings with an empty ground floor do not have a 2nd penthouse floor. These buildings constitute 10% of the whole Beyoğlu Preservation Area.
23	Att.1= Business-Shopping	Att.13= No 2nd Basement	0.9870	0.4150	98% of the buildings with ground floor business-shopping do not have a 2nd basement floor. These buildings constitute 41% of the whole Beyoğlu Preservation Area.
24	Att.1= Residential	Att.16= No 2nd Penthouse	0.9870	0.3210	98% of the buildings with ground floor residential use do not have a 2nd penthouse floor. These buildings constitute 41% of the whole Beyoğlu Preservation Area.
25	Att.1= Empty	Att.8= No 7th Floor	0.9890	0.1050	98% of the buildings with an empty ground floor have less than 7 floors. These buildings constitute 10% of the whole Beyoğlu Preservation Area.
26	Att.1= Empty	Att.13= No 2nd Basement	0.9920	0.1050	99% of the buildings with an empty ground floor do not have a 2nd basement floor. These buildings constitute 10% of the whole Beyoğlu Preservation Area.
27	Att.1= Residential	Att.8= No 7th Floor	0.9970	0.3240	99% of the buildings with ground floor residential use have less than 7 floors. These buildings constitute 32% of the whole Beyoğlu Preservation Area.
28	Att.1= Business-Shopping	Att.14= No 3rd Basement	0.9970	0.4190	99% of the buildings with ground floor business-shopping do not have a 3rd basement floor. These buildings constitute 41% of the whole Beyoğlu Preservation Area.
29	Att.1= Residential	Att.7= No 6th Floor	0.9980	0.3210	99% of the buildings with ground floor residential use have less than 6 floors. These buildings constitute 32% of the whole Beyoğlu Preservation Area.
30	Att.1= Empty	Att.9= No 8th Floor	0.9980	0.1060	99% of the buildings with an empty ground floor have less than 8 floors. These buildings constitute 10% of the whole Beyoğlu Preservation Area.
31	Att.1= Empty	Att.10= No 9th Floor	0.9980	0.1060	99% of the buildings with an empty ground floor have less than 9 floors. These buildings constitute 10% of the whole Beyoğlu Preservation Area.
32	Att.1= Empty	Att.17= No 3rd Penthouse	0.9990	0.1060	99% of the buildings with an empty ground floor do not have a 2nd basement floor. These buildings constitute 10% of the whole Beyoğlu Preservation Area.

>>>

RULE	ANTECEDENT	CONSEQUENT	CONFIDENCE	SUPPORT	DESCRIPTION OF RULE
33	Att.1= Residential	Att.17= No 3rd Pent-house	0.9990	0.3250	99% of the buildings with ground floor residential use do not have a 3rd penthouse floor. These buildings constitute 32% of the whole Beyoğlu Preservation Area.
34	Att.1= Business-Shop-ping	Att.17= No 3rd Penthouse	0.9990	0.4200	99% of the buildings with ground floor business-shopping do not have a 3rd penthouse floor. These buildings constitute 42% of the whole Beyoğlu Preservation Area.
35	Att.1= Residential	Att.9= No 8th Floor	1.0000	0.3250	100% of the buildings with ground floor residential use have less than 8 floors. These buildings constitute 32% of the whole Beyoğlu Preservation Area.
36	Att.1= Residential	Att.10= No 9th Floor	1.0000	0.3250	100% of the buildings with ground floor residential use have less than 9 floors. These buildings constitute 32% of the whole Beyoğlu Preservation Area.
37	Att.1= Business-Shop-ping	Att.11= No 10th Floor	1.0000	0.4200	100% of the buildings with ground floor business-shopping have less than 10 floors. These buildings constitute 42% of the whole Beyoğlu Preservation Area.
38	Att.1= Residential	Att.11= No 10th Floor	1.0000	0.3250	100% of the buildings with ground floor residential use have less than 10 floors. These buildings constitute 32% of the whole Beyoğlu Preservation Area.
39	Att.1= Empty	Att.11= No 10th Floor	1.0000	0.1060	100% of the buildings with an empty ground floor have less than 10 floors. These buildings constitute 10% of the whole Beyoğlu Preservation Area.
40	Att.1= Empty	Att.14= No 3rd Basement	1.0000	0.1060	100% of the buildings with an empty ground floor do not have a third basement floor. These buildings constitute 10% of the whole Beyoğlu Preservation Area.

TABLE 5.3 Association rules between Att.1 and 44 other building attributes in the Beyoğlu Preservation Area with over 70% confidence.

In order to frame a more general conclusion based on Table 5.3, eight statements have been inferred based on observation of the given association rules. Thus, an important number of buildings in the Beyoğlu Preservation Area,

- with ground floor residential use have less than 4 floors (Association Rules Nos. 38, 36, 35, 29, 27, 14, 9),
- with ground floor residential use also have 1st or 2nd floor residential use (Association Rules Nos. 15, 7). This gives an indication of possible clustering of residential use within the buildings,
- with 1st floor residential use also have ground floor residential use (Association Rule No. 6). This gives an indication of possible clustering of residential use within the buildings,
- with 1st, 2nd or 3rd floor business-shopping also have ground floor business-shopping (Association Rules Nos. 19, 17, 16). This gives an indication of possible clustering of business-shopping use within the buildings,
- with an empty (unused) ground floor have less than 5 floors (Association Rules Nos. 39, 31, 30, 25, 20),
- with ground floor business-shopping have a medium level of maintenance conditions (Association Rules Nos. 2, 3),

- with ground floor residential or business-shopping use have no empty floors i.e. are fully occupied (Association Rules Nos. 4, 8),
- with ground floor residential or business-shopping are privately owned (Association Rules Nos. 10, 13).

To conclude, the reason behind the existence of associations among the categories of the ground floor use and certain other attributes demands another exploratory step that is beyond the scope of this thesis. In terms of a general evaluation of the results, it may be concluded that the values of certain attributes have an effect on the occurrence of certain categories of ground floor use (Sökmenoğlu, Çağdaş, & Sarıyıldız, 2012). These results provide an indication of the composition of data and the existence of buildings with all floors in residential use and/or business-shopping. It should be emphasized that even though some associations between different attributes may be obvious to the analyst in observing the thematic maps of the Beyoğlu Preservation Area or the Beyoğlu Preservation Area Building Features Database built from it, most of these would be impossible to discover simply by visual inspection. This is because the database is so large that it is not possible to detect these patterns without computational analysis. Moreover, even though some associations may be obvious to the eye of the analyst, it is not possible to objectively quantify them without applying Association Rule Analysis.

As a final remark, it should be noted that comparing the results of Association Rule Analysis and Naïve Bayes Classification analysis is insignificant for one simple reason. Even though they both operate as classification algorithms, Naïve Bayes Classification analysis covers a larger area of the database and therefore analyzes a more complex task than Association Rule Analysis, which is more focused. Naïve Bayes Classification analysis considers all the values of one attribute to predict all the values of another, whereas Association Rule Analysis considers the co-occurrence of one specific value of an attribute in association with a specific value of another. Thus, broadly speaking, the prediction accuracy provided by Naïve Bayes Classification can be considered a function of all the possible confidence results provided by Association Rule Analysis for each attribute value. Hence, Naïve Bayes Classification and Association Rules operate in a parallel but not directly comparable way.

§ 5.1.2.4 Test (4): Are there any recurring patterns of floorspace use within the buildings in the Beyoğlu Preservation Area?

The results of the previous Test (3) provide an indication of the existence of buildings in the Beyoğlu Preservation Area in which all the floors are dedicated to residential and/or business-shopping use. To investigate this, a clustering method available in RapidMiner was applied in this test to identify floorspace use patterns within the buildings (This will be referred as vertical floorspace use patterns). Specifically, the analysis implements a clustering algorithm with 10 attributes concerning floorspace use data (Att.1-10; from ground floor to 9th floor use). Basement and penthouse floor use data was excluded to keep the results straightforward.

Clustering analysis is used to partition a set of data items into a set of classes in such a way that items with similar features are gathered together. Clustering is best used to find groups of items that are similar, such as identifying subgroups of customers with similar buying behaviour from a given data set of customers. The clustering methodology was explained in further detail in Section 3.5 (Data mining Methods and Operators Implemented in the Thesis). The RapidMiner screenshot in Figure 5.35 illustrates the data mining process.

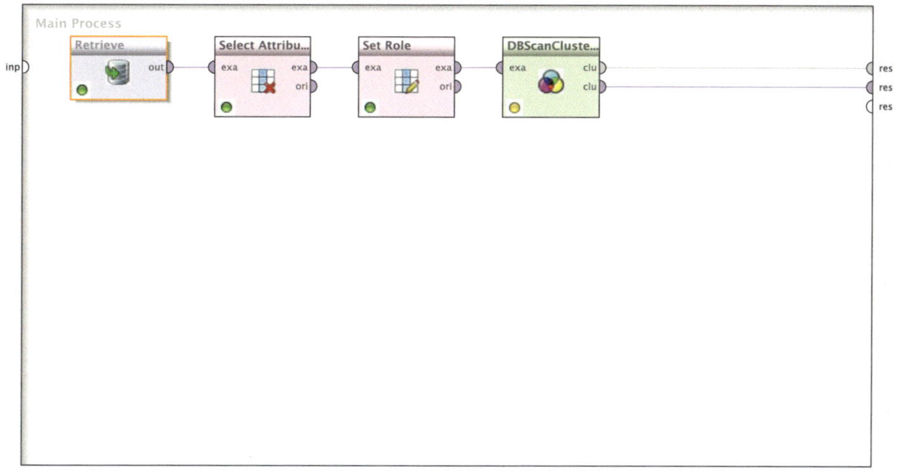

FIGURE 5.35 Clustering process in RapidMiner with DBSCAN Clustering Operator.

This process consists of applying a DBSCAN Clustering Operator. After several tests, the parameters of the DBSCAN algorithm are set as follows: epsilon is set to 1, the number of minimum points is defined as 5, and the measure type for measuring the distance between the points is set to Nominal distance. When the number of minimum points is set to 5 and the epsilon to 1 or a value lower than 1 (i.e., 0.5, 0.1, 0.05) the algorithm finds the same 131 clusters. When the epsilon is set to a value greater than 1 (i.e., 2, 3, 4) the algorithm fails and only returns 2 clusters. When the epsilon is set to 5 the algorithm completely fails to properly cluster the given dataset. A small number of minpoints was chosen to find a large number of small and fine detailed clusters: with larger numbers, larger and fewer clusters and more noise would be generated.

With the above parameters, 131 different clusters were found in 11,984 buildings and 638 buildings were clustered as noise. Therefore, there are 130 relevant clusters, 23 of which contain more than 100 buildings (approx. 1% of the whole data set). Table 5.4 provides information on the 23 most populated clusters in the Beyoğlu Preservation Area containing more than 100 buildings.

CLUSTERS	ATT.1	ATT.2	ATT.3	ATT.4	ATT.5	ATT.6	ATT.7	ATT.8	ATT.9	ATT.10	#
4	Residen-tial	Residen-tial	Residen-tial	No 3rd floor	No 4th floor	No 5th floor	No 6th floor	No 7th floor	No 8th floor	No 9th floor	1276
6	Residen-tial	Residen-tial	Residen-tial	Residen-tial	No 4th floor	No 5th floor	No 6th floor	No 7th floor	No 8th floor	No 9th floor	928
7	Residen-tial	Residen-tial	No 2nd Floor	No 3rd floor	No 4th floor	No 5th floor	No 6th floor	No 7th floor	No 8th floor	No 9th floor	745
0	NOT CLUSTERED										638
1	Other	No 1st floor	No 2nd Floor	No 3rd floor	No 4th floor	No 5th floor	No 6th floor	No 7th floor	No 8th floor	No 9th floor	578
8	Residen-tial	Residen-tial	Residen-tial	Residen-tial	Residen-tial	No 5th floor	No 6th floor	No 7th floor	No 8th floor	No 9th floor	554
22	Business-Shop-ping	Business-Shop-ping	No 2nd Floor	No 3rd Floor	No 4th floor	No 5th floor	No 6th floor	No 7th floor	No 8th floor	No 9th floor	471
25	Business-Shop-ping	Business-Shop-ping	Business-Shop-ping	Business-Shop-ping	Business-Shop-ping	No 5th floor	No 6th floor	No 7th floor	No 8th floor	No 9th floor	457
19	Business-Shop-ping	Business-Shop-ping	Business-Shop-ping	No 3rd floor	No 4th floor	No 5th floor	No 6th floor	No 7th floor	No 8th floor	No 9th floor	455
18	Business-Shop-ping	No 1st floor	No 2nd Floor	No 3rd floor	No 4th floor	No 5th floor	No 6th floor	No 7th floor	No 8th floor	No 9th floor	420
26	Business-Shop-ping	Business-Shop-ping	Business-Shop-ping	Business-Shop-ping	No 4th floor	No 5th floor	No 6th floor	No 7th floor	No 8th floor	No 9th floor	433
Clusters	Att.1	Att.2	Att.3	Att.4	Att.5	Att.6	Att.7	Att.8	Att.9	Att.10	#
93	Socio-cultu-ral Infra-structure	No 1st floor	No 2nd Floor	No3rd floor	No 4th floor	No 5th floor	No 6th floor	No 7th floor	No 8th floor	No 9th floor	408
105	Empty	Empty	Empty	No 3rd floor	No 4th floor	No 5th floor	No 6th floor	No 7th floor	No 8th floor	No 9th floor	299
30	Business-Shop-ping	Residen-tial	Residen-tial	Residen-tial	No 4th floor	No 5th floor	No 6th floor	No 7th floor	No 8th floor	No 9th floor	297
27	Business-Shop-ping	Residen-tial	Residen-tial	No 3rd Floor	No 4th floor	No 5th floor	No 6th floor	No 7th floor	No 8th floor	No 9th floor	287
106	Empty	Empty	Empty	Empty	No 4th floor	No 5th floor	No 6th floor	No 7th floor	No 8th floor	No 9th floor	240

>>>

CLUSTERS	ATT.1	ATT.2	ATT.3	ATT.4	ATT.5	ATT.6	ATT.7	ATT.8	ATT.9	ATT.10	#
36	Business-Shopping	Residential	Residential	Residential	Residential	No 5th floor	No 6th floor	No 7th floor	No 8th floor	No 9th floor	237
21	Business-Shopping	Business-Shopping	Business-Shopping	Business-Shopping	Business-Shopping	Business-Shopping	No 6th floor	No 7th floor	No 8th floor	No 9th floor	219
108	Empty	Empty	No 2nd Floor	No 3rd Floor	No 4th floor	No 5th floor	No 6th floor	No 7th floor	No 8th floor	No 9th floor	213
9	Residential	Residential	Residential	Residential	Residential	Residential	No 6th floor	No 7th floor	No 8th floor	No 9th floor	150
131	Open Space	No 1st floor	No 2nd Floor	No 3rd floor	No 4th floor	No 5th floor	No 6th floor	No 7th floor	No 8th floor	No 9th floor	139
5	Residential	No 1st floor	No 2nd Floor	No 3rd floor	No 4th floor	No 5th floor	No 6th floor	No 7th floor	No 8th floor	No 9th floor	139
110	Empty	Empty	Empty	Empty	Empty	No 5th floor	No 6th floor	No 7th floor	No 8th floor	No 9th floor	123
Clusters	Att.1	Att.2	Att.3	Att.4	Att.5	Att.6	Att.7	Att.8	Att.9	Att.10	#
131	Open Space	No 1st floor	No 2nd Floor	No 3rd floor	No 4th floor	No 5th floor	No 6th floor	No 7th floor	No 8th floor	No 9th floor	139
5	Residential	No 1st floor	No 2nd Floor	No 3rd floor	No 4th floor	No 5th floor	No 6th floor	No 7th floor	No 8th floor	No 9th floor	139
110	Empty	Empty	Empty	Empty	Empty	No 5th floor	No 6th floor	No 7th floor	No 8th floor	No 9th floor	123
38	Business-Shopping	Empty	Empty	Empty	No 4th floor	No 5th floor	No 6th floor	No 7th floor	No 8th floor	No 9th floor	114

TABLE 5.4 23 most populated clusters in the Beyoğlu Preservation Area.

The DBSCAN Clustering Operator performs successful clustering. In Table 5.5 the clusters found by the algorithm are compared with the contents of the actual database.

	NUMBER OF BUILDINGS	
CLUSTERS	found by the DBSCAN algorithm	(existing)
Cluster 4	1250	1276
Cluster 6	930	928
Cluster 7	737	745
Cluster 1	574	578
Cluster 8	552	554
Cluster 22	460	471
Cluster 25	457	457
Cluster 19	455	513
Cluster 26	433	433
Cluster 18	420	420
Cluster 93	408	408
Cluster 105	299	299
Cluster 30	297	297
Cluster 27	273	287
Cluster 106	242	240
Cluster 36	237	237
Cluster 21	218	219
Cluster 108	213	213
Cluster 9	151	150
Cluster 131	139	139
Cluster 5	136	139
Cluster 110	123	123
Cluster 38	114	114

TABLE 5.5 Comparing clustering results with the real dataset.

The GIS map in Figure 5.36 displays the main cluster, Cluster 4, consisting of buildings with 3 floors (ground, 1st and 2nd floors), all of which are residential.

FIGURE 5.36 GIS map of the most dominant floorspace use clusters in the Beyoğlu Preservation Area, consisting of 1,276 buildings.

The series of GIS maps of the Beyoğlu Preservation Area in Figures 5.37-40 display the 23 main clusters and one map showing all the clusters, plus buildings that are not clustered (i.e. considered as noise).

FIGURE 5.37 Clusters 4, 6, 7, 1, 8 and 22.

Cluster 25:
Business-Shopping, Business-Shopping, Business-Shopping, Business-Shopping, Business-Shopping (457 buildings)

Cluster 19:
Business-Shopping, Business-Shopping, Business-Shopping (455buildings)

Cluster 26:
Business-Shopping, Business-Shopping, Business-Shopping, Business-Shopping (433 buildings)

Cluster 18:
Business-Shopping (420 buildings)

Cluster 93:
Sociocultural Infrastructure (408 buildings)

Cluster 105:
Empty, Empty, Empty (299 buildings)

FIGURE 5.38 Clusters 25, 19, 26, 18, 93 and 105.

Cluster 30:
Business-Shopping, Residential, Residential, Residential (297 buildings)

Cluster 27:
Business-Shopping, Residential, Residential (273 buildings)

Cluster 106:
Empty, Empty, Empty, Empty (242 buildings)

Cluster 36:
Business-Shopping, Residential, Residential, Residential, Residential (237 buildings)

Cluster 21:
Business-Shopping, Business-Shopping, Business-Shopping, Business-Shopping, Business-Shopping, Business-Shopping (218 buildings)

Cluster 108:
Empty, Empty (213 buildings)

FIGURE 5.39 Clusters 30, 27, 106, 36, 21 and 108.

Cluster 9:
Residential, Residential, Residential, Residential, Residential, Residential (151 buildings)

Cluster 131:
Open Space (139 buildings)

Cluster 5:
Residential (136 buildings)

Cluster 110:
Empty, Empty, Empty, Empty, Empty (123 buildings)

Cluster 38:
Business-Shopping, Empty, Empty, Empty (114 buildings)

All the clusters (in red), buildings not clustered in grey (638 buildings)

FIGURE 5.40 Clusters 9, 131, 5, 110, 38 and Buildings Not Clustered.

The results of the clustering analysis reveal the most significant vertical floorspace use patterns in the Beyoğlu Preservation Area by scanning 11,984 buildings in terms of their functional uses. The maps displaying clusters show the invisible informal neighbourhoods of the Beyoğlu Preservation Area in terms of floorspace use patterns. This was mentioned previously in Chapter (4), while explaining the theoretical background of this research. In applying data mining methods, new types of natural territories may appear instead of formal boundaries (official neighbourhood boundaries drawn up by the municipality on the maps). These kinds of patterns cannot be revealed by simple queries or GIS analysis functions. As suggested by the approach used in this thesis, the integration of RapidMiner and GIS as two different platforms provides a more sophisticated reading of the database and enables some previously unknown information on the composition of the Beyoğlu Preservation Area Building Features Database to appear.

The clustering process described above takes a few minutes of computation time on an ordinary computer and it is almost impossible to conduct an analysis involving this amount of data without computation. In the case of the Beyoğlu Preservation Area, since we have a general idea of the composition of the district, the accuracy of these results can be evaluated. Therefore, in this case, data mining analysis helps to scientifically validate insights. In other cases involving previously unknown districts, it is evident that such an analysis would uncover previously unknown clustering patterns in an efficient way with a high level of accuracy.

The same clustering analysis is implemented to determine vertical floorspace use patterns, in the different neighbourhoods of the Beyoğlu Preservation Area, namely Karaköy, Cihangir and Tarlabaşı. The image in Figure 5.41 illustrates these patterns in these neighbourhoods and in the Beyoğlu Preservation Area, in the form of building sections.

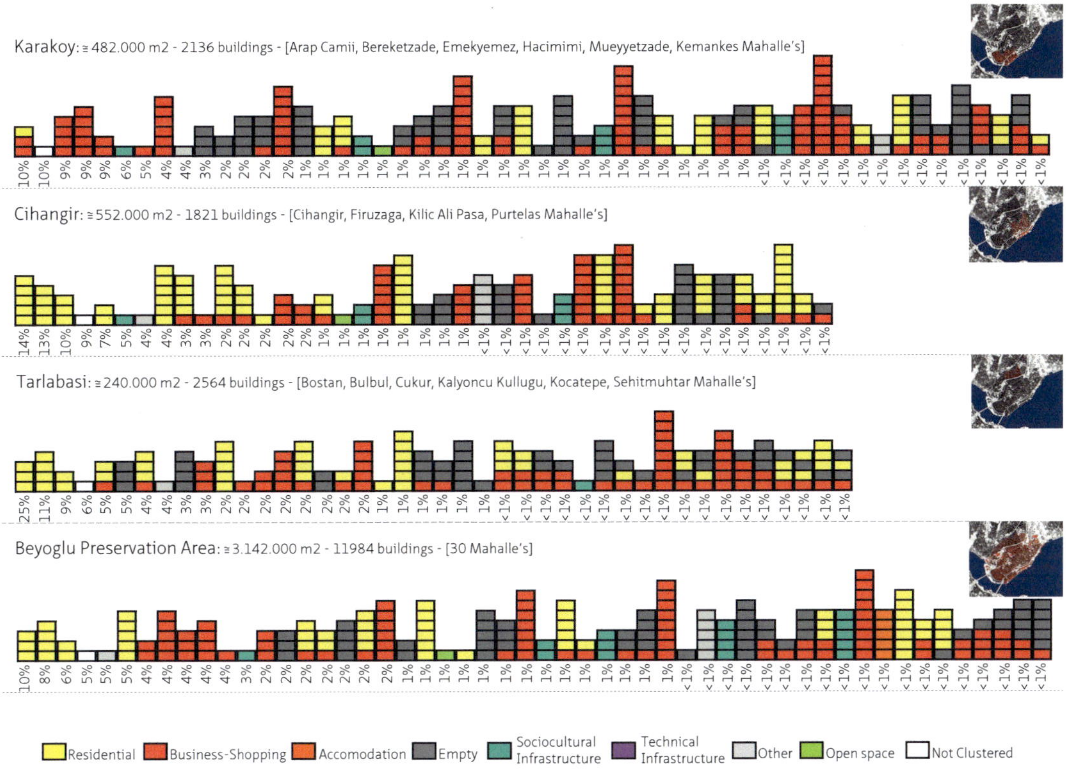

FIGURE 5.41 Vertical floorspace use patterns, in Karaköy, Cihangir, Tarlabaşı and the Beyoğlu Preservation Area, illustrated in the form of building sections.

Figure 5.41 allows us to compare the floorspace use characteristics of the different neighbourhoods. On the basis of this figure it can be inferred that;

- Karaköy mostly contains buildings with business-shopping functions and there are a significant number of empty buildings in comparison with the Beyoğlu Preservation Area and other neighbourhoods. Karaköy does not seem to have a good mixture of functions. Compared to the Beyoğlu Preservation Area and other neighbourhoods, Karaköy is the most different neighbourhood in terms of vertical floorspace use patterns and contains higher buildings in comparison to Cihangir and Tarlabaşı.
- Cihangir mostly contains buildings with residential functions but there are a significant number of business-shopping functions, as well. There are also a considerable number of buildings with business-shopping functions on the ground floor and residential functions on the upper floors. This is a mixed-use district.
- Tarlabaşı mostly contains buildings with residential functions but there are also a significant number of business-shopping functions. However, there are not many buildings with business-shopping functions on the ground floor and residential functions on the upper floors, as in Cihangir. This suggests that the residential and

business-shopping functions might be clustered in different parts of the and that Tarlabaşı has no mixed-use streets. There are also a significant number of empty buildings (more than in Cihangir), and the buildings have fewer floors than in the other districts.
- The Beyoğlu Preservation Area's most dominant clusters are residential buildings, although the second most dominant function is business-shopping, which is more prevalent than in Cihangir and Tarlabaşı.
- Apart from these observations concerning the individual districts, one general important point concerning empty buildings is that the buildings are either completely empty or their first floors are dedicated to business-shopping, while the upper floors are empty. Residential buildings do not have empty floors.

All these results reveal site-specific characteristics of the urban context under analysis. This information can be used to define the problems concerning the use of floorspace and make decisions on how and where to intervene. This is exemplified during the course of the Tarlabaşı Datascope workshop (see section (5.3) for more details).

§ 5.1.3 A critical review of the implementation

This section summarizes and evaluates the work carried out in Implementation (1).

It includes the implementation of the KDPM for urban analysis, previously introduced in Chapter (4) (see Figure 4.1), in the context of the Beyoğlu Preservation Area. It began by describing how the generic model was adapted to analyze the data contained in the traditional thematic maps of the Beyoğlu Preservation Area. It then provided details of how the Beyoğlu Preservation Area Building Features Database was formulated. Finally it presented 4 different tests that were carried out by applying 3 different data mining methods, namely Naïve Bayes Classification, Association Rule Analysis and DBSCAN Clustering. These tests allowed us to focus on Research Question (2) and investigate the kind of information patterns and relationships that can be extracted from the traditional thematic maps of the Beyoğlu Preservation Area by implementing a knowledge discovery approach to urban analysis through data mining using the KDPM for urban analysis. How these patterns and relationships can be represented was also investigated.

Test (1) was carried out by implementing a Naïve Bayes Classification to explore relationships between different categories of ground floor use and 44 other attributes of the buildings in the whole Beyoğlu Preservation Area and its three neighbourhoods (Tarlabaşı, Cihangir and Karaköy) and to determine whether the ground floor use category can be predicted using other attributes of the buildings and vice versa. The results, in the form of predictive powers, are illustrated in a series of polar graphs visualizing the similarities and differences between the Beyoğlu Preservation Area, Tarlabaşı, Cihangir and Karaköy. This test allowed us to rank the relationships between different attributes and compare different urban environments from this perspective.

It should be emphasized that although these results indicate a certain relationship between the use of ground floor and relevant predictors for this attribute, there is no causality argument based on the relative prediction capabilities of the attributes. Critically speaking, an in-depth analysis of why these attributes are relevant in predicting the use of ground floor for buildings in the Beyoğlu Preservation Area would be needed to supplement this test. This test provides objective grounds for formulating questions on causality: 'why do certain attributes affect the occurrence of certain categories of ground floor use?' However, this was beyond the scope of the research, as it focused primarily on how to implement a knowledge discovery approach to urban analysis to explore different kinds of patterns and relationships that can be discovered using data mining methods.

One interesting application of the Naïve Bayes Classification would be to predict unknown values based on existing relationships within the urban environment. This is exemplified in Implementation (3).

Test (1) was an implementation of the Bayes classification in a two-dimensional manner, measuring one-to-one relationships. It should be noted that multi-dimensional (one-to-many) applications of the Naïve Bayes Classification may cause problems with urban data because the naïve assumption could affect the accuracy of the classification. There are approaches which increase the accuracy of Bayesian classifiers with spatial data by eliminating this assumption, but this discussion is beyond the scope of this thesis. Moreover, as previously mentioned, it is widely agreed that Naïve Bayes classifiers can perform well even with correlated data attributes (Domingos & Pazzani, 1997; Ibrahim & Bennett, 2014; Qi & Zhu, 2003).

In Test (2) a Naïve Bayes Classification was carried out in full awareness of this fact, testing the combined effect of multiple attributes (with the highest level of prediction accuracy) in predicting the categories of ground floor use. Using the available data, the aim was to measure the highest possible prediction power in predicting the use of ground floor for the buildings in the Beyoğlu Preservation Area and to investigate whether the prediction accuracy for different categories of the ground floor use could be increased. As previously mentioned, accounting for the effects of spatial autocorrelation could have had an effect on the accuracy of the model.

In a similar vein, an interesting application would be to test a combination of the most powerful attributes in terms of predicting the categories of the ground floor use with attributes that might be particularly complementary (e.g. the dominant ground floor use surrounding the buildings within a certain distance; the pedestrian flow within the street where the building is located etc.) to see whether this combination could increase the prediction accuracy of the uses that registered low predictability (e.g., business-shopping, socio-cultural and technical infrastructures). Unfortunately, these attributes were not available. However, this application was used elsewhere to measure the patterns of ground floor use based on spatial adjacency and floorspace use patterns within buildings in Cihangir by implementing the KDPM for urban analysis (Sökmenoğlu & Sönmez, 2013). However, the application was not included here, as it is still in a preliminary stage.

Test (3) was conducted to test the Association Rules Classification method. The aim was to capture the associations between the categories of ground floor use (Att.1) for the buildings and forty-four other attributes, one by one. Association Rule Analysis enabled the attribute values in the Beyoğlu Preservation Area Building Features Database that occur together to be detected. It was therefore different from the Naïve Bayes Classification, allowing a descriptive type of 'relational urban knowledge' of building features to be captured. Frequent itemsets were discovered within the database by interpreting the association rules that gave some indication of possible clusters of residential and business-shopping uses within buildings in the Beyoğlu Preservation Area.

As acknowledged in the first two tests, the causality behind the data mining results demands further study, which is beyond the scope of this thesis. Again, this data mining application could be used to formulate questions concerning the causality behind the association rules for different categories of ground floor use and certain other attributes.

The descriptive nature of the association rules given in probabilistic terms makes them particularly interesting in terms of testing how they can be used to support architects, urban designers and urban planners. Accordingly, Implementation (2) would make use of this method to support the development of urban intervention proposals for the regeneration of Tarlabaşı.

Test (4) was carried out by testing a data mining clustering method in order to reveal the most significant vertical floorspace use patterns in the buildings of the Beyoğlu Preservation Area. This involved scanning 11,984 buildings in terms of their functional uses. The previous test, applying association rule analysis, indicated the existence of clusters of residential and business-shopping uses within the buildings in the Beyoğlu Preservation Area, and this final test enabled us to identify these vertical floorspace use patterns. Clustering analysis was also carried out for the Karaköy, Cihangir and Tarlabaşı neighbourhoods and the clusters uncovered are displayed in the form of building sections. This allowed for an alternative illustration of the selected urban environments and a comparative evaluation of the vertical floorspace use clusters.

It is important to acknowledge that, depending on their intensity, even though these clusters can sometimes be more or less evident to the eye of the analyst, they cannot be objectively identified by simple queries or GIS analysis functions. Moreover, if applied in previously unknown districts, and/or where the clusters are not so intense/obvious, the clustering analysis will uncover previously unknown and/or non-obvious patterns. One interesting test would be to cluster floorspace use data with other attributes that can be generated through topology-based urban analysis methods, e.g. space syntax (Hillier & Hanson, 1984) or place syntax (Stahle, Marcus, & Karlström, 2007), etc.

These tests helped us to investigate Research Question (2) by exploring the kind of information patterns and relationships that can be extracted from the traditional thematic urban analysis maps for the Beyoğlu Preservation Area, implementing the KDPM for urban analysis. Additionally, these tests also revealed certain issues concerning the knowledge discovery through data mining approach and the KDPM for urban analysis:

- The process of converting data from pdf to the CAD drawing format, as depicted in Figure 5.2, is not always straightforward. Some inconsistencies in the vector graphics editor software result in the loss of some data whilst layering the attributes;
- The data formulation phase was time-consuming due to the large amount of data to be processed; it would be better to automate this phase if the model is to be applied in practice;
- Even though GIS provides a number of spatial analysis tools, there may be a need to design and implement problem-specific custom-made spatial analysis tools within GIS and this demands programming skills which regular architects or urban planners do not have;
- In terms of its application and evaluation, data mining requires statistical knowledge, both for selecting the appropriate algorithms and for interpreting the results and, once again, this is not one of the regular skills architects or planners possess. Expert support is therefore needed[3], although the user-friendly software and community support are helpful and encouraging for non-expert data mining analysts;
- The Beyoğlu Preservation Area Building Features Database represents only certain available aspects of this urban environment but not the complete reality. It is a data-driven approach and the unavailability of more sophisticated types of data (temporal, social, demographic, economic, etc.) is one of the major limitations of this approach. In particular, the inclusion of temporal data would allow the dynamism of the urban environment to be captured for research. However, as previously mentioned, the KDPM for urban analysis describes a generic procedure and the model can therefore

3 As mentioned earlier I am grateful to Ceyhun Burak Akgül (PhD from the Electrical and Electronic Engineering Department at Télécom ParisTech Signals-Images and Boğaziçi University EE/BUSIM) for his support in implementing data mining methods and techniques.

be implemented elsewhere with more comprehensive databases. Nevertheless, it should be acknowledged that reality is infinitely complex and choices always have to be made about how much detail to include and how much to generalize or approximate (Goodchild, 2006) ;

- The underlying causes of the relationships and patterns discovered requires further analysis, which is beyond the scope of this thesis. However, these tests clearly demonstrate that data mining can support analysts in formulating questions on causality and such questions are potentially valuable in urban design, planning and decision-making;
- It is important to acknowledge that the results of data mining analysis cannot be interpreted as 'relational urban knowledge' without being validated by the analyst. These information patterns and relationships will only have the potential to be interpreted as 'relational urban knowledge' and support urban design, planning and decision-making if found 'useful' or 'valuable' by the analyst. In other words, the way in which these results are used is strongly dependent on the interests of the researchers or practitioners;
- These analyses definitely cannot reveal all that is hidden in the urban environment but, as the Conclusion Chapter emphasises, these kinds of information, based on the relational particularities of specific urban environments, may constitute a valuable site-specific background for urban design and planning projects (Sökmenoğlu, Çağdaş, & Sarıyıldız, 2011a);

Despite these difficulties and limitations, Implementation (1) demonstrates that the adaptation of the knowledge discovery process using data mining to urban data analysis developed in this thesis performs successfully. Data mining algorithms reveal the hidden patterns and relationships in building features in the Beyoğlu Preservation Area. Exporting these findings into a GIS platform allows new maps to be generated. These maps show where these patterns are located in space which, in turn, leads to further discovery. The KDPM for urban analysis as a whole allows for an in-depth analysis and better understanding of an urban environment by breaking its complexity down into patterns and relationships.

Finally, in addition to the three types of data mining methods, namely Naïve Bayes Classification, Association Rule Analysis and DBSCAN Clustering, other methods, such as Support Vector Machine and Decision Trees, would be worth implementing. Support Vector Machine (SVM), for instance, is a widely used method for regression and classification of numerical data and there are also hybrid approaches that combine SVM with different optimization techniques, such as Particle Swarm Optimization and Evolutionary Algorithms. Another commonly employed data mining method that could be applied to urban data is the Decision Tree, which can be used for classification of both nominal and numerical data. Decision Trees are easy to interpret, very good at handling categorical features, and able to capture nonlinear relations and would therefore be interesting to apply to urban data. In addition, Neural Networks could prove interesting for predictions although, unlike Naïve Bayes Classifications, Neural Networks do not identify interrelations between variables from which predictions are calculated. Obviously, when using the available data the implementation of spatial data mining algorithms would be also appropriate, although as previously discussed in section (3.4), within the scope of this thesis the decision was made to apply conventional data mining algorithms after computing spatial relationships (i.e. certain topological and distance relationships) in the data pre-processing phase, using GIS spatial analysis methods. Finally, if time-based data had been available, spatio-temporal data mining algorithms could also have been implemented.

The next chapter looks at how the results of such a process could be used in developing intervention proposals for urban regeneration. The chapter which follows introduces an implementation showing how the KDPM for urban analysis can contribute towards developing urban intervention proposals for the regeneration of Tarlabaşı neighbourhood, located in the Beyoğlu Preservation Area

§ 5.2 Implementation (2) Informing the Development of Intervention Proposals for Urban Regeneration

This section focuses on Research Question (3) by providing an example of how a knowledge discovery approach to urban analysis through data mining can contribute towards the development of intervention proposals for urban regeneration.
The problem of the regeneration of Tarlabaşı was selected as the subject for Implementation (2). Tarlabaşı, which is a very low-income district in the Beyoğlu Preservation Area, is one of the richest historical city-centre neighbourhoods in Istanbul in terms architectural heritage. The boundaries of Tarlabaşı are shown in Figure 5.42.

FIGURE 5.42 Tarlabaşı buildings shown in red.

The regeneration of Tarlabaşı is one of the most widely criticized applications of the Master Plan for the Beyoğlu Preservation Area and is a central theme of the discussions regarding the overloaded urban transformation agenda for Istanbul. Limited by the available data, an alternative to the heavily criticized transformation project, namely the Tarlabaşı renewal project initiated by the Istanbul Metropolitan Municipality and Beyoğlu Municipality is proposed here. The renewal project, which is currently under construction, is essentially criticized for not preserving the existing architectural, social and economic characteristics of this historical neighbourhood by destroying its original community and land use patterns. Therefore, a regeneration approach aiming at creating a mixed-use + mixed-user profile + mixed-income neighbourhood, whilst preserving original patterns of ground floor use in Tarlabaşı, is proposed. The main purpose of this approach, which will be explained in more detail in Table 5.9, is to regenerate Tarlabaşı by allowing different social profiles to live in this neighbourhood while still preserving its low-income local residents and original patterns of patterns of ground floor use.

GIS, data mining and evolutionary computation methods are combined to implement this approach. The computational process is shown in Figure 5.43.

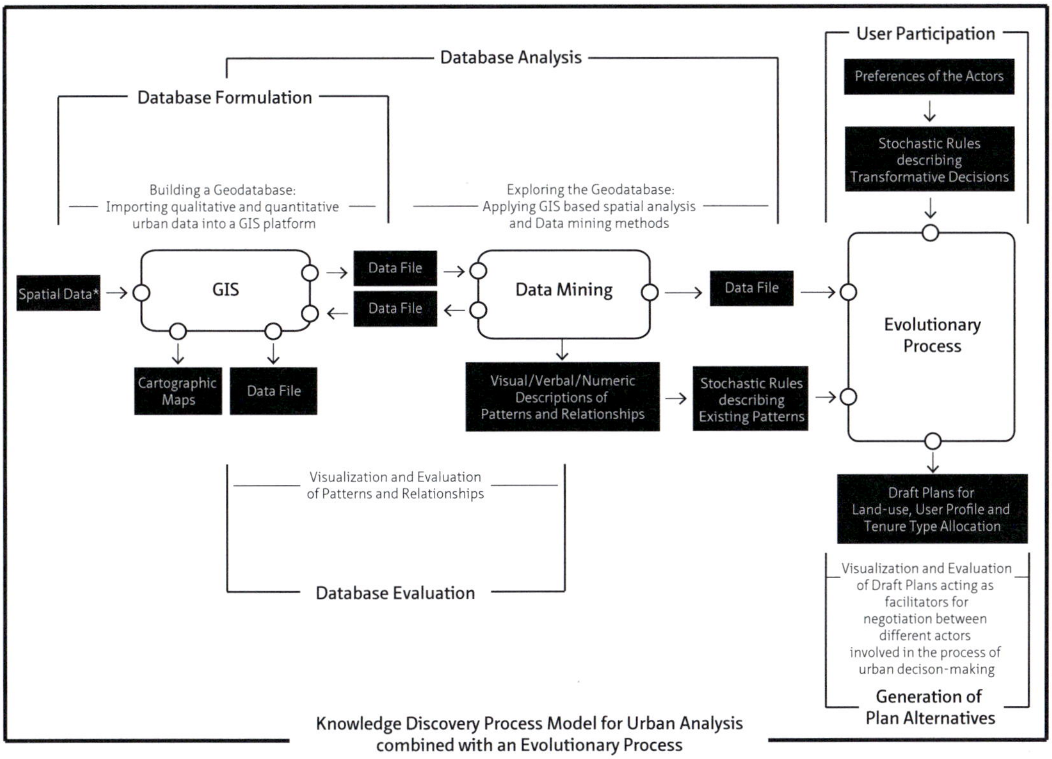

FIGURE 5.43 Knowledge Discovery Process Model (KDPM) for urban analysis combined with an evolutionary process.

The process depicted above combines GIS, data mining and evolutionary computation and demonstrates how the KDPM for urban analysis can support the formulation of urban intervention proposals in the form of draft plans for ground floor use, user type and tenure type allocation. The knowledge discovery process implemented with the KDPM for urban analysis (shown in Figure 4.1, Chapter 4) is extended by the addition of the evolutionary process component. As shown in Figure 5.43, the patterns and relationships discovered through the implementation of the data mining algorithms are formulated in the form of stochastic rules and used to guide the evolutionary process. The different preferences of the actors (users) are also expressed in the form of stochastic rules describing transformative decisions, again to be used to guide the evolutionary process. In specific terms, these rules are used for fitness measurements of an Evolutionary Algorithm. The Evolutionary Algorithm processes these conflicting rules and generates draft plans for ground floor use, user profile and tenure-type allocation, which verify these rules as far as possible. In terms of the development of urban intervention proposals, this computational process offers two important contributions:

1 The KDPM for urban analysis enables the existing patterns and relationships between attributes to be quantified in the form of stochastic rules, which reflect site-specific particularities of the urban environment under investigation. These rules are used to guide the evolutionary process and preserve the site-specific characteristics.

2 With further study and elaboration, this computational process, which combines the KDPM for urban analysis with Evolutionary Computation, can be transformed into a generic model which provides a way for user participation in inner city urban regeneration processes. The evolutionary component of this overall computational process may be considered to enable overlapping and conflicting urban intervention proposals made by different actors to direct the transformation process. Draft plans produced by the evolutionary process may be seen as facilitators for negotiation between the different actors involved in the process of transformation.

The following sections begin with an introduction to the general background to urban transformation policy in Istanbul. Information is then provided on the Master Plan for the Beyoğlu Preservation Area and the Tarlabaşı Renewal Project, followed by a description of other contemporary approaches, with a focus on the Dutch context which inspired the formulation of the key principles and strategies for the alternative regeneration approach to Tarlabaşı proposed here. The approach to the regeneration of Tarlabaşı is then introduced and the computational process required to implement this approach is described. The section concludes with a critical evaluation of this implementation, possible future research directions and the possible contributions such an approach can offer to the development of intervention proposals for urban regeneration.

§ 5.2.1 Urban transformation policy in Istanbul

Urban transformation projects have been seriously transformed Istanbul since the 1980s but it is only in the last decade that the state has discovered the potential of the historic city centre of Istanbul as a source of economic profit. Municipalities are taking unbridled advantage of the economic benefits of investing in city centres, focusing on profit. Although it is a process that should address the greater complexities to prevent social and spatial segregation of low-income local residents, urban regeneration in Istanbul involves the physical renovation and transformation of land use which openly aims to displace the urban poor. All the issues, including the historical, cultural, social and architectural aspects relating to the original identity of the place, should be considered when developing urban policies for transformation. In fact, it is advantageous in economical and functional terms to carefully preserve all these aspects of urban identity, each of which contributes to the potential of the others.

There are enormous problems with the way in which urban transformation is approached in Turkey. These may be summarized as:

- The lack of any tradition of scientific and professional approaches in urban transformation projects. In general, leading professionals and advanced tools and methods are not included in policy-making and planning processes. The contemporary vision of strategic planning and community development is overlooked.
- The lack of any tradition of collaborative urban transformation processes that includes local people and users of cities in the design, planning decision-making processes. Bottom-up processes are not preferred and, in general, urban renewal only takes place as a top-down process.
- Policy-makers usually approach urban transformation as a political and economic instrument, not with the aim of serving the welfare of the public but to increase urban land values.
- There is little communication between the different institutions responsible for urban transformation, meaning that decisions taken on different levels are not integrated.
- The definition of urban transformation is to a large extent limited to physical concerns; the social and cultural aspects of the transformation process are disregarded.

In addition to all these issues, a recent law has been introduced (in 2005) to speed up the application of urban transformation projects, known as the "Law on the protection and Revitalization of Deteriorated Historical and Cultural Immovable Assets through Renovation and Regeneration"; Article 5366 (Yıpranan Tarihî ve Kültürel Taşınmaz Varlıkların Yenilenerek Korunması ve Yaşatılarak Kullanılması Hakkında Kanun) (Resmi Gazete, 2005). Under Article 5366, the state acquired an enormous power in determining the future of currently devastated historic and cultural districts. Used by the government to bypass existing legal barriers, the law has created a market for profiteering by investors and developers.

This law has massive implications for the transformation of Istanbul's city centre. As widely emphasized in literature on the subject, the law has enabled large-scale real estate projects to be undertaken in heritage sites in the name of urban regeneration (Ahunbay, 2007; Dincer, 2008; Gunay, 2010; "Joint ICOMOS/UNESCO (WHC) Expert Mission Report: Historic Areas of Istanbul (Turkey) (C356)," 6–11 April, 2006; Kuban, 2007; "Report of the Joint UNESCO World Heritage Centre/ICOMOS Reactive Monitoring Mission to the Historic Areas of Istanbul World Heritage Site ", 8 -13 May 2008).

The current urban transformation trends in Istanbul are driven mainly by neo-liberal economics and politics, resulting only in economic profits for the investors. Urban transformation in Istanbul is not only active in historic inner city neighbourhoods (20% of the entire historic peninsula is under urban transformation, on the legal basis of Article 5366) (Aksoy, 2008) but also in the transformation of "gecekondu" (shantytown/squatter) neighbourhoods (Kucukcekmece, Gungoren, Zeytinburnu, Sisli,

Tuzla). Hardly any of the current urban transformation projects have any interest in public accountability and social goals. Unfortunately, they focus mainly on the physical transformation of the dilapidated building stock and there is hardly any commitment to the social development of the neighbourhoods subjected to the urban transformation process, although all the transformation projects have serious and almost irreversible social and physical implications. Unfortunately, the approach to urban regeneration in Turkey is based on segregation, "facilitated through segregated urban spaces, segregated communities and segregated institutions" (Gunay, 2010, p. 1179).

§ 5.2.2 The Master Plan for the Beyoğlu Preservation Area and implementation of the Tarlabaşı renewal project

Tarlabaşı is a historic district in the Beyoğlu Preservation Area which dates from the mid-16th century, when it was a settlement for non-Muslim diplomats during the Ottoman period in Istanbul. Over time it was transformed into a lower-middle class, non-Muslim (mainly Jewish, Armenian and Greek people) neighbourhood consisting mainly of craftsmen, smaller merchants, businessmen and diplomats working in the embassies and companies in and around Istiklal Caddesi, the Beyoğlu Preservation Area's most vibrant avenue. Following the establishment of the Turkish Republic in 1923, several political events, such as the exchange of Anatolian Greeks for the Greek Turkish population under the Treaty of Lausanne, the heavy Wealth Tax (Varlık Vergisi) which targeted non-Muslim citizens in 1942, and the Cyprus crisis in 1955, led non-Muslim citizens to leave Istanbul, as well as Tarlabaşı. Rural migration in the early 1950s affected the demographics of Istanbul, and the space left by the non-Muslim citizens in Tarlabaşı began to be filled by young male immigrants arriving from cities throughout Anatolia looking for employment. In the 1980s, the radical urban restructuring of Istanbul under neo-liberal policies led to the demolition of 360 historic buildings to create the six-lane Tarlabaşı Boulevard and this final act of destruction (in 1988) cut the physical connection between Tarlabaşı and the other parts of Beyoğlu. The latest transformation measure for Tarlabaşı is known as the Tarlabaşı Renewal Project, led by the Beyoğlu Municipality. The Tarlabaşı Renewal Project, which involves the demolition of almost 300 historic buildings and pedestrianization of the Tarlabaşı Boulevard by diverting traffic to underground tunnels, is currently under construction. It is just one of the many urban transformation projects initiated by the AK Party (AKP - the governing party) serving solely as an instrument for generating economic profits. In Turkey, a totally new period began when the AKP came to power in 2002. AKP urban policies focus mainly on making a profit from urban land and this, of course, stems from the urgent need to generate economic resources in the current period of global economic depression. The following section provides further details of the political aspects and one-sided economic benefits of the Tarlabaşı renewal project. The images in Figure 5.44 show the past and present state of the Tarlabaşı streets.

FIGURE 5.44 Tarlabaşı streets in the past ("Burasi Tarlabaşı mi?,") and in 2014 under demolition ("Streets of Tarlabaşı Istanbul," 2012)

The Tarlabaşı district is the current hot spot for urban transformation in Istanbul, which started with the Master Plan for the Beyoğlu Preservation Area prepared by the Department of Housing and Urban Development of the Istanbul Metropolitan Municipality. The master plan was first presented on 21.05.2009 on a 1/5000 scale, then on a 1/1000 scale in 21.12.2010. The Master Plan for the Beyoğlu Preservation Area is shown in Figure 5.45.

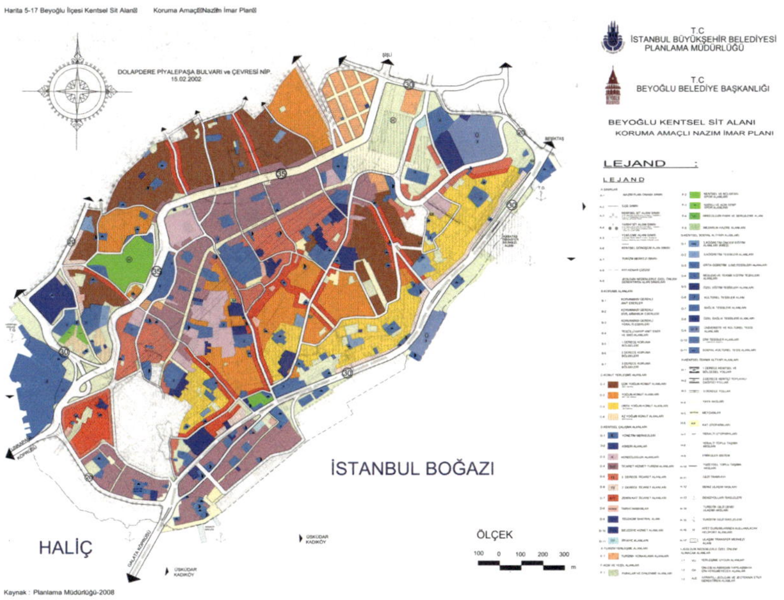

FIGURE 5.45 The 2008 Master Plan for the Beyoğlu Preservation Area produced by the Istanbul Metropolitan Municipality ("1/5000 ölçekli Beyoğlu İlçesi,Kentsel Sit Alanı Koruma Amaçlı Uygulama İmar Planı," 2010).

In the report accompanying the plan, some neighbourhoods in the Beyoğlu Preservation Area (the Cezayir dead-end street, Tophane area, Galata Tower and surroundings, historic buildings in the Beyoğlu Preservation Area and its surroundings, some urban blocks in Bedrettin mahallesi and Tarlabaşı) are declared "Renewal Areas" on the basis of the aforementioned Article 5366.

Tarlabaşı is one of these areas: in 2006, the Turkish Cabinet officially declared a 20,000m2 part of the neighbourhood an "Urban Renewal Area". The "Tarlabaşı renewal project is the first application of this law in the Beyoğlu Preservation Area. The implications of Article 5366, as identified by Aksoy (2008), can be re summarized as:

- Districts declared "Urban Renewal Areas" on the basis of Article 5366 can be demolished and re-built or renovated in order to incorporate new functions, such as housing, commerce, culture, tourism and social infrastructures.
- Empowered by Article 5366, the municipality can appoint private firms as the designers, planners and constructors of urban renewal projects. This could easily be considered advantageous, but most of the time, in Turkey, private firms have no concerns about protecting the rights of the local communities and their spatial and cultural commodities. In addition, private firms have no interest in communication and participatory planning, which is a serious problem.
- In order to bypass the complications of the expropriation process, Article 5366 offers municipalities a shortcut for the expropriation of individual properties in the name of public interest.
- Article 5366 overrules the public authority in charge of preserving cultural and natural assets on the basis of Article 2863. A commission in charge of urban renewal areas can take over the duties of the preservation committee.

In 2007, the tender was awarded to the GAP Construction Company belonging to Çalık Holding. Residents and owners of houses in Tarlabaşı were only informed of the tender and planned demolition of their properties in 2008 and were forced to leave the neighbourhood. The alternative offered by the municipality was for them to move to the newly built TOKI (Social Housing Administration of Turkey) high-rise blocks in Kayabaşı, a satellite city in a development zone on the outskirts of the Istanbul, a two-hour bus ride away from Tarlabaşı. However, the inhabitants of Tarlabaşı were too poor to afford the mortgages for the Kayabaşı apartments (Constanze Letsch, 2011). The Kayabasi satellite city is shown in Figure 5.46.

FIGURE 5.46 Kayabasi satellite city (Lewis, 2011).

The image of Tarlabaşı in Figure 5.47 shows how different the life of Tarlabaşı residents is and how this contrasts with the lifestyle provided by the Kayabasi satellite city.

FIGURE 5.47 Tarlabaşı streets before the evacuation (Harris, 2012).

Figures 5.48 and 5.49 show the present state of Tarlabaşı after evacuation of the residents.

FIGURE 5.48 Tarlabaşı streets after the evacuation, picture by the author.

FIGURE 5.49 Empty buildings in Tarlabaşı after the evacuation, picture by the author.

In the report accompanying the plan, Tarlabaşı is defined as a very problematic and unsafe residential area inhabited by low and very low-income communities, with 'undesirable' local, small-scale manufacturing and commercial activities.

The main goals of the project are defined as follows in the report:

- Physical Renovation: To renovate all the deteriorated building stock and infrastructures by protecting the historic urban character but also creating a new lifestyle in the area, taking the needs of the contemporary world into account.
- Economical Vitalization: Tourism, services and commercial activities will be promoted to improve the image of Tarlabaşı.
- Social improvement: The project will help integrate the people of Tarlabaşı into the city. The current inhabitants of the neighbourhood will also benefit from the improvements to the area. The Municipality of Beyoğlu will implement a social policy that will protect the assets of all parties and establish a social institute to support the Tarlabaşı residents during the renovation process. The constructor will provide financial support, such as subsidized rents, and offer job opportunities in the new Tarlabaşı ("1/1000 ölçekli Beyoğlu İlçesi,Kentsel Sit Alanı Koruma Amaçlı Uygulama İmar Planı Raporu," 2010).

However, the Beyoğlu Municipality only focused on physical renovation and economic vitalization, with the plans for social improvement remaining on paper. The social improvement measures for local residents that were promised in the report have never been implemented. Therefore, the execution of the plan turned out to consist of physical interventions and transformations to the functions of buildings that favoured economic profits for municipalities and private organizations. The transformation of functional use has been planned in an exclusive manner, not for the local residents of Tarlabaşı but for the new profile envisaged by the municipality. In fact, this is explicitly stated by the municipality in the images of the project that were distributed: residential blocks and shopping malls that the locals of the rundown Tarlabaşı could never afford. For whom was the Tarlabaşı renewal planned? Clearly it was not destined for the low-income residents of Tarlabaşı. The applied interventions of the master plan can be summarized as follows:

- The plots facing the Tarlabaşı Avenue will accommodate commercial-service-tourism activities and the rest of the neighbourhood will be residential, as it used to be originally.
- Tarlabaşı Boulevard will be pedestrianized and an underground tunnel will be built to divert traffic below street level (http://www.Beyoğlubuyukdonusum.com/Tarlabaşı). Finally, a major construction project started in 2012 after three years of preparation, including the evacuation and relocation of the Tarlabaşı people. The total project area has a footprint of 20.000m2 and contains 9 blocks and 278 historic buildings (210

of which are listed as civil architectural heritage buildings). Figure 5.50 shows the boundaries of the Tarlabaşı renewal project.

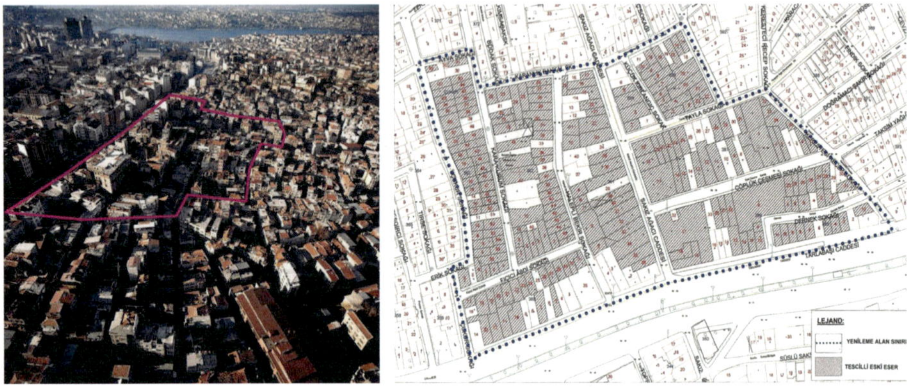

FIGURE 5.50 Boundaries of the Tarlabaşı renewal project (http://www.Beyoğlubuyukdonusum.com/Tarlabaşı).

However, the total area of the Tarlabaşı neighbourhood is around 240.000 m2 and it contains approximately 2000 buildings. Figure 5.51 and Figure 5.52 show the renovation plans for one of the nine blocks to be renovated under the Tarlabaşı renewal project.

FIGURE 5.51 Boundaries of the Tarlabaşı renewal project and a computer-generated image of Block 360 (http://www.Beyoğlubuyukdonusum.com/Tarlabaşı).

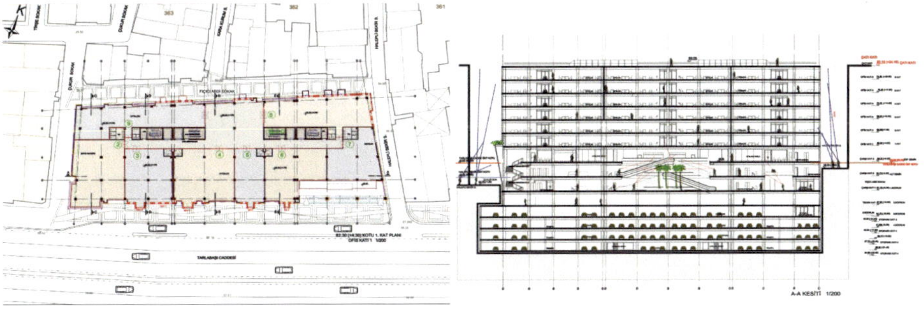

FIGURE 5.52 Block number 360 and its plans and sections (http://www.Beyoğlubuyukdonusum.com/Tarlabaşı).

Essentially the municipality proposes to get rid of the urban poor and the original Levantine architectural features of the neighbourhood by relocating its inhabitants and demolishing its slim, four-storey bow-fronted homes and narrow streets to build 15-storey buildings containing upmarket residences, offices and shopping malls. This perspective is clear in the words of the current mayor of Beyoğlu, Ahmet Misbah Demircan, "Tarlabaşı Boulevard, currently lined with cheap hotels that rent rooms by the hour, wig shops and smaller businesses, will become "the Champs-Elysées of Istanbul" (C. Letsch, 2011). The Tarlabaşı renewal project has been seriously criticized by scholars and NGOs, mainly for being a fragmentary, project-based approach to urban regeneration which ignores the rights of the original Tarlabaşı residents, forces them to leave the neighbourhood and destroys the historical architectural features. Further details of the main critical issues regarding the project are provided in Table 5.6.

ISSUES	CLARIFICATION
Municipality ignored the public interest	Beyoğlu Municipality assigned all its responsibilities to the private sector by appointing a private firm to prepare the design and the tender documents, which later also became the constructor of the Tarlabaşı renewal project, with a share of 58%. The share of the individual owners of the properties was 42%. Furthermore, Article 5366 guaranteed that the complications of the expropriation process could be bypassed by the immediate expropriation of individual properties in the name of the public interest, which effectively granted unilateral power to the municipality (Dincer, 2008). The public interest, literally, was not protected by the law and was clearly disregarded by the municipality. The Beyoğlu Municipality acted as a facilitator for the private sector to solve conflicts in the renewal process. Negotiations between the individual owners of the properties and the private sector were based solely on economic profit (Aksoy, 2008). The municipality, which was supposed to represent the public interest, assigned all its power to the private sector.
Unlimited power is given to the private sector	The obligation to use public resources to renovate and preserve the civil architecture of Tarlabaşı, based on Article 5266 (Law on the Preservation of Cultural and Natural Assets), is overruled by Article 5366. On the basis of Article 5366, in the case of Tarlabaşı, all the capital needed to construct the renewal project has been provided by the private sector. This has conferred unlimited power on the private sector and transformed the Tarlabaşı renewal process into an ordinary, unexceptional construction project (Dincer, 2008).

>>>

ISSUES	CLARIFICATION
Aimed at social and spatial segregation	The ultimate aim of the Tarlabaşı renewal project, as it is nowadays being implemented, is to create a totally new Tarlabaşı with a new high-income resident profile. In fact, this is explicitly stated in the urban renewal plan reports prepared by the municipality and the private sector ("Beyoğlu Ilcesi Tarlabaşı 1. Etap Yenileme Alani Yenileme Avan ve Uygulama Projesinin Hazirlanmasi ve Uygulanmasi Isi Idari Sartnamesi," 2007). Therefore, the social and spatial segregation of low-income, marginalized people is a primary goal of the process. However, the project should have been planned as a long-term rehabilitation and regeneration process by including all the residents in the decision-making process (Aksoy, 2008). The Tarlabaşı renewal project as it is today is no more than a demolition and rebuilding project aimed at generating economic profit without any concern for social or cultural issues. The tool for renewal is the physical architectural project and its economic value as a real estate product, the target of the renewal is the new high-income profile citizen and no role is assigned for the local residents of Tarlabaşı in this scenario. Moreover, the current residents of Tarlabaşı are mainly large low-income families, most of whom are tenants (71%), in informal employment with no social security According to research carried by the Tarlabaşı Community Centre, 66% of the residents of Tarlabaşı have no social security (http://www.Tarlabaşı.org/en/). Therefore, it would appear to be impossible for the local residents to find affordable housing and there are no government regulations for rent subsidies which would prevent their removal from the urban renewal area. The local residents of Tarlabaşı are the most disadvantaged party in the renewal process (Aksoy, 2008).
Destruction of the historic architectural features	The buildings in Tarlabaşı are small houses with 3 or 4 floors, densely packed into narrow streets and specifically designed for low-income residents. The historical heritage of Tarlabaşı is a very dense, low-income urban lifestyle. The current renewal project disregards and destroys these original urban characteristics, creating larger plots by joining multiple narrow plots together to provide new functional uses and new users (Aksoy, 2008). Only the facades of the buildings are preserved in the urban renewal process, not the typological architectural characteristics of the historic buildings that constitute the essence of the urban patterns, such as block characteristics, building depth and height, roof characteristics and street-building relationships (Akin, 2008; Dincer, 2008). In building an over-scaled (in comparison to the size of the original buildings) office, commercial and high-income residential complex with no connection at all to the existing socio-demographic, cultural and spatial patterns of Tarlabaşı, this project is changing the image of the Beyoğlu Preservation Area and Tarlabaşı by erasing the existing social and cultural identities of the place. However, the era of demolishing historical heritage and re-building its replica has come to an end and urban regeneration should now aim to preserve the collective memory of the residents by maintaining the evidence of time (Dincer, 2008).
A fragmentary, short-term vision	The Tarlabaşı renewal project is not an integral vision of transformation but a fragmentary, project-oriented approach, which has a short-term vision. The actual renewal area is 3% of the whole Tarlabaşı district and the plan for renewal does not contain any information on what is going to happen to the rest of Tarlabaşı (Aksoy, 2008). This is not an acceptable approach for an urban regeneration process, as it has no connection to the rest of Tarlabaşı, or to the Beyoğlu Preservation Area or Istanbul. Urban renewal projects may have various implications on different scales and these should be carefully studied and the possible consequences tested (Dincer, 2008).
Decreasing population density	The population density in the Tarlabaşı renewal area is between 4703 and 6366 persons per hectare (information provided in the analysis reports of the Beyoğlu Municipality Planning Department). The renewal project, on the other hand, is planned for 1867 people (Aksoy, 2008). Increasing population density is, however, a principle of contemporary inner-city regenerations.
No participation or documentation	In principle, the most important thing is to question who the transformation is for and preserve every party's right to the city (Harvey, 2008). In order to implement this principle, urban renewal should be developed as a well-documented transparent process, organized and managed in a democratic way and open to public participation (Dincer, 2008). The process of transformation and the way in which it is implemented should include users in the decision-making and design process. This will obviously ensure more democratic processes and increase the chance of the projects being more sustainable. In the case of Tarlabaşı none of the parties concerned, namely the inhabitants of the district and the local NGOs, are included in the decision-making process and the project is designed and applied via top-down decisions. However, today the contemporary approach to urban transformation works both as a bottom-up and top-down process to foster more democratic processes that encourage participation and collective decision-making.

TABLE 5.6 Main Criticisms of the Tarlabaşı Renewal Project initiated by the Istanbul Metropolitan Municipality and Beyoğlu Municipality.

The transformation concept in the Beyoğlu Preservation Area and in Tarlabaşı defined by Beyoğlu Municipality is considered only within the context of tourism and this restricted approach only results in higher urban land prices and social exclusion. This neo-liberal type of urban transformation can offer nothing but short-term economic profits for the investors and developers, at the expense of seriously damaging all the tangible and intangible elements of the city, its architectural heritage and the local residents, including all their socio-cultural localities.

In contrast to the Tarlabaşı transformation project led by the Istanbul Metropolitan Municipality and Beyoğlu Municipality, the current concept of design, planning and decision-making in urban transformation are changing dramatically. The new trends in urban transformation approaches, specifically in the Dutch context, will be discussed in the following section.

§ 5.2.3 New trends in urban transformation projects; the Dutch experience

Urban renewal measures first started with slum clearance. Slum clearance dates back to the 19th century when the main motivation was to curb the unhealthy and disorderly urban lifestyle in cities. In western culture, slum clearance projects began in the USA and the UK in the 1930s, driven mainly by concerns about public health and safety. The first slum clearance project in the USA, known as "the tower in the park" strategy based on demolishing traditional old buildings and urban patterns, was seen as a way of combating all the physical and social problems of urban life (Stouten, 2010). However, it transpired that the level of crime and violence was higher in the "tower in the park" than it had been in the old tenement streets (Stouten, 2010).

In the 1950s the term 'slum clearance' was replaced by 'urban renewal' in the USA and the American Housing Act of 1949, designed to encourage slum clearance and residential development, was copied by many western European countries as an approach to combating the decay in inner cities (Stouten, 2010). The 1949 American Housing Act came to be used as a device for displacing socially and radically undesirable groups in favour of prestige projects (Friedland, 1982; Harloe, 1995) (as cited in Stouten, 2010, p. 26).

Since the 1950s, the definition, methods and focus of urban renewal have been constantly changing due to economic, social and political drivers. The approach to urban renewal has been revitalized, affected by industrialization, modernization, economic growth and decline, privatization, globalization, post-industrialization and other factors, and differs from country to country. In the Netherlands, urban regeneration, a term associated with reducing socio-economic inequalities, was adopted after 1990 and urban renewal has become one of the elements in this process.

The contemporary approach to urban regeneration, as defined by (Roberts, 2004, p. 17), involves;

A comprehensive and integrated vision and action aimed at the resolution of urban problems and seeking to bring about a lasting improvement in the economic, physical, social and environmental condition of an area that has been subjected to change. (as cited in Stouten, 2010, p. 28)

Integral urban regeneration and strategic planning is the core of contemporary visions of urban regeneration. Strategic planning as defined by Stouten (2010) means breaking with the more inward-looking approach of the past and replacing it with an outward-looking approach involving measures that take general economic and social developments into greater consideration, whilst also taking environmental aspects into account. Unlike fragmentary, project-oriented, short-term visions (Stouten, 2010), an integral vision for solving urban problems aims to provide sustainable improvements to economic, social and physical conditions by recognizing the relevant factors and sectors in urban design and planning. Contemporary definitions emphasise that urban regeneration is a continuous process of negotiation between various interests and actors, which aims to provide sustainable renovation and refurbishment of the city.

FEATURES OF SUSTAINABILITY	CRITERIA FOR SUSTAINABILITY
Physical Quality of Housing	Flexibility in relation to different lifestyles, use value of the dwelling.
Housing Provision	Accessibility, availability, affordability for all social groups.
Urban Design	Good quality - easily maintainable - housing and residential environment. Flexibility in relation to multi-functionality e.g., reuse of office buildings for housing, reuse of brown fields, minimization of travel, spatial conditions for high-quality public transport.
Social Structure	Avoiding social exclusion, displacement of disadvantaged groups, reducing social inequalities; attractive environment, strong pull for a range of social groups, mixture of socio-economic and ethnic groups; respect and bridging of plural identities; ability to reduce violence and crime.
Economic Structure	Flourishing economic base built on long-term commitments; a broad range of workers; networked or ability to link up; creation of added value.
Governance	Decentralization of power; flexible process; active and institutionalized forms of partnerships including housing associations, organization of local residents, tenants, and owner-occupiers, local entrepreneurs, schools etc.; new forms of citizen participation and interactive democracy with the help of the internet and new media; top-down vision and bottom-up emphasis on inclusion.
Urban Planning	Strategic planning, including community-led development; accessible public spaces, compact city, provision of a wide range of amenities including a strong mix of housing.

TABLE 5.7 Aspects of sustainable urban renewal and sustainable communities, redrawn from Stouten (2010) p. 185.

In the case of Rotterdam, sustainable urban renewal and community development is the most recent name for urban renewal and regeneration processes, as proposed by Stouten (2010). This term emphasizes the ultimate aim of physical and social sustainability and the inclusion of communities within the process, bridging the physical, social and economic aspects of the renewal process. The features of sustainable urban renewal and community development, which have strongly inspired the approach to the regeneration of the Tarlabaşı district explored in this thesis, are shown in Table 5.7, as listed by Stouten (2010).

The examples of Rotterdam's Oude Noorden, Amsterdam's Eastern Docklands and the Dutch experience of urban renewal and regeneration in general were sources of inspiration in developing the approach used in this thesis to the regeneration of the Tarlabaşı district, given that the Netherlands is a relatively strong welfare state compared to many western countries and Turkey. Unlike Turkey, in the Dutch context, the state's contribution to improving housing and residential environments seriously considers the risk of spatial and social segregation. Even though the Netherlands has experienced a fundamental change in socio-economic policy since 2000 (Stouten, 2010), due to the withdrawal of the welfare state and the adoption of neo-liberal government policies, the experience of urban regeneration in the Netherlands is still very important, given its long and significantly strong tradition of recognizing the right to housing. In the Netherlands, housing is seen as one of the basic needs of the citizens and one of the basic duties of the state. The Dutch government organizations mainly responsible for providing rented social housing, known as Housing Associations, own about 75% of the three million rented homes in the Netherlands (http://www.government.nl/issues/housing/rented-housing).

Specifically, the urban development process in Rotterdam described by Stouten (2010), which began in the 1950s, offers many valuable experiences. Rotterdam's approach to urban renewal, providing a relatively significant level of integration of social, economic and housing policies, is considered a good example for other cities in the Netherlands and elsewhere in Europe (Stouten, 2010).

The basic principles of the urban renewal and regeneration processes in Rotterdam as examined through the work of Stouten (2010) are listed and briefly explained below. Even though the contents of these principles may sometimes partially overlap, they all point to different aspects of the process that are crucial. These principles and strategies, explained in detail in Table 5.8, have had a significant influence on developing this approach, which is aiming at creating a mixed-use + mixed-user profile + mixed-income neighbourhood whilst preserving the original patterns of ground floor use inTarlabaşı.

PRINCIPLES	CLARIFICATION
Avoiding social and spatial segregation	If particular care and the necessary measures are not taken, urban renewal can cause social and spatial segregation by leading to the forced re-housing of the current residents. Above all, urban renewal should aim to avoid the forced removal and displacement of the lowest paid or ethnically different members of society by providing affordable housing and social development. Renewed housing stock, after rehabilitation, should remain accessible to local residents, who are mostly low-income groups. Moreover, the issue of ethnicity should be defined as one of the distinguishing and special characteristics of the neighbourhoods and should be carefully maintained. The principle of housing allocation rules was applied in the Oude Noorden urban renewal process to avoid segregation of the current low-income and ethnically different residents. These allocation rules were based on the 85%-15% principle; in 85% of the modernized or new housing priority was given to those who were in urgent need of accommodation and who came from the area, whilst the remaining 15% went to those in similar need from other areas and other parts of the city, with the highest priority given to those in need due to the demolition or amalgamation of dwellings as part of urban renewal (Stouten, 2010). As explained by Stouten (2010), avoiding the displacement of low-income groups was a central feature of Rotterdam's approach to urban renewal. "People moving house is not, in itself, the problem that leads to new agendas but it becomes a problem if moving increases inequalities between different social groups" (Stouten, 2010) p. 184.
Encouraging the involvement of residents in the urban renewal processes	Urban renewal is a multi-dimensional process involving physical and environmental aspects, social and community issues and areas such as employment, education, housing etc. The multiple concerns and interests of diverse actors can give rise to conflicts. Urban renewal should be defined as a democratic negotiation process in which every actor should participate. It is crucial to develop a full consensus between all the parties involved in order to sustain the regeneration process. Residents, however, should be recognized as the primary actors involved in the process and their presence should be ensured by the governmental or legal organizations.
Tracking new lifestyles and how society changes	Urban regeneration concerns bringing new activities to the urban renewal area to increase the dynamism of the neighbourhood and promote diversity as an important component of urban life. It is therefore important to track the new urban lifestyles and how the composition of the population, infrastructure and social networks change within a society. The growing demand for dwellings for single people and two-person households, for instance, is a result of changing lifestyles.
Establishing social and spatial relationships between the urban renewal area and the rest of the city	The scale of operation in an urban renewal process changes from a neighbourhood to a regional and even a national scale. This is a multifaceted operation in which different policies should be integrated, and is also a process full of conflicts requiring cooperation between the different parties from different scales and contexts. Thus, it is very important to maintain a holistic approach by considering the functioning of the neighbourhood under transformation in relation to the city's housing market and the social-spatial relationships of the area in relation to other surrounding areas of the city. The possible future effects of urban transformation plans should be carefully investigated before they are implemented.
Defining urban renewal as a process, not a product	Urban renewal is more than the physical rehabilitation of the building stock, and includes strategic social and economic actions and policies. It is a "process, not a product" (Stouten, 2010) p. 148 that must be managed. It therefore also includes management of the newly built and renewed housing stock, as well as management of the long-term social and political measures in the regeneration plan.
Linking physical deprivation to social causes	Providing a social perspective on urban renewal complements physical improvements to housing and residential environments. Linking physical deprivation to its social causes (such as unemployment, physical and spiritual poverty, sickness, old age, disability, discrimination and inadequate housing) is crucial for the success of the urban renewal process. The urban renewal process therefore should include efforts to overcome social problems and should normalize the social and economic position of the residents. A social perspective might include activities such as fighting unemployment (e.g., strengthening small and medium-sized business, paying special attention to retailing, commercial services and tourism, developing new forms of industrial activity, deregulation and priority for spatial development, experimental projects for creating jobs such as the Big City Policy at the end of the 1990s), improving levels of education, fighting insecurity in public areas experienced by both residents and visitors and improving the quality of health care (Stouten, 2010). Nevertheless, social and economic measures taken in the neighborhood level, cannot be sufficient to solve the problem of physical and social deprivation, because many aspects of this problem, "such as poverty and unemployment, are structural", meaning that the solutions extend beyond the local area and borough (Feddama & Hulsbergen, 1991; Stouten, 1995, 2010; VROM-Raad, 1999) (as cited in Stouten, 2010, p. 126).

>>>

PRINCIPLES	CLARIFICATION
Sustainable development as an objective in urban renewal	In the 1990s, in Western European countries including the Netherlands sustainable development was included as an objective in urban renewal. This brought an end to the short-term, ad hoc project-based approach adopted before the 1990s and opened up a totally new way of approaching urban renewal. A more comprehensive and integrated vision of the renewal of cities emerged, directed towards sustainable improvement (Roberts, 2004; Stouten, 2010). Since then, ideas such as maintaining plural identities and bridging them, avoiding social exclusion and participation and cooperation have been defined as important principles in any urban renewal process that aims to create a sustainable city.
Preserving the character and atmosphere of the area	When it became clear that the strategies based on demolishing traditional old buildings and urban patterns failed to resolve the physical and social problems of the urban context under renewal, strategies based on preservation and renovation began to be applied. As explained by Stouten (2010), in the contemporary urban renewal processes in Rotterdam, the strategy is to maintain the original urban fabric and specific characteristics of the residential environment, at least whenever the structural conditions and programmatic considerations permit. It should be understood that the collective memory of the residents is something that is strongly linked to the original urban fabric, with all its physical and social components.
Maintaining the functional mix, promoting mixed-use to preserve dynamism	Since the 1960s, especially following Jane Jacobs's influential book - The Death and Life of Great American Cities - mixed-use has become a very important concept; "a fine-grain mixing of diverse uses creates vibrant and successful neighbourhoods" (Jacobs, 1961). She defines mixed-use as one of the conditions required to generate diversity in a city district (Sökmenoğlu & Sönmez, 2013). In the case of Rotterdam Oude Noorden, maintaining the functional mix on the high streets and the broad distribution of working-class accommodation undoubtedly ensured that the atmosphere of the area remained lively (Stouten, 2010). It is therefore important to identify basic principles to reduce the functional dispersal of businesses/shops and dwellings, based on the particular features of the residential area, such as mixing housing and work functions or placing local shops within reasonable walking distance. Moreover, in order to maintain the existing land use (principally housing) patterning is one strategy that preserves the character of the area. The concept of the Compact City (dating from the 1990s) is another strategy that promotes mixed-use in inner-city urban renewal, supporting the principle of sustainability. The compact city strategy gives priority to the "revitalization of city centres, high densities, mixed functions and the promotion of public transport, with urban development concentrated in public transport interchanges and, assist in sustainable development, thus limiting the use of cars and pollution and keeping the loss of the countryside to a minimum" (Breheny, 1999) (as cited in Stouten, 2010, p. 97).
Urban renewal progresses by small projects rather than large modernization projects	As explained by Stouten (2010) since they involve too many communal decisions, large-scale modernization projects are difficult to manage and may not easily provide room for manoeuvre, if desired. Moreover, because of their scale they can have massive impacts on the urban context under transformation, which might not be reversible. Small projects, however, can be more easily manoeuvred and allow for the involvement of individual wishes more than large-scale projects. Urban renewal progressing by small urban interventions might also enable feedback from residents and the city's complex networks and mechanisms to be measured. Thus, urban renewal strategies might be renewed while urban renewal is still in progress. Above all, as society is under constant transformation, it is not acceptable any more to approach urban renewal as a strictly defined planning measure. Instead, strategic and flexible planning is seen as a necessity in order to achieve physical and social sustainability. Large-scale projects are too definite, while small-scale interventions based on customized strategies allow for a flexible process.
Customization of urban renewal	The physical, social, economic and cultural aspects of each district will be different from each other. Each specific district has its own genuine character and will require different types of intervention for different types of problems. Specific locations, because of their situation within the city, may be suitable for specific types of uses and users. Therefore, urban renewal does not present one single formula for any district or city, and customization of the urban renewal process is very important in terms of being able to respond to the needs of different districts. This is also a crucial principle, which helps achieve the goal of sustainability.

>>>

PRINCIPLES	CLARIFICATION
Encouraging a balanced population with regard to different income groups (mixed-income and mixed-user profile)	At the end of the 1970s, the imbalance in the composition of the population was seen as a major problem by the municipality of Rotterdam (GemeenteRotterdam, 1977) (as cited in Stouten, 2010, p. 166) Therefore, in addition to a concern to improve and replace the old housing stock and urban fabric, urban renewal also aimed to change the composition of the population in these areas (Stouten, 2010). Encouraging a balanced population in terms of different income levels, ethnicity, age and profession is a very important principle of sustainable urban development. Any imbalance in the composition of the population can be adjusted by aiming for a mixed-income and mixed-demographic neighbourhood. In addition to providing measures to maintain a balanced level of income, urban renewal has to include special strategies for the elderly, one-person and two-person households, students and communes, as well as minority groups from different ethnic backgrounds. As Stouten (2010) explains, many measures were taken to maintain a balanced composition, such as keeping the existing housing stock, giving priority to social housing for urban renewal to avoid the forced re-housing of current residents on the grounds of income, balancing age distribution in the long term, and providing housing for a reasonable proportion of special population groups such as minorities from different ethnic and religious backgrounds. A strategy of housing differentiation has been adopted in the Oude Nooren urban renewal process. Housing differentiation was promoted within the housing stock by a greater variety of housing typologies, housing size, price and type of financing to match the heterogeneity of the population more effectively (Stouten, 2010). Stouten (2010) also explains that although it is difficult to express and quantify particular demand characteristics and translate them into housing characteristics, it is still possible to produce housing types that are flexible enough to suit several different lifestyles. Flexibility was defined as the extent to which a dwelling could be adjusted to suit the way in which the needs of its users change over time (Eldonk & Fassbinder, 1990; Hellgardt, 1988) (as cited in Stouten, 2010, p. 155). Creating different living areas for people with different lifestyles, flexibility and the option of running different housing programs within the same floor plans were the basic architectural principles behind the housing differentiation strategy. As explained by Stouten (2010) in the case of Rotterdam the process of deregulation and differentiation is known to provide a significant stimulus for organizations at city and area level to satisfy housing needs. The differentiation of basic typologies in the housing supply greatly increased its diversity and, according to Stouten (2010), this is an important precondition for sustainability. The housing program and tenure-type was also highly differentiated in the transformation of the Eastern Harbour District in Amsterdam to create user-profile diversity (Buurman et al., 2006).

TABLE 5.8 CaptionHere

These main principles of urban renewal and regeneration in the Dutch context, which mainly aim for a sustainable development in urban transformation by preserving the socio-demographic and architectural characteristics of the neighbourhoods, constitute the essential points considered whilst developing our approach to the regeneration of Tarlabaşı. More details will be provided in the following section.

§ 5.2.4 An approach to the regeneration of Tarlabaşı supported by the knowledge discovery approach to urban analysis through data mining and evolutionary computation

Based on the criticisms of the current renewal project initiated by the Istanbul Metropolitan Municipality and Beyoğlu Municipality and inspired by the experiences of the Netherlands, in particular the renewal and regeneration of Rotterdam's Oude Noorden area, an alternative approach has been formulated in this thesis for the regeneration of Tarlabaşı. This section introduces the approach, which aims to achieve a mixed-use + mixed-user profile + mixed-income neighbourhood whilst preserving its existing resident and patterns of ground floor use.

The basis of the approach, briefly framed above, is clarified in detail in Table 5.9, with reference to the key principles and strategies adopted.

PRINCIPLES	STRATEGIES
Avoiding social and spatial segregation	A strategy of **tenure-type differentiation** that will create a **mixed-income profile** as an instrument to combat the displacement of low-income local residents of Tarlabaşı and avoid the current social and cultural segregation resulting from the project initiated by the Istanbul Metropolitan Municipality and Beyoğlu Municipality. The Tarlabaşı locals are mostly large, low-income families and a housing **differentiation** program can therefore be implemented as part of the regeneration process to provide them with suitable housing.
Encouraging a balanced population composition with regard to different user groups (mixed-income and mixed-user profile) Tracking new lifestyles and how society changes Establishing social and spatial relationships between the urban renewal area and the rest of the city	In Tarlabaşı, there is a need to balance the composition of the population in terms of different income levels, ethnicity, age, profession and social status as a first step towards sustainable community development. Therefore, there is a need to implement a strategy to create a mixed-income and mixed-user profile neighbourhood. An approach that considers the functioning of Tarlabaşı with regard to the city's housing demand is important. Changes in the household composition within the city and the country indicate that there is a demand for small flats for one or two person households and specially designed housing for elderly and disabled people. Thus, the demands of such 'special needs' groups can be met, whilst also increasing social diversity in the Tarlabaşı community. Integrating special target groups and maintaining a mixed-user profile can also be an instrument for reducing marginalization in Tarlabaşı, not by excluding these individuals (refugees, prostitutes, drug addicts) but by positively changing their social environment. A program for housing differentiation can be a means of implementing the physical transformation of the housing stock.
Preserving the character and atmosphere of the area Maintaining the functional mix and promoting mixed-use to preserve dynamism	Maintaining the existing composition of building use is a strategy that preserves the character and atmosphere of Tarlabaşı. Maintaining the existing spatial distribution of uses can serve as a key instrument for preserving the socio-spatial networks in the neighbourhood. Moreover, maintaining a balanced mixed use in decaying city centres is also known as a means of providing urban vitality. Therefore, implementing a model to support balanced mixed use as well as small local businesses and production next to housing is a necessary strategy for Tarlabaşı.
Customization of urban renewal	The proximity of Tarlabaşı to important university campuses is a special characteristic of the area that can be used as an instrument for developing the community. As mentioned by Stouten (2010) the strategy of using the area as a "springboard", emphasizing the development of special target groups, has been an important feature of the Oude Noorden strategic plan since 1999. Developing a young student community in Tarlabaşı may help achieve the social objectives of transformation as well as the **mixed-user profile**. The inclusion of a student community could create vitality and prevent social decline, as well as helping to regenerate the atmosphere of the place and renew its identity within the city. A young community can bring a new creative energy to the area.

TABLE 5.9 Key principles and strategies for the regeneration of Tarlabaşı.

The approach used in this thesis to the regeneration of Tarlabaşı, which is detailed in Table 5.9, may be summarized as:

- Allowing low-income local residents to be a part of the "new" Tarlabaşı by following a mixed-income principle through a tenure-type differentiation strategy: Tenure differentiation includes three types of tenure, targeting low, middle and upper-middle income groups (subsidized rented, privately rented and owner-occupied housing).

A business-type differentiation is also implemented to allow local businesses (run by local residents) to remain in the neighbourhood. Two types of business use are defined: regular and local business. Other types of ground floor use cover those which already exist in the neighbourhood.

Allowing different social profiles to live in the "new" Tarlabaşı by following a mixed-user profile principle through a housing differentiation strategy: The housing differentiation strategy promotes six types of housing, targeting different types of user (regular residential, student housing and housing for 1-2 person households, families with children, the elderly and the disabled). Each user type requires a different housing type and the existing housing stock in Tarlabaşı can be renewed in accordance with user preferences by means of architectural interventions (e.g., access arrangements, floor plan layout modifications, etc.). Since there are three very important university campuses close to the district, this strategy particularly promotes student housing to allow students to form another social group in the "new" Tarlabaşı. In fact, the presence of young university students in Tarlabaşı is already evident in a few areas, and the rents are affordable. Figure 5.53 shows a map of the Beyoğlu Preservation Area and its surroundings, showing the three university campuses.

FIGURE 5.53 Map of the Beyoğlu Preservation Area and its surroundings, showing the three university campuses: Istanbul Technical University (ITU), Mimar Sinan University (MSGSU) and Bilgi University.

Maintaining original patterns of ground floor use to preserve socio-spatial networks in the neighbourhood by following a mixed-use principle: The following types of uses already exist in Tarlabaşı: residential, business-shopping, social and technical infrastructures, accommodation, open spaces and other uses. The factors that influence the use of ground floor (i.e. relationships between the use of ground floor and other building attributes) and the intensity of the existing types of use will be preserved as much as possible. Moreover, as previously explained, in order to increase diversity, residential use is differentiated to enable different user-profiles to live in Tarlabaşı, and business-shopping use is differentiated to enable local small-scale business types to remain in the neighbourhood.

Table 5.10 summarizes how the mixed-use, mixed-profile and mixed-income principles materialise within the context of this implementation.

MIXED-USE			MIXED-USER PROFILES	MIXED-INCOME
Use Type	Use Differentiation	Differentiation Strategy	Users Type	Tenure Type
Residential	Residential	Housing differentiation strategy	Existing Tarlabaşı Residents	Subsidized rented tenure
	Student housing		Students	Privately rented tenure
	Housing for 1-2 person households		1-2 person households	Owner occupied tenure
	Housing for families with children		Families with children	
	Housing for the elderly		The elderly	
	Housing for the disabled		The disabled	
Business-Shopping	Business-Shopping	Business differentiation strategy		
	Local Business			
Accommodation				
Sociocultural infrastructures				
Technical infrastructures				
Other				
Open spaces				

TABLE 5.10 Framework for mixed-use, mixed-user profile and mixed-income strategies.

In order to implement this approach to the regeneration of Tarlabaşı, a computational process that combines GIS, data mining and evolutionary computation (previously introduced in Figure 5.43) was developed to allocate ground floor use (some of the rules also allocate a use category for 1st and 2nd floors but floorspaceuse allocation mainly concerns ground floor), user profile and tenure-type (based on income). This computational process consists of identifying and applying three types of allocation rules, acting as ground floor use, user profile and tenure-type allocation determinants:

- Existing Rules (E-type rules); used to preserve the original patterns of ground floor use in Tarlabaşı (acting as floorspace use and user-profile allocation determinants). These rules are determined by means of data mining analysis by applying the KDPM for urban analysis.
- Intervention Rules (I-type rules); used to fill the empty floors based on existing patterns of ground floor use (residential/business-shopping) in Tarlabaşı (acting as floorspace use allocation determinants). These rules are determined by means of data mining analysis by applying the KDPM for urban analysis.
- Designer Rules (D-type rules); used to transform Tarlabaşı, based on mixed-use, mixed-profile and mixed-income principles (acting as floorspace use, user profile and tenure-type allocation determinants). The author identifies these rules, but in the generic process (see Figure 5.43) they will be determined by the actors involved in the transformation based on their different preferences.

The E and I-type rules active in the computational process are identified from an analysis of a GIS database consisting of the buildings in Tarlabaşı, which is a subset of the Beyoğlu Preservation Area Building Features Database. This Tarlabaşı Building Features Database contains 2136 buildings and 45 attributes associated with the buildings. A total area of 240.000m2 is subject to transformation. Figure 5.54 contains a map showing Tarlabaşı coloured in red. The focus of the municipality for the renewal, however, is outlined as a polygon in dashed lines.

FIGURE 5.54 Map showing Tarlabaşı coloured in red: the polygon in dashed lines is the renewal area.

The attributes of the buildings active in this computational process, their value range and the rule type they are associated with are shown in Table 5.11.

ATTRIBUTES	VALUES	ASSOCIATED RULE TYPES D	I	E
Att.1 Ground floor use	Residential (R), Business-Shopping (B), Accommodation (A), Empty (E), Sociocultural Infrastructure (S), Other (O), Student Housing (SH), 1-2 person Household (1-2P), Family with Children (F), Elderly (El), Disabled (D), Local Business (LB)	x	x	x
Att.2 1st Floor use	Residential (R), Business-Shopping (B), Accommodation (A), Empty (E), Sociocultural Infrastructure (S), Other (O), Student Housing (SH), 1-2 person Household (1-2P), Family with Children (F), Elderly (El), Disabled (D), Local Business (LB)	x	x	
Att.3 2nd Floor use	Residential (R), Business-Shopping (B), Accommodation (A), Empty (E), Sociocultural Infrastructure (S), Other (O), Student Housing (SH), 1-2 person Household (1-2P), Family with Children (F), Elderly (El), Disabled (D), Local Business (LB)	x		
Att.12 1st Basement Floor use	No Basement (No), Business-Shopping (B), Residential (R), Other (O), Empty (E), Accommodation (A), Sociocultural Infrastructure (S)		x	
Att.15 1st Penthouse use	No 1st Roof (No), Business-Shopping (B), Residential (R), Other (O), Empty (E), Accommodation (A), Sociocultural Infrastructure (S)		x	
Att.21 Building Maintenance Conditions	Medium, Bad, Good, Unknown, Ruined	x		
Att.22 Building Construction Style	RC, Masonry, Other, Wood, No Structure	x		
Att.24 Ownership	Private, Other	x		
Att.25 Historical Registry (intensity)	Not Available, %0-10 registered, %10-20 registered, %20-30 registered, %30-40 registered, %40-50 registered, %50-60 registered, %60-70 registered, %70-80 registered, %80-90 registered, %90-100 registered	x		
	NA, %0-10, %10-20, %20-30, %30-40, %40-50, %50-60, %60-70, %70-80, %80-90, %90-100			
Att.27 Historical Registry of Buildings	Not Available (NA), Registered Monuments (RM), Registered Civil Architecture (RCA)	x		
Att.28 Building Footprint	0-19 m2 (I), 20-75 m2 (II), 76-150 m2 (III), 151-18.000 m2 (IV)	x		
Att.33 Distance to Kabatas	{0-526 m (I), 527-841 m (II), 842-1106 m (III), 1107-1335 m (IV), 1336-1576 m (V), 1577-1839 m (VI), 1840-2259 m (VII)		x	x
Att.34 Distance to Taksim	{0-450 m (I), 451-693 m (II), 694-919m (III), 920-1178m (IV), 1179-1453m (V), 1454-1728m (VI), 1729-2071m (VII)		x	x
Att.38 Slope Code	0,1,2,3,4,5, 6,7,8,9	x		
Att.39 Land Height	0-11m (11), 12-21m (21), 22-31m (31), 32-41m (41), 42-51m (51), 52-61m (61), 62-71m (71)		x	x
Att.40 Number of Floors	1, 2, 3, 4, 5, 6, 7, 8, 9	x	x	x
Att.41 Basement (With or without)	No Basement (No), 1 Basement (1), 2 Basements (2)	x	x	x
Att.44 Street hierarchy	3rd Level, 2nd Level, 1st Level	x	x	x
Att.45 Land Price	0-74.6 TL/m2 (1), 74.7-152.24 TL/m2 (2), 152.25-276.12 TL/m2 (3), 276.13-480.02 TL/m2 (4), 480.03-806.28 TL/m2 (5), 806.29-1357.91 TL/m2 (6), 1357.92-2358.17 TL/m2 (7), 2358.18-3639.26 TL/m2 (8), 3639.27-6940.83 TL/m2 (9), 6940.84-17928.15 TL/m2 (10)	x	x	x
Att.46 Tenure-type (a new attribute created to implement D-type rules)	Socially rented (Srent), Privately Rented (Prent), Owner-occupier (Owner)	x		

TABLE 5.11 Attributes of the buildings active in the computational process, their value range and the associated rule type.

The following paragraphs, present the details of the computational process implemented to identify and apply the allocation rules.

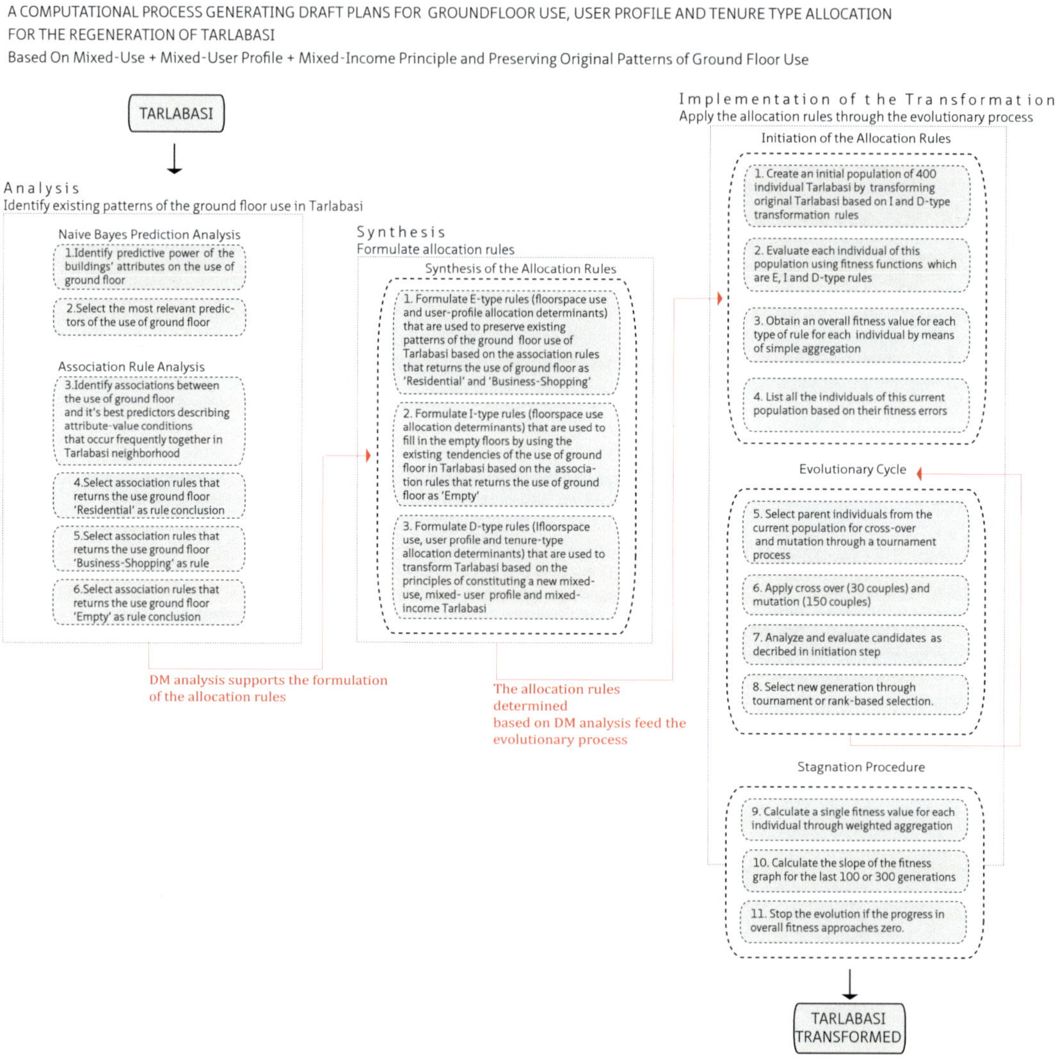

FIGURE 5.55 Computational process implemented to support the generation of draft plans for the regeneration of Tarlabaşı

Various complementary computational methods and techniques were applied in order to create this approach to the regeneration of Tarlabaşı. The KDPM for urban analysis was used to extract existing relations and patterns concerning the use of ground floor in Tarlabaşı (E and I-type rules) and this "relational knowledge of building features" was used to support the generation of the draft plans, together with the new transformative decisions (D-type rules) defined by the author. The existing patterns and relationships, together with the transformative intervention decisions, were implemented using an evolutionary process. The whole computational process implemented to support the formulation of the intervention proposals for the regeneration of Tarlabaşı is shown in detail in Figure 55.

As seen in Figure 5.55, the computational process consists of three major phases:

1. The Analysis Phase: analysis of the database to identify the existing patterns of ground floor in Tarlabaşı (the KDPM for urban analysis is applied here),
2. The Synthesis Phase: the formulation of the allocation rules,
3. The Implementation Phase: the application of the allocation rules using an evolutionary process to carry out the generation of the draft plans for the regeneration of Tarlabaşı .

§ 5.2.4.1 Analysis Phase

One of the main principles in the formation of the new Tarlabaşı is to preserve the existing relationships between ground floor use and other building attributes. The analysis phase therefore consists of the discovery of the existing patterns of ground floor use in Tarlabaşı by means of Bayes Classification and Association Rule Analysis applied sequentially. Bayes Classification allows us to filter out the relevant attributes for further analysis to explore the co-occurrence patterns using the Association Rule method. The Tarlabaşı Building Features Database is considerably large and, as mentioned in the previous chapter, Association Rule algorithms may produce a large number of patterns in such databases. Hence, the Bayes Classification serves as an elimination process for identifying the most relevant attributes, subsequently explored using Association Rule Analysis.

The first step is therefore to analyse how the use of ground floor in Tarlabaşı is related to other building attributes by applying a Bayes Classification. This analysis measures the predictive power of attributes (one-by-one) over the use of ground floor and it was postulated that this predictive power of one attribute over another is a measure of the relationship between the two variables. Implementing Bayes Classification enables the relationship between the use of ground floor and other attributes to be ranked whilst avoiding explicit functional dependency modelling and/or probabilistic modelling (otherwise the specific models chosen would have to be justified and validated - a task beyond the scope of this thesis).

By applying the Bayes Classification, 17 attributes were identified with a predictive power of over 50%, and 13 attributes were selected that were relevant to our approach. These 13 attributes are the best relevant predictors of ground floor use in the buildings in Tarlabaşı, as shown in Table 5.12.

ATTRIBUTES	PREDICTIVE POWER*
Att.2 1st Floor use	73.96%
Att.12 1st Basement floor	66.41%
Att.3 2nd Floor use	64.36%
Att.41 Basement (with or without)	56.31%
Att.44 Street hierarchy	54.07%
Att.40 Number of Floors	53.34%
Att.39 Land Height	52.95%
Att.33 Distance to Kabatas	52.07%
Att.15 1st Penthouse use	51.88%
Att.45 Land Price	51.88%
Att.34 Distance to Taksim	51.78%
Att.21 Building Maintenance Conditions	51.73%
Att.22 Building Construction Material	50.51%

TABLE 5.12 Best predictors of ground floor use for buildings in Tarlabaşı and their prediction accuracy, on a scale ranging from 100% to 50% (*overall prediction accuracy of the attributes for the use of ground floor of the buildings in Tarlabaşı).

After identifying the best predictors of ground floor use, the following step involves the application of Association Rule Analysis to describe these relationships in the form of probabilistic co-occurrence rules. The Association Rule Analysis describes the attribute-value conditions that frequently occur together in the original Tarlabaşı neighbourhood. After analyzing each attribute's associations with the use of ground floor, three types of Association Rules were selected that were relevant to our approach:

- Association Rules with the rule consequent "ground floor use: residential"
- Association Rules with the rule consequent "ground floor use: business-shopping"
- Association Rules with the rule consequent "ground floor use: empty"

The Association Rules with the rule consequent "ground floor use: residential" are shown in Table 5.13.

RULE ANTECEDENT	RULE CONSEQUENT	SUPPORT	CONFIDENCE	RULE DESCRIPTION
Att.41 = 1 Basement	Att.1 = Residential	30.03%	67.13%	67.13% of the buildings with 1 basement floor have ground floor residential use. These buildings constitute 30.03% of the whole Tarlabaşı district.
Att.39 = 41	Att.1 = Residential	15.17%	66.16%	66.16% of the buildings that are located 32-41 meters above sea level have ground floor residential use. These buildings constitute 15.17% of the whole Tarlabaşı district.
Att.45 = 1	Att.1 = Residential	11.86%	65.80%	65.8% of the buildings that are priced below 74.6 TL/m2 have ground floor residential use. These buildings constitute 11.86% of the whole Tarlabaşı district.
Att.34 = IV	Att.1 = Residential	14.86%	59.16%	59.16% of the buildings that are 920-1178 meters from Taksim Square have ground floor residential use. These buildings constitute 14.86% of the whole Tarlabaşı district.
Att.40 = 2	Att.1 = Residential	8.85%	56.61%	56.61% of the buildings with 2 floors have ground floor residential use. These buildings constitute 8.85% of the whole Tarlabaşı district.
Att.33 = V	Att.1 = Residential	16.65%	55.82%	55.82% of the buildings that are 1336-1576 meters from Taksim Square have ground floor residential use. These buildings constitute 16.65% of the whole Tarlabaşı district.
Att.39 = 31	Att.1 = Residential	12.36%	55.81%	55.81% of the buildings that stand 22-31 meters above sea level have ground floor residential use. These buildings constitute 12.36% of the whole Tarlabaşı district.
Att.45 = 2	Att.1 = Residential	24.69%	53.87%	53.87% of the buildings that are priced between 74.7-152.24 TL/m2 have ground floor residential use. These buildings constitute 24.69% of the whole Tarlabaşı district.
Att.44 = 3rd Level	Att.1 = Residential	42.51%	52.71%	52.71% of the buildings that are located in 3rd level streets have ground floor residential use. These buildings constitute 42.51% of the whole Tarlabaşı district.

TABLE 5.13 Association Rules with rule consequent "ground floor use: residential" (a description of the values of the attributes can be found in Table 5.11).

The Association Rules with the rule consequent "ground floor use: business-shopping" are presented in Table 5.14.

RULE ANTECEDENT	RULE CONSEQUENT	SUPPORT	CONFIDENCE	RULE DESCRIPTION
Att.44 = 1st Level	Att.1 = Business-Shopping	3.63%	91.18%	91.18% of the buildings that are located in 1st level streets have ground floor business-shopping. These buildings constitute 3.63% of the whole Tarlabaşı district.
Att.45 = 7	Att.1 = Business-Shopping	3.98%	88.70%	88.7% of the buildings that are priced over 6940.84 TL/m2 have ground floor business-shopping. These buildings constitute 3.98% of the whole Tarlabaşı district.
Att.40 = 5	Att.1 = Business-Shopping	5.93%	63.87%	63.87% of the buildings that have 5 floors have ground floor business-shopping. These buildings constitute 5.93% of the whole Tarlabaşı district.
Att.45 = 4	Att.1 = Business-Shopping	4.33%	59.04%	59.04% of the buildings that are priced between 276.13-480.02 TL/m2 have ground floor business-shopping. These buildings constitute 4.33% of the whole Tarlabaşı district.
Att.39 = 71	Att.1 = Business-Shopping	3.04%	57.78%	57.78% of the buildings that stand 62-71 meters above sea level have ground floor business-shopping. These buildings constitute 3.04% of the whole Tarlabaşı district.
Att.44 = 2nd Level	Att.1 = Business-Shopping	8.15%	53.05%	53.05% of the buildings that are located in 2nd level streets have ground floor business-shopping. These buildings constitute 8.15% of the whole Tarlabaşı district.

TABLE 5.14 Association Rules with rule consequent "ground floor use: business-shopping" (Description of the values of the attributes can be found in Table 5.11).

The Association Rules with the rule consequent "ground floor use: residential" and "ground floor use: business-shopping" were used unchanged to formulate the E-type rules, which were then used to preserve the existing Tarlabaşı patterns of ground floor use. The Association Rules with the rule consequent "ground floor use: empty" are shown in Table 5.15.

RULE ANTECEDENT	RULE CONSEQUENT	SUPPORT	CONFIDENCE	RULE DESCRIPTION
Att.39 = 71	Att.1 = Empty	1.05%	20.00%	20% of the buildings that stand 71 meters above sea level have an empty ground floor. These buildings constitute 1.05% of the whole Tarlabaşı district.
Att.39 = 61	Att.1 = Empty	2.65%	19.10%	19/10% of the buildings that stand 52-61 meters above sea level have an empty ground floor. These buildings constitute 2.65% of the whole Tarlabaşı district.
Att.33 = III	Att.1 = Empty	4.10%	17.80%	17.80% of the buildings that are 842-1106 meters away from the Kabatas ferry terminal have an empty ground floor. These buildings constitute 4.10% of the whole Tarlabaşı district.

>>>

RULE ANTECEDENT	RULE CONSEQUENT	SUPPORT	CONFIDENCE	RULE DESCRIPTION
Att.34 = II	Att.1 = Empty	5.54%	16.92%	16.92% of the buildings that are 451-693 meters away from Taksim Square have an empty ground floor. These buildings constitute 4.10% of the whole Tarlabaşı district.
Att.39 = 51	Att.1 = Empty	3.20%	14.88%	14.88% of the buildings that stand 42-51 meters above sea level have an empty ground floor. These buildings constitute 3.20% of the whole Tarlabaşı district.
Att.40 = 2	Att.1 = Empty	2.18%	13.97%	13.97% of the buildings that have 2 floors have an empty ground floor. These buildings constitute 2.18% of the whole Tarlabaşı district.
Att.40 = 4	Att.1 = Empty	3.39%	13.64%	13.64% of the buildings that have 4 floors have an empty ground floor. These buildings constitute 3.39% of the whole Tarlabaşı district.
Att.12 = No Base-ment	Att.1 = Empty	7.18%	13.06%	13.06% of the buildings that have no basement floor have an empty ground floor. These buildings constitute 7.18% of the whole Tarlabaşı district.
Att.15 = No 1st Penthouse	Att.1 = Empty	8.97%	12.93%	12.93% of the buildings that have no penthouse floor have an empty ground floor. These buildings constitute 7.18% of the whole Tarlabaşı district.
Att.45 = 1	Att.1 = Empty	2.26%	12.55%	12.55% of the buildings that are priced below 74.6TL/m2 have an empty ground floor. These buildings constitute 2.26% of the whole Tarlabaşı district.
Att.45 = 2	Att.1 = Empty	5.73%	12.51%	12.51% of the buildings that are priced between 74.6-152.24 TL/m2 have an empty ground floor. These buildings constitute 5.73% of the whole Tarlabaşı district.
Att.40 = 3	Att.1 = Empty	4.84%	12.49%	13.64% of the buildings that have 3 floors have an empty ground floor. These buildings constitute 3.39% of the whole Tarlabaşı district.
Att.44 = 3rd Level	Att.1 = Empty	9.98%	12.38%	12.38% of the buildings that are located in 3rd level streets have an empty ground floor. These buildings constitute 9.98% of the whole Tarlabaşı district.
Att.44 = 2nd Level	Att.1 = Empty	1.83%	11.93%	11.93% of the buildings that are located in 2nd level streets have an empty ground floor. These buildings constitute 1.83% of the whole Tarlabaşı district.
Att.33 = IV	Att.1 = Empty	5.58%	11.83%	11.83% of the buildings that are 1107-1335 meters away from the Kabatas ferry terminal have an empty ground floor. These buildings constitute 5.58% of the whole Tarla-başı district.
Att.34 = III	Att.1 = Empty	4.45%	10.87%	10.87% of the buildings that are 694-919 meters away from Taksim have an empty ground floor. These buildings constitute 4.45% of the whole Tarlabaşı district.
Att.1 = Business-Shopping	Att.2 = Empty	3.78%	10.85%	10.85% of the buildings that use the ground floor for busi-ness-shopping have an empty first floor. These buildings constitute 3.78% of the whole Tarlabaşı district.
Att.41 = 1 Base-ment	Att.1 = Empty	4.84%	10.81%	10.81% of the buildings that have 1 basement floor have an empty ground floor. These buildings constitute 4.84% of the whole Tarlabaşı district.
Att.39 = 41	Att.1 = Empty	2.22%	9.69%	9.69% of the buildings that stand 32-41 meters above sea level have an empty ground floor. These buildings constitute 2.22% of the whole Tarlabaşı district.

>>>

RULE ANTECEDENT	RULE CONSEQUENT	SUPPORT	CONFIDENCE	RULE DESCRIPTION
Att.39 = 31	Att.1 = Empty	1.83%	8.27%	8.27% of the buildings that stand 22-31 meters above sea level have an empty ground floor. These buildings constitute 1.83% of the whole Tarlabaşı district.
Att.33 = V	Att.1 = Empty	2.38%	7.97%	7.97% of the buildings that are 1577-1839 meters away from the Kabatas ferry terminal have an empty ground floor. These buildings constitute 2.38% of the whole Tarlabaşı district.
Att.39 = 21	Att.1 = Empty	1.09%	7.87%	7.87% of the buildings that stand 12-21 meters above sea level have an empty ground floor. These buildings constitute 1.09% of the whole Tarlabaşı district.
Att.34 = IV	Att.1 = Empty	1.87%	7.45%	7.45% of the buildings that are 920-1178 meters away from Taksim have an empty ground floor. These buildings constitute 1.87% of the whole Tarlabaşı district.
Att.1 = Business-Shopping	Att.15 = Empty	1.87%	5.37%	5.37% of the buildings that use the ground floor for business-shopping have an empty penthouse floor. These buildings constitute 1.87% of the whole Tarlabaşı district.

TABLE 5.15 Association Rules with rule consequent "ground floor use: empty" (description of the values of the attributes can be found in Table 5.11).

§ 5.2.4.2 Synthesis Phase

This is the phase where allocation rules (E, I and D-type rules) are formulated. The Association Rules with the rule consequent "ground floor use: residential" and "ground floor use: business-shopping" (see Table 5.13 and 5.14) were used to formulate the E-type rules that preserve the existing patterns in Tarlabaşı in the evolutionary process. The E-type rules are shown in Table 5.16.

R#	RULE ANTECEDENT (IF) (X)	DECISION (THEN) (Y)	PROBABILITY	DECISION (THEN)	PROBABILITY	PROBABILITY FOR NUMBER OF BUILDINGS VERIFYING BOTH X AND Y/TOTAL NUMBER OF BUILDINGS
E1	Att.45 = 7	Att.1 = random {B, LB}	88.70%	Att.1 = random {R, A, E, S, O}	11.30%	3.98%
E2	Att.40 = 5	Att.1 = random {B, LB}	63.87%	Att.1 = random {R, A, E, S, O}	36.13%	5.93%
E3	Att.45 = 4	Att.1 = random {B, LB}	59.04%	Att.1 = random {R, A, E, S, O}	40.96%	4.33%
E4	Att.39 = 71	Att.1 = random {B, LB}	57.78%	Att.1 = random {R, A, E, S, O}	42.22%	3.04%
E5	Att.44 = 2nd Level	Att.1 = random {B, LB}	53.05%	Att.1 = random {R, A, E, S, O}	46.95%	8.15%

>>>

R#	RULE ANTECEDENT (IF) (X)	DECISION (THEN) (Y)	PROBABILITY	DECISION (THEN)	PROBABILITY	PROBABILITY FOR NUMBER OF BUILDINGS VERIFYING BOTH X AND Y/TOTAL NUMBER OF BUILDINGS
E6	Att.41 = 1 Basement	Att.1 = random {R, Stu, 1-2P, F, El, D}	67.13%	Att.1 = random {B, A, E, S, O}	32.87%	30.03%
E7	Att.39 = 41	Att.1 = random {R, Stu, 1-2P, F, El, D}	66.16%	Att.1 = random {B, A, E, S, O}	33.84%	15.17%
E8	Att.45 = 1	Att.1 = random {R, Stu, 1-2P, F, El, D}	65.80%	Att.1 = random {B, A, E, S, O}	34.20%	11.86%
E9	Att.34 = IV	Att.1 = random {R, Stu, 1-2P, F, El, D}	59.16%	Att.1 = random {B, A, E, S, O}	40.84%	14.86%
E10	Att.40 = 2	Att.1 = random {R, Stu, 1-2P, F, El, D}	56.61%	Att.1 = random {B, A, E, S, O}	43.39%	8.85%
E11	Att.33 = V	Att.1 = random {R, Stu, 1-2P, F, El, D}	55.82%	Att.1 = random {B, A, E, S, O}	44.18%	16.65%
E12	Att.39 = 31	Att.1 = random {R, Stu, 1-2P, F, El, D}	55.81%	Att.1 = random {B, A, E, S, O}	44.19%	12.36%
E13	Att.45 = 2	Att.1 = random {R, Stu, 1-2P, F, El, D}	53.87%	Att.1 = random {B, A, E, S, O}	46.13%	24.69%
E14	Att.44 = 3rd Level	Att.1 = random {R, Stu, 1-2P, F, El, D}	52.71%	Att.1 = random {B, A, E, S, O}	47.29%	42.51%

TABLE 5.16 Existing Rules (E-type rules) generated, based on the Association Rules given in Tables 5.13 and 5.14 (Rules for preserving existing patterns of residential and business-shopping uses).

The descriptions of the E-type rules are listed below:

- E1 rule: Ground floors of the 88.70% of the buildings with a land price of over 6940.84 TL/m^2 will be randomly allocated for business-shopping or local business. These buildings will constitute 3.98% of the whole Tarlabaşı district. The remaining 11.30% will be randomly allocated for one of the following uses: residential, accommodation, empty, social-infrastructure, other.
- E2 rule: Ground floors of the 63.87% of the buildings with 5 floors will be randomly allocated for business-shopping or local business. These buildings will constitute 5.93% of the whole Tarlabaşı district. The remaining 36.13% will be randomly allocated for one of the following uses: residential, accommodation, empty, social-infrastructure, other.
- E3 rule: Ground floors of the 59.04% of the buildings with a land price of 276.13-480.02 TL/m^2 will be randomly allocated for business-shopping or local business. These buildings will constitute 4.33% of the whole Tarlabaşı district. The remaining 40.96% will be randomly allocated for one of the following uses: residential, accommodation, empty, social-infrastructure, other.
- E4 rule: Ground floors of the 57.78% of the buildings that stand 62-71 meters above sea level will be randomly allocated for business-shopping or local business. These

buildings will constitute 3.04% of the whole Tarlabaşı district. The remaining 42.22% will be randomly allocated for one of the following uses: residential, accommodation, empty, social-infrastructure, other.

- E5 rule: Ground floors of the 53.05% of the buildings that are located in 2nd level streets will be randomly allocated for business-shopping or local business. These buildings will constitute 8.15% of the whole Tarlabaşı district. The remaining 46.95% will be randomly allocated for one of the following uses: residential, accommodation, empty, social-infrastructure, other.
- E6 rule: Ground floors of the 67.13% of the buildings with one basement floor will be randomly allocated for one of the housing types: residential, student housing, 1-2 person households, families with children, housing for the elderly, housing for the disabled. These buildings will constitute 30.03% of the whole Tarlabaşı district. The remaining 32.87% will be randomly allocated for one of the following uses: business-shopping, accommodation, empty, social-infrastructure, other.
- E7 rule: Ground floors of the 66.16% of the buildings that stand 32-41 meters above sea level will be randomly allocated for one of the housing types: residential, student housing, 1-2 person households, families with children, housing for the elderly, housing for the disabled. These buildings will constitute 15.17% of the whole Tarlabaşı district. The remaining 33.84% will be randomly allocated for one of the following uses: business-shopping, accommodation, empty, social-infrastructure, other.
- E8 rule: Ground floors of the 65.80% of the buildings with a land price of less than 74.6TL/m2 will be randomly allocated for one of the housing types: residential, student housing, 1-2 person households, families with children, housing for the elderly, housing for the disabled. These buildings will constitute 11.86 % of the whole Tarlabaşı district. The remaining 34.20% will be randomly allocated for one of the following uses: business-shopping, accommodation, empty, social-infrastructure, other.
- E9 rule: Ground floors of the 59.16% of the buildings that are 920-1178 meters away from Taksim will be randomly allocated for one of the housing types: residential, student housing, 1-2 person households, families with children, housing for the elderly, housing for the disabled. These buildings will constitute 14.86 % of the whole Tarlabaşı district. The remaining 40.84% will be randomly allocated for one of the following uses: business-shopping, accommodation, empty, social-infrastructure, other.
- E10 rule: Ground floors of the 56.61% of the buildings with two floors will be randomly allocated for one of the housing types: residential, student housing, 1-2 person households, families with children, housing for the elderly, housing for the disabled. These buildings will constitute 8.85 % of the whole Tarlabaşı district. The remaining 43.39% will be randomly allocated for one of the following uses: business-shopping, accommodation, empty, social-infrastructure, other.
- E11 rule: Ground floors of the 55.82% of the buildings that are 1577-1839 meters away from the Kabatas ferry terminal will be randomly allocated for one of the housing types: residential, student housing, 1-2 person households, families with children,

housing for the elderly, housing for the disabled. These buildings will constitute 16.65 % of the whole Tarlabaşı district. The remaining 44.18% will be randomly allocated for one of the following uses: business-shopping, accommodation, empty, social-infrastructure, other.

- E12 rule: Ground floors of the 55.81% of the buildings that stand 22-31 meters above sea level will be randomly allocated for one of the housing types: residential, student housing, 1-2 person households, families with children, housing for the elderly, housing for the disabled. These buildings will constitute 12.36 % of the whole Tarlabaşı district. The remaining 44.19% will be randomly allocated for one of the following uses: business-shopping, accommodation, empty, social-infrastructure, other.
- E13 rule: Ground floors of the 53.87% of the buildings with a land price of 74.6-152.24 TL/m^2 will be randomly allocated for one of the housing types: residential, student housing, 1-2 person households, families with children, housing for the elderly, housing for the disabled. These buildings will constitute 24.69 % of the whole Tarlabaşı district. The remaining 46.13% will be randomly allocated for one of the following uses: business-shopping, accommodation, empty, social-infrastructure, other.
- E14 rule: Ground floors of the 52.71% of the buildings that are located in 3rd level streets will be randomly allocated for one of the housing types: residential, student housing, 1-2 person households, families with children, housing for the elderly, housing for the disabled. These buildings will constitute 42.51 % of the whole Tarlabaşı district. The remaining 47.29% will be randomly allocated for one of the following uses: business-shopping, accommodation, empty, social-infrastructure, other.

I-type rules are the rules that allocate new use to empty floors. The Association Rules with rule consequent "ground floor use: empty" (see Table 5.13) were used to determine the buildings that require intervention and existing tendencies of floorspace use in the ground floor are used to define the form of intervention. Existing tendencies are basically determined by the association of each attribute (associated with empty ground floors, see Table 5.15) with other categories of use (see Appendix D). In this way, the empty floors are allocated to business-shopping, residential or other uses based on the existing allocation patterns of ground floor use in Tarlabaşı. The I-type rules are given in Table 5.17.

R#	RULE ANTECEDENT (IF)	RULE CONSEQUENT (THEN)	DECISION (THEN)	PROBABILITY	DECISION (THEN)	PROBABILITY
I1	Att.39 = 71	Att.1 = Empty	Att.1= Business-Shopping	57.78%	Att.1= random {R, A, S, O}	42.22%
I2	Att.39 = 61	Att.1 = Empty	Att.1= Business-Shopping	43.54%	Att.1= random {R, A, S, O}	56.46%
I3	Att.33 = III	Att.1 = Empty	Att.1 = Business-Shopping	44.58%	Att.1= random {R, A, S, O}	55.42%
I4	Att.34 = II	Att.1 = Empty	Att.1 = Residential	39.21%	Att.1= random {A, S}	17.88%
			Att.1 = Business-Shopping	38.86%		
			Att.1 = Other	4.05%		
I5	Att.39 = 51	Att.1 = Empty	Att.1 = Business-Shopping	36.30%	Att.1= random {A, S, O}	21.05%
			Att.1 = Residential	42.65%		
I6	Att.40 = 2	Att.1 = Empty	Att.1 = Residential	56.61%	Att.1= random {A, S, O}	14.96%
			Att.1 = Business-Shopping	28.43%		
I7	Att.40 = 4	Att.1 = Empty	Att.1 = Residential	43.73%	Att.1= random {A, S, O}	15.20%
			Att.1 = Business-Shopping	41.07%		
I8	Att.12 = No Base-ment	Att.1 = Empty	Att.1 = Business-Shopping	46.49%	Att.1= random {R, A, S}	45.56%
			Att.1 = Other	7.95%		
I9	Att.15 = No 1st Roof	Att.1 = Empty	Att.1 = Residential	43.62%	Att.1= random {A, S}	14.05%
			Att.1 = Business-Shopping	36.09%		
			Att.1 = Other	6.24%		
I10	Att.45 = 1	Att.1 = Empty	Att.1 = Residential	65.80%	Att.1= random {B, A, S, O}	34.20%
I11	Att.45 = 2	Att.1 = Empty	Att.1 = Residential	53.87%	Att.1= random {A, S}	13.44%
			Att.1 = Business-Shopping	28.09%		
			Att.1 = Other	4.60%		
I12	Att.40 = 3	Att.1 = Empty	Att.1 = Business-Shopping	26.99%	Att.1= random {R, A, S, O}	73.01%
I13	Att.44 = 3rd Level	Att.1 = Empty	Att.1 = Residential	52.71%	Att.1= random {A, S}	13.24%
			Att.1 = Business-Shopping	28.63%		
			Att.1 = Other	5.42%		
I14	Att.44 = 2nd Level	Att.1 = Empty	Att.1 = Business-Shopping	53.05%	Att.1= random {R, A, S, O}	46.95%
I15	Att.45 = 3	Att.1 = Empty	Att.1 = Business-Shopping	44.39%	Att.1= random {A, S, O}	16.99%
			Att.1 = Residential	38.62%		

>>>

R#	RULE ANTECEDENT (IF)	RULE CONSEQUENT (THEN)	DECISION (THEN)	PROBABILITY	DECISION (THEN)	PROBABILITY
I16	Att.33 = IV	Att.1 = Empty	Att.1 = Residential	49.13%	Att.1= random {A, S}	12.99%
			Att.1 = Business-Shopping	33.00%		
			Att.1 = Other	4.88%		
I17	Att.34 = III	Att.1 = Empty	Att.1 = Residential	48.43%	Att.1= random {A, S}	11.91%
			Att.1 = Business-Shopping	35.27%		
			Att.1 = Other	4.39%		
I18	Att.1 = Business-Shopping	Att.2 = Empty	Att.2 = Business-Shopping	36.13%	Att.1= random {R, A, S, O}	63.87%
I19	Att.41 = 1 Basement	Att.1 = Empty	Att.1 = Residential	67.13%	Att.1= random {A, S, O}	12.03%
			Att.1 = Business-Shopping	20.84%		
I20	Att.39 = 41	Att.1 = Empty	Att.1 = Residential	66.16%	Att.1= random {A, S, O}	13.26%
			Att.1= Business-Shopping	20.58%		
I21	Att.39 = 31	Att.1 = Empty	Att.1 = Business-Shopping	29.75%	Att.1= random {R, A, S}	65.32%
			Att.1 = Other	4.93%		
I22	Att.33 = V	Att.1 = Empty	Att.1 = Residential	55.82%	Att.1= random {A, S}	9.01%
			Att.1 = Business-Shopping	30.33%		
			Att.1 = Other	4.84%		
I23	Att.39 = 21	Att.1 = Empty	Att.1 = Business-Shopping	47.47%	Att.1= random {A, S, O}	11.80%
			Att.1 = Residential	40.73%		
I24	Att.34 = IV	Att.1 = Empty	Att.1 = Residential	59.16%	Att.1= random {A, S}	8.23%
			Att.1 = Business-Shopping	27.33%		
			Att.1 = Other	5.28%		
I25	Att.1 = Business-Shopping	Att.15 = Empty	Att.15 = Residential	18.34%	Att.1= random {A, S, O}	77.30%
			Att.15 = Business-Shopping	4.36%		

TABLE 5.17 Intervention Rules (I-type rules) for empty floors.

The descriptions of I-type rules are as follows:

- I1 rule: Empty ground floors of the 57.78% of the buildings that stand 71 meters above sea level will be allocated for business-shopping use. The remaining buildings will be randomly allocated for one of the following uses: residential, accommodation, sociocultural infrastructure, other.
- I2 rule: Empty ground floors of the 43.54% of the buildings that stand 52-61 meters above sea level will be allocated for business-shopping use. The remaining buildings will be randomly allocated for one of the following uses: residential, accommodation, sociocultural infrastructure, other.
- I3 rule: Empty ground floors of the 44.58% of the buildings that are 842-1106 meters away from the Kabatas ferry terminal will be allocated for business-shopping use. The remaining buildings will be randomly allocated for one of the following uses: residential, accommodation, sociocultural infrastructure, other.
- I4 rule: Empty ground floors of the 39.21% of the buildings that are 451-693 meters away from Taksim Square will be allocated for residential use, 38.86% of them will be allocated for business-shopping use and 4.05% will be allocated for other use. The remaining buildings will be randomly allocated for accommodation or sociocultural infrastructures.
- I5 rule: Empty ground floors of the 36.30% of the buildings that stand 42-51 meters above sea level will be allocated for business-shopping use and 42.65% will be allocated for residential use. The remaining buildings will be randomly allocated for accommodation, sociocultural infrastructure or other use.
- I6 rule: Empty ground floors of the 56.61% of the buildings with 2 floors will be allocated for residential use and 28.43% will be allocated for business-shopping use. The remaining buildings will be randomly allocated for one of the following uses: accommodation, sociocultural infrastructure or other.
- I7 rule: Empty ground floors of the 43.73% of the buildings with 4 floors will be allocated for residential use and 41.07% will be allocated for business-shopping use. The remaining buildings will be randomly allocated for one of the following uses: accommodation, sociocultural infrastructure or other.
- I8 rule: Empty ground floors of the 46.49% of the buildings that have no basement floor will be allocated for business-shopping use and 7.95% will be allocated for other use. The remaining buildings will be randomly allocated for one of the following uses: residential, accommodation or sociocultural infrastructure.
- I9 rule: Empty ground floors of the 43.62% of the buildings that have no penthouse floor will be allocated for residential use, 36.09% for business-shopping use and 4.60% for other use. The remaining buildings will be randomly allocated for accommodation or sociocultural infrastructures.
- I10 rule: Empty ground floors of the 65.80% of the buildings that are priced below 74.6TL/m^2 will be allocated for residential use. The remaining buildings will be randomly allocated for one of the following uses: business-shopping, accommodation, sociocultural infrastructure or other.

- I11 rule: Empty ground floors of the 53.87% of the buildings that are priced between 74.6 - 152.24 TL/m² will be allocated for residential use, 28.09% for business-shopping use and 4.6% for other use. The remaining buildings will be randomly allocated for accommodation or sociocultural infrastructure.
- I12 rule: Empty ground floors of the 26.99% of the buildings with 3 floors will be allocated for business-shopping use. The remaining buildings will be randomly allocated for one of the following uses: residential, accommodation, sociocultural infrastructure or other.
- I13 rule: Empty ground floors of the 52.71% of the buildings that are located in 3rd level streets will be allocated for residential use, 28.63% for business-shopping and 5.42% of them for other use. The remaining buildings will be randomly allocated for accommodation or sociocultural infrastructures.
- I14 rule: Empty ground floors of the 53.05% of the buildings that are located in 2nd level streets will be allocated for business-shopping use. The remaining buildings will be randomly allocated for one of the following uses: residential, accommodation, sociocultural infrastructure or other.
- I15 rule: Empty ground floors of the 44.39% of the buildings that are priced between 152.245 and 276.12 TL/m² will be allocated for business-shopping use and 38.62% will be allocated for residential use. The remaining buildings will be randomly allocated for one of the following uses: accommodation, sociocultural infrastructure or other.
- I16 rule: Empty ground floors of the 49.13% of the buildings that are 1107-1335 meters away from the Kabatas ferry terminal will be allocated for residential use, 33% for business-shopping use and 4.88% for other use. The remaining buildings will be randomly allocated for accommodation or sociocultural infrastructure
- I17 rule: Empty ground floors of the 48.43% of the buildings that are 694-919 meters away from Taksim will be allocated for residential use, 35.27% for business-shopping use and 4.39% for other use. The remaining buildings will be randomly allocated for accommodation or sociocultural infrastructure.
- I18 rule: Ground floors of the 36.13% of the buildings that use their ground floors for business-shopping and have their first floors empty will be allocated for business-shopping use. The remaining buildings will be randomly allocated for one of the following uses: residential, accommodation, sociocultural infrastructure or other.
- I19 rule: Empty ground floors of the 67.13% of the buildings with 1 basement floor will be allocated for residential use and 20.84% of them for business-shopping use. The remaining buildings will be randomly allocated for one of the following uses: accommodation, sociocultural infrastructure or other.
- I20 rule: Empty ground floors of the 66.16% of the buildings that stand 32-41 meters above sea level will be allocated for residential use and 20.58% for business-shopping use. The remaining buildings will be randomly allocated for one of the following uses: accommodation, sociocultural infrastructure or other.
- I21 rule: Empty ground floors of the 29.75% of the buildings that stand 22-31 meters above sea level will be allocated for business-shopping use and 20.58% of them for

other use. The remaining buildings will be randomly allocated for one of the following uses: residential, accommodation, sociocultural infrastructure.

- I22 rule: Empty ground floors of the 55.82% of the buildings that are 1577-1839 meters away from the Kabatas ferry terminal will be allocated for residential use, 30.33% will be allocated for business-shopping use and 4.84% of them will be allocated for other use. The remaining buildings will be randomly allocated for accommodation or sociocultural infrastructure.
- I23 rule: Empty ground floors of the 47.47% of the buildings that stand 12-21 meters above sea level will be allocated for business-shopping use and 40.73% for residential use. The remaining buildings will be randomly allocated for one of the following uses: accommodation, sociocultural infrastructure or other.
- I24 rule: Empty ground floors of the 59.16% of the buildings that are 920-1178 meters away from Taksim will be allocated for residential use, 27.33% for business-shopping use and 5.28% for other use. The remaining buildings will be randomly allocated for one of the following uses: accommodation or sociocultural infrastructure.
- I25 rule: Ground floors of the 18.34% of buildings that use their ground floors for business-shopping and have their penthouse empty will be allocated for residential use and 4.36% of them for business-shopping use. The remaining buildings will be randomly allocated for one of the following uses: accommodation, sociocultural infrastructure or other.

Finally, the D-type rules used to modify the original Tarlabașı were formulated by the author in accordance with the approach adopted: creating a mixed-use, mixed-user profile and a mixed-income Tarlabașı. Hence, the task of the D-type rules is to regulate the functional use of the buildings, user-profiles and tenure-types based on this approach. In general terms, if this computational process is taken as a generic model for urban regeneration, the D-type rules can be defined as the transformative decisions provided by the relevant actors involved in the transformation process, according to their preferences. The D-type rules are transformative acts that may contain conflicts of interests affecting the different parties. User participation is provided by processing the D-type rules using evolutionary computation (see Figure 5.43).

Table 5.18- 23 shows the definition and justification of the D-type rules. As seen in Table 5.18-23, there are six types of transformative decisions concerning the allocation of mixed-user profile and mixed-tenure, from which the D-type rules are derived.

RULE ANTECEDENT (IF)	Att.28=II			
	Att.40=2 or Att.40=3			
	Att.22 =Masonry or Att.22 =Wood			
	Att.24=Private			
	Att. 25 = %50-60 registered or Att.25= %60-70 registered or Att.25= %70-80 registered or Att.25= %80-90 registered or Att.25= %90-100 registered			
DECISION (THEN)	Att.1= 1-2P	Att.46= Srent	Att.46= Prent	Att.46= Owner
PROBABILITY	40%	50%	10%	40%
DECISION (THEN)	Att.1=S	Att.46= Srent	Att.46= Prent	Att.46= Owner
PROBABILITY	5%	90%	0%	10%
DECISION (THEN)	Att.1=Stu	Att.46= Srent	Att.46= Prent	Att.46= Owner
PROBABILITY	40%	85%	10%	5%
DECISION (THEN)	Att.1=random {B, A, O}			
PROBABILITY	15%			

Rule Description

Ground floors of the 40% of privately owned masonry or wooden buildings with a ground floor surface area of 20 to 75 m2 and 2 or 3 floors, located in blocks where more than 50% of the buildings are registered as civil architecture will be allocated as 1-2 person household residential accommodation. 50% of these buildings will have subsidized rents, 10% will be privately rented and 40% owner occupied.

Ground floors of the 5% of privately owned masonry or wooden buildings with a ground floor surface area of 20 to 75 m2 and 2 or 3 floors, located in blocks where more than 50% of the buildings are registered as civil architecture, will be allocated as social infrastructures. 90% of these buildings will have subsidized rents and 10% will be owner occupied.

Ground floors of the 40% of privately owned masonry or wooden buildings with a ground floor surface area of 20 to 75 m2 and 2 or 3 floors, located in blocks where more than 50% of the buildings are registered as civil architecture, will be allocated as social infrastructures. 85% of these buildings will have subsidized rents, 10% will be privately rented and 5% owner occupied.

Ground floors of the 15% of privately owned masonry or wooden buildings with a ground floor surface area of 20 to 75 m2 and 2 or 3 floors located in blocks where more than 50% of the buildings are registered as civil architecture will be randomly allocated for business-shopping, accommodation or other use.

Rule justification

The floorspace use allocation agenda is to transform the ground floors of the 85% of small, privately owned wooden or masonry detached houses located in blocks with a rich stock of civil architecture into 1 or 2 person households, student residences or socio-cultural infrastructures.

TABLE 5.18 D1 rules (431 buildings in Tarlabaşı are eligible for D1 rules).

RULE ANTECEDENT (IF)	Att.28=III			
	Att.40=2 Att.40=3 Att.40=4			
	Att.22 =Masonry Att.22 =Wood			
	Att.24=Private			
	Att.25= %50-60 registered or Att.25= %60-70 registered or Att.25= %70-80 registered or Att.25= %80-90 registered or Att.25= %90-100 registered			
	Att.27=Registered Civil Architecture			
DECISION (THEN)	Att.1= F	Att.46= Srent	Att.46= Prent	Att.46= Owner
PROBABILITY	80%	50%	20%	30%
DECISION (THEN)	Att.1=random {B, A, S, O}			
PROBABILITY	20%			

RuleDescription

Ground floors of the 80% of privately owned masonry or wooden listed buildings with a ground floor surface area of 76 to 150 m2 and 2, 3 or 4 floors, located in blocks where more than 50% of the buildings are registered as civil architecture will be allocated as family housing. 50% of these buildings will have subsidized rents socially rented, 20% will be privately rented and 30% owner occupied.

Ground floors of the 20% of privately owned masonry or wooden listed buildings with a ground floor surface between 76 and 150 m2 and 2-3 or 4 floors, located in blocks where more than 50% of the buildings are registered as civil architecture will be randomly allocated as business-shopping, accommodation, social infrastructures or other use.

Rule justification

The floorspace use allocation agenda is to transform ground floors of the 80% of the privately owned, medium-sized, architecturally valuable wooden or masonry buildings located in blocks with a rich stock of listed civil architecture into family housing.

TABLE 5.19 D2 rules (618 buildings in Tarlabaşı are eligible for D2 rules).

RULE ANTECEDENT (IF)	Att.38=0 Att.38=1			
	Att.22=RC			
	Att.27=Not Available			
	Att.21=Bad Att.21=Medium			
	Att.41=No basement			
	Att.45<3			
DECISION(THEN)	Att.1= El	Att.46= Srent	Att.46= Prent	Att.46= Owner
PROBABILITY	40%	70%	10%	20%
DECISION (THEN)	Att.1= D	Att.46= Srent	Att.46= Prent	Att.46= Owner
PROBABILITY	40%	70%	10%	20%
DECISION (THEN)	Att.1=random {B, A, S, O, Stu, 1-2P}			
PROBABILITY	20%			

Rule Description

Ground floors of the 40% of unlisted reinforced concrete buildings in poor or average condition with no basement, with a land value below the average for the neighbourhood and not located on a slope will be allocated as housing for the elderly. 70% of these buildings will have subsidized rents, 10% will be privately rented and 20% owner occupied.

Ground floors of the 40% of the unlisted reinforced concrete buildings in poor or average condition with no basement, with a land value below the average for the neighbourhood and not located on a slope will be allocated as housing for the disabled. 70% of these buildings will have subsidized rents, 10% will be privately rented and 20% owner occupied.

Ground floors of the 20% of the unlisted reinforced concrete buildings in bad or average condition with no basement, with a land-value below the average for the neighbourhood, and not located on a slope will be randomly allocated as 1-2 person housing, student housing, business-shopping, accommodation, social infrastructures or other use.

Rule justification

The floorspace use allocation agenda is to transform ground floors of the 80% of deteriorated unlisted reinforced concrete buildings with a relatively low land value suitable for elderly and disabled people (i.e. without basements and standing on a gentle slope) by demolishing and rebuilding them in compliance with housing standards for the elderly and disabled.

TABLE 5.20 D3 rules (105 buildings in Tarlabaşı are eligible for D3 rules).

RULE ANTECEDENT (IF)	Att.1=Business-Shopping			
	Att.2=Residential			
	Att.44=3rd level			
DECISION (THEN)	Att.1= LB	Att.46= Srent	Att.46= Prent	Att.46= Owner
PROBABILITY	65%	60%	30%	10%
DECISION (THEN)	Att.1=random {B, A, S, O, Stu, 1-2P, F}			
PROBABILITY	10%			

Rule Description

Ground floors of the 65% of the buildings located in 3rd level streets, which use the ground floor for business-shopping and the 1st floor for residential purposes will be allocated for local business. 60% of these buildings will have subsidized rents, 40% will be privately rented and 10% owner occupied.

Ground floors of the 10% of the buildings located in 3rd level streets, which use the ground floor for business-shopping and the 1st floor for residential purposes will be randomly allocated as 1-2 person housing, student housing, family housing, business-shopping, social infrastructures or other use.

Ground floors of the 25 % of the buildings located in 3rd level streets, which use the ground floor as business-shopping, and the 1st floor for residential purposes will stay as they are, allocated to business-shopping.

Rule justification

The floorspace use allocation agenda is to create a local business function, which will be protected by the policy. This involved identifying buildings with a high probability of local business use on the ground floor and transforming the ground floors of this 65% of the buildings into local business use.

TABLE 5.21 D4 rules (267 buildings in Tarlabaşı are eligible for D4 rules).

RULE ANTECEDENT (IF)	Att.1=Business-Shopping			
	Att.2=Business-Shopping			
	Att.3=Empty			
DECISION (THEN)	Att.3= 1-2P	Att.46= Srent	Att.46= Prent	Att.46= Owner
PROBABILITY	40%	50%	30%	20%
DECISION (THEN)	Att.3= Stu	Att.46= Srent	Att.46= Prent	Att.46= Owner
PROBABILITY	40%	50%	30%	20%
DECISION (THEN)	Att.1=B			
PROBABILITY	20%			

Rule Description

40% of the buildings with an empty second floor that use the ground and 1st floors for business-shopping will be allocated as 1-2 person household housing. 50% of these buildings will have subsidized rents, 30% will be privately rented and 20% owner occupied.

40% of the buildings with an empty second floor that use the ground and 1st floors for business-shopping will be allocated as student housing. 50% of these buildings will have subsidized rents, 30% will be privately rented and 20% owner occupied.

20% of the buildings that have an empty second floor and use the ground and 1st floors for business-shopping will be allocated as business-shopping.

Rule justification

The floorspace use allocation agenda is to fill the empty floors of buildings mainly used for business-shopping, mostly (80%) by young-user profiles such as 1-2 person households or students, to increase the mixed-use percentage in the neighbourhood. The remaining 20% will be reserved for business-shopping so that some buildings will be totally occupied by business-shopping.

TABLE 5.22 D5 rules (17 buildings in Tarlabaşı are eligible for D5 rules).

RULE ANTECEDENT (IF)	Att.1=Business-Shopping			
	Att.2=Empty			
DECISION (THEN)	Att.2= 1-2P	Att.46= Srent	Att.46= Prent	Att.46= Owner
PROBABILITY	40%	50%	30%	20%
DECISION (THEN)	Att.2= Stu	Att.46= Srent	Att.46= Prent	Att.46= Owner
PROBABILITY	40%	50%	30%	20%
DECISION (THEN)	Att.1=random {B, F}			
PROBABILITY	20%			

Rule Description

40% of the buildings with an empty first floor, which use the ground floor for business-shopping, will be allocated as 1-2 person housing. 50% of these buildings will have subsidized rents, 30% will be privately rented and 20% owner occupied.

40% of the buildings with an empty first floor, which use the ground floor for business-shopping, will be allocated as student housing. 50% of these buildings will have subsidized rents, 30% will be privately rented and 20% owner occupied.

20% of the buildings with an empty first floor, which use the ground floor for business-shopping, will be randomly allocated as business-shopping or family housing.

Rule justification

The floorspace use allocation agenda is to fill the empty floors of buildings, which use the ground floor for business-shopping, mostly (80%) by young-user profiles such as 1-2 person households or students, to increase the mixed-use percentage in the neighbourhood. Either family housing or business-shopping will fill the remaining 20%. Most of the upper floors of the buildings that use the ground floor for business-shopping will be converted to mainly residential use.

TABLE 5.23 D6 rules (50 buildings in Tarlabaşı are eligible for D6 rules).

The D1 rule set is created to transform the ground floors of the 85% of small, privately owned wooden or masonry detached houses located in blocks with a rich stock of civil architecture into 1 or 2 person households, student residences or socio-cultural infrastructures. Accordingly:

- Ground floors of the 40% of privately owned masonry or wooden buildings with a ground floor surface area of 20 to 75 m^2 and 2 or 3 floors, located in blocks where more than 50% of the buildings are registered as civil architecture will be allocated as 1-2 person household residential accommodation. 50% of these buildings will have subsidized rents, 10% will be privately rented and 40% owner occupied.
- Ground floors of the 5% of privately owned masonry or wooden buildings, with a ground floor surface area of 20 to 75 m^2 and 2 or 3 floors located in blocks where more than 50% of the buildings are registered as civil architecture will be allocated as social infrastructures. 90% of these buildings will have subsidized rents and 10% will be owner occupied.
- Ground floors of the 40% of privately owned masonry or wooden buildings with a ground floor surface area of 20 to 75 m^2 and 2 or 3 floors located in blocks where more than 50% of the buildings are registered as civil architecture will be allocated as social infrastructures. 85% of these buildings will have subsidized rents, 10% will be privately rented and 5% owner occupied.
- Ground floors of the 15% of privately owned masonry or wooden buildings with a ground floor surface area of 20 to 75 m^2 and 2 or 3 floors located in blocks where more

than 50% of the buildings are registered as civil architecture will be randomly allocated for business-shopping, accommodation or other use.

- The D2 rule set is created to transform the ground floors of the 80% of privately owned, medium-sized, architecturally valuable wooden or masonry buildings located in blocks with a rich stock of listed civil architecture into family housing. Accordingly:
- Ground floors of the 80% of privately owned masonry or wooden listed buildings with a ground floor surface area of 76 to 150 m^2 and 2, 3 or 4 floors, located in blocks where more than 50% of the buildings are registered as civil architecture will be allocated as family housing. 50% of these buildings will have subsidized rents, 20% will be privately rented and 30% owner occupied.
- Ground floors of the 20% of privately owned masonry or wooden listed buildings with a ground floor surface between 76 and 150 m^2 and 2-3 or 4 floors, located in blocks where more than 50% of the buildings are registered as civil architecture will be randomly allocated as business-shopping, accommodation, social infrastructures or other use.

The D3 rule set is created to transform the ground floors of 80% of the deteriorated, unlisted, reinforced concrete buildings with a relatively low land value which are suitable for elderly and disabled people (i.e. buildings without basements that stand on a gentle slope) by demolishing and rebuilding them in compliance with housing standards for the elderly and disabled. Accordingly:

- Ground floors of the 40% of unlisted reinforced concrete buildings in poor or average condition with no basement, with a land value below the average for the neighbourhood and not located on a slope will be allocated as housing for the elderly. 70% of these buildings will have subsidized rents, 10% will be privately rented and 20% owner occupied.
- Ground floors of the 40% of unlisted reinforced concrete buildings in poor or average condition with no basement, with a land value below the average for the neighbourhood and not located on a slope will be allocated as housing for the disabled. 70% of these buildings will have subsidized rents, 10% will be privately rented and 20% owner occupied.
- Ground floors of the 20% of unlisted reinforced concrete buildings in bad or average condition with no basement, with a land-value below the average for the neighbourhood, and not located on a slope will be randomly allocated as 1-2 person housing, student housing, business-shopping, accommodation, social infrastructures or other use.

The D4 rule set creates a local business function (e.g. grocery store, tea and coffee house, small workshop etc.) that will be protected by the policy. This rule set involved identifying the most suitable buildings for local business use on the ground floor and transforming the ground floors of the 65% of these buildings into local business use. Accordingly:

- Ground floors of the 65% of buildings located in 3rd level streets which use the ground floor for business-shopping and the 1st floor for residential purposes will be allocated for local business. 60% of these buildings will have subsidized rents, 40% will be privately rented and 10% owner occupied.
- Ground floors of the 10% of buildings located in 3rd level streets which use the ground floor for business-shopping and the 1st floor for residential purposes will be randomly allocated as 1-2 person housing, student housing, family housing, business-shopping, social infrastructures or other use.
- Ground floors of the 25 % of buildings located in 3rd level streets which use the ground floor as business-shopping and the 1st floor for residential purposes will stay as they are, allocated to business-shopping.

The D5 rule set is created to fill the empty floors of buildings mainly used for business-shopping, mostly (80%) by young-user profiles such as 1-2 person households or students, to increase the mixed-use percentage in the neighbourhood. The remaining 20% will be reserved for business-shopping so that some buildings will be totally occupied by business-shopping. Accordingly:

- 40% of the buildings with an empty second floor that use the ground and 1st floors for business-shopping will be allocated as 1-2 person household housing. 50% of these buildings will have subsidized rents, 30% will be privately rented and 20% owner occupied.
- 40% of the buildings with an empty second floor that use the ground and 1st floors for business-shopping will be allocated as student housing. 50% of these buildings will have subsidized rents, 30% will be privately rented and 20% owner occupied.
- 20% of the buildings that have an empty second floor and use the ground and 1st floors for business-shopping will be allocated as business-shopping.

The D6 rule set is created to allocate young-user profiles (such as 1-2 person households or students) to the empty floors of the buildings that use the ground floor for business-shopping. 80% of these buildings would be allocated to young-user profiles and this would increase the mixed-use percentage in the neighbourhood. Either family housing or business-shopping will be allocated to the remaining 20%. Most of the upper floors of the buildings that use the ground floor for business-shopping will be converted to residential use. Accordingly:

- 40% of the buildings with an empty first floor which use the ground floor for business-shopping will be allocated as 1-2 person housing. 50% of these buildings will have subsidized rents, 30% will be privately rented and 20% owner occupied.
- 40% of the buildings with an empty first floor which use the ground floor for business-shopping, will be allocated as student housing. 50% of these buildings will have subsidized rents, 30% will be privately rented and 20% owner occupied.
- 20% of the buildings with an empty first floor which use the ground floor for business-shopping will be randomly allocated as business-shopping or family housing.

§ 5.2.4.3 Implementation Phase

This phase involves the transformation of Tarlabaşı by means of an Evolutionary Algorithm. The ground floor use, user-profile and tenure-type allocation rules (E, I and D-type rules) described in the previous phase are implemented using an evolutionary process to carry out the regeneration of Tarlabaşı. The evolutionary process acts as a negotiation platform for the E, I and D-type rules (which might conflict with each other). Thus, if this computational process which supports the development of urban intervention proposals for the regeneration of Tarlabaşı is taken as a generic model, evolutionary computation can be considered as an important component of this process which can facilitate the inclusion of different intervention ideas, belonging to different participants, in the course of generating intervention proposals. A colleague of the author, N. Onur Sönmez (PhD candidate at ITU& TU Delft, the Design Informatics Chair, Faculty of Architecture), supported this part of the thesis by programming the Evolutionary Algorithm that is implemented here in Python programming language. The following paragraphs explain the details of this implementation.

An Evolutionary Algorithm was designed to carry out a sample urban transformation process. In this evolutionary process, the Tarlabaşı district is represented as a series of critical attributes for all the buildings in the district (i.e. the Tarlabaşı Building Features Database). These attributes are transformed using the three types of Association Rules (E, I and D-type rules) for fitness measurements.

Before describing the process in detail, certain important parameters of the evolutionary process should be noted in advance. These parameters and their possible values (the final, most efficient parameter combinations) are given in Table 5.24.

PARAMETER NAME	PARAMETER VALUE
Population number (number of candidates, N)	400
Maximum tour (generation count)	1500 to 5000
Number of crossover couples	30
Mutation number (number of individuals to be mutated)	150
Stability stop slope	-0.00015
Stability check for the last n generations	n= 300 generations
Crossover selection operator	Tournament
n-point crossover rate	0.1 (0.1 of rows are exchanged)
Mutation selection operator	Tournament
Mutation rate (probability for number of buildings/rows)	0.01
Attribute mutation rate (probability for number of attributes to be mutated for each selected row)	0.25
Overall mutation rate	0.01x0.25 = 0.0025
New population selection operator	"rank selection" or "tournament"
Fitness packages	"intervene", "existing" ("fitness_existing_xyt", "fitness_existing_xyx"), "designer" (primary and secondary/nested)
Fitness weights	[1., 1., .0025]
Attributes taken into account for evaluations:	["Att.1", "Att.2", "Att.3", "Att.12", "Att.15", "Att.21", "Att.22", "Att.24", "Att.25","Att.27","Att.28","Att.33","Att.34","Att.38"," Att.39","Att.40","Att.41","Att.42","Att.44","Att.45","Att.46"]
Attributes that are mutated (unmasked attributes)	['Att.1', 'Att.2', 'Att.3', 'Att.15', 'Att.46']

TABLE 5.24 Parameter combination for the evolutionary process for of Tarlabaşı.

The following paragraphs describe how the evolutionary process, which consists of the initiation, fitness evaluation, evolution and stagnation phases, was carried out. Figure 5.56 (a fragment of Figure 5.55 showing the workflow of the evolutionary process only) describes the flow of the process.

FIGURE 5.56 Implementation of the evolutionary process to transform Tarlabaşı.

Initiation of the first set of candidates

In the initiation phase of the Evolutionary Algorithm, a population consisting of N candidates (the number of candidates is the population number N given in Table 5.24: the value of this parameter depends on the complexity of the problem and is limited by performance considerations) is initiated through N distinct and comprehensive mutations of the initial matrix of a given district (Tarlabaşı). This set of initiatory mutations is not carried out randomly. Two series of rules (I-type and D-type rules) are applied sequentially over the initial matrix representing original Tarlabaşı. The buildings that meet the conditions of these rules are mutated. If applied once, this procedure (all the I-type and D-type rules applied sequentially) creates one candidate. In order to generate all the candidates, the procedure is repeated N times. If the number of candidates is 400, as shown in Table 5.24, this means that this procedure was repeated 400 times, each time over the original Tarlabaşı and 400 different candidates were obtained as a result.

Through initiation, a population of N alternative Tarlabaşı districts is obtained which are closer to the desired new situation, although none are in the exact desired state. Evolution takes the form of negotiating and reconciling the attribute values in the matrices so that a final Tarlabaşı is produced that reflects all the evaluation rules (E, I and D-type rules) as far as possible (I and D-type rules are used both for initiation and for evaluation). The mutation procedure of the initiation process is described in detail below.

For example, Table 5.25 shows the I-type rule I4.

CONDITIONS	CONDITIONS	ACTION ALTERNATIVES	PROBABILITY	ACTION FOR REMAINING PROBABILITY D = 100 −(A+B+C)
Att.34 = II	Att.1 = Empty	Att.1 = Residential	39.21% (a)	Random {Accommodation, Sociocultural infrastructure}
		Att.1 = Business-Shopping	38.86% (b)	Random {Accommodation, Sociocultural infrastructure}
		Att.1 = Other	4.05% (c)	Random {Accommodation, Sociocultural infrastructure}

TABLE 5.25 Intervention rule I4.

For each row (building) in the matrix for a new candidate (initially the Tarlabaşı matrix itself), the list of I-type rules is randomly re-shuffled (to avoid bias). Then, for each rule in the shuffled list:

– First, the conditions are first checked, one by one;

– Secondly, if all the conditions are met, the action defined in the rule is applied to the row (building). This usually implies the alteration of the given attribute in a stochastic manner, according to the given probabilities.

In the example rule in Table 5.25, the alteration will be applied according to the probabilities (residential: 39.21%, business-shopping: 38.86%, other: 4.05%, random {accommodation, sociocultural infrastructure}: remaining probability), meaning that one of the options in the given action is probabilistically chosen and applied. It should be noted that as these rules are not independent (the condition parts are partially overlapping - all the buildings under mutation are empty buildings), each newly applied rule may override and change/disrupt the changes made by the previous one. For this reason, a maximum of one rule is applied to each building/matrix row and, if a rule is applied, the procedure continues with the next row/building. This also explains why it is not possible to produce the desired attribute value distributions with this initiation procedure alone.

A similar procedure is applied for the D-type rules and an example for D-type rule D1 is given in Table 5.26:

CONDITIONS (EQUALS)	Att.28= II				
CONDITIONS (EITHER /OR)	Att.40= 2	Att.40= 3			
CONDITIONS (EITHER /OR)	Att.22 =Masonry	Att.22 =Wood			
CONDITIONS (EQUALS)	Att.24= Private				
CONDITIONS (ONE AMONGST MANY)	Att.25= %50-60 registered	Att.25= %60-70 registered	Att.25= %70-80 registered	Att.25= %80-90 registered	Att.25= %90-100 registered
ACTION ALTERNATIVE	**Att.1= 1-2P (If you change Att.1 to 1-2P, also change Att. 46 as follows)**	Att.46= Srent	Att.46= Prent	Att.46= Owner	
PROB.	**40%**	50%	10%	40%	
ACTION ALTERNATIVE	**Att.1= S**	Att.46= Srent	Att.46= Prent	Att.46= Owner	
PROB.	**5%**	90%	0%	10%	
ACTION ALTERNATIVE	**Att.1= Stu**	Att.46= Srent	Att.46= Prent	Att.46= Owner	
PROB.	**40%**	85%	10%	5%	
ACTION FOR REMAINING PROBABILITY D = 100 –(A+B+C)	**Random {B, A, O}**				
PROB.	**15%**				

TABLE 5.26 Designer rule D1.

The D-type rules are applied after I-type rules to all the rows/buildings. The following procedure is used for the D-type rules for each row (building) of a new candidate matrix (the new matrix already altered by the I-type rules), and then for each rule in the D-type rules list:

- First, the conditions are checked one by one;
- If all the conditions are met, the action defined in the rule is applied.

This is a little more complicated, yet similar. First, the initial rule (the bold rows in the example) is applied probabilistically, as in the I-type rules, meaning that one of the options in the given action is probabilistically chosen and applied. Each of these options may have secondary rules assigned to them. If there is a secondary action for that option, this action is also carried out in the same way.

The D-type rules list is not shuffled as in the I-type rules, since the condition parts are different, making it clear that they would apply to different buildings. However, it still appears possible that a prior rule application could change a building in such a way that it becomes eligible for a following rule, which is not an important problem in this context.

The fitness evaluation phase compares each member of this population in terms of its compliance with E-type, I-type and D-type rules. After the initiation phase, each member of the population is evaluated. The evaluation process is as follows:

Firstly, for each rule, a candidate Tarlabaşı is compared with the desired state defined by the rule. This amounts to finding the difference between the desired and existing ratios or percentages. These differences are treated as errors and thus an error value is obtained for each rule.

The evaluation considers each of the rule lists, namely E-type rules, I-type rules and D-type rules as distinct packages.

An example E-type rule is shown in Table 5.27.

RULE ANTECEDENT (IF)	/condition X	Att.41 = 1 Basement
RULE CONSEQUENT (THEN)	/condition Y	Att.1 = {R, Stu, 1-2P, F, El, D}
SUPPORT	/interpretation: probability for Number of buildings verifying both X and Y/Total Number of buildings	30.03%
CONFIDENCE	/interpretation: probability for Number of buildings verifying both X and Y/Number of buildings verifying X	67.13%
ELSE	/remaining probability uniformly shared amongst	Random {B, A, E, S, O}

TABLE 5.27 E-type Rule E6.

In order to apply these rules as evaluative rules, the items in the rules are interpreted as described in the Table 5.27. For fitness calculation, for each rule:

- The whole matrix is traversed to find the rows/buildings that meet the conditions X and/or Y;
- In this sub-selection only, the following ratios are calculated:
    1. Number of buildings verifying both X and Y/total number of buildings,
    2. Number of buildings verifying both X and Y/number of buildings verifying X;
- Each of these ratios are then subtracted from the respective values given in the rule to find two error values for the individual/candidate Tarlabaşı district, according to this rule, i.e. the deviance of the candidate from the desired condition;
- For each of the rules, the two error values are stored within the lists;
- After all the error values have been calculated, they are added together (equally weighted) and averaged to find an overall/unified value for the E-type rules 'package'.

In the case of I-type rules, again searching through the rows and checking for the conditions identifies the sub-samples/sub-selections. Then, within this sample, the value distribution for the given attributes is found and the values found for the candidate are subtracted from the desired/target values. This is explained using the Table 5.28 (see the rule I4 given in Table 5.25).

ATTRIBUTE CONDITION	DESIRED/TARGET DISTRIBUTION
Att.1 = Residential	39.21% (a)
Att.1 = Business-Shopping	38.86% (b)
Att.1 = Other	4.05% (c)

TABLE 5.28 Distribution for Att.1.

For example, if the ratio of residential use for Att.1 is found to be 45%, the error value is |39.21 - 45|=5.79. This step is repeated for all the options and the errors are summed up.

- The error values for each of the rules are stored within lists;
- After all the error values have been calculated, they are added together (equally weighted) and averaged to find an overall/unified value for the I-type rules 'package'.

The D-type rules are similar, but in this case the secondary distributions are also calculated. As the secondary rules are nested within a higher-level rule, the errors are calculated for the sub-selection of a sub-selection. Accordingly, the error values identified are multiplied with the coefficient/probability of the option they are linked to, to scale their weights proportionally. However, in the end, the error values identified for secondary rules are treated as first level rules, in order to balance the effect of each rule on the evolution of the population. This results in a list of rules that includes both first and second level rules. These are then averaged out to find a single error value for the D-type rules.

Evolutionary cycle

The evolutionary cycle follows the initial fitness evaluation of all members of the population. The evolutionary cycle starts by selecting parent individuals to apply mutation and crossover (i.e. variation operators). This procedure is called parent selection and is carried out using a tournament process in which randomly selected individuals compete over each of the three fitness values. The individual with more (in this case two) wins will be selected to apply mutation and cross-over. Two parameters are required for the parent selection procedure: the number of individuals to be mutated (mutation number) and the number of cross-over couples, as given in Table 5.24 (e.g. in the case of Test 55 -will be introduced later-, we start with a population of 400 individuals and 150 of them are mutated – 30 of them are selected as cross-over couples). Through mutation and crossover, new individuals are obtained and added to the candidate population.

In the case of mutation, a set of candidate Tarlabaşı districts are first selected through tournament selection (according to the "mutation number" given in Table 5.24 as desired by the designer), then, for each candidate:

- A number of buildings/rows are selected (according to the given probability for the number of buildings: the "mutation rate", given in Table 5.24) and for each building:
    - A number of attributes are randomly selected from the unmasked attribute list according to a pre-given rate (probability) for the number of attributes (the "attribute mutation rate", given in Table 5.24),
- These are randomly (uniform probability) changed to another value within the range of that attribute.

The probability for a building undergoing mutation ("mutation rate"), multiplied by the probability of an attribute to be modified ("attribute mutation rate") determines the amount of mutated genes, i.e. the "overall mutation rate" (each value within a candidate matrix is a gene).

In the case of cross-over, a set of parent pairs (of candidate Tarlabaşı districts) is first selected using tournament selection. Then, for each couple;

- A list of row numbers is calculated through random sampling, according to a crossover ratio, which is between [0-1] (the "n-point crossover" operator, given in Table 5.24)
- The rows indicated by these numbers are extracted from both parents.
- The rows from the first parent are placed over the remaining rows of the second parent.

This is repeated again in reverse order so that there are two children candidates/ districts, each with a set of rows taken from other parents.

Following this step (i.e. obtaining new individuals through mutation and crossover and adding them to the candidate population), another selection procedure (i.e. new generation selection) is carried out to select a new generation of individuals from all the candidates, i.e. the existing candidates and the new set of individuals generated through cross-over and mutation (in the case of Test 55, a new set of 400 individuals will be selected from among 400+150=650 individuals). Two different approaches were used to select the new generation, namely tournament and rank-based selection, with the tournament method being the same as parent selection.

In the rank-based version, three error values, resulting from the evaluation of each member of this population in terms of its compliance with E-type, I-type and D-type rules, are used to rank the individuals/candidates. In this case, in order to monitor the overall progression of the process, the single error values of the E, I and D-type rules are totalled and averaged with a weighted aggregation. In fact, this aggregated/unified fitness value can be used to carry out the process as a single-objective evolution. In this case, different weights can be adjusted by the analyst-designer to tune the effects of the rule sets. For instance, if the aim is for the D-type rules to have more impact on the evolutionary process, the weight of the error average of the D-type rules can be increased accordingly. This is done by changing the fitness weights parameter given in Table 5.24 (e.g. in the case of Test 55, explained further in Figures 5.57-60, the weights are chosen to scale the average fitness errors of the different rule types. The E-type rule average fitness error decreases from 2.4% to 0.25%, the D-type rule average fitness error decreases from 82% to 50% and the I-type rule average fitness error decreases from 3.3% to 2.2%. Accordingly, the E- and I-type rule weights are adjusted to 1 and the D-type rule weight is adjusted to 0.025 to scale all the average fitness errors. In our implementation, this balancing action was carried out solely to monitor the overall process, i.e. to check for stagnation.)

In the rank-based version, the rank of each individual was calculated separately for each fitness rule type. These individuals were listed according to their minimum ranks. Starting with the highest available minimum rank, a desired number of individuals were selected. If a series of individuals occupies the same minimum-rank level, the rank values of each individual are summed up and the individuals are ordered in terms of the resulting values. Thus, the algorithm displays a tendency to select individuals that are averagely fine for all three fitness types. The individuals with a high fitness value for only a few of the fitness rule types but a very low value for others are not likely to be selected.

Stagnation / stopping criterion

The evolutionary cycle continues until a predefined number of generations are reached or the process stagnates (stops improving the fitness values). In the stagnation check, as described above, a single fitness value is calculated for each individual through weighted aggregation, which attempts to equalize the effect of each fitness type. In order to check how the evolution proceeds through generations, the slope of the fitness graph was calculated for the last 100 or 300 generations. This value represents the speed of the progress in overall fitness: the higher the slope, the greater the speed. If the slope approaches zero, this shows that the evolution has almost stopped. The algorithm stops automatically if the slope drops below a pre-specified threshold. The values for these process parameters were determined after a series of trials.

The results obtained were consistent, indicating that the algorithm operates successfully. One test (Test 55) was selected to illustrate the process. Test 55 starts with a population number of 400. In each generation, 30 couples are selected for crossover and 150 candidates for mutation. Rank-based selection is implemented for the new generation selection. The evolutionary process continued for 909 generations. Figure 5.57 shows the process graph for the overall fitness. It should be noted that the error value is simply taken as negative fitness and therefore a decrease in error means an increase in fitness.

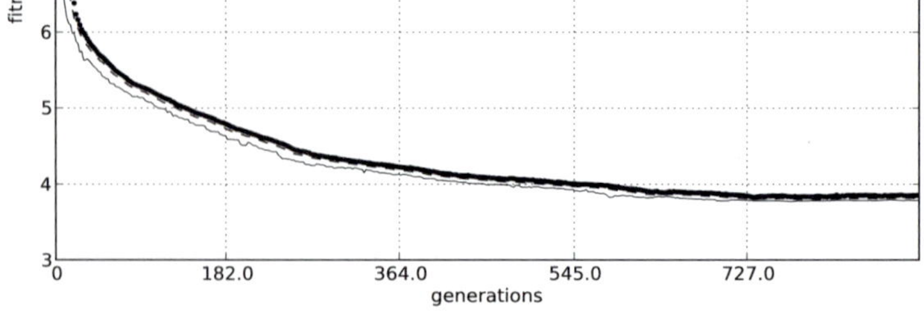

FIGURE 5.57 Overall fitness graph (aggregated error) of an evolution iterated over 909 generations (population: 400 members).

It can be observed in Figure 5.57 that at around 750 generations the process stagnated and a few hundred generations later evolution stopped. However, as can be seen in Figure 5.59, the D-type rules were still improving, at the expense of an increase in average I-type error. Despite improving D-type rules, the process was weakening compliance with I-type rules. The two movements cancelled each other out and the overall fitness value stagnated. The weights used in the aggregation of overall fitness have an effect on this balance. Separate process graphs depicting the average errors of each rule type were also produced. Figure 5.58 shows the fitness graph for the E-type rules.

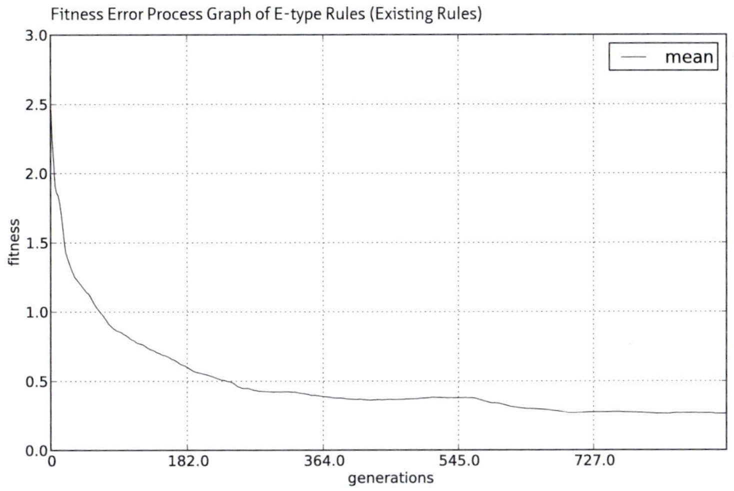

FIGURE 5.58 Process graph for the fitness (average error) of E-type rules.

In Figure 5.58, it can be seen that the average error for E-type rules decreases through the generations and tends to stabilize at around 0.25%. Starting from around 2.4%, the average error decreases to 0.25% in the 909th generation. Figure 5.59 shows the average error of D-type rules over the generations.

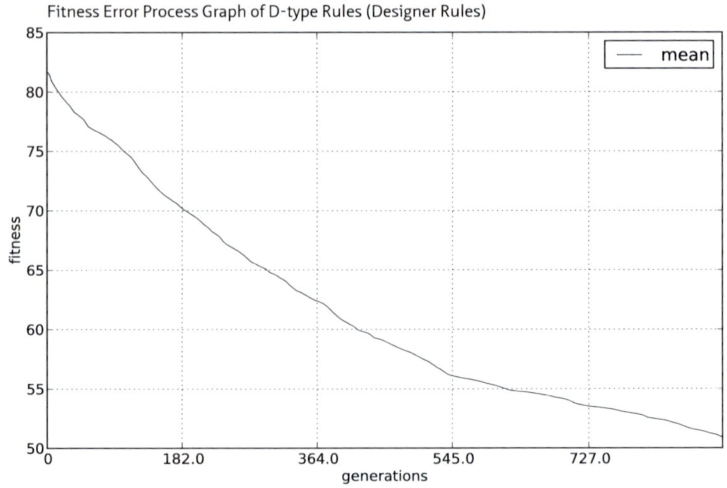

FIGURE 5.59 Process graph for the fitness (average error) of E-type rules.

In Figure 5.59, it can be seen that the average error for D-type rules decreases dramatically and continuously over the generations. Starting at around 82%, the average error decreases to 50% in the 909th generation. Figure 5.60 shows the average error for I-type rules over the generations.

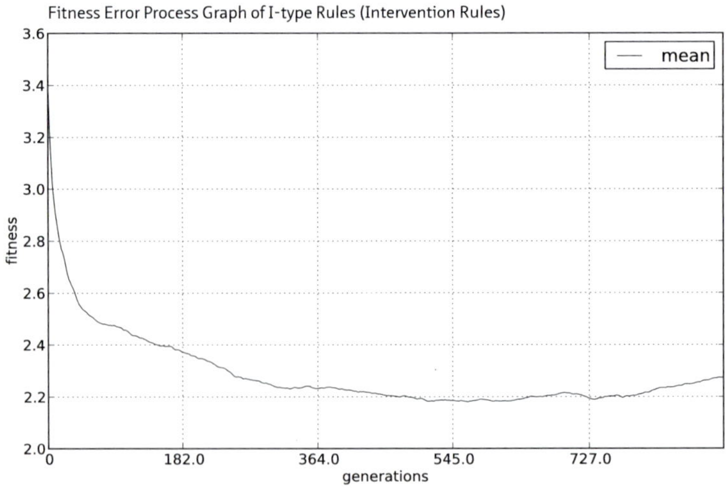

FIGURE 5.60 Process graph for the fitness errors of I-type rules.

The fitness graph for I-type rules is not as consistent as the ones for the previous rules and its behaviour changes slightly at around generation 550, probably because the I-type rules conflict with the E-type and D-type rules, and the process exploits the consistent decrease in D-type rules to decrease the overall error, even when this results in an increase in I-type rule errors. Starting at around 3.3%, the average error decreases to 2.2% in the 545th generation, after which the decrease stops and the error tends to increase slowly through further generations to around 2.3% in the 909th generation. Process graphs for each single rule for Test 55 can be observed in Appendix E. It should be noted that although the average error for all rule types decreased, this does not mean that each single rule has improved. It should also be added that, if required, the evolutionary process can be manipulated in favour of the D-type rules so that the fitness error values of the D-type rules can be decreased at the expense of increasing the fitness error values of the E-type and I-type rules.

Test 55, explained above, was carried out using the rank-based selection operator to select the new generations. However, as previously stated, a tournament selection operator was also tested. The evolutionary behaviour of the tournament and rank-based versions are not dramatically different but there is one important difference: the rank-based version strongly favours candidates that are at least averagely fine for all rule types simultaneously. A candidate that has a low ranking in a single rule type will simply not be selected.

Figure 5.61 presents two rank-based tests side by side, in which a consistent and stable process can be observed and Figure 5.62 shows two tests for tournament selection. As can be seen in Figure 5.62, the use of tournament selection to select new parents appears unstable and converges at worse error values, which makes the rank-based version preferable.

Rank-based approach for new generation selection (test 54)

Rank-based approach for new generation selection (test 55)

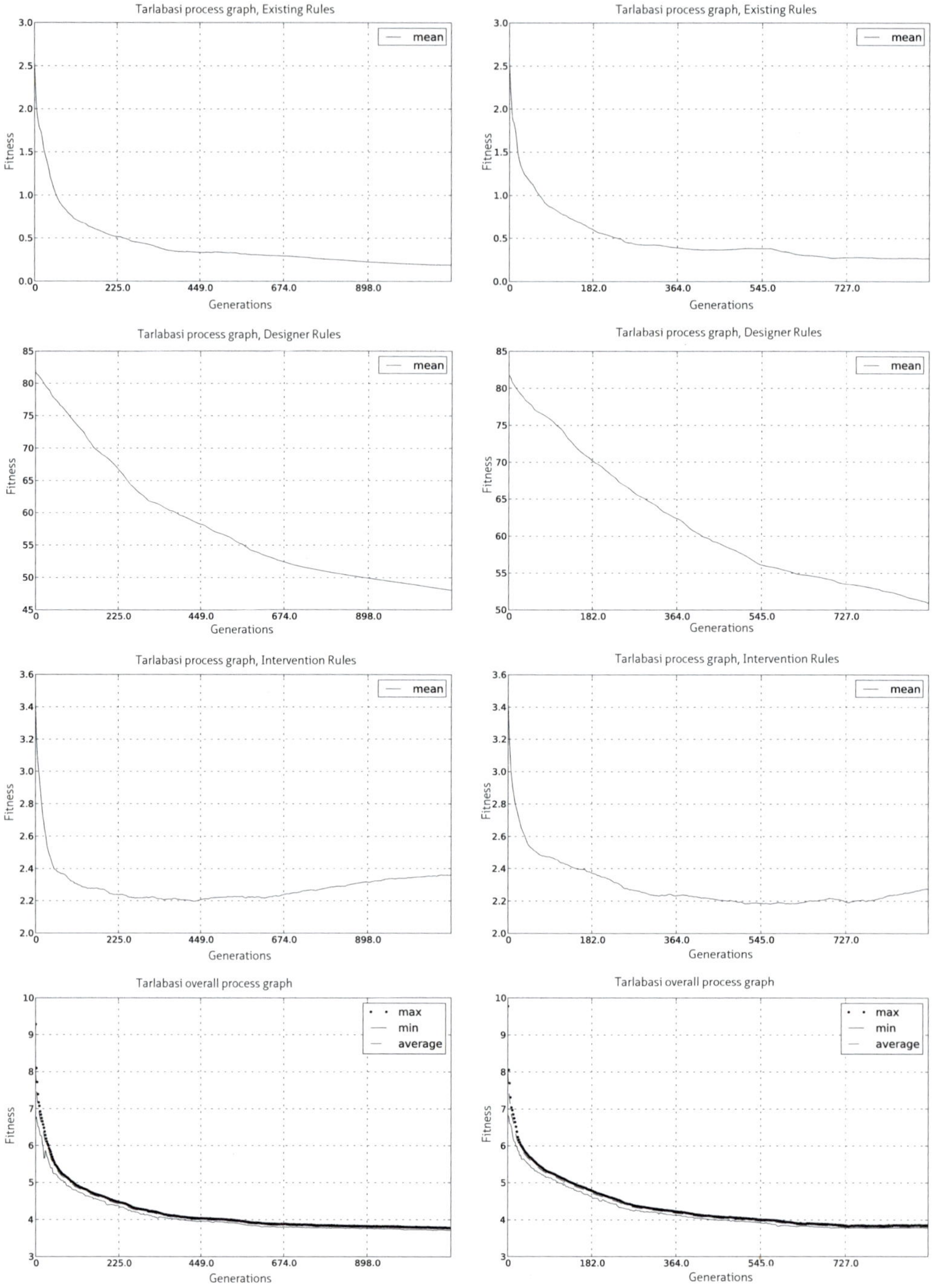

FIGURE 5.61 Two tests using a rank-based approach for new generation selection: Test 55 and Test 56.

Tournament approach for new generation selection (test 52)

Tournament approach for new generation selection (test 62)

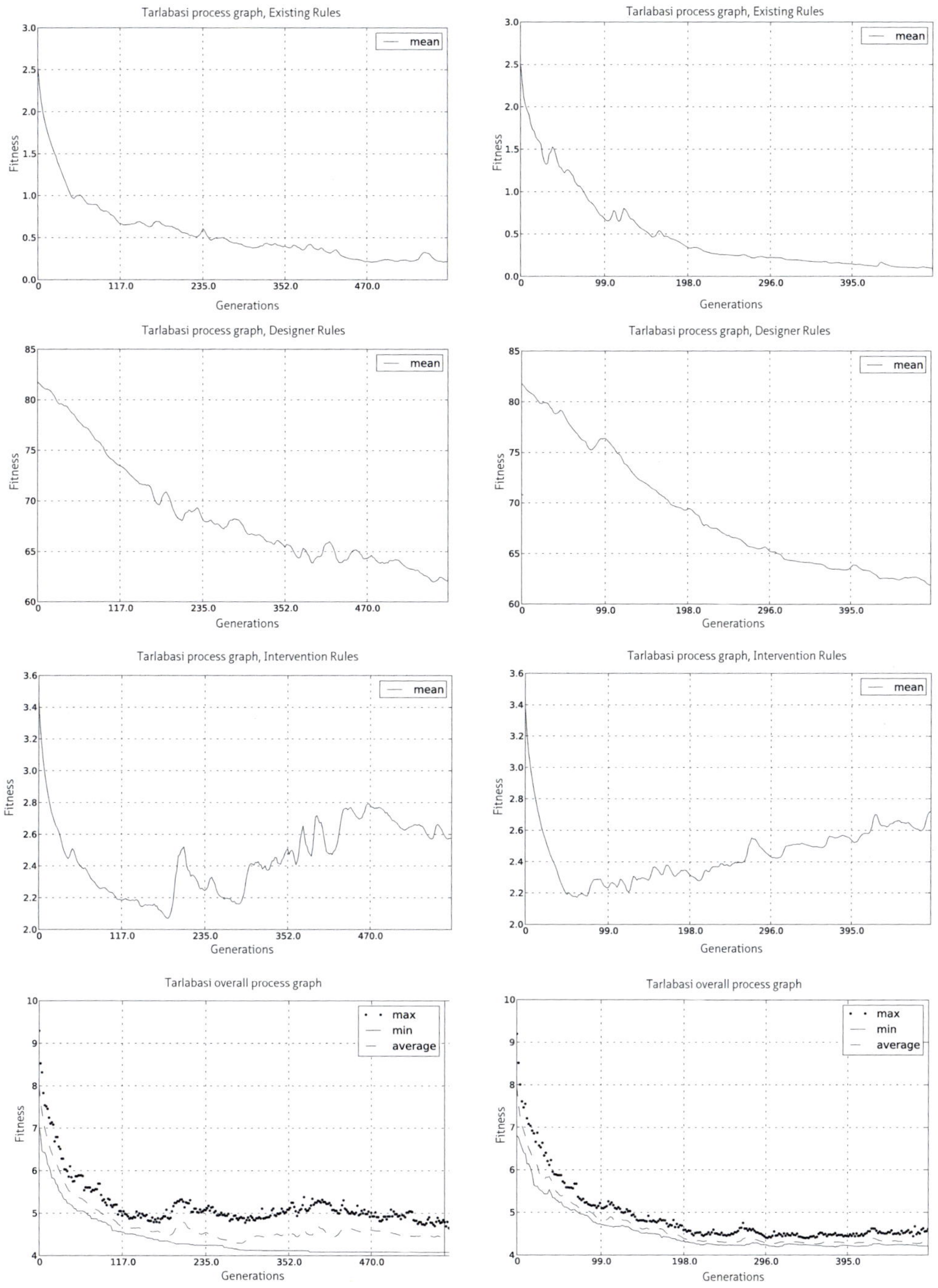

FIGURE 5.62 Two tests based on the tournament approach for new generation selection: Test 52 and Test 62.

The output of the evolutionary process is a test file in csv format: a new dataset for the new transformed or regenerated Tarlabaşı. The series of tables below compare the new Tarlabaşı and the original one to examine the extent of the transformation that has taken place during the evolutionary process. The following attributes were all transformed in the evolutionary process: Att.1 (ground floor use), Att.2 (1st floor use), Att.3 (2nd floor use), Att.15 (1st penthouse use) and Att. 46 (Tenure-type, a new attribute created for ownership allocation). However, because a relatively small number, namely Att.2, Att.3 and Att.15, were transformed, the following paragraphs mainly focus on evaluating the transformation of Att. 1 and the development of Att. 46. Figure 5.63 shows the distribution of ground floor use categories for the new and original Tarlabaşı.

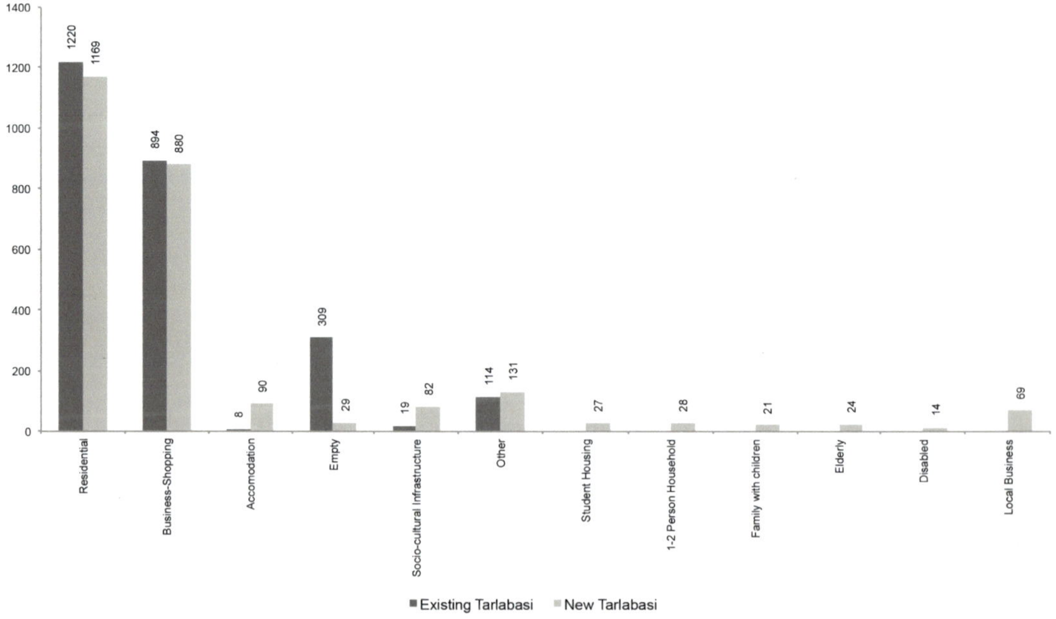

FIGURE 5.63 Distribution of Att.1 (ground floor use) for the new and original Tarlabaşı.

As seen in Figure 5.63, a mixed-user profile strategy based on housing type and business type differentiation is implemented throughout the evolutionary process and, as a result, new types of housing (housing for students, 1-2 person households, families with children, the elderly and the disabled) and local business categories are developed in the new Tarlabaşı. It may be assumed that these new types are valid not only for the ground floors of the buildings, but also for the whole building. This transformation is achieved by implementing the D-type rules. The amounts of these new types of housing and businesses are relatively small in comparison to the Tarlabaşı neighbourhood as a whole. However, by using a weighted aggregation approach, with higher weighting, the dominance of the D-type rules could be achieved. Moreover, introducing new D-type rules which would be defined in accordance with the objectives of the researcher, may also affect how the transformation of Tarlabaşı takes place. Apart from developing new types of use, there is also a significant decrease in the number of empty floors (309 empty floors in the original Tarlabaşı and 29 empty in the new one), achieved by implementing the I-type rules responsible for filling empty floors based on the original trends for residential and business-shopping uses. Finally, the total amount of residential and business-shopping uses remains more or less the same (1220 residential floors in the original Tarlabaşı and 1169 regular residential floors plus 114 new types of residences in the new one, 894 business-shopping use in the original Tarlabaşı and 880 regular business-shopping floors plus 69 local business in the new one), achieved by implementing the E-type rules which are used to preserve the original patterns of ground floor use in Tarlabaşı. The amount of sociocultural infrastructure and accommodation use has increased, based on the implementation of both E- and I-type rules but, if required, excluding them from the rules could prevent this. In addition, certain buildings which are important for strategic reasons can be masked during the evolutionary process, if necessary, in order to preserve them in their original form. More importantly, it should be emphasized that the process is not only about preserving the amount of uses but also the relationships that exist between different features of the buildings in this neighbourhood and establishing new relationships by taking advantage of the local features of Tarlabaşı.

Figure 5.64 contains a map of Tarlabaşı showing the new distribution of housing.

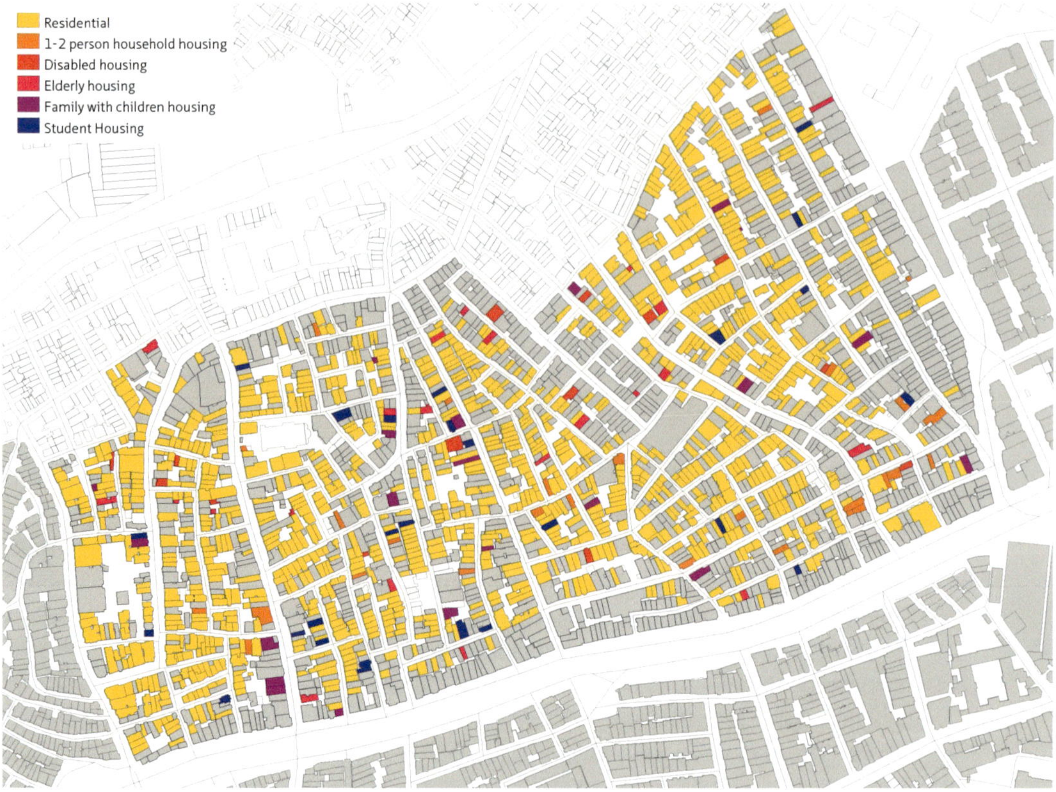

FIGURE 5.64 Distribution of housing types in the new Tarlabaşı (after evolution).

Figure 5.65 presents a map of Tarlabaşı showing residential uses that are transformed into another type of use during the evolutionary process.

FIGURE 5.65 GIS map showing residential uses that are transformed into another type of use during the evolutionary process (blue) and residential buildings (all housing types: 1-2 person households, disabled, elderly, families with children and students) in the new Tarlabaşı (yellow).

Figure 5.66 presents a map of Tarlabaşı showing the new distribution of business-shopping in Tarlabaşı.

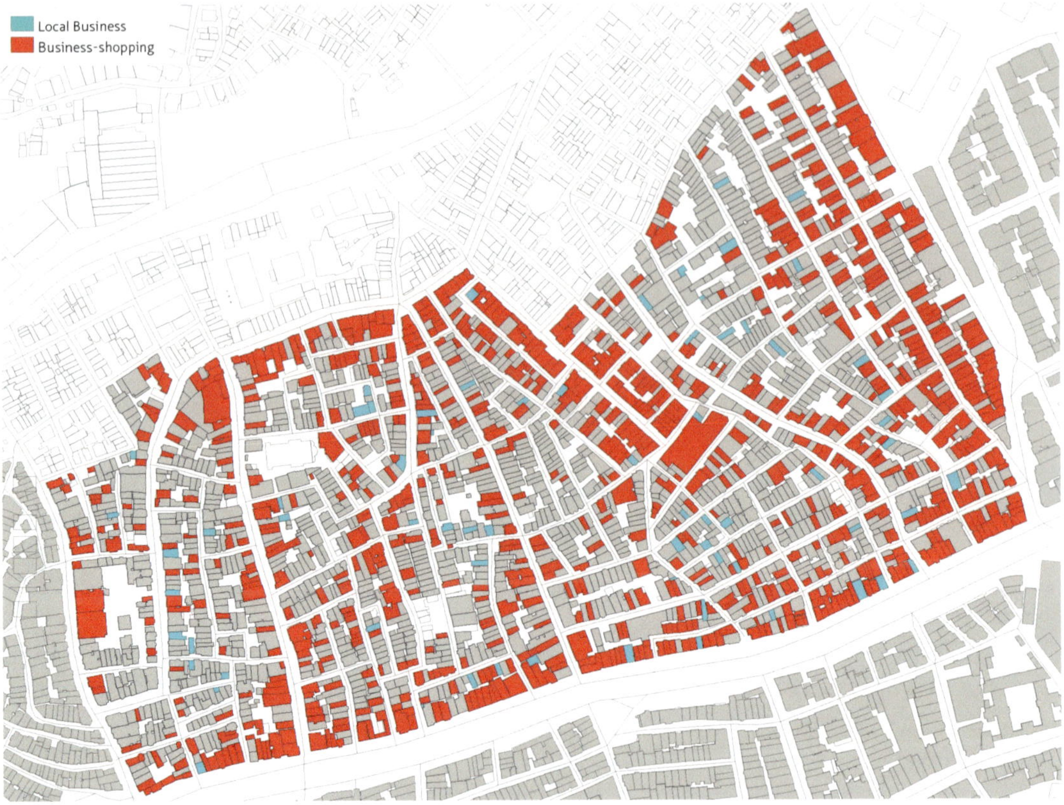

FIGURE 5.66 Distribution of business types in the new Tarlabaşı (after evolution).

Figure 5.67 contains a map of Tarlabaşı showing business-shopping uses that are transformed into another type of use during the evolutionary process.

FIGURE 5.67 GIS map showing business-shopping uses that are transformed into another type of use during the evolutionary process (blue) and business-shopping uses (all business types included: business-shopping and local business) in the new Tarlabaşı (red).

The details of this evolution, namely how residential and business-shopping uses are transformed, can be seen in Figure 5.68.

Evolution of Business-shopping use			
Original Tarlabasi	**->**	**Tarlabasi After Evolution**	**Number of Buildings**
Business-shopping	->	Business-shopping	726
Business-shopping	->	Socio-cultural infrastructure	28
Business-shopping	->	Accomodation	25
Business-shopping	->	Local business	20
Business-shopping	->	Residential	17
Business-shopping	->	Other	15
Business-shopping	->	1-2 Person household	14
Business-shopping	->	Student housing	14
Business-shopping	->	Empty	11
Business-shopping	->	Elderly housing	9
Business-shopping	->	Family with children housing	9
Business-shopping	->	Disabled housing	6

Evolution of Residential use			
Original Tarlabasi	**->**	**Tarlabasi After Evolution**	**Number of Buildings**
Residential	->	Residential	1062
Residential	->	Local business	40
Residential	->	Accomodation	24
Residential	->	Business-shopping	22
Residential	->	Other	15
Residential	->	Empty	13
Residential	->	Student housing	10
Residential	->	1-2 Person household	9
Residential	->	Family with children housing	8
Residential	->	Socio-cultural infrastructure	7
Residential	->	Elderly housing	6
Residential	->	Disabled housing	4

FIGURE 5.68 Transformation of residential and business-shopping use through the evolutionary process (726 buildings remained the same for business-shopping use, 1062 buildings remained the same for residential use).

It should be noted here that the transformation of the residential and business-shopping uses to 'empty' is an undesired outcome that results from the E-type rules used to preserve the existing patterns in Tarlabaşı during the evolutionary process. However it can be fixed in many ways, e.g. by preventing the Evolutionary Algorithm from assigning 'empty use'. Figure 5.69 shows the distribution of Att.46 (tenure-type) for the new Tarlabaşı: (Att.46 does not exist in the original Tarlabaşı, but was introduced as part of this approach to allow for mixed-income residents. This attribute is therefore absent in the graph below for the original Tarlabaşı.)

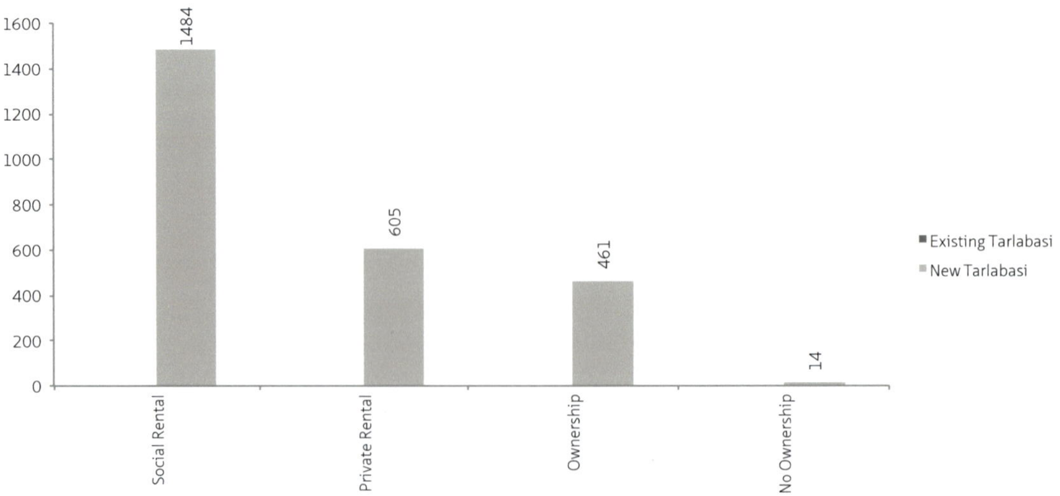

FIGURE 5.69 Distribution of Att.46 (tenure-type) for the new Tarlabaşı.

As Figure 5.69 shows, there are three types of tenure in the new Tarlabaşı, namely subsidized-rented, privately rented and owner-occupied, achieved by implementing D-type rules. Only 14 buildings (labelled as no ownership) could not be transformed. Figure 5.70 presents a map of Tarlabaşı showing the new tenure-type distribution in Tarlabaşı.

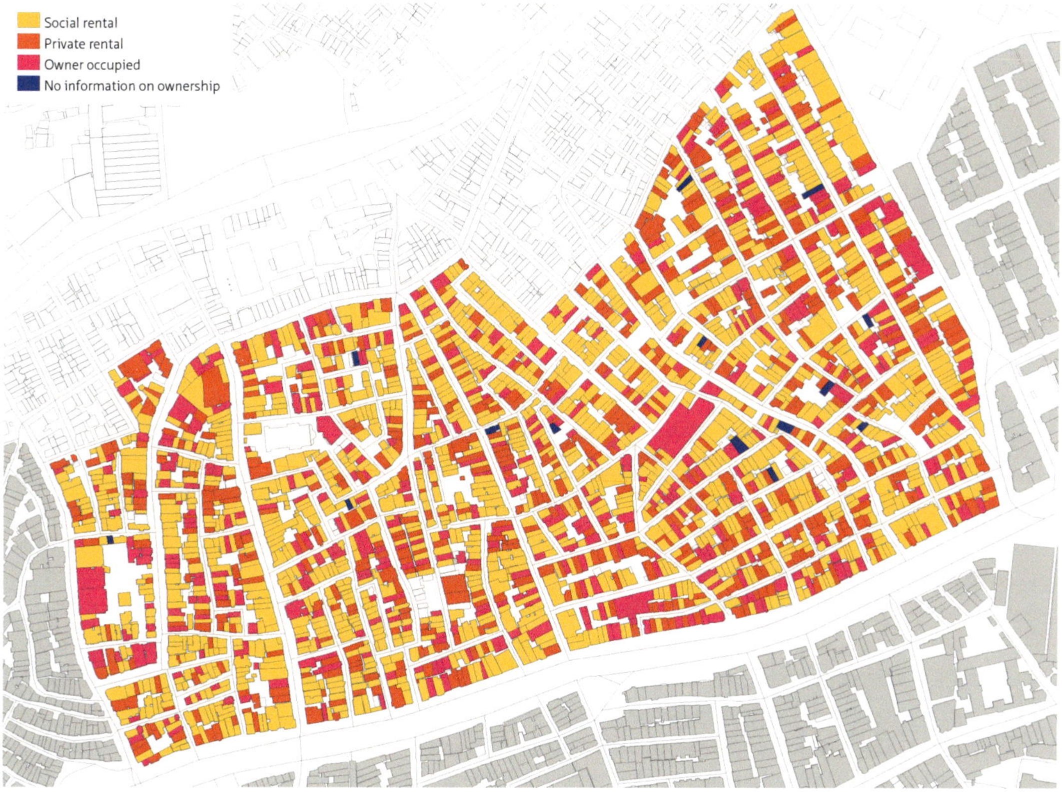

FIGURE 5.70 Tenure-type distribution in the new Tarlabaşı (after evolution).

On the basis of these observations, the implementation of data mining analysis and an Evolutionary Algorithm based on the rules found by data mining, the analysis proved successful in creating a mixed-use + mixed-user profile + mixed-income Tarlabaşı while preserving the existing patterns of ground floor use of the neighbourhood. As a result, it may be stated that Implementation (2) appears to be a promising preliminary example both for preserving the existing social atmosphere and ground floor use characteristics of a neighbourhood whilst transforming it, and for creating a process that allows for negotiation between conflicting transformative ideas.

§ 5.2.5 A critical review of the implementation

This section summarizes and evaluates the work conducted in Implementation (2).

This implementation was developed to investigate Research Question (3). It involves the implementation of KDPM for urban analysis in combination with an evolutionary process and aims to test the extent to which the knowledge discovery approach to urban analysis through data mining developed in this thesis can enhance the urban analysis process for Tarlabaşı and support the development of urban intervention proposals for the regeneration of this neighbourhood. As stated previously, the Tarlabaşı neighbourhood located in the Beyoğlu Preservation Area is currently undergoing urban renewal, involving mass demolition and large-scale construction work that fails to respect the existing architectural and urban patterns and economic and social networks. Limited by the available data, an alternative regeneration approach to the heavily criticized transformation project developed by the Beyoğlu Municipality is proposed, creating a mixed-use + mixed-user profile + mixed-income neighbourhood while preserving existing patterns of ground floor use. A computational process combining GIS, data mining and evolutionary computation was developed to apply this regeneration approach, using a GIS database consisting of the buildings in Tarlabaşı (2136 buildings and 45 attributes associated with the buildings, representing a total area of 240.000 m2). The computational process consists of three phases:

1 In the Analysis Phase, the KDPM for urban analysis was used to explore the existing patterns of ground floor use that would be preserved. Each attribute's associations with the use of ground floor were investigated in order to identify these patterns. Two different methods of data mining were applied in succession: Naïve Bayes Classification and Association Rule Analysis. Naïve Bayes Classification was used to rank the relationships between different attributes and the use of ground floor in terms of their predictive powers. The attributes that were most powerful in predicting the use of ground floor were considered the most relevant ones for Association Rule Analysis. Association Rule Analysis, in turn, identified each relevant attribute's associations with the use of ground floor in the form of probabilistic co-occurrence rules. Three types of association rules that are relevant to this regeneration approach (i.e. creating a mixed-use, mixed-user profile and mixed-income Tarlabaşı while preserving existing patterns of ground floor use) were selected for formulating allocation rules (acting as floorspace use, user profile and tenure-type allocation determinants) to feed the evolutionary process: association rules that produce 'Residential', 'Business-shopping' and 'Empty' ground floor use.

2 In the Synthesis Phase, the selected association rules were processed to formulate the rules (E, I and D-type rules) that would be used as input for the evolutionary process. The association rules that produce 'Residential' and 'Business-Shopping' ground floor

use revealed the existing patterns of ground floor use and were used to formulate the E-type rules that preserve these patterns. The association rules that produce 'Empty' ground floor use were used to formulate the I-type rules designed to allocate new use to empty ground floors based on the existing patterns of ground floor use in Tarlabaşı. Finally, the author formulated D-type rules designed to transform Tarlabaşı based on the proposed regeneration approach. In principle, the D-type rules can be said to be the transformative intervention decisions of different actors (e.g., Tarlabaşı residents, policy makers etc.) shaped by their conflicting preferences. These rules regulate the functional use of the buildings, user profiles and tenure-types.

3 In the Implementation Phase, E, I and D-type rules formulated in a stochastic manner were used as input for the evolutionary process. The Evolutionary Algorithm programmed by a colleague of the author (N. Onur Sönmez, PhD candidate at ITU& TU Delft, the Design Informatics Chair, Faculty of Architecture) in the Python programming language transforms Tarlabaşı using these rules for fitness measurements. The evolutionary process therefore acts as a negotiation platform between overlapping and conflicting urban intervention decisions (formulated in the form of stochastic rules), preserving existing patterns of ground floor use as well as implementing the different preferences of the actors. As a result, this computational process generates draft plans for ground floor use, user profile and tenure-type allocation for Tarlabaşı which verify these urban intervention decisions (i.e. the given rules) as far as possible. While the KDPM for urban analysis made it possible to objectively identify some of the site-specific particularities of Tarlabaşı in terms of patterns of ground floor use, the evolutionary process ensured the preservation of these site-specific characteristics as far as possible, as well as implementing new transformative intervention decisions.

The output of the evolutionary process is a dataset in the form of a text file representing the new Tarlabaşı transformed according to the regeneration approach. This database is further examined by means of descriptive graphics and GIS maps to explore the extent of the transformation that has taken place during the evolutionary process. On the basis of these examinations, the computational process that enables the existing characteristics of floorspace use in the ground floors of the buildings in Tarlabaşı to be preserved whilst transforming the neighborhood according to the regeneration approach proved successful. Although this process (involving the implementation of the KDPM for urban analysis and an Evolutionary Algorithm which is guided by the results of the analysis model) is tailored for the regeneration problem in Tarlabaşı, with further research it could be transformed into a generic model which can provide a way to support user participation in inner-city urban regeneration processes and enables the desired characteristics of the urban environment that is subject to transformation to be preserved.

Although this computational process successfully transforms Tarlabașı according to the given aims, some important questions should be addressed in a critical review of the outputs and how to approach them:

- The evolutionary process generates multiple solutions with similar fitness values; what should be done about the hundreds of similar solutions? How should one be selected from them? How can the "result" be interpreted?

  At the end of the evolutionary process the algorithm selects the "most fit solution" and provides the data file (a text file in csv format) of this "best Tarlabașı". However, this is only one solution, and an evolutionary process generates multiple solutions, with similar fitness values although, from the point of view of individual buildings, the alternative solutions may be different. Evaluating these multiple solutions and selecting the one that is most appealing thus becomes a major challenge. But is this really the objective? In fact, this is a general issue regarding evolutionary methods, although the problem can be discussed within the specific context of this research.

  First of all, the implementation conducted here enables draft plans (ground floor use, user-profile and tenure-type allocation plans) to be generated which apply the stated aim of creating a mixed-use, mixed-income, mixed-tenure Tarlabașı while preserving its existing patterns of ground floor use as far as possible. The goal here is not to generate a single solution but to produce alternative solutions that can be further discussed and elaborated by the actors involved in the transformation (e.g. local residents in Tarlabașı, policy makers, developers, etc.). By their very nature, urban transformation processes never offer one good solution that is appealing to everyone. Therefore, the fact that the Evolutionary Algorithm generates multiple solutions does not contradict the nature of this problem. Due to conflicting interests, the problem of urban transformation is a nontrivial problem that cannot be solved simply by applying everyone's wishes, although ideally all parties should be satisfied as far as possible and the evolutionary process does address this. Outputs shaped by conflicting interests must be considered facilitator drafts for negotiation between the different actors involved in the process of regeneration. The evolutionary process is a draft producer, a generator of alternative solutions to deal with the nontrivial problem of urban transformation. Even though different drafts will contain different solutions in terms of individual buildings, the issue of which draft is actually chosen is not a crucial concern, since the draft is the starting point for an in-depth process of negotiation between parties and different actors will intervene in the draft plans whilst negotiating. Therefore, more than one draft plan should be discussed in detail, and it may even be possible to combine the alternatives that are most interesting from the point of the individual actors. Thus, the evolutionary process as implemented in this context facilitates collaboration and negotiation and is a means of achieving the complex task of satisfying the conflicting interests of all parties as far as possible.

- How does the evolutionary process support the participation of users in the course of generating draft plan proposals?

  The answer to this question is already answered by the previous one. Once more, it should be emphasized that the draft plans generated by the evolutionary process aim to reconcile the contradicting interests of the actors as far as possible. Therefore the process of evolution itself can be described as a negotiation process that takes place between different parties. For user participation to be effective in the real sense, further negotiation between users is naturally required, and this would begin by using the alternative solutions, which are already negotiated to a certain extent through the evolutionary process.

- How could the evolutionary process be improved, in terms of evaluating the outputs generated and enhancing its capacity to facilitate user participation?

  The data file generated by the evolutionary process, which represents the new Tarlabaşı, does not provide enough input for the evaluation process. It therefore requires a component that generates visual material and database statistics (as was the case in this implementation) for the results to be easily understandable and usable. One future objective could be to develop a visualization component that produces maps and descriptive graphs of the generated outputs, which is needed to evaluate and interpret the alternative drafts in a practical way. In fact, this is an essential requirement if the aim is to implement such a process in urban practice.

  Moreover, a simultaneous visualization component which displays the evolution as it iterates can facilitate the evaluation of the results as well as enhance user participation and collaboration between actors. This component would display the interaction between the conflicting interests of the actors during the evolution. This would prevent the evolutionary process from turning into a 'black-box' and the actors would understand the complexities of the process better. It would also enable the actors to interpret the evolution as an exploratory process through which they would be able to observe the interaction between the different interests and thus evaluate their approaches. In addition, it could be used to develop interactive variants of the evolutionary approach to enable the actors to intervene in the process, thereby becoming pro-active in shaping it.

  Re-designing the Evolutionary Algorithm to implement Interactive Evolutionary Computation would be one interesting option. Recent research has focused on making the process of evolution "more efficient through automating or augmenting the capabilities of designers" (Secretan et al, 2011, p.37) by involving them into the evolutionary process, a process known as Interactive Evolutionary Computation (Takagi, 2001). In Interactive Evolutionary Computation, users select the parents of the next generation and, as the process runs again and again, the population evolves to satisfy their preferences. Interactive Evolutionary Computation is defined as "an artificial evolution guided by human direction" and is known to be "well-suited to domains in which success and failure are subjective and difficult to formalize" (Secretan et al, 2011, p.37). This system could provide a platform that would encourage users to participate and contribute to the evolutionary process for the regeneration of Tarlabaşı.

– How do the KDPM for urban analysis and the application of data mining algorithms contribute to the development of urban intervention proposals?

  The KDPM contributes to urban analysis by describing a process, which enables the analyst to quantify patterns, and relationships that can be valuable in understanding the site-specific characteristics of the urban environment under investigation. In this way, the KDPM for urban analysis assists in the discovery of 'relational urban knowledge' concerning building features that can be put into action in generating draft plans for urban intervention. Therefore, this model does not function as a solution generator or decision-maker, since making decisions is a human task. The information patterns and relationships discovered by implementing the KDPM for urban analysis have to be evaluated, validated and interpreted by the human researchers and pratctitioners and then put into operation.

– What are the most critical issues concerning this implementation?

  Critically speaking, a few important points need to be acknowledged before moving to the next implementation:

  Most importantly, this implementation postulates that the 'relational urban knowledge' concerning building features obtained in the form of patterns and relationships between the use of ground floor and other building attributes which are extracted by implementing the KDPM for urban analysis, is valuable enough to preserve. Although this hypothesis is open to discussion, it is a fact that this 'relational urban knowledge' of building features consists of site-specific characteristics. The existing allocation of uses in the ground floors of the buildings in Tarlabaşı is self-organized to a great extent due to the absence of government auditing of urban planning in Turkey, meaning that it is mainly formed by a historical process continuously shaped by economic, political, social and cultural dynamics. Therefore, Tarlabaşı can be considered mostly a "self-organized quarter", which is why, in principle, the author considers that the patterns and relationships between the use of ground floor and other attributes are valuable enough to preserve.

  Another critical issue that would be interesting and necessary to analyse is the relations between the spatial configuration of Tarlabaşı (e.g. space syntax analysis) and patterns of ground floor use allocation, as well as the interrelations between different uses of ground floor in terms of their spatial adjacency, using this knowledge to produce ground floor use allocation plans. A study of this kind has already been produced by the author for Cihangir and a conference paper on the subject has been published (Sökmenoğlu & Sönmez, 2013). However, the study is not included in this thesis because it is still in a preliminary stage. The patterns of ground floor use of Cihangir were explored by focusing on reciprocal relationships involving housing and commercial uses, based on spatial adjacency (horizontal patterns) and floorspace use patterns within the buildings (vertical patterns). Reciprocal relationships between housing and commercial uses were measured by implementing the KDPM for urban analysis and were tested to determine whether they could be re-generated using the Evolutionary Algorithm implemented in this study.

Another limitation of this implementation is the fact that the data is limited to what was obtained from the thematic urban analysis maps for the Master Plan of the Beyoğlu Preservation Area. In particular, the lack of data concerning the demographic, social and economic characteristics of the population was a major obstacle to explore and demonstrate the real potential of the knowledge discovery approach to urban analysis through data mining. In addition, the data mining methods that were applied depended on the type of data that was available: with additional types of data, other methods could have been tested.

It is also important to emphasise that neither the key principles and strategies (listed in Table 5.7) defining this approach to the regeneration of Tarlabaşı nor the computational process that was used to implement the approach can fully cover all the aspects of this transformation process. The process is undoubtedly much more complex; urban regeneration itself is not only a topic of interest to academics involved in urban studies but is also a pressing issue with regard to politics and public wealth, and has been seriously criticized in terms of democracy and justice. Although the regeneration process applied here has a limited scope and is limited by the available data, it may be regarded as a preliminary model for a more detailed and holistic regeneration of Tarlabaşı. With further study, this process could be expanded to include other aspects and become more holistic.

As a final remark, it is important to state that poverty is the most crucial problem that has to be faced in Tarlabaşı, as in most other urban transformation processes. Poverty is a social and political fact, and urban planning or design alone cannot solve this deeply rooted, complex, multifaceted problem. Creating an egalitarian society not only requires reducing differences in income levels but also developing policies that provide for social integration and prevent social exclusion. The approach developed in this thesis aims to create a new Tarlabaşı that allows for the existence of low-income groups alongside wealthier groups. However, it should be clearly acknowledged that this alone is not sufficient to solve all the social and economic problems as well as the major overall problem of poverty.

- How does this implementation contribute to urban research?

Approximately 90% of urban planning and design concerns interventions in the existing urban fabric (Stouten, 2010) and so it is extremely important to work on transforming existing urban environments. Through refinement, and further research to create a more detailed and holistic approach, the computational process demonstrated here can offer a generic model for the regeneration of existing (in particular historic) urban environments. This implementation contributes to studies of urban regeneration by focusing on the following two topics, which are relevant and much needed in the current urban research agenda:

  - Research on how to identify and preserve the existing character of urban environments: The KDPM for urban analysis enables site-specific particularities of the urban environment under investigation to be explored. Implementation of the KDPM for urban analysis specifically responds to the following key principles designated for the regeneration of Tarlabaşı: "preserving the character and atmosphere of the area and maintaining the functional mix" and "promoting mixed-use to preserve dynamism" (see Table 5.9)
  - Research on participatory planning processes that reflect the multiple concerns and interests of the various actors: The evolutionary phase of this overall computational process provides a means of negotiation between different actors. The algorithm uses the overlapping and conflicting urban intervention decisions of different actors as measurements of fitness and aims to verify them as far as possible. The Evolutionary Algorithm thus enables different opinions to direct the transformation process. Implementation of the evolutionary process specifically responds to the key principle designated for the regeneration of Tarlabaşı; "encouraging the involvement of residents in the urban renewal processes" (see Table 5.9). However this contribution is rather limited. This is mainly because the topic of user participation was not in the scope of the thesis and therefore a more in depth investigation of the concept was not performed.

Based on these contributions, it can be argued that Implementation (2) exemplified how quantitative/computational methods can help us to deal with humanistic concerns in urban planning. As previously mentioned in Chapter (2), this is one of the most important lines of research in urban studies: can we bridge the gap between humanistic and positivistic approaches, through the use of ICT based approaches?

Nowadays, humanistic approaches to urban studies conceptualize methods that are pluralistic, democratic, sensitive to social, cultural and environmental matters, communicative, participatory and context-sensitive, and they focus more on relations and processes than on objects and forms. Conversely, analytical/quantitative approaches are struggling to find new tools and methods to develop pragmatic solutions, mostly for the quantitative problems of cities and citizens. In order to provide measures to achieve economic, social, cultural and ecological sustainability in our cities, we need to find instruments that can support us in establishing common ground between these divergent concerns and methods in humanistic and positivist approaches. This implementation exemplifies that the combined use of data mining and evolutionary computation could offer such an instrument and could be used to create an approach towards urban planning that reflects humanistic concerns.

To conclude, despite the difficulties and limitations mentioned in the previous paragraphs, the implementation demonstrates that the adaptation of the knowledge discovery process through data mining to urban data analysis developed in this thesis performs successfully in informing the development of urban intervention proposals in the form of draft plans in an urban regeration process by revealing site-specific characteristics.

The following implementation is based on an international student workshop, exemplifying how the KDPM for urban analysis combined with parametric urban analysis techniques can enhance the urban analysis process and assist students in the development of urban intervention proposals for the regeneration of Tarlabașı.

§ 5.3 Implementation (3) Evaluation in an International Student Workshop

This section introduces an international student workshop, namely the Tarlabașı Datascope workshop, which focused on exploring the capabilities and limitations of the knowledge discovery approach to urban analysis through data mining, combined with parametric methods and techniques, to support urban intervention scenarios for the regeneration of Tarlabașı (http://Tarlabașıdatascope.wordpress.com/). Particular importance was placed on introducing a variety of data mining methods, in order to investigate the usability of data mining analysis methods and techniques for students and Research Question (3), namely the extent to which these methods can enhance the urban analysis process and support the development of intervention proposals for urban regeneration. Feedback from the students and our observations provide clues to the capabilities and limitations of the knowledge discovery approach to urban analysis through data mining proposed in this thesis, as well as the possibilities for future developments.

In the following sub-sections, the scope, goals, programme and agenda of the workshop are introduced, followed by a detailed description of the students' work. Finally, an evaluation of the workshop is presented, based on participant surveys and our inferences.

§ 5.3.1 Goals of the Tarlabaşı Datascope workshop

The Tarlabaşı Datascope workshop ran from 13 May to 20 May 2014, attended by 13 participants who were architecture and urban design and planning students (4th and 5th year undergraduates and MSc and PhD students) and was mainly organized to test the knowledge discovery approach to urban analysis through data mining proposed in this thesis, in an educational context. The workshop was organized at the Istanbul Technical University Faculty of Architecture (Architectural Design Computing Graduate Program) in collaboration with TU Delft and TU Lisbon and was led by the author of this thesis together with Pirouz Nourian (PhD candidate and instructor at TU Delft, Faculty of Architecture, Department of Architectural Engineering + Technology, Chair of Design Informatics) and José Nuno Beirao (PhD in Urban Design at TU Delft, the Design Informatics Chair, Faculty of Architecture). The author developed the outline of the Tarlabaşı Datascope workshop on the basis of this PhD study. The structure and content of the workshop was developed in collaboration with José Nuno Beirao and Pirouz Nourian, based on their PhD research. Apart from the main instructors, Ceyhun Burak Akgül (PhD in Electrical and Electronic Engineering at Télécom ParisTech Signals-Images and at Boğaziçi University EE/BUSIM, http://www.cba-research.com/) joined the workshop to give an introductory lecture on the main features, methods and techniques of knowledge discovery through data mining.

The goal of the workshop was to propose urban intervention scenarios for Tarlabaşı, a rundown historical neighbourhood in Istanbul, also the subject of the previously introduced Implementation (2). As stated in the previous section, the Tarlabaşı neighbourhood is currently undergoing urban renewal, involving mass demolition and large-scale construction work led by the Beyoğlu Municipality. The approach to urban renewal applied by the municipality has been heavily criticized for failing to respect the existing architectural and urban patterns and economic and social networks. The workshop therefore aimed to produce alternative urban intervention scenarios to demonstrate how Tarlabaşı could be transformed without destroying its original social and spatial characteristics.

Accordingly, it was very important to identify the site-specific particularities of Tarlabaşı in order to incorporate them into urban intervention strategies. Various computational urban analysis methods and techniques were therefore introduced as a toolset to enable various aspects of the site to be identified. The tools and techniques that were introduced were based on GIS, data mining and parametric design, implemented in RapidMiner, QuantumGIS, Rhino 5, Grasshopper (Cheetah Plug-in designed by Pirouz Nourian and Samaneh Rezvani) Slingshot, Postgres PgAdmin and PostGIS. Within the context of the workshop, the toolset was tested to determine how it could be used to support the development of urban intervention proposals involving an inner-city urban regeneration problem. The poster for the workshop can be found in Appendix F.

§ 5.3.2 Agenda of the Tarlabaşı Datascope workshop

Students worked intensively in the workshop for 8 days. The workshop process and workflow is shown in Table 5.29.

TARLABAŞI DATASCOPE WORKSHOP	
Day 1: Monday, May 13th	
09:30-10:00	Registration, installation
10:00-11:00	Lecture [intro+context]: Urban transformation in Tarlabaşı - A. Sökmenoğlu
12:00-16:00	Tarlabaşı Site Visit
16:00-18:00	Studio [identification of the problems]
Day 2: Tuesday, May 14th	
09:30-10:15	Lecture [tools] A. Sökmenoğlu & C. B. Akgul - Data Mining
10:30-11:15	Lecture [tools] P. Nourian – Parametric Design
11:30-12:15	Lecture [tools] J. Beirão - Parametric Urban Design
14:00-16:00	Studio [computational analysis] Data mining techniques and applications - A.Sökmenoğlu & C. B. Akgul
16:30-...	Studio [problem definitions + intervention scenario development]
Day 3: Wednesday, May 15th	
09:30-10:30	1st Presentations [problems + intervention scenarios]
11:00-13:00	Studio [computational design] Configurative Design (Analysis, Synthesis and some hints on Evaluation) - P. Nourian
14:30-16:30	Studio [computational analysis] Parametric urban design tools; density indicators and their calculation in Grasshopper. Available urban design variables in a Grasshopper test models. Guidance for scenario exploration - J. Beirão
17:00-...	Studio [integration of computational analysis themes with scenario developments]
Day 4: Thursday, May 16th	
09:30-11:30	2nd Presentations [computational analysis + intervention scenarios]
12:00-...	Studio [computational analysis + synthesis]
Day 5: Friday, May 17th	
09:30-12:30	Studio [computational analysis + synthesis]
16:00-18:00	3rd Presentations [computational analysis + synthesis + intervention scenarios]
Day 6: Saturday May 18th	
13:00-17:30	Studio [computational analysis + synthesis + intervention scenarios]
Day 7: Sunday May 19th	
13:00-17:30	Studio [computational analysis + synthesis + intervention scenarios]
Day 8: Monday, May 20th	
09:30-12:30	Studio [computational analysis + synthesis + intervention scenarios]
14:00-18:00	Final Presentations [computational analysis + synthesis + intervention scenarios]

TABLE 5.29 Programme for the Tarlabaşı Datascope Workshop.

The workshop began with a detailed lecture given by the author introducing:

- The urban context: Tarlabaşı.
- Details and implications of the Tarlabaşı renewal project led by the Beyoğlu Municipality.
- Workshop Agenda: proposing alternative scenarios for the regeneration of Tarlabaşı.

Following the introductory lecture, a site visit was organized to identify the problems by actually experiencing the atmosphere of Tarlabaşı. At the site, the participants also visited the Tarlabaşı Community Centre, operating under the Tarlabaşı Community Support Association to provide educational, social and psychological support for the Tarlabaşı residents (http://www.Tarlabaşı.org/en/). A lecture was given by the sociologist Nese Erdilek (Bilgi University, Centre for Migration Research), the chair of the Tarlabaşı Community Centre, introducing the characteristics of the inhabitants of Tarlabaşı, their problems and the implications of the Tarlabaşı renewal project for them, followed by a discussion on the physical and social problems of the site.

The next step was an intensive analysis of Tarlabaşı using the data associated with the components of the urban environments (buildings and streets) provided by us. The participants were given data on the following features of the site:

- Ground floor use of buildings
- 1st floor use of buildings
- 2nd floor use of buildings
- 3rd floor use of buildings
- Building footprint
- Land price of buildings
- Number of floors in buildings
- Street network
- Topographical data

Computational analysis themes given by the instructors were classified into three themes by applying the techniques introduced in the workshop:

- Patterns of floorspace use in the buildings of Tarlabaşı
- Network analysis
- Pedestrian access / walkability analysis

After introducing the generic process of the KDPM for urban analysis and the data mining analysis carried out in this study, participants got familiar with RapidMiner and got an idea of what kind of analysis can be implemented using RapidMiner and how one can use the findings of this analysis in developing urban intervention proposals. Together with the author, participants first identified the patterns of floorspace use in the buildings in Tarlabaşı. Data mining floorspace use data of the buildings enabled the participants to explore the existing patterns in the neighbourhood and identify the programmatic needs to support the formulation of a list of program requirements to be considered as needs or opportunities for urban intervention. Then, following the generic process described by the KDPM for urban analysis, participants started to interact with RapidMiner by themselves and explored their own queries with the support of the author (see Figures 5.71 and 5.72). Depending on their particular interests, participants applied clustering analysis to identify some floorspace use clusters in the buildings and Naïve Bayes analysis to predict the use of the empty floors, based on the existing patterns (More information is provided later). These techniques were presented in detail in Section 3.5 (Data Mining Methods and Operators Implemented in the Thesis).

FIGURE 5.71 A participant interacts with the interface of the RapidMiner.

FIGURE 5.72 A participant examines the results of a clustering analysis implemented in RapidMiner.

In addition, Pirouz Nourian introduced the use of Rhino-Grasshopper and the Cheetah plug-in designed for urban network analysis. Cheetah, a computational tool suite designed for urban network analysis, is a plug-in for configurative analysis and design. Cheetah tools measure network distances for pedestrians, considering topographic impedance (the difficulty of walking uphill), aggregate walking distances, and the suitability of urban buildings in terms of their ease of pedestrian access to an arbitrary list of places deemed important by the user/designer. With Cheetah, designers can use the objective measures of actual walking distance and also insert their own inter-subjective understandings of a neighbourhood to mark 'important places' and their corresponding level of importance in the analyses, if necessary. Cheetah tools can help to build an overview of the accessibility of a neighbourhood for pedestrians (Nourian, 2013). The Tarlabaşı street network was constructed and analyzed in terms of different measures such as closeness, centrality and choice, using the Cheetah plug-in (see Figure 5.73). Pedestrian access/walkability analysis in specific urban nodes and activities was also enabled through the implementation of the same tools and techniques. Pedestrian access from urban blocks to vital services was measured and a gradient of measures visualized.

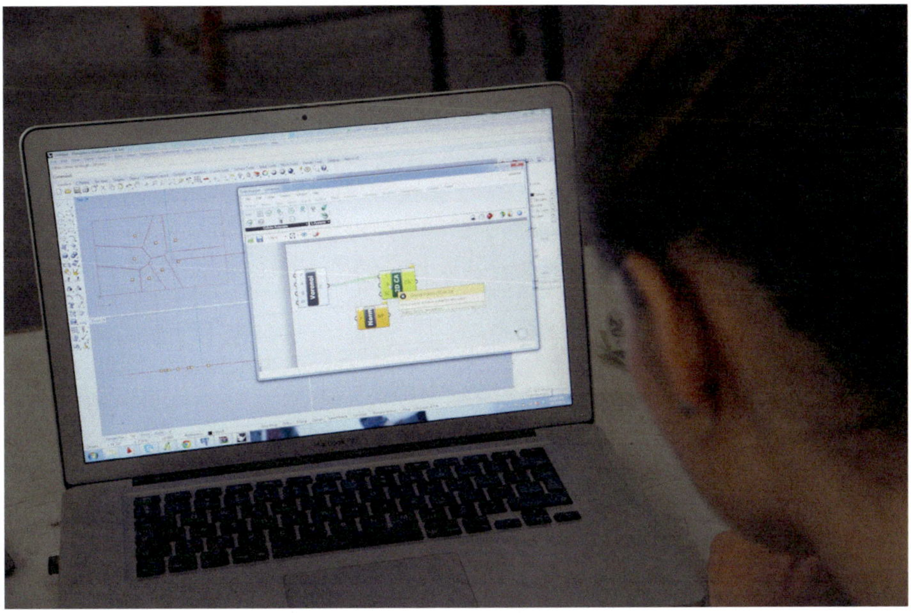

FIGURE 5.73 A participant interacts with Cheetah plug-in.

In addition to analyzing the existing data and given themes of computational urban analysis, students were encouraged to come up with ideas on what to analyze, based on their findings regarding the problems of the urban context, such as the lack of open spaces, lack of sunlight, connectivity problems for Tarlabaşı and its neighbouring districts, and conflicts between pedestrians and cars.

After the analysis stage, students were asked to propose a framework for synthesizing the findings of the analysis, based on their approach to the regeneration of Tarlabaşı. In order to do so, they first had to develop a strategic scenario and urban intervention proposals. On the basis of the various analyses and their specific approach, the students therefore proposed:

- A general strategic scenario for the regeneration of Tarlabaşı;
- Urban intervention and design proposals, such as new buildings, new functions and new public spaces, that would enable them to produce this strategic scenario.

The students' work is presented in detail in the next section.

§ 5.3.3 Work produced by the students

In total, 13 architecture or urbanism students from the 4th and 5th years of undergraduate, MSc and PhD courses attended the workshop and were grouped into teams of 3 or 4 people (see Figure 5.74). Working intensively for eight days, they developed different urban intervention scenarios for the regeneration of Tarlabaşı by implementing data mining and Cheetah methods and techniques to support the formulation of their strategic scenarios. The work produced by each team is explained and evaluated in detail in the following paragraphs. Firstly, their conceptual ideas are introduced, then the whole process is analyzed in detail in table format under seven headings (concept, problems, strategic scenario, intervention, analysis, synthesis and conclusion) and finally the work is evaluated in terms of use of analysis tools and achievements in providing solutions to the problems they had identified.

FIGURE 5.74 Tutors and participants.

The first team, "Team: Diversity; Tarlabaşı Interven[func]tion", was made up of four students; Ayse Colakoglu (MSc student in Architectural Design Computing, ITU), Zuzanna Koltowska (MArch student, Warsaw University of Technology), Tolga Karasay (MSc student in Architectural Design Computing, ITU), Omer Cavusoglu (PhD student in Architectural Design Computing, ITU).

FIGURE 5.75 First slide from "Team: Diversity; Tarlabaşı Interven[func]tion".

Their first slide introducing their conceptual idea is shown in Figure 5.75.

"Team: Diversity; Tarlabaşı Interven[func]tion" focused on the theme of creating diversity in spatial and social terms. Their work is analyzed in detail in association with their final presentation slides (given in the Appendix G) in Table 5.30.

MAIN STEPS AND OUTPUTS IN THE PROCESS	DESCRIPTION
Concept	To make Tarlabaşı a more diverse area in social and spatial terms. (Slide 2)
Problems	There are problems with connectivity to Istiklal Street and the lack of attractiveness and public spaces. (Slide 2)
Strategic Scenario	To spatially and socially connect Istiklal Street and Tarlabaşı; -by providing more diverse urban activities which might attract more people -by introducing a new cultural axis from Istiklal Street to Bilgi University which passes by two main churches (Slide 2) -by activating the existing social infrastructure and re-activating empty historical civil architecture by transforming it into new public spaces (Slide 2)
Intervention	To implement a mixed-use allocation plan and improve the street network performance (Slide 2)
Analysis	- Visualization of ground floor use in Tarlabaşı: the predominant residential and business-shopping functions are measured in Excel (Slide 3) - Identification of the maximum and minimum percentage of commercial use on ground floors of buildings (Slide 3) - Clustering analysis for floorspace use patterns within the buildings in Tarlabaşı using data mining (Slide 4) - Mapping of the most dominant clusters in GIS (Slides 5,6,7,8) - Proximity (buffer zone) analysis in GIS to determine buildings 75 metres away from the two main churches. (Slide 9) -Clustering analysis for floorspace use patterns within the buildings in the two buffer zones. (Slides 9 and 10) - Mapping the most dominant clusters within the buffer zones in GIS (Slides 9 and 10) -Accessibility analysis using the Cheetah plug-in in Grasshopper Rhinoceros to measure accessibility of public buildings (Slide 11) - GIS query to identify new public spaces: historical buildings which are completely empty are selected for reactivation as new public spaces to provide public facilities (Slides 12 and 13) - Network analysis using the Cheetah plug-in to measure the performance of the whole Tarlabaşı network after the introduction of new public buildings (Slides 14 and 15) - Analysing network connection performance to improve the path from the bus stop to the churches by implementing the shortest path analysis tool (Slide 17)
Synthesis	- Based on the analysis measuring the diversity of mixed-use in the area, a certain amount of residential/commercial/other use is identified (Slide 3) -The location of new public buildings is identified (Slides 12, 13, 14, 15) -The network connectivity performance of the cultural axis is increased by adding new connections to the street network (Slide 16 and 17)
Conclusion	- A new ground floor use allocation plan is introduced, based on the mixed-use principle explored in the analysis (Slides 18 and 19) - A new network of public buildings is created in such a way that the performance of the street network is increased (Slides 12, 13, 14, 15) - A new cultural axis is introduced as an attraction for Tarlabaşı (Slides 16 and 17) - A pedestrian path passing by the two main cultural attractions (churches) is highlighted and improved by adding new connections to the street network and changing the location of the bus stop (Slides 16 and 17) - The building blocks previously demolished (in 1988 are re-created to spatially connect Tarlabaşı with the rest of the Beyoğlu Preservation Area (Slide 20) - A GIS-based irregular cellular automata model is planned but not successfully implemented due to time limitations (Slide 21)

TABLE 5.30 Analysis of the work produced by "Team: Diversity; Tarlabaşı Interven[func]tion".

As seen in Table 5.30, "Team: Diversity; Tarlabaşı Interven[func]tion" is concerned with the problems of connectivity between Tarlabaşı and Istiklal Street, its lack of attractiveness and public spaces. As a strategic solution to these problems, they focus on providing more diverse urban activities to attract more people. They introduce a new cultural axis from Istiklal Street to Bilgi University passing by two churches, which are important historical places of interest, and they plan to re-activate empty historical buildings listed as civil architectural heritage by transforming them into new public spaces. The intervention strategy is to implement a mixed-use allocation scenario and improve the street network performance by making use of the urban analysis tools provided.

A variety of analyses were carried out, using GIS, data mining and Cheetah and explained in detail in Table 5.30 above. These methods were used both to measure the existing properties of the urban environment and to evaluate the performance of the new Tarlabaşı after the interventions. This was critical and, in fact, demonstrated the utility of the analysis tools, both for understanding the existing situation and evaluating the performance of the new interventions. The intervention decisions (new public buildings and new street connections) were regularly tested using network analysis in Cheetah. The team also used data mining intensively to understand and measure the mixed-use patterns of Tarlabaşı and operationalized this information in order to decide on the amount of mixed-use allocation they would introduce.

As a response to the problems of Tarlabaşı, and in order to implement their concept of creating a more socially and spatially diverse area, the team came up with a new ground floor use allocation plan based on the mixed-use principle, namely a new network of public buildings to boost the street network performance, and a new cultural attraction axis which is well connected to Istiklal Street. In addition to these interventions based on the analysis and synthesis process, they also introduced the idea of re-building the buildings previously demolished (in 1988) to open up the six-lane Tarlabaşı Boulevard and re-create the spatial connection between Tarlabaşı and the Beyoğlu Preservation Area. They even started to work on a cellular automata model to implement the mixed-use allocation plan by automation, but this had to remain as an idea due to time limitations.

"Team: Diversity; Tarlabaşı Interven[func]tion" was very enthusiastic about the workshop, especially the computational urban analysis tools and methods, and therefore experimented with many ways of using them. The way in which they used these tools was very consistent with their scenario and they were able to build up a logical and robust connection between the analysis and synthesis processes. Their general concept and solutions to the problems of Tarlabaşı were also realistic and elegant, making efficient use of the local context by activating the existing potential, such as emphasizing the cultural aspects (churches) and the importance of the connection between the Beyoğlu Preservation Area and Dolapdere via Tarlabaşı.

The second team, "Team: Public Network of Tarlabaşı" was made up of three students; Dila Sel (MSc student in Architectural Design Computing, ITU), Ezgi Bastug (MSc student in Architectural Design Computing, ITU), Mutlu Gungor (MSc student in Architectural Design Computing, ITU).

Their first slide introducing their conceptual idea is shown in Figure 5.76.

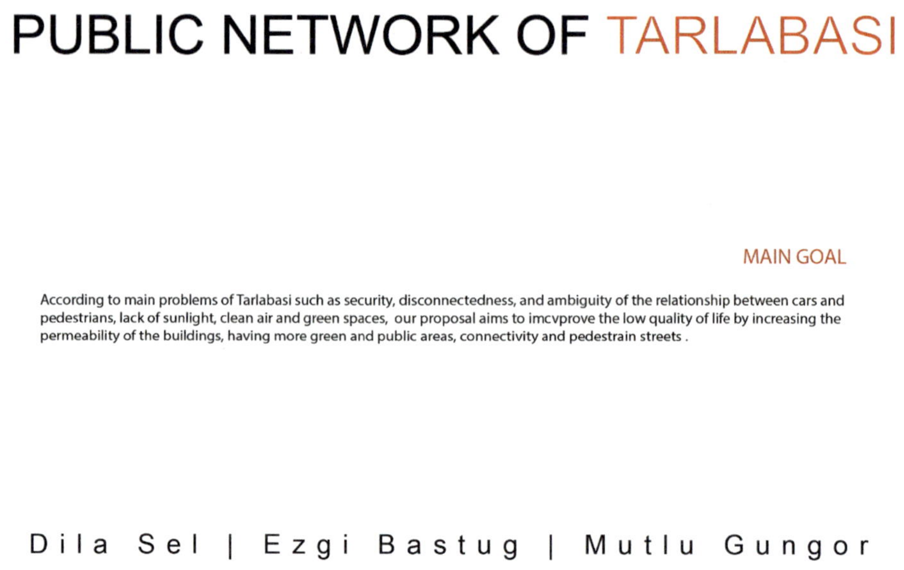

FIGURE 5.76 First slide from "Team: Public Network of Tarlabașı".

"Team: Public Network of Tarlabașı" focused on creating a new green public space network in Tarlabașı to improve the quality of life. Their work is analyzed in detail in association with their final presentation slides (given in the Appendix H) in Table 5.31.

MAIN STEPS AND OUTPUTS IN THE PROCESS	DESCRIPTION
Concept	Improving the quality of life in Tarlabaşı by introducing a new green public network (Slide 1)
Problems	There are problems with disconnectivity, car-pedestrian conflicts, security, lack of sunlight, green spaces and clean air (Slide 1)
Strategic Scenario	-To create a new network of green public spaces by opening semi-public courtyards to the public (Slides 2, 3, 4) -To replace the ground floors of non-historical buildings with public spaces (Slides 2, 3, 4) -To restore historical buildings and reconstruct ruined historical buildings as new public buildings, including various functions to improve social interaction (Slides 2, 3, 4)
Intervention	To create a new network of public green spaces by re-evaluating the existing courtyards inside the blocks of buildings, increasing block permeability and adding new connections to the existing street network in Tarlabaşı (Slide 1)
Analysis	- GIS query to identify buildings with different land-price values and empty ground floors (Slide 5) - Data mining clustering analysis to identify how non-historical buildings with all floors empty and in ruins or in bad condition are clustered, based on their floor number (Slides 6 and 7) - Data mining Naïve Bayes analysis to predict the use of the ground floors of empty buildings based on the existing patterns of ground floor use in Tarlabaşı (Slide 9) - Analysis of the existing courtyards, parks and passages by means of their geometry and footprint (Slide 8) - Analysis of the existing street network and exploration of how network connectivity changes by adding new attraction points, using the Cheetah analysis plug-in (Slide 11) - Analysis to identify buildings within 8 minutes of walking distance from the selected green spaces using the Cheetah analysis plug-in (Slide 10) - GIS query to identify the "all empty" buildings and non-historical buildings with empty ground floors, to select the spots where new street connections will be added to the existing street network (Slide 13) - Street network analysis with the Cheetah analysis plug-in to identify buildings within 8 minutes of walking distance from the courtyards before and after adding new street connections (Slide 14) -Buildings within 3 minutes walking distance from the courtyard were identified by street network analysis using the Cheetah plug-in, and the distribution of floorspace use and average number of floors of these buildings was calculated (Slide 17)
Synthesis	- Existing courtyards are transformed into parks and passages based on their geometry and footprint: rectangular spaces are transformed into passages, square spaces larger than 300 m2 are kept as courtyards and those smaller than 300 m2 are transformed into parks (Slides 8, 10, 11) - New street connections are added to the existing street network (Slides 12 and 13) - New buildings are built on the site of the empty non-historical buildings with one extra floor. The ground floors of these buildings (originally empty ground floors) are transformed into public space to allow for the permeability of the blocks to the courtyards, the total area of open spaces is increased to 8% and the accessible open spaces are increased to 23% (Slide 16) - The functional organization of the courtyard is defined based on the average number of floors and the land floorspace use distribution of the building stock around the courtyard: if the surroundings are more residential, the courtyard is organized as a park; if more commercial, the courtyard is organized as a commercial open space (Slide 17)
Conclusion	A new public green space network is created in Tarlabaşı: small parks, green courtyards and passages create a new pedestrian route with better network connectivity (Slide 15)

TABLE 5.31 Analysis of the work produced by "Team: Public Network of Tarlabaşı".

As seen in Table 5.31, the "Team: Public Network of Tarlabaşı" is concerned with the problem of the disconnectivity of Tarlabaşı, car-pedestrian conflicts, security and lack of sunlight, green spaces and fresh air. As a strategic solution to these problems they introduced the idea of creating a new network of public green spaces by opening semi-public courtyards for public use. In order to make this possible, they proposed reconstructing ruined non-historical buildings by increasing the number of floors, so that the ground floors of the new buildings could be dedicated to public use and the new extra floor could be given an appropriate function. Their main focus was on the creation of a new network of public green spaces, namely courtyards, parks and passages, in a way that would also increase street network connectivity.

They carried out a variety of analyses using GIS, data Mining and Cheetah, explained in detail in Table 5.31, and used GIS to make queries and to filter data. They implemented a data mining clustering analysis to identify different clusters of floorspace use within the buildings located in the selected part of the database and used this information to make decisions on physical interventions. Unlike the other teams, they also implemented another type of data mining analysis previously discussed in this thesis, namely Naïve Bayes Classification, to predict the use of empty ground floors based on the existing patterns of ground floor use in Tarlabaşı. The team used Cheetah analysis to objectively measure street network connectivity after the new connections has been introduced.

As a solution to the problem of the lack of green public spaces they introduced a new network of three types of green spaces and managed to increase the street network connectivity of the neighbourhood. In order to do so, they made use of both data mining and Cheetah in a complementary way to identify the locations of the physical interventions. Although they did not provide any solutions for the other problems they identified, their original idea of creating a network of public green spaces was very interesting and their scenario was consistent. This was a very small-scale intervention idea but it made sense and was appreciated by the instructors and audience. "Team: Public Network of Tarlabaşı" used the analysis tools intensively whilst developing their intervention proposals, and the analysis and synthesis processes were neatly connected.

The third team, named "Team: Social Network in Tarlabaşı", consisted of three students; Dilara Hos (4th year Architecture student, ITU), Marija Cvetinovic (PhD student in Urban Planning and Participatory Processes, Ecole Polytechnique Federale de Lausanne), Yagiz Soylev (4th year Architecture student, ITU).

Their first slide introducing their conceptual idea is shown in Figure 5.77.

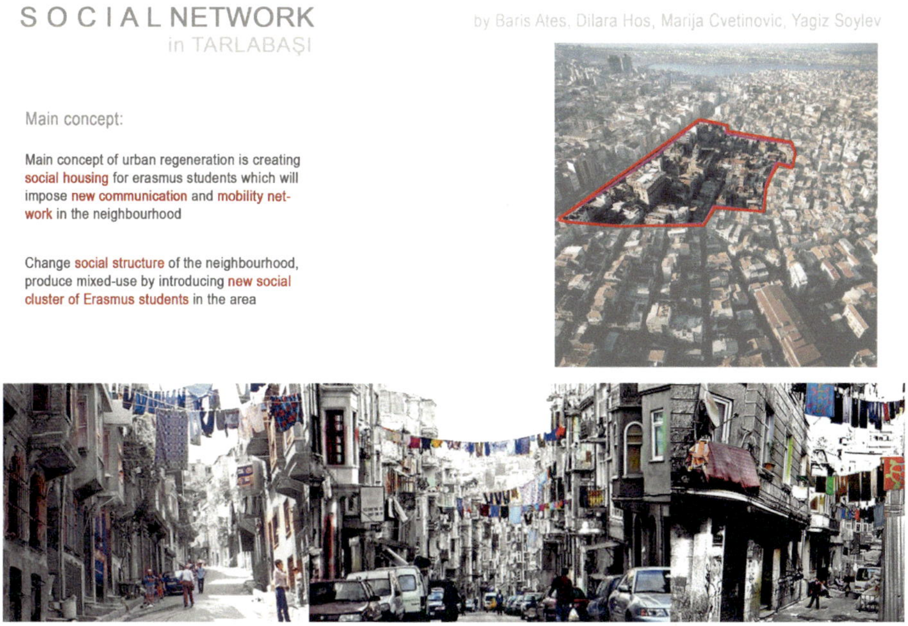

FIGURE 5.77 First slide from "Team: Social Network in Tarlabaşı".

"Team: Social Network in Tarlabaşı" focused on intervening in the social structure of Tarlabaşı by creating social housing for Erasmus exchange students in order to create a new communications and mobility network. Their work is analyzed in detail in association with their final presentation slides (included in Appendix I) in Table 5.32.

MAIN STEPS AND OUTPUTS IN THE PROCESS	DESCRIPTION
Concept	To intervene in the social structure of Tarlabaşı by creating social housing for Erasmus Students, which will create a new communication and mobility network in Tarlabaşı. (Slide 1)
Problems	There are problems with connectivity, attractiveness and the lack of focal points. (Slide 2)
Strategic Scenario	To introduce a new social class of Erasmus students and a new student social housing function in Tarlabaşı, in order to develop a new identity for the neighbourhood by creating a new social network. This new social network will attract new people, increase interaction between locals and newcomers and provide new job opportunities for the locals. (Slides 3 and 4)
Intervention	To transform appropriate existing buildings into social housing for Erasmus students. (Slide 4)
Analysis	- Vicinity analysis using the Cheetah plug-in in Rhinoceros to identify the locations which are best connected to the three important nodes; Taksim Square, the Tarlabaşı bus stop and the Tepebasi bus stop (Slide 6) - GIS query to identify the buildings which are most suitable for transforming into social housing for Erasmus students; buildings which are not registered as civil architecture + in ruined or bad condition + with a footprint of less than 50 m2 (Slide 7) - Data mining analysis to explore theclusters of floorspace use within the buildings in the areas identified through superimposition of vicinity analysis and GIS queries. (Slides 6 and 8)
Synthesis	Identification of buildings to be transformed into social housing for Erasmus students based on data mining clustering analysis: clusters of residential buildings and buildings containing empty floors are selected. (Slides 7 and 8)
Conclusion	- Proposal for a bottom-up, time-based urban development process based on small scale interventions, maintaining the original urban patterns of the neighbourhood (Slide 9) -A non-invasive integrated transformation program which aims to rehabilitate the social structure of the neighbourhood by introducing students as a new social user class; (Slide 9) -The amount of mixed-use is maintained and promoted, and the existing multi-functional blocks of buildings along the Tarlabaşı Boulevard are preserved (Slide 9) - A block in which most of the buildings are already empty is identified as a future transformation hot spot where new functions can be developed (Slide 9) -A couple of building blocks are identified as a centre for a future local attraction (Slide 9)

TABLE 5.32 Analysis of the work produced by "Team: Social Network in Tarlabaşı".

As seen in Table 5.32, the "Team: Social Network in Tarlabaşı" is mainly concerned with the problem of social connectivity between Tarlabaşı and the rest of the city, and the lack of attractiveness and focal points in the neighbourhood. As a strategic solution to this problem, they introduced the idea of creating a new social group in Tarlabaşı i.e. exchange students on the Erasmus programme (European Community Action Scheme for the Mobility of University Students) and proposed to provide student social housing for them. In this way, they aimed to create a new social network which would increase interaction between locals and newcomers. This interaction would, they claimed, subsequently attract new people, provide new job opportunities for locals and increase social connectivity between Tarlabaşı and the rest of Istanbul. In order to achieve this, they transformed appropriate existing buildings into social housing for exchange students on the Erasmus programme.

The team also carried out a variety of analyses using GIS, data mining and Cheetah, explained in detail in Table 5.32 above. They used the analysis tools in a complementary way in order to identify locations for the student social housing. They carried out a vicinity analysis using the Cheetah plug-in to identify the locations that were best connected to the important transportation nodes and GIS queries to select the buildings to be demolished and reconstructed in accordance with their criteria. In addition, they used data mining clustering analysis to identify the clusters of floorspace use within the buildings located in the superimposed area of selected blocks, and vicinity analysis. In this way they narrowed down the solution space, firstly by implementing a Cheetah analysis and GIS filtering, followed by a data mining clustering analysis, which served as a tool to explore the floorspace use characteristics of the solution space. Like the others, this team also operationalized the results of the analysis process for generating intervention proposals for the regeneration of Tarlabaşı.

"Team: Social Network in Tarlabaşı" was able to produce a valuable strategy for combating the social disconnection between Tarlabaşı and Istanbul. Apart from the physical intervention agenda, which was the focus of the work, they also introduced important ideas about the regeneration problem in Tarlabaşı. They proposed a bottom-up, time-based approach to urban regeneration based on micro-scale interventions and produced a non-invasive program aimed at rehabilitating social aspects which could, in turn, have an effect on improving the spatial problems. With these proposals, "Team: Social Network in Tarlabaşı" made a very valuable contribution to the workshop discussions.

The fourth team, named "Team: Raise your Head", consisted of three students; Cosku Cinkilic (Architect, recent graduate of the Architecture Department, ITU), Derya Karaali (MArch student in Architectural Design, Bilgi University), Ecem Ergin (MArch student in Architectural Design, ITU)

Their first slide introducing their conceptual idea is shown in Figure 5.78.

FIGURE 5.78 First slide from "Team: Raise your Head".

"Team: Raise your Head" focused on creating new meeting places both for the inhabitants of Tarlabaşı and for newcomers. Their work is analyzed in detail in association with their final presentation slides (included in Appendix J) in Table 5.33.

MAIN STEPS AND OUTPUTS IN THE PROCESS	DESCRIPTION
Concept	To create meeting places for the inhabitants of Tarlabaşı and incoming social classes (Slide 1)
Problems	There are problems of light due to the physical configuration (narrow streets) and high density of the neighbourhood, and no axes for safe pedestrian routes (Slides 2 and 3)
Strategic Scenario	To create a new type of public space on the top floors, namely top follies to improve social communication between the inhabitants and incoming social classes. Top floor public spaces will serve as meeting places for the public and prevent social decline by introducing new ways of communicating and socializing. The top follies project will be applied step-by-step and developed gradually over time. This will allow for improvements to the project, based on feedback from the locals (Slides 6, 8, 9)
Intervention	To create a new type of public space on the top floors, namely top follies, which have more sunlight than at street level and are much more spatially intimate. (Slides 8 and 9)
Analysis	- GIS query to identify business-shopping use and empty floors (Slides 4 and 5) - Proximity analysis using the Cheetah plug-in in Rhinoceros to measure the proximity of the buildings to the entrance of business axes and to entrance points to Istiklal Avenue (Slide 11) - GIS analysis to classify the proximity of the Tarlabaşı buildings to the entrance of business axes and to entrance points to Istiklal Avenue (Slide 12) - GIS query to identify buildings within the first proximity zone (class) with a maximum of 4 floors and an empty top floor. (Slide 12)
Synthesis	-The streets where buildings with business-shopping functions on the ground floor and an empty top floor are clustered and selected as the main business axes, based on GIS queries (Slides 4 and 5) -The zone with the highest proximity to the entrance of the business axes and the entrance points to Istiklal Avenue, based on the proximity analysis using the Cheetah plug-in in Rhinoceros, is selected as the first intervention zone where the top follies will be located (Slides 8, 11, 12)
Conclusion	- Main business axes are created and emphasized (Slide 14) -Top follies are created as a new public space for Tarlabaşı inhabitants (Slide 14) - A new pedestrian route following the top follies is introduced as an attraction for Tarlabaşı (Slide 14) - A cable car line is proposed from Tarlabaşı to Dolapdere (Slides 13 and 14)

TABLE 5.33 Analysis of the work produced by "Team: Raise your Head".

As seen in Table 5.33, "Team: Raise your Head" was mainly concerned with the problem of sunlight at street level and therefore built up their strategic scenario by creating a new kind of public space on the top floors of the buildings, named 'top follies'. 'Top follies' would receive enough sunlight and, more importantly, would serve as a meeting place for the inhabitants of Tarlabaşı. "Team: Raise your Head" claimed that an intervention of this kind could improve communications and socio-cultural exchanges between social classes and prevent social decline. Therefore, during the workshop they focused on finding appropriate locations for the top follies. They did not experiment with the analysis tools as much as the other groups due to the fact that they were still taking exams in addition to attending the workshop, so they could not participate as intensively as the others. Nevertheless, they made use of GIS and the

Cheetah plug-in, as explained in detail in Table 5.33. They used GIS to make queries and filter data and identified the main commercial axes within the neighbourhood based on these queries. They also used Cheetah proximity analysis to measure the proximity of the buildings to the entrance of the main commercial axes and the entrance points of the Istiklal Avenue. Unlike the other groups, they used a GIS-based classification method to classify the proximity measurement which they implemented with Cheetah and identified various proximity zones. Finally, they proposed to build the 'top follies' in the buildings located around the main commercial axes which had empty top floors. They proposed a time-based implementation of their ideas, in which the zone with the closest proximity to the entrance of the main commercial axes and the entrance points of the Istiklal Avenue was selected as the initial intervention zone where the first 'top follies' would be located. Subsequently, they proposed to develop this intervention strategy over time, based on user feedback, in other areas in Tarlabaşı. They also proposed a new pedestrian walkway for the 'top follies' as an added attraction for the neighbourhood. Although they did not provide a clear definition and detailed scenario for the functioning of the 'top follies', in principle this was an interesting and inspiring approach, involving a micro-scale urban intervention without major construction work.

The following section is dedicated to an evaluation of the workshop, firstly through an analysis of the questionnaire completed by the students, and secondly, a self-evaluation of the workshop by the author, in order to highlight the achievements and the limitations of the analysis tools and the workshop process as a whole.

§ 5.3.4 Students' evaluations of the Tarlabaşı Datascope workshop

A questionnaire was prepared for the students to evaluate the workshop. The results of the questionnaire are shown in Table 5.34.

QUESTION	AVERAGE GRADE
Computational Urban Analysis tools supported participants in making decisions whilst developing their intervention goals	(4) A Lot
Computational Urban Analysis tools were very helpful in the scenario development process	(4) A Lot
The use of different computational platforms and techniques in a complementary way enabled participants to develop their intervention ideas in better-informed way	(4) A Lot
During the design process, Computational Urban Analysis tools were helpful for understanding the urban problems	(3) Moderately
During the design process, Computational Urban Analysis tools were helpful for understanding the urban context	(3) Moderately
During the design process, Computational Urban Analysis tools were helpful for developing a background for the design agenda	(4) A Lot
During the design process, Computational Urban Analysis tools were helpful for developing urban intervention proposals	(4) A Lot
During the design process, Computational Urban Analysis tools were helpful for producing supporting information	(4) A Lot
During the design process, Computational Urban Analysis tools were helpful for land-allocation for different functions	(4) A Lot
During the design process, Computational Urban Analysis tools were helpful for creativity	(3) Moderately
During the design process, Computational Urban Analysis tools were helpful for productivity	(4) A Lot
During the design process, Computational Urban Analysis tools were helpful for quality	(4) A Lot
During the design process, Computational Urban Analysis tools were helpful for saving time	(4) A Lot
Computational Urban Analysis tools function as a design tool	(3) Moderately
Computational Urban Analysis tools function as a design assistant	(5) A great deal

TABLE 5.34 Results of the participant questionnaire.

The questionnaire also included open questions. The students' answers were edited slightly to correct the English language errors without changing the meaning of the comments. The open questions and student answers are listed below:

Student answers to this question: "What kind of additional computational analysis tools would be good?" included:

- Time-based data and time-based analysis tools
- Data on social aspects of the site and tools to analyze social data
- Analysis tools for measuring environmental performance
- Integrated tools for topography and sunlight
- Analysis tools for section level versus plan level analysis
- Analysis tools for topological aspects

The second question was "How would you evaluate the contribution of data mining applications in developing your intervention scenarios?" Student answers to this question included positive reactions to the contribution of data mining such as:

- "It helped us with clustering the selected data by GIS."
- "Data mining is very good for creating clustering."
- "Clustering contributed a great deal towards organizing the GIS results and improving the scenario with the chosen filters."
- "It helped us to produce the classification of functional distribution."
- "Data mining provides us with information which is hard to obtain without automation."
- "The main contribution of data mining is analyzing the area in terms of saving time, obtaining certain data and viewing all the data in a schema."
- "With it is easier to see or visualize your connections."
- "It helps us to make sense of our data and provides us with a helpful classification."
- "It is very important for categorizing, clustering the data identified or developing patterns."
- "It is very valuable for understanding complex uses of the spaces. Also I think it is a very valuable evaluation tool (e.g. data visualization)."
- "The data mining application helped me to find my way around a confusing data list. It should be used in all projects. It helps us to understand the city much better than directly looking at separate plans or data lists."

The third question was: "How would you evaluate the contribution of the Cheetah applications in developing your intervention scenarios?" Student answers to this question included positive reactions to the contribution of the Cheetah plug-in in Rhinoceros and Grasshopper, such as:

- "One very important aspect of the Cheetah plug-in is that it enables us to play around with the possible street configurations."
- "It helps with making decisions about design solutions, it narrows down the choice."
- "Proximity, vicinity and walking distances according to topography helped us to decide our intervention spots."
- "Walking distance analysis worked slowly, the most important contribution is connectivity analysis."
- "Walking distance analysis was very helpful."
- "Cheetah is a real time-saver, with easy connections and a well-designed and detailed structure. It's nice to have a tool that can give you instant feedback, on the basis of which you can change your concept."

All of the students answered "yes" to the question: "Do you plan to work with these tools in your future projects?"

The next question was, "Describe your overall impressions: how was the workshop for you? Please include comments for each of the above questions, with a particular focus on your impressions of the computational urban analysis tools and their contribution to scenario development and the floorspace use allocation process." There were two main criticisms, mainly concerning lack of time and difficulty in learning to use the tools in such a short time. Some students stated that they needed more time to produce better solutions and that it was quite challenging to adapt to the computational tools. We received very positive answers about their overall impressions, such as:

- "The idea of combining different tools is very good but quite complex"
- "The workshop is very rich in content, offering an innovative approach and opportunity to combine urban planning with urban design in a more elaborate and detailed vision of urban development."
- "The tools were helpful for improving scenarios and proving ideas. The connections between the tools were complicated. Understanding how and where to use each tool and how to combine them with urban ideas was challenging."
- "The tools were very suitable for analyzing physical aspects."
- "It is more important to decide what to do with the tools than how to use them. In the end your project does not end any earlier, but you do it with more detailed information."

§ 5.3.5 A critical review of the implementation

This sub-section summarizes and evaluates the work conducted in Implementation (3).

An international student workshop focusing on the regeneration of Tarlabaşı, located in the Beyoğlu Preservation Area, was carried out to extend the investigation of the Research Question (3) "How could this 'relational urban knowledge' support architects, urban designers or urban planners whilst developing intervention proposals for urban regeneration?" As stated earlier, Tarlabaşı is currently facing a heavily criticized urban renewal process which is destroying the site-specific characteristics of this inner-city urban neighbourhood. The workshop (Tarlabaşı Datascope) involved the implementation of KDPM for urban analysis in combination with parametric urban analysis techniques and aimed to test the extent to which these methods can enhance an urban analysis process and support the development of urban intervention proposals.

Tarlabaşı Datascope was organized at the Istanbul Technical University Faculty of Architecture in collaboration with ITU, TU Delft and TU Lisbon and was led by the author, Pirouz Nourian (PhD candidate and instructor at TU Delft, Faculty of

Architecture, Department of Architectural Engineering + Technology, Chair of Design Informatics) and José Nuno Beirao (PhD in Urban Design at TU Delft, the Design Informatics Chair, Faculty of Architecture). The author developed the outline of the workshop, based on the work carried out in this thesis study. The structure and content of the workshop was developed in collaboration with José Nuno Beirao and Pirouz Nourian, based on their PhD research.

Within the scope of this 8-day workshop, 13 architecture and urban design and planning students (4th and 5th year undergraduates and MSc and PhD students) were asked to produce alternative urban regeneration scenarios to demonstrate how Tarlabaşı could be sensitively transformed by small-scale interventions without causing serious damage to its original social and spatial characteristics. Hence, they were asked to identify the site-specific particularities of Tarlabaşı by making use of the computational urban analysis and synthesis methods and techniques that were provided. These methods and techniques involved the implementation of KDPM for urban analysis and a set of parametric urban analysis tools (Cheetah Plug-in) designed by Pirouz Nourian and Samaneh Rezvani and developed using Grasshopper-Rhinoceros software. The operations were conducted in various software platforms involving RapidMiner, QuantumGIS, Rhino 5, Grasshopper, Slingshot, Postgres PgAdmin and PostGIS. The computational analysis mainly included the implementation of the KDPM for urban analysis for clustering floorspace use in the buildings and floorspace use prediction and the implementation of the Cheetah Plug-in for street network analysis and pedestrian access / walkability analysis.

Following the computational analysis, which enabled the students to undertake an in-depth exploration of the site-specific characteristics of Tarlabaşı, they were asked to produce a general strategic scenario for the regeneration of Tarlabaşı and to materialize this scenario. The students came up with urban intervention and design proposals based on their findings regarding the potential and problems of the urban context.

The students reacted positively to the use of data mining methods and techniques, which they found valuable in terms of enabling them to make sense of the urban data provided, through clustering and classification. They acknowledged that it would have been too complex and perhaps impossible to discover the patterns of floorspace use in the buildings of Tarlabaşı without the implementation of the KDPM for urban analysis. TThey found the Cheetah plug-in creative and helpful in developing their intervention decisions. Overall, they found this toolset of computational methods and techniques supportive in the course of developing urban intervention proposals but also quite challenging to learn to use in a short period of time.

Although from the author's point of view, the workshop was beneficial in terms of investigating Research Question (3), demonstrating how the knowledge discovery approach to urban analysis through data mining proposed in this thesis can support the development of intervention proposals for urban regeneration, some important questions should be addressed in order to provide a critical review of this implementation:

- How did the knowledge discovery approach to urban analysis through data mining support the students in making decisions whilst developing urban intervention proposals?

In the Tarlabaşı Datascope workshop three teams of students efficiently used the knowledge discovery approach to urban analysis through data mining in the course of generating urban intervention proposals. The role of the data mining analysis in each team's proposal development process is reviewed in detail below:

"Team: Diversity; Tarlabaşı Interven[func]tion" aimed to make Tarlabaşı a more diverse area, both in social and spatial terms. Accordingly, they decided to implement a mixed-use strategy, which would make Tarlabaşı more diverse in spatial terms and attractive in social terms. To achieve this, they first needed to understand the existing patterns of floorspace use in the buildings: what kind of clusters there were and how they were distributed spatially. They therefore implemented a clustering analysis for the whole neighbourhood. In this way, they identified how floorspace use is clustered within the buildings (vertical floorspace use patterns) and mapped the results in GIS. Based on the findings of this data mining application, they were able to synthesize their intervention ideas: they identified 'how much' mixed-use they wanted to achieve (i.e. how many buildings would be residential, how many of them would be commercial, and how many of them would be used for other purposes), based on the existing trends of ground floor use, and they detected the parts of the neighbourhood which are relatively weak in terms of mixed-use and would thus be subject to intervention. They also implemented clustering analysis for specific spots which they marked important. This gave them a clear understanding of the floorspace use configurations around these spots, and accordingly they decided which buildings to transform in terms of floor space usage. As a result, they introduced a mixed-use allocation plan for the ground floors of the buildingd in Tarlabaşı, which can be used as a regeneration intervention for the neighborhood and which they were able to produce supported by the results of the data mining analysis.

"Team: Public Network of Tarlabaşı" aimed to improve the quality of life in Tarlabaşı by introducing a new green public network. Accordingly they decided to create new public spaces by opening semi-public courtyards, introducing new ground floor public spaces and public buildings. To achieve this, they implemented clustering analysis to identify how the vacant non-historical buildings and vacant buildings in ruins or in bad condition were clustered, based on their floor number. From the findings of this data mining application, they were able to synthesize their intervention ideas: they identified which ground floors would be allocated for public use (to create a passage from the street to the courtyards) and how many floors these buildings would contain when reconstructed. Additionally, they implemented clustering analysis to identify the functional organization around these buildings and used this information in deciding the functional use of the courtyards; they allocated a use for the courtyards in accordance with the existing patterns of flooruse in the buildings around them. Moreover, they also implemented Naïve Bayes Classification to assign new functions to the empty ground floors based on the existing patterns of ground floor use in Tarlabaşı. More specifically, they used the Naïve Bayes Classification model to assign a new class label to the empty ground floors, as if empty floors were records with an unknown class label. 1st floor use was used as the predictor variable and the ground floor use as the variable to be labelled/predicted. The model was trained with the dataset consisting of instances whose class labels were known and the learnt function was used to predict the class label of these 'unknown' records, which were empty floors. As a final output, they introduced a proposal for the regeneration of Tarlabaşı that creates a number of new public spaces in the neighbourhood, which they were able to produce supported by the result of the data mining analysis.

"Team: Social Network in Tarlabaşı" aimed to intervene in the social structure of Tarlabaşı by introducing a new social group of students. Accordingly they decided to create new social housing, mainly for Erasmus students, by transforming some of the existing buildings. To achieve this they needed to find out which buildings were most suitable for transformation. Using Cheetah analysis and GIS queries they identified the buildings with a footprint of less than 50 m2 which were not registered as civil architecture or were in ruins or in bad condition, and were best connected to transportation nodes around the neighbourhood. They then implemented a clustering analysis to explore the clusters of floorspace use in the buildings located in these areas. Based on these data mining findings, they were able to synthesize their intervention ideas: they found out that the most appropriate buildings to transform into social housing were residential buildings and buildings with empty floors located in these areas. As a result, they introduced a proposal for the regeneration of Tarlabaşı focusing on the rehabilitation of the social structure of the neighbourhood, which they were able to produce supported by the results of the data mining analysis.

– Considering the work produced by the student teams in the course of the Tarlabaşı Datascope workshop, what are the benefits and limitations of implementing the knowledge discovery approach to urban analysis through data mining proposed in this thesis?

The emphasis of the workshop was on developing a context-sensitive approach to the regeneration of Tarlabaşı, which would be implemented through small-scale interventions. Both the data mining and Cheetah methods and techniques that were provided responded very well to this context-sensitive approach and enabled the students to identify some of the micro-scale characteristics of Tarlabaşı in order to incorporate them into their urban intervention strategies. The students evaluated this feature of the data mining and Cheetah methods and techniques very positively. In fact, the variety of Tarlabaşı urban intervention strategies developed by the students and the potential in their work for further development demonstrates that these methods and techniques support building context-sensitive approaches in the course of developing urban intervention proposals by enabling site-specific patterns and relations between multiple dimensions of micro-scale urban components to be discovered in urban neighbourhoods.

However, in addition to the above-mentioned comments, there are also some significant limitations. In terms of the content of the workshop, one important limitation, also mentioned by the participants, was the lack of data on the temporal, social and demographic aspects of Tarlabaşı. This kind of information would be extremely interesting in terms of measuring how physical, economic and spatial aspects are related to socio-demographical aspects. As mentioned in the evaluation of Implementation (2), the unavailability of relevant data is a major limitation on producing more interesting results that can support the development of urban intervention proposals using the knowledge discovery approach to urban analysis through data mining.

– How did the combination of GIS, data mining and the Cheetah plug-in perform and how could this be improved?

The integration of GIS and data mining worked through the exchange of data files, without any great difficulties and it is especially interesting to visualize the results of the data mining analysis in GIS, as most of the students did. Data mining methods are suitable for analysing GIS-based databases, since they offer clustering and classification methods which complement the GIS spatial analysis tools and techniques. In addition, the combined use of GIS, data mining and the parametric toolset provided by the Cheetah plug-in allowed students to investigate the details of the urban configuration, both in terms of ground floor use and street networks, which is a rather unusual implementation in urban analysis. However, the whole process was not fully automated, meaning that there were no seamless connections between the analysis tools that were introduced. Information is mainly exchanged between the different computational analysis platforms through a database file. Technically, an online link connecting this database file to all the platforms could be established, enabling the whole process to become fully automated. This workshop clearly shows how and why a fully automated computational urban analysis, synthesis and design process would be very interesting and supportive. The Tarlabaşı Datascope workshop is a step towards the CIM concept, and the ways in which the participants used the analysis tools, their approach and their evaluation of the methods offered important feedback in terms of how urban researchers and practitioners can benefit from such a fully automated platform, namely a platform for CIM.

A shorter version of this workshop, named Urban Datascope, was held at eCAADe 2013, at TU Delft (http://urbandatascope.wordpress.com/) (http://ecaade2013.bk.tudelft.nl/).

– How does this implementation contribute to this thesis and to urban research in general?

The most important contribution of this workshop with regard to this thesis was that through this experience we were able to test the reactions of the students to the KDPM for urban analysis (how they made use of it, and whether they found it supportive whilst developing urban intervention proposals). In our opinion, the fact that they captured the real aim of data mining, which is the discovery of hidden relationships and information patterns that cannot be found by SQL-style querying and data filtering methods, is very important. The way in which they implemented the knowledge discovery approach to urban analysis through data mining proposed in this thesis also allowed us to investigate Research Question (3), i.e. the idea that this approach, if applied accordingly, facilitates, guides and supports the development of intervention proposals for urban regeneration.

To conclude, in addition to contributing to this thesis in terms of investigating the potential ways of using the proposed knowledge discovery approach to urban analysis through data mining whilst developing urban intervantion proposals. Implementation (3), allowed us to combine data mining with parametric urban analysis techniques. One aspect that could not be achieved within this workshop, due to a full agenda and time limitations, was to add the measurements that were found through the implementation of the Cheetah Plug-in to the Tarlabaşı database. If implemented, this would make it possible to mine the configurative aspects of the urban environments, together with other available features of the buildings. This could have resulted in the discovery of very interesting patterns and relationships, especially among the morphological and spatial features and floorspace use data. This implementation contributed to the general research on urban regeneration by demonstrating how 'relational urban knowledge' concerning building features can be discovered and utilized in the course of developing urban intervention proposals. Moreover, the variety of small-scale intervention approaches that can be formulated for the regeneration of Tarlabaşı by making use of its site-specific characteristics was an important contribution to the general debate on how an alternative to the heavily criticized transformation project developed by the Beyoğlu Municipality could be developed.

§ 5.4 Conclusion

Chapter (5) has mainly examined the extent to which a knowledge discovery approach to urban analysis through data mining can enhance an urban analysis process and support the development of intervention proposals for urban regeneration. The KDPM for urban analysis, previously presented in Chapter (4), was applied in the Beyoğlu Preservation Area in Istanbul. Three implementation of this model were executed in order to investigate the research questions under study. Implementation (1) investigated the kind of patterns and relationships that can be extracted from the traditional thematic maps of the Beyoğlu Preservation Area by implementing a knowledge discovery approach to urban analysis through data mining and how these patterns and relationships can be represented. Implementation (2) and (3) focused on how a knowledge discovery approach to urban analysis through data mining can contribute towards the development of urban intervention proposals for the regeneration of the Tarlabaşı district in the Beyoğlu Preservation Area. Implementation (2), executed the KDPM for urban analysis together with Evolutionary Computation in order to produce an alternative approach to the regeneration of Tarlabaşı. Implementation (3) implemented the KDPM for urban analysis via an international workshop. Participants implemented this model with parametric urban analysis techniques and produced urban intervention proposals for the regeneration of Tarlabaşı. Three implementations exposed the capabilities and limitations of this approach. In particular, Implementation (2) and (3) have revealed that the major contribution of data mining is to expose the site-specific characteristics of urban environments in a useful way, thus enabling a context-sensitive process to be planned.

The next chapter reviews what has been achieved in this thesis, identifies the main outputs and contributions, pinpoints the limitations of the knowledge discovery approach to urban analysis through data mining proposed in this thesis and proposes possible future research paths.

6 Conclusion

This study developed and implemented a knowledge discovery approach through data mining in the field of urban data analysis. In particular, the knowledge discovery approach through data mining was used to reveal the 'knowledge' that is implicitly stored in the conventional thematic maps of the Beyoğlu Preservation Area (used as the basis of the 2008 Master Plan for the Beyoğlu Preservation Area, prepared by the Istanbul Metropolitan Municipality) and demonstrated how this 'knowledge' can become utilizable in producing regeneration proposals for a deteriorated neighbourhood in the Beyoğlu Preservation Area (Tarlabaşı).

Developments in large-scale computing and performance, together with new techniques and automated tools for data collection and analysis, are opening up promising opportunities for urban data analysis. Motivated by these recent advances in computer science and ICT, the main driving force behind the research was to investigate how this may contribute to urban analysis. Accordingly, the overall aim of the thesis was the development of a knowledge discovery approach to urban analysis; a domain-specific adaptation of the generic process of knowledge discovery using data mining defined by Fayyad et al. (1996b).

On a more specific level, the thesis aimed towards 'knowledge discovery' in traditional thematic maps published in 2008 by the Istanbul Metropolitan Municipality as a basis of the Master Plan for the Beyoğlu Preservation Area, which is one of the most important historical inner-city neighbourhoods in Istanbul. These thematic urban analysis maps, which represent urban components, namely buildings, streets, neighbourhoods and their various attributes such as floorspace use in the buildings, land price, population density or historical importance, constitute a detailed data source. Yet they do not really extend our knowledge of Beyoğlu Preservation Area beyond documenting its current state and they have hardly any connection to the intervention decisions presented in the plan. Using a knowledge discovery approach through data mining, could help to discover the 'useful' and 'valuable' information patterns hidden in these maps and such 'knowledge' could become operational in the course of developing intervention proposals for urban regeneration.

In accordance with the stated aims, three connected research questions were formulated:

- **Research Question (1):** Can we develop a general process model to adapt the generic process of knowledge discovery using data mining for urban data analysis?

A *'Knowledge Discovery Process Model for Urban Analysis'*, namely the *KDPM*, was developed as an answer to the Research Question (1). This urban analysis process model is a domain-specific adaptation of the generic process of knowledge discovery in databases defined by Fayyad et al. (1996b) in the field of urban analysis. The KDPM for urban analysis describes a general process of database formulation, analysis and evaluation for extracting information patterns and relationships from urban data by combining GIS and data mining functionalities. In other words, this computational process enables urban databases to be analyzed in order to extract 'relational urban knowledge'. 'Relational urban knowledge' is a term employed in this thesis to refer to the potentially 'useful' and/or 'valuable' patterns and relationships that can be discovered in urban databases by implementing data mining methods and techniques.

– **Research Question (2):** What kind of information patterns and relationships can be extracted from the traditional thematic maps of the Beyoğlu Preservation Area by further developing and implementing this model?

The KDPM for urban analysis was further developed to construct a GIS database, namely *the Beyoğlu Preservation Area Building Features Database,* mainly from the thematic maps of the Master Plan for the Beyoğlu Preservation Area and was implemented to explore information patterns and relationships between the different features of buildings in the Beyoğlu Preservation Area and its three main neighbourhoods, Cihangir, Karaköy, and Tarlabaşı. Three different types of data mining methods, namely Naïve Bayes Classification, Association Rule Analysis and Clustering, were tested in order to explore the range of 'relational urban knowledge' concerning building features which could be discovered by implementing this urban analysis model. The results of these tests provided an *insight into the information patterns hidden in the Beyoglu Preservation Area Building Features Database* and constituted the answer to the Research Question (2) by exposing the form of relations and patterns that can be found using different data mining methods. In specific, Naïve Bayes Classification revealed the power of one or many building attributes over the categories of another building attribute and this was postulated as a measure of the relationship between these two attributes of the buildings in the Beyoğlu Preservation Area. Association Rule Analysis, for its part, revealed co-ocurence relationships between attributes of the buildings in the Beyoğlu Preservation Area and informed about how frequently the attributes co-occur in the database. These are highly descriptive quantitative outputs and found to be useful for being employed as input for other computational methods. Finally, clustering method grouped the buildings in the Beyoğlu Preservation Area based on their floorspace use attributes and provided information about the patterns of building use in the area. These findings were visualized using GIS and other representation techniques and were used to compare these urban environments. Visual representation added great value to the results, since it makes them more understandable and interpretable, and enables further inferences and comparisons to be formulated.

- **Research Question (3):** How could this 'relational urban knowledge' support architects, urban designers or urban planners whilst developing intervention proposals for urban regeneration?

To provide an answer to this research question, the KDPM for urban analysis was implemented in two different implementations, which both aimed to investigate how the model could be used whilst developing urban intervention proposals for the regeneration of the Tarlabaşı neighbourhood located in the Beyoğlu Preservation Area. This historical neighbourhood is currently undergoing a heavily criticized urban renewal process which displaces the low-income local residents to create a new Tarlabaşı for high-income residents and destroys the original land use patterns. In order to address this problem using the limited data available from the thematic maps, an alternative regeneration approach was developed in the course of Implementation (1). This approach aimed to generate draft plans for ground floor use, user profile and tenure-type allocation which would create a mixed-use + mixed-user profile + mixed-income Tarlabaşı whilst preserving the existing patterns of ground floor use in the buildings of the neighbourhood. A computational process combining KDPM for urban analysis with an Evolutionary Algorithm (programmed in Python programming language by N. Onur Sönmez) was designed and used to implement this approach. The input for this process was the original ground floor use allocation plan of the neighbourhood. In this process, the task of the KDPM for urban analysis was to identify some of the existing patterns of ground floor use in the buildings (i.e. 'relational urban knowledge' concerning building features) hidden in this plan. The task of the evolutionary algorithm, on the other hand, was to transform this plan to reflect the regeneration approach imposed by the author, whilst also preserving the existing patterns of ground floor use as far as possible. The output of this process was the draft plans for ground floor use, user profile and tenure-type allocation. In this way, the KDPM for urban analysis, combined with an evolutionary process, supported the development of urban intervention proposals for the regeneration of Tarlabaşı. This *computational process, which generates allocation plans for ground floor use, user-profile and tenure-type, using GIS and data mining functionalities with evolutionary computation,* together with the generated plans provided an answer to the Research Question (3). This implementation helped us to exemplify how the 'relational urban knowledge' concerning building features discovered by implementing a knowledge discovery approach to urban analysis through data mining can assist architects, urban designers or urban planners in generating intervention proposals for urban regeneration.

In order to extend the investigation of Research Question (3), the author organized an international student workshop, The Tarlabaşı Datascope workshop together with his colleagues (Pirouz Nourian and Jose Nuno Beirao as organizers and instructors and Ceyhun Burak Akgül as a guest lecturer). The workshop focused on exploring computational urban analysis and synthesis methods and techniques to support the development of urban intervention proposals for the regeneration of Tarlabaşı. In this workshop, students developed context-sensitive solutions for the urban regeneration problem in Tarlabaşı by making use of data mining and other computational analysis techniques run in the Cheetah plug-in developed in Rhino-Grasshopper by Pirouz Nourian and Samaneh Rezvani (i.e. Network analysis and Pedestrian Access / Walkability analysis). This process and the urban intervention proposals proposed by students also provided an answer to the Research Question (3). Limited by the available data, students used data mining analysis in order to reveal the patterns and relationships hidden in multiple layers of information, understand the site-specific micro-scale features of Tarlabaşı in detail, and synthesize their intervention proposals. This workshop enabled us to investigate how students with no expertise in data mining approached these techniques and tools, and to test whether the knowledge discovery approach to urban analysis through data mining is really supportive and beneficial whilst developing urban intervention proposals in real-life cases.

The following section lists all the outputs of the thesis (the main ones highlighted above and other outputs) by reviewing how they contribute to the general agenda for urban studies and explaining the scientific and societal contributions of this thesis.

§ 6.1 Outputs of the Thesis and Scientific and Societal Contributions

The main outputs of the thesis and their contributions to the domain of urban research are evaluated as follows:

- *The urban studies timeline:* The literature survey for this research produced an Urban Studies timeline which includes brief reviews of some of the ideas and works that have been most influential in the development of urban theory and practice. A number of inferences about the evolution of urban theory and practice were drawn from an examination of this timeline. Although these inferences can be considered speculative and incomplete, they still contribute to the general research on the evolution of approaches, objectives, and focal points in the field of urban theory and practice in general and in the field of urban analysis in particular. The Urban Studies timeline can be developed further in the future.
- *A concept for approaching cities:* the city as a 'data mine': This thesis conceptually defines the city as a 'data mine', a conceptual approach that emphasizes the city as the source of a tremendous amount and incredible range of data which, if investigated, could facilitate a better understanding of urban environments. This approach provides a conceptual basis for researchers who are interested in building data-driven approaches for urban analysis, and for those working in the field of urban analytics. Chapter (4), Section (4.1) explains the details of this approach.

- *A KDPM for urban analysis*: A KDPM for urban analysis, which is basically a domain-specific adaptation of the generic process of knowledge discovery in databases through data mining, was developed in this research. The model describes a semi-automated process of database formulation, analysis and evaluation for extracting information patterns and relationships from urban data. The KDPM for urban analysis suggests that GIS functionalities can be used to formulate a database, and GIS and data mining can be used in a complementary way to analyse the database and evaluate the outcomes. The model illustrates how the output of a GIS platform can become the input for a data mining platform and vice versa. This results in an interlinked analytical process and a more sophisticated analysis of urban data therefore becomes possible. In Implementation (2) the model was extended and applied specifically to demonstrate how to analyze data contained in the thematic maps using data mining methods. Implementations (2) and (3) also illustrated how the KDPM for urban analysis can be combined with other quantitative/computational approaches. Obviously, other studies have implemented data mining methods and techniques in combination with GIS technology. In fact, it is natural to combine these two technologies in analyzing spatial data. However, as far as this research reveals, none of these projects have presented and implemented a process model that describes how to use GIS and data mining functionalities in a complementary way. Furthermore, to the best of the author's knowledge, no previous research has been conducted into the implementation of data mining methods to extract 'knowledge' from thematic maps traditionally used for urban analysis. Another important feature of the model is that it is simple enough to encourage urban researchers and practitioners (who have no expertise in data mining, GIS and spatial statistics) to use data mining in their work. Overall, the model contributes to the general agenda of urban analysis by presenting a method for implementing advanced data-driven analysis. The KDPM for urban analysis in general, and the extended version of this model (with evolutionary algorithm) in particular, can be re-used to analyze other urban environments and the model is therefore a utilizable output of this thesis. Moreover, the model has the potential to support CIM research, which is currently a relevant research topic (this is discussed further in section 6.3.1). Chapter (4), Section (4.2) explains the details of the model.
- *The Beyoğlu Preservation Area Building Features Database:* This research produced a GIS database for the Beyoğlu Preservation Area using official thematic maps of the Beyoğlu Preservation Area provided by the Istanbul Metropolitan Municipality in the form of pdf files. These files contain information about the floorspace use in buildings, population density of the building blocks, floor-space index, historical register of buildings, slope of buildings location etc. Constructing this database from scratch was the most time-consuming part of the study. First, each of the thematic maps was separately transformed from a pdf to a drawing file using vector editor software. All the drawing files were then preprocessed and cleaned using a CAD application. Next, they were incorporated into a GIS application and combined in the form of a georeferenced GIS file with layers and the associated database. By performing Join operations some of the topological relationships between the buildings and other components of the

maps (building blocks, streets, official neighbourhood boundaries) were computed and attributed to the buildings. Finally, the database was enhanced using GIS spatial analysis tools (to calculate building footprints and a number of distance relationships for buildings with important transportation nodes and meeting points in the Beyoğlu Preservation Area) and land-price data obtained from Beyoğlu Municipality was added. As a result, the Beyoğlu Preservation Area Building Features database, which consists of 11,984 buildings and their 45 spatial and non-spatial attributes, was constructed. One of the originalities of this thesis stems from applying data mining methods to such a comprehensive GIS database, constructed from a range of actual micro-scale data representing multiple features attributed to buildings. The Beyoğlu Preservation Area Building Features Database, which was built during the course of this thesis, relies on actual and official data and will be available to the public for use in further research after the publication of this thesis. In this way, the thesis also contributes to scientific research material on the Beyoğlu Preservation Area and the Beyoğlu Preservation Area Building Features Database is also a utilizable output of this thesis. Chapter (5), Section (5.1) explains the details of the Beyoğlu Preservation Area Building Features Database.

- *Insight into the information patterns hidden in the Beyoğlu Preservation Area Building Features Database:* Implementing the KDPM for urban analysis enabled information patterns and relationships between building features in the Beyoğlu Preservation Area and its three neighbourhoods, Cihangir, Karaköy and Tarlabaşı, to be explored. This was performed by applying three different types of data mining methods and the findings were discussed, cartographically visualized in GIS and represented in the form of graphics. The Naïve Bayes Classification was applied to determine whether the category of the ground floor use was predictable using other building attributes and vice versa. The results were gathered in the form of predictive powers. By applying Association Rule Analysis the associations between the categories of ground floor use (Att.1) of the buildings and forty-four other attributes were captured, one by one. The results produced the attribute values in the Beyoğlu Preservation Area Building Features Database that occur together. Using DBSCAN clustering analysis the most significant vertical floorspace use patterns in the buildings in the Beyoğlu Preservation Area were identified. Chapter 5, Section 5.1 explains the details of this study.
- *An alternative approach to the regeneration of the Tarlabaşı neighbourhood:* In contrast to the destructive approach developed by the Istanbul Metropolitan Municipality and Beyoğlu Municipality, limited by the data available in the Beyoğlu Preservation Area Building Features Database, this research developed an alternative approach to the regeneration of Tarlabaşı that aimed to be more sensitive to the existing social and spatial characteristics of the neighbourhood. The essence of this approach lies in creating a mixed-use + mixed-user profile + mixed-income Tarlabaşı, whilst preserving the existing patterns of ground floor use in the buildings of the neighbourhood. The basis of this approach can be briefly summarized as: (1) allowing low-income local residents to be part of the 'new' Tarlabaşı, following a mixed-income principle with a tenure-type differentiation strategy, (2) enabling different social profiles to live in the

'new' Tarlabaşı, following a mixed-user profile principle with a housing differentiation strategy and (3) maintaining the original patterns of building use to preserve socio-spatial networks in the neighbourhood, following a mixed-use principle. To be more specific, a tenure-type differentiation strategy was developed to promote three types of tenure, targeting low, middle and upper-middle income groups. A business-type differentiation strategy was also introduced to enable local business types (run by local residents) remain in the neighbourhood. A housing differentiation strategy was developed to provide six types of housing (for regular families, student housing, 1-2 person households, families with children and housing for the elderly and disabled). Finally a mixed-use principle was established which would preserve the intensity of the existing types of uses in the groundf loors and some of the relationships between ground floor use and -other building attributes. All these strategic decisions led to the formulation of a set of rules, which were processed using a computational process to generate alternative ground floor use, user-profile and tenure-type allocation plans for Tarlabaşı. The computational process is explained below. This output contributes to the ongoing discussion on how to approach the problem of urban regeneration in Tarlabaşı in particular, and in inner-city contexts in general.

– *A computational process which generates allocation plans for ground floor use, user-profile and tenure-type, using GIS and data mining functionalities with evolutionary computation:* In order to implement the regeneration approach described above, this study developed a computational process that combines GIS and data mining functionalities with an Evolutionary Algorithm. In other words, the KDPM for urban analysis, which describes a semi-automated process of database formulation, analysis and evaluation, was extended to include a generative phase involving the use of an Evolutionary Algorithm. The overall process involved the successive application of Naïve Bayes classification, association rule analysis and an evolutionary algorithm to a subset of the Beyoğlu Preservation Area Building Features Database representing the Tarlabaşı neighbourhood. The input of this computational process was the existing ground floor use allocation plan of the Beyoğlu Preservation Area. First, this plan was analyzed using data mining methods to identify the original lpatterns of ground floor use. Next, this information was used to generate two set of rules: rules which would be used to allocate a new use category to empty ground floors based on the existing patterns of ground floor use in Tarlabaşı, and rules which would be used to preserve the existing allocation of uses in the ground floors of the buildings in the neighbourhood. These rules were then used for fitness measurements for an evolutionary algorithm, together with other fitness measurements (concerning user-profile and tenure-type) defined by the author and based on the regeneration approach. As a result, the algorithm transformed the existing ground floor use allocation plan in accordance with the given rules and assigned user-profile and tenure-type information for each building. In this way, a number of ground floor use, user profile and tenure-type allocation plans for Tarlabaşı were generated. During the computational process, data mining exposed the site-specific characteristics of Tarlabaşı, thus enabling a context-sensitive process to be planned. At the same time, the evolutionary computation applied within this computational process, executed the transformation, preserving the existing characteristics of Tarlabaşı as requested. In this study, the author defined the fitness measurements used in the evolutionary process. However, in a generic implementation of this computational process, the conflicting interests of the different actors involved in the transformation can shape these fitness measurements and to a certain extent, the evolutionary phase of the process can support user participation. Therefore, with further development, this process can lead to a generic model for developing more context-sensitive proposals in the course of urban regeneration processes. This implementation has also a limited contribution to the general research on how to enable user participation in developing urban interventions. Moreover, in demonstrating how to use the outputs of the knowledge discovery process through data mining in developing intervention proposals for urban regeneration, it also contributes to the data mining research domain. To the best of our knowledge, no prior research has exemplified how to make use of data mining findings whilst developing urban intervention proposals. Using these findings for fitness measurements for an Evolutionary Algorithm to produce allocation plans for ground floor use, user-profile and tenure-type is the most original contribution of this computational process. Hence, this process is also an important utilizable output of this thesis. Another significant aspect of this implementation is that it exemplifies how ICT-based analytical/ quantitative methods (i.e. the combined use of data mining and evolutionary methods) can be used to create an approach to urban planning that incorporates humanistic concerns. Chapter (5), Section (5.2) explains the details of this computational process.

- *A set of strategic urban intervention ideas/proposals for the regeneration of Tarlabaşı, developed by students:* This output was generated during the course of the Tarlabaşı Datascope workshop, which was organized to test the KDPM for urban analysis with students. The participants developed a set of strategic urban intervention proposals for the regeneration of Tarlabaşı. Limited by the availabile data in the Beyoğlu Preservation Area Building Features Database, the proposals formulated by the students exemplify how a context-sensitive alternative to the destructive urban renewal project developed by the Beyoğlu Municipality and Istanbul Metropolitan Municipality could be achieved. In this way, the workshop contributes to the general debate on the regeneration of Tarlabaşı by demonstrating how small-scale intervention strategies based on context-sensitive approaches could be developed. In addition, the workshop exemplifies how the knowledge discovery approach to urban analysis proposed in this thesis can be complemented by parametric urban analysis techniques and how the outcomes of the data mining analysis can be used in developing urban intervention proposals. It also adds to the students' knowledge by introducing advanced computational techniques for urban analysis, namely data mining and complementary methods (i.e. Network analysis and Pedestrian access / walkability analysis implemented using the Cheetah plug-in developed in Rhino-Grasshopper by Pirouz Nourian and Samaneh Rezvani). Thus, the workshop enabled the usability and utility of computational urban analysis methods to be investigated in relation to a real and contemporary urban regeneration problem. Moreover, the evaluation of the workshop by the students demonstrates that the KDPM for urban analysis aroused enthusiasm for using data mining in their work. Chapter (5), Section (5.3) explains the details of the Tarlabaşı Datascope workshop.

Having examined the particular contributions of the outcomes of the thesis, the overall scientific and societal contributions of this thesis study will now be presented:

- Knowledge discovery in databases, an interdisciplinary domain of data analysis involving methods related to artificial intelligence, machine learning, statistics and database systems, is being used in a wide range of disciplines, mainly in business analytics, health research, science and engineering, but has rarely been applied to the analysis of urban data. Therefore, the overall scientific contribution of this thesis is to provide guidance for the targeted researchers and practitioners on how to implement this relatively new approach to data analysis with urban data and use the findings to inform the development of intervention proposals for urban regeneration.
- The essential societal contribution of this thesis is the evidence that by implementing the knowledge discovery approach to urban analysis through data mining, urban analysis can become more operational in supporting the development of intervention proposals for urban regeneration. This approach enables what is termed 'relational urban knowledge' to be discovered, which can be very valuable for urban practitioners, enabling them to identify the characteristics of a given environment and evaluate how their interventions can adapt to this environment. One of the most important failures in urban intervention processes is usually ignoring the site-specific particularities of urban environments. In such cases, urban intervention projects generally produce unintentional consequences, such as the failure of physical and policy-based interventions to adapt to their environments. Using a knowledge discovery approach to urban analysis through data mining, researchers and practitioners can see patterns beyond raw data which can help them develop an insight into situations before proposing any intervention. The conflict between design and planning projects and the existing interrelations of an urban environment can be minimized in the light of the 'relational urban knowledge' that can be gathered from this environment. As exemplified in this thesis, this 'knowledge' can support architects, urban designers or urban planners whilst building more context-sensitive approaches in urban regeneration processes. Studies supported by the proposed approach can lead to better informed design and planning proposals and thus improve the quality of built environments.

The limitations concerning the implementation of the knowledge discovery approach to urban analysis through data mining developed in this thesis are reviewed in the following sections.

§ 6.2 Limitations of Implementing the Knowledge Discovery Approach to Urban Analysis through Data Mining

The implementations that were conducted validated our approach but also exposed its limitations. In this section, the limitations of the knowledge discovery approach to urban analysis through the application of data mining methods with regard to its application and operability in developing intervention proposals for urban regeneration are discussed in a critical review of the concept of the city as a 'data mine' and the model, the KDPM for urban analysis.

§ 6.2.1 A critical review of the concept of city as a 'data mine'

The concept of the city as a 'data mine' is strongly influenced by recent developments in computation science and ICT. These developments have made large quantities of data available to researchers, together with feasible methods and techniques for storing and processing this data. Cities are also enormous sources of data and information that can be collected digitally. One of the major challenges facing researchers and practitioners of urban studies is therefore to make use of this data to shape the future of cities. The concept of the city as a 'data mine' is grounded in this requirement, which is prominent in the current urban studies agenda. Although this conceptual approach is promising in terms of providing a basis for building a data-driven approach to urban analysis, design and planning, there are certain limitations and difficulties with regard to its implementation:

- Despite the impressive developments and increasing interest in data collection and analysis methods, there are still serious problems involved in accessing multi-dimensional and micro-scale urban data. This constitutes the major limitation of the concept, as it is entirely dependent on the availability of large amounts of diverse data.
- Within this thesis, the unavailability of social, demographic, cultural and time-based data represented an important limitation in terms of demonstrating the variety of ways in which the concept can enhance our knowledge of cities. This type of human-related data is essential to a full investigation of whether data mining methods can support an approach to humanistic concerns in urban planning. Furthermore, it is important to acknowledge that a large amount of information and data emerging from cities cannot be converted into a digital database, and it is this which, in fact, constitutes the most serious weakness of our conceptual approach and the KDPM for urban analysis. However, the ability of data mining methods to process temporal and non-conventional data formats such as text-mining, image-mining, audio mining, video

mining etc. suggests promising research paths which are worth testing (discussed in section 6.3.2).

- In addition, the importance of collecting, storing and sharing urban data for tracking changes in urban environments has not yet been recognized by the urban authorities in Turkey, which is data-poor in comparison to many other countries. It is extremely important to store urban data to construct and document the memory of urban space, as well as to allow for scientific research based on real data. On the other hand, caution should be exercised in terms of public and individual rights concerning the ethics and politics of data collection, storing and sharing. The problems concerning data sharing in Turkey are considerable. Privacy is always an important underlying reason for these problems, but another serious reason is the lack of any culture of open-source information and knowledge sharing. This issue has hindered this research in many ways, by blocking access to many interesting data types. This is, again, an important limitation on the applicability of this concept and model, since they are entirely data-driven. This discussion, however, is beyond the scope of this thesis. The knowledge discovery approach to urban analysis through data mining will not really be applicable in Turkey until a data collection, storing and sharing culture is established.

Nevertheless, the knowledge discovery approach to urban analysis through data mining and the associated concept and model developed in this thesis constitutes a promising basis for urban analysis, as there is a strong likelihood that these limitations will decrease over time.

§ 6.2.2 A critical review of the urban analysis model: the KDPM for urban analysis

The KDPM for urban analysis was developed on the basis of the concept of the city as a 'data mine' and aims to explore information patterns and relationships hidden in this 'data mine' by applying a knowledge discovery approach involving data mining methods and techniques. As seen in the implementation of the model in the Beyoğlu Preservation Area, the model also presents certain limitations and difficulties, mostly resulting from technical weaknesses. The limitations resulting from the KDPM for urban analysis are:

- The database formulation phase (see Figure 5.2 depicting how the KDPM for urban analysis is applied to the Beyoğlu Preservation Area), including selecting the appropriate data, pre-processing it and transforming it into the correct format for the analysis phase, can be very time-consuming. As the Istanbul Metropolitan Municipality did not provide GIS files, the database had to be created from scratch and this was very lengthy process. However, had GIS files been available, the formulation of an appropriate database to apply data mining analysis would have been much easier and quicker. Therefore, since creating a database from scratch demands so much time and labour, it does not seem feasible to implement this model in practice without sufficient human resources or the availability of GIS files for the urban environment under investigation. In addition, within the scope of this thesis, since the database preparation took so long, the range of data mining methods could not be extended in the analysis phase and only the Naïve Bayes Classification, Association Rule Analysis and DBSCAN Clustering methods could be tested.

- Despite the user-friendly data mining software, which provides a good level of technical support for analysts, selecting the appropriate data analysis technique still requires some level of expertise in data mining. This is heavily dependent on the type of data that is available and the research question under investigation. Therefore, the applicability of the KDPM for urban analysis requires some training in data mining methods and techniques by testing a variety of data. Moreover, as was the case in this thesis, expert support is needed in order to be able to decide on the methods and techniques to use with different types of data to investigate different types of questions and evaluate the outcomes.
- Most of the data mining software tailored to the analysis of spatial data is rare and barely accessible to non-professionals. These tools are mostly designed for expert users, such as geoscientists and computer scientists specializing in spatial data analysis. As previously mentioned, this thesis particularly aimed to target the community of architects, urban designers and planners who have no-expertise in spatial data analysis. The KDPM for urban analysis was therefore implemented using regular open-source data mining software (RapidMiner) with high visual quality and a user-friendly interface design. This meant that the database had to be formatted to suit the classic data mining algorithms available in the RapidMiner platform. RapidMiner demands a flat data file and this also had an impact on shaping the structure of the model.
- In applying the KDPM for urban analysis, although it is very interesting to use GIS as a tool to visualize the results of the data mining analysis, the lack of a fully automated process for linking GIS to data mining software is a major difficulty for the analyst. It is therefore necessary to create a fully automated process to enable this model to be applied easily in practice. This also represents a contribution towards the concept of CIM (elaborated in the next section) [4].

Despite these difficulties and limitations regarding the use of the KDPM in urban analysis, the future for capturing, storing and analyzing data is highly promising and there is growing scientific interest in this field. This trend provides indications for future improvements to methods, techniques and tools that may help scientists to overcome most of these limitations.

4 Work in this line of research features in Malerba et al. (2009).

§ 6.3 Future Research Paths

§ 6.3.1 City Information Modelling (CIM)

The KDPM for urban analysis mainly implements the combined use of data mining and GIS methods and techniques and was applied as a semi-automated process. In addition, the process that the model suggests was extended to include evolutionary computation in Implementation (2) and applied together with parametric urban analysis tools in Implementation (3). The experience resulting from these implementations provides some feedback on the kind of features a CIM platform could include and how a CIM platform could support urban design and planning. On the basis of these experiences, it can be anticipated that a CIM platform should allow for fully automated online data collection, data management, data storing, data analysis, data visualization and design implementation. Creating a seamless flow of information without any loss seems to be the most critical challenge in establishing a CIM platform. As we have seen, in implementing the KDPM for urban analysis, the exchange of information between data mining and GIS is handled without great difficulty by importing and exporting the data files. Online sharing of the same database could help to turn this semi-automated information flow into a fully automated process.

Figure 6.1 shows the basic steps in a computational urban design and planning process, confirming that data mining methods and techniques are applicable in the Data Analysis and Design Evaluation Phases.

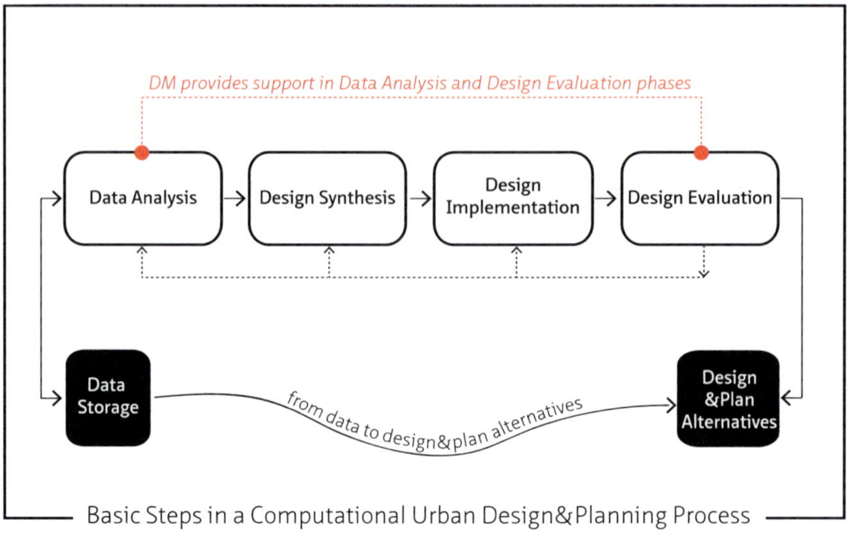

FIGURE 6.1 Basic steps in a computational urban design and planning process.

The proposed scheme shown above depicts a workflow starting with the analysis of data and ending with the generation of design and planning alternatives. This process is rarely linear and can contain loops between steps, as indicated by the black dashed lines. Different computational methods, techniques and tools can be activated in each step of the process. Data mining, GIS-based methods, topology-based methods, density-based methods and other computational methods and techniques can be activated in the data analysis step. Proceeding to the next step of design synthesis from data analysis mainly involves activating the human decision-making process, creating strategies based on the outcomes of the analysis process and general agenda. The implementation of the design or planning decisions can be established via a CAD and visual programming platform, and the design alternatives generated could once again be evaluated by implementing the same data analysis methods and techniques. Therefore, data mining can support both the Data Analysis and Design Evaluation Phases in urban design and planning processes.

A CIM platform should establish this process (i.e. Figure 6.1) by integrating various computational methods and techniques. Accordingly, the integration of data mining within these processes and the interoperability of data mining with other computational methods obviously appear to be important future lines of research. In addition, research into the use of data mining methods and techniques with various types of urban data is required in CIM research (discussed in the next sub-section).

§ 6.3.2 Towards data mining non-conventional urban data

It is highly important to acknowledge that we cannot 'mine' everything. the findings discoverable by knowledge discovery through data mining are limited by the relevant data that is collectable and available. It may be limited simply by the unavailability of relevant data (not everything can be represented in data tables, some data is inaccessible due to privacy and security issues, some is simply not up to date, etc.). Another limitation concerns the problems regarding data collection (inconsistencies in data due to incorrect collection methods), and a third may involve difficulties in organizing the data in the form of data tables. On the other hand, even if high-quality and highly-relevant data is processed using the most accurate methods, the results of the data mining are still not understandable and utilizable without domain knowledge and a clear purpose. The creativity and common sense of the humans are always the most decisive factors in interpreting the results of knowledge discovery using data mining methods and techniques and in making them utilizable.

In this thesis, data mining methods and techniques applicable to the database were implemented, which was constructed mainly from traditional thematic maps of the Beyoğlu Preservation Area. However, there are other methods and techniques that could allow the user to work with more complex types of data that cannot be structured in a data table format. It is likely that the application of such methods will be highly important and popular in urban studies in the near future.

Mining time series data (data that is collected at discrete points in time), for instance, is one of the most exciting applications in data mining and could produce very valuable results if applied to explore the ever-changing composition of cities. Furthermore, the data mining of non-conventional data gathered from cities in the form of images, texts, visual and audio recordings, etc. could also generate very interesting results. Thus, one future research path would obviously be to experiment with how this type of non-conventional urban data could be collected and mined, and therefore what type of 'knowledge' it could produce. However, methods such as text mining or image mining, which allow for the analysis of such data, remain technically challenging and this should be taken into consideration when planning future research. Some insights into applying these methods to urban analysis are given below:

- Text mining is typically used to classify or cluster large document collections such as news articles, web pages, etc. or to mine 'opinions' in questionnaires or summarised texts. The objective of text mining is to obtain useful information from unstructured data, such as paragraphs of texts. One potential application of text mining in the field of urban studies would be to mine the 'opinions' of the city dwellers on a certain subject (e.g. an urban intervention project, an architectural competition for a public building, the performance of a certain place in the city etc.) This data could be collected through a system that allows for online participation, in order to obtain a large database. Text mining by analysing opinions would lead to the discovery of subjective knowledge, which is valuable for humanistic urban studies. Moreover, it is very likely that such a text mining application would enhance user participation in urban design and planning by enabling valuable insights to be discovered from the preferences of users.

- Image mining is typically used in medical image mining, satellite image mining, face recognition, visual surveillance, etc. The objective of image mining is to produce useful information by distinguishing between images. One potential application of image mining in the field of urban studies would be to identify city dweller behaviour patterns in a certain place in the city i.e. how people interact with each other and with the physical environment. This could facilitate the ranking of certain performative aspects of these places (e.g. the success and failure of buildings or urban spots in terms of their physical and morphological configurations, potential ways of interacting with these places, etc.) This would lead to the discovery of a user-specific type of knowledge through data mining, which could constitute a very valuable input for architectural design, urban design and planning, and humanistic urban studies.
- Mining time series data concerning spatial locations (spatial time-series) is mainly used for prediction purposes, such as traffic management, atmosphere surveillance, environmental protection etc. The objective of mining time series data is to produce valuable information by investigating how the data changes over time. The application of mining spatial time series data for purposes other than prediction could also generate interesting results. For instance, one potential application would be to explore the crowdedness of urban life and how the crowdedness of certain places in the city changes at different times of the day. This application could support our understanding of the drivers of human mobility and urban vitality, enable us to compare the similarities and dissimilarities between different places in the city and discover anomalies or unexpected occurrences. Similar applications would respond to the arguments of post-structuralist approaches to urban studies mentioned in Chapter (2) and lead to a dynamic-active concept of cities instead of a static-passive concept.

In addition to testing these data mining techniques, research into how various types of urban data can be collected and processed so that data mining methods can be applied, and the post-processing of the outputs of data mining (e.g. evaluation, visualization, etc. of the results) are important topics for future research.

In the future, it is highly likely that the analysis of the massive flows of 'big data' enabled by the 'intelligent' technologies embedded into the built environment could lead to the discovery of an unprecedented type of knowledge of the interaction between places and people. This knowledge will be exceptional because it will be constructed from an analysis of data that tracks the instant behaviour of individuals in real and virtual spaces. The extraction, elaboration and utilization of this type of knowledge has the potential to provide common research ground for positivistic approaches (mostly focusing on quantitative aspects of the cities, such as formal and functional properties and applying "hard"/quantitative methods with a mathematical base) and humanistic approaches (mostly focusing on qualitative aspects of the cities, such as social, economic and cultural properties and applying "soft"/qualitative methods) in urban studies by revealing how the qualitative and quantitative dimensions of cities interact with each other. This, in turn, may offer new opportunities for fighting urban problems, and is related to the current scientific debate on whether the "new quantitative revolution[5]" is an opportunity for a rapprochement between the different concerns of positivistic and humanistic approaches to urban studies, or whether it is just a re-evaluation of the quantification of the world (see, for instance, Cresswell (2014); Johnston et al. (2014a); Johnston et al. (2014b); Wyly (2014)).

§ 6.4 Final Evaluation of the Thesis

The knowledge discovery approach to urban analysis through data mining presented in this thesis allowed for a semi-automated, data-driven analysis of an urban environment without relying on any existing theories. This approach supported the exploration of site-specific information patterns and relationships between the multiple dimensions of a micro-scale urban component i.e. the building. Although fully acknowledging that we cannot represent every aspect of a city in a database, the thesis still successfully demonstrated that a knowledge discovery approach to urban analysis through data mining can help us to develop site-specific insights into urban environments. This approach can therefore support architects, urban designers and urban planners whilst developing context-sensitive intervention proposals for urban regeneration.

In conclusion, it should be noted that this research could lead to much more exciting results if were possible to access more interesting types of data. In other words, the unavailability of social, demographic, cultural and time-based data of any type on the urban environment being studied was a serious drawback in terms of demonstrating the variety of ways in which a knowledge discovery approach to urban analysis through data mining could enrich our current knowledge of cities.

5 The period between the 1950s and 1960s, when the application of mathematical and statistical techniques to geographical data was highly popular, is described as the 'quantitative revolution' by Burton (1963). Accordingly the phrase, the "new quantitative revolution" refers to the growing interest in the application of recent quantitative methods, which are more sophisticated than those used in the 1960s.

References

1/1000 ölçekli Beyoğlu İlçesi,Kentsel Sit Alanı Koruma Amaçlı Uygulama İmar Planı. (2010). Retrieved June 12, 2012, from http://www.Beyoğlu.bel.tr/download/KENTSEL_SiT_ALANi_U.i.P.pdf

1/1000 ölçekli Beyoğlu İlçesi,Kentsel Sit Alanı Koruma Amaçlı Uygulama İmar Planı Raporu. (2010). Retrieved March 13, 2013, from http://www.Beyoğlu.bel.tr/download/Beyoğlu_imar_plan_raporu.doc

Agrawal, R., Imielinski, T., & Swami, A. (1993). Mining association rules between sets of items in large databases, *Proceedings of the ACM SIGMOD Conference on Management of Data* (pp. 207–216).

Agrawal, R., & Srikant, R. (1994). Fast Algorithms for Mining Association Rules. In Bocca, Jarke & Zaniolo (Eds.), *Proceedings of the 20th International COnference on Very Large Databases, Santiago de Chile*: Morgan Kaufmann.

Ahunbay, Zeynep. (2007). Tarihi Istanbul ve koruma kurullarindan koparilan yenileme alanlari [The renewal sites that bypass the historic Istanbul and protection boards]. *Mimar.ist*(26), 65–68.

Akin, Nur. (2008). Bir Sergi Uzerine Gorusler: Tarlabaşı Gelecegini Paylasiyor. *Mimarist*(29), 13-14. *Tarlabaşı Yenileme Projesi: Kuresel Istanbul'un Yeni Kent Siyaseti*, 8 Octobre 2008 Sess. (2008).

Akthar, F. , & Hahne, C. (2012). *RapidMiner 5 Operator Reference* Retrieved fromhttp://docs.rapidi.com/files/rapidminer/RapidMiner_OperatorReference_en.pdf

Alexander, C., Ishikawa, S., Silverstein, M., Jacobson, M., Fiksdahl-King, I., & Angel, S. (1977). *A Pattern Language: Towns, Buildings, Construction (Center for Environmental Structure)* Oxford University Press.

Alexander, C., Silverstein, M. , Angel, S. , Ishikawa, S., & Abrams, D. (1975). *The Oregon Experiment (Center for Environmental Structure)* Oxford University Press.

Alexander, Christopher. (1965). A City is not a Tree *Architectural Forum, 122*(1-2), 58-62

Alexander, Christopher. (1979). *The timeless way of building*. New York: Oxford University Press.

Alexander, Christopher. (1987). *A New Theory of Urban Design*. New York: Oxford University Press.

Allen, John, Massey, Doreen B., & Cochrane, Allan. (1998). *Rethinking the region*. New York: Routledge.

Allen, P. (1997). *Cities and Regions as Self-Organizing Systems: Models of Complexity*. London: Taylor and Francis.

Altartouria, A., & Jolmaa, A. (2013). *A Naive Bayes classifier for modeling distributions of the common reed in Southern Finland.* Paper presented at the 20th International Congress on Modelling and Simulation, Adelaide, Australia.

Appice, A., Berardi, M., Ceci, M., & Malerba, D. (2005). Mining and Filtering Multi-level Spatial Association Rules with ARES. *Foundations of Intelligent Systems Lectures on Computer Science, 3488*, 342-353.

Appice, A., Ceci, M., Lanza, A., Lisi, F. A., & Malerba, D. (2003). Discovery of spatial association rules in geo-referenced census data: A relational mining approach. *Intelligent Data Analysis, 7*, 541-566.

Appleyard, Donald. (1979). *The Environment as a social symbol: Within a theory of environmental action and perception*: Institute of Urban & Regional Development, University of California.

Aurigi, Alessandro. (2005). *Making the digital city : the early shaping of urban Internet space*. Aldershot, Hants, England ; Burlington, VT: Ashgate.

Barnes, Trevor J. (2000). Inventing economic geography in Anglo-America, 1889-1960 In E. Sheppard & T. J. Barnes (Eds.), *A companion to economic geography* (pp. 11-26). Oxford: Blackwell.

Barnes, Trevor J. (2003). The place of locational analysis: a selective and interpretive history. *Prog Hum Geogr, 27*(1), 69-95.

Barnett, V., & Lewis, T. (1994). *Outliers in Statistical Data* (3rd ed.). Chichester: John Wiley & Sons.

Batty, Michael. (1976). *Urban modelling : algorithms calibrations, predictions*. Cambridge ; New York: Cambridge University Press.

Batty, Michael. (2005). *Cities and complexity : understanding cities with cellular automata, agent-based models, and fractals*. Cambridge, Mass.: MIT Press.

Batty, Michael. (2008). Fifty Years of Urban Modeling: Macro-Statics to Micro-Dynamics. In S. Albeverio, Andrey, D., Giordano, P., Vancheri, A. (eds.) (Ed.), *The Dynamics of Complex Urban Systems: an Interdisciplinary Approach* (pp. 1-20): Physica-Verlag Heidelberg.

Batty, Michael, Axhausen, K., Fosca , G., Pozdnoukhov , A., Bazzani , A., Wachowicz, M., . . . Portugali, Y. (2012). Smart Cities of the Future. *European Physical Journal Special Topics, 214*, 481-518.

Batty, Michael, & Longley, P. A. (1994). *Fractal Cities: A Geometry of Form and Function*. San Diego, CA: Academic Press.

Behnisch, M., & Ultsch, A. (2008). Urban Data Mining Using Emergent SOM. In C. Preisach, Burkhardt, H., Schmidt-Thieme L., Decker, R. (eds.) (Ed.), *Data Analysis, Machine Learning and Applications*. Berlin, Heidelberg: Springer

Behnisch, M., & Ultsch, A. . (2009). Urban data-mining: spatiotemporal exploration of multidimensional data. *Building Research & Information, 37*(5), 520-532.

Beirao, J. N., Montenegro, N., & Arrobas, P. (2012). *City Information Modelling: parametric urban models including design support data*. Paper presented at the 2ª Conferência do PNUM Morfologia Urbana nos Países Lusófonos, Instituto Universitário de Lisboa.

Bernstein, S. J., & Mellon, W.G. . (1978). *Selected Readings in Quantitative Urban Analysis*: Pergamon Press.

Beyoğlu Ilcesi Tarlabaşı 1. Etap Yenileme Alani Yenileme Avan ve Uygulama Projesinin Hazirlanmasi ve Uygulanmasi Isi Idari Sartnamesi. (2007). Retrieved March 13, 2013, from http://www.Beyoğlubuyukdonusum.com/images/pdf/idari_sartname.pdf

Birant, D., & Kut, A. (2007). ST-DBSCAN: An algorithm for clustering spatial–temporal data. *Data and Knowledge Engineering, 60*, 208-221.

Bogorny, V. (2006). *Enhancing Spatial Association Rule Mining in Geographic Databases.* (PhD), Universidade Federal Do Rio Grande Do Sul, Porto Alegre.

Bogorny, V., Palma, A.T. , Engel, P. , & Alvares, L.O. . (2006). Weka-gdpm: Integrating classical data mining toolkit to geographic information systems *SBBD Workshop on Data Mining Algorithms and Applications, WAAMD 2006* (pp. 9–16).

Bogorny, V., & Tietbohl, A. (2006). Extending the Weka Data Mining Toolkit to support Geographic Data Preprocessing. Porto Alegre: Universidade Federal Rio Grande Do Sul Instituto De Informatica.

Boyer, Christine (1994). *The City of Collective Memory: Its Historical Imagery and Architectural Entertainments*. Cambridge: MIT Press.

Breheny, M. (1999). *Counterurbanisation and Sustainable Urban Form*. Paper presented at the Globalization, Urban Form and Governance, Delft, Faculty of Architecture: Sector Urban Renewal and Urban Management.

Breiman, Leo. (2001). Statistical Modeling: The Two Cultures. *Statistical Science, 21*(3), 199–231.

Breskvar Zaucer, L., Zupan, B., & Golobic, M. (2010). Formal Interpretation of Preference Maps: A Data Mining Approach. In Buhmann, Pietsch & Kretzler (Eds.), *Proceedings of digital landscape architecture 2010: Anhalt University of Applied Sciences* (pp. 87-99). Berlin: Wichmann

Bunge, W. (1962). *Theoretical Geography (1st edn.)*. Lund, Sweden: Gleerup.

Burasi Tarlabaşı mi?). Retrieved March 13, 2013, from http://wowturkey.com/forum/viewtopic.php?t=53830

Burton, Ian. (1963). The Quantitative Revolution and Theoretical Geography. *Canadian Geographer, VII*(4), 151-162.

Buurman, Marlies , Hulsman, Bernard , Ibelings, Hans , Jolles, Allard , Melet, Ed, & Schaap, Ton. (2006). *Eastern Harbour District Amsterdam Urbanism and Architecture*. Rottertam: NAI Publishers.

Castells, Manuel. (1996). *The Rise of The Network Society*. Oxford: Blackwell.

Ceci, Michelangelo (2005). *Naive Bayesian Learning from Structural Data.* (PhD), Università degli Studi di Bari, Italy.

Celik, M., Dadaser Celik, F., & Dokuz, A. S. (2011). Anomaly Detection in Temperature Data Using DBSCAN Algorithm *Proceedings of the International Symposium on Innovations in Intelligent Systems and Applications (INISTA)*: IEEE

Chawla, S., Shekhar, S., Wu, W.L., & Ozesmi, U. (2001). *Modeling spatial dependencies for mining geospatial data.* Paper presented at the 1st SIAM International Conference on Data Mining, Arlington, VA.

Chawla, S., Shekhar, S., Wu, W.L., & Tan, X. (2000). Spatial Data Mining: An emerging tool for policy makers. *CURA REPORTER*. Retrieved July 25, 2008, from http://www.cura.umn.edu/reporter/00-Sep/article2.pdf

Chen, J., Chen, W., Yu, J., & Yang, Z. (2011). Comparisons with Spatial Autocorrelation and Spatial Association Rule Mining *IEEE International Conference on Spatial Data Mining and Geographical Knowledge Services (ICSDM)* (pp. 32-37).

Christopoulou, K. (2009). *A Geographic Knowledge Discovery Approach to Property Valuation.* (PhD Thesis), UCL.

Cios, Krzysztof J. , Pedrycz, Witold , Swiniarski, Roman W. , & Kurgan, Lukasz A. . (2007). *Data Mining A Knowledge Discovery Approach*. New York: Springer.

Cresswell, Tim. (2014). Déjà vu all over again: Spatial science, quantitative revolutions and the culture of numbers. *Dialogues in Human Geography, 4*(1), 54-58. doi: 10.1177/2043820614525715

Cullen, G. (1961). *The Concise Townscape*. London: Architectural Press.

Demsar, U. (2006). *Data Mining of Geospatial Data: Combining Visual and Automatic Methods.* (PhD Thesis), KTH.

Dicken, P., & Malmberg, A. (2001). Firms in territories: A relational perspective. *Economic Geography, 77*, 345–363.

Dickens, P. (1981). The hut and the machine: towards a social theory of architecture. *Architectural Design, 51*(1), 32-45.

Dincer, I. (2008). Kentsel koruma ve yenileme sorunlarini ornekler uzerinden tartismak [To Discuss Urban Conservation and Renewal Problems Through Case Studies]. http://www.planlama.org/new/planlama.org-yazilari/kentsel-koruma-ve-yenileme-sorunlarini-ornekler-uzerinden-tartismak-suleymaniyeve-Tarlabaşı.html

Doel, M. A. (1999). *Poststructuralist Geographies: The Diabolical Art of Spatial Science*: Edinburgh University Press.

Domingos, P., & Pazzani, M. . (1997). On the optimality of the simple bayesian classifiee under zero-one loss. *Machine Learning, 29*(2-3), 1-30.

Doxiadis, C. A. (1968). *EKISTICS: An Introduction to the Science of Human Settlements*: Oxford University Press.

Duda, R. O., Hart, P. E., & Stork, D. G. . (2000). *Pattern Classification* (2nd ed.): Wiley.

Eldonk, J. van, & Fassbinder, H. (1990). *Flexible Fixation*. Assen: Van Gorcum.

Fayyad, U. M., Piatetsky-Shapiro, G., & Smyth, P. (1996a). From data mining to knowledge discovery: An Overview. In U. Fayyad, G. Piatetsky-Shapiro, P. Smyth & R. Uthurusamy (Eds.), *Advances in Knowledge Discovery and Data Mining* (pp. 1-30): AAAI Press.

Fayyad, U. M., Piatetsky-Shapiro, G., & Smyth, P. (1996b). From Data Mining to Knowledge Discovery: An Overview. *AI Magazine, 17*, 37-54.

Feddama, R., & Hulsbergen, E. (1991). *Grooотstedelijke werkloosheid, ideologie en realiteit*. Delft: TU Delft Publicatiebureau Bouwkunde.

Friedland, R. . (1982). *Power and Crisis in the City: Corporations, Unions and Urban Policy*. London and Basingstoke: Macmillan Press ltd.

Geddes, P. (1915). *Cities in Evolution*. London: Williams Press.

GemeenteRotterdam. (1977). *Ontwerp Structuurplan Binnen de Ruit* Rotterdam: Gemeente Rotterdam.

Gil, J., Beirão, J., Montenegro, N., & Duarte, J. (2010). *Assessing Computational Tools for Urban Design*. Paper presented at the eCAADe 2010 Conference: Future Cities, ETH Zurich.

Gil, J., Montenegro, N., Beirao, J. N., & Duarte, J. P. (2009). *On the Discovery of Urban Typologies: Data Mining the Multi dimensional Character of Neighbourhoods*. Paper presented at the eCAADe 2009 Conference, Istanbul Technical University.

Goodchild, M. F. . (2006). Afterword: From Systems to Science. In M. Kennedy (Ed.), *Introducing Geographic Information Systems with ArcGIS*: John Wiley&Sons, INC.

Graham, Stephen, & Healey, Patsy. (1999). Relational concepts of space and place: Issues for planning theory and practice. *European Planning Studies, 7*(5), 623-646. doi: http://dx.doi.org/10.1080/09654319908720542

Gray, Jim. (2005). Foreword. In I. H. Witten, Frank E. (Ed.), *Data Mining: Practical Machine Learning Tools and Techniques*: Morgan Kaufmann.

Gunay, Zeynep. (2010). Conservation versus Regeneration?: Case of European Capital of Culture 2010 Istanbul. *European Planning Studies, 18*(8), 1173-1186.

Güting, R. H. (1994). An Introduction to Spatial Database Systems. *The International Journal on Very Large Data Bases, 3*(4), 357-399.

Hall, P. (1998). *Cities in Civilisation*. London: Weidenfeld and Nicolson.

Hamilton, A., Wang, H., Tanyer, A. M., Arayici, Y., Zhang, X., & Song, Y. (2005). Urban information model for city planning. *Journal of Information Technology in Construction*(10: Special Issue From 3D to nD modelling), 55-67.

Han, J., & Kamber, M. (2001). *Data Mining: Concepts and Techniques*: Morgan Kaufmann.

Han, J., & Kamber, M. (2006). *Data mining : concepts and techniques* (2nd ed.). Amsterdam ; Boston San Francisco, CA: Elsevier; Morgan Kaufmann.

Han, J., Koperski, K., & Stefanovic, N. (1997). GeoMiner: a system prototype for spatial data mining. In J. M. Peckman, S. Ram & M. Franklin (Eds.), *Proceedings of the 1997 ACM SIGMOD international conference on Management of data* (pp. 553-556). Tucson, AZ, USA.

Hanna, S. (2007). Automated Representation of Style by Feature Space Archetypes: Distinguishing Spatial Styles from Generative Rules. *International Journal of Architectural Computing, 5*(1), 2-23.

Harloe, M. (1995). *The People's Home*. Oxford: Blackwell.

Harris, Randy. (2012). Tarlabaşı area. Retrieved March 13, 2013, from http://500px.com/photo/16512057

Harrison, C., Eckman, B., Hamilton, R., Hartswick, P., Kalagnanam, J., Paraszczak, J., & P., Williams. (2010). Foundations for smarter cities. *BM Journal of Research and Development, 54*(1).

Harvey, David. (1969). *Explanation in Geography*. London: Edward Arnold.

Harvey, David. (1973). *Social justice and the city*. London,: Edward Arnold.

Harvey, David. (1982). *The Limits to Capital*. Oxford: Blackwell

Harvey, David. (1985). *The Urbanization of Capital: Studies in the History and Theory of Capitalist Urbanization* Oxford: Blackwell.

Harvey, David. (1996). *Justice, Nature and the Geography of Difference*. Oxford: Blackwell.

Harvey, David. (2008). The right to the city. *New Left Review, 53*, 23–40.

Healey, Patsy. (2007). *Urban Complexity and Spatial Strategies: Towards a Relational Planning for Our Times* UK: Routledge in conjunction with The Royal Town Planning Institute.

Hellgardt, M. (1988). *Der Typologische Austausch*. Delft: DUP.

Hillier, B., & Hanson, J. (1984). *The Social Logic of Space* (Vol. 2). Cambridge: Cambridge University Press

Howard, Ebenezer. (1946). *Garden Cities of To-Morrow*. London: Faber and Faber (Original: 1902).

Hwang, S.W. (1996). The implications of the nonlinear paradigm for integrated environmental desig and planning. *Journal of Planning Literature, 11*(2), 167—180.

Ibrahim, Adamu M., & Bennett, B. (2014). The Assessment of Machine Learning Model Performance for Predicting Alluvial Deposits Distribution. *Procedia Computer Science*(36), 637-642.

Jacobs, Jane. (1961). *The death and life of great American cities*. New York: Random House.

Jain, A., & Dubes, R. (1988). *Algorithms for Clustering Data*. New Jersey: Prentice Hall.

Johnson-Marshall, Percy (1966). *Rebuilding Cities from Medieval to Modern Times (Original, in Italian)*: Edinburgh U.P.

Johnston, R., Harris, R., Jones, K., D., Manley., Sabel, C. E, & Wang, W. W. (2014a). Mutual misunderstanding and avoidance, misrepresentations and disciplinary politics: spatial science and quantitative analysis in (United Kingdom) geographical curricula. *Dialogues in Human Geography, 4*(1), 3-25. doi: 10.1177/2043820614525706

Johnston, R., Harris, R., Jones, K., Manley, D., Sabel, C. E, & Wang, W. W. (2014b). One step forward but two steps back to the proper appreciation of spatial science. *Dialogues in Human Geography, 4*(1), 59-69. doi: 10.1177/2043820614526818

Joint ICOMOS/UNESCO (WHC) Expert Mission Report: Historic Areas of Istanbul (Turkey) (C356). (6–11 April, 2006). Retrieved June 24, 2014, from whc.unesco.org/archive/2006/mis356-2006.pdf

Jones, Martin. (2009). Phase space: geography, relational thinking, and beyond. *Prog Hum Geogr, 33*(4), 487-506.

Jović, A., Brkić, K. , & Bogunović, N. . (2014). An overview of free software tools for general data mining. In Biljanovic, Butkovic, Skala, Golubic, Cicin-Sain, Sruk, Ribaric, Gros, Vrdoljak, Mauher & Cetusic (Eds.), *37th International Convention on Information and Communication Technology, Electronics and Microelectronics (MIPRO)* (pp. 1112-1117): IEEE.

Karthikeyan, T., & Manikandaprabhu, P. (2015). Analyzing Urban Area Land Coverage Using Image Classification Algorithms. In Jain, Behera, Mandal & Mohapatra (Eds.), *Proceedings of the International Conference on Computational Intelligence In Data Mining (CIDM), Smart Innovation, Systems and Technolgies 32* (Vol. 2, pp. 439-449). India: Springer.

Khemlani, L. (2005). Hurricanes and their Aftermath: How Can Technology Help? Retrieved 27 May, 2010, from http://www.aecbytes.com/buildingthefuture/2005/Hurricane-TechHelp_pr.html

Kononenko, I. (1993). Inductive and Bayesian learning in medical diagnosis. . *Applied Artificial Intelligence, 7*, 317-337.

Koperski, K. , & Han, J. . (1995). Discovery of Spatial Association Rules in Geographic Information Databases *Proceedings of the 4th International Symposium on Advances in Spatial Databases*: Springer-Verlag.

Kostof, S. (1991). *The City Shaped: Urban Patterns and Meanings Through History* Boston: Little, Brown and Co.

Kotsiantis, Sotiris, & Kanellopoulos, Dimitris. (2006). Association Rules Mining: A Recent Overview *GESTS International Transactions on Computer Science and Engineering, 32*(1), 71-82.

Kotu, V., & Deshpande, B. (2015). *Predictive Analytics and Data Mining: Concepts and Practice with RapidMiner*. USA: Morgan Kaufmann.

Krier, Rob. (1979). *Urban Space*. New York: Rizzoli.

Kuban, Dogan (2007, February 18 2007). Istanbul kirsal kultur baskenti [Istanbul rural capital of culture]. , *Cumhuriyet*.

Kumar, M. N., Venkatesan, Dr. , & Prabhu, D. M. (2014). Integration of Classification and Clustering for the Analysis of Spatial Data. *International Journal of Advanced Research in Computer Engineering & Technology, 3*(12), 4086-4096.

Kuok, C., Fu, A.-C., & Wong, M. (1998). Mining fuzzy association rules in databases. *SIGMOD Record, 27*, 41–46.

Kurgan, Lukasz A., & Musilek, Peter. (2006). A survey of Knowledge Discovery and Data Mining process models. *The Knowledge Engineering Review, 21*(1), 1-24. doi: 10.1017/S0269888906000737

Land, S., & Fischer, S. (2013). RapidMiner 5. Retrieved June 24, 2013, from http://docs.rapidi.com/files/academic/RapidMiner_RapidMinerInAcademicUse_en.pdf

Lefebvre, H. (1970). *The Urban Revolution*: University of Minnesota Press.

Lefebvre, H. (1970). *La révolution urbaine*. Paris: Gallimard.

Letsch, C. (2011). Tarlabaşı is Renewed. *Near East Quarterly* 2013, from http://www.neareastquarterly.com/index.php/2011/06/11/Tarlabaşı-is-renewed/?output=pdf

Letsch, Constanze. (2011). The house that TOKI built. Retrieved March 13, 2013, from http://www.Tarlabaşıistanbul.com/2011/03/the-house-that-toki-built/

Lewis, Jonathan. (2011). Tarlabaşı-Kayabasi. Retrieved March 2013, from http://jonathanlewis.photoshelter.com/gallery-image/Tarlabaşı-blog-Kayabasi-

Liu, W., & Seto, K. C. (2008). Using the ART-MMAP neural network to model and predict urban growth: a spatiotemporal data mining approach. *Environment & Planning B: Planning & Design, 35*(2), 296 – 317.

Lynch, K. (1960). *The Image of the City* United States of America: MIT Press.

Lynch, K. (1981). *A Theory of Good City Form*. Cambridge, MA: MIT Press.

Malerba, D., Esposito, F. , Lanza, A. , Lisi, F.A. , & Appice, A. (2003). Empowering a GIS with inductive learning capabilities: The case of ingens. *Journal of Computers, Environment and Urban Systems, 27*, 265–281.

Malerba, D., Lanza, A., & Appice, A. (2009). Leveraging the Power of Spatial Data Mining to Enhance the Applicability of GIS Technology. In H. J. Miller & J. Han (Eds.), *Geographic Data Mining and Knowledge Discovery* (Second ed.). New York: CRC Press.

Marshall, Stephen. (2004). *Streets and Patterns: The Structure of Urban Geometry*: Routledge.

Marshall, Stephen. (2009). *Cities Design and Evolution*. Abingdon, Oxon: Routledge.

Massey, D. (1992). Politics and space/time. *New Left Review, 196*, 65–84.

Massey, D. (1998). *Power-geometries and the politics of space-time*. Hettner-Lecture. Department of Geography, University of Heidelberg, Heidelberg.

May, M., & Savinov, A. A. (2003). Spin!-an enterprise architecture for spatial data mining. In V. Palade, R. J. Howlett & L. C. Jain (Eds.), *KES, Lecture Notes in Computer Science* (Vol. 2773, pp. 510–517): Springer, Berlin.

Miller, H. J. (2004). Geographic Data Mining and Knowledge DiscoveryHandbook of Geographic Information Science. In J. P. Wilson & A. S. Fotheringham (Series Eds.): Blackwell. Retrieved from http://www.geog.utah.edu/%7Ehmiller/research.html.

Miller, H. J., & Han, J. (2001). Geographic data mining and knowledge discovery, An overview. In H. J. Miller H. J. (Ed.), *Geographic data mining and knowledge discovery*: Taylor & Francis.

Moholy-Nagy, S. (1968). *The Matrix of Man*. London: Pall-Mall.

Možina, M., Demšar, J., Kattan, M. , & Zupan, B. (2004). Nomograms for visualization of naive Bayesian classifier *Proceedings of the Principles and Practice of Knowledge Discovery in Databases Conference (PKDD-2004)* (pp. 337-348). Pisa.

Mukhlash, I., & Sitohang, B. (2007). Spatial Data Preprocessing for Mining Spatial Association Rule with Conventional Association Mining Algorithms *Proceedings of the International Conference on Electrical Engineering and Informatics Institut Teknologi* (pp. 531-534). Bandung, Indonesia

Mumford, L. (1961). *The City in History*. New York: Harcourt, Brace, Jovanovich.

Nijkamp, P. (1980). *New Developments in multidimensional geographical data and policy analysis* Paper presented at the Paper presented ath the Colloquium on Theoretical and Quantitative Geography, Cambridge. ftp://zappa.ubvu.vu.nl/19800011.pdf

Norberg-Schulz, Christian. (1980). *Genius Loci: Towards a Phenomenology of Architecture*: Rizzoli.

Nourian, Pirouz. (2013). CONFIGURBANIST. Retrieved September 12, 2014, from https://sites.google.com/site/pirouznourian/configurbanist

O'Sullivan, David, & Unwin, David. (2003). *Geographic Information Analysis* New Jersey: John Wiley&Sons Inc.

Park, Robert E. , Burgess, Ernest W. , & McKenzie, Roderick D. . (1925). *The City* The University of Chicago Press.

Peca, I., Fuchs, G., Vrotsou, K., Andrienko, N., & Andrienko, G. (2012). Scalable Cluster Analysis of Spatial Events. In K. Matkovic & G. Santucci (Eds.), *Proceedings of the International Workshop on Visual Analytics* (pp. 2-6): The Eurographics Association.

Perez-Gomez, Alberto. (1983). *Architecture and the Crisis of Modern Science*. Cambridge, Massachusetts: MIT Press.

Phelps, N., & Waley, P. (2004). Capital versus the districts: A tale of one multinational company's attempt to disembed itself. *Economic Geography, 80*, 191–215.

Portugali, Juval. (2006). Complexity Theory as a link between space and place. *Environment & Planning A, 38*(4), 647-664.

Portugali, Juval. (2011). *Complexity, cognition and the city*. Heidelberg ; New York: Springer.

Portugali, Juval. (2012). Complexity Theories of Cities: Achievements, Criticism and Potentials. In H. M. J. Portugali, E. Stolk, E. Tan (Ed.), *Complexity Theories of Cities Have Come of Age: An Overview with Implications to Urban Planning and Design*. Heidelbeg: Springer.

Price, David. (1994). Projects 1981 - 1991. *Urban Design, 2014*(52: Gordon Cullen).

Qi, F., & Zhu, A. (2003). Knowledge discovery from soil maps using inductive learning. *International Journal Geographical Information Science, 17*(8), 771-795.

Quinlan, J. (1993). *C4.5: Programs for Machine Learning*. San Francisco, CA, USA: Morgan Kaufmann Publishers.

Reffat, R. (2010). *A Decision Support System of Discovering Architectural Patterns using Data Mining*. Paper presented at the Design Decision Support Systems.

Report of the Joint UNESCO World Heritage Centre/ICOMOS Reactive Monitoring Mission to the Historic Areas of Istanbul World Heritage Site (8 -13 May 2008). Retrieved June 24, 2014, from whc.unesco.org/document/100746

Resmi Gazete. (2005). Law on the protection and Revitalization of Deteriorated Historical and Cultural Immovable Assets through Renovation and Regeneration, *Resmi Gazete*.

Roberts, P. (2004). The Evolution, Definition and Purpose of Urban Regeneration. In P. Roberts & H. Sykes (Eds.), *Urban Regeneration: A handbook: 9-37*. London, Thousand Oaks and New Delhi: Sage Publications.

Rowe, C., & Koetter, F. (1978). *Collage City*. Cambridge: The MIT Press.

Sahli, Nabil, & Jabeur, Nafaa. (2010). Knowledge Discovery and Reasoning in Geospatial Applications. In M. M. Gaber (Ed.), *Scientific Data Mining and Knowledge Discovery Principles and Foundations* (pp. 251-269): Springer.

Santhisree, K., Damodaram, A., Appaji, S., & NagarjunaDevi, D. (2010). Web Usage Data Clustering using Dbscan algorithm and Set similarities. In B. Werner (Ed.), *Proceedings of the International Conference on Data Storage and Data Engineering* (pp. 220-224). Bangalore, India: IEEE Computer Society.

Sassen, Sassika. (2011). Talking Back to Your Intelligent City. Retrieved 1 May, 2013, from http://whatmatters.mckinseydigital.com/cities/talking-back-to-your-intelligent-city,

Shekhar, S., Evans, M. R., Kang, J. M., & Mohan, P. (2011). Identifying patterns in spatial information: A survey of methods. *Wiley Interdisciplinary Reviews: Data Mining and Knowledge Discovery, 1*(3), 193-214.

Shekhar, S., Gandhi, V., Zhang, P., & Vatsavai, R. R. (2009). Availability of Spatial Data Mining Techniques. In A. S. Fotheringham & P. A. Rogerson (Eds.), *The Sage Handbook of Spatial Analysis*. London: Sage Publications.

Shekhar, S., Zhang, P., Huang, Y. , & Vatsavai, R. R. (2003). Trends in Spatial Data Mining. In H. Kargupta & A. Joshi (Eds.), *Data Mining: Next Generation Challenges and Future Directions*: AAAI/MIT Press.

Sitte, Camillo. (1945). *The Art of Building Cities: Building According to its Artistic Fundamentals*. New York: Reinhold (Original: 1889).

Sökmenoğlu, A., & Çağdaş, G. (2006). Transformations created by ICKT on the architectural design and its education. *ITU A/Z Journal, 3*(1-2), 37-52.

Sökmenoğlu, A., Çağdaş, G., & Sarıyıldız, S. (2010). Exploring the Patterns and Relationships of Urban Attributes by Data Mining. In L. H. Gerhard Schmitt, Luc Van Gool, Frédéric Bosché, Remo Burkhard, Suzanne Colemann, Jan Halatsch, Michael Hansmeyer, Silke Konsorski-Lang, Antje Kunze et al. (Ed.), *Future cities: 28th eCAADe Conference Proceedings, 15-18 September 2010* (pp. 873-881). ETH Zurich, Switzerland: ETH Zurich.

Sökmenoğlu, A., Çağdaş, G., & Sarıyıldız, S. (2011). Application of Data Mining In Micro-scale Urban Feature Analysis. In T. Cheng, P. Longley, C. Ellul & A. Chow (Eds.), Proceedings of the 11th International Conference on GeoComputation, 20-22 july 2011 (pp. 154-160). University College London, UK: University College London.

Sökmenoğlu, A., Çağdaş, G., & Sarıyıldız, S. (2011a). A Multi-Dimensional Exploration of Urban Attributes by Data Mining. In P. Leclercq, Heylighen, A., and Martin, G. (Ed.), *Designing together - CAADFutures 2011, Proceedings of the 14th International conference on Computer Aided Architectural Design, 4-8 July 2011* (pp. 333-349). Liege, Belgium: Les Éditions de l'Université de Liège.

Sökmenoğlu, A., Çağdaş, G., & Sarıyıldız, S. (2012). Exploring Relationships of an Urban System: BeyoğluProceedings of the International Planning History Society Conference "Cities, nations and regions in planning history", 15-18 July 2012. Sao Paulo, Brasil: Faculty of Architecture and Urbanism, University of Sao Paulo. Retrieved from http://www.fau.usp.br/15-iphs-conference-saopaulo2012/abstractsAndPapersFiles/Sessions/30/Sökmenoğlu.pdf.

Sökmenoğlu, A., & Sönmez, N. Onur (2013). Exploring Reciprocal Relationships of Land-Uses in a Historical Mixed-Use Quarter of Istanbul. In R. Stouffs & S. Sarıyıldız (Eds.), *Computation and Performance: 31st eCAADe Conference Proceedings, 18-20 September 2013* (Vol. 1, pp. 301-310). Delft, The Netherlands: eCAADe and Delft University of Technology Faculty of Architecture.

Spriergegen, Paul D. (1965). *Urban Design: The Architecture of Towns and Cities* New York: McGraw-Hill.

Stahle, A., Marcus, L., & Karlström, A. (2007). Place Syntax Tool—GIS Software for Analysing Geographic Accessibility with Axial Lines *New Developments in Space Syntax Software* (pp. 35–42).

Stojanovski, Tan. (2013). *City information modeling (CIM) abd urbanism: blocks, connections. territories, people and situations.* Paper presented at the SimAUD'13, San Diego, CA, USA.

Stouten, Paul. (1995). *Urban Renewal in Transition*. Delft: Publicatiebureau Bouwkunde.

Stouten, Paul. (2010). *Changing Contexts in Urban Regeneration: 30 Years of Modernisation in Rotterdam*. Amsterdam: Techne Press.

Streets of Tarlabaşı Istanbul. (2012). Retrieved March 2013, from http://www.spreephoto.de/wp-content/uploads/2012/05/streets-of-Tarlabaşı-istanbul.jpg

Sumathi, N., Geetha, R., & Bama, S. S. (2008). Spatial Data Mining - Techniques Trends And Its Applications. *Journal of Computer Applications, 1*(4), 28-30.

Sunley, Peter. (2008). Relational Economic Geography: A Partial Understanding or a New Paradigm? *Economic Geography, 84*(1), 1-20.

Tafuri, M. (1976). *Architecture and Utopia: Design and Capitalist Development*. Cambridge, MA: MIT Press.

Takagi, H. (2001). Interactive Evolutionary Computation: Fusion of the Capacities of EC Optimization and Human Evaluation. *IEEE, 89*(9), 1275–1296.

Tan, Pang-Ning , Steinbach, Michael , & Kumar, Vipin (2005). *Introduction to Data Mining* Boston, MA, USA Addison-Wesley Longman Publishing Co., Inc.

Tang, H., & McDonald, S. (2002). *Integrating GIS and Spatial Data Mining Technique for Target Marketing of University Courses.* Paper presented at the Symposium on Geospatial Theory, Processing and Applications, Ottowa.

Thompson, G. . (2003). *Between hierarchies and markets: The logic and limits of network forms of organization*. Oxford, U.K.: Oxford University Press.

Thrift, Nigel (1999). Steps to an Ecology of Place. In A. J. S. P. Massey D (Ed.), *Human Geography Today* (pp. 295–323). Cambridge: Polity Press.

Thrift, Nigel (2002a). The Future of Geography. *Geoforum, 33*, 291-298.

Thrift, Nigel, & French, S. (2002b). The automatic production of space. *Transactions of the Institute of British Geographers, 27*(3), 309–335. doi: doi: 10.1111/1475-5661.00057

Tobler, W. R. . (1979). Cellular Geography. In Gale & Olsson (Eds.), *Philosophy in Geography*. Dordrecht, Reidel.

Tschumi, B. (1996). *Architecture and Disjunction*. Cambridge, MA: MIT Press.

Verhein, F. , & Chawla, S. (2006). Mining spatio-temporal association rules, sources, sinks, stationary regions and horoughfares in object mobility databases *Database Systems for Advanced Applications* (pp. 187-201).

Verma, M., Srivastava, M., Chack, N. , Diswar, A. K., & Gupta, N. (2012). A Comparative Study of Various Clustering Algorithms in Data Mining. *International Journal of Engineering Research and Applications (IJERA), 2*(3), 1370-1384.

VROM-Raad. (1999). *Stad en Wijk: verscheillen maken kwaliteit. Visie op de stad*. Den Haag: VROM-Raad.

Wagner, Otto. (1988). *Modern Architecture: A Guidebook for His Students to This Field of Art (Texts & Documents)*. Los Angeles: Getty Research Institute.

Wirth, Louis (1938). Urbanism as a Way of Life. *The American Journal of Sociology, 44*(1), 1-24.

Witten, I. H., & Frank, E. (2005). *Data Mining: Practical Machine Learning Tools and Techniques*: Morgan Kaufmann.

Wyly, Elvin. (2014). The new quantitative revolution. *Dialogues in Human Geography, 4*(1), 26-38. doi: 10.1177/2043820614525732

Yang, Z., Ju, F., & Shao, B. (2012). Research on Integration of Spatial Data Mining and GIS Based on Component Technology. In G. Lee (Ed.), *Advances in Computational Environment Science Selected papers from 2012 International Conference on Environment Science (ICES 2012), Australia, Melbourne, 15-16 January, 2012* (pp. 161-167). Berlin Heidelberg: Springer

Appendices

Appendix A Urban Studies Timeline

URBAN STUDIES TIMELINE	
1	**First Ordnance Survey map, the 1-inch Map of Kent – 1801** Urban mapping, and mapping as a general means of representing urban phenomena, is one of the most influential urban analysis techniques in the history of urban studies. In the UK, the Ordnance Survey was authorized by the Treasury in 1841 to produce town plans and by 1892 urban Britain had been mapped on a scale sufficient to show such details as the size of a doorstep, as explained by Joyce (2003) and Murdoch (2006). Mapping techniques enabled urban space to be visualized in completely new ways, which, in a certain sense, made it more tangible but also oversimplified it. Thus, the various entities, complex processes and relationships between them, which create urban space, were rendered on paper. Early urban visualization technologies specifically directed the planning professional's attention towards topographical rather than topological space. As suggested by Murdoch (2006), the use of maps not only allowed for a 'natural' and 'neutral' appreciation of urban space but also introduced a certain formality into understanding spatial relations: the study of the city as a formal composition of physical entities, as an analysis of urban morphology.
2	**"The Art of Building Cities: Building According to its Artistic Fundamentals", book by Camillo Sitte - 1889** The first seminal textbook on urban design (Cuthbert, 2006), written by architect Camillo Sitte. The publication of the book marks the beginning of a new period in the field of city planning. Camillo Sitte was against the functionalist modern style of urban design, its methods such as the "gridiron system, the radial system, and the triangular system" (Sitte, 1889) and its emphasis on designing in favour of the automobile. Sitte (1889) instead proposed to observe the design principles that can be found in the streets and buildings of medieval cities. Cuthbert (2006, p. 56) argues that he proposed a contextual approach to the study of urban form, which was often argued to embody the arguments of medieval urbanism and seen as "a retreat into historism". Contextualism, originating in the Vienna School, adopts a form-based approach, since its philosophy is built up from urban forms. Known as an architectural discourse that opposes rationalism, contextualism debates on the impossibility of creating new urban forms, since all urban forms are already present. (Cuthbert, 2006, p. 56). Contextualism propose to study "historically defined typologies" and use these design principles to plan cities, and they strongly criticize "the sterile zoning practices of state-sponsored regulation" (Cuthbert, 2006, p. 56).
3	**The "Linear City Concept" by Arturo Soria y Mata – 1892** The first modern town planning vision, introducing the idea that the whole city must be planned or designed as a building.
4	**"Modern Architecture", book by Otto Wagner – 1896** This book introduces what is "modern", a rational vision of architecture and cities in contrast to historicism. Deeply opposed to the vision of contextualism, rationalism is grounded on functionalism and argues that history has little importance while creating new urban forms, since these have to be designed in accordance with the new social agendas (Cuthbert, 2006, p. 56). Cuthbert (2006, p. 56) argues that the conflicting approaches of Camillo Sitte and Otto Wagner towards the design of the Vienna city centre symbolises the two different visions, which dominated the 20th century.
5	**The "Garden City Concept" by Ebenezer Howard – 1898** The concept of garden cities is introduced for the first time in the book by Howard entitled "To-morrow: A Peaceful Path to Real Reform". Later on, in 1902, the book is published again as" Garden Cities of Tomorrow". The book is a major reference and had a great effect on planning practice: many "garden cities" have been constructed all around the world. According to Oudenampsen (2013) the concept of the garden city is basically "a solution for the urban crisis that followed the agricultural depression in the late 19th century". It is a utopian city proposal, combining the qualities of urban and rural life; "There are in reality not, as is constantly assumed, two alternatives – town life and country life – but a third alternative, in which all the advantages of the most energetic and active town life, with all the beauty and delight of the country, may be secured in perfect combination." (Howard, 1946, p. 46). Howard's proposal not only concerned the organization of the physical form of cities but also outlined a new socio-economic system; "it was a third socio-economic system, superior both to Victorian capitalism and to bureaucratic, centralized socialism" (Peter Hall & Ward, 1998, p. 25). Nevertheless, according to Cuthbert (2006, p. 246), Garden City has to be seen as an urban design proposal, since it is mainly concerned with the urban form. Howard's proposal was an ideal model for a city of 1,000 acres with 32,000 inhabitants, surrounded by an agricultural land of 5,000 acres. Factories were on the outer ring of the town and connected to the city centre by a railway line. The garden city concept promoted land-use zoning and the functional separation of everyday activities.

>>>

URBAN STUDIES TIMELINE	
6	"Une Cite Industrielle, a modernist utopian city design proposal" by Tony Garnier – 1904 A design proposal for an ideal industrial city with 35,000 inhabitants, introducing socialist ideas and the functional separation of daily activities.
7	Establishment of the Royal Town Planning Institute in London – 1914 The profession of town planning is institutionalized; town planning is recognized as a new and specific area of expertise.
8	"Cities in Evolution: an introduction to the town planning movement and to the study of civics", book by Patrick Geddes – 1915 Patrick Geddes explains the foundations of urban growth on the basis of Darwin's theory of natural selection. His ideas "became established through the imposition of a top-down 'organic' order in city and regional planning associated with the work of Patrick Abercrombie, one of Geddes' best-known followers" (Batty & Marshall, 2009, p. 552). Abercrombie's approach was "rooted in 'physicalism', a perspective that assumed social problems could be solved by manipulating the physical built environment." (Batty & Marshall, 2009, p. 552). According to Batty and Marshall (2009), Geddes interpreted evolution as "primarily driven from within an organism, rather than by external agency (as in natural selection) and he emphasized the importance of cooperation (on a scale ranging from cells to societies), which ultimately triumphed over competition. According to this view, cities were the ultimate expression of social union and evolution" (Geddes & Thomson, 1889, 1911) (as cited in Batty and Marshall, 2009, p. 556).
9	The "Frankfurt School", or Institute for Social Research, founded by a group of Marxist intellectuals in Germany – 1923 The "Frankfurt School" is one of the most influential institutions in the development of Marxist theory and its leading figures included Max Horkheimer, Theodor Adorno, Walter Benjamin and Jürgen Habermas. Cuthbert (2006, p. 58) explains that "the Frankfurt school was essentially concerned with the 'deep structures' driving society", combining the philosophical principles of Marxism and Freudian social physiology. Cuthbert (2006) argues that the work of Theodore Adorno, introducing the concept of the "culture industry", and Walter Benjamin had a significant influence on the research concerning the study of city form and urban life. According to Cuthbert (2006), the most important contribution originating from the Frankfurt School was the idea that the forms found in art and architecture should be understood as a "code language for processes taking place in society" (Held, 1980, p. 80) (as cited in Cuthbert, 2006, p. 58).
10	"Radiant City (La Ville Radieuse) Masterplan", first introduced in 1924 and published in 1933 by Le Corbusier A vision of an ideal city, introducing high-density housing typologies and standardization in accordance with modernist ideals.
11	"The City", book by Robert E. Park, Ernest W. Burgess and Roderick D. McKenzie, members of the urban research programme (urban sociology) at the University of Chicago Department of Sociology - 1925 This book presents a theory of urban ecology which proposes that cities are just like natural ecosystems which are ruled by the principles of evolution (as defined by Darwin) and the most important principle which shapes cities is the force of competition. The Concentric Zone model proposed by Park and Burgess illustrates the spatial organization of urban areas, explaining that the cities would take shape according to the forces of competition for land and resources. And this will inevitably cause a social and spatial differentiation.
12	"The Hochhausstadt (a utopian high-rise city)", designed by Ludwig Hilberseimer – 1927 The Hochhausstadt (high-rise city) designed by the urban planner Ludwig Hilberseimer, who was also teaching at the Bauhaus in Dessau, is a utopian city plan. It is a materialization of the idea of "the metropolis as a molar machine", "involving large-scale social, technical and economic systems intercommunicating with architectural elements..." (Hays, 1992, p. 173) (as cited in Cuthbert, 2006, p. 61). The plan proposes different levels of transportation for car and pedestrian traffic and "identical high rise structures organized in uniform blocks along the grid created by transportation routes" ("Paper Architecture: Visionary Structures on the Printed Page," 2011).
13	First CIAM Congress (The International Congresses of Modern Architecture): founding members included Le Corbusier – 1928 The architectural principles of the Modern Movement are formalized and spread via the CIAM Congress. Very briefly, the main argument of the Modern Movement is "the view of architecture as a mediator for improving the world and fighting social problems through the design of buildings and through urban planning" ("CIAM's La Sarraz Declaration," 1928).
14	4th CIAM Congress, entitled "The Functional City" – 1933 The idea of applying modern methods of architectural analysis and planning to the whole city is introduced and discussed during the 4th CIAM Congress, entitled "The Functional City". This was a new approach to planning which challenged the dominant orthodox vision. Thirty-four cities are analyzed and solutions to their urban problems are proposed. The essential influence on cities is determined as "functional order": "the chaotic division of land, resulting from sales, speculations, inheritances, must be abolished by a collective and methodical land policy" ("CIAM's La Sarraz Declaration," 1928). The Athens Charter, published in 1943 by Le Corbusier, includes the outcomes of the Congress and contains observations, studies and remedial measures for planning cities.

>>>

URBAN STUDIES TIMELINE

15	**"Urbanism as a way of Life", article published in the American Journal of Sociology by Louis Wirth, one of the leading urban sociologists and an influential figure in the Chicago School of Sociology – 1938** The primary focus of this article is a sociological definition of the city which introduces sociological proposals for academic urban research, focusing on population size, density, and demographic heterogeneity. Wirth's approach to social and spatial relationships is bidirectional; "...physical mechanisms of the city are not isolated phenomena unrelated to the city as a social entity, but are affected by and affect the urban mode of life." (Wirth, 1938, p. 20)
16	**"Country of London Plan" by Sir Leslie Patrick Abercrombie and John Henry Forshaw – 1943** The official plan produced to guide the development and reconstruction of London after World War II, which combines the principle of communal organization with the principle of functional differentiation.
17	**Establishment of the Regional Science Association - 1954** The Regional Science Association is founded in December 1954 by the economist Walter Isard, together with a group of academics from economics, geography, city planning, political science and rural sociology. Their approach is termed regional science; "a discipline (which) concerns the careful and patient study of social problems with regional or spatial dimensions, employing diverse combinations of analytical and empirical research'' (Isard, 1975, p. 2). This definition is elaborated further: "Regional science is primarily [a] social science. It is concerned with the study of man and (the) spatial forms which his continuous interaction with, and adaptation to, the physical environment take. Regional science concentrates its attention upon human behaviour and institutions; and, unlike geography, it is much more confined to scientific analyses of social processes, giving much less attention to spatial detail and associated physical and biological elements.'' (Isard, 2003, p. 188) (as cited in Donaghy, 2014, p. 82). Walter Isard's three important books (Location and Space Economy, in 1956, Industrial Complex Analysis and Regional Development, in 1959, and, Methods of Regional Analysis, in 1960), and the establishment of the Journal of Regional Science in 1958 had great importance for the recognition of the Regional Science and the Regional Science Department in the University of Pennsylvania was established in 1958 (Boyce, 2004). According to Donaghy (2014, p. 82), regional science mainly focus on "social problems with regional or spatial dimensions" and this make it an applied science. Moreover the uniqueness of regional science is argued to derive from its emphasis on the use of ''diverse combinations of analytical and empirical research'' (Isard, 1975, p. 2) (as cited in Donaghy, 2014, p. 82). Boyce (2004) argues that the social sciences are essential for regional science but it is also an interdisciplinary field, drawing on work from various disciplines including engineering, the physical sciences, and even the humanities.
18	**Cumbernauld, a new town designed in Scotland, UK – 1956** One of the most important new towns planned according to the Modernist New Town vision in the UK and known to be one of the least-loved examples of post-war planning. In 1993, DoCoMoMo listed it as one of the sixty key monuments of post-war architecture.
19	**First Urban Design Conference, held at the Graduate School of Design at Harvard University – 1956** "Urban design" was first used as a distinctive term during the First Urban Design Conference, held at the Graduate School of Design at Harvard University. The conference announcement invited the participants to explore "the role of the planner, architect, and landscape architect in the design and development of cities." (R. Marshall, 2009)
20	**CIAM Congress ends – 1959** The last CIAM congress, held in the Netherlands.
21	**"The Image of the City", book by Kevin Lynch – 1960** A very important book on the evaluation of city form. The criterion of imageability; "quality in a physical object which gives it a high probability of evoking a strong image in any given observer" (Lynch, 1960, p. 9) is introduced and its potential value in urban design is demonstrated by Lynch. Another concept introduced by the book is "the legibility of the city", defined as "the ease with which [a city's] parts can be recognized and can be organized into a coherent pattern" (Lynch, 1960, pp. 2-3). The quality of "legibility" not only helps citizens to find their way around, but is also important in ensuring their "emotional and physical well-being". The book argues that the underlying elements of city form that create "the identity and structure" of the city are paths, edges, nodes, landmarks and districts and that in order to plan imageable cities it is important for urban designers to understand how people perceive these elements.
22	**Archigram, formed at the Architecture Association in London by six architects and designers, Peter Cook, Warren Chalk, Ron Herron, Dennis Crompton, Michael Webb and David Greene – 1960** Archigram created projects that proposed a radical and utopian perspective on city planning by developing a robust critique of the Modern vision. Between 1960 and 1974, it developed iconic utopian projects such as such as The Plug-in City, The Walking City and The Instant City.

>>>

URBAN STUDIES TIMELINE	
23	"The City in History: Its Origins, Its Transformations, and Its Prospects", by Lewis Mumford – 1961 The book is one of the best known books on the history of the city but is limited to western culture. Focusing on the forms and functions of the city and the purposes that have emerged from this, Mumford (1961, p. 11) claims that "If we would lay a new foundation for urban life, we must understand the historic nature of the city, and distinguish between its original functions, those that have emerged from it, and those that may still be called forth". According (Mumford, 1961) the historical development of man and the forms and functions of the city are associated and Cuthbert (2006) argues that this perspective implies a chronological way of thinking about the city form.
24	"The Death and Life of Great American Cities", book by Jane Jacobs – 1961 This book is one of the most influential books to criticize the oversimplified study of urban phenomena and the Modern town planning vision. Jacobs (1961) claims that modern planning theory had failed to grasp the complex and unpredictable interactions that occur between differing activities in urban space. It offers a robust critique of zoning activities, proposing a mix of diverse uses to create vibrant and successful neighbourhoods. It was through Jane Jacobs's book in particular that the idea of urban complexity was popularized and linked to the complexity theories and/or the science of complexity began to emerge in the 1960s, in the field of physics. Jacobs proposes to take inspiration from complexity theories, specifically the concept of 'organized complexity' in dynamic systems, in order to understand urban complexity and diversity. Jacobs had a great influence on the generation of new planning theorists, since system analysts as well as urban planners were interested in urban studies. Her approach opened up new methods for urban studies, such as modelling urban systems using new computer technologies.
25	"The Concise Townscape", book by Thomas Gordon Cullen – 1961 Introduces the concept of the "townscape", proposing a new vision of urban design which places great emphasis on visual perception and how this can influence the physical environment and human experience. The idea behind the concept of "townscape" is to approach urban environments as a form of landscape. Unlike the Modernist vision, the importance of designing public space is strongly emphasized.
26	"Theoretical Geography", book by William Bunge - 1962 Theoretical Geography first appeared in 1962 and it is claimed to be "perhaps the seminal text of the spatial-quantitative revolution." (Cox, 2001, p. 71) (cited in Goodchild, 2008, p. 1) The book contends for the benefits of "quantification and formal reasoning in statistical inference" (Goodchild, 2008). Bunge pioneered methods and models that were later refined via GIS (geographical information systems). Goodchild (2008, p. 13) states that the "central place theory had evolved into location-allocation", and "optimal routing and geodesics" gave rise to "corridor location". Moreover, his ideas on "spatial similarity" led to "spatial autocorrelation metrics" and "the fields of spatial statistics and geostatistics" (Goodchild, 2008, p. 13). The period between the 1950s and 1960s is described as a 'quantitative revolution' by Burton (1963). It marked the beginning of the use of numerical techniques for analysis and description in geography and spatial research. Burton (1963) argues that this is "a radical transformation of the spirit and purpose" of geography. The quantitative revolution started with the birth of spatial science, which first appeared in America. American spatial science began in around 1955 and is associated with the Universities of Washington and Iowa, and later Chicago, Northwestern, Michigan and Ohio (Barnes, 2000, 2003). At the time, the field of geography was in crisis and accused of not being scientific, mainly because it was perceived as overly descriptive. Searching for a nomothetic geography and encouraged by developments in computing science, geographers started to make use of mathematical formulations taken from various disciplines. They borrowed "gravity" and "entropy-maximizing models" from physics, "urban land use models" and "social physics" from sociology and land economics, and "network and graph theory and the analysis of topological forms incorporated into transportation studies" from geometry (Pooler, 1977) (as cited in Barnes, 2003, p. 94). Furthermore, over time they also started to develop their own specific mathematical approaches to geography (e.g. spatial autocorrelation) and geographical statistics (spatial statistics-geostatistics) emerged as an offshoot of statistics.

>>>

URBAN STUDIES TIMELINE

27	**"Locational Analysis in Human Geography", book by Peter Haggett – 1965** Haggett's book draws heavily on the works of the leading scientists of the location theory: Johann Von Thünen (the concentric model of agricultural land use), Walter Christaller (the central place model), Alfred Weber (theory of the location of industries) and August Lösh (nested central place hierarchy). Haggett defines locational analysis as "a mathematically and numerically based study and explanation of location and spatial distribution drawing upon the traditions of location theory within economics" (Haggett, 1965, p. 13), and "the 'neglected geometrical tradition' of geography" (Barnes, 2003, p. 71; Haggett, 1965, pp. 15-16). He introduced the idea of mathematical model building in geography as "an ideal representation of reality in order to demonstrate certain of its properties" (Haggett, 1965, p. 19). His book is focused on a model type which "simplifies the complexities of location and spatial distribution using mathematical forms of representation and connects to the 'properties' of reality by using analytical techniques" (Barnes, 2003, p. 71). Haggett's book is seen as very important in providing a framework for the new techniques and aims of geographical study (Jones, 1956) (cited in Barnes, 2003, p. 152). His ideas and the model building activities were incorporated into the discipline of planning (see, for example, Models in Planning by Lee in 1973 and Urban and Regional Models in Geography and Planning by Wilson in 1964) (Charlton, 2008). The book is considered to be an early intervention in the attempt by geography to restyle itself as a spatial science (Charlton, 2008).
28	**"Urban Design: The Architecture of Towns and Cities", book by Paul D. Spriergegen - 1965** Cuthbert (2006) argues that the idea that cities develop over time is essential for this work and this implies a chronological way of thinking about the form of the city. The interpretation of the history of cities is given in a "diachronic and atheoretical" fashion and the work mainly focus on "the architectural (and landscape architectural) object" (Cuthbert, 2006, p. 27).
29	**"A City is not a Tree", article by Christopher Alexander – 1965** A robust critique of the modern town planning vision for being unable to grasp the full complexity of existing urban patterns. Comparing the structural organization of man-made cities with natural cities by abstracting them into structures, Alexander demonstrates that artificial cities are all designed as tree-like structures. He proposes a "semilattice structural organization as a potentially much more complex and subtle structure than the tree", as a guiding organizational principle for planning cities (Alexander, 1965, p. 382).
30	**"Rebuilding Cities from Medieval to Modern Times", book by Percy Johnson Marshall – 1966** An examination of how existing cities can be rebuilt based on Modernist principles.
31	**"Matrix of Man: Illustrated History of Urban Environment", book by Moholy-Nagy – 1968** The purpose of this book is to represent "the evolution of the fundamental types of urban form in terms of mythicoreligious, cosmological, social and economic history" (Condit, 1969, p. 253). This book adopts a perspective that focuses on form and function as the essence of explaining cities. Cuthbert (2006, p. 29) defines it as a typological approach towards the study of urban form, which views the "historical process as a series of typologies", as an investigation of the reasons behind the emergence of different typologies of urban form and their functional evolution over time.
32	**"Geographic Information System for Regional Planning", article by Roger Tomlinson – 1968** The first known use of the term "Geographic Information System" (GIS) was introduced by Roger Tomlinson, who developed the first GIS for the CLI (Canada Land Inventory). Tomlinson (1968) defines GIS as a computational system for the storage and manipulation of land data. Batty, Dodge, Jiang, and Smith (1998) argues that since the late 1950s, digital computing have dramatically shaped the fields architecture and urban planning. "In urban planning, the process of computerization began earlier with municipal information systems and land-use transportation modelling, whereas dramatic developments in urban research began in the late 1980s and 1990s in terms of tools for visualizing and representing information, particularly in the form of geographic information systems (GIS) with desktop packages such as ArcView and MapInfo becoming standard, almost routine practice" (Batty et al., 1998, p. 1). Geographical Information Systems (GIS) can essentially be seen as the synthesis of cartography, statistical analysis and database technology. GIS play a key role in making use of spatial data by providing a means of generating, modifying, managing, analyzing and visualizing spatial data. The key contribution of GIS, above and beyond the functions provided by other forms of software such as cartographic mapping or computer aided design packages, lies in the analysis of spatial data (Lloyd, 2010).
33	**"Ekistics: the science of human settlements", book by C.A. Doxiadis - 1968** Ekistics is the "science of human settlements" as described by Doxiadis. Doxiadis (1968) defines the whole range of human settlements as "a very complex system of five elements - nature, man, society, shells (i.e. buildings) and networks", and interrelationships involving these five elements form human settlements: "It is a system of natural, social, and man-made elements which can be seen in many ways - economic, social, political, technological, and cultural. For this reason only the widest possible view can help us to understand it." (Doxiadis, 1970, p. 1)

>>>

URBAN STUDIES TIMELINE	
34	**"Explanation in Geography (1969)", book by David Harvey – 1969** A very important book with a central emphasis on the importance of scientific explanation in geographical studies. This book is about "the ways in which geographical understanding and knowledge can be acquired and the standards of rational argument and inference that are necessary to ensure that the process is reasonable" (Harvey, 1969, p. viii). Harvey underlines the importance of the theory and argues that the lack of identity in geography is mainly due to the lack of a theoretical body of knowledge; "Without theory we cannot hope for controlled, consistent and rational explanation of events. Without theory we can scarcely claim to know our own identity" (Harvey, 1969, p. 486) Although his main concern is methodology not philosophy, he refers to philosophers of science, a field of knowledge mostly ignored by geographers. Explanation in geography is seen as a "pioneering exploration of 'scientific method' for geography and its philosophical underpinnings" and it is also "one of the first substantive geographical engagements with social science" (Johnston, 2008a, p. 31).
35	**"General System Theory: Foundations, Development, Applications", book by Ludwig von Bertalanffy – 1968** Systems theory is: "the transdisciplinary study of the abstract organization of phenomena, independent of their substance, type, or spatial or temporal scale of existence. It investigates both the principles common to all complex entities, and the (usually mathematical) models which can be used to describe them." (Heylighen & Joslyn, 1992, paragraph 1) Heylighen and Joslyn (1992) argue that the theory of systems developed by Von Bertalanffy (1969) was both a "reaction against reductionism and an attempt to revive the unity of science": "He emphasized that real systems are open to, and interact with, their environments, and that they can acquire qualitatively new properties through emergence, resulting in continual evolution. Rather than reducing an entity (e.g. the human body) to the properties of its parts or elements (e.g. organs or cells), systems theory focuses on the arrangement of and relations between the parts, which connect them into a whole (cf. holism). This particular organization determines a system, which is independent of the concrete substance of the elements (e.g. particles, cells, transistors, people, etc.). Thus, the same concepts and principles of organization underlie the different disciplines (physics, biology, technology, sociology, etc.), providing a basis for their unification." (Heylighen & Joslyn, 1992, paragraph 2)
36	**"La Revolution Urbaine (The Urban Revolution)", book by Henri Lefebvre – 1970** Lefebvre (1970) criticizes simplistic and physicalist methods of analyzing and designing cities that do not consider their social and economic dimensions. He emphasises that urban epistemology plays no role in contemporary urbanism and sees it as a major hindrance to solving urban problems.
37	**Demolition of the Pruitt–Igoe housing blocks – 1972** The demolition of the Pruitt–Igoe housing blocks in St Louis, Missouri is announced as the "death of modernism" by Charles Jenks. The Pruitt–Igoe housing blocks, designed in accordance with the CIAM ideal of the "Functional City", later faced serious problems of poverty, crime, and segregation.
38	**"La question Urbaine" (The Urban Question: Marxist Approach), book by Manuel Castells - 1972** Castells explores the relationships between spatial forms and economic processes such as administration, consumption, exchange and production. Castells' main argument is that urban structures are produced and maintained by political and economic interests. His perspective constructs a more sophisticated adaptation of Marxist theory within urban theory and design, defined as the birth of Urban Spatial Theory by Cuthbert (2006).
39	**"Models in planning: an introduction to the use of quantitative models in planning", book by Colin Lee – 1972** Urban Planning was soon affected by the "quantitative revolution" and the rise of spatial science. Colin Lee was one of the first authors to introduce mathematical modelling into planning in his well-known book "Models in Planning". He explains his motivation as the increasing interest in the use of quantitative models in urban and regional planning since the mid 1960s. The book is aimed at students and professionals working in the field of planning who have a limited knowledge of mathematics and statistics and introduces the contribution that models can make to the work of the planner. The principles underlying the design and use of models and the mathematical context of modelling are examined in detail. Basic forms of the most frequently used spatial models are introduced, namely "linear models", "gravity models", the "Lowry model" and "optimizing models". The objective of the book, as defined by Lee (1972, p. ix), is "to provide an introduction to some of the techniques which are being used to construct urban and regional models for students and practicing planners with a limited numerate background." The focus of the book is not mathematical analysis, but understanding the structure of the models.
40	**"Social Justice and the City", book by David Harvey – 1973** Harvey (1973, p. 9) underlines the relevance of social justice in "the application of spatial and geographical principles to urban and regional planning". The "interpenetration between social processes and spatial form" is deeply discussed and space is defined as a "social dimension".

>>>

URBAN STUDIES TIMELINE	
41	"The Oregon Experiment", book by Christopher Alexander, Murray Silverstein, Shlomo Angel, Sara Ishikawa, and Denny Abrams - 1975 This is the third volume in the series introducing the Pattern Language theory and describes a community-based planning process for the University of Oregon. This experimental planning process gave rise to a new theory of architecture and planning, namely pattern language.
42	"Urban modelling: algorithms calibrations, predictions", book by Michael Batty - 1976 The subject of this book is urban modelling. The field of urban modelling is "concerned with designing, building and operating mathematical models of urban phenomena, typically cities and regions" (Batty, 1976). Batty (1976) describes urban modelling as the logical outcome of a systems approach to planning. (Batty, 1976, p. xx) lists the motivations for the development of urban models as such: -"understanding urban phenomena through analysis and experiment" -"helping planners, politicians and the community to predict, prescribe and invent the urban future" -"demonstrating the limitations of theory and the potential of simulation in education"
43	"Architecture and Utopia: Design and Capitalist Development", book by Tafuri – 1976 Written by one of the best known critics of modern architecture, this book adopts a Marxist approach to architecture and its relation to the city and society. The main focus is the "identification of the tasks which capitalist development has taken away from architecture" (Tafuri, 1976, p. ix) It argues that the practice of architecture has become an instrument of the capitalist system and thus cannot have a social mission and possess transformative power.
44	"A Pattern Language: Towns, Buildings, Construction", book by Christopher Alexander, Sara Ishikawa and Murray Silverstein from the Center for Environmental Structure at Berkeley, California, with Max Jacobson, Ingrid Fiksdahl-King and Shlomo Angel – 1977 The second volume in the series introducing Pattern Language theory, a new theory of architecture and planning providing a catalogue of patterns as solutions to common design problems. The pattern language is introduced as a guiding language to enable anyone to design a building, or components of a built environment. Alexander et al. (1977) explains their ideas as such: "The core idea behind the formulation of the theory is that people should design their own houses, streets and communities, since most of the wonderful places in the world were not made by architects but by the people". J. Price (1999) argues that patterns as a method caught the imagination of the object-oriented programming community and the book was particularly influential in architectural computation.
45	"Collage City", book by Colin Rowe and Fred Koetter – 1978 Cuthbert (2006, p. 32) argues that the idea of "urban design history as a process of assembling and integrating fragments and the assumption of discontinuity rather than order" began with Collage City by Rowe and Koetter (1978), which questions the study of urban form without referring to "the social and psychological processes that inform it". It represents utopia as metaphor and the Collage City as the solution for fighting the disintegration of modern architecture (Rowe & Koetter, 1978).
46	"Timeless Way of Building", book by Christopher Alexander – 1979 The first volume in the series introducing the Pattern Language theory. The idea of complexity in urban research (urban complexity on a theoretical level) is emphasized and the simplistic way of thinking about cities and planning is criticized.
47	"Urban Space", book by Rob Krier – 1979 This book criticizes new military technologies, the ideal cities of the 20th century, and 19th century industrial building for destroying the traditional concept of urban space and its structure. From an in-depth analysis of the morphological and typological elements of traditional urban space, Krier operationalizes this knowledge to suggest a classification of urban space and introduces this work as a guide for urban planners and urban designers. The concept of urban space is defined on the basis of its formal characteristics, without imposing aesthetic criteria (Krier, 1979).
48	"The Environment as a social symbol", book by Donald Appleyard – 1979 "The Environment as a social symbol" draws attention to the importance of the symbolic meanings embedded in the built environment . Cuthbert (2006) views this as an important move beyond the functional approach to the symbolic content of the environment. Cuthbert (2006) argues that this book played an important role and by 1980 cultural aspects of space began to be considered.

>>>

49	**"Genius Loci: Towards a Phenomenology of Architecture", book by Christian Norberg-Schulz – 1979** This book is one of the most important books on architectural theory to be heavily influenced by Heidegger's phenomenology. Norberg-Schulz introduces phenomenology as a way out of the impasse created by analytical 'scientific' concepts unable to describe the qualitative totalities of cities. He introduces his book as a first step towards a phenomenology of architecture; a philosophy which understands architecture in existential terms. He criticizes the 'scientific' agenda of urban planning and architects and its disregard for the "everyday life-world" basic properties of human existence and "spirit of places (genius loci)", stating that "the conquest of the existential dimension is the main purpose of the book". (Norberg-Schulz, 1980, p. 5). Norberg-Schulz also emphasises that the book is concerned with the psychic implications of architecture, rather than its functional dimension.
50	**"A Theory of Good City Form", book by Kevin Lynch – 1981** The main focus of this book is the "interrelation of human purpose and the city form" (Lynch, 1981, p. 343). Through the history of cities, Lynch identifies three distinct types of normative theory- "cosmic, machine and organic " - each of which he finds either problematic or limited when applied to contemporary society (Larice & Macdonald, 2012, p. 229). Instead of these analogies, he proposes a normative theory of "good city form" based on five aspects of "performance", namely "vitality", "sense", "fit", "access" and "control", together with two "meta-criteria" – "efficiency" and "justice" – which are used to evaluate these dimensions.
51	**The Hut and the Machine: towards a social theory of architecture, article by Peter Dickens – 1981** Cuthbert (2006, p. 41) observes that Dickens adopts a "Marxist perspective on architecture as social closure and ideological production". The book claims that architecture and urban planning are a form of social production and they have to be understood in terms of their interactions with other forms of social production.
52	**"The Limits to Capital", book by David Harvey - 1982** This book is argued to be an important contribution for the studies concerning what Harvey terms "historical-geographical materialism", which can be seen as an extension of Marxist studies (Johnston, 2008b). The books seeks "to integrate the financial (temporal) and geographical (global and spatial) aspects to accumulation within the overall framework of Marx's argument in a holistic and dialectical rather than segmented and analytical way." (Harvey, 2006, p. x). "Dealing with the spatial aspects of countering the problems of overproduction and underconsumption" (Johnston, 2008b, p. 941), this book is seen by Cuthbert (2006) as one of the important works of "new urban studies" in the late 1970s and early 1980s: The task of New Urban Studies was to "reconstruct urban social theory concerned with urban planning as part of the state apparatus because of its role in the social control and regulation of urban space" (Cuthbert, 2006, p. 9).
53	**"Great Planning Disasters", book by Peter Geoffrey Hall – 1982** Peter Hall provides an in-depth analysis of the great planning disasters of the 1970s by evaluating the decisions of professional bureaucrats, community activists, and politicians involved in these processes. As he explains, the book does not claim to explain how to avoid new disasters, but demonstrates that planning involves complex relationships between different stakeholders and thus a different form of knowledge to architectural knowledge is required for decision-making and city planning.
54	**"The Social Logic of Space", book by Bill Hillier, Julienne Hanson – 1984** An attempt to "synthesize the entire field of urban design" (Cuthbert, 2006, p. 6), space syntax theory is introduced as a representation of a syntax for the morphic language of human spatial organization (Hillier & Hanson, 1984). It is defined by the authors as both a theory of the constructability of spatial order (a theory of morphology) and a theory of how abstract descriptions may be retrieved from it (a theory of abstract knowability) (Hillier & Hanson, 1984). Space syntax theory and methodology provide tools to describe and quantitatively measure spatial configurations of urban space. Street layout spatial structures are represented as axial maps with axial lines i.e. the longest lines of sight that cover all the open spaces in the study area. The syntactical properties of space (Hillier & Hanson, 1984), such as "integration", "connectivity", and "intelligibility", are calculated by means of the "axial map". "Space organization and social encounter patterns are morphic languages" and "the construction of a social theory of space organization therefore becomes a question of understanding the relations between the principles of pattern generation in both" (Hillier & Hanson, 1984, p. 50). According to the authors, the most original contribution of the space syntax theory is to expose the essential relationships between the social, economic and environmental performance of places and their spatial configuration. Moreover they also argue that space syntax research demonstrated that spatial layout directly affects movement, land use, safety, land value and carbon emissions (http://www.spacesyntax.com/).

>>>

55	**"Architecture and the Crisis of Modern Science", book by Alberto Perez-Gomez – 1983** The crisis in modern science, as described by Perez-Gomez, derives from the; "simultaneous beliefs in the possibility of obtaining rational and fixed solutions to all aspects of human knowledge and the subjectivity of human perceptions...the Cartesian split between objective truth and subjective opinion, between body and mind, and rejection of myth, poetry, and art as legitimate and primary forms of knowledge...This acute and unprecedented division between science and art, reason and poetry, architecture and engineering...produced evils brought about by the transformation of architectural theory into an instrument of technological domination that excluded metaphysics" (Perez-Gomez, 1983, pp. 314-315) (cited in Mark, 1984, p. 900). Perez-Gomez (1983) criticizes functionalism and formalism in architecture for dividing the objective and subjective realms of human reality and claims that even Marxist approaches believe that structure can be separated from meaning. He argues that only phenomenology, with its rediscovery of the primacy of perception, has been capable to overcome the fundamental problem of architecture, namely the loss of existential meaning (Perez-Gomez, 1983).
56	**"The City of Collective Memory: Its Historical Imagery and Architectural Entertainments", book by Christine Boyer - 1994** Boyer criticizes the "perspective of white, middle-class architects and planning professionals who worry in a depoliticized fashion about a city's competitiveness in the global restructuring of capital" (Boyer, 1994, p. 4) and explores the possibility of revitalising the public realm by capturing the individual and collective memories of communities, questioning whether the individuals involved in the process would become more politically active (Hodder, 1996). The importance of Boyer's book lies in its emphasis on the significant role of communities in the making of urban space.
57	**"The Potential of Glasgow City Centre", report by Gordon Cullen – 1985** The Glasgow project can be described as an application of the "Townscape" theory to the city of Glasgow. This approach assumes that the way to increase the economic competitiveness of a city lies in enriching its visual appeal. The aim of the Glasgow project was to attract investment into the city of Glasgow, which was in competition with Edinbugh, by increasing its allure and reputation (D. Price, 1994). The solution proposed by Cullen was to "devise a programme of "implosion" initiated by raising the visual and spatial attraction of the centre to a point where it would become the only logical place to relocate and redevelop" (D. Price, 1994).
58	**"The Urbanization of Capital: Studies in the History and Theory of Capitalist Urbanization", book by David Harvey - 1985** In this Marxist reading of urbanization shaped by capitalism, Harvey's main objective is ''to bring spatial relations and geographical phenomena explicitly into the main corpus of Marxian thought and to trace the effects of such an insertion upon our interpretations of fundamental concepts'' (Harvey, 1985, p. 34). The "semiotic nature of the built environment and the relationship between labour, capital and the urban landscape" is also emphasized through the book; "Capital represents itself in the form of a physical landscape created in its own image, created as use values to enhance the progressive accumulation of capital..." (Harvey, 1985, p. 25) (cited in Cuthbert, 2006, p. 69).
59	**First IJCAI workshop on Knowledge Discovery in Databases - 1987** Data mining which originates from machine learning and statistics is a well-established discipline within the fields of artificial intelligence (AI) and knowledge engineering (KE) (Coenen, 2011, p. 25). The first IJCAI (International Joint Conference on Artificial Intelligence) workshop on Knowledge Discovery in Databases was organized in 1987 at Detroit MI, USA. Data mining started to be more popular by the 1990s (Coenen, 2011). Conferences of data mining including the ACM SIGKDD annual conference in 1995 and the European PKDD and Pacific/Asia PAKDD conferences in 1997, significantly increased the popularity of this discipline among researchers (Coenen, 2011). One of the most widely used definitions of KDD is proposed by Fayyad, Piatetsky-Shapiro, and Smyth (1996a, p. 30) as the "nontrivial process of identifying valid, novel, potentially useful, and ultimately understandable patterns in data". According to Fayyad et al. (1996a, p. 28), knowledge discovery refers to "the overall process of discovering useful knowledge from data", and data mining is the key component and refers to a "particular step in this process", namely the "application of specific algorithms to extract patterns (models) from data".
60	**"A New Theory of Urban Design" by Christopher Alexander – 1987** Defines a specific theory of urban design, introducing "organicness" not as an analogy but as a structural quality of old towns. The sense of wholeness found in the organic old towns is identified as the departure point for this new theory of urban design. Alexander (1987, p. 3) argues that: "The task of creating wholeness in the city can only be dealt with as a process. It cannot be solved by design alone...the process above all is responsible for wholeness...not merely the form". The book explores the establishment of a new theory to deal with creating "a suitable process for the city to become whole again." Alexander (1987, p. 3).

>>>

URBAN STUDIES TIMELINE

61 "The Informational City: Information Technology, Economic Restructuring, and the Urban-Regional Process", book by Manuel Castells – 1989

The restructuring of the capitalist system and new technologies related to collecting and sharing information has transformed cities in a dramatic way and Castells coins a new term for this, namely "the informational city". The concept of the "informational city" is defined as the spatial expression of a new form of social organization that is made up of technology, cultural information and social information, as well as their interaction (Castells, 1989). The concept is not directly related to information technologies.

62 "The City Shaped: Urban Patterns and Meanings Through History", book by Kostof – 1991

The focus of this work is the history of the "vital contest between socio-economic change" (Kostof, 1991, p. 41) and the physical form of the city. He underlines the importance of the socio-cultural meanings of physical urban patterns: "Without the force of tradition and a consolidated social agenda, unsupervised city-making will succumb to disorder" (Kostof, 1991, p. 64).

63 "Politics and Space/Time", article by Doreen Massey – 1992

Massey introduces her own alternative view of space, namely relational space. Moving away from "the notion of society as a kind of 2D or 3D slice that moves through time" and rejecting the "dichotomous dualism" of space/time, she places an emphasis on the "inseparability of time and space and on the need to think in terms of space/time" (Massey, 1992 p. 84). She conceptualizes space as "constructed out of interrelations, as the simultaneous coexistence of social interrelations and interactions at all spatial scales, from the most local level to the most global." (Massey, 1992 p. 80). She also rejects the unidirectional approach of conceptualizing space as purely a form of social relation, arguing that the "spatial is socially constituted...and the social is spatially constituted too." (Massey, 1992 p. 70). She refers to the concepts of "spatial order and chaos" and "unintended consequences" in terms of spatial arrangements reminiscent of the terminology of complexity science, evolution and emergence in a Darwinian sense. Her definition of "relational space" and the conceptual framework for space/time is one of the most important and earliest contributions to the general discourse of "relational space" and post-structuralism.

64 "Complexity: The Emerging Science at the Edge of Order and Chaos", book by Mitchell Waldrop - 1992

Waldrop introduces complexity as an entirely new and still developing branch of scientific thinking that aims to move beyond the linear, reductionist approach that has dominated science since Newton (Waldrop, 1992). Complexity science focuses on the study of "complex self-organizing adaptive systems" that are made up of many independent agents who interact and adapt to each other and to their environment (Dare, 2000). Complex systems produce the phenomenon of emergence; "a system behaving as more than the sum of its parts" (Gershenson, 2008). As defined by Gershenson (2008, p. preface), a complex system is a system "in which elements interact and affect each other so that it is difficult to separate the behaviour of individual elements". Examples of complex systems are "a cell composed of interacting molecules", "a brain composed of interacting neurons", "a market composed of interacting merchants", "an ant colony", "the Internet", "a city", "an ecosystem", "traffic", "weather and crowds" Gershenson (2008). Gershenson (2008, p. preface) argues that "in each of these systems, the state of one element partly depends on the state of the other elements and, in turn, affects them. This makes it difficult to study complex systems using traditional linear and reductionist approaches." Complexity science provides new tools and methods for studying complex systems, thus re-framing and enlarging our understanding of the world. Gershenson (2008) notes that the status of complexity as a science is still being debated but, nevertheless, the study of complexity incorporates scientific features and has been also used as a problem-solving method. Similarly, Haken (2012, p. 19) mentions that "current complexity theory is not a monolithic theory" but rather a toolkit which includes various methods for dealing with complex systems.

65 First Congress for the New Urbanism in USA – 1993

The Congress for the New Urbanism was founded in 1993 by a group of architects (Peter Calthorpe, Andrés Duany, Elizabeth Moule, Elizabeth Plater-Zyberk, Stefanos Polyzoides and Dan Solomon). Their mission is "to change the practices and standards of urban design and development to support healthy regions and diverse, complete neighbourhoods" (http://www.cnu.org/history). They underline the importance of physical design as a supporting framework for planning, recognizing that "physical solutions by themselves will not solve social and economic problems" (http://www.cnu.org/history). They are committed to "reestablishing the relationship between the art of building and the making of community, through citizen-based participatory planning and design" ("Charter of the New Urbanism," 2001). New Urbanism describes the fundamental qualities of urban places in diverse scales (from regional scale to the scale of individual buildings). The importance of walkability, human-scale neighbourhoods, mixed-use, sustainability and public space are particularly underlined.

>>>

URBAN STUDIES TIMELINE	
66	"Fractal Cities: A Geometry of Form and Function", book by Michael Batty and Paul Longley - 1994 Fractal Cities by Michael Batty and Paul Longley is one of the first books to introduce complexity science into urban research. The book is based on a view of the world as complex: "chaotic, discontinuous, irregular in its superficial physical form but (...) beneath this first impression lies an order which is regular, unyielding and of infinite complexity." (Batty & Longley, 1994, p. v). The focus of the book is the application of fractal geometry in cities, arguing that "cities are fractal in form and that much of our pre-existing urban theory is a theory of the fractal city" (Batty & Longley, 1994, p. vi).
67	"Justice, Nature and the Geography of Difference", book by David Harvey – 1996 This book defines the foundational concepts for defining space-time, place and nature and argues that our understanding of them is related to the production of geographical differences. Harvey's basic argument is that "spatial and ecological differences are constituted by and constuitive of socio-ecological and political-economic processes" (Harvey, 1996, p. 6). The book represents a relational approach to geography in which the fundamental concepts of geography are represented through social practices, in relation to each other. For Harvey (1996), the relational perspective defines discrete spaces and places as "dynamic configurations of relative "permanences" within the overall spatio-temporal dynamics of ecological processes" (Harvey, 1996, p. 294). For example, he believes that "learning to see the world from multiple positions - if such an exercise is possible - then becomes a means to better understand how the world as a totality works" (Harvey, 1996, p. 284). He argues for "dialectic relationalism" (Sunley, 2008, p. 15); "While I accept the general argument that process, flux, and flow should be given a certain ontological priority in understanding the world, I also want to insist that this is precisely the reason why we should pay so much attention to what I will later call the 'permanences' that surround us and help solidify and give meaning to our lives. Furthermore, while it is formally true that everything can be reduced to flows... we are in daily practice surrounded by things, institutions, discourses and even states of mind of such relative permanence and power that it would be foolish not to acknowledge those evident qualities." (Harvey, 1996, pp. 7-8).
68	The School of Geography at the University of Leeds hosts the first international conference on 'GeoComputation' – 1996 The School of Geography at the University of Leeds hosted the first international conference on 'GeoComputation' in 1996. The term "Geocomputation" was first used by Openshaw and Abrahart (1996, p. 665) as "the process of applying computing technology to geographical problems". It is an interdisciplinary area employing non-conventional data analysis techniques (different than conventional statistical methods) in the field of spatial data analysis. Moreover, advanced computational techniques such as cellular automata, agent-based systems, genetic algorithms and neural networks are frequently used in the field of Geocomputation.
69	"Architecture and Disjunction", book by Bernard Tschumi – 1996 Tschumi's book is an attempt to build a new definition for architecture based on its relations to "everyday life, movement and action" by applying the principles of deconstruction. He argues that "deconstructing a given program meant showing that the program could challenge the very ideology it implied" and in this way "one may be able to design the conditions that will make it possible for this nonhierarchical nontraditional society to happen." (Tschumi, 1996, p. 199).
70	"The Rise of The Network Society", book by Manuel Castells – 1996 The first book in a trilogy entitled "The Information Age: Economy, Society and Culture" by sociologist Manuel Castells, introducing the concept of networks as the main driver of social life: "Our exploration of emergent social structures across domains of human activity and experience leads to an over-arching conclusion: as an historical trend, dominant functions and processes in the Information Age are increasingly organized around networks. Networks constitute the new social morphology of our societies, and the diffusion of networking logic substantially modifies the operation and outcomes in processes of production, experience, power, and culture. While the networking form of social organization has existed in other times and spaces, the new information technology paradigm provides the material basis for its pervasive expansion throughout the entire social structure." (Castells, 1996, p. 500).
71	First international journal of Urban Design; Urban Design International - 1996 Urban Design International is the first truly international network for researchers and practitioners involved in the multi-disciplinary tasks of urban design and management (http://www.palgrave-journals.com/udi/index.html).

>>>

URBAN STUDIES TIMELINE	
72	"Cities and Regions as Self-Organizing Systems: Models of Complexity", book by Peter Allen – 1997 Cities and Regions as Self-Organizing Systems by Peter Allen (1997) was one of the pioneering works involved in introducing complexity science into urban research. The book applies complex systems theory to the spatial evolution of patterns of human settlement and economic activity (Prigogine, 1997). Prigogine (1997) argues that the science of complexity overcomes the splitting of science into 'two cultures' (Snow, 1964) and Allen's work is an important contribution to the new dialogue between human sciences and concepts which originated in the natural sciences. The kinds of models described in the book are represented as an exploration of the strategic possibilities potentially open to the system. Allen (1997, p. 291) emphasizes that "diversity, flexibility and pluralism are in general to be encouraged, and that plans which might seriously reduce these, should be examined and tested very thoroughly before being adopted."
73	"Power-geometries and the politics of space-time: Hettner-Lectures", book by Doreen Massey – 1998 The relational approach adopted by Massey (1998 p. 28) takes space as space to be "a product of the interrelations running through different spatial scales", as a "sphere of the possibility of multiplicity" which is "never closed, never fixed, and always in the process of becoming, as relations unfold."
74	"Cities in Civilization", book by Peter Hall – 1998 A book on urban history which takes form and function as the essence of explaining cities. P. Hall (1998) explores cities in order to understand the forces that make them creative, particular and exceptional at a particular time in history, generalizing "the commonality these places share".
75	The non-representational theory of geography, introduced and elaborated by Nigel Thrift in various works such as Spatial Formations (1996) and Steps to an Ecology of Place - 1999 Nigel Thrift is one of the most influential figures working mainly on the reconceptualization of space within geographical theory under the post-structuralist influence. Following the work of Deleuze and Foucault, he developed a non-representational theory which advocates exploring "relational rather than representational understandings" (Thrift, 1999) in urban studies. This idea is based on an acceptance of the view that "we cannot extract a representation of the world because we are slap bang in the middle of it, co-constructing it with numerous human and non-human others for numerous ends" (Thrift, 1999, pp. 296-297). As Foucault and Deleuze's post-structuralist way of thinking is concerned with what lies beyond the text and focuses on embodied practices, object worlds and their relational structure, Thrift's post-structuralist geography focuses on the multiplicity of relations emerging from 'our' embodiment in space and time, beyond stabile representations of topographical space.
76	"Towards an Urban Renaissance", report by Richard Rogers – 1999 Towards an Urban Renaissance is a report written by the Urban Task Force UK, chaired by architect Richard Rogers. Their mission was to identify strategic principles for sustainable urban development to guide the governmental planning authorities in England (Rogers, 1999). Urban task force specifically addressed three challenges: "the decline of regional inner-city areas and communities"; "the official prediction of the need for 4 million additional households"; "suburban sprawl consuming greenfield sites at an alarming rate, causing social and economic decline within inner-city areas" (Rogers, 1999). The report offers strategic advice for solving these problems and particularly emphasizes the importance of design and design-led urban regeneration processes, the involvement of communities in decision-making processes, planning at neighbourhood level, improving non-car transport etc. (Rogers, 1999)
77	"Space-time, 'science' and the relationship between physical geography and human geography", article by Doreen Massey – 1999 Massey claims that complexity theory ("an unresolved paradigm") may have serious impacts on the future of cities. Thrift (2002a, p. 295) states that one of the most interesting expectations concerning the contribution of complexity theory is mentioned by Massey (1999a, 2000) namely that complexity theory has the potential to create a new rapprochement between human and physical geography, which are becoming divided.
78	"Poststructuralist Geographies: The Diabolical Art of Spatial Science", book by Marcus Doel – 1999 This book adopts a post-structuralist approach and introduces the concept of "pointillism". The conventional cartographic representations, as and conceptualizations of urban space in the form of classification maps, which are used as the basis for urban analysis, do not extend beyond observing the current state of the system in question. Doel (1999) describes this method of urban analysis as the mapping of surface phenomena into regular classification units and defines it as a "pointillist" approach, based on the illusion of urban features as points, which ignores the relational nature of urban space; "...just as in geography, the fundamental illusion is the autonomy and primacy of the point" (Doel, 1999, p. 32). With regard to pointillism, Doel (1999) criticizes the practice of enumerating the properties and attributes of various spatial entities in order to map surface phenomena into regular units of classification. In Doel's view, this kind of thinking creates a superficial quality by clinging to the surface of what actually takes place (Doel, 1999).

>>>

URBAN STUDIES TIMELINE	
79	"The Future of Geography", article by Nigel Thrift in Geoforum No. 33 – 2002 Thrift observes that ICT brings new geographical concepts and possibilities; "The world is becoming doubly geographical.. I now work a lot on the social impacts of new telecommunications technologies. What is striking there is how the geographical data and techniques needed to produce and track such telecommunication systems (the kind of data and techniques used by GIS and GPS, and the like) is itself becoming a part of the production of new and fast growing geographies, from the myriad of interconnections of the world-wide web to the new possibilities of "hyper coordination" arising from wireless technologies like mobile phone or radio frequency identification tags. In turn, these information geographies are producing new geographical possibilities..." (Thrift, 2002a, p. 294).
80	"Hurricanes and their Aftermath: How Can Technology Help?" article by Khemlani – 2005 CIM (City Information Modelling), as a concept, first appeared in 2005, described by Khemlani (2005) as; "an extension of the BIM concept to neighbourhood and city level that is able to capture all the critical data relating to a city's geographical location, topology, major roads, bridges, buildings etc. in an intelligent format, creating a highly accurate and detailed digital replica which can be subjected to sophisticated analysis and simulations to support more holistic decision-making". CIM does not exist yet as a platform but is a conceptual idea that describes an adaptation of the BIM (Building Information System) for cities.
81	"Cities and Complexity: Understanding Cities with Cellular Automata, Agent-Based Models, and Fractals", book by Michael Batty – 2005 The key theme of this book is "the notion that cities in particular and urban development in general emerge from the bottom-up and that the spatial order at more aggregate scales can be explained only in this way." (Batty, 2005, p. 6). The book is based on an understanding of cities being influenced by complexity sciences and applies its methods and concepts to urban research. It presents agent-based models (ABM) and cellular automata (CA) models, simulating specific urban situations.
82	"Complexity Theory as a link between space and place", article by Juval Portugali – 2006 Portugali (2006, p. 651) claims that "theories of complex systems" can "bridge the two cultures of geography" which are the quantitative and the qualitative geographies.
83	"The form of cities: political economy and urban design", book by Alexander Cuthbert - 2006 Cuthbert (2006, p. 6) introduces the idea that "urban design should be located within the spatial political economy rather than architectural determinism, policy, planning or the generalized anarchy of ideas within mainstream urban design". In the search for a substantial theoretical foundation for urban design, Cuthbert (2006, p. 7) therefore proposes to consider spatial political economy as a "meta-narrative" ("with a powerful intellectual base dating back to Adam Smith, Hegel and Marx") which can combine spatial studies developed under the direction of diverse disciplines such as "social science, geography, cultural studies, economics, architecture, art history", and "existential positions such as feminism and sustainability".
84	"Urban Complexity and Spatial Strategies: Towards a Relational Planning for Our Times", book by Patsy Healey – 2007 This book offers an analysis of planning practices in three countries in terms of governance, institutions, strategy and relational geography, and presents "a way of thinking about what it means to think and act strategically with respect to the governance of place." (Healey, 2007, p. 287). Healey develops "a relational approach to the governance of the 'places' of urban areas" by emphasizing "the value of recognizing multiplicity, diversity and heterogeneity" (Healey, 2007, p. 287). She argues that "in a relational understanding urban areas are understood as geographical spaces transacted by very many webs of relations that weave across, in and around each other, generating nodes of activity and identifiable places with distinctive social and physical qualities" (Healey, 2007, p. 190). Healey emphasizes that "the recognition of the complexity of the relations that co-exist and transect in urban areas and the range of governance processes which affect how these relations evolve" (Healey, 2007, p. 266) is very important in understanding the nature of spaces and places.
85	First issue of the interdisciplinary journal of Urban Design and Planning – 2008 The journal aims to be an inter-disciplinary journal; "addressing urban design and planning, and bridging between these and the other built environment disciplines". Marshall (2008) proposes that this implies an approach that ranges from urban design (e.g. urban blocks and quarters) to planning (e.g. whole settlements or regions).

>>>

86	**"The right to the city", article by David Harvey – 2008** Harvey (2008, pp. 1-2) argues that social life and preferences are not independent of the configuration of the city we live in and introduces the notion of the "right to the city" i.e. "the freedom to make and remake our cities and ourselves", which he thinks is "the most precious yet most neglected of our human rights": "The question of what kind of city we want cannot be divorced from that of what kind of social ties, relationship to nature, lifestyles, technologies and aesthetic values we desire. The right to the city is far more than the individual liberty to access urban resources: it is a right to change ourselves by changing the city. It is, moreover, a common rather than an individual right since this transformation inevitably depends upon the exercise of a collective power to reshape the processes of urbanization." (Harvey, 2008, p. 1).
87	**"Cities, Design and Evolution", book by Stephen Marshall – 2009** S. Marshall (2009) defines the city as a collection of different component entities with their own agendas which are able to create a functional order in the absence of any design or planning. He uses the concepts of emergence and evolution to build a framework that suggests the possibility of functional urban order. He rejects the conventional metaphors and analogies, which misrepresent part-whole relationships and assume that a city is a designable object. Instead he introduces the idea of the city as a super-unit: a collection of components that contains units and sub-units: the city as an ecosystem. The main difference from the organic metaphor is that the ecosystem analogy of the city includes the idea of collectivity as a new kind of dimensionality, which introduces the concept of interaction, the idea of change, transformation and adaptation over time and an explanation for how urban order emerges.
88	**First Conference on Complexity Theory of Cities (CTC): Complexity Theories of Cities Have Come of Age – 2009** 'Complexity Theories of Cities Have Come of Age' is the first conference to focus on the application of complexity theory in the domain of spatial research. Chaired by Juval Portugali and Han Meyer, the conference took place in TU Delft. The central theme of the conference was to discuss the effects of complexity theory methods and tools for planning and urban design and how CTC can contribute to solving the central questions of 21st century cities and urbanism. Following the conference, a book entitled: "Complexity Theories of Cities Have Come of Age: An Overview with Implications for Urban Planning and Design" was published in 2012. The book includes a detailed discussion by Portugali (2012) on the "achievements, criticism and potential of CTC" in the last three decades. As claimed by Peter Allen, complex systems thinking provides us a new foundation for understanding the reality of the world and hopefully CTC models will constitute a new ground for policy development. In particular, CTC models may help us to develop more insight on how the "bio-physical part of the system (the hydrology, soils, vegetation, ecology, physical infrastructure, etc.) is linked dynamically to the human part of the system that is driving the exploitation of resources, both natural and human". Allen (2012, p. 87). This in turn may help us in building strategies for sustainable urban development.
89	**"Complexity, cognition and the city", book by Juval Portugali – 2011** Since the late 1990s, urban complexity has begun to be addressed from the perspective of the complexity sciences and this new area of study has been referred to as "complexity theories of cities (CTC)" by Portugali in his book entitled: "Complexity, cognition and the city". The book studies the convergence of three fields of science; complexity, cognition and the city. Portugali (2011) identifies two main problems in the application of complexity theories in the field of urban research. Firstly; "CTC have almost lost their connection with the core of urban studies, that is, they have become more a branch of complexity theories" Secondly; "by treating cities as inanimate physical complex systems, CTC can verify existing complexity theories but cannot add to them new dimensions that might typify human complex systems but not inanimate physical systems." (Portugali, 2011, p. 3). Therefore the aim of the book, as presented by Portugali, is to demonstrate how CTC can fully contribute to urban studies and "how it can contribute to mainstream complexity theory" (Portugali, 2011, p. 3). He claims that the answer lies in linking complexity, cognition and the city.
90	**"Smart City", a research project associated with the FuturICT, one of the six pilot projects of The Future and Emerging Technologies (FET) Flagships of the European Commission – 2012** The Smart City, is a research project associated with the FuturICT project, which is an initiative that aims to "develop Information and Communications Technologies that will provide scientists, governmental officials and citizens with a planetary scale computer called a Living Earth Platform" (http://www.futurict.eu/). FuturICT is one of the six pilot projects of The Future and Emerging Technologies (FET) Flagships of the European Commission ("Joining forces in Europe to target futuristic technologies," 2011). Batty et al. (2012, p. 484) define the concept of the smart city as one, which "revolves around the need to coordinate and integrate technologies that had previously been developed in isolation but have clear operational synergies and need to be linked in order to take advantage of many new opportunities to improve the quality of life." The main idea behind smart cities is to improve the quality of transportation, healthcare, communication, energy, water and waste etc. services and provide sustainable urban development.

Bibliography

Alexander, C., Ishikawa, S., Silverstein, M., Jacobson, M., Fiksdahl-King, I., & Angel, S. (1977). *A Pattern Language: Towns, Buildings, Construction (Center for Environmental Structure)* Oxford University Press.

Alexander, C., Silverstein, M. , Angel, S. , Ishikawa, S., & Abrams, D. (1975). *The Oregon Experiment (Center for Environmental Structure)* Oxford University Press.

Alexander, Christopher. (1965). A City is not a Tree *Architectural Forum, 122*(1-2), 58-62

Alexander, Christopher. (1979). *The timeless way of building*. New York: Oxford University Press.

Alexander, Christopher. (1987). *A New Theory of Urban Design*. New York: Oxford University Press.

Allen, P. (1997). *Cities and Regions as Self-Organizing Systems: Models of Complexity*. London: Taylor and Francis.

Allen, P. (2012). Cities: the Visible Expression of Co-evolving Complexity. In J. Portugali, H. Meyer, E. Stolk & E. Tan (Eds.), *Complexity Theories of Cities Have Come of Age: An Overview with Implications to Urban Planning and Design* (pp. 67-89): Springer.

Appleyard, Donald. (1979). *The Environment as a social symbol: Within a theory of environmental action and perception*: Institute of Urban & Regional Development, University of California.

Barnes, Trevor J. (2000). Inventing economic geography in Anglo-America, 1889-1960 In E. Sheppard & T. J. Barnes (Eds.), *A companion to economic geography* (pp. 11-26). Oxford: Blackwell.

Barnes, Trevor J. (2003). The place of locational analysis: a selective and interpretive history. *Prog Hum Geogr, 27*(1), 69-95.

Batty, Michael. (1976). *Urban modelling : algorithms calibrations, predictions*. Cambridge ; New York: Cambridge University Press.

Batty, Michael. (2005). *Cities and complexity : understanding cities with cellular automata, agent-based models, and fractals*. Cambridge, Mass.: MIT Press.

Batty, Michael, Axhausen, K., Fosca , G., Pozdnoukhov , A., Bazzani , A., Wachowicz, M., . . . Portugali, Y. (2012). Smart Cities of the Future. *European Physical Journal Special Topics, 214*, 481-518.

Batty, Michael, Dodge, M., Jiang, B., & Smith, A. (1998). GIS and Urban Design. Retrieved June 2014, from http://www.casa.ucl.ac.uk/urbandesifinal.pdf

Batty, Michael, & Longley, P. A. (1994). *Fractal Cities: A Geometry of Form and Function*. San Diego, CA: Academic Press.

Batty, Michael, & Marshall, Stephen. (2009). The evolution of cities: Geddes, Abercrombie and the new physicalism. *Town Planning Review, 80*(6), 551-574.

Boyce, D. . (2004). A short history of the field of Regional Science. *Regional Science, 83*, 31-57.

Boyer, Christine (1994). *The City of Collective Memory: Its Historical Imagery and Architectural Entertainments*. Cambridge: MIT Press.

Bunge, W. (1962). *Theoretical Geography (1st edn.)*. Lund, Sweden: Gleerup.

Burton, Ian. (1963). The Quantitative Revolution and Theoretical Geography. *Canadian Geographer, VII*(4), 151-162.

Castells, Manuel. (1972). *La Question Urbaine* Paris: Maspero.

Castells, Manuel. (1977). *The Urban Question: A Marxist Approach*. London: Edward Arnold.

Castells, Manuel. (1989). *The Informational City: Information Technology, Economic Restructuring, and the Urban-Regional Process* Oxford: Blackwell.

Castells, Manuel. (1996). *The Rise of The Network Society*. Oxford: Blackwell.

Charlton, Martin (2008). Locational Analysis in Human Geography (1965): Peter Haggett. In P. Hubbard, R. Kitchin & A. Valentine (Eds.), *Key Texts in Human Geography*: SAGE.

Charter of the New Urbanism. (2001). Retrieved June 22, 2014, from http://www.cnu.org/charter

CIAM's La Sarraz Declaration. (1928). Retrieved June 20, 2014, from http://modernistarchitecture.wordpress.com/2011/09/08/ciams-la-sarraz-declaration-1928/

Coenen, Frans. (2011). Data mining: past, present and future *The Knowledge Engineering Review, 26*(1), 25-29.

Condit, Carl W. (1969). Matrix of Man: An Illustrated History of the Urban Environment by Sibyl Moholy-Nagy Book Reviews. *Isis, 60*(2), 253-255.

Cox, K. R. (2001). Classics in human geography revisited: Bunge, W., Theoretical Geography Commentary 1. . *Prog Hum Geogr, 25*(1), 71-73.

Cullen, G. (1961). *The Concise Townscape*. London: Architectural Press.

Cuthbert, Alexander R. (2006). *The form of cities : political economy and urban design*. Malden, MA ; Oxford: Blackwell Pub.

Dare, Robert. (2000). Book Review Complexity: the Emerging Science at the Edge of Order and Chaos

Waldrop, M. (1992). *Complexity* New York: Simon and Schuster.

Dickens, P. (1981). The hut and the machine: towards a social theory of architecture. *Architectural Design, 51*(1), 32-45.

Doel, M. A. (1999). *Poststructuralist Geographies: The Diabolical Art of Spatial Science*: Edinburgh University Press.

Donaghy, Kieran P. (2014). Walter Isard's Evolving Sense of the Scientific in Regional Science. *International Regional Science Review, 37*(1), 78-95

Doxiadis, C. A. (1968). *EKISTICS: An Introduction to the Science of Human Settlements*: Oxford University Press.

Doxiadis, C. A. (1970). Ecistics the Science of Human Settlements. *Science, 170*(3956).

Fayyad, U. M., Piatetsky-Shapiro, G., & Smyth, P. (1996a). From data mining to knowledge discovery: An Overview. In U. Fayyad, G. Piatetsky-Shapiro, P. Smyth & R. Uthurusamy (Eds.), *Advances in Knowledge Discovery and Data Mining* (pp. 1-30): AAAI Press.

Geddes, P. (1915). *Cities in Evolution*. London: Williams Press.

Geddes, P., & Thomson, J. A. (1911). *Evolution*. London: Williams and Norgate.

Gershenson, C. (2008). *Complexity-5 questions*. Copenhagen: Automatic Press.

Goodchild, M. F. (2008). Theoretical Geography (1962): William Bunge. In P. Hubbard, R. Kitchin & G. Valentine (Eds.), *Key Texts in Human Geography* (pp. 9-16). Los Angeles: SAGE.

Haggett, Peter. (1965). *Locational Analysis in Human Geography*. London: Edward Arnold.

Haken, H. (2012). An Overview with Implications to Urban Planning and Design. In H. M. eds. J. Portugali, E. Stolk, E. Tan (Ed.), *Complexity Theories of Cities Have Come of Age*. Heidelbeg: Springer.

Hall, P. (1998). *Cities in Civilisation*. London: Weidenfeld and Nicolson.

Hall, Peter , & Ward, Colin (1998). *Sociable Cities: The Legacy of Ebenezer Howard*. Chichester: John Wiley.

Harvey, David. (1969). *Explanation in Geography*. London: Edward Arnold.

Harvey, David. (1973). *Social justice and the city*. London,: Edward Arnold.

Harvey, David. (1985). *The Urbanization of Capital: Studies in the History and Theory of Capitalist Urbanization* Oxford: Blackwell.

Harvey, David. (1996). *Justice, Nature and the Geography of Difference*. Oxford: Blackwell.

Harvey, David. (2006). Introduction *The Limits to Capital*. London: Verso.

Harvey, David. (2008). The right to the city. *New Left Review, 53*, 23–40.

Hays, M. K. (1992). *Modernism and the Posthumanist Subject: The Architecture of Hannes Meyer and Ludwig Hilberseimer*. Cambridge, MA: MIT Press.

Healey, Patsy. (2007). *Urban Complexity and Spatial Strategies: Towards a Relational Planning for Our Times* UK: Routledge in conjunction with The Royal Town Planning Institute.

Held, D. (1980). *Introduction to Critical Theory : Horkheimer to Habermas*. Berkeley: University of California Press.

Heylighen, F., & Joslyn, C. (1992). What is Systems Theory? Retrieved June 2014, from http://pespmc1.vub.ac.be/SYSTHEOR.html

Hillier, B., & Hanson, J. (1984). *The Social Logic of Space* (Vol. 2). Cambridge: Cambridge University Press

Hodder, Robert. (1996). Reviews : The City of Collective Memory: Its Historical Imagery and Architectural Entertainments M. Christine Boyer *Journal of Planning Education and Research, 16*(September), 71-73.

Howard, Ebenezer. (1946). *Garden Cities of To-Morrow*. London: Faber and Faber (Original: 1902).

Isard, W. (1975). *Introduction to Regional Science*: Prentice Hall.

Isard, W. (2003). *History of Regional Science and the Regional Science Association International: The Beginnings and Early History*: Springer.

Jacobs, Jane. (1961). *The death and life of great American cities*. New York: Random House.

Johnson-Marshall, Percy (1966). *Rebuilding Cities from Medieval to Modern Times (Original, in Italian)*: Edinburgh U.P.

Johnston, R. (2008a). Explanation in Geography (1969): David Harvey. In P. Hubbard, R. Kitchin & A. Valentine (Eds.), *Key Texts in Human Geography*. Los Angeles: SAGE.

Johnston, R. (2008b). The Limits to Capital by David Harvey; The New Imperialism by David Harvey; A Brief History of Neoliberalism by David Harvey; Spaces of Global Capitalism by David Harvey. *Annals of the Association of American Geographers, 98*(4), 941-948.

Joining forces in Europe to target futuristic technologies. (2011). Retrieved June 23, 2014, from http://www.fet11.eu/about/fet-flagships

Jones, E. (1956). Cause and Effect in Human Geography. *Ann. Assoc. Am. Geog., 46*, 369- 377.

Joyce, P. (2003). *The Rule of Freedom: Liberalism and the Modern City*. London: Verso.

Khemlani. (2005). Hurricanes and their Aftermath: How Can Technology Help? Retrieved 27 May, 2010, from http://www.aecbytes.com/buildingthefuture/2005/Hurricane-TechHelp_pr.html

Kostof, S. (1991). *The City Shaped: Urban Patterns and Meanings Through History* Boston: Little, Brown and Co.

Krier, Rob. (1979). *Urban Space*. New York: Rizzoli.

Larice, M., & Macdonald, E. (2012). The Urban Design Reader. In M. Larice & E. Macdonald (Eds.), *The Urban Design Reader* (pp. 229-234).

Lee, Colin. (1972). *Models in planning: an introduction to the use of quantitative models in planning* (Vol. 4): Pergamon Press.

Lefebvre, H. (1970). *The Urban Revolution*: University of Minnesota Press.

Lloyd, C. D. (2010). *Spatial Data Analysis An Introduction for GIS users*: Oxford University Press.

Lynch, K. (1960). *The Image of the City* United States of America: MIT Press.

Lynch, K. (1981). *A Theory of Good City Form*. Cambridge, MA: MIT Press.

Mark, Robert (1984). Architecture and the Crisis of Modern Science by Alberto Pérez-Gómez. *Technology and Culture, 25*(4), 900-902.

Marshall, Richard. (2009). The Elusiveness of Urban Design: The Perpetual Problem of Definition and Role in Urban Design In A. Krieger & W. S. Saunders (Eds.), *Urban Design* (pp. 38-57). Minneapolis: University of Minnesota Press

Marshall, S. (2008). Retrieved June 2014, from http://www.icevirtuallibrary.com/docserver/fulltext/udap161-001.pdf?expires=1407247378&id=id&accname=guest&check
sum=2F6220ECFFF3749B505705DA5BCB44DF

Marshall, Stephen. (2009). *Cities Design and Evolution*. Abingdon, Oxon: Routledge.

Massey, D. (1992). Politics and space/time. *New Left Review, 196*, 65–84.

Massey, D. (1998). *Power-geometries and the politics of space-time*. Hettner-Lecture. Department of Geography, University of Heidelberg, Heidelberg.

Massey, D. (1999a). Space-time, 'science' and the relationship between physical geography and human geography. *Transactions of the Institute of British Geographers, 24*(261–276).

Moholy-Nagy, S. (1968). *The Matrix of Man*. London: Pall-Mall.

Mumford, L. (1961). *The City in History*. New York: Harcourt, Brace, Jovanovich.

Murdoch, Jon. (2006). *Post-structuralist Geography: A Guide to Relational Space*. London: Sage Publications Ltd.

Norberg-Schulz, Christian. (1980). *Genius Loci: Towards a Phenomenology of Architecture*: Rizzoli.

Openshaw, S., & Abrahart, R. J. (1996). *Geocomputation*. Paper presented at the 1st International Conference on GeoComputation University of Leeds, UK.

Oudenampsen, Merijn (2013). Retracing the Garden City. http://merijnoudenampsen.org/2013/04/03/retracing-the-garden-city/

Paper Architecture: Visionary Structures on the Printed Page. (2011). Retrieved June 8, 2014, from http://www.artic.edu/aic/resources/resource/2084

Park, Robert E. , Burgess, Ernest W. , & McKenzie, Roderick D. . (1925). *The City* The University of Chicago Press.

Perez-Gomez, Alberto. (1983). *Architecture and the Crisis of Modern Science*. Cambridge, Massachusetts: MIT Press.

Pooler, J.A. (1977). The origins of the spatial tradition in geography: an interpretation. *Ontario Geography 11*, 56-83.

Portugali, Juval. (2006). Complexity Theory as a link between space and place. *Environment & Planning A, 38*(4), 647-664.

Portugali, Juval. (2011). *Complexity, cognition and the city*. Heidelberg ; New York: Springer.

Portugali, Juval. (2012). Complexity Theories of Cities: Achievements, Criticism and Potentials. In H. M. J. Portugali, E. Stolk, E. Tan (Ed.), *Complexity Theories of Cities Have Come of Age: An Overview with Implications to Urban Planning and Design*. Heidelbeg: Springer.

Price, David. (1994). Projects 1981 - 1991. *Urban Design, 2014*(52: Gordon Cullen).

Price, Jonathan. (1999). Christopher Alexander's Pattern Language. *IEEE TRANSACTIONS ON PROFESSIONAL COMMUNICATION, 42*(2, JUNE), 117-122.

Prigogine, I. (1997). Foreword *Cities and Regions as Self-Organizing Systems: Models of Complexity by P. Allen*. London: Taylor and Francis.

Rogers, R. (1999). Urban Task Force. Retrieved June 23, 2014, from http://www.richardrogers.co.uk/Asp/uploadedFiles/Image/2832_urban_task_force_research/1999/RSHP_A_JS_2832_L_E_MP.pdf

Rowe, C., & Koetter, F. (1978). *Collage City*. Cambridge: The MIT Press.

Sitte, Camillo. (1889). Modern Systems. Artistic Limitation of Modern City Planning Retrieved July 10, 2014, from http://urban-planning.library.cornell.edu/DOCS/sitte.htm

Sitte, Camillo. (1945). *The Art of Building Cities: Building According to its Artistic Fundamentals*. New York: Reinhold (Original: 1889).

Snow, C. P. (1964). *The two cultures: and a second look* (2d ed.). Cambridge,: University Press.

Spriergegen, Paul D. (1965). *Urban Design: The Architecture of Towns and Cities* New York: McGraw-Hill.

Sunley, Peter. (2008). Relational Economic Geography: A Partial Understanding or a New Paradigm? *Economic Geography, 84*(1), 1-20.

Tafuri, M. (1976). *Architecture and Utopia: Design and Capitalist Development*. Cambridge, MA: MIT Press.

Thrift, Nigel (1999). Steps to an Ecology of Place. In A. J. S. P. Massey D (Ed.), *Human Geography Today* (pp. 295–323). Cambridge: Polity Press.

Thrift, Nigel (2002a). The Future of Geography. *Geoforum, 33*, 291-298.

Tomlinson, R. F. (1968). A Geographic Information System for Regional Planning. Retrieved June 2014, from http://gisandscience.files.wordpress.com/2012/08/1-a-gis-for-regional-planning_ed.pdf

Tschumi, B. (1996). *Architecture and Disjunction*. Cambridge, MA: MIT Press.

Von Bertalanffy, Ludwig. (1969). *General System Theory: Foundations, Development, Applications* (Revised edition March 17, 1969 ed.): George Braziller Inc.

Wagner, Otto. (1988). *Modern Architecture: A Guidebook for His Students to This Field of Art (Texts & Documents)*. Los Angeles: Getty Research Institute.

Waldrop, M. (1992). *Complexity* New York: Simon and Schuster.

Wirth, Louis (1938). Urbanism as a Way of Life. *The American Journal of Sociology, 44*(1), 1-24.

Appendix B Beyoğlu Preservation Area Building Features Database

BEYOĞLU PRESERVATION AREA BUILDING FEATURES DATABASE					
Attributes		Urban Entity	Attribute Value Type	Attribute Category	Statistics
Att.1	Ground Floor use	Building Floor	Qualitative (8 categories)	Socio-economic	mode = Business-Shopping (5035), least = Technical Infrastructure (39)
Att.2	1st Floor use	Building Floor	Qualitative (8 categories)	Socio-economic	mode = Residential (4961), least = Technical Infrastructure (11)
Att.3	2nd Floor use	Building Floor	Qualitative (8 categories)	Socio-economic	mode = Residential (4303), least = Technical Infrastructure (6)
Att.4	3rd Floor use	Building Floor	Qualitative (8 categories)	Socio-economic	mode = No 3rd Floor (6077), least = Technical Infrastructure (2)
Att.5	4th Floor use	Building Floor	Qualitative (8 categories)	Socio-economic	mode = No 4th Floor (8368), least = Technical Infrastructure (3)
Att.6	5th Floor use	Building Floor	Qualitative (8 categories)	Socio-economic	mode = No 5th Floor (10612), least = Technical Infrastructure (1)
Att.7	6th Floor use	Building Floor	Qualitative (8 categories)	Socio-economic	mode = No 6th Floor (11424), least = Technical Infrastructure (1)
Att.8	7th Floor use	Building Floor	Qualitative (8 categories)	Socio-economic	mode = No 7th Floor (11726), least = Other (2)
Att.9	8th Floor use	Building Floor	Qualitative (8 categories)	Socio-economic	mode = No 8th Floor (11885), least = Other (1)
Att.10	9th Floor use	Building Floor	Qualitative (8 categories)	Socio-economic	mode = No 9th Floor (11962), least = Accomodation (5)
Att.11	10th Floor use	Building Floor	Qualitative (8 categories)	Socio-economic	mode = No 10th Floor (11981), least = Business-Shopping (1)
Att.12	1st Basemen floor uset	Building Floor	Qualitative (8 categories)	Socio-economic	mode = No Basement (7197), least = Technical Infrastructure (9)
Att.13	2nd Basement floor use	Building Floor	Qualitative (8 categories)	Socio-economic	mode = No 2nd Basement (11717), least = Accomodation (7)
Att.14	3rd Basement floor use	Building Floor	Qualitative (8 categories)	Socio-economic	mode = No 3rd Basement (11935), least = Technical Infrastructure (2)
Att.15	1st Penthouse floor use	Building Floor	Qualitative (8 categories)	Socio-economic	mode = No 1st Roof (8862), least = Other (22)
Att.16	2nd Penthouse floor use	Building Floor	Qualitative (8 categories)	Socio-economic	mode = No 2nd Roof (11804), least = Other (1)
Att.17	3rd Penthouse floor use	Building Floor	Qualitative (8 categories)	Socio-economic	mode = No 3rd Roof (11973), least = Empty (2)
Att.18	Neighborhood (Mahalle)	Neigborhood	Qualitative (30 categories)	Location Name	mode = SEHITMUHTAR_Neighborhood (693), least = OMER_AVNI_MAHALLESI (4)

	Attribute Value Range	Data Source
	Other (712), Residential (3895), Business-Shopping (5035), Accomodation (154), Sociocultural Infrastructure (736), Empty (1273), Technical Infrastructure (39), Open Space (140)	Istanbul Metropolitan Municipality
	No 1st Floor (1629), Residential (4961), Business-Shopping (3061), Other (124), Accomodation (168), Empty (1502), Sociocultural Infrastructure (389), Technical Infrastructure (11), Open Space (139)	Istanbul Metropolitan Municipality
	No 2nd Floor (3345), Residential (4303), Empty (1381), Accomodation (162), Business-Shopping (2258), Sociocultural Infrastructure (291), Other (99), Technical Infrastructure (6), Open Space (139)	Istanbul Metropolitan Municipality
	No 3rd Floor (6077), Residential (2697), Empty (1027), Accomodation (143), Business-Shopping (1619), Sociocultural Infrastructure (196), Other (84), Technical Infrastructure (2), Open Space (139)	Istanbul Metropolitan Municipality
	No 4th Floor (8368), Empty (596), Residential (1418), Business-Shopping (1137), Sociocultural Infrastructure (117), Accomodation (136), Technical Infrastructure (3), Other (70), Open Space (139)	Istanbul Metropolitan Municipality
	No 5th Floor (10612), Residential (414), Business-Shopping (546), Sociocultural Infrastructure (52), Empty (256), Accomodation (93), Technical Infrastructure (1), Other (10)	Istanbul Metropolitan Municipality
	No 6th Floor (11424), Residential (90), Business-Shopping (279), Sociocultural Infrastructure (24), Empty (95), Technical Infrastructure (1), Accomodation (68), Other (3)	Istanbul Metropolitan Municipality
	No 7th Floor (11726), Residential (27), Business-Shopping (137), Sociocultural Infrastructure (15), Empty (30), Accomodation (47), Other (2)	Istanbul Metropolitan Municipality
	No 8th Floor (11885), Empty (12), Business-Shopping (48), Residential (2), Sociocultural Infrastructure (6), Accomodation (30), Other (1)	Istanbul Metropolitan Municipality
	No 9th Floor (11962), Business-Shopping (10), Empty (7), Accomodation (5)	Istanbul Metropolitan Municipality
	No 10th Floor (11981), Business-Shopping (1), Accomodation (2)	Istanbul Metropolitan Municipality
	No Basement (7197), Business-Shopping (1497), Other (315), Empty (587), Residential (2218), Sociocultural Infrastructure (94), Technical Infrastructure (9), Accomodation (67)	Istanbul Metropolitan Municipality
	No 2nd Basement (11717), Other (8), Residential (148), Business-Shopping (67), Empty (17), Technical Infrastructure (8), Sociocultural Infrastructure (12), Accomodation (7)	Istanbul Metropolitan Municipality
	No 3rd Basement (11935), Other (3), Residential (25), Business-Shopping (7), Empty (4), Technical Infrastructure (2), Sociocultural Infrastructure (3), Accomodation (5)	Istanbul Metropolitan Municipality
	No 1st Roof (8862), Residential (1884), Business-Shopping (552), Empty (507), Other (22), Accomodation (76), Sociocultural Infrastructure (81)	Istanbul Metropolitan Municipality
	No 2nd Roof (11804), Residential (78), Empty (38), Business-Shopping (37), Accomodation (19), Sociocultural Infrastructure (7), Other (1)	Istanbul Metropolitan Municipality
	No 3rd Roof (11973), Residential (4), Accomodation (5), Empty (2)	Istanbul Metropolitan Municipality
	KOCATEPE_Neighborhood (501), GUMUSSUYU_Neighborhood (484), BULBUL_Neighborhood (646), CIHANGIR_Neighborhood (491), CATMALIMESCIT_Neighborhood (307), SEHITMUHTAR_Neighborhood (693), BOSTAN_Neighborhood (234), KALYONCU_KULLUGU_Neighborhood (442), KATIP_MUSTAFA_CELEBI_Neighborhood (439), BEDRETTIN_Neighborhood (285), SAHKULU_Neighborhood (353), CUKUR_Neighborhood (562), HACIMIMI_Neighborhood (438), KILICALIPASA_Neighborhood (412), KEMANKES_Neighborhood (400), KULOGLU_Neighborhood (397), PURTELAS_Neighborhood (324), TOMTOM_Neighborhood (462), YAHYAKAHYA_Neighborhood (476), EVLIYACELEBI_Neighborhood (110), FIRUZAGA_Neighborhood (594), OMER_AVNI_Neighborhood (422), SURURI_Neighborhood (293), KAMERHATUN_Neighborhood (259), ASMALIMESCIT_Neighborhood (330), EMEKYEMEZ_Neighborhood (372), ARAPCAMI_Neighborhood (313), BEREKETZADE_Neighborhood (308), MUEYYETZADE_Neighborhood (305), HUSEYINAGA_Neighborhood (328), OMER_AVNI_MAHALLESI (4)	Istanbul Metropolitan Municipality

>>>

BEYOĞLU PRESERVATION AREA BUILDING FEATURES DATABASE					
Attributes		Urban Entity	Attribute Value Type	Attribute Category	Statistics
Att.19	Population Density (Person/Ha)	Building Block	Quantitative (10 categories)	Socio-demographic	mode = 1000-1500P_HA (2300), least = 200-300P_HA (517)
Att.20	Presence in the Bosphorus Silhouette	Building	Qualitative (2 categories)	Cultural-historic-economic	mode = Disturbing (185), least = Present (7)
Att.21	Building Maintenance Conditions	Building	Qualitative (5 categories)	Architectural-physical	mode = Medium (8044), least = Ruined (235)
Att.22	Building Construction Material	Building	Qualitative (4 categories)	Architectural-physical	mode = Masonry (7557), least = Other (66)
Att.23	Empty Floor Ratio in the Building	Building	Quantitative (8 categories)	Socio-economic	mode = Fully Occupied (8243), least = No Floor (137)
Att.24	Ownership	Building	Qualitative (25 categories)	Socio-economic	mode = Private (9541), least = Other (2443)
Att.25	Historical Registry (intensity)	Building Block	Qualitative (10 categories)	Cultural-historic	mode = %10-20 registered (1872), least = %90-100 registered (192)
Att.26	Floor Space Index (FSI)	Building Block	Quantitative (9 categories)	Architectural-morphological	mode = 3.00-4.00 (3842), least = 7.50+ (24)
Att.27	Historical Registry of Buildings	Building	Qualitative (3 categories)	Cultural-historic	mode = Not Available (7623), least = Registered Monuments (576)
Att.28	Building Footprint	Building	Quantitative (7 categories)	Architectural-physical	avg = 126.818 +/- 346.171
Att.29	Distance to Dolmabahce	Building	Quantitative (7 categories)	Spatial-topological	avg = 1561.519 +/- 523.598
Att.30	Distance to Galata Bridge	Building	Quantitative (7 categories)	Spatial-topological	avg = 1230.008 +/- 529.917
Att.31	Distance to Galata Tower	Building	Quantitative (7 categories)	Spatial-topological	avg = 993.074 +/- 489.584
Att.32	Distance to Galatasaray	Building	Quantitative (7 categories)	Spatial-topological	avg = 642.615 +/- 255.615
Att.33	Distance to Kabatas	Building	Quantitative (7 categories)	Spatial-topological	avg = 1273.475 +/- 466.770
Att.34	Distance to Taksim	Building	Quantitative (7 categories)	Spatial-topological	avg = 1036.111 +/- 484.985
Att.35	Distance to Tepebasi	Building	Quantitative (7 categories)	Spatial-topological	avg = 719.322 +/- 304.994
Att.36	Distance to Tunel	Building	Quantitative (7 categories)	Spatial-topological	avg = 840.742 +/- 403.011
Att.37	Distance to Unkapani	Building	Quantitative (7 categories)	Spatial-topological	avg = 1303.062 +/- 530.636
Att.38	Slope Code	Building	Quantitative (9 categories)	Spatial-topographical	mode = 1 (4790), least = 9 (4)
Att.39	Land Height (elevation from the sea level)	Building	Quantitative (8 categories)	Spatial-topographical	mode = 61 (2087), least = 11 (690)
Att.40	Number of Floors	Building	Quantitative (12 categories)	Architectural-physical	mode = 3 (2740), least = 11 (1)

	Attribute Value Range	Data Source
	200-300P_HA (517), 0-100P_HA (1122), No Density (2038), 1000-1500P_HA (2300), 100-200P_HA (960), 300-500P_HA (1245), 500-750P_HA (909), 2000-_P_HA (675), 1500-2000P_HA (1159), 750-1000P_HA (1045)	Istanbul Metropolitan Municipality
	Disturbing (185), Present (7)	Istanbul Metropolitan Municipality
	Medium (8044), Bad (2365), Good (997), Unknown (343), Ruined (235)	Istanbul Metropolitan Municipality
	RC (3916), Masonry (7557), Other (66), Wood (229), No Structure (136)	Istanbul Metropolitan Municipality
	Fully Occupied (8243), %40-59 empty (556), %20-39 empty (859), %1-19 empty (442), All Empty (1065), %60-79 empty (386), %80-99 empty (156), No Floor (137)	Istanbul Metropolitan Municipality
	Private (9541), Other (2443)	Istanbul Metropolitan Municipality
	%20-30 registered (1830), %50-60 registered (1062), %60-70 registered (1242), %10-20 registered (1872), %0-10 registered (1220), %70-80 registered (611), %40-50 registered (1237), %30-40 registered (1662), %90-100 registered (192), %80-90 registred (224)	Istanbul Metropolitan Municipality
	3.00-4.00 (3842), 5.00-7.50 (874), 4.00-5.00 (1814), 2.00-3.00 (3790), 1.00-2.00 (1222), 0.00-0.50 (120), 0.50-1.00 (125), 7.50+ (24), No KAKS (94)	Istanbul Metropolitan Municipality
	Not Available (7623), Registered Monuments (576), Registered Civil Architecture (3785)	Istanbul Metropolitan Municipality
	[0.120 ; 17928.150] {0-34 m2, 35-48 m2, 49-61 m2, 62-81m2, 82-114 m2, 115-187 m2, 187-17928 m2}	computed in GIS (polygon geometry calculation)
	[67.927 ; 2645.240] {67-687 m., 688-1068 m., 1069-1361 m., 1362-1666 m., 1667-1975 m., 1976-2268 m., 2269-2645 m.}	computed in GIS with Hawth's Tools add-on
	[42.260 ; 2373.590] {42-441m., 442-773 m., 774-1098 m., 1099-1369 m., 1370-1606 m., 1607-1859 m., 1860-2373 m.}	computed in GIS with Hawth's Tools add-on
	[0.000 ; 2220.369] {0-348 m., 349-615 m., 616-899 m., 900-1146 m., 1147-1370m., 1371-1632 m., 1633-2219 m.}	computed in GIS with Hawth's Tools add-on
	[0.000 ; 1509.233] {0-293 m., 294- 451 m., 452-588 m., 588-721 m., 722-872 m., 873-1048 m., 1049-1508 m.}	computed in GIS with Hawth's Tools add-on
	[0.000 ; 2259.720] {0-562 m., 563-841 m., 842-1106 m., 1107-1335m., 1336-1576 m., 1577-1839 m., 1840-2259 m.}	computed in GIS with Hawth's Tools add-on
	[0.000 ; 2072.183] { 0-450 m., 451-693 m., 694-919m., 920-1178, 1179-1453m., 1454-1728m., 1729-2071m.}	computed in GIS with Hawth's Tools add-on
	[40.440 ; 1822.421] {40-359 m., 360-535 m., 536-704 m., 705-867 m., 868-1039 m., 1040-1275 m., 1276-1821 m.}	computed in GIS with Hawth's Tools add-on
	[0.000 ; 2075.647] {0-332 m., 333-547 m., 548-770 m,. 771-1005 m,. 1006-1230 m., 1231-1501 m., 1502-2074 m.}	computed in GIS with Hawth's Tools add-on
	[116.220 ; 2691.352] {166-562 m., 563-894 m., 895-1191 m., 1192-1462 m., 1463-1720 m., 1721-2037 m., 2038-2691 m.}	computed in GIS with Hawth's Tools add-on
	1 (4790), 4 (2751), 7 (365), 6 (690), 8 (969), 0 (621), 5 (873), 3 (587), 2 (334), 9 (4)	Istanbul Metropolitan Municipality
	71 (1440), 41 (1808), 61 (2087), 51 (1367), 11 (690), 21 (1421), 31 (1844), 1 (1327)	Istanbul Metropolitan Municipality
	1 (1628), 4 (2444), 5 (1963), 2 (1719), 3 (2740), 6 (780), 7 (289), 8 (145), 9 (73), 10 (17), 11 (1), Other (185)	Istanbul Metropolitan Municipality

>>>

BEYOĞLU PRESERVATION AREA BUILDING FEATURES DATABASE						
Attributes		Urban Entity	Attribute Value Type	Attribute Category	Statistics	
Att.41	Basement (with or without)	Building	Qualitative (4 categories)	Architectural	mode = No Basement floor (7197), least = 3 Basement floor (49)	
Att.42	Penthouse (with or without)	Building	Qualitative (4 categories)	Architectural	mode = No Penthouse floor(8862), least = 3 Penthouse floor (11)	
Att.43	Streets	Building	Qualitative (52 categories)	Location Name	mode = 3rd Level (8627), least = Doktor Bedii Gorbon Sokak (8)	
Att.44	Street Hierarchy	Building	Qualitative (3 categories)	Socio-economic	mode = 3rd Level (8627), least = 1st Level (598)	
Att.45	Land Price	Street	Quantitative (12 categories)	Economic	avg = 969.620 +/- 1600.324	

	Attribute Value Range	Data Source
	No Basement floor (7197), 1 Basement floor (4521), 3 Basement floor (49), 2 Basement floor (217)	Istanbul Metropolitan Municipality
	No Penthouse floor (8862), 2 Penthouse floor (168), 1 Penthouse floor (2943), 3 Penthouse floor (11)	Istanbul Metropolitan Municipality
	3rd Level (8627), Istiklal Caddesi (233), Meclis-i Mebusan Caddesi (185), Tarlabaşı Caddesi (181), Siraselviler Caddesi (141), Sakizagaci Caddesi (132), Kalyoncu Kullugu Caddesi (127), Mesrutiyet Caddesi (93), Turan Caddesi (93), Bogazkesen Caddesi (83), Ismet Inonu Caddesi (79), Kemeralti Caddesi (78), Defterdar Yokusu (77), Laleci Caddesi (75), Kumbaraci Yokusu (73), Galipdede Caddesi (66), Yenicarsi Caddesi (64), Omer Hayyam Caddesi (63), Aynalicesme Caddesi (61), Taksim Caddesi (57), Refik Saydam Caddesi (56), TersaneVe-SabahattinEvren Caddesi (53), Gunesli Sokak (49), Kemankes Caddesi (48), Sipahi Firini Sokak (48), Akyol Sokak (46), ... and 21 more ... , Civici Sokak (27), Susam Sokak (24), Mete Caddesi (19), Coskun Sokak (18), Selime Hatun Sokak (18), Mexelik Sokak (17), Zambak Sokak (17), Maliye Caddesi (16), Bolahenk Sokak (15), Hamambasi Caddesi (15), Havuzdegirmeni Sokak (15), Karabas Mektebi Sokak (15), Altin Bilezik Sokak (14), Arikan Sokak (14), Gumruk Sokak (14), Hayrat Sokak (13), Osmanli Sokak (13), Tali Sokak (13), AskerOcagi Caddesi (12), IlkBelediye Caddesi (12), Laleciler Caddesi (12), Tozkoparan Mezarlik Sokak (12), Sabuncu Sokak (11), Ayni Alibaba Sokak (10), Nilufer Sokak (9), Doktor Bedii Gorbon Sokak (8)	Istanbul Metropolitan Municipality
	3rd Level (8627), 2nd Level (2759), 1st Level (598)	Istanbul Metropolitan Municipality
	[43.000 ; 8611.000]{43-86; 97-140; 151-183; 194-258; 269-388; 398-592; 646-891; 915-1238; 1292-1830; 1938-2691; 2906-4306; 5382-8611}	Beyoğlu Municipality

Appendix C Naive Bayes Classification Results for label attribute 'ground floor use'

NAIVE BAYES CLASSIFICATION RESULTS FOR LABEL ATTRIBUTE 'GROUND FLOOR USE'.		
Predictors	Ground floor use attribute values	Performance metrics
Att.2 1st Floor use	Overall Prediction Accuracy	74.74%
	Recall for class: Other	96.19%
	Recall for class: Residential	95.40%
	Recall for class: Business-Shopping	58.29%
	Recall for class: Accomodation	97.40%
	Recall for class: Socio-Cultural Infrastructure	41.71%
	Recall for class: Empty	79.34%
	Recall for class: Technical Infrastructure	25.64%
	Recall for class: Open Space	99.29%
Att.3 2nd Floor use	Overall Prediction Accuracy	63.03%
	Recall for class: Other	13.82%
	Recall for class: Residential	76.50%
	Recall for class: Business-Shopping	62.50%
	Recall for class: Accomodation	95.00%
	Recall for class: Socio-Cultural Infrastructure	29.85%
	Recall for class: Empty	64.22%
	Recall for class: Technical Infrastructure	9.52%
	Recall for class: Open Space	100%
Att.4 3rd Floor use	Overall Prediction Accuracy	53.72%
	Recall for class: Other	12.35%
	Recall for class: Residential	99.59%
	Recall for class: Business-Shopping	41.10%
	Recall for class: Accomodation	87.50%
	Recall for class: Socio-Cultural Infrastructure	15.56%
	Recall for class: Empty	0.00%
	Recall for class: Technical Infrastructure	0.00%
	Recall for class: Open Space	100%

>>>

NAIVE BAYES CLASSIFICATION RESULTS FOR LABEL ATTRIBUTE 'GROUND FLOOR USE'.		
Predictors	**Ground floor use attribute values**	**Performance metrics**
Att.5 4th Floor use	Overall Prediction Accuracy	47.75%
	Recall for class: Other	10%
	Recall for class: Residential	99.74%
	Recall for class: Business-Shopping	28.04%
	Recall for class: Accomodation	83.75%
	Recall for class: Socio-Cultural Infrastructure	9.69%
	Recall for class: Empty	0.00%
	Recall for class: Technical Infrastructure	4.76%
	Recall for class: Open Space	100%
Att.6 5th Floor use	Overall Prediction Accuracy	42.69%
	Recall for class: Other	1.18%
	Recall for class: Residential	5.07%
	Recall for class: Business-Shopping	95.38%
	Recall for class: Accomodation	58.75%
	Recall for class: Socio-Cultural Infrastructure	3.32%
	Recall for class: Empty	0.00%
	Recall for class: Technical Infrastructure	0.00%
	Recall for class: Open Space	0.00%
Att.7 6th Floor use	Overall Prediction Accuracy	42.37%
	Recall for class: Other	0.59%
	Recall for class: Residential	1.33%
	Recall for class: Business-Shopping	98.49%
	Recall for class: Accomodation	43.75%
	Recall for class: Socio-Cultural Infrastructure	0.77%
	Recall for class: Empty	0.00%
	Recall for class: Technical Infrastructure	0.00%
	Recall for class: Open Space	0.00%
Att.8 7th Floor use	Overall Prediction Accuracy	42.32%
	Recall for class: Other	0.29%
	Recall for class: Residential	0.00%
	Recall for class: Business-Shopping	99.88%
	Recall for class: Accomodation	31.25%
	Recall for class: Socio-Cultural Infrastructure	0.51%
	Recall for class: Empty	0.00%
	Recall for class: Technical Infrastructure	0.00%
	Recall for class: Open Space	0.00%

>>>

NAIVE BAYES CLASSIFICATION RESULTS FOR LABEL ATTRIBUTE 'GROUND FLOOR USE'.		
Predictors	Ground floor use attribute values	Performance metrics
Att.9 8th Floor use	Overall Prediction Accuracy	42.19%
	Recall for class: Other	0.00%
	Recall for class: Residential	0.00%
	Recall for class: Business-Shopping	100%
	Recall for class: Accomodation	21.25%
	Recall for class: Socio-Cultural Infrastructure	0.00%
	Recall for class: Empty	0.00%
	Recall for class: Technical Infrastructure	0.00%
	Recall for class: Open Space	0.00%
Att.10 9th Floor use	Overall Prediction Accuracy	41.96%
	Recall for class: Other	0.00%
	Recall for class: Residential	0.00%
	Recall for class: Business-Shopping	100%
	Recall for class: Accomodation	3.75%
	Recall for class: Socio-Cultural Infrastructure	0.00%
	Recall for class: Empty	0.00%
	Recall for class: Technical Infrastructure	0.00%
	Recall for class: Open Space	0.00%
Att.11 10th Floor use	Overall Prediction Accuracy	41.91%
	Recall for class: Other	0.00%
	Recall for class: Residential	100%
	Recall for class: Business-Shopping	0.00%
	Recall for class: Accomodation	0.00%
	Recall for class: Socio-Cultural Infrastructure	0.00%
	Recall for class: Empty	0.00%
	Recall for class: Technical Infrastructure	0.00%
	Recall for class: Open Space	0.00%
Att.12 1st Basement floor use	Overall Prediction Accuracy	62.43%
	Recall for class: Other	0.00%
	Recall for class: Residential	55.20%
	Recall for class: Business-Shopping	95.18%
	Recall for class: Accomodation	45.00%
	Recall for class: Socio-Cultural Infrastructure	13.01%
	Recall for class: Empty	29.71%
	Recall for class: Technical Infrastructure	0.00%
	Recall for class: Open Space	0.00%

>>>

NAIVE BAYES CLASSIFICATION RESULTS FOR LABEL ATTRIBUTE 'GROUND FLOOR USE'.		
Predictors	Ground floor use attribute values	Performance metrics
Att.13 2nd Basement floor use	Overall Prediction Accuracy	43.31%
	Recall for class: Other	0.00%
	Recall for class: Residential	3.74%
	Recall for class: Business-Shopping	99.92%
	Recall for class: Accomodation	6.25%
	Recall for class: Socio-Cultural Infrastructure	2.04%
	Recall for class: Empty	0.00%
	Recall for class: Technical Infrastructure	0.00%
	Recall for class: Open Space	0.00%
Att.14 3rd Basement floor use	Overall Prediction Accuracy	42.11%
	Recall for class: Other	0.00%
	Recall for class: Residential	0.46%
	Recall for class: Business-Shopping	100.00%
	Recall for class: Accomodation	3.75%
	Recall for class: Socio-Cultural Infrastructure	0.00%
	Recall for class: Empty	0.00%
	Recall for class: Technical Infrastructure	0.00%
	Recall for class: Open Space	0.00%
Att.15 1st Penthouse use	Overall Prediction Accuracy	49.40%
	Recall for class: Other	2.35%
	Recall for class: Residential	33.54%
	Recall for class: Business-Shopping	88.77%
	Recall for class: Accomodation	47.50%
	Recall for class: Socio-Cultural Infrastructure	7.65%
	Recall for class: Empty	0.00%
	Recall for class: Technical Infrastructure	0.00%
	Recall for class: Open Space	0.00%
Att.16 2nd Penthouse use	Overall Prediction Accuracy	42.24%
	Recall for class: Other	0.00%
	Recall for class: Residential	1.54%
	Recall for class: Business-Shopping	99.12%
	Recall for class: Accomodation	12.50%
	Recall for class: Socio-Cultural Infrastructure	0.51%
	Recall for class: Empty	0.00%
	Recall for class: Technical Infrastructure	0.00%
	Recall for class: Open Space	0.00%

>>>

NAIVE BAYES CLASSIFICATION RESULTS FOR LABEL ATTRIBUTE 'GROUND FLOOR USE'.		
Predictors	Ground floor use attribute values	Performance metrics
Att.17 3rd Penthouse use	Overall Prediction Accuracy	41.92%
	Recall for class: Other	0.00%
	Recall for class: Residential	0.00%
	Recall for class: Business-Shopping	99.96%
	Recall for class: Accomodation	2.50%
	Recall for class: Socio-Cultural Infrastructure	0.00%
	Recall for class: Empty	0.00%
	Recall for class: Technical Infrastructure	0.00%
	Recall for class: Open Space	0.00%
Att.18 Neighborhood (Mahalle)	Overall Prediction Accuracy	55.64%
	Recall for class: Other	0.00%
	Recall for class: Residential	78.39%
	Recall for class: Business-Shopping	71.72%
	Recall for class: Accomodation	0.00%
	Recall for class: Socio-Cultural Infrastructure	0.00%
	Recall for class: Empty	0.00%
	Recall for class: Technical Infrastructure	0.00%
	Recall for class: Open Space	2.90%
Att.19 Population Density (Person/Ha)	Overall Prediction Accuracy	57.43%
	Recall for class: Other	0.00%
	Recall for class: Residential	88.68%
	Recall for class: Business-Shopping	68.06%
	Recall for class: Accomodation	0.00%
	Recall for class: Socio-Cultural Infrastructure	0.00%
	Recall for class: Empty	0.00%
	Recall for class: Technical Infrastructure	0.00%
	Recall for class: Open Space	0.00%
Att.20 Presence in the Bosphorus Silhouette	Overall Prediction Accuracy	41.92%
	Recall for class: Other	0.00%
	Recall for class: Residential	0.00%
	Recall for class: Business-Shopping	99.96%
	Recall for class: Accomodation	0.00%
	Recall for class: Socio-Cultural Infrastructure	0.51%
	Recall for class: Empty	0.00%
	Recall for class: Technical Infrastructure	0.00%
	Recall for class: Open Space	0.00%

>>>

NAIVE BAYES CLASSIFICATION RESULTS FOR LABEL ATTRIBUTE 'GROUND FLOOR USE'.		
Predictors	Ground floor use attribute values	Performance metrics
Att.21 Building Maintenance Conditions	Overall Prediction Accuracy	44.28%
	Recall for class: Other	0.00%
	Recall for class: Residential	0.00%
	Recall for class: Business-Shopping	98.69%
	Recall for class: Accomodation	0.00%
	Recall for class: Socio-Cultural Infrastructure	0.00%
	Recall for class: Empty	17.41%
	Recall for class: Technical Infrastructure	0.00%
	Recall for class: Open Space	95.65%
Att.22 Building Construction Material	Overall Prediction Accuracy	44.09%
	Recall for class: Other	5.29%
	Recall for class: Residential	4.15%
	Recall for class: Business-Shopping	98.65%
	Recall for class: Accomodation	0.00%
	Recall for class: Socio-Cultural Infrastructure	0.00%
	Recall for class: Empty	0.00%
	Recall for class: Technical Infrastructure	0.00%
	Recall for class: Open Space	95.65%
Att.23 Empty Floor ratio in the building	Overall Prediction Accuracy	51.65%
	Recall for class: Other	0.00%
	Recall for class: Residential	11.67%
	Recall for class: Business-Shopping	91.52%
	Recall for class: Accomodation	0.00%
	Recall for class: Socio-Cultural Infrastructure	0.00%
	Recall for class: Empty	80.03%
	Recall for class: Technical Infrastructure	0.00%
	Recall for class: Open Space	98.55%
Att.24 Ownership	Overall Prediction Accuracy	41.91%
	Recall for class: Other	0.00%
	Recall for class: Residential	0.00%
	Recall for class: Business-Shopping	100.00%
	Recall for class: Accomodation	0.00%
	Recall for class: Socio-Cultural Infrastructure	0.00%
	Recall for class: Empty	0.00%
	Recall for class: Technical Infrastructure	0.00%
	Recall for class: Open Space	0.00%

>>>

NAIVE BAYES CLASSIFICATION RESULTS FOR LABEL ATTRIBUTE 'GROUND FLOOR USE'.		
Predictors	Ground floor use attribute values	Performance metrics
Att.25 Historical Registry (intensity)	Overall Prediction Accuracy	48.25%
	Recall for class: Other	0.00%
	Recall for class: Residential	40.96%
	Recall for class: Business-Shopping	83.27%
	Recall for class: Accomodation	0.00%
	Recall for class: Socio-Cultural Infrastructure	0.00%
	Recall for class: Empty	0.00%
	Recall for class: Technical Infrastructure	0.00%
	Recall for class: Open Space	0.00%
Att.26 Floor Space Index (FSI)	Overall Prediction Accuracy	48.53%
	Recall for class: Other	4.12%
	Recall for class: Residential	46.24%
	Recall for class: Business-Shopping	78.02%
	Recall for class: Accomodation	0.00%
	Recall for class: Socio-Cultural Infrastructure	8.16%
	Recall for class: Empty	0.00%
	Recall for class: Technical Infrastructure	0.00%
	Recall for class: Open Space	0.00%
Att.27 Historical Registry of Build-ings	Overall Prediction Accuracy	44.73%
	Recall for class: Other	0.00%
	Recall for class: Residential	0.00%
	Recall for class: Business-Shopping	98.01%
	Recall for class: Accomodation	0.00%
	Recall for class: Socio-Cultural Infrastructure	55.87%
	Recall for class: Empty	0.00%
	Recall for class: Technical Infrastructure	0.00%
	Recall for class: Open Space	0.00%
Att.28 Building Footprint	Overall Prediction Accuracy	37.62%
	Recall for class: Other	0.00%
	Recall for class: Residential	91.30%
	Recall for class: Business-Shopping	17.84%
	Recall for class: Accomodation	0.00%
	Recall for class: Socio-Cultural Infrastructure	4.59%
	Recall for class: Empty	0.00%
	Recall for class: Technical Infrastructure	0.00%
	Recall for class: Open Space	7.25%

>>>

NAIVE BAYES CLASSIFICATION RESULTS FOR LABEL ATTRIBUTE 'GROUND FLOOR USE'.		
Predictors	Ground floor use attribute values	Performance metrics
Att.29 Distance to Dolmabahce	Overall Prediction Accuracy	40.05%
	Recall for class: Other	0.00%
	Recall for class: Residential	43.57%
	Recall for class: Business-Shopping	61.69%
	Recall for class: Accomodation	0.00%
	Recall for class: Socio-Cultural Infrastructure	0.00%
	Recall for class: Empty	0.00%
	Recall for class: Technical Infrastructure	0.00%
	Recall for class: Open Space	0.00%
Att.30 Distance to Galata Bridge	Overall Prediction Accuracy	44.53%
	Recall for class: Other	0.00%
	Recall for class: Residential	69.07%
	Recall for class: Business-Shopping	52.53%
	Recall for class: Accomodation	0.00%
	Recall for class: Socio-Cultural Infrastructure	0.00%
	Recall for class: Empty	0.00%
	Recall for class: Technical Infrastructure	0.00%
	Recall for class: Open Space	0.00%
Att.31 Distance to Galata Tower	Overall Prediction Accuracy	44.59%
	Recall for class: Other	0.00%
	Recall for class: Residential	64.52%
	Recall for class: Business-Shopping	56.23%
	Recall for class: Accomodation	0.00%
	Recall for class: Socio-Cultural Infrastructure	0.00%
	Recall for class: Empty	0.00%
	Recall for class: Technical Infrastructure	0.00%
	Recall for class: Open Space	0.00%
Att.32 Distance to Galatasaray	Overall Prediction Accuracy	48.87%
	Recall for class: Other	0.00%
	Recall for class: Residential	69.99%
	Recall for class: Business-Shopping	62.17%
	Recall for class: Accomodation	0.00%
	Recall for class: Socio-Cultural Infrastructure	0.00%
	Recall for class: Empty	0.00%
	Recall for class: Technical Infrastructure	0.00%
	Recall for class: Open Space	0.00%

>>>

NAIVE BAYES CLASSIFICATION RESULTS FOR LABEL ATTRIBUTE 'GROUND FLOOR USE'.		
Predictors	Ground floor use attribute values	Performance metrics
Att.33 Distance to Kabatas	Overall Prediction Accuracy	42.96%
	Recall for class: Other	0.00%
	Recall for class: Residential	22.99%
	Recall for class: Business-Shopping	84.63%
	Recall for class: Accomodation	0.00%
	Recall for class: Socio-Cultural Infrastructure	0.00%
	Recall for class: Empty	0.00%
	Recall for class: Technical Infrastructure	0.00%
	Recall for class: Open Space	0.00%
Att.34 Distance to Taksim	Overall Prediction Accuracy	41.64%
	Recall for class: Other	0.00%
	Recall for class: Residential	55.50%
	Recall for class: Business-Shopping	56.16%
	Recall for class: Accomodation	0.00%
	Recall for class: Socio-Cultural Infrastructure	0.00%
	Recall for class: Empty	0.00%
	Recall for class: Technical Infrastructure	0.00%
	Recall for class: Open Space	0.00%
Att.35 Distance to Tepebasi	Overall Prediction Accuracy	43.76%
	Recall for class: Other	0.00%
	Recall for class: Residential	29.49%
	Recall for class: Business-Shopping	81.44%
	Recall for class: Accomodation	0.00%
	Recall for class: Socio-Cultural Infrastructure	35.20%
	Recall for class: Empty	95.69%
	Recall for class: Technical Infrastructure	0.00%
	Recall for class: Open Space	1.45%
Att.36 Distance to Tunel	Overall Prediction Accuracy	44.09%
	Recall for class: Other	0.00%
	Recall for class: Residential	44.14%
	Recall for class: Business-Shopping	70.89%
	Recall for class: Accomodation	0.00%
	Recall for class: Socio-Cultural Infrastructure	0.00%
	Recall for class: Empty	0.00%
	Recall for class: Technical Infrastructure	0.00%
	Recall for class: Open Space	0.00%

>>>

NAIVE BAYES CLASSIFICATION RESULTS FOR LABEL ATTRIBUTE 'GROUND FLOOR USE'.		
Predictors	Ground floor use attribute values	Performance metrics
Att.37 Distance to Unkapani	Overall Prediction Accuracy	43.62%
	Recall for class: Other	0.00%
	Recall for class: Residential	60.98%
	Recall for class: Business-Shopping	56.67%
	Recall for class: Accomodation	0.00%
	Recall for class: Socio-Cultural Infrastructure	0.00%
	Recall for class: Empty	0.00%
	Recall for class: Technical Infrastructure	0.00%
	Recall for class: Open Space	0.00%
Att.38 Slope Code	Overall Prediction Accuracy	45.39%
	Recall for class: Other	0.00%
	Recall for class: Residential	25.86%
	Recall for class: Business-Shopping	88.21%
	Recall for class: Accomodation	0.00%
	Recall for class: Socio-Cultural Infrastructure	0.00%
	Recall for class: Empty	0.00%
	Recall for class: Technical Infrastructure	0.00%
	Recall for class: Open Space	0.00%
Att.39 LandHeight (elevation from the sea level)	Overall Prediction Accuracy	48.80%
	Recall for class: Other	0.00%
	Recall for class: Residential	47.62%
	Recall for class: Business-Shopping	79.41%
	Recall for class: Accomodation	0.00%
	Recall for class: Socio-Cultural Infrastructure	0.00%
	Recall for class: Empty	0.00%
	Recall for class: Technical Infrastructure	0.00%
	Recall for class: Open Space	0.00%
Att.40 Number of Floors	Overall Prediction Accuracy	45.94%
	Recall for class: Other	0.00%
	Recall for class: Residential	52.74%
	Recall for class: Business-Shopping	68.54%
	Recall for class: Accomodation	2.50%
	Recall for class: Socio-Cultural Infrastructure	0.00%
	Recall for class: Empty	0.00%
	Recall for class: Technical Infrastructure	0.00%
	Recall for class: Open Space	0.00%

>>>

NAIVE BAYES CLASSIFICATION RESULTS FOR LABEL ATTRIBUTE 'GROUND FLOOR USE'.		
Predictors	Ground floor use attribute values	Performance metrics
Att.41 Basement (with or without)	Overall Prediction Accuracy	50.67%
	Recall for class: Other	0.00%
	Recall for class: Residential	66.10%
	Recall for class: Business-Shopping	69.49%
	Recall for class: Accomodation	0.00%
	Recall for class: Socio-Cultural Infrastructure	0.00%
	Recall for class: Empty	0.00%
	Recall for class: Technical Infrastructure	0.00%
	Recall for class: Open Space	0.00%
Att.42 Penthouse (with or without)	Overall Prediction Accuracy	41.91%
	Recall for class: Other	0.00%
	Recall for class: Residential	0.00%
	Recall for class: Business-Shopping	99.92%
	Recall for class: Accomodation	2.50%
	Recall for class: Socio-Cultural Infrastructure	0.00%
	Recall for class: Empty	0.00%
	Recall for class: Technical Infrastructure	0.00%
	Recall for class: Open Space	0.00%
Att.43 Streets	Overall Prediction Accuracy	45.49%
	Recall for class: Other	1.18%
	Recall for class: Residential	94.52%
	Recall for class: Business-Shopping	34.73%
	Recall for class: Accomodation	0.00%
	Recall for class: Socio-Cultural Infrastructure	0.00%
	Recall for class: Empty	0.64%
	Recall for class: Technical Infrastructure	0.00%
	Recall for class: Open Space	0.00%
Att.44 Street Hierachy	Overall Prediction Accuracy	43.96%
	Recall for class: Other	0.00%
	Recall for class: Residential	85.39%
	Recall for class: Business-Shopping	38.51%
	Recall for class: Accomodation	0.00%
	Recall for class: Socio-Cultural Infrastructure	0.00%
	Recall for class: Empty	0.00%
	Recall for class: Technical Infrastructure	0.00%
	Recall for class: Open Space	0.00%

>>>

NAIVE BAYES CLASSIFICATION RESULTS FOR LABEL ATTRIBUTE 'GROUND FLOOR USE'.		
Predictors	Ground floor use attribute values	Performance metrics
Att.45 Land Price	Overall Prediction Accuracy	51.22%
	Recall for class: Other	0.00%
	Recall for class: Residential	97.24%
	Recall for class: Business-Shopping	46.59%
	Recall for class: Accomodation	0.00%
	Recall for class: Socio-Cultural Infrastructure	0.00%
	Recall for class: Empty	0.00%
	Recall for class: Technical Infrastructure	0.00%
	Recall for class: Open Space	0.00%

Appendix D Formulation of the I-type rules that allocate new use to empty floors

FORMULATION OF THE I-TYPE RULES THAT ALLOCATE NEW USE TO EMPTY FLOORS.											
Buildings that will be intervened in					Form of intervention			Basis of Intervention (Association Rules that shows the tendencies in data)			
R#	Rule Premise	Rule Conclusion	Support	Confidence	Intervention	Probability	ELSE {}	Rule Premise	Rule Conclusion	Support	Confidence
I1	Att.39 = 71	Att.1 = Empty	1.05%	20.00%	Att.1= Business-Shopping	57.78%	random {R, A, S, T, O}	Att.39 = 71	Att.1 = Business-Shopping	3.04%	57.78%
I2	Att.39 = 61	Att.1 = Empty	2.65%	19.10%	Att.1= Business-Shopping	43.54%	random {R, A, S, T, O}	Att.39 = 61	Att.1 = Business-Shopping	6.05%	43.54%
I3	Att.33 = III	Att.1 = Empty	4.10%	17.80%	Att.1 = Business-Shopping	44.58%	random {R, A, S, T, O}	Att.33 = III	Att.1 = Business-Shopping	10.26%	44.58%
I4	Att.34 = II	Att.1 = Empty	5.54%	16.92%	Att.1 = Residential	39.21%	random {A, S, T}	Att.34 = II	Att.1 = Residential	12.83%	39.21%
					Att.1 = Business-Shopping	38.86%	random {A, S, T}	Att.34 = II	Att.1 = Business-Shopping	12.71%	38.86%
					Att.1 = Other	4.05%	random {A, S, T}	Att.34 = II	Att.1 = Other	1.33%	4.05%
I5	Att.39 = 51	Att.1 = Empty	3.20%	14.88%	Att.1 = Business-Shopping	36.30%	random {A, S, T, O}	Att.39 = 51	Att.1 = Business-Shopping	7.80%	36.30%
					Att.1 = Residential	42.65%	random {A, S, T, O}	Att.39 = 51	Att.1 = Residential	9.17%	42.65%
I6	Att.40 = 2	Att.1 = Empty	2.18%	13.97%	Att.1 = Residential	56.61%	random {A, S, T, O}	Att.40 = 2	Att.1 = Residential	8.85%	56.61%
					Att.1 = Business-Shopping	28.43%	random {A, S, T, O}	Att.40 = 2	Att.1 = Business-Shopping	4.45%	28.43%
I7	Att.40 = 4	Att.1 = Empty	3.39%	13.64%	Att.1 = Residential	43.73%	random {A, S, T, O}	Att.40 = 4	Att.1 = Residential	10.88%	43.73%
					Att.1 = Business-Shopping	41.07%	random {A, S, T, O}	Att.40 = 4	Att.1 = Business-Shopping	10.22%	41.07%

>>>

FORMULATION OF THE I-TYPE RULES THAT ALLOCATE NEW USE TO EMPTY FLOORS.											
Buildings that will be intervened in					Form of intervention			Basis of Intervention (Association Rules that shows the tendencies in data)			
R#	Rule Premise	Rule Conclusion	Support	Confidence	Intervention	Probability	ELSE {}	Rule Premise	Rule Conclusion	Support	Confidence
I8	Att.12 = No Basement	Att.1 = Empty	7.18%	13.06%	Att.1 = Business-Shopping	46.49%	random {R, A, S, T}	Att.12 = No Basement	Att.1 = Business-Shopping	25.55%	46.49%
					Att.1 = Other	7.95%	random {R, A, S, T}	Att.12 = No Basement	Att.1 = Other	4.37%	7.95%
I9	Att.15 = No 1st Roof	Att.1 = Empty	8.97%	12.93%	Att.1 = Residential	43.62%	random {A, S, T}	Att.15 = No 1st Roof	Att.1 = Residential	30.27%	43.62%
					Att.1 = Business-Shopping	36.09%	random {A, S, T}	Att.15 = No 1st Roof	Att.1 = Business-Shopping	25.04%	36.09%
					Att.1 = Other	6.24%	random {A, S, T}	Att.15 = No 1st Roof	Att.1 = Other	4.33%	6.24%
I10	Att.45 = 1	Att.1 = Empty	2.26%	12.55%	Att.1 = Residential	65.80%	random {B, A, S, T, O}	Att.45 = 1	Att.1 = Residential	11.86%	65.80%
I11	Att.45 = 2	Att.1 = Empty	5.73%	12.51%	Att.1 = Residential	53.87%	random {A, S, T}	Att.45 = 2	Att.1 = Residential	24.69%	53.87%
					Att.1 = Business-Shopping	28.09%	random {A, S, T}	Att.45 = 2	Att.1 = Business-Shopping	12.87%	28.09%
					Att.1 = Other	4.60%	random {A, S, T}	Att.45 = 2	Att.1 = Other	2.11%	4.60%
I12	Att.40 = 3	Att.1 = Empty	4.84%	12.49%	Att.1 = Business-Shopping	26.99%	random {R, A, S, T, O}	Att.40 = 3	Att.1 = Business-Shopping	10.45%	26.99%
I13	Att.44 = 3rd Level	Att.1 = Empty	9.98%	12.38%	Att.1 = Residential	52.71%	random {A, S, T}	Att.44 = 3rd Level	Att.1 = Residential	42.51%	52.71%
					Att.1 = Business-Shopping	28.63%	random {A, S, T}	Att.44 = 3rd Level	Att.1 = Business-Shopping	23.09%	28.63%
					Att.1 = Other	5.42%	random {A, S, T}	Att.44 = 3rd Level	Att.1 = Other	4.37%	5.42%
I14	Att.44 = 2nd Level	Att.1 = Empty	1.83%	11.93%	Att.1 = Business-Shopping	53.05%	random {R, A, S, T, O}	Att.44 = 2nd Level	Att.1 = Business-Shopping	8.15%	53.05%
I15	Att.45 = 3	Att.1 = Empty	2.89%	11.86%	Att.1 = Business-Shopping	44.39%	random {A, S, T, O}	Att.45 = 3	Att.1 = Business-Shopping	10.80%	44.39%
					Att.1 = Residential	38.62%	random {A, S, T, O}	Att.45 = 3	Att.1 = Residential	9.40%	38.62%

>>>

FORMULATION OF THE I-TYPE RULES THAT ALLOCATE NEW USE TO EMPTY FLOORS.											
Buildings that will be intervened in					Form of intervention			Basis of Intervention (Association Rules that shows the tendencies in data)			
R#	Rule Premise	Rule Conclusion	Support	Confidence	Intervention	Probability	ELSE {}	Rule Premise	Rule Conclusion	Support	Confidence
I16	Att.33 = IV	Att.1 = Empty	5.58%	11.83%	Att.1 = Business-Shopping	33.00%	random {A, S, T}	Att.33 = IV	Att.1 = Business-Shopping	15.56%	33.00%
					Att.1 = Other	4.88%	random {A, S, T}	Att.33 = IV	Att.1 = Other	2.30%	4.88%
					Att.1 = Residential	49.13%	random {A, S, T}	Att.33 = IV	Att.1 = Residential	23.17%	49.13%
R#	Rule Premise	Rule Conclusion	Support	Confidence	Intervention	Probability	ELSE {}	Rule Premise	Rule Conclusion	Support	Confidence
I17	Att.34 = III	Att.1 = Empty	4.45%	10.87%	Att.1 = Residential	48.43%	random {A, S, T}	Att.34 = III	Att.1 = Residential	19.81%	48.43%
					Att.1 = Business-Shopping	35.27%	random {A, S, T}	Att.34 = III	Att.1 = Business-Shopping	14.43%	35.27%
					Att.1 = Other	4.39%	random {A, S, T}	Att.34 = III	Att.1 = Other	1.79%	4.39%
I18	Att.1 = Business-Shopping	Att.2 = Empty	3.78%	10.85%	Att.2 = Business-Shopping	36.13%	random {R, A, S, T, O}	Att.1 = Business-Shopping	Att.2 = Business-Shopping	12.60%	36.13%
I19	Att.41 = 1 Basement	Att.1 = Empty	4.84%	10.81%	Att.1 = Residential	67.13%	random {A, S, T, O}	Att.41 = 1 Basement	Att.1 = Residential	30.03%	67.13%
					Att.1 = Business-Shopping	20.84%	random {A, S, T, O}	Att.41 = 1 Basement	Att.1 = Business-Shopping	9.32%	20.84%
I20	Att.39 = 41	Att.1 = Empty	2.22%	9.69%	Att.1= Business-Shopping	20.58%	random {A, S, T, O}	Att.39 = 41	Att.1 = Business-Shopping	4.72%	20.58%
					Att.1 = Residential	66.16%	random {A, S, T, O}	Att.39 = 41	Att.1 = Residential	15.17%	66.16%
I21	Att.39 = 31	Att.1 = Empty	1.83%	8.27%	Att.1 = Other	4.93%	random {R, A, S, T}	Att.39 = 31	Att.1 = Other	1.09%	4.93%
					Att.1 = Business-Shopping	29.75%	random {R, A, S, T}	Att.39 = 31	Att.1 = Business-Shopping	6.59%	29.75%

>>>

FORMULATION OF THE I-TYPE RULES THAT ALLOCATE NEW USE TO EMPTY FLOORS.											
Buildings that will be intervened in					Form of intervention			Basis of Intervention (Association Rules that shows the tendencies in data)			
R#	Rule Premise	Rule Conclusion	Support	Confidence	Intervention	Probability	ELSE {}	Rule Premise	Rule Conclusion	Support	Confidence
I22	Att.33 = V	Att.1 = Empty	2.38%	7.97%	Att.1 = Residential	55.82%	random {A, S, T}	Att.33 = V	Att.1 = Residential	16.65%	55.82%
					Att.1 = Business-Shopping	30.33%	random {A, S, T}	Att.33 = V	Att.1 = Business-Shopping	9.05%	30.33%
					Att.1 = Other	4.84%	random {A, S, T}	Att.33 = V	Att.1 = Other	1.44%	4.84%
I23	Att.39 = 21	Att.1 = Empty	1.09%	7.87%	Att.1 = Residential	40.73%	random {A, S, T, O}	Att.39 = 21	Att.1 = Residential	5.66%	40.73%
					Att.1 = Business-Shopping	47.47%	random {A, S, T, O}	Att.39 = 21	Att.1 = Business-Shopping	6.59%	47.47%
I24	Att.34 = IV	Att.1 = Empty	1.87%	7.45%	Att.1 = Residential	59.16%	random {A, S, T}	Att.34 = IV	Att.1 = Residential	14.86%	59.16%
					Att.1 = Business-Shopping	27.33%	random {A, S, T}	Att.34 = IV	Att.1 = Business-Shopping	6.86%	27.33%
					Att.1 = Other	5.28%	random {A, S, T}	Att.34 = IV	Att.1 = Other	1.33%	5.28%
I25	Att.1 = Business-Shopping	Att.15 = Empty	1.87%	5.37%	Att.15 = Residential	18.34%	random {A, S, T, O}	Att.1 = Business-Shopping	Att.15 = Residential	6.40%	18.34%
					Att.15 = Business-Shopping	4.36%	random {A, S, T, O}	Att.1 = Business-Shopping	Att.15 = Business-Shopping	1.52%	4.36%

Appendix E Fitness Error Graphs for E type, I-Type and D-type R

R#	Rule Antecedent (if) (X)	Decision (then) (Y)	Probability*	Decision (then)	Probability	Probability** for Number of buildings verifying both X and Y/Total Number of buildings
E1	Att.45 = 7	Att.1 = random {B, LB}	88.70%	Att.1 = random {R, A, E, S, O}	11.30%	3.98%

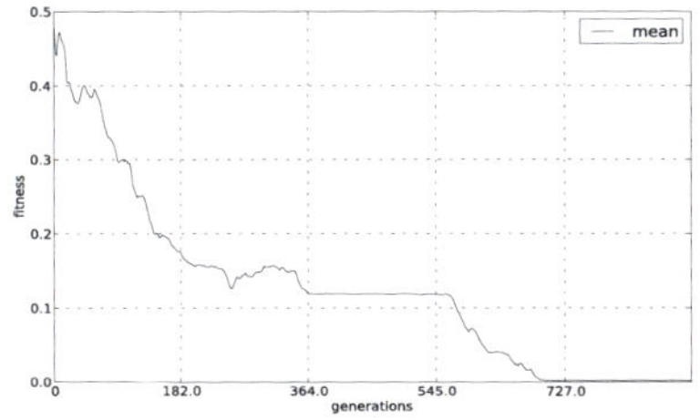

Fitness error graph for Probability*

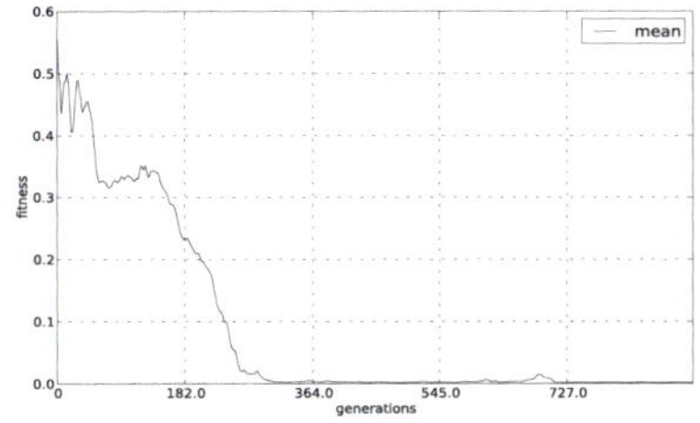

Fitness error graph for Probability**

R#	Rule Antecedent (if) (X)	Decision (then) (Y)	Probability*	Decision (then)	Probability	Probability** for Number of buildings verifying both X and Y/Total Number of buildings
E2	Att.40 = 5	Att.1 = random {B, LB}	63.87%	Att.1 = random {R, A, E, S, O}	36.13%	5.93%

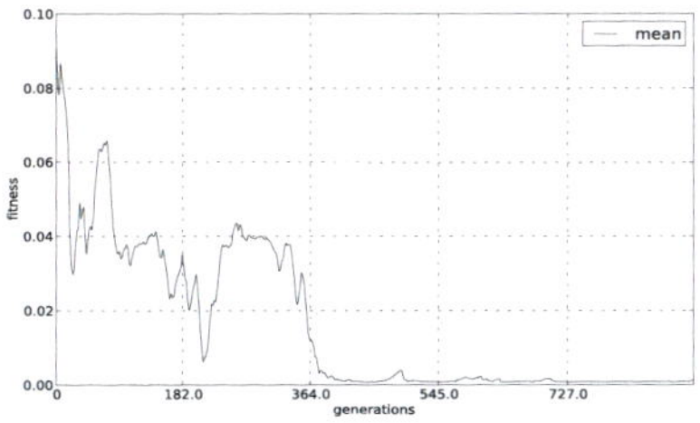

Fitness error graph for Probability*

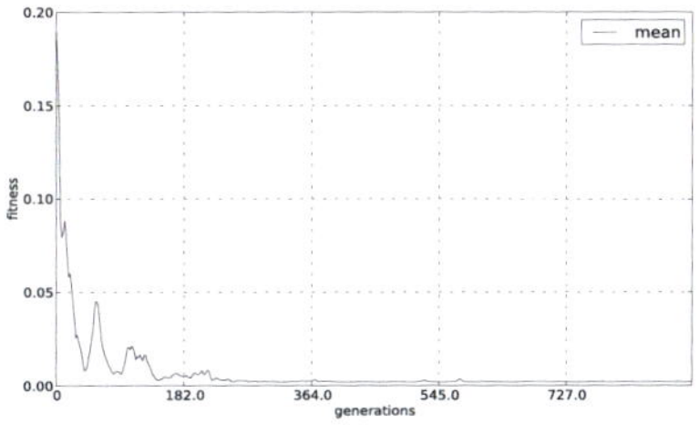

Fitness error graph for Probability**

R#	Rule Antecedent (if) (X)	Decision (then) (Y)	Probability*	Decision (then)	Probability	Probability** for Number of buildings verifying both X and Y/Total Number of buildings
E3	Att.45 = 4	Att.1 = random {B, LB}	59.04%	Att.1 = random {R, A, E, S, O}	40.96%	4.33%

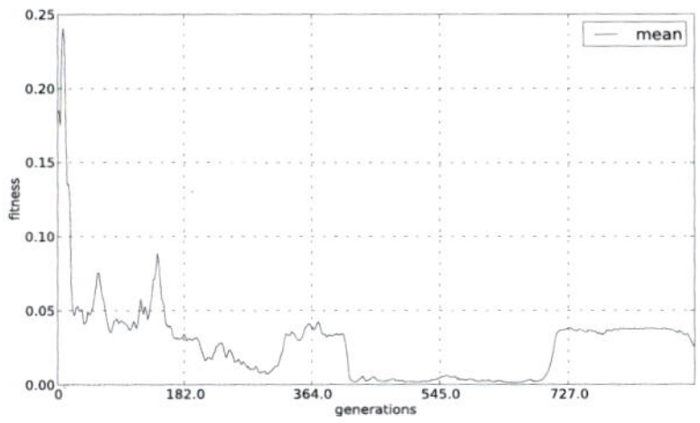

Fitness error graph for Probability*

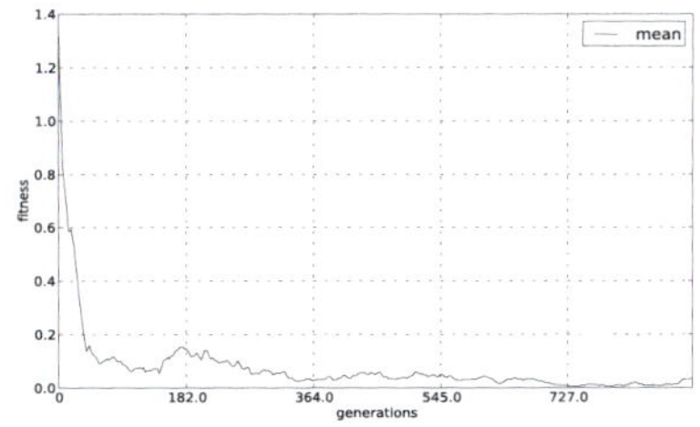

Fitness error graph for Probability**

FIGURE APP.E.1 Fitness error graphs for E1, E2 and E3

R#	Rule Antecedent (if) (X)	Decision (then) (Y)	Probability*	Decision (then)	Probability	Probability** for Number of buildings verifying both X and Y/Total Number of buildings
E4	Att.39 = 71	Att.1 = random {B, LB}	57.78%	Att.1 = random {R, A, E, S, O}	42.22%	3.04%

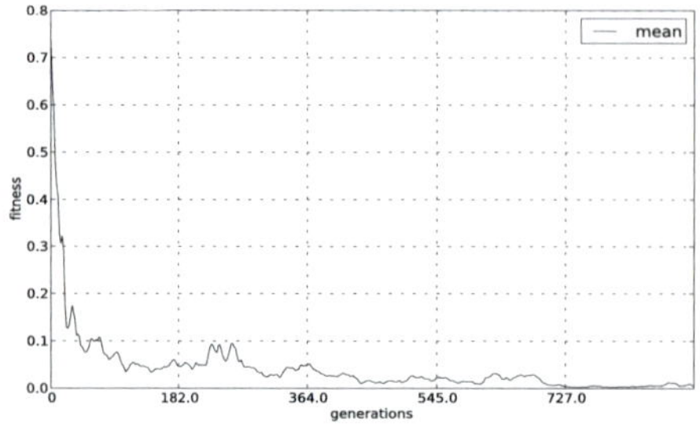

Fitness error graph for Probability*

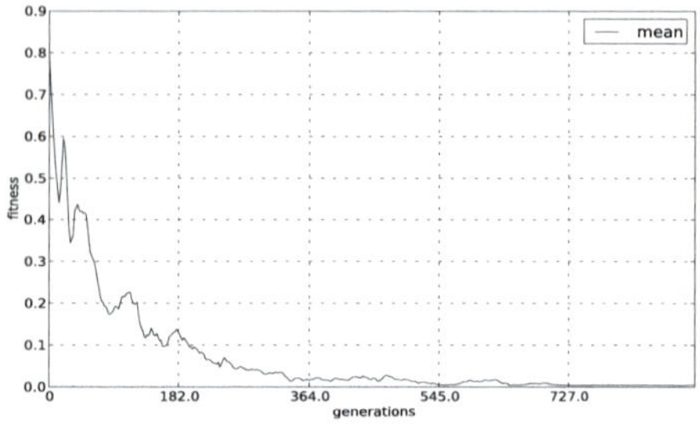

Fitness error graph for Probability**

R#	Rule Antecedent (if) (X)	Decision (then) (Y)	Probability*	Decision (then)	Probability	Probability** for Number of buildings verifying both X and Y/Total Number of buildings
E5	Att.44 = 2nd Level	Att.1 = random {B, LB}	53.05%	Att.1 = random {R, A, E, S, O}	46.95%	8.15%

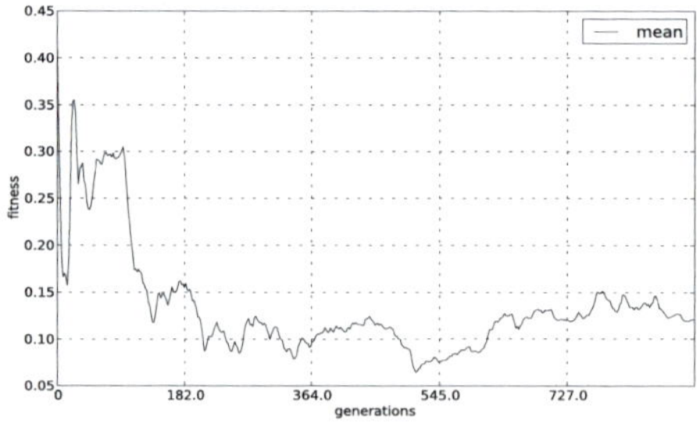

Fitness error graph for Probability*

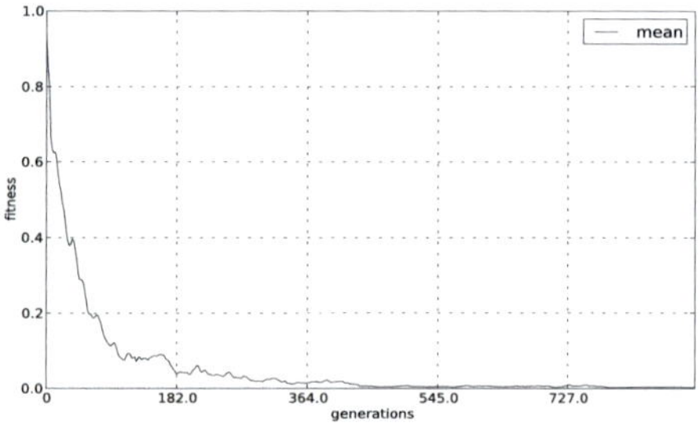

Fitness error graph for Probability**

R#	Rule Antecedent (if) (X)	Decision (then) (Y)	Probability*	Decision (then)	Probability	Probability** for Number of buildings verifying both X and Y/Total Number of buildings
E6	Att.41 = 1 Basement	Att.1 = random {R, Stu, 1-2P, F, El, D}	67.13%	Att.1 = random {B, A, E, S, O}	32.87%	30.03%

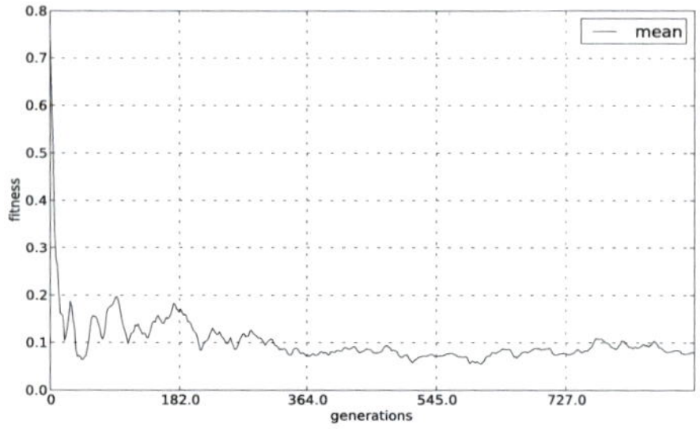

Fitness error graph for Probability*

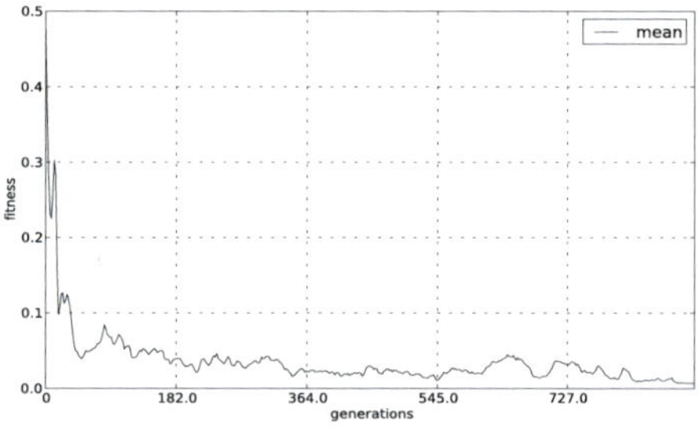

Fitness error graph for Probability**

FIGURE APP.E.2 Fitness error graphs for E4, E5 and E6

R#	Rule Antecedent (if) (X)	Decision (then) (Y)	Probability*	Decision (then)	Probability	Probability** for Number of buildings verifying both X and Y/Total Number of buildings
E7	Att.39 = 41	Att.1 = random {R, Stu, 1-2P, F, El, D}	66.16%	Att.1 = random {B, A, E, S, O}	33.84%	15.17%

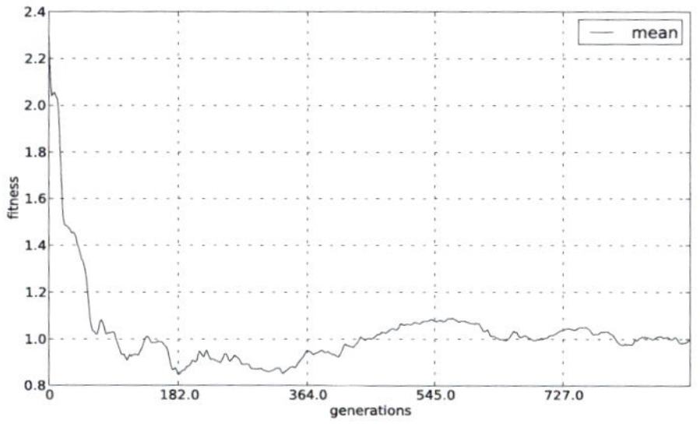

Fitness error graph for Probability*

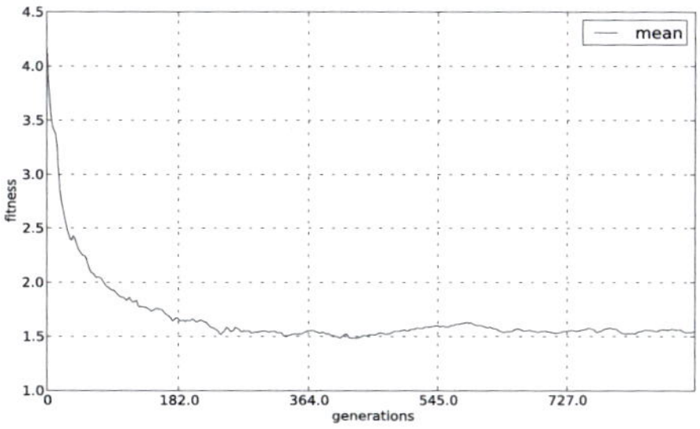

Fitness error graph for Probability**

R#	Rule Antecedent (if) (X)	Decision (then) (Y)	Probability*	Decision (then)	Probability	Probability** for Number of buildings verifying both X and Y/Total Number of buildings
E8	Att.45 = 1	Att.1 = random {R, Stu, 1-2P, F, El, D}	65.80%	Att.1 = random {B, A, E, S, O}	34.20%	11.86%

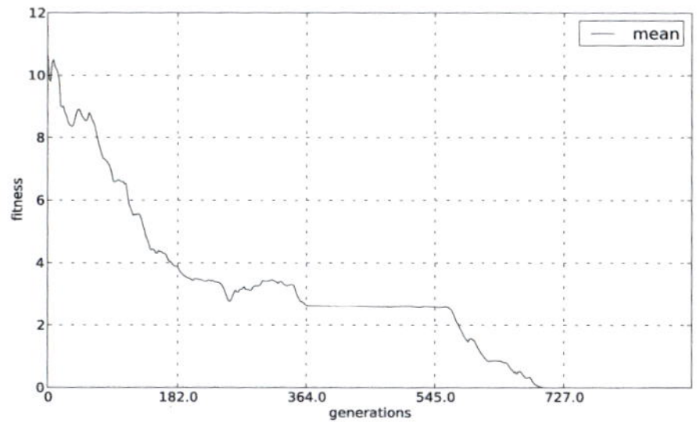

Fitness error graph for Probability*

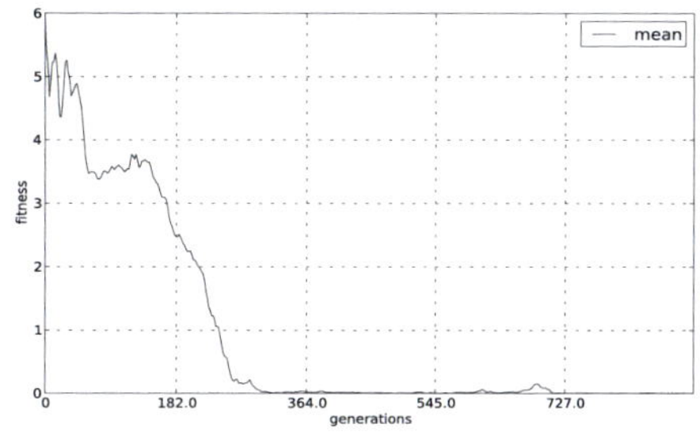

Fitness error graph for Probability**

R#	Rule Antecedent (if) (X)	Decision (then) (Y)	Probability*	Decision (then)	Probability	Probability** for Number of buildings verifying both X and Y/Total Number of buildings
E9	Att.34 = IV	Att.1 = random {R, Stu, 1-2P, F, El, D}	59.16%	Att.1 = random {B, A, E, S, O}	40.84%	14.86%

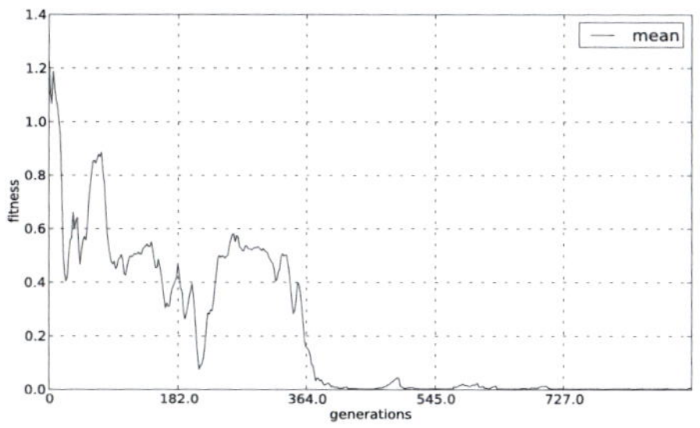

Fitness error graph for Probability*

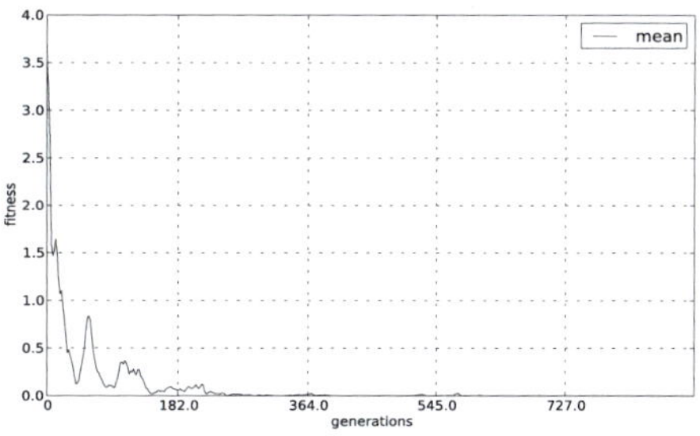

Fitness error graph for Probability**

FIGURE APP.E.3 Fitness error graphs for E7, E8 and E9

R#	Rule Antecedent (if) (X)	Decision (then) (Y)	Probability*	Decision (then)	Probability	Probability** for Number of buildings verifying both X and Y/Total Number of buildings
E10	Att.40 = 2	Att.1 = random {R, Stu, 1-2P, F, El, D}	56.61%	Att.1 = random {B, A, E, S, O}	43.39%	8.85%

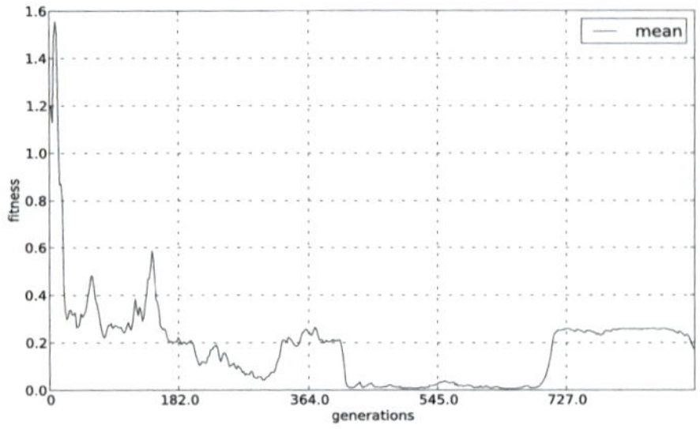

Fitness error graph for Probability*

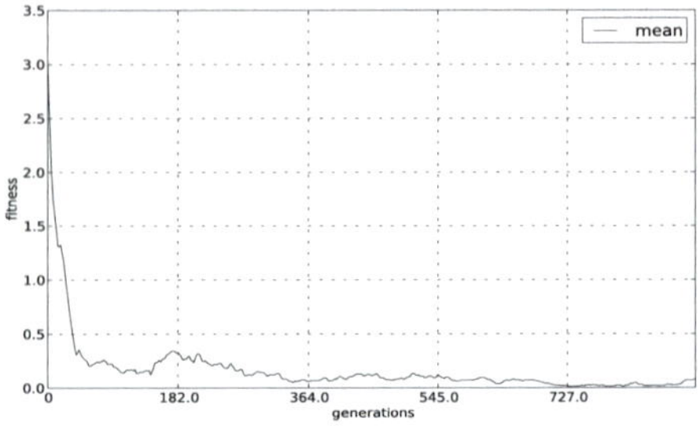

Fitness error graph for Probability**

R#	Rule Antecedent (if) (X)	Decision (then) (Y)	Probability*	Decision (then)	Probability	Probability** for Number of buildings verifying both X and Y/Total Number of buildings
E11	Att.33 = V	Att.1 = random {R, Stu, 1-2P, F, El, D}	55.82%	Att.1 = random {B, A, E, S, O}	44.18%	16.65%

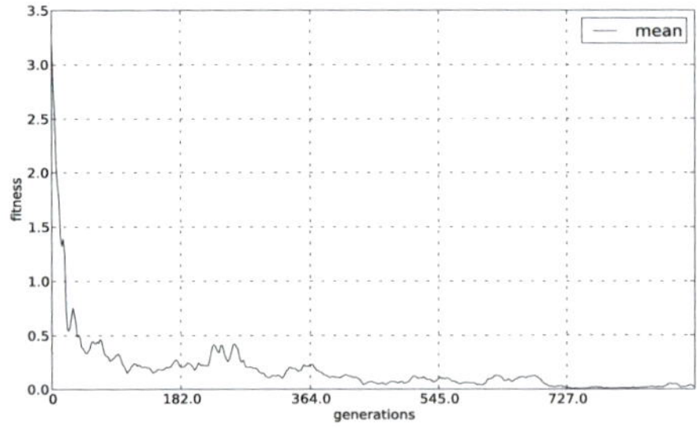

Fitness error graph for Probability*

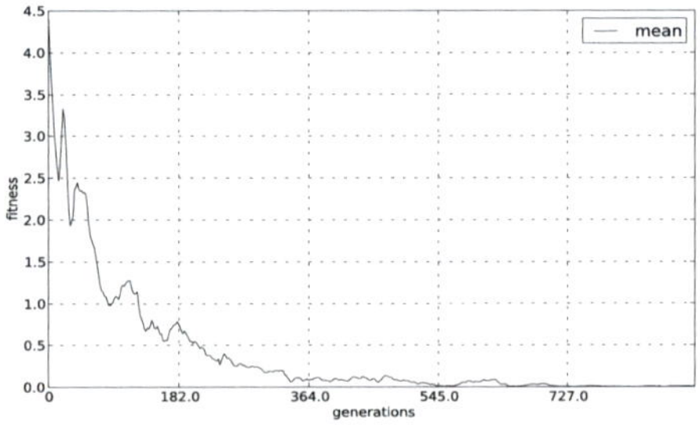

Fitness error graph for Probability**

R#	Rule Antecedent (if) (X)	Decision (then) (Y)	Probability*	Decision (then)	Probability	Probability** for Number of buildings verifying both X and Y/Total Number of buildings
E12	Att.39 = 31	Att.1 = random {R, Stu, 1-2P, F, El, D}	55.81%	Att.1 = random {B, A, E, S, O}	44.19%	12.36%

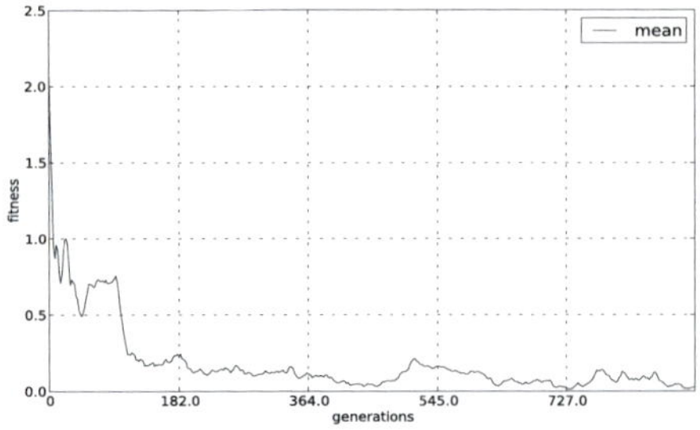

Fitness error graph for Probability*

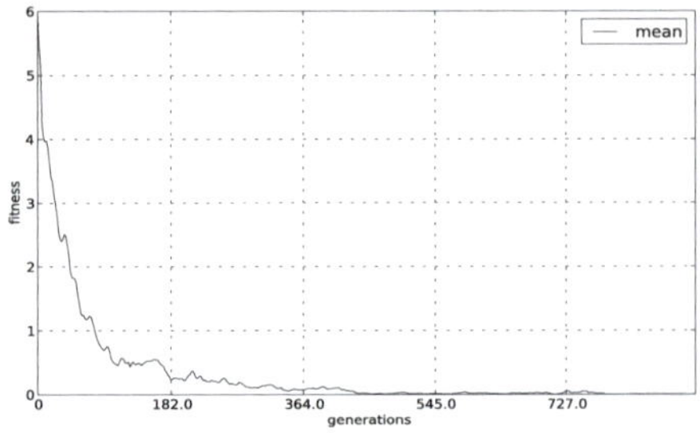

Fitness error graph for Probability**

FIGURE APP.E.4 Fitness error graphs for E10, E11 and E12

R#	Rule Antecedent (if) (X)	Decision (then) (Y)	Probability*	Decision (then)	Probability	Probability** for Number of buildings verifying both X and Y/Total Number of buildings
E13	Att.45 = 2	Att.1 = random {R, Stu, 1-2P, F, El, D}	53.87%	Att.1 = random {B, A, E, S, O}	46.13%	24.69%

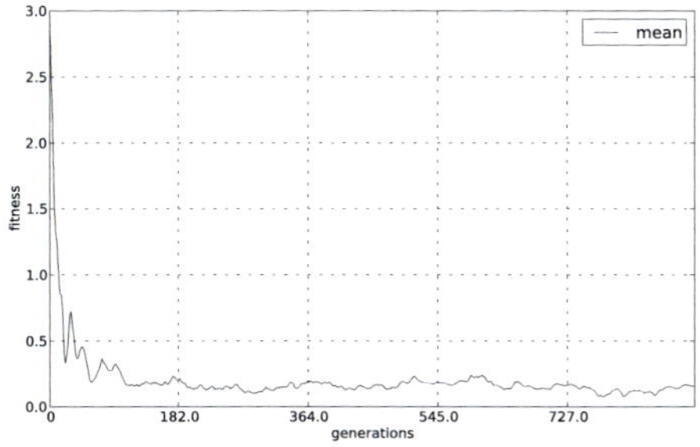

Fitness error graph for Probability*

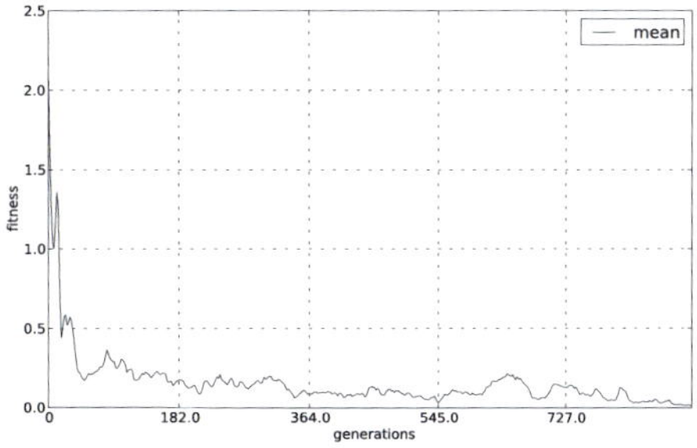

Fitness error graph for Probability**

R#	Rule Antecedent (if) (X)	Decision (then) (Y)	Probability*	Decision (then)	Probability	Probability** for Number of buildings verifying both X and Y/Total Number of buildings
E14	Att.44 = 3rd Level	Att.1 = random {R, Stu, 1-2P, F, El, D}	52.71%	Att.1 = random {B, A, E, S, O}	47.29%	42.51%

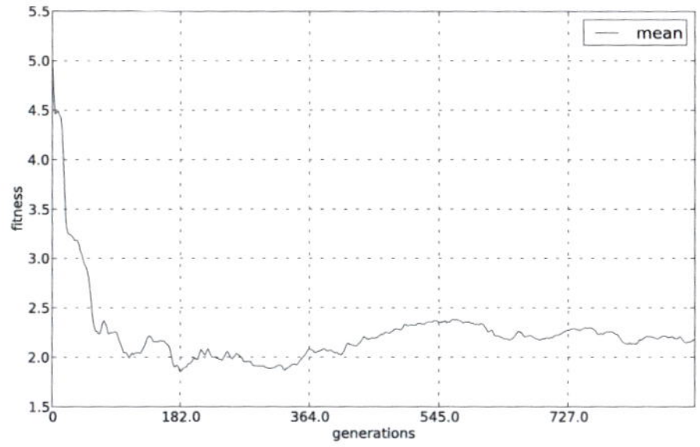

Fitness error graph for Probability*

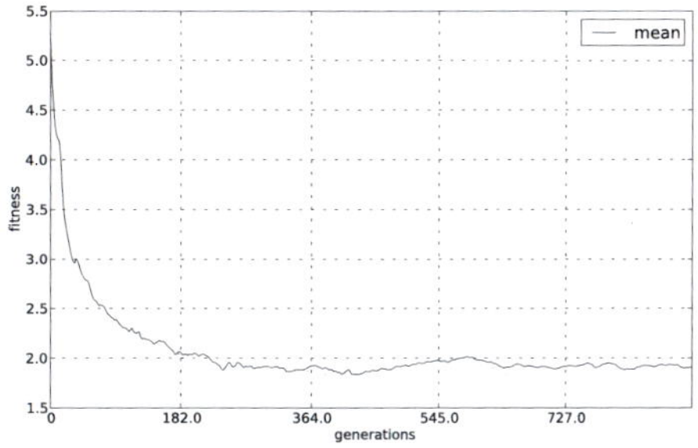

Fitness error graph for Probability**

FIGURE APP.E.5 Fitness error graphs for E13, E14

R#	Rule Antecedent (if)	Rule Consequent (then)	Decision (then)	Probability*	Decision (then)	Probability
I1	Att.39 = 71	Att.1 = Empty	Att.1= Business-Shopping	57.78%	Att.1= random {R, A, S, O}	42.22%

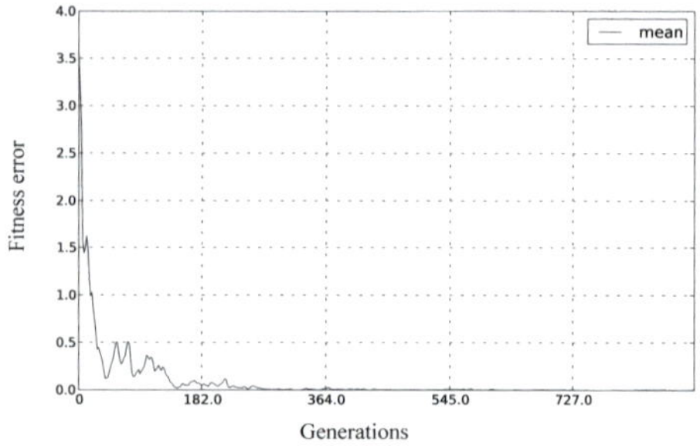

Fitness error graph for Probability*

R#	Rule Antecedent (if)	Rule Consequent (then)	Decision (then)	Probability*	Decision (then)	Probability
I2	Att.39 = 61	Att.1 = Empty	Att.1= Business-Shopping	43.54%	Att.1= random {R, A, S, O}	56.46%

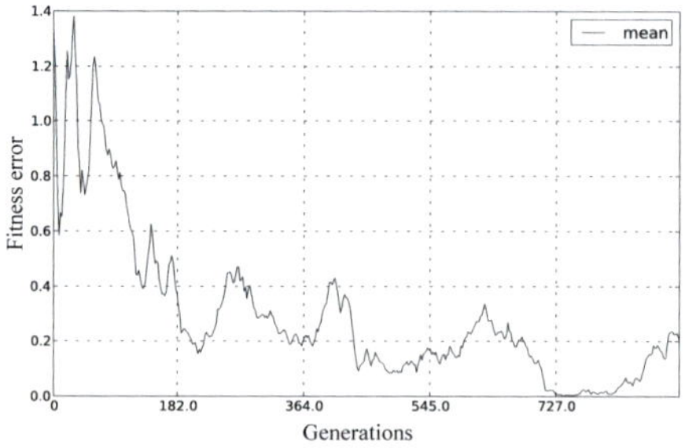

Fitness error graph for Probability*

R#	Rule Antecedent (if)	Rule Consequent (then)	Decision (then)	Probability*	Decision (then)	Probability
I3	Att.33 = III	Att.1 = Empty	Att.1 = Business-Shopping	44.58%	Att.1= random {R, A, S, O}	55.42%

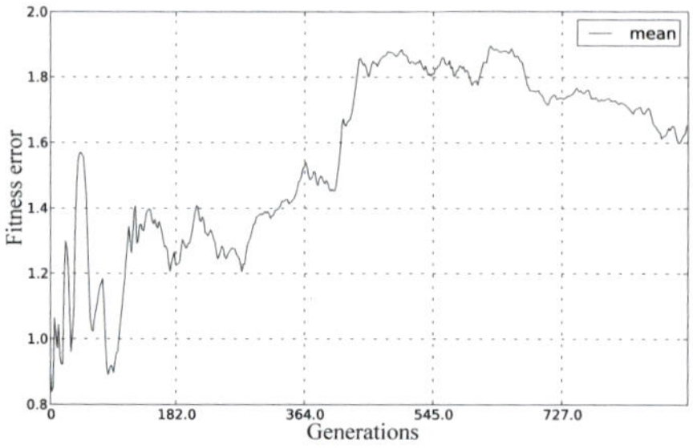

Fitness error graph for Probability*

FIGURE APP.E.6 Fitness error graphs for I1, I2 and I3

R#	Rule Antecedent (if)	Rule Consequent (then)	Decision (then)	Probability*	Decision (then)	Probability
I4.1			Att.1 = Residential	39.21%		
I4.2	Att.34 = II	Att.1 = Empty	Att.1 = Business-Shopping	38.86%	Att.1= random {A, S}	17.88%
I4.3			Att.1 = Other	4.05%		

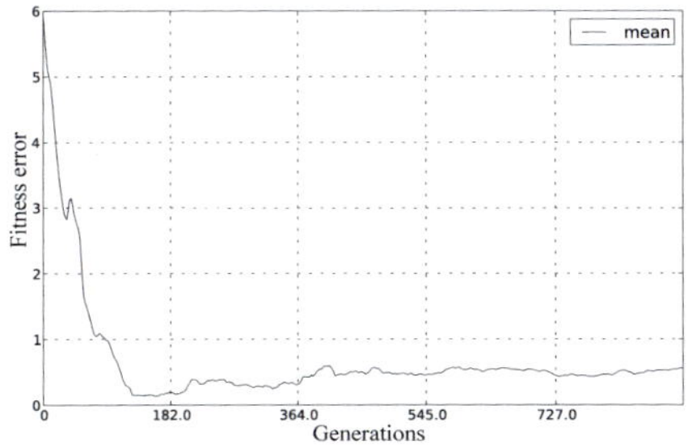

Fitness error graph for Probability* (Rule I4.1)

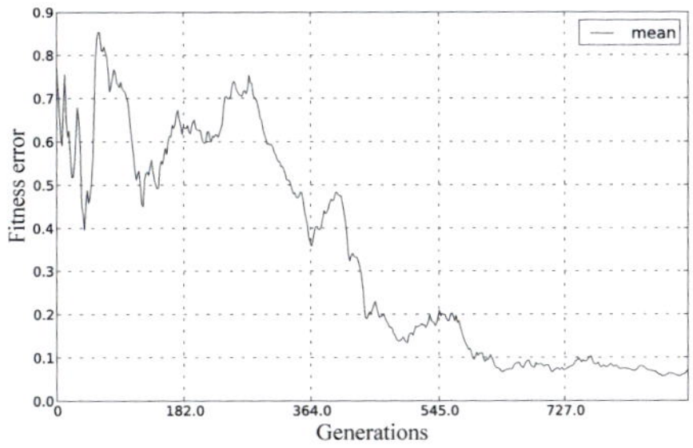

Fitness error graph for Probability* (Rule I4.2)

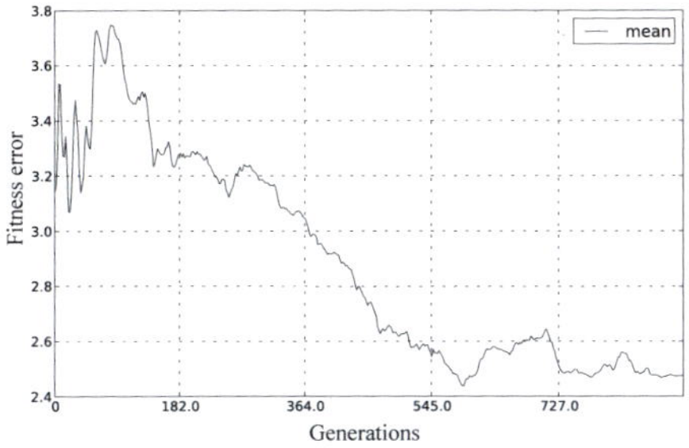

Fitness error graph for Probability* (Rule I4.3)

R#	Rule Antecedent (if)	Rule Consequent (then)	Decision (then)	Probability*	Decision (then)	Probability
I5.1	Att.39 = 51	Att.1 = Empty	Att.1 = Business-Shopping	36.30%	Att.1= random {A, S, O}	21.05%
I5.2			Att.1 = Residential	42.65%		

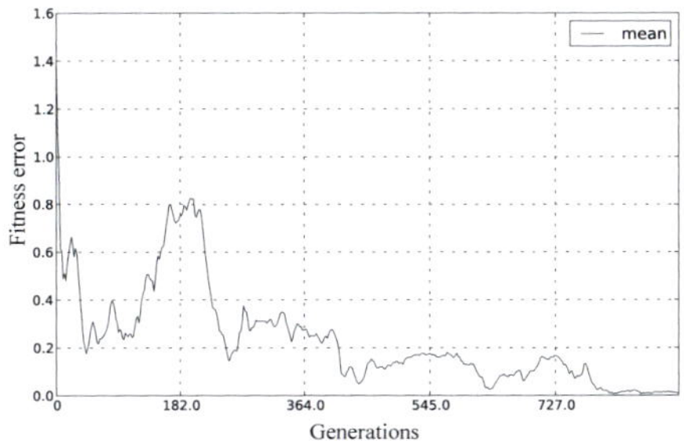

Fitness error graph for Probability* (Rule I5.1)

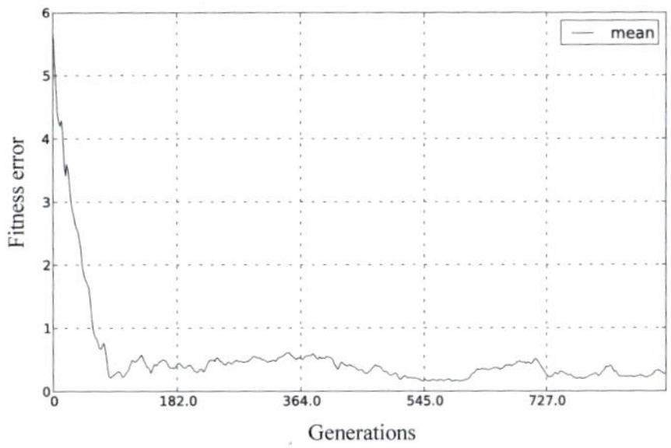

Fitness error graph for Probability* (Rule I5.2)

FIGURE APP.E.7 Fitness error graphs for I4, I5

R#	Rule Antecedent (if)	Rule Consequent (then)	Decision (then)	Probability*	Decision (then)	Probability
I6.1	Att.40 = 2	Att.1 = Empty	Att.1 = Residential	56.61%	Att.1= random {A, S, O}	14.96%
I6.2			Att.1 = Business-Shopping	28.43%		

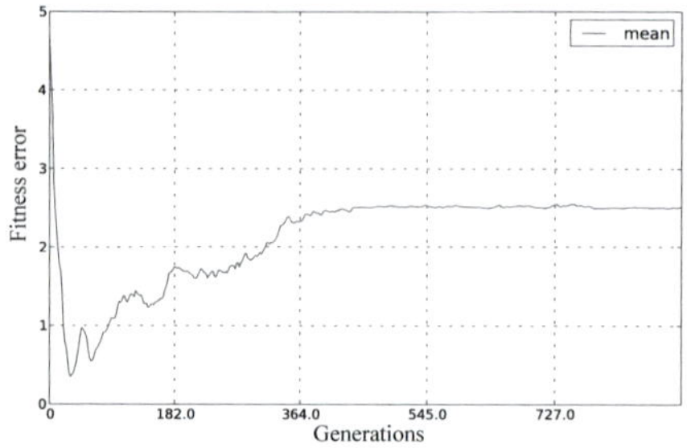

Fitness error graph for Probability* (Rule I6.1)

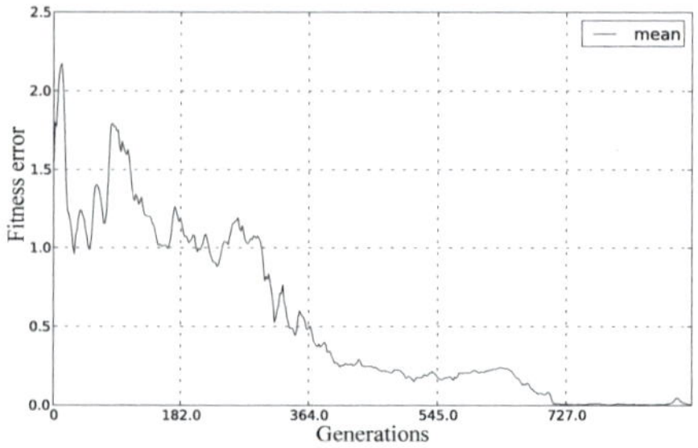

Fitness error graph for Probability* (Rule I6.2)

R#	Rule Antecedent (if)	Rule Consequent (then)	Decision (then)	Probability*	Decision (then)	Probability
I7.1	Att.40 = 4	Att.1 = Empty	Att.1 = Residential	43.73%	Att.1= random {A, S, O}	15.20%
I7.2			Att.1 = Business-Shopping	41.07%		

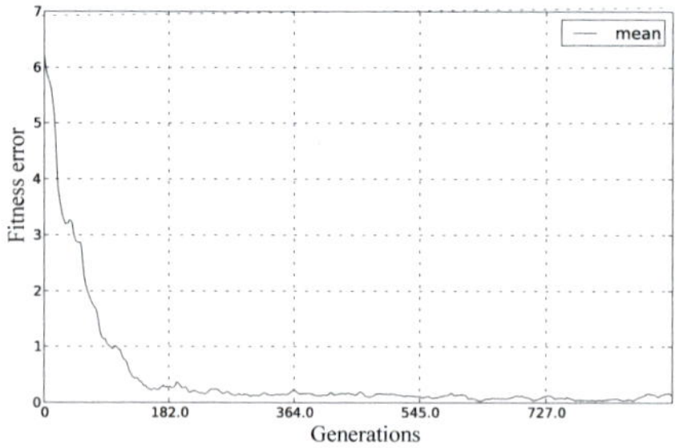

Fitness error graph for Probability* (Rule I7.1)

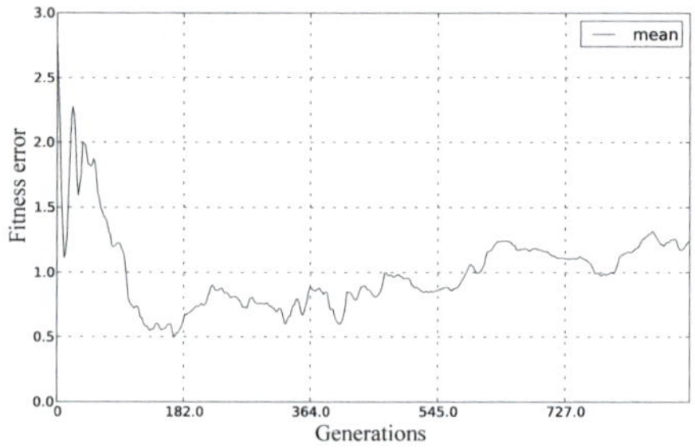

Fitness error graph for Probability* (Rule I7.2)

R#	Rule Antecedent (if)	Rule Consequent (then)	Decision (then)	Probability*	Decision (then)	Probability
I8.1	Att.12 = No Basement	Att.1 = Empty	Att.1 = Business-Shopping	46.49%	Att.1= random {R, A, S}	45.56%
I8.2			Att.1 = Other	7.95%		

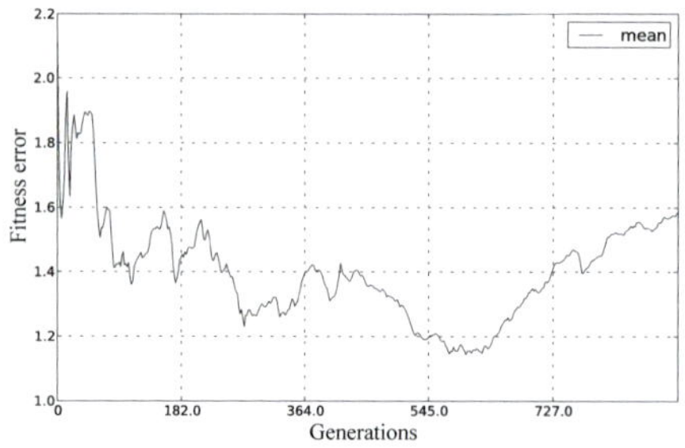

Fitness error graph for Probability* (Rule I8.1)

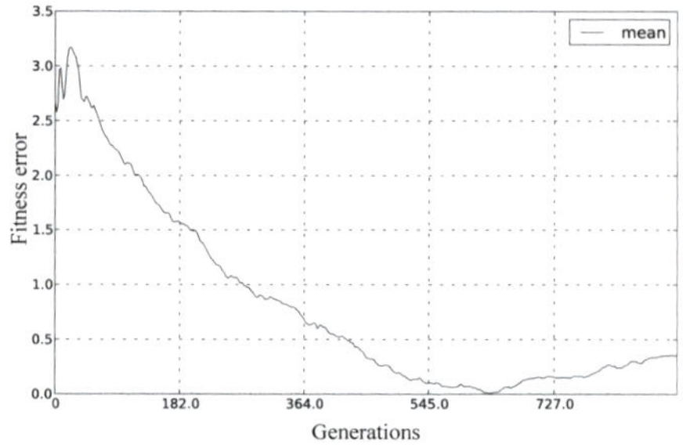

Fitness error graph for Probability* (Rule I8.2)

FIGURE APP.E.8 Fitness error graphs for I6, I7 and I8

R#	Rule Antecedent (if)	Rule Consequent (then)	Decision (then)	Probability*	Decision (then)	Probability
I9.1			Att.1 = Residential	43.62%		
I9.2	Att.15 = No 1st Roof	Att.1 = Empty	Att.1 = Business-Shopping	36.09%	Att.1= random {A, S}	14.05%
I9.3			Att.1 = Other	6.24%		

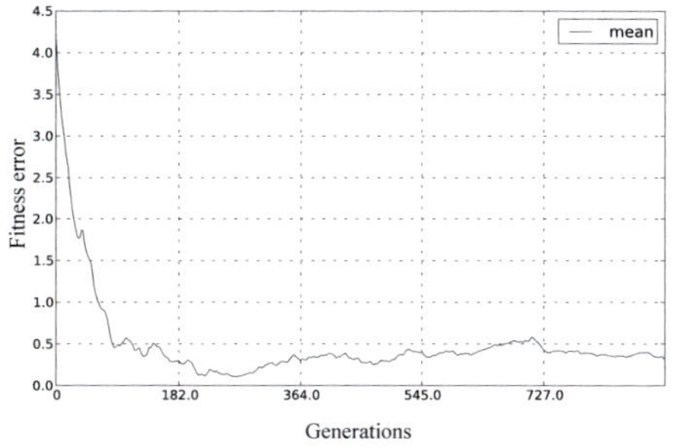

Fitness error graph for Probability* (Rule I9.1)

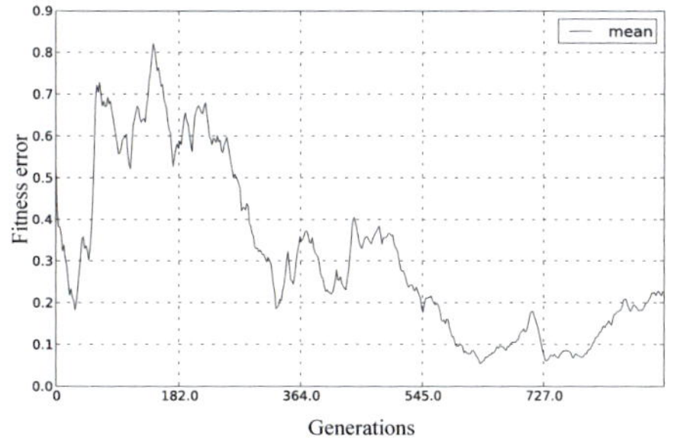

Fitness error graph for Probability* (Rule I9.2)

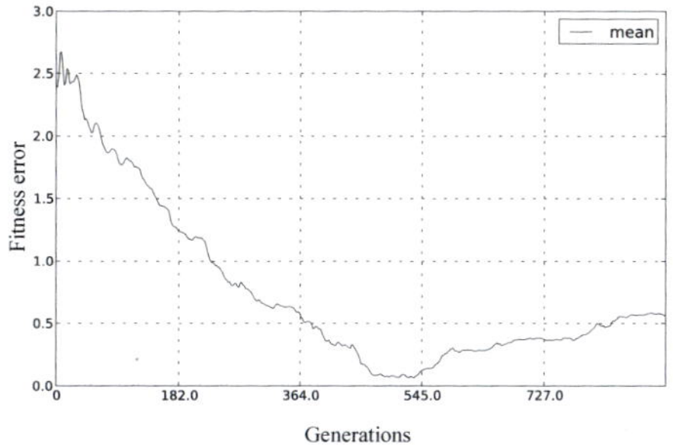

Fitness error graph for Probability* (Rule I9.3)

R#	Rule Antecedent (if)	Rule Consequent (then)	Decision (then)	Probability*	Decision (then)	Probability
I10	Att.45 = 1	Att.1 = Empty	Att.1 = Residential	65.80%	Att.1= random {B, A, S, O}	34.20%

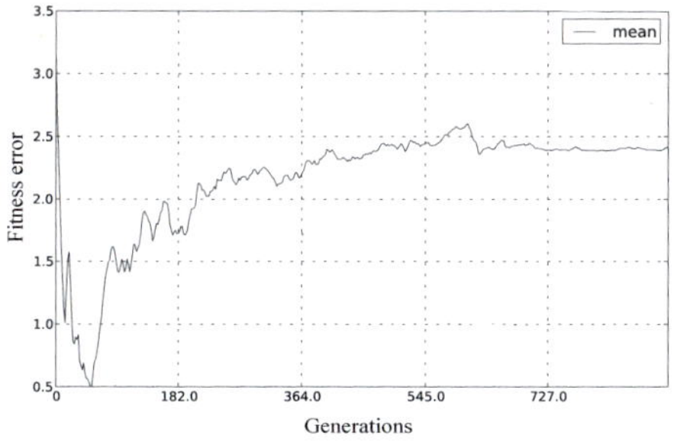

Fitness error graph for Probability* (Rule I10.1)

FIGURE APP.E.9 Fitness error graphs for I9, I10

R#	Rule Antecedent (if)	Rule Consequent (then)	Decision (then)	Probability*	Decision (then)	Probability
I11.1			Att.1 = Residential	53.87%		
I11.2	Att.45 = 2	Att.1 = Empty	Att.1 = Business-Shopping	28.09%	Att.1= random {A, S}	13.44%
I11.3			Att.1 = Other	4.60%		

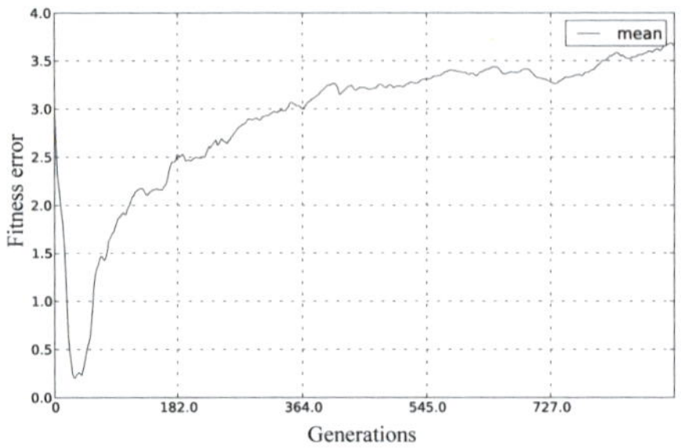

Fitness error graph for Probability* (Rule I11.1)

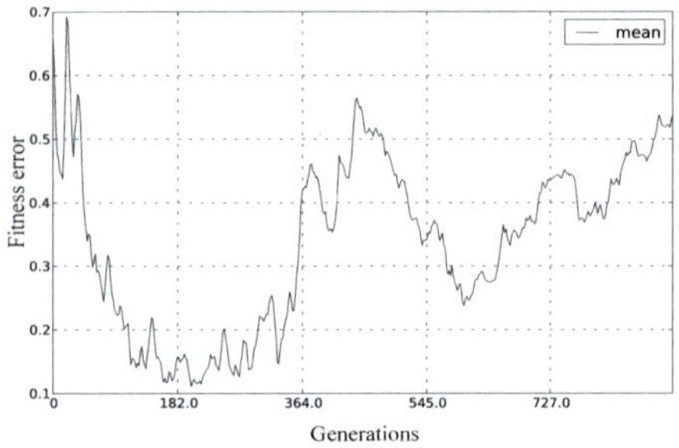

Fitness error graph for Probability* (Rule I11.2)

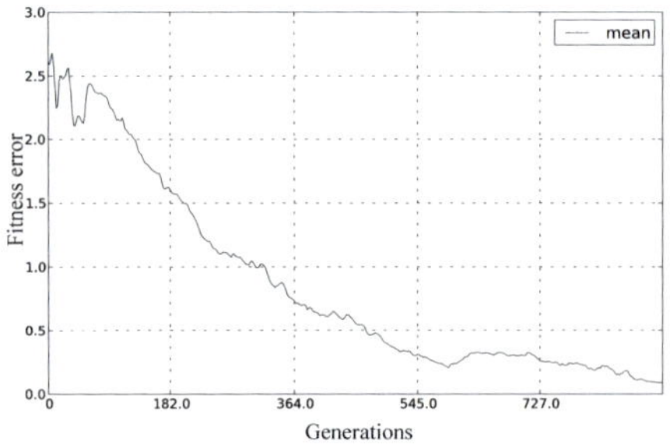

Fitness error graph for Probability* (Rule I11.3)

R#	Rule Antecedent (if)	Rule Consequent (then)	Decision (then)	Probability*	Decision (then)	Probability
I12	Att.40 = 3	Att.1 = Empty	Att.1 = Business-Shopping	26.99%	Att.1= random {R, A, S, O}	73.01%

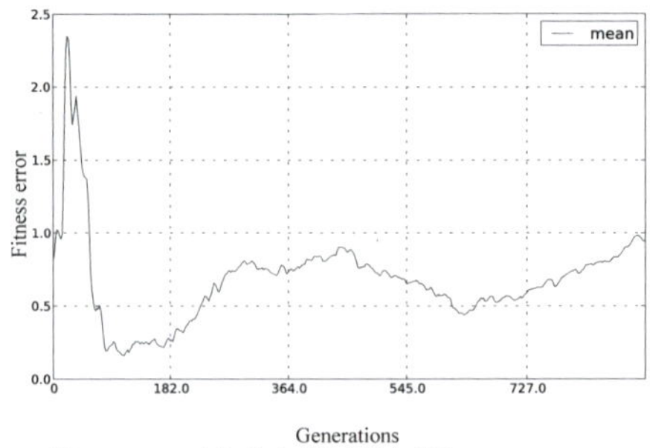

Fitness error graph for Probability* (Rule I12)

FIGURE APP.E.10 Fitness error graphs for I11, I12

R#	Rule Antecedent (if)	Rule Consequent (then)	Decision (then)	Probability*	Decision (then)	Probability
I13.1			Att.1 = Residential	52.71%		
I13.2	Att.44 = 3rd Level	Att.1 = Empty	Att.1 = Business-Shopping	28.63%	Att.1= random {A, S}	13.24%
I13.3			Att.1 = Other	5.42%		

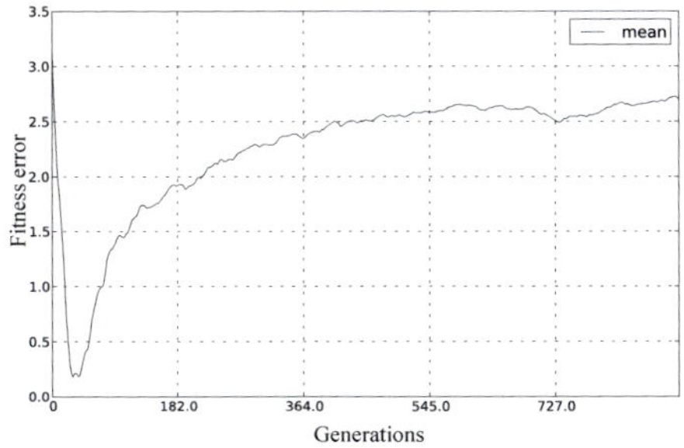

Fitness error graph for Probability* (Rule I13.1)

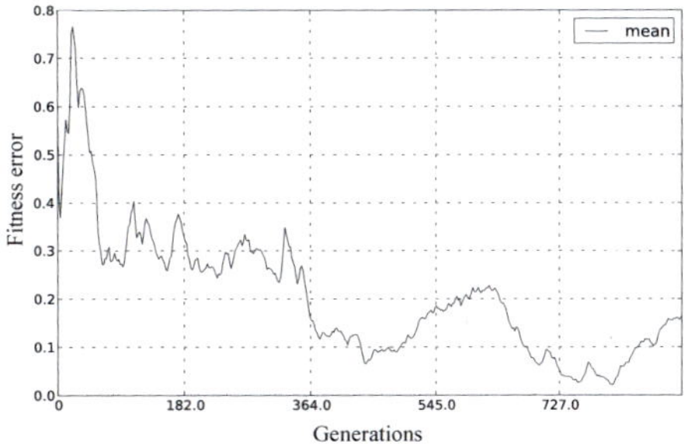

Fitness error graph for Probability* (Rule I13.2)

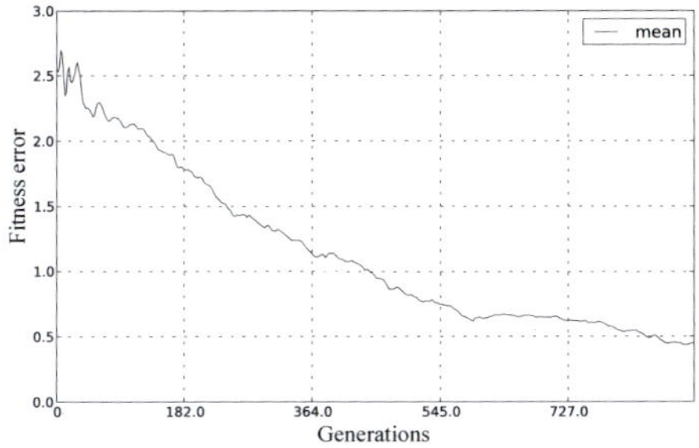

Fitness error graph for Probability* (Rule I13.3)

R#	Rule Antecedent (if)	Rule Consequent (then)	Decision (then)	Probability*	Decision (then)	Probability
I14	Att.44 = 2nd Level	Att.1 = Empty	Att.1 = Business-Shopping	53.05%	Att.1= random {R, A, S, O}	46.95%

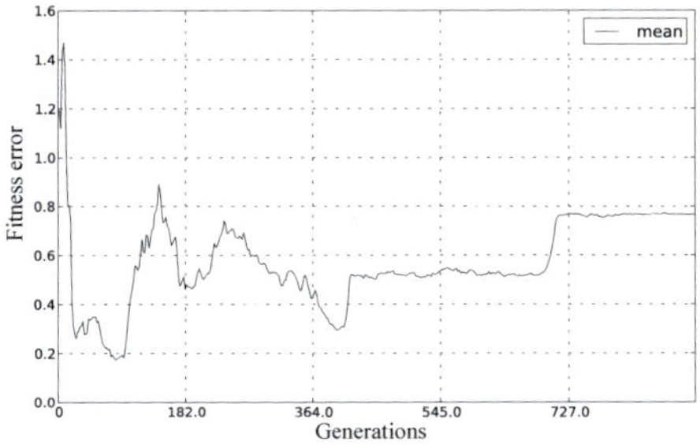

Fitness error graph for Probability* (Rule I14)

FIGURE APP.E.11 Fitness error graphs for I13, I14

R#	Rule Antecedent (if)	Rule Consequent (then)	Decision (then)	Probability*	Decision (then)	Probability
I15.1	Att.45 = 3	Att.1 = Empty	Att.1 = Business-Shopping	44.39%	Att.1= random {A, S, O}	16.99%
I15.2			Att.1 = Residential	38.62%		

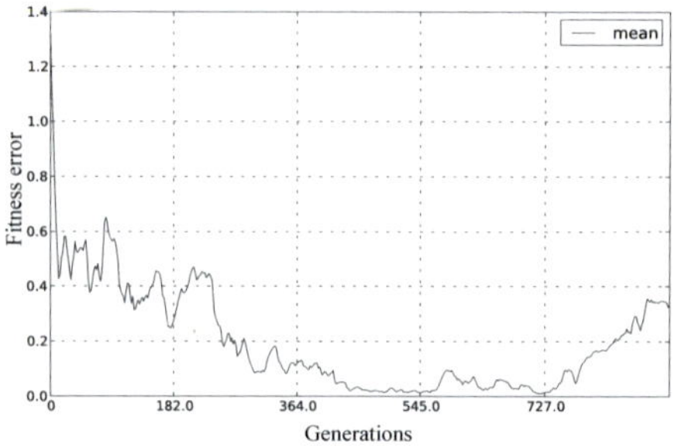

Fitness error graph for Probability* (Rule I15.1)

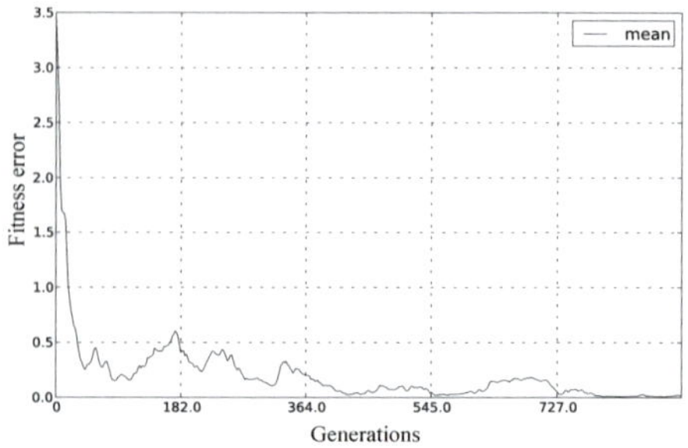

Fitness error graph for Probability* (Rule I15.2)

R#	Rule Antecedent (if)	Rule Consequent (then)	Decision (then)	Probability*	Decision (then)	Probability
I16.1	Att.33 = IV	Att.1 = Empty	Att.1 = Residential	49.13%	Att.1= random {A, S}	12.99%
I16.2			Att.1 = Business-Shopping	33.00%		
I16.3			Att.1 = Other	4.88%		

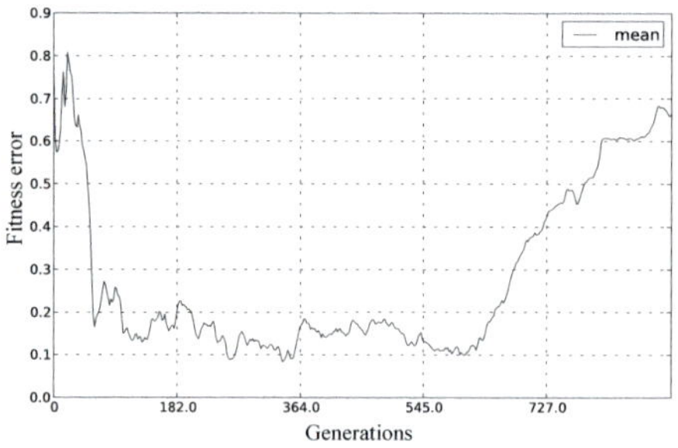

Fitness error graph for Probability* (Rule I16.1)

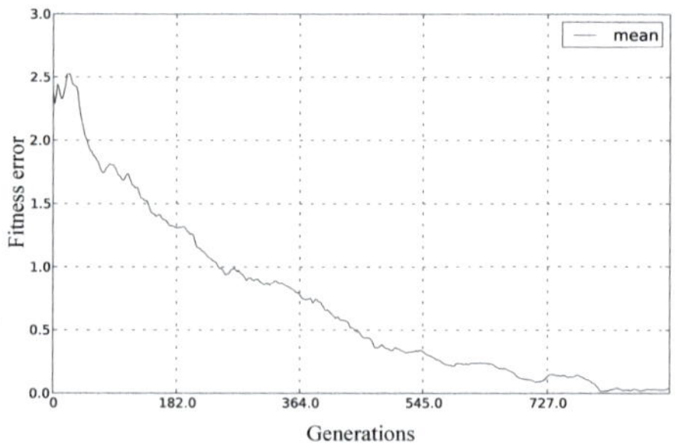

Fitness error graph for Probability* (Rule I16.2)

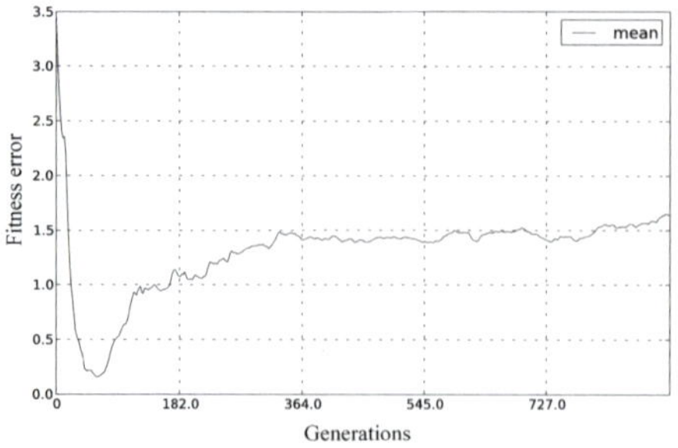

Fitness error graph for Probability* (Rule I16.3)

FIGURE APP.E.12 Fitness error graphs for I15, I16

R#	Rule Antecedent (if)	Rule Consequent (then)	Decision (then)	Probability*	Decision (then)	Probability
I17.1			Att.1 = Residential	48.43%		
I17.2	Att.34 = III	Att.1 = Empty	Att.1 = Business-Shopping	35.27%	Att.1= random {A, S}	11.91%
I17.3			Att.1 = Other	4.39%		

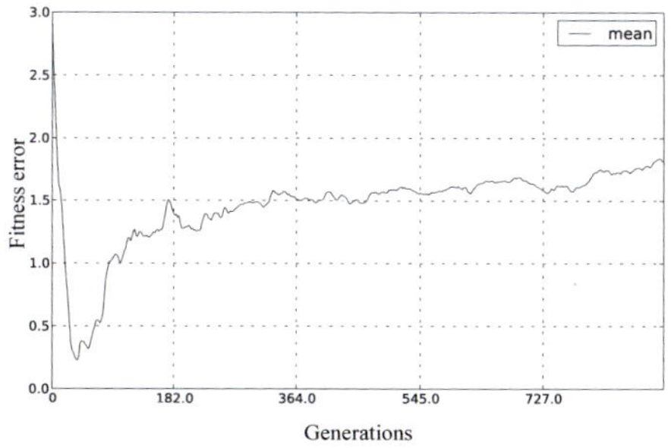

Fitness error graph for Probability* (Rule I17.1)

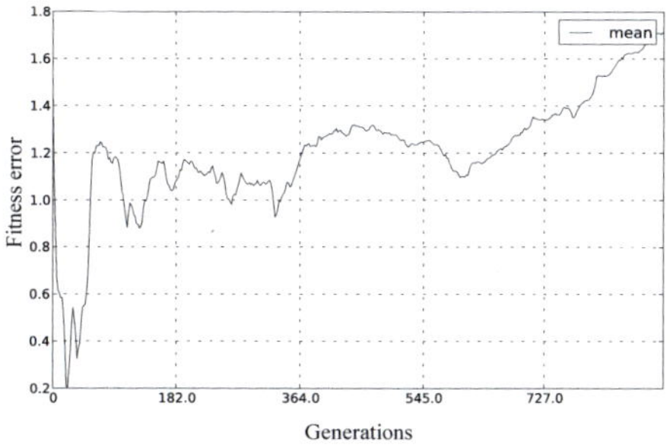

Fitness error graph for Probability* (Rule I17.2)

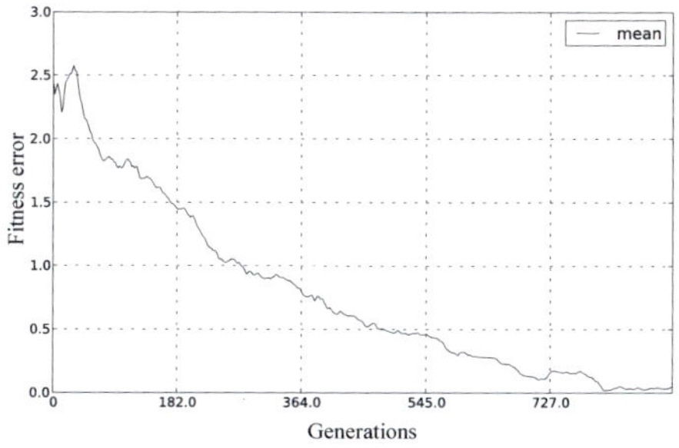

Fitness error graph for Probability* (Rule I17.3)

R#	Rule Antecedent (if)	Rule Consequent (then)	Decision (then)	Probability*	Decision (then)	Probability
I18	Att.1 = Business-Shopping	Att.2 = Empty	Att.2 = Business-Shopping	36.13%	Att.1= random {R, A, S, O}	63.87%

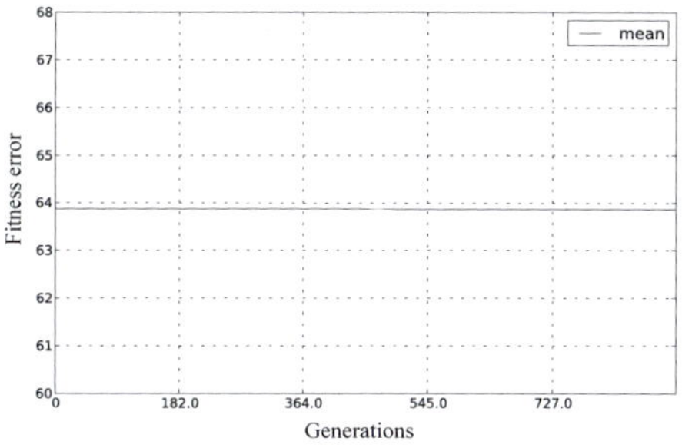

Fitness error graph for Probability* (Rule I18)

FIGURE APP.E.13 Fitness error graphs for I17, I18

R#	Rule Antecedent (if)	Rule Consequent (then)	Decision (then)	Probability*	Decision (then)	Probability
I19.1	Att.41 = 1 Basement	Att.1 = Empty	Att.1 = Residential	67.13%	Att.1= random {A, S, O}	12.03%
I19.2			Att.1 = Business-Shopping	20.84%		

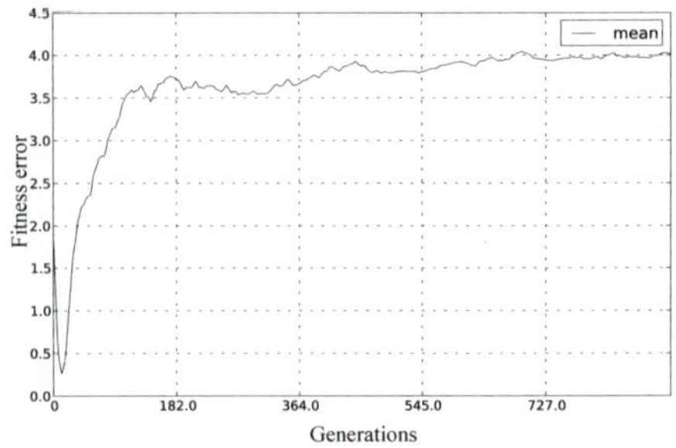

Fitness error graph for Probability* (Rule I19.1)

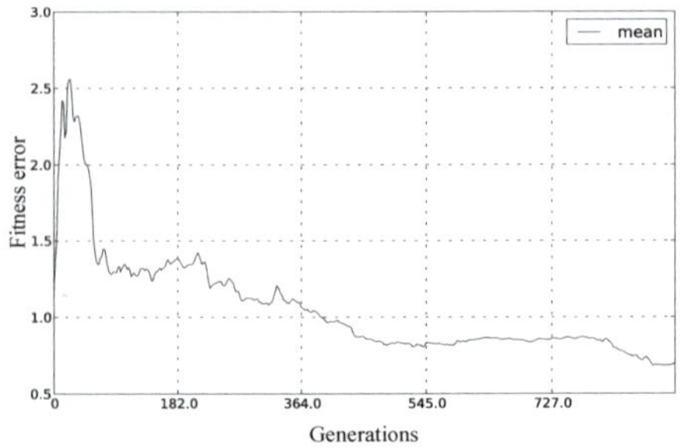

Fitness error graph for Probability* (Rule I19.2)

R#	Rule Antecedent (if)	Rule Consequent (then)	Decision (then)	Probability*	Decision (then)	Probability
I20.1	Att.39 = 41	Att.1 = Empty	Att.1 = Residential	66.16%	Att.1= random {A, S, O}	13.26%
I20.2			Att.1=Business-Shopping	20.58%		

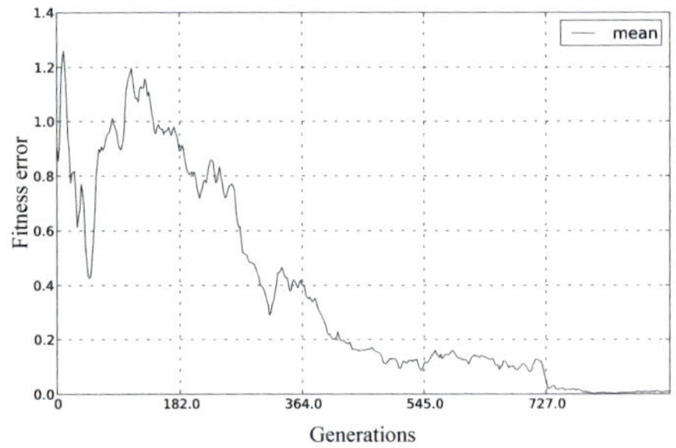

Fitness error graph for Probability* (Rule I20.1)

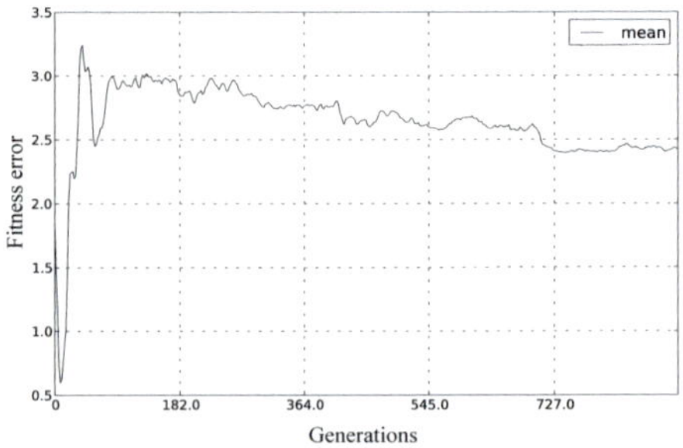

Fitness error graph for Probability* (Rule I20.2)

R#	Rule Antecedent (if)	Rule Consequent (then)	Decision (then)	Probability*	Decision (then)	Probability
I21.1	Att.39 = 31	Att.1 = Empty	Att.1 = Business-Shopping	29.75%	Att.1= random {R, A, S}	65.32%
I21.2			Att.1 = Other	4.93%		

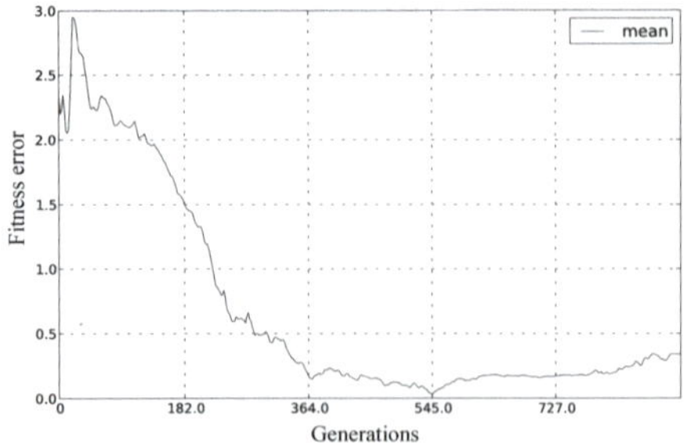

Fitness error graph for Probability* (Rule I21.1)

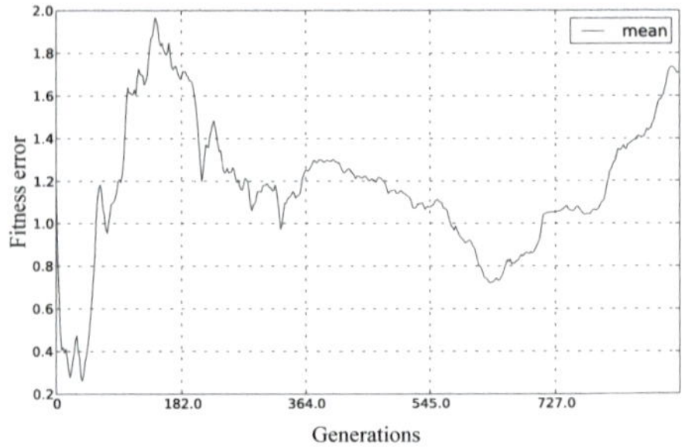

Fitness error graph for Probability* (Rule I21.2)

FIGURE APP.E.14 Fitness error graphs for I19, I20, I21

R#	Rule Antecedent (if)	Rule Consequent (then)	Decision (then)	Probability*	Decision (then)	Probability
I22.1			Att.1 = Residential	55.82%		
I22.2	Att.33 = V	Att.1 = Empty	Att.1 = Business-Shopping	30.33%	Att.1= random {A, S}	9.01%
I22.3			Att.1 = Other	4.84%		

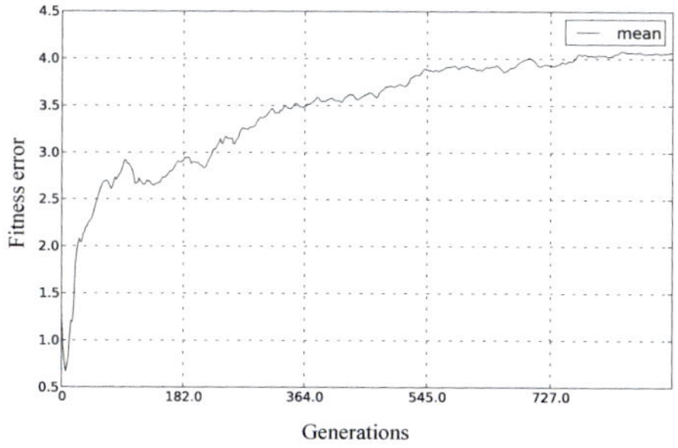

Fitness error graph for Probability* (Rule I22.1)

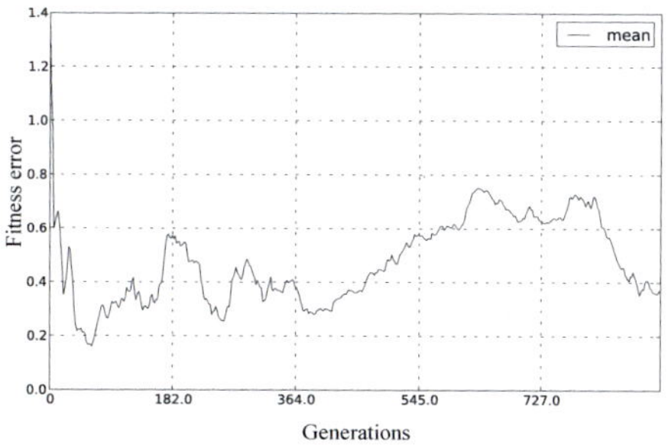

Fitness error graph for Probability* (Rule I22.2)

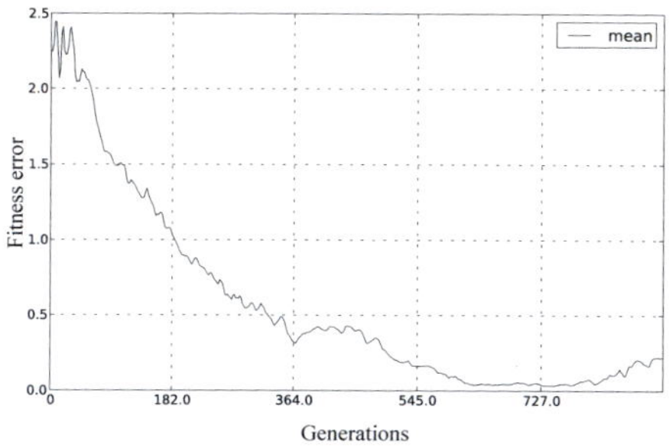

Fitness error graph for Probability* (Rule I22.3)

R#	Rule Antecedent (if)	Rule Consequent (then)	Decision (then)	Probability*	Decision (then)	Probability
I23.1	Att.39 = 21	Att.1 = Empty	Att.1 = Business-Shopping	47.47%	Att.1= random {A, S, O}	11.80%
I23.2			Att.1 = Residential	40.73%		

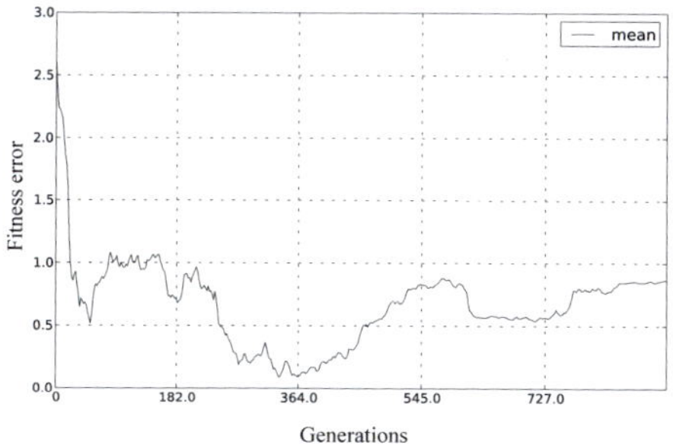

Fitness error graph for Probability* (Rule I23.1)

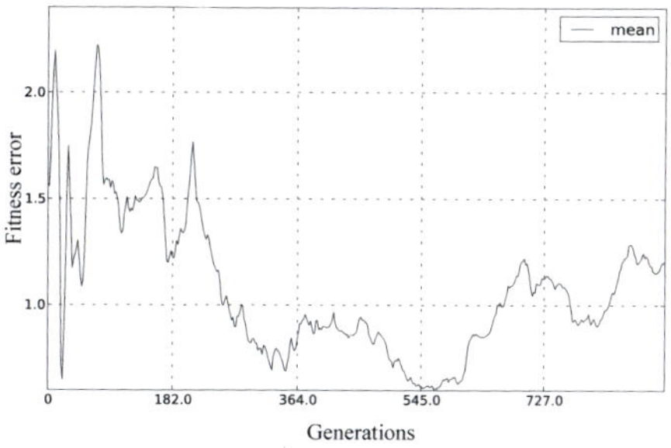

Fitness error graph for Probability* (Rule I23.2)

FIGURE APP.E.15 Fitness error graphs for I22, I23

R#	Rule Antecedent (if)	Rule Consequent (then)	Decision (then)	Probability*	Decision (then)	Probability
I24.1			Att.1 = Residential	59.16%		
I24.2	Att.34 = IV	Att.1 = Empty	Att.1 = Business-Shopping	27.33%	Att.1= random {A, S}	8.23%
I24.3			Att.1 = Other	5.28%		

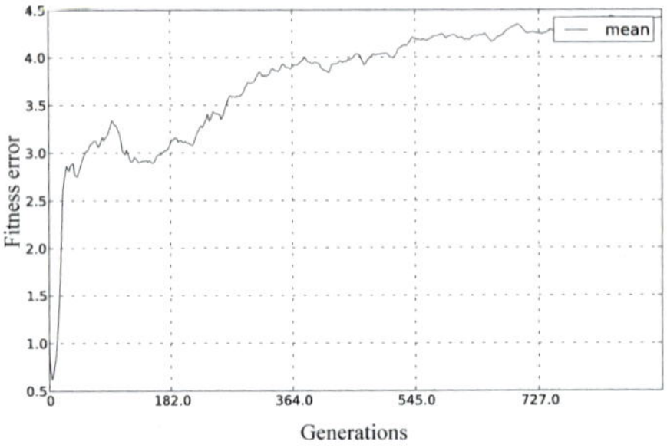

Fitness error graph for Probability* (Rule I24.1)

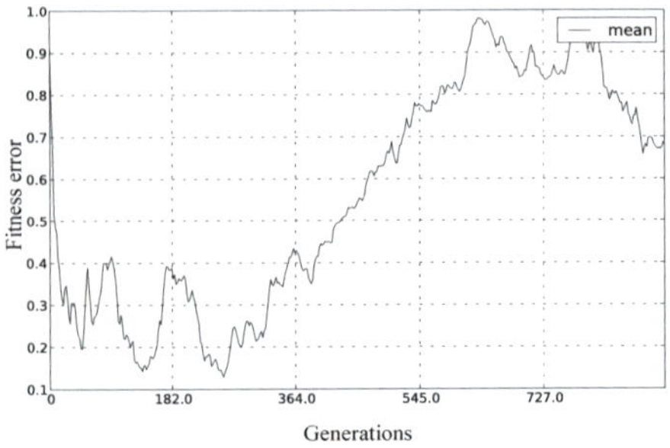

Fitness error graph for Probability* (Rule I24.2)

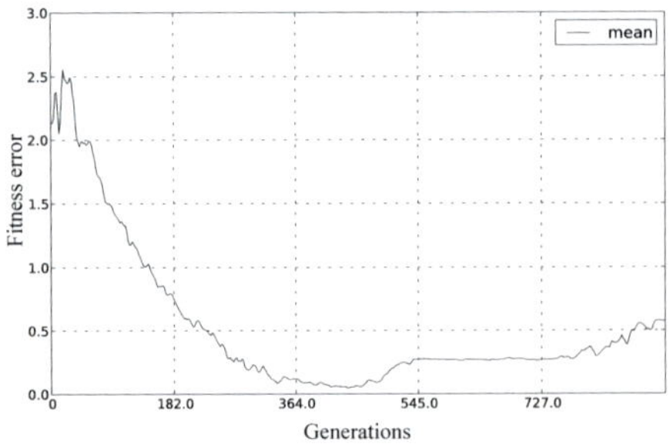

Fitness error graph for Probability* (Rule I24.3)

R#	Rule Antecedent (if)	Rule Consequent (then)	Decision (then)	Probability*	Decision (then)	Probability
I25.1	Att.1 = Business-Shopping	Att.15 = Empty	Att.15 = Residential	18.34%	Att.1= random {A, S, O}	77.30%
I25.2			Att.15 = Business-Shopping	4.36%		

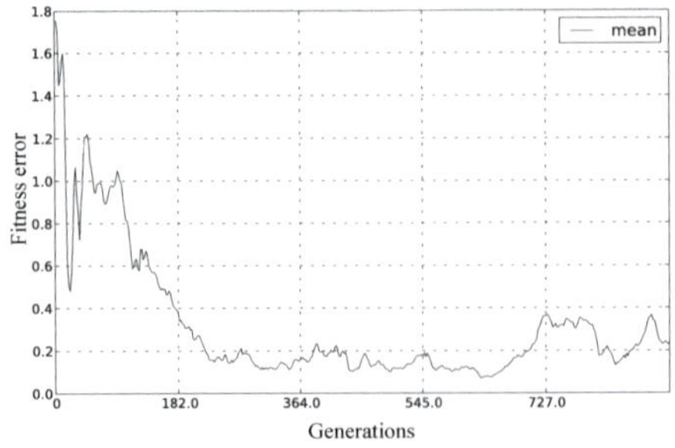

Fitness error graph for Probability* (Rule I25.1)

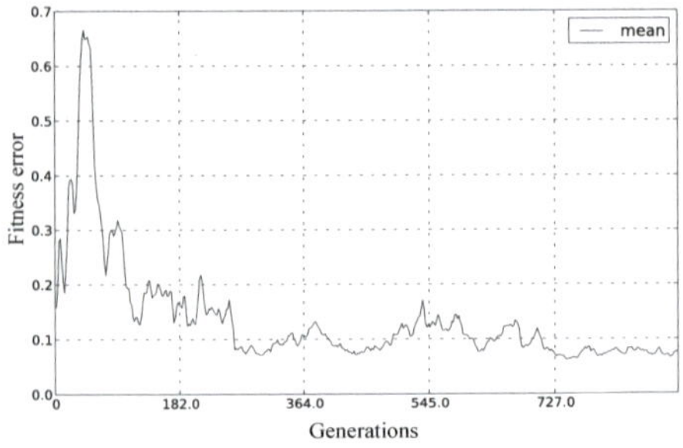

Fitness error graph for Probability* (Rule I25.2)

FIGURE APP.E.16 Fitness error graphs for I24, I25

Rule Antecedent (if)					Decision (then)	Probability	Decision (then)	Probability	Decision (then)	Probability	Decision (then)	Probability
Att.28=II	Att.40=2 or Att.40=3	Att.22 =Masonry or Att.22 =Wood	Att.24=Private	Att. 25 = %50-60 registered or Att.25= %60-70 registered or Att.25= %70-80 registered or Att.25= %80-90 registered or Att.25= %90-100 registered	Att.1=1-2P Att.46=Srent Att.46=Prent Att.46=Owner D1.a	40% 50% 10% 40%	Att.1=S Att.46=Srent Att.46=Prent Att.46=Owner D1.b	5% 90% 0% 10%	Att.1=Stu Att.46=Srent Att.46=Prent Att.46=Owner D1.c	40% 85% 10% 5%	Att.1=random {B, A, O}	15% D1

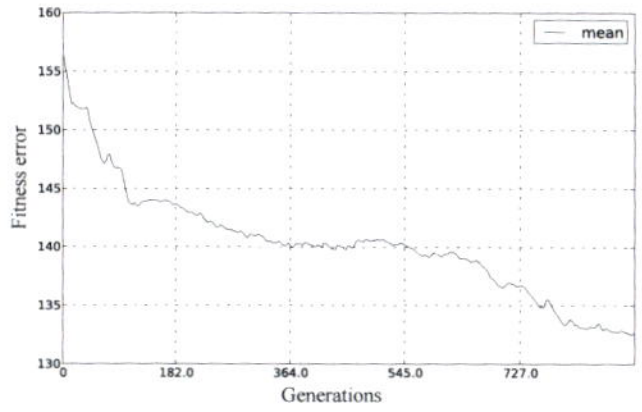

Fitness error graph for D1

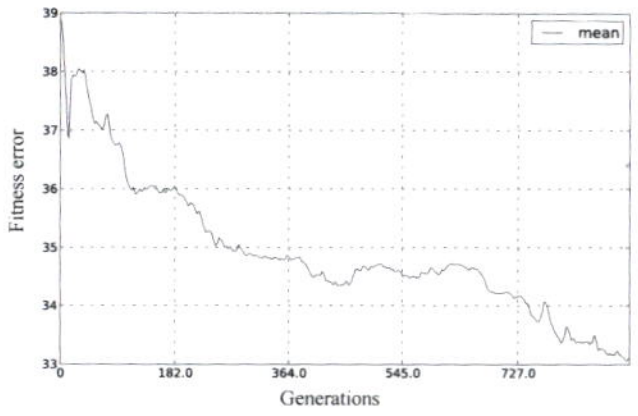

Fitness error graph for D1.a

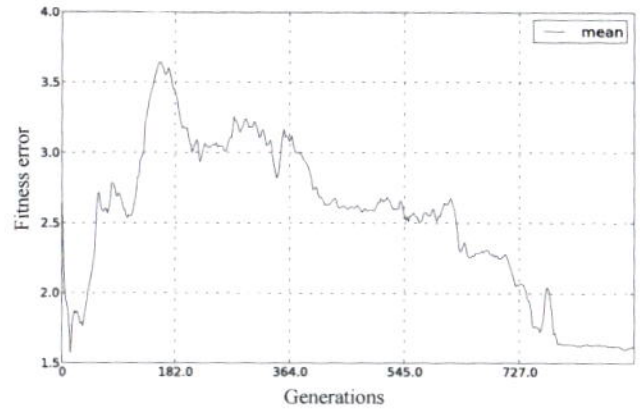

Fitness error graph for D1.b

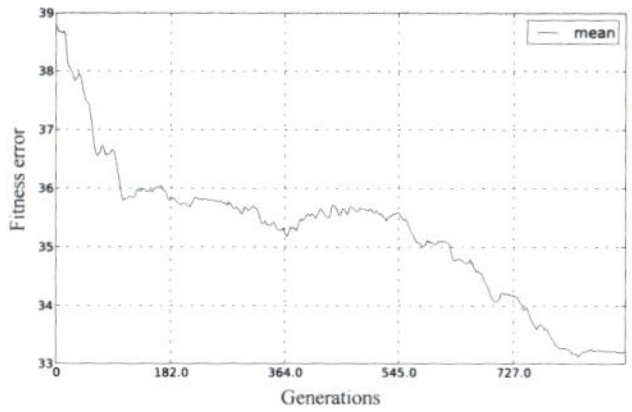

Fitness error graph for D1.c

FIGURE APP.E.17 Fitness error graph for D1

Rule Antecedent (if)						Decision (then)	Probability	Decision (then)	Probability
Att.28=III	Att.40=2 Att.40=3 Att.40=4	Att.22 =Masonry Att.22 =Wood	Att.24=Private	Att.25= %50-60 registered or Att.25= %60-70 registered or Att.25= %70-80 registered or Att.25= %80-90 registered or Att.25= %90-100 registered	Att.27=Registered Civil Architecture	Att.1=F Att.46=Srent Att.46=Prent Att.46=Owner D2.a	80% 50% 20% 30%	Att.1=random {B, A, S, O}	20% D2

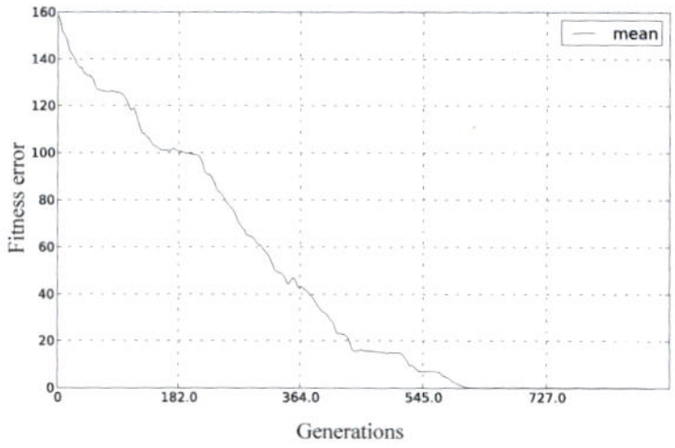

Fitness error graph for D2

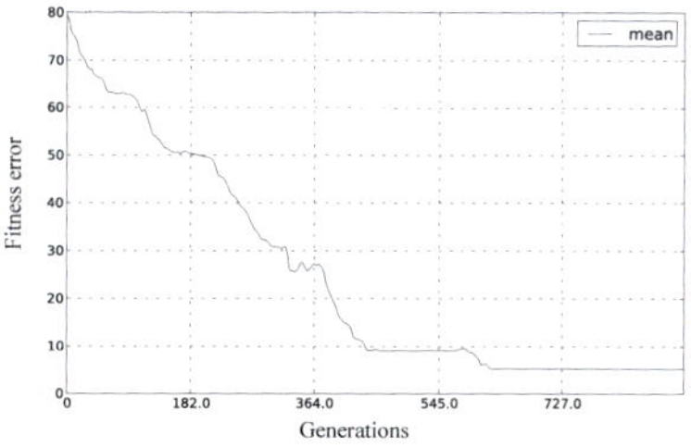

Fitness error graph for D2.a

FIGURE APP.E.18 Fitness error graph for D2

Rule Antecedent (if)	Decision(then)	Probability	Decision (then)	Probability	Decision (then)	Probability
Att.38=0 Att.22=RC Att.27=Not Available Att.21=Bad Att.41=No basement Att.45<3	Att.1=El	40%	Att.1= D	40%	Att.1=random {B, A, S, O, Stu, 1-2P}	20%
Att.38=1 Att.21=Medium	Att.46=Srent	70%	Att.46=Srent	70%		
	Att.46=Prent	10%	Att.46=Prent	10%		
	Att.46=Owner	20%	Att.46=Owner	20%		

D3.a D3.b D3

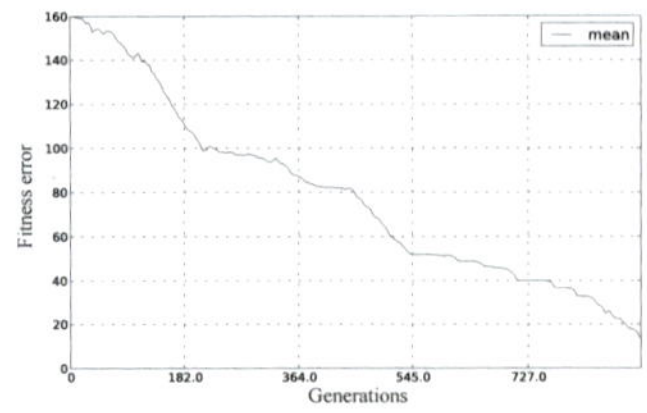

Fitness error graph for D3

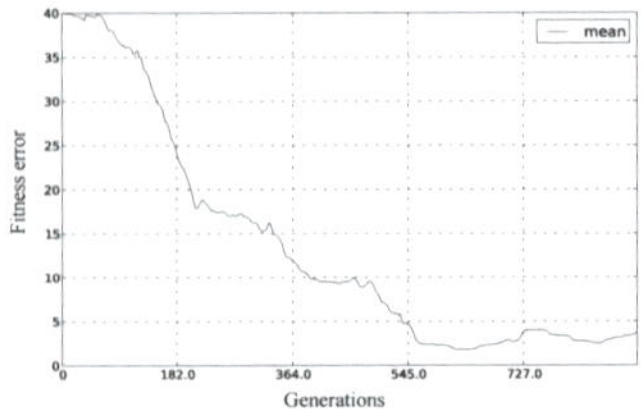

Fitness error graph for D3.a

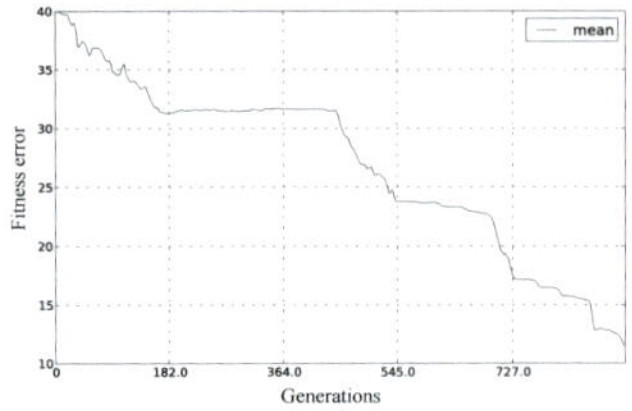

Fitness error graph for D3.b

FIGURE APP.E.19 Fitness error graph for D3

Rule Antecedent (if)	Decision (then)	Probability	Decision (then)	Probability
Att.1=Business-Shopping **Att.2**=Residential **Att.44**=3rd level	**Att.1**=LB	65%	**Att.1**=random {B, A, S, O, Stu, 1-2P, F}	10%
	Att.46=Srent	60%		
	Att.46=Prent	30%		
	Att.46=Owner	10%		

D4.a D4

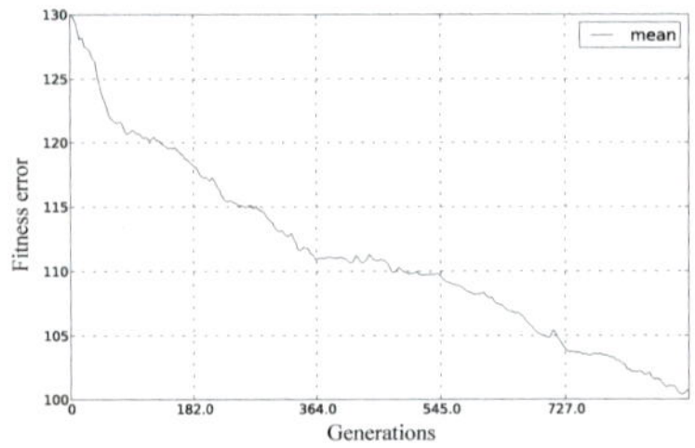

Fitness error graph for D4

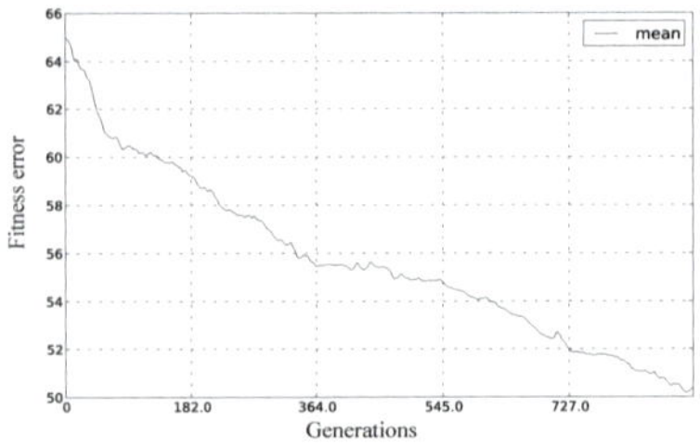

Fitness error graph for D4.a

FIGURE APP.E.20 Fitness error graph for D4

Rule Antecedent (if)			Decision (then)	Probability	Decision (then)	Probability	Decision (then)	Probability
Att.1=Business-Shopping	Att.2=Business-Shopping	Att.3=Empty	Att.3=1-2P	40%	Att.3=Stu	40%	Att.1=B	20%
			Att.46=Srent	50%	Att.46=Srent	50%		D5
			Att.46=Prent	30%	Att.46=Prent	30%		
			Att.46=Owner	20%	Att.46=Owner	20%		
				D5.a		D5.b		

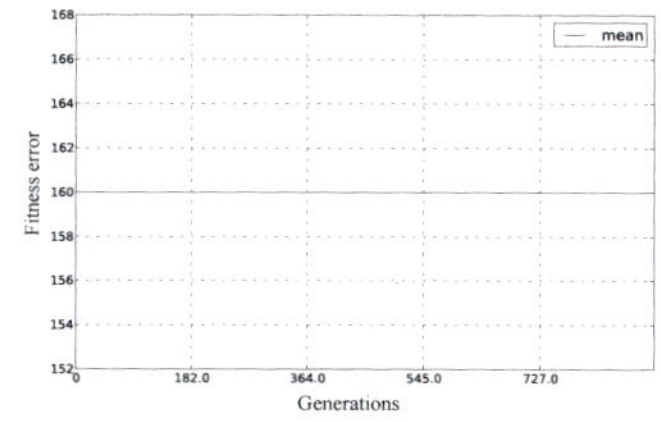

Fitness error graph for D5

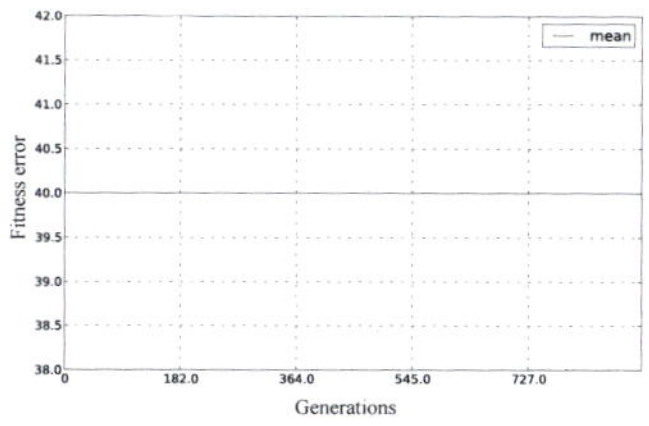

Fitness error graph for D5.a

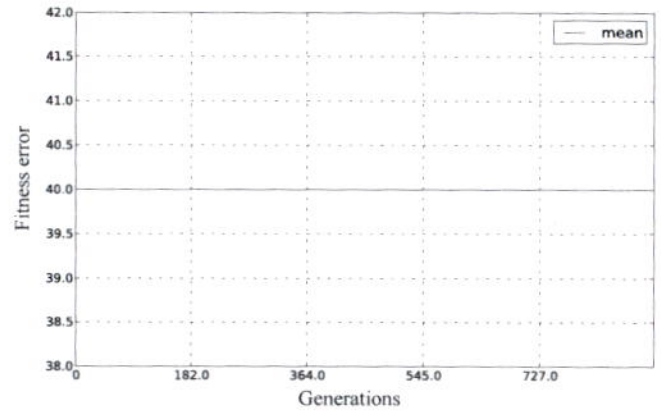

Fitness error graph for D5.b

FIGURE APP.E.21 Fitness error graph for D5

Rule Antecedent (if)		Decision (then)	Probability		Decision (then)	Probability		Decision (then)	Probability
Att.1=Business-Shopping	Att.2=Empty	Att.2=1-2P	40%		Att.2=Stu	40%		Att.1=random {B, F}	20%
		Att.46=Srent	50%		Att.46=Srent	50%			D6
		Att.46=Prent	30%		Att.46=Prent	30%			
		Att.46=Owner	20%	D6.a	Att.46=Owner	20%	D6.b		

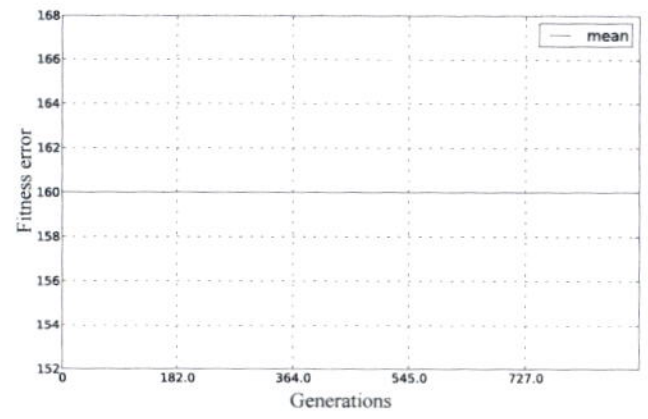

Fitness error graph for D6

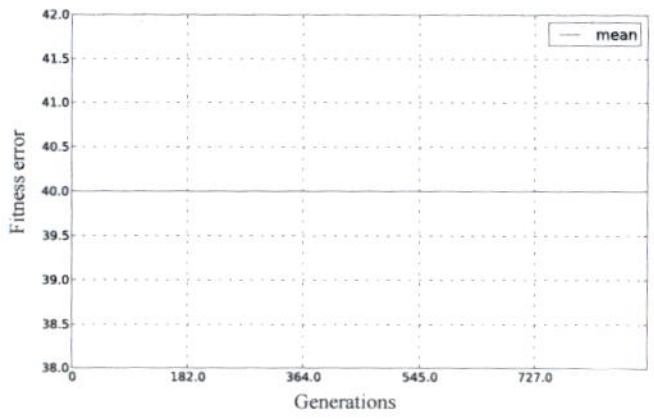

Fitness error graph for D6.a

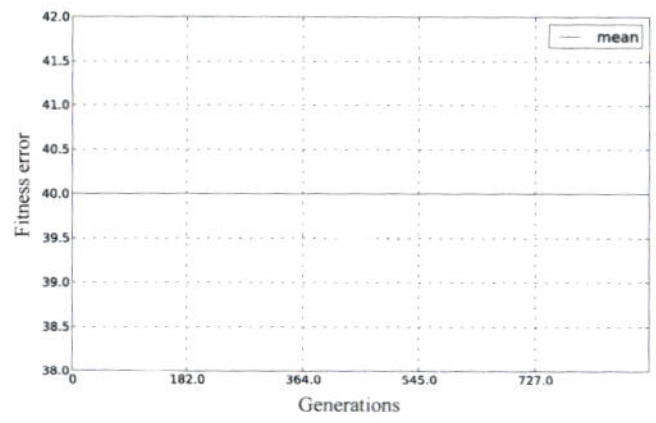

Fitness error graph for D6.b

FIGURE APP.E.22 Fitness error graph for D6

Appendix F Tarlabaşı Datascope Workshop Poster

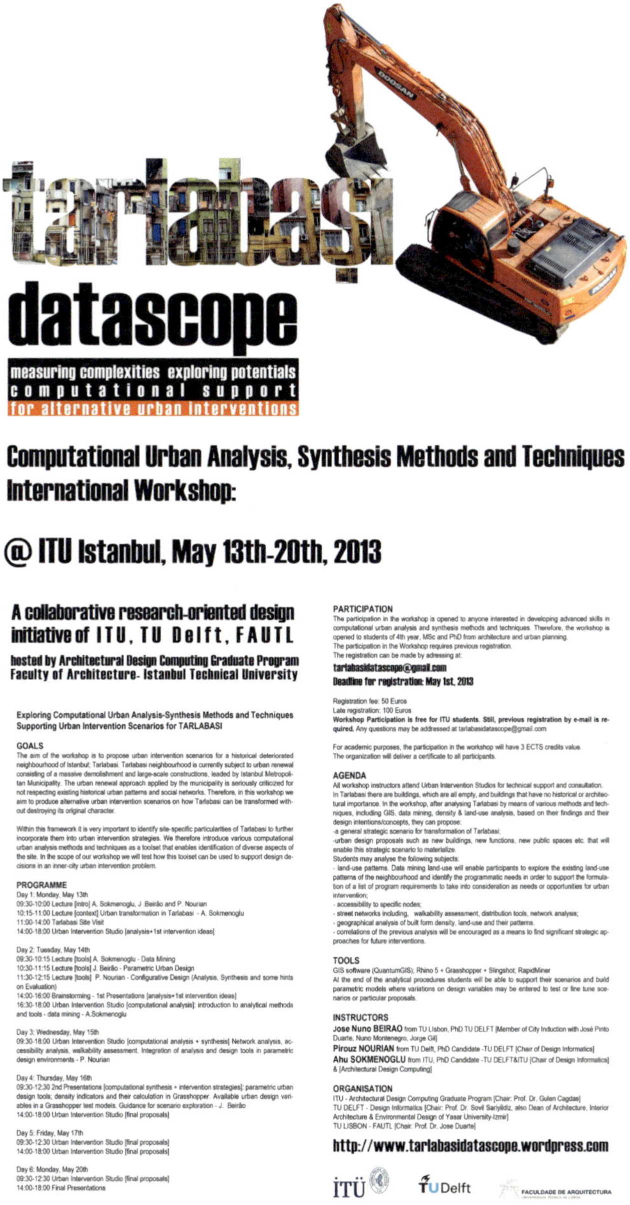

FIGURE APP.F.1 Tarlabaşı Datascope workshop poster

Appendix G Presentation slides of "Team: Diversity; Tarlabaşı Interven[func]tion"

Slide 1

Tarlabaşı Interven[func]tion

Team | Diversity

Ayşe Çolakoğlu Istanbul Technical University
Zuzanna Julia Kołtowska Warsaw University of Technology
Tolga Karasay Istanbul Technical University
Ömer Halil Çavuşoğlu Istanbul Technical University

Urban Inverventions in Tarlabaşı
Computational Urban Analysis, Synthesis Methods and Techniques International Workshop: 20.05.2013

Slide 2

Design | First Ideas of Our Proposal

How to make Tarlabaşı more socially diverse area?

The goal is to spatially and socially connect Istiklal Street and Tarlabaşı. We should provide more diversity of activities, which attract people. Empty and non-historical plots can be find on the site, so their functions could be easily transformed to public or open spaces.

Rhinoceros-Grasshopper used as a base to computational process

Cheetah for using Network Analysis to locate green or open spaces based on some previously defined rules.

Rapid Miner for identifying building types according to land uses.

DB_Import for selecting empty buildings, public functions, non-historical buildings in Grasshopper

Quantum GIS for mapping the analysis via query.

ARC GIS used for Buffer Zone analysis.

FIGURE APP.G.1 Slides 1 and 2

Slide 3

Analysis | land use

The purpose of land use analysis is to detect existing diversity ratios in Tarlabaşı to balance diversity. The ground floor level's function of Tarlabaşı and two counter-characteristic block were selected to identify the diversity.

to find distribution of land uses

↓ QuantumGIS

intervention area ground floor land use analysis

max commercial ratio at ground floor: %68
min commercial at ground floor ratio: %11
avarage commercial at ground floor: %35

intervention area ground floor land use analysis

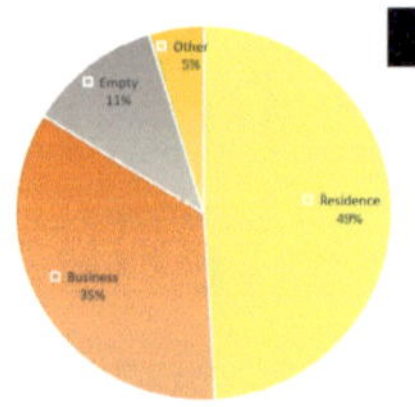

land use distribution of tarlabaşı

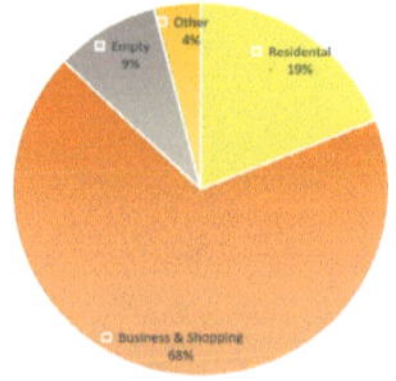

land use distribution of highly commercial block

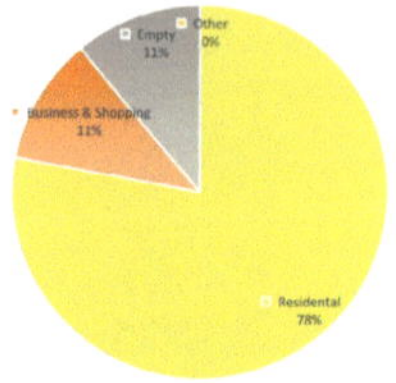

land use distribution of highly residential block

Slide 4

Analysis | land use of buildings in Tarlabaşı

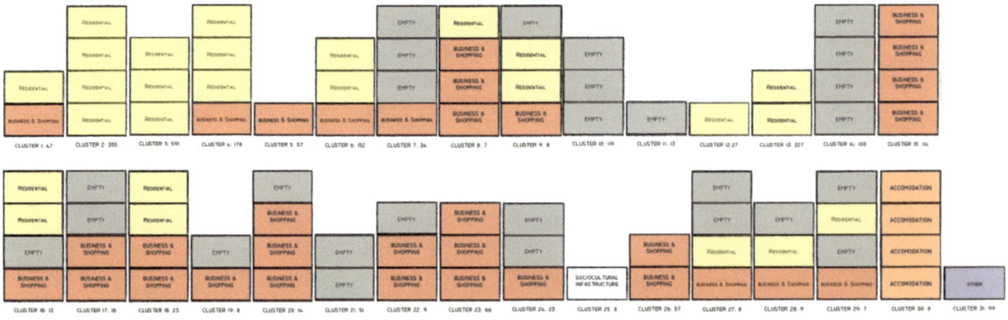

building types of Tarlabaşı

Cluster Code	Item Numbers	Ground Floor Function	First Floor Function	Second Floor Function	Third Floor Function
Cluster 1	47	Business & Shopping	Residential	-	-
Cluster 2	355	Residential	Residential	Residential	Residential
Cluster 3	591	Residential	Residential	Residential	-
Cluster 4	178	Business & Shopping	Residential	Residential	Residential
Cluster 5	57	Business & Shopping	-	-	-
Cluster 6	152	Business & Shopping	Residential	Residential	-
Cluster 7	34	Business & Shopping	Empty	Empty	Empty
Cluster 8	7	Business & Shopping	Business & Shopping	Business & Shopping	Residential
Cluster 9	8	Business & Shopping	Residential	Residential	Empty
Cluster 10	119	Empty	Empty	Empty	-
Cluster 11	13	Empty	-	-	-
Cluster 12	27	Residential	-	-	-
Cluster 13	227	Residential	Residential	-	-
Cluster 14	100	Empty	Empty	Empty	Empty
Cluster 15	114	Business & Shopping	Business & Shopping	Business & Shopping	Business & Shopping
Cluster 16	13	Business & Shopping	Empty	Residential	Residential

Cluster Code	Item Numbers	Ground Floor Function	First Floor Function	Second Floor Function	Third Floor Function
Cluster 17	16	Business & Shopping	Business & Shopping	Empty	Empty
Cluster 18	23	Business & Shopping	Business & Shopping	Residential	Residential
Cluster 19	8	Business & Shopping	Empty	-	-
Cluster 20	14	Business & Shopping	Business & Shopping	Business & Shopping	Empty
Cluster 21	51	Empty	Empty	-	-
Cluster 22	9	Business & Shopping	Business & Shopping	Empty	-
Cluster 23	66	Business & Shopping	Business & Shopping	Business & Shopping	-
Cluster 24	23	Business & Shopping	Empty	Empty	-
Cluster 25	8	Sociocultural Infastructure	-	-	-
Cluster 26	57	Business & Shopping	Business & Shopping	-	-
Cluster 27	8	Business & Shopping	Residential	Empty	Empty
Cluster 28	9	Business & Shopping	Residential	Empty	-
Cluster 29	7	Business & Shopping	Empty	Residential	Empty
Cluster 30	8	Accomodation	Accomodation	Accomodation	Accomodation
Cluster 31	99	Other	-	-	-

list of building types

FIGURE APP.G.2 Slides 3 and 4

Slide 5

Analysis | land use of buildings in Tarlabaşı

c_3: 591 (Residential, Residential, Residential)

c_2: 355 (Residential, Residential, Residential,Residential)

According to the results of Rapid miner, we have 8 major building types. The clusters are mapped via using QuantumGIS. The most common building type is cluster 3 with 591 buildings, the second one is the cluster 2 with 355 buildings. Both of them consist of residential facilities which are located generally in the middle of the district.

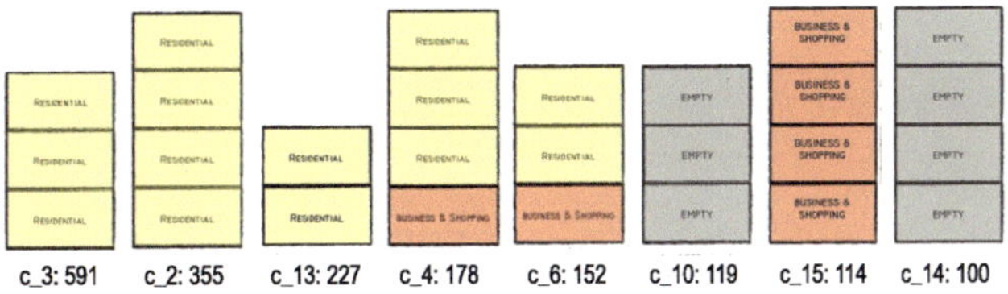

most common building types of Tarlabaşı

Slide 6

Analysis | land use of buildings in Tarlabaşı

c_13: 227 (Residential, Residential)

c_4: 178 (Business & Shopping, Residential, Residential, Residential)

227 building in Tarlabaşı belongs to the cluster 13. Due to their residential function, they are also located mostly back site of the district. On the other hand, cluster 4 which has commercial function at the ground floor is distributed to whole side almost homogeniously.

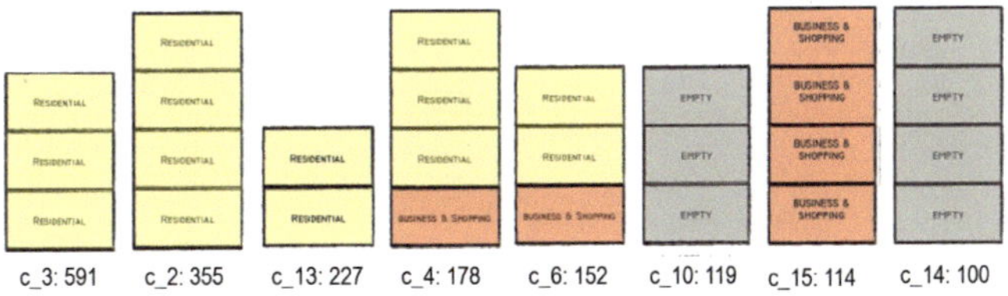

most common building types of Tarlabaşı

FIGURE APP.G.3 Slides 5 and 6

Analysis | land use of buildings in Tarlabaşı

Slide 7

c_6: 152 (Business & Shopping, Residential, Residential)

c_10: 119 (Empty, Empty, Empty)

Cluster 6 has commercial function at the ground floor distributed to whole site almost homogeniously but some blocks don't have this type of buildngs. There are also existing but empty buildings inside the territory at about 152 item.

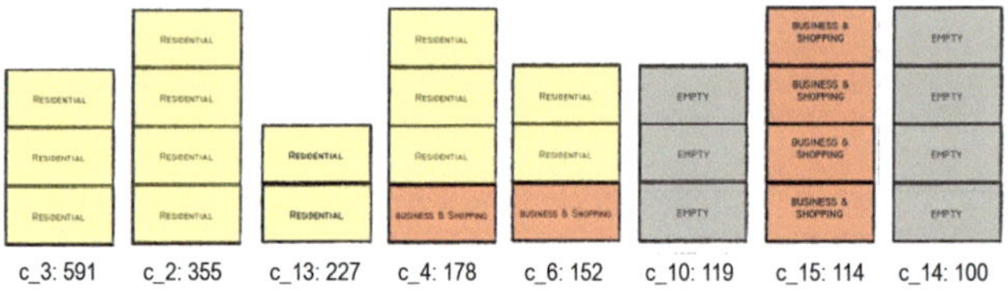

most common building types of Tarlabaşı

Analysis | land use of buildings in Buffer Zone

Slide 8

buffer zone analysis

Cluster Code	Item Numbers	Ground Floor Function	First Floor Function	Second Floor Function	Third Floor Function
Cluster 2	74	Residential	Residential	Residential	Residential
Cluster 3	130	Residential	Residential	Residential	
Cluster 4	43	Business & Shopping	Residential	Residential	Residential
Cluster 5	8	Business & Shopping	-	-	
Cluster 6	26	Business & Shopping	Residential	Residential	
Cluster 7	7	Business & Shopping	Empty	Empty	Empty
Cluster 10	23	Empty	Empty	Empty	
Cluster 12	6	Residential	-	-	
Cluster 13	25	Residential	Residential	-	
Cluster 14	13	Empty	Empty	Empty	Empty
Cluster 15	8	Business & Shopping	Business & Shopping	Business & Shopping	Business & Shopping
Cluster 25	6	Sociocultural Infastructure	-	-	- - - -
Cluster 31	22	Other	-	-	

list of building types

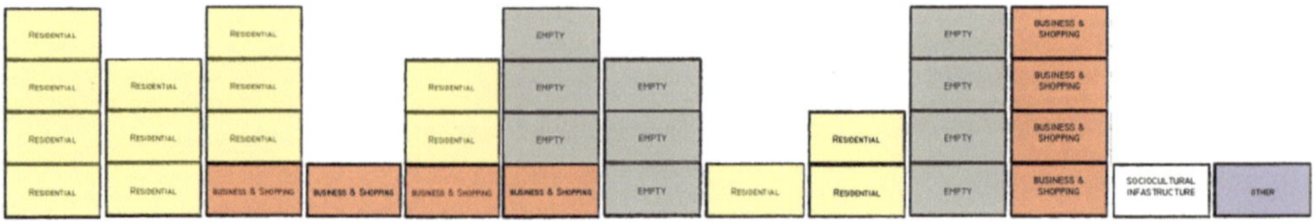

building types of Tarlabaşı

FIGURE APP.G.4 Slides 7 and 8

Slide 9

Analysis | land use of buildings in Buffer Zone

buffer zone analysis

Cluster Code	Item Numbers	Ground Floor Function	First Floor Function	Second Floor Function	Third Floor Function
Cluster 2	74	Residential	Residential	Residential	Residential
Cluster 3	130	Residential	Residential	Residential	
Cluster 4	43	Business & Shopping	Residential	Residential	Residential
Cluster 5	8	Business & Shopping	-	-	
Cluster 6	26	Business & Shopping	Residential	Residential	
Cluster 7	7	Business & Shopping	Empty	Empty	Empty
Cluster 10	23	Empty	Empty	Empty	
Cluster 12	6	Residential	-	-	
Cluster 13	25	Residential	Residential	-	
Cluster 14	13	Empty	Empty	Empty	Empty
Cluster 15	8	Business & Shopping	Business & Shopping	Business & Shopping	Business & Shopping
Cluster 25	6	Sociocultural Infastructure	-	-	- - - -
Cluster 31	22	Other	-	-	

list of building types

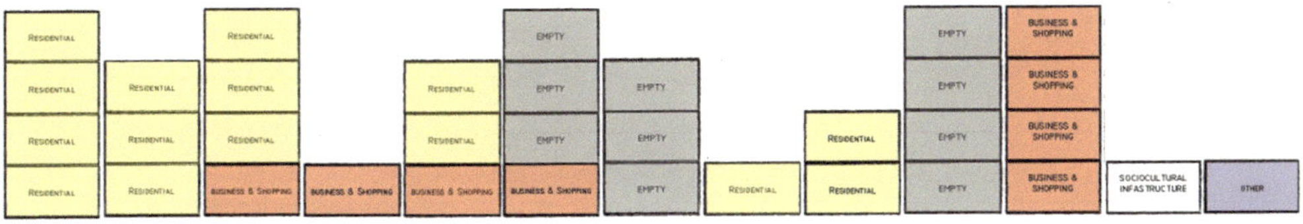

building types of Tarlabaşı

Slide 10

Analysis | land use of buildings in Buffer Zone

Buffer Zone analysis targets to identify diversity and building function ratios of Aya Constantine and Meryem Ana Assyrian Church in Tarlabaşı which are main nodes of our main cultural axes from İstiklal Street to Bilgi University. Buffer zone's centre points are churces and their radius are 75m. Buffer zone analysis is created by using ArcGIS and clusters demonstrated in Rapid Miner as 13 types of clusters. The most common 3 ones have mostly residential functions. Buffer zone analysis results are used for deciding the allocation to new functions to these zones.

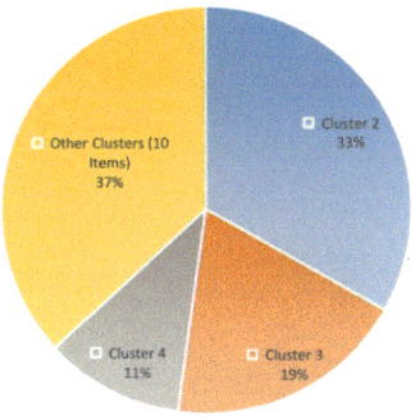

distribution of clusters in buffer zone

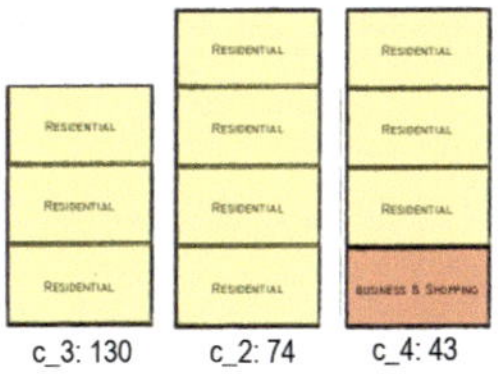

most common building types of Buffer Zone

c_3: 130 (Residential, Residential, Residential)

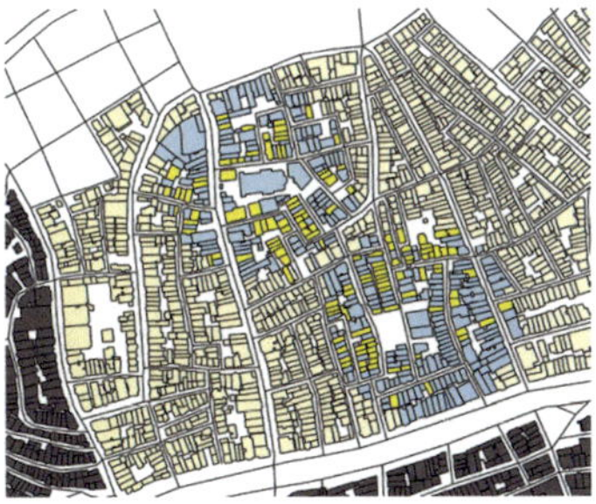

c_2: 74 (Residential, Residential, Residential, Residential)

c_4: 43 (Business, Residential, Residential, Residential)

FIGURE APP.G.5 Slides 9 and 10

FIGURE APP.G.6 Slides 11 and 12

FIGURE APP.G.7 Slides 13 and 14

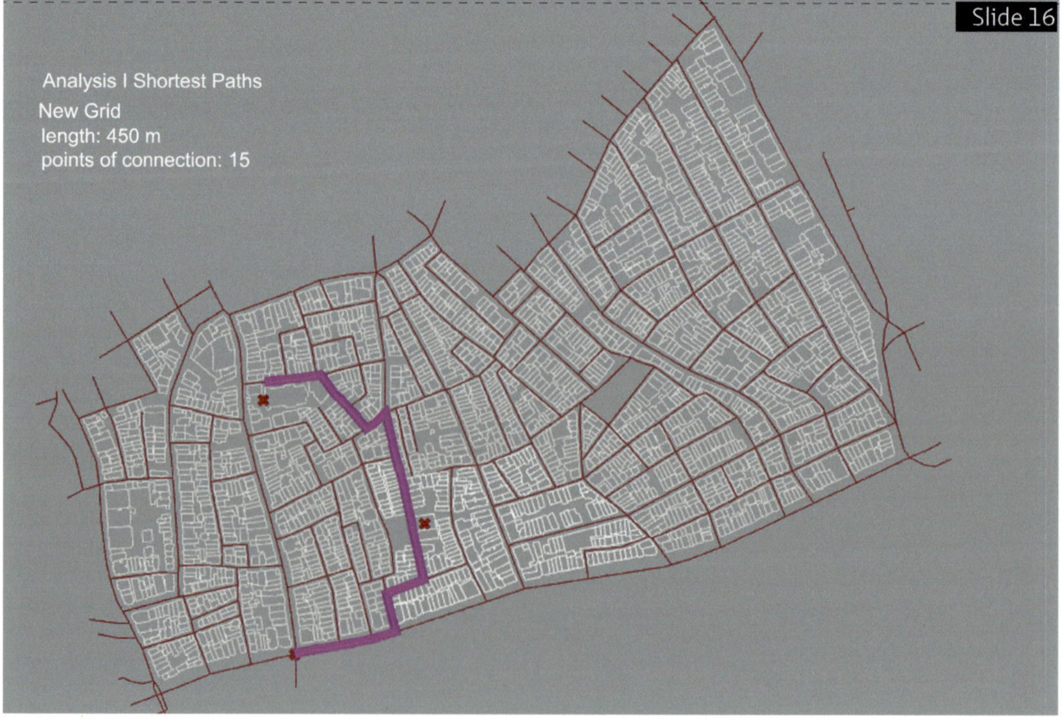

FIGURE APP.G.8 Slides 15 and 16

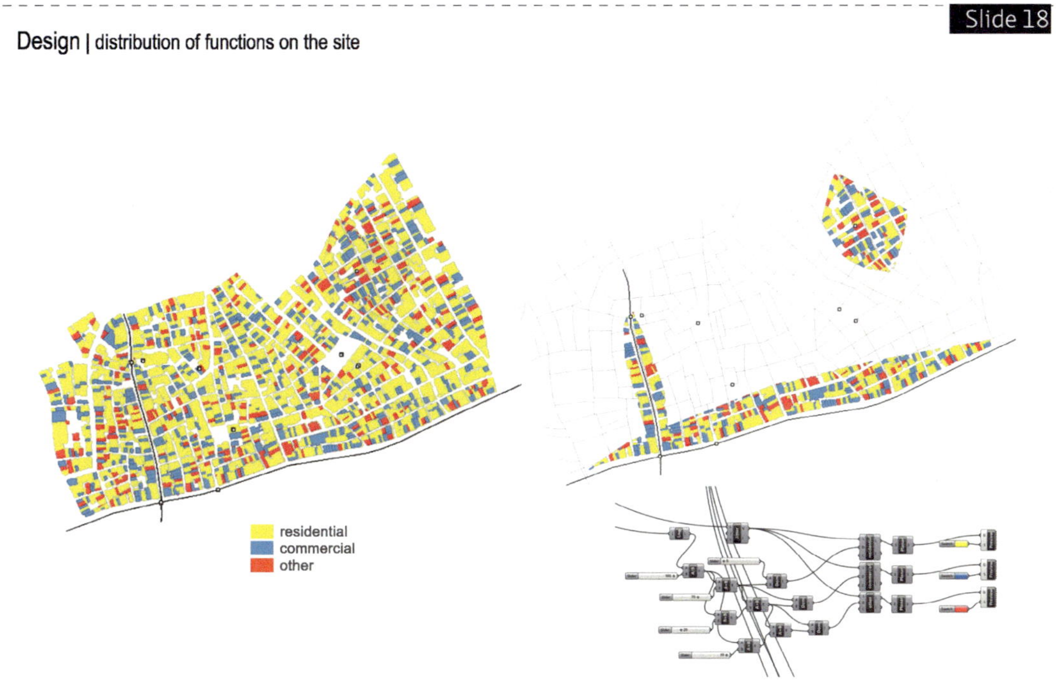

FIGURE APP.G.9 Slides 17 and 18

Slide 19

Design | distribution of functions on the site

existing function distribution

proposal function distribution

Slide 20

Design | Connection of Two Region by Redesigning Tarlabaşı Boulevard

FIGURE APP.G.10 Slides 19 and 20

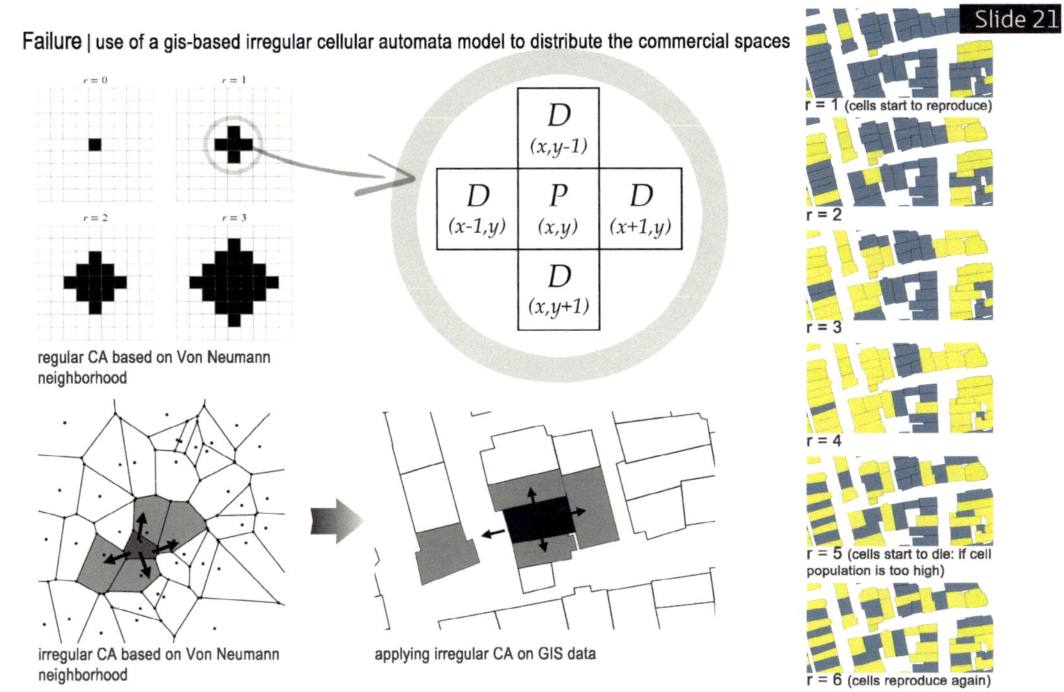

FIGURE APP.G.11 Slide 21

Appendix H Presentation slides of "Team: Public Network of Tarlabaşı"

Slide 1

PUBLIC NETWORK OF TARLABASI

MAIN GOAL

According to main problems of Tarlabasi such as security, disconnectedness, and ambiguity of the relationship between cars and pedestrians, lack of sunlight, clean air and green spaces, our proposal aims to imcvprove the low quality of life by increasing the permeability of the buildings, having more green and public areas, connectivity and pedestrain streets .

D i l a S e l | E z g i B a s t u g | M u t l u G u n g o r

Slide 2

DESIGN PRINCIPLES

Street types
- Main Streets
- Side Streets
- Pedestrian Streets
- Stairs

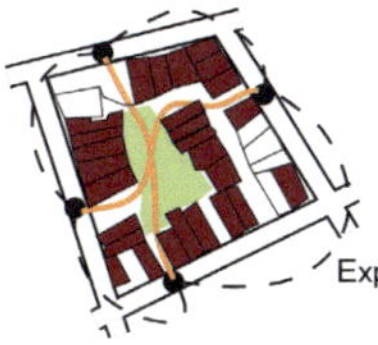

Block Types
Mono Blocks
Facade Organization
Courtyard

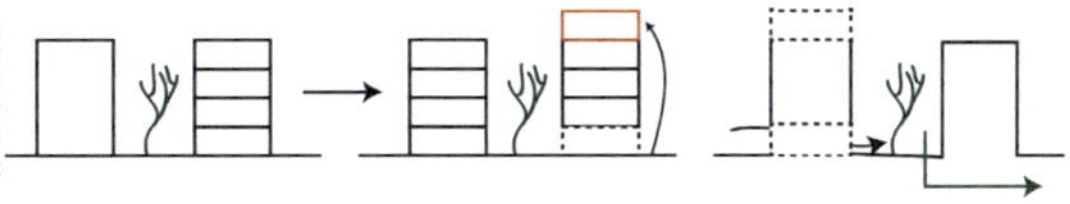

FIGURE APP.H.1 Slides 1 and 2

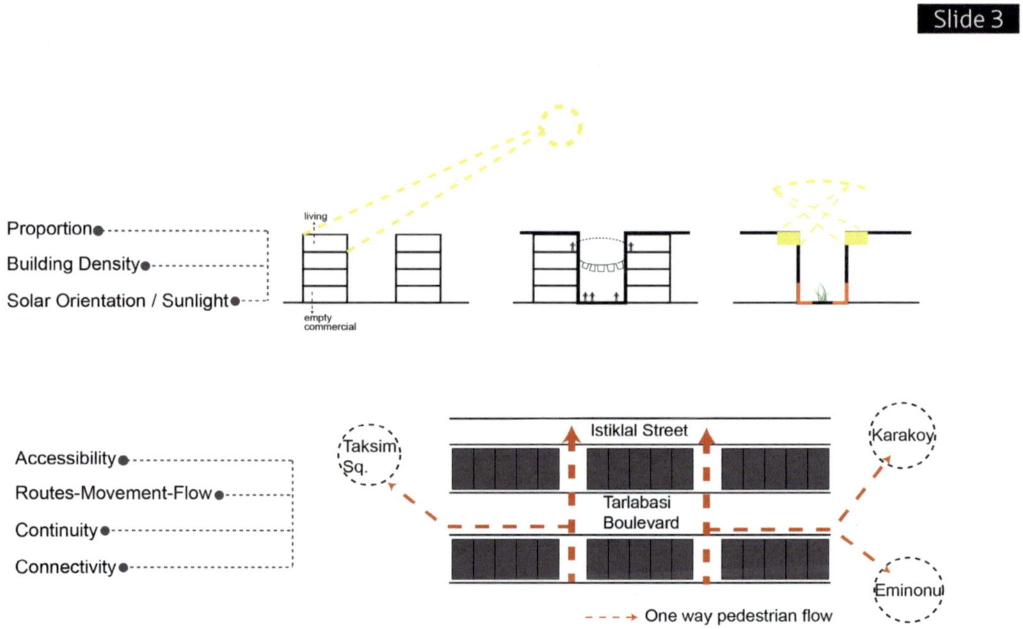

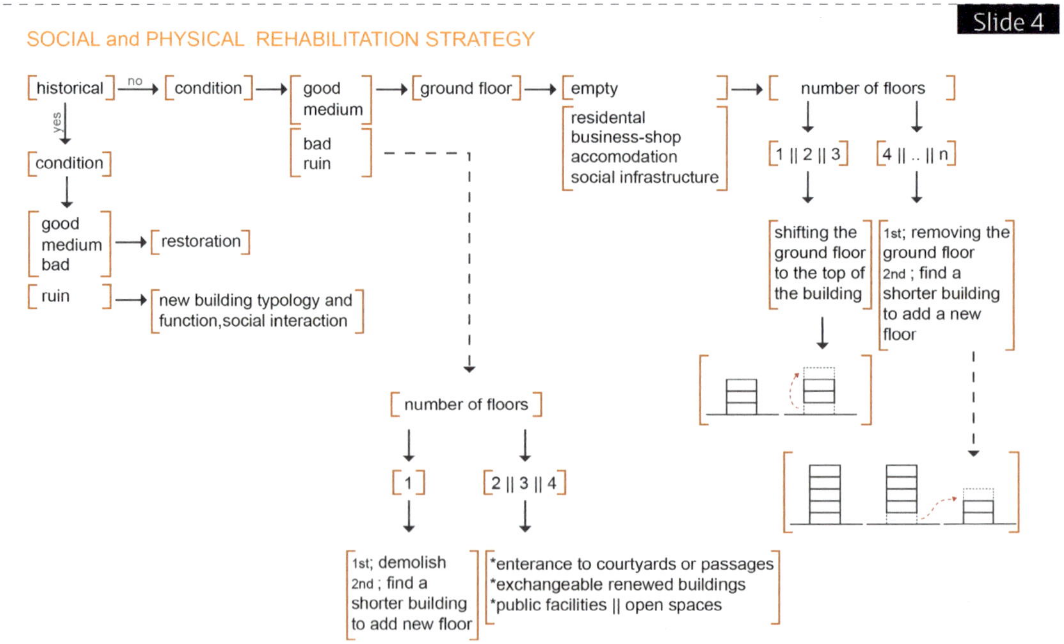

FIGURE APP.H.2 Slides 3 and 4

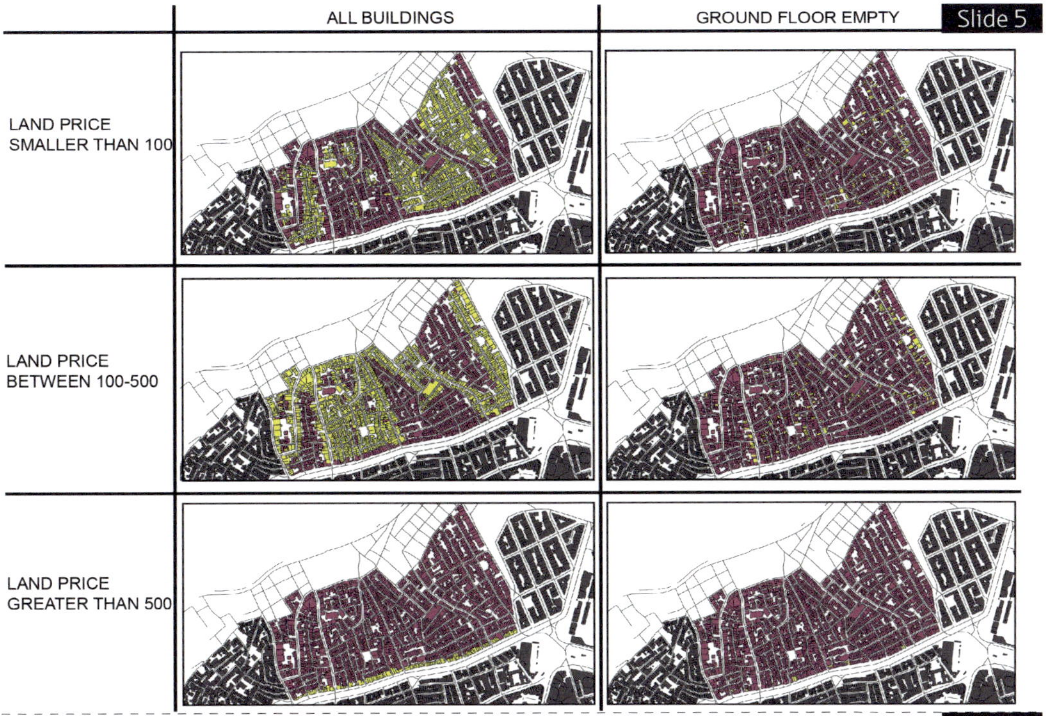

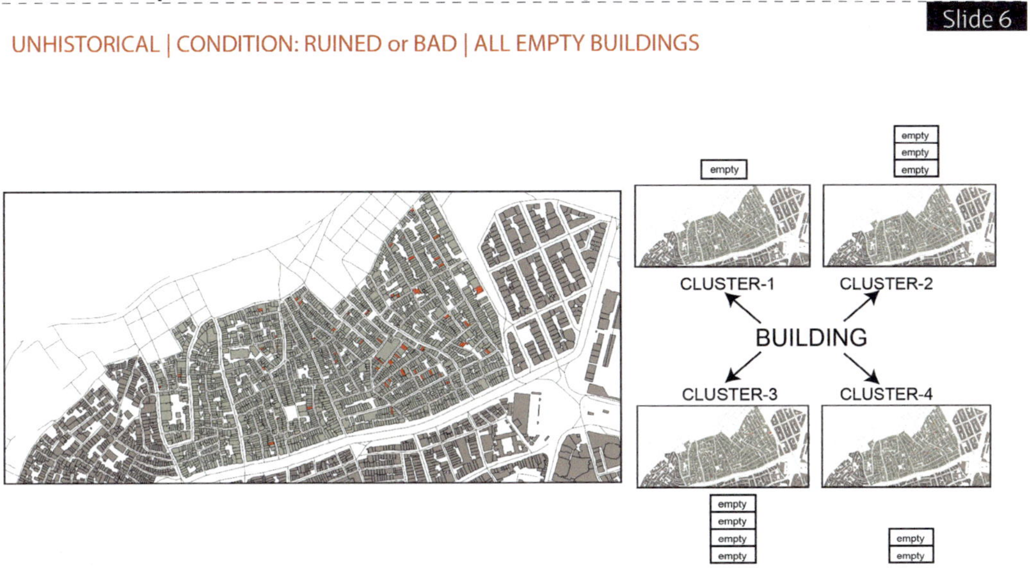

FIGURE APP.H.3 Slides 5 and 6

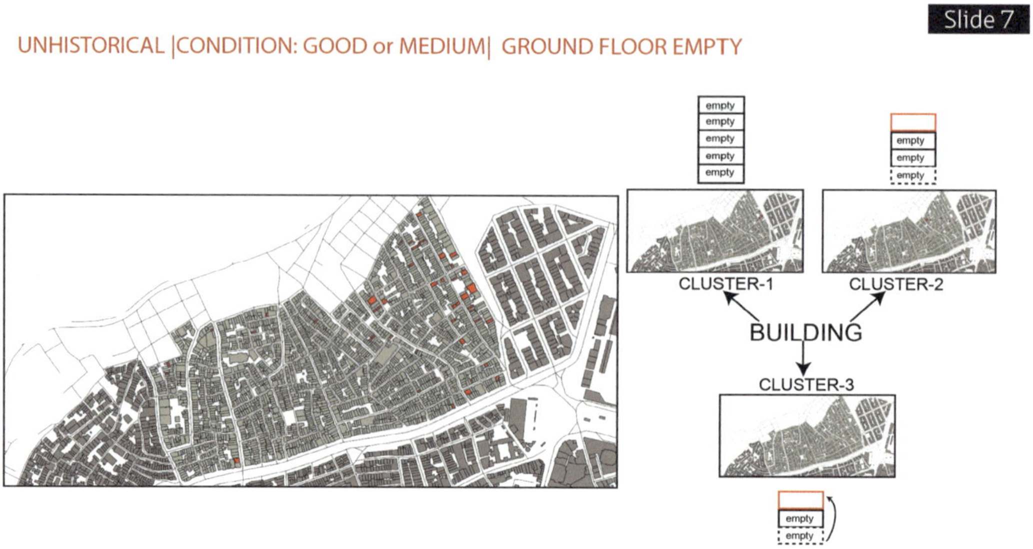

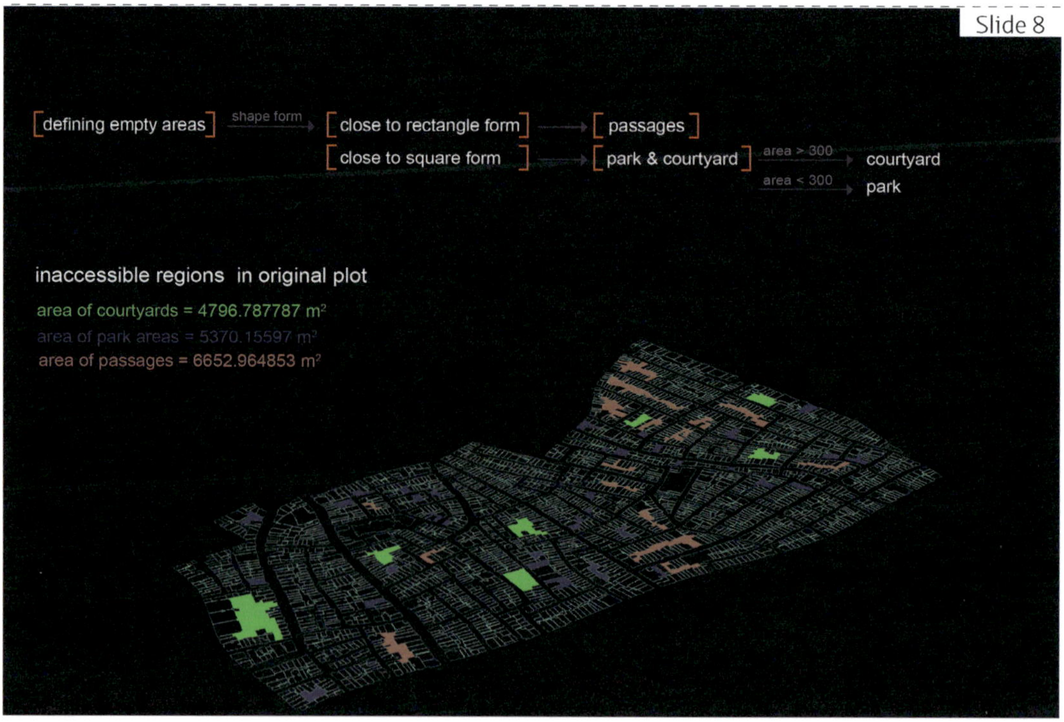

FIGURE APP.H.4 Slides 7 and 8

Slide 9

PREDICTING LAND USE OF EMPTY GROUND FLOOR

IDNO_BLDG	PREDICTED G_F	GROUND FLOOR
10053.0	Business-Shopping	Empty
10142.0	Business-Shopping	Empty
9911.0	Business-Shopping	Empty
9893.0	Residential	Empty
10090.0	Residential	Empty
10065.0	Residential	Empty
10146.0	Residential	Empty
9735.0	Residential	Empty
9794.0	Residential	Empty
9877.0	Residential	Empty
10042.0	Residential	Empty
10143.0	Residential	Empty
10205.0	Residential	Empty
9946.0	Residential	Empty

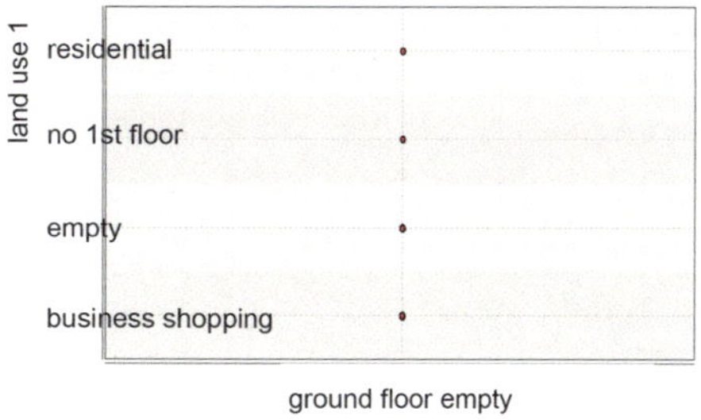

accuracy

	true Business-Shopping	true Residential	true Sociocultural Infrastructure	true Other	true Accomodation	class precision
pred. Business-Shopping	322	1	2	1	0	98.77%
pred. Residential	408	1176	2	5	0	73.92%
pred. Sociocultural Infrastructure	5	0	5	0	0	50.00%
pred. Other	58	27	8	109	0	53.96%
pred. Accomodation	2	0	0	0	8	80.00%
class recall	40.50%	97.67%	29.41%	94.78%	100.00%	

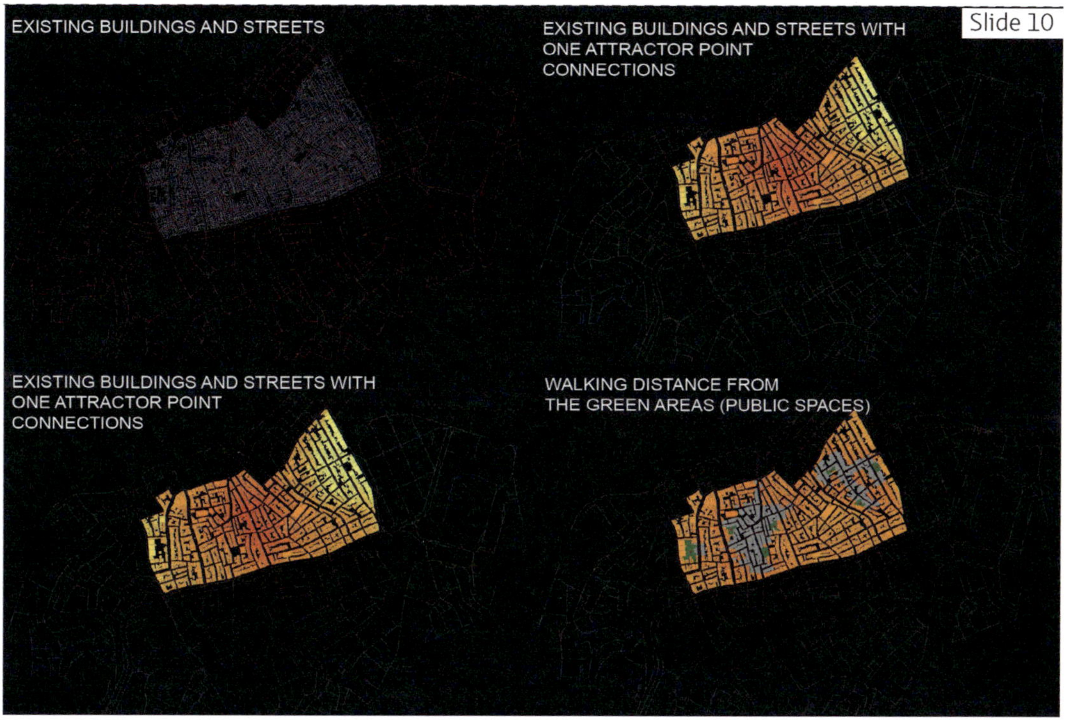

FIGURE APP.H.5 Slides 9 and 10

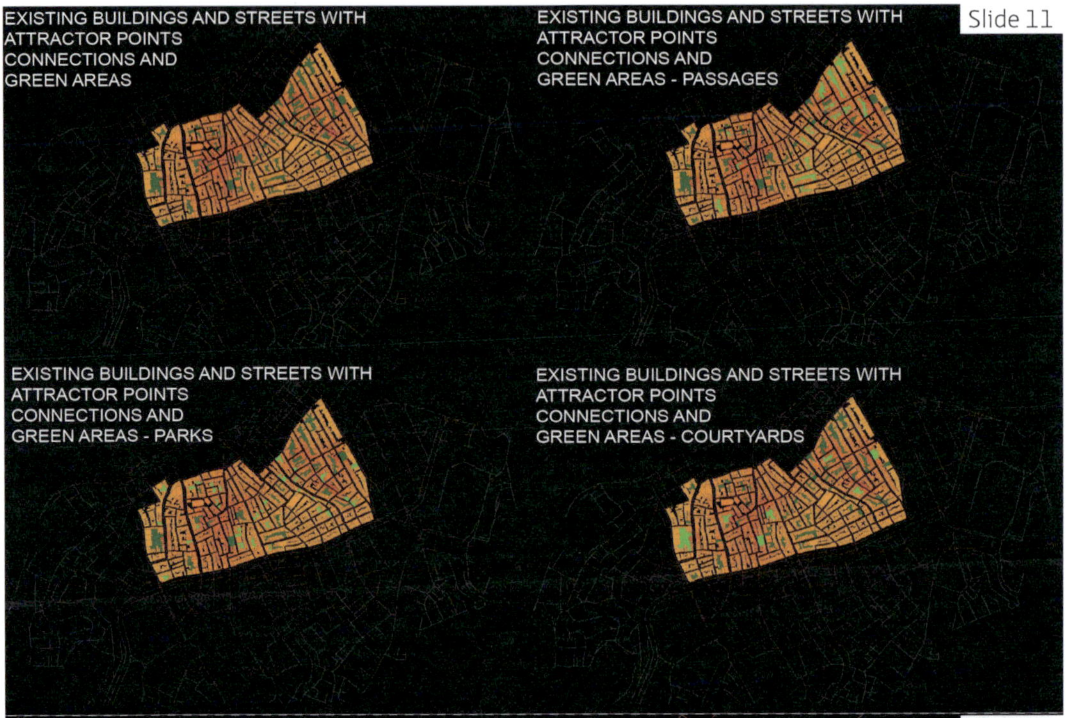

FIGURE APP.H.6 Slides 11 and 12

FIGURE APP.H.7 Slides 13 and 14

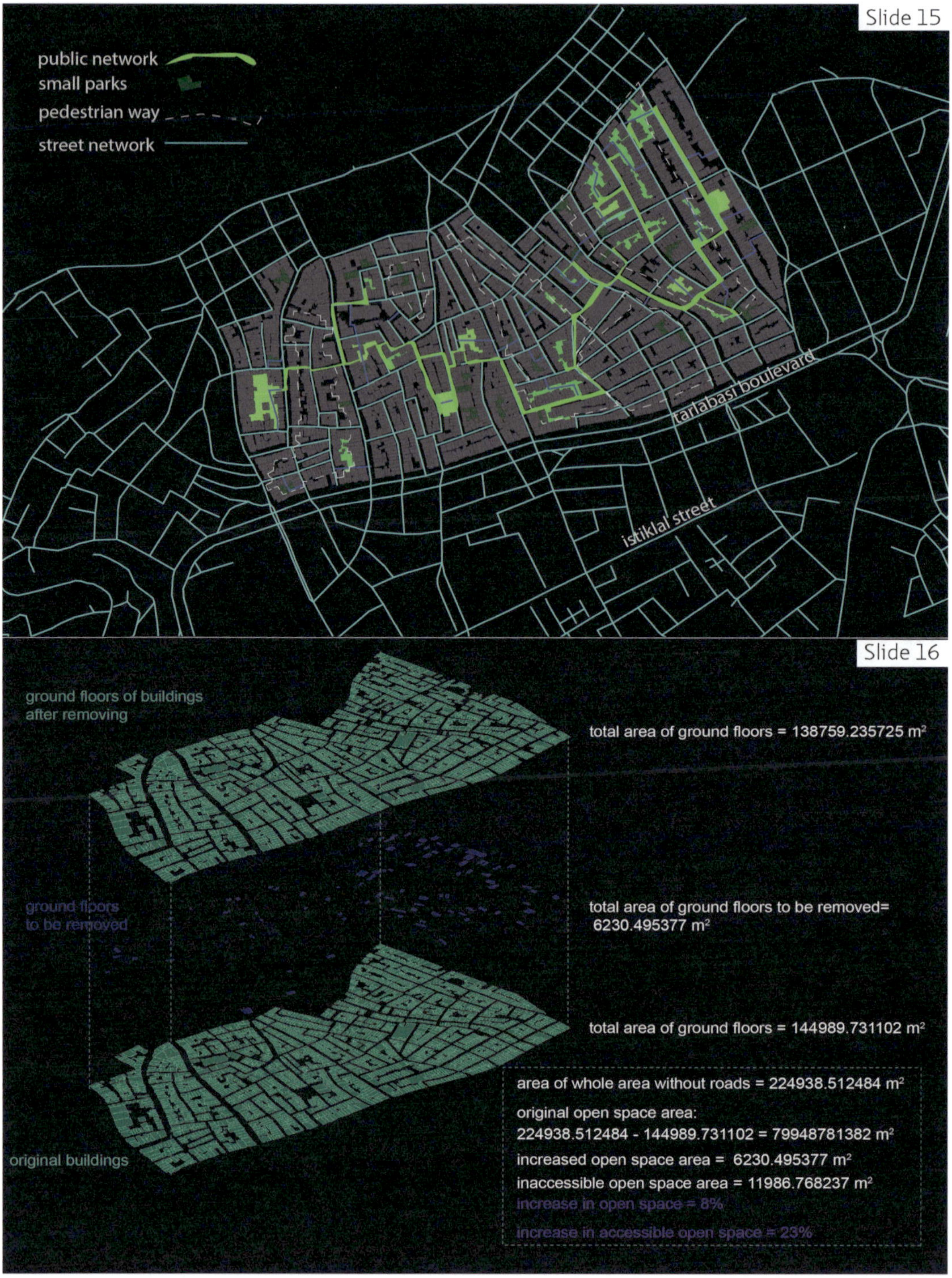

FIGURE APP.H.8 Slides 15 and 16

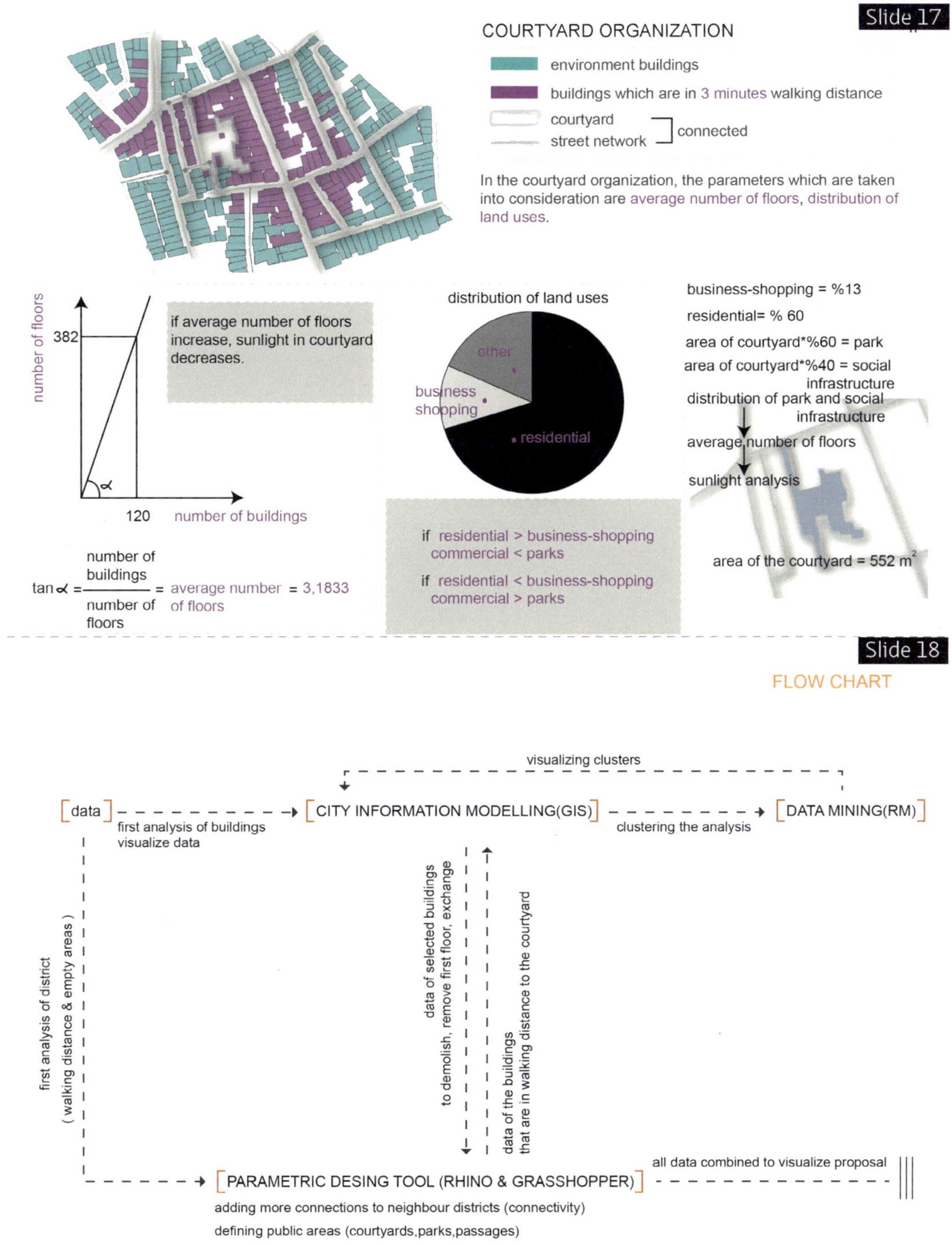

FIGURE APP.H.9 Slides17 and 18

Slide 19

CRITICS

The tools that are used during the workshop help us to analyse not only the district but also the buildings' informations. The city planning or urban regeneration projects can be easily improved by these analysis that are provided by these design tools (City Information Modelling-GIS, Data Mining-RM, Parametric Design Tool-Rhinoceros & Grasshopper). These analysis cannot reflect the social life in the district. Due to this, the urban regeneration projects cannot be considered without relation between the social life and these analysis.

FIGURE APP.H.10 Slide 19

Appendix I Presentation slides of "Team: Social Network in Tarlabaşı"

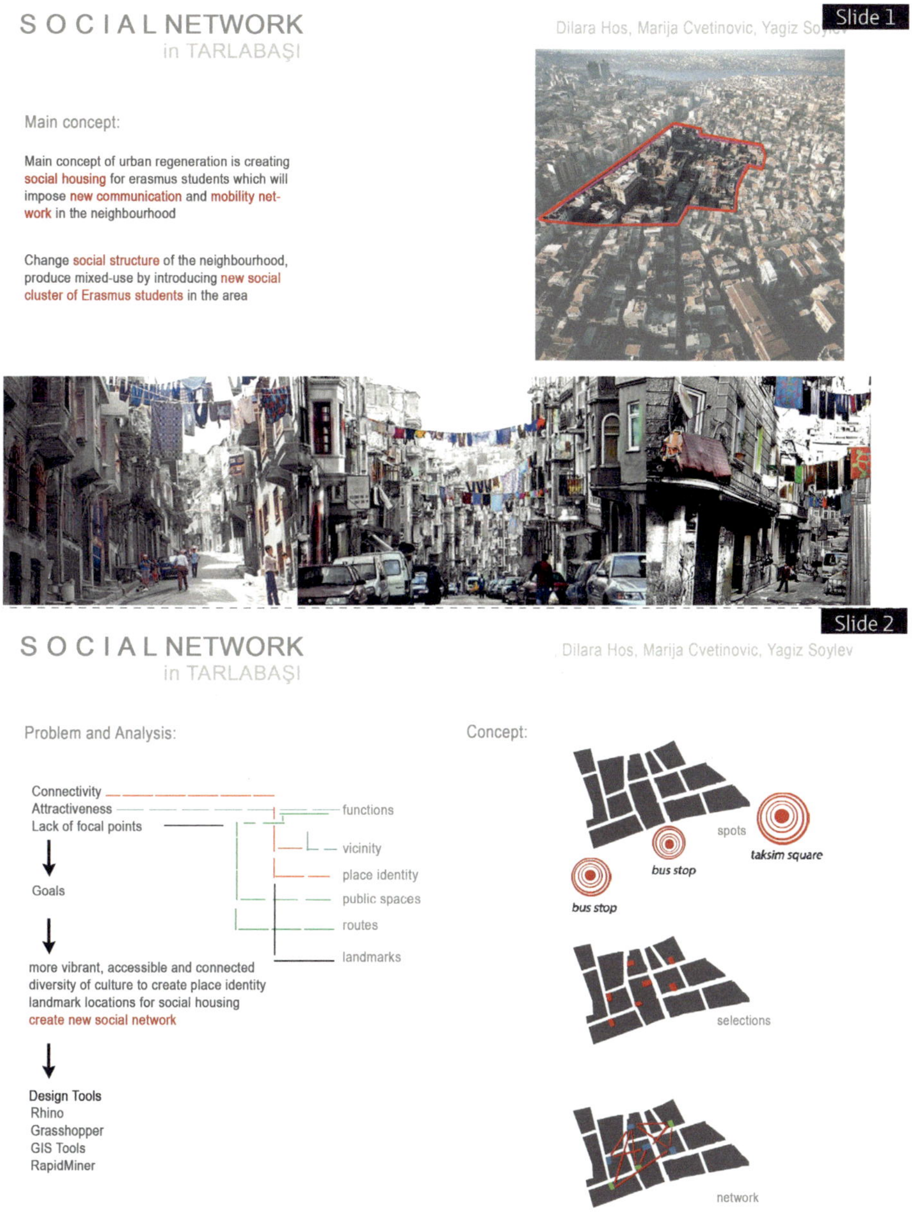

FIGURE APP.I.1 Slides 1 and 2

Slide 3

S O C I A L NETWORK
in TARLABAŞI

Dilara Hos, Marija Cvetinovic, Yagiz Soylev

Strategy:

Introduce new social cluster and new function in the area in order to develop place identity for specify areas and introduce corresponding social network among these locations

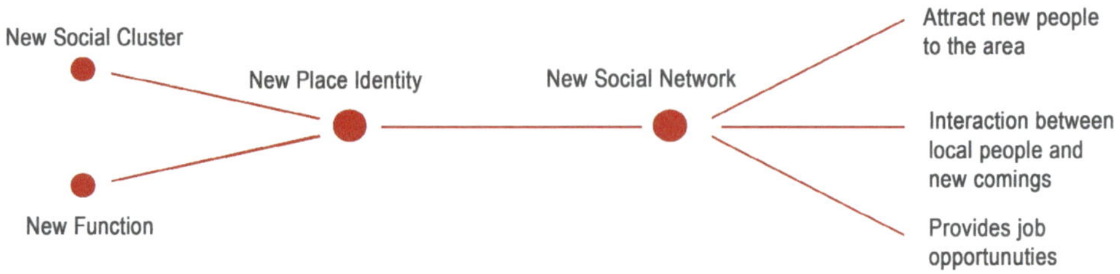

Slide 4

S O C I A L NETWORK
in TARLABAŞI

Dilara Hos, Marija Cvetinovic, Yagiz Soylev

Scenario:

Provide locations & functions for contact creation
Definition of spots for the network

Increase the interaction between local and new comings

FIGURE APP.I.2 Slides 3 and 4

S O C I A L NETWORK
in TARLABAŞI

Dilara Hos, Marija Cvetinovic, Yagiz Soylev

Slide 5

Data Flow:

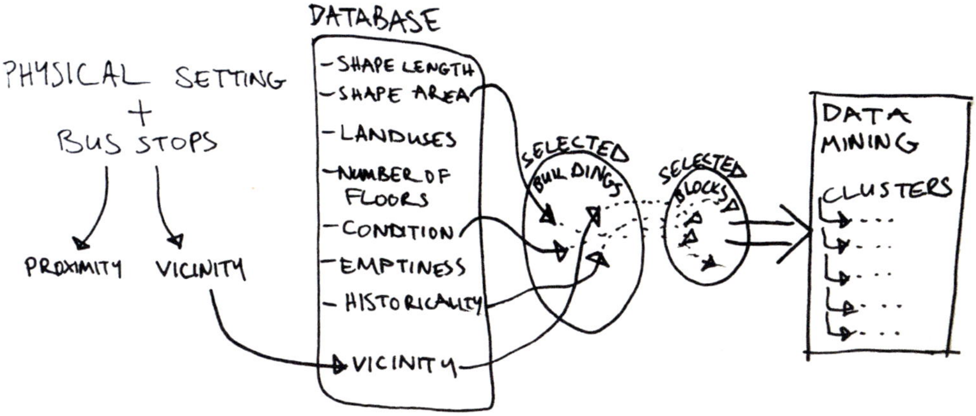

S O C I A L NETWORK
in TARLABAŞI

by Baris Ates, Dilara Hos, Marija Cvetinovic, Yagiz Soylev

Slide 6

Program: **1st Step-** Vicinity

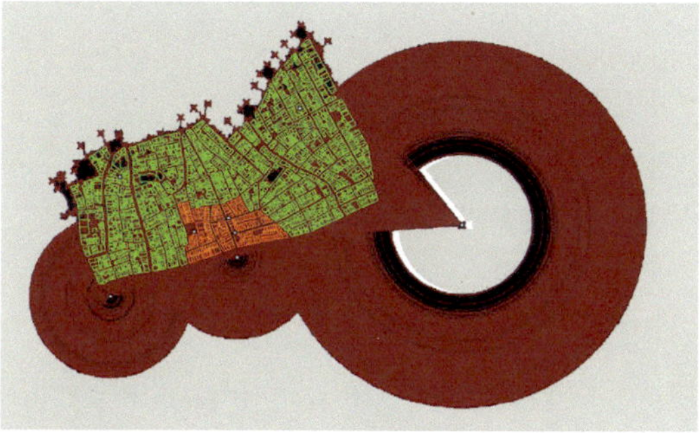

Three spots are chosen in order to locate the housing in a strategic position.

Spatial representation of vicinity gradient from Cheetah

FIGURE APP.I.3 Slides 5 and 6

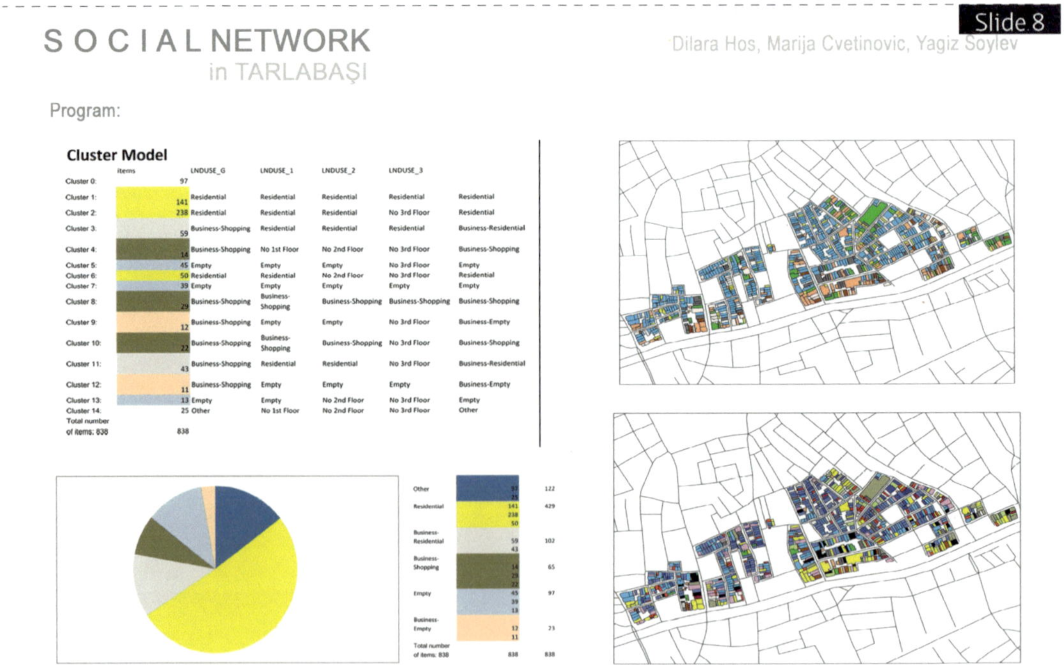

	items	LNDUSE_G	LNDUSE_1	LNDUSE_2	LNDUSE_3	
Cluster 0:	97					
Cluster 1:	141	Residential	Residential	Residential	Residential	Residential
Cluster 2:	238	Residential	Residential	Residential	No 3rd Floor	Residential
Cluster 3:	59	Business-Shopping	Residential	Residential	Residential	Business-Residential
Cluster 4:	14	Business-Shopping	No 1st Floor	No 2nd Floor	No 3rd Floor	Business-Shopping
Cluster 5:	45	Empty	Empty	Empty	No 3rd Floor	Empty
Cluster 6:	50	Residential	Residential	No 2nd Floor	No 3rd Floor	Residential
Cluster 7:	39	Empty	Empty	Empty	Empty	Empty
Cluster 8:	29	Business-Shopping	Business-Shopping	Business-Shopping	Business-Shopping	Business-Shopping
Cluster 9:	12	Business-Shopping	Empty	Empty	No 3rd Floor	Business-Empty
Cluster 10:	22	Business-Shopping	Business-Shopping	Business-Shopping	No 3rd Floor	Business-Shopping
Cluster 11:	43	Business-Shopping	Residential	Residential	No 3rd Floor	Business-Residential
Cluster 12:	11	Business-Shopping	Empty	Empty	Empty	Business-Empty
Cluster 13:	13	Empty	Empty	No 2nd Floor	No 3rd Floor	Empty
Cluster 14:	25	Other	No 1st Floor	No 2nd Floor	No 3rd Floor	Other
Total number of items: 838	838					

Other	97 25	122
Residential	141 238 50	429
Business-Residential	59 43	102
Business-Shopping	14 29 22	65
Empty	45 39 13	97
Business-Empty	12 11	23
Total number of items: 838	838	838

FIGURE APP.I.4 Slides 7 and 8

Slide 9

S O C I A L NETWORK
in TARLABAŞI

Dilara Hos, Marija Cvetinovic, Yagiz Soylev

Conclusion:

- bottom-up step-by-step urban transformation: flexibility of t he development model
- small scale renovation projects: keeping the design pattern of the area (new buildings for Erasmus students are all smaller, less than 50m2)
- non-invasive integrated rehabilitation: rebuilding social structure (new layer of users and visitors for this area)
- rebalancing usage patterns for the area: new network of urban actors support the development of new functions for the area
- creating local landmarks with mixed-use functions

Slide 10

S O C I A L NETWORK
in TARLABAŞI

Dilara Hos, Marija Cvetinovic, Yagiz Soylev

Future Scenario

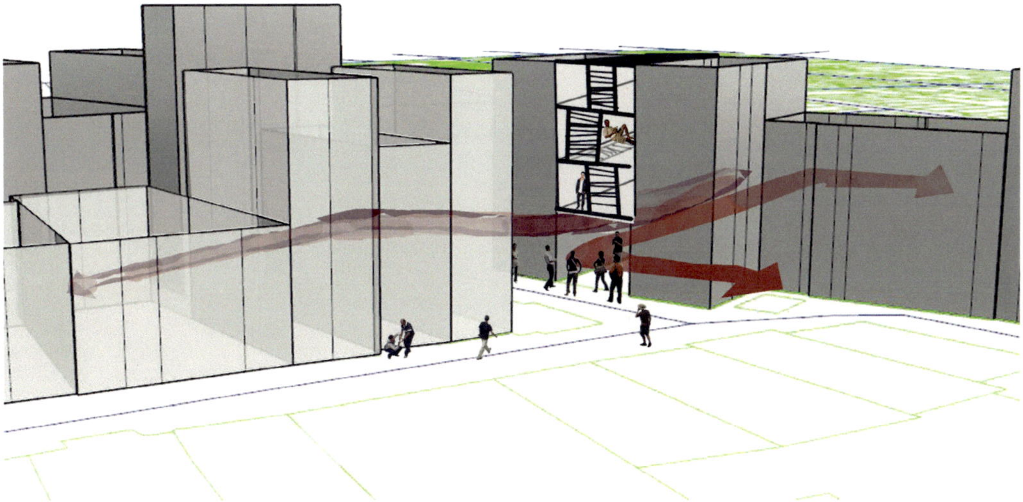

FIGURE APP.I.5 Slides 9 and 10

Appendix J Presentation slides of "Team: Raise your Head"

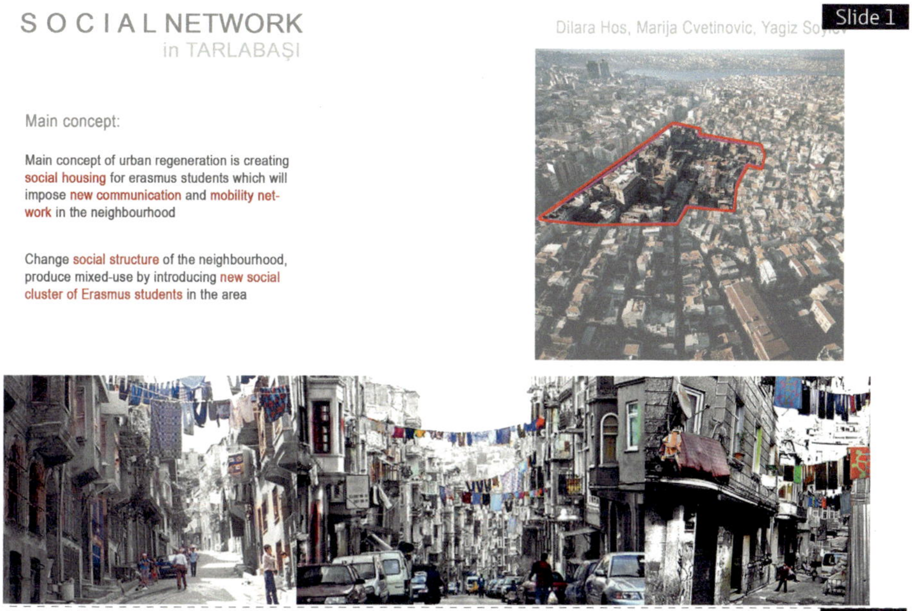

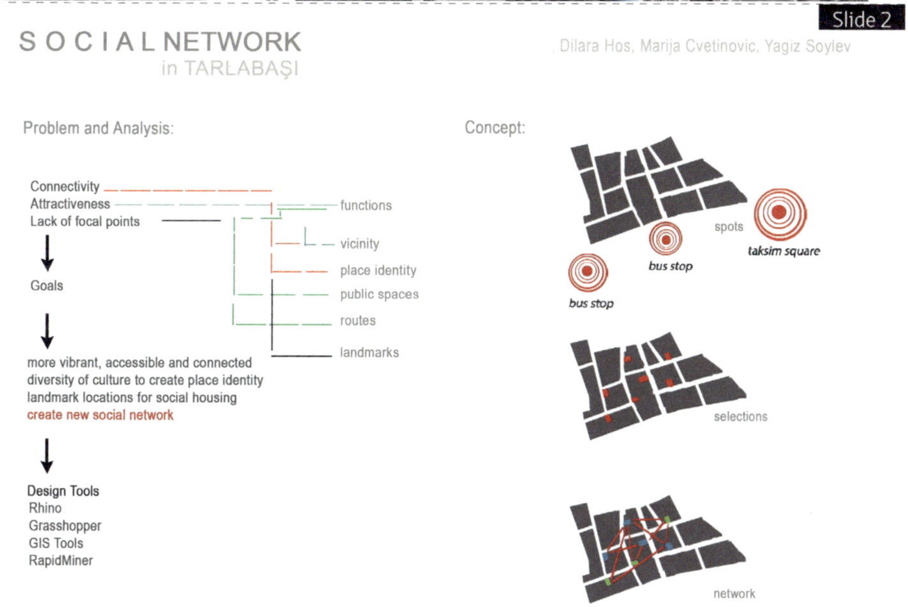

FIGURE APP.J.1 Slides 1 and 2

Slide 3

-The intervention area is located on north side of a high slope of Beyoglu Region.

-Site did not get enough light for comfortable living.

-There are no specialized main axes for safe walk.

Slide 4

Analysis

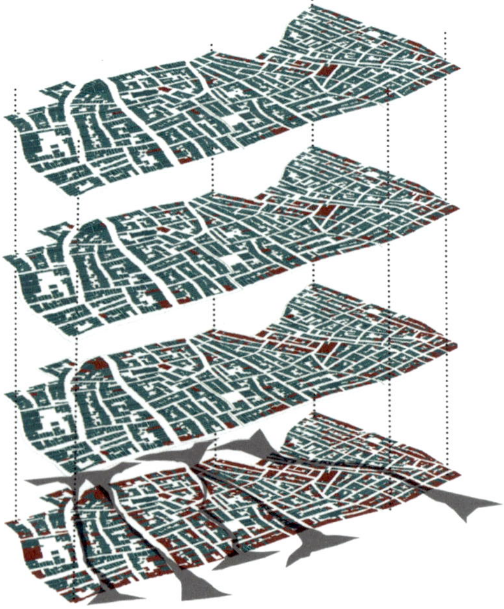

landuse shema
bussiness-shopping usage

FIGURE APP.J.2 Slides 3 and 4

Slide 5

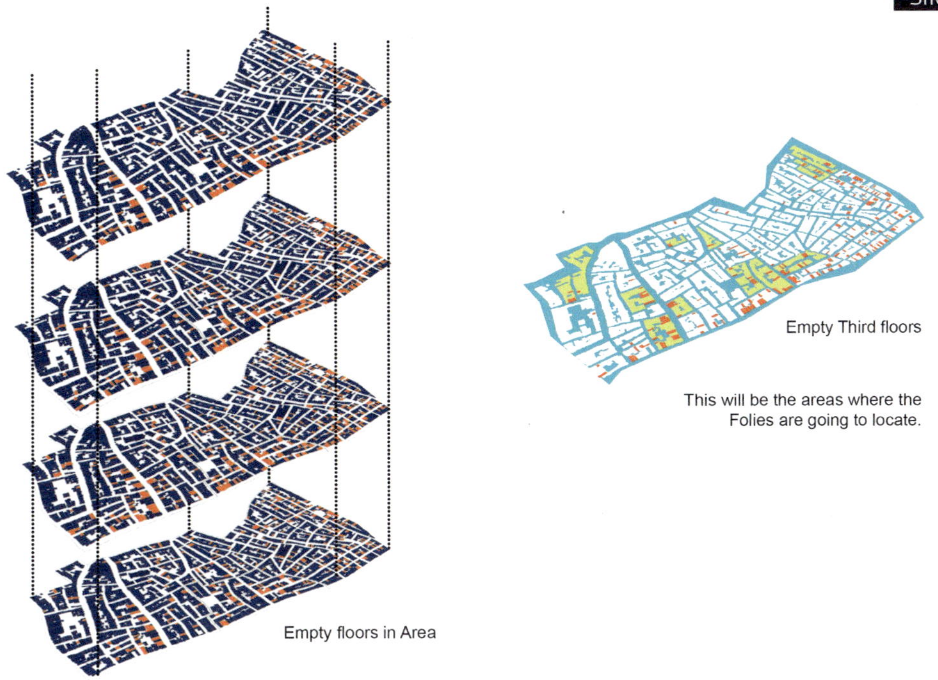

Slide 6

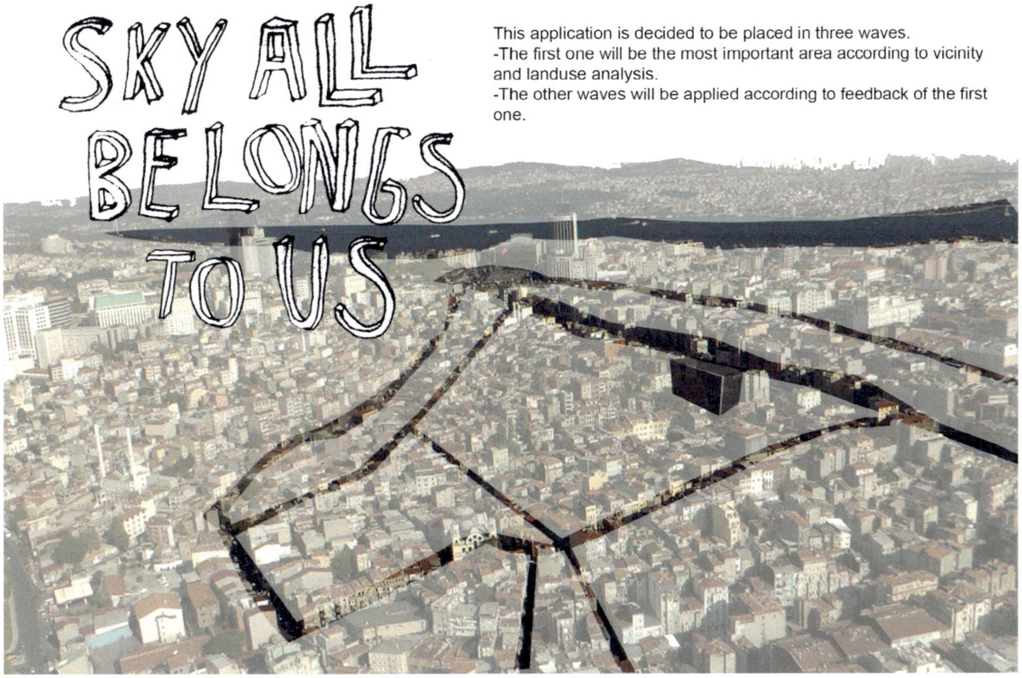

FIGURE APP.J.3 Slides 5 and 6

Slide 7

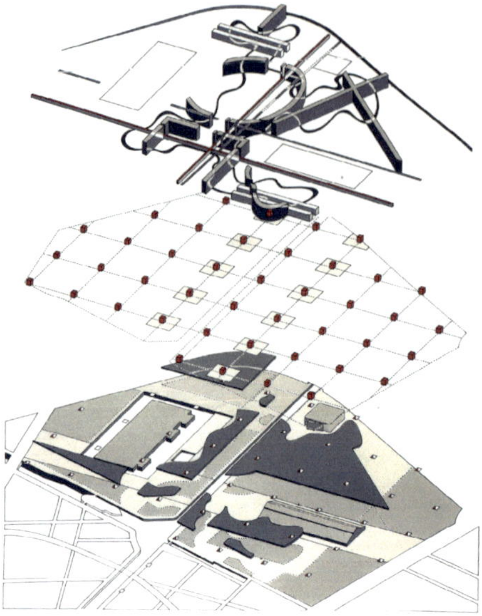

Bernard Tschumi

Slide 8

What's the solution?

-To specify a path according to vicinity analysis and to place folies on the building roofs among this path

What is the aim of the folies?

-the inhabitants do not have enough space in their homes and spend their times on the streets. These folies will provide more light and clean alternative socialising spaces for them.

How will it contribute to inhabitants dailylife?

-citizens will notice the folies walking on the streets and start to look for them and riddle the network

In which way the folies can be placed?

-Vicinity according to Tarlabaşı Boulevard and İstiklal Avenue

-Among the business lines between İstiklal Avenue and Kasımpaşa District

FIGURE APP.J.4 Slides 7 and 8

Slide 9

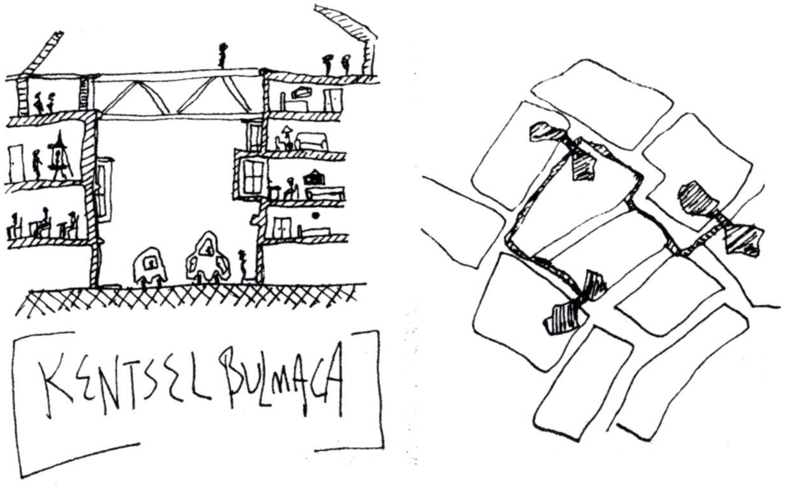

Drawing of concept idea

Slide 10

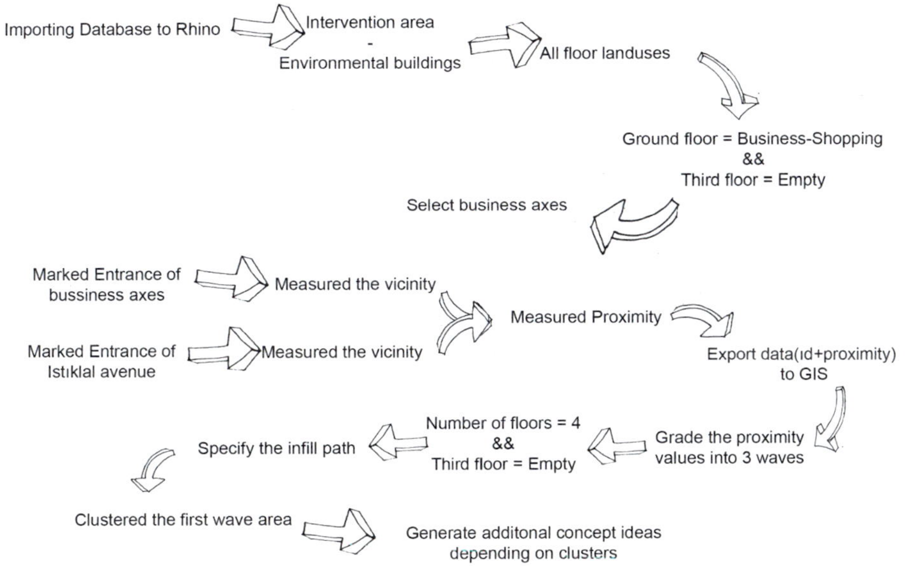

Process Diagram

FIGURE APP.J.5 Slides 9 and 10

Slide 11

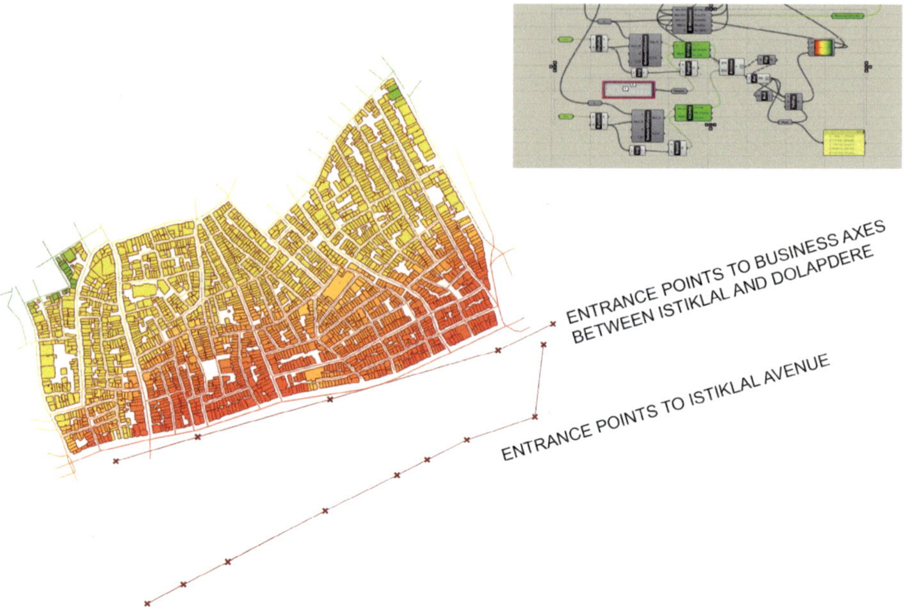

Slide 12

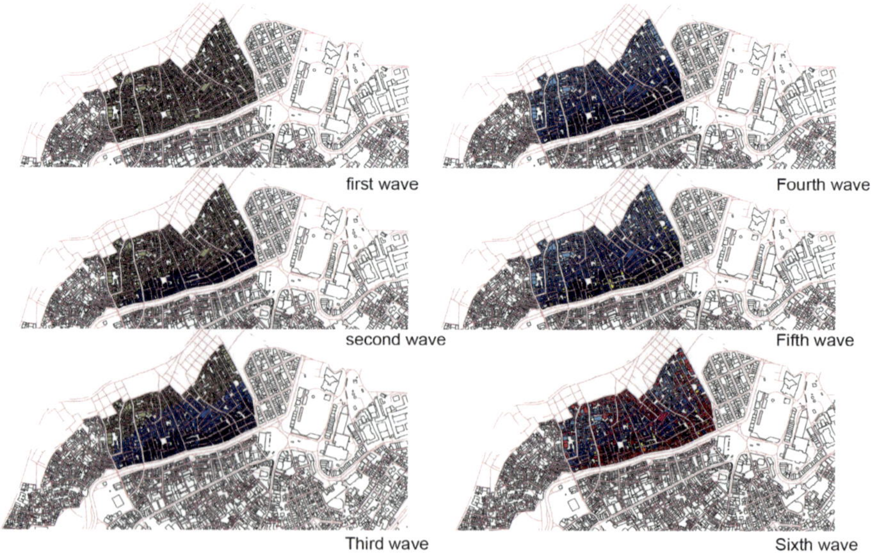

Quantum GIS Analysis

FIGURE APP.J.6 Slides 11 and 12

Slide 13

Alternative solution to Tarlabası network

Slide 14

In conclusion,

Since we cannot predict the certain results of urban redevelopment, we suggest our plan as an experiment.

We suggest regeneration of Tarlabaşı District, encountering inhabitants with a new social class without displacing inhabitants and demolishing historical buildings. However, we would like to realize this plan in three stages to see the result and continue developing.

A city is composed of different social and phsical relations, even the small interventions can end up unexpectedly.

Therefore the plan spreads over a time and will progress according to feedbacks.

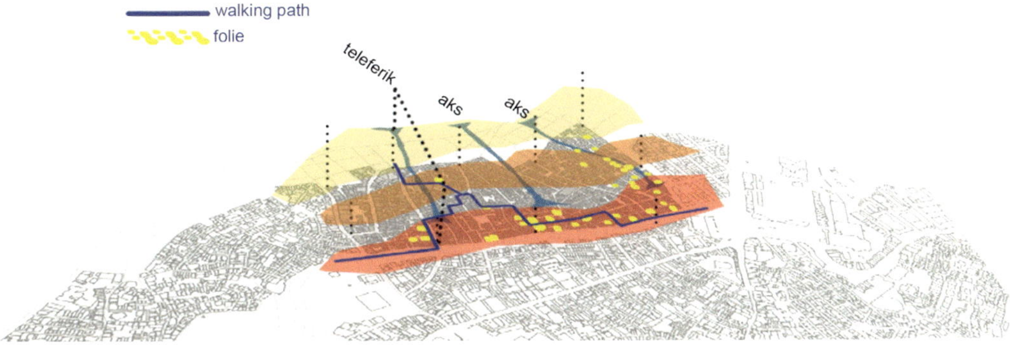

FIGURE APP.J.7 Slides 13 and 14

Slide 15

FIGURE APP.J.8 Slide 15

Curriculum vitae

Name Surname: Ahu Sökmenoğlu Sohtorik
Place and Date of Birth: 22.05.1978
E-Mail: ahuSökmenoğlu@yahoo.com

Education

B.Sc.: Istanbul Technical University, Department of Architecture
M.Sc. : Istanbul Technical University, Institute of Informatics, Architectural Design Computing Graduate Program

Professional experience and rewards

Architect, (2003-2004) MEDA Architects
Architect, (2004-2005) NET Mimarlık
Research assistant, (from 2005 on) İTÜ Faculty of Architecture, Dept. of Arch.

Publications, presentations and patents on the thesis

Sökmenoğlu, A., & Çağdaş, G. (2006). Transformations created by ICKT on the architectural design and its education. *ITU A|Z Journal, 3*(1-2), 37-52.

Sökmenoğlu, A., Çağdaş, G., & Sarıyıldız, S. (2010). Exploring the Patterns and Relationships of Urban Attributes by Data Mining. In L. H. Gerhard Schmitt, Luc Van Gool, Frédéric Bosché, Remo Burkhard, Suzanne Colemann, Jan Halatsch, Michael Hansmeyer, Silke Konsorski-Lang, Antje Kunze et al. (Ed.), *Future cities: 28th eCAADe Conference Proceedings, 15-18 September 2010* (pp. 873-881). ETH Zurich, Switzerland: ETH Zurich.

Sökmenoğlu, A., Çağdaş, G., & Sarıyıldız, S. (2011). Application of Data Mining In Micro-scale Urban Feature Analysis. In T. Cheng, P. Longley, C. Ellul & A. Chow (Eds.), Proceedings of the 11th International Conference on GeoComputation, 20-22 july 2011 (pp. 154-160). University College London, UK: University College London.

Sökmenoğlu, A., Çağdaş, G., & Sarıyıldız, S. (2011). A Multi-Dimensional Exploration of Urban Attributes by Data Mining. In P. Leclercq, Heylighen, A., and Martin, G. (Ed.), *Designing together - CAADFutures 2011, Proceedings of the 14th International conference on Computer Aided Architectural Design, 4-8 July 2011* (pp. 333-349). Liege, Belgium: Les Éditions de l'Université de Liège.

Sökmenoğlu, A., Çağdaş, G., & Sarıyıldız, S. (2012). Exploring Relationships of an Urban System: BeyoğluProceedings of the International Planning History Society Conference "Cities, nations and regions in planning history", 15-18 July 2012. Sao Paulo, Brasil: Faculty of Architecture and Urbanism, University of Sao Paulo. Retrieved from http://www.fau.usp.br/15-iphs-conference-sao-paulo-2012/abstractsAndPapersFiles/Sessions/30/Sökmenoğlu.pdf.

Sökmenoğlu, A., & Sarıyıldız, S. (2013). Computational Contribution in Contemporary Urban Issues. In A. Gospodini (Ed.), *Proceedings of the International Conference on "Changing Cities": Spatial, morphological, formal & socio-economic dimensions, June 18-21 2013,* (pp. 696-705). Skiathos, Greece: Department of Planning and Regional Development, School of Engineering, University of Thessaly.

Sökmenoğlu, A., & Sönmez, N. Onur (2013). Exploring Reciprocal Relationships of Land-Uses in a Historical Mixed-Use Quarter of Istanbul. In R. Stouffs & S. Sarıyıldız (Eds.), *Computation and Performance: 31st eCAADe Conference Proceedings, 18-20 September 2013* (Vol. 1, pp. 301-310). Delft, The Netherlands: eCAADe and Delft University of Technology Faculty of Architecture.

Other publications, presentations and patents

Hirschberg, U. **Sökmenoğlu**, A., Gürbüz, E., Alaçam, S., Çağdaş, G. (2012). Architectural Design Education through A Workshop: Experimenting with Digital Media. In B. B. Hisarlıgil, S. Locke & O. Turen (Eds.), *MIMED Forum IV: Flexibility in Architectural Education* (pp. 298-314). Newcastle upon Tyne, UK: Cambridge Scholar Publishing.

Avcı, O., & **Sökmenoğlu**, A. (2011). Renkli Karşılama Mekanı. *XXI*(103), 67-71.

Sökmenoğlu, A., & Akgül, C. B. (2010). Exploring the Patterns and Trends of Socio-spatial Activities of Architecture Student Community in Istanbul by Data Mining. In L. H. Gerhard Schmitt, Luc Van Gool, Frédéric Bosché, Remo Burkhard, Suzanne Colemann, Jan Halatsch, Michael Hansmeyer, Silke Konsorski-Lang, Antje Kunze et al. (Ed.), *Future cities: 28th eCAADe Conference Proceedings, 15-18 September 2010* (pp. 143-150). Zurich, Switzerland: ETH Zurich.

Sökmenoğlu, A., & Çağdaş, G. (2010). Mimarlık Eğitiminde Deneysel Yaklaşımlar: Bütünleşik Tasarım Atölyesi *Mimarlıkta Sayısal Tasarım 2010-Teknolojiler, Yöntemler ve Bilgi Yönetimi, May 10 2010* (pp. 51-54). Istanbul, Turkey: Yıldız Technical University Faculty of Architecture.

Sökmenoğlu, A., & Turkkan, S. (2009). Digital Monumentality in/for Public Spaces. In G. Çağdaş & B. Colakoglu (Eds.), *Computation: the New Realm of Architectural Design, 27th eCAADe Conference Proceedings, 16-19 September 2009* (pp. 835-843). Istanbul, Turkey: Istanbul Technical University.

Sökmenoğlu, A., & Turkkan, S. (2007). *Public Aesthetics, Power and New Media*. Paper presented at the International Conference Power & Space: Transforming the Contemporary City, December 6-8 2007, Cambridge University, UK.

Sökmenoğlu, A., & Çağdaş, G. (2007). *Graduate Education on Architectural Design Computing at Faculty of Architecture, ITU*. Paper presented at the TMMOB_Mimarlar Odası Mimarlik ve Eğitim Kurultayı IV-Mimarlık Eğitiminde Bilgisayarla Tasarım, Bütünleşik Yaklaşımlar, 23 March 2007, Middle East Technical University Faculty of Architecture, Ankara, Turkey.

Sökmenoğlu, A., Ayanoğlu, M., & Çağdaş, G. (2006). A Parametrical Shape Grammar Model for Generating Bedestens; a Classical Ottoman Period Commerce Building Type. In V. Bourdakis & D. Charitos (Eds.), *Communicating Space(s): 24th eCAADe Conference Proceedings, 6-9 September 2006* (pp. 308-312). Volos, Greece: University of Thessaly.

Sökmenoğlu, A., & Çağdaş, G. (2006). Enformayon ve İletişim Teknolojileri Etkisinde Mimari Tasarım Yaklaşımları. In H. Alpay Er, S. Timur, L. N. E. Arıburun, H. H. Bağlı, A. O. İlhan, A. Z. Turan, G. Turan, E. Küçüksayraç & A. Enşici (Eds.), *3rd National Design Congress: Türkiye'de Tasarımı Tartışmak, June 19-22, 2006* (pp. 476-487). İstanbul, Turkey: ITU Industrial Design Department.

Dülgeroğlu Yüksel, Y. & **Sökmenoğlu**, A. (2006). İstanbul'un Kültür Aksında Bir Sergileme Modülü Tasarımı". *Stüdyo Dergisi, 3*. http://www.studyomim.itu.edu.tr/sayi3/sergileme_modulu_tasarimi.pdf

Sökmenoğlu, A., & Çağdaş, G. (2005). Enformasyon ve İletişim Teknolojileri Etkisinde Kentsel Yaşam, Mekan ve Sürdürülebilirlik *World's Urban Planners Day, 29th Colloquim, 8 November 2005* (pp. 283-293). İstanbul, Turkey İstanbul Technical University, Faculty of Architecture.

Sökmenoğlu, A., Çağdaş, G. (2004). Transforming Architecture in The light of IT and Creative Educational Approaches Guiding on The Way Future. In A. Dikbas (Ed.), *itc@edu: Third International Workshop on Construction Information Technology in Education, September 7, 2004* (pp. 115-131). İstanbul, Turkey: İTÜ Yayınları.

Made in the USA
Las Vegas, NV
03 November 2026

57423445R00243